Commentary on the
NICOMACHEAN ETHICS

Library of Living Catholic Thought

VOLUME I

ST. THOMAS AQUINAS

Commentary on the NICOMACHEAN ETHICS

TRANSLATED BY

C. I. LITZINGER, O.P.

Library of Living Catholic Thought

VOLUME I

HENRY REGNERY COMPANY
Chicago

Nihil Obstat: Urban Voll, O.P., S.T. Lr.
Anthony D. Lee, O.P., S.T. Lr.

Imprimi Potest: W. D. Marrin, O.P., P.G., S.T.D.
Prior Provincialis, St. Joseph's Province

Nihil Obstat: Francis Conway, O.P., S.T. Lr.
Diocesan Censor Deputatus

Imprimatur: ✠ Richard Cardinal Cushing
Archbishop of Boston
January 15, 1964

To the memory of

Donald J. McMahon, O.P.

THE DIVISION OF THE TEN

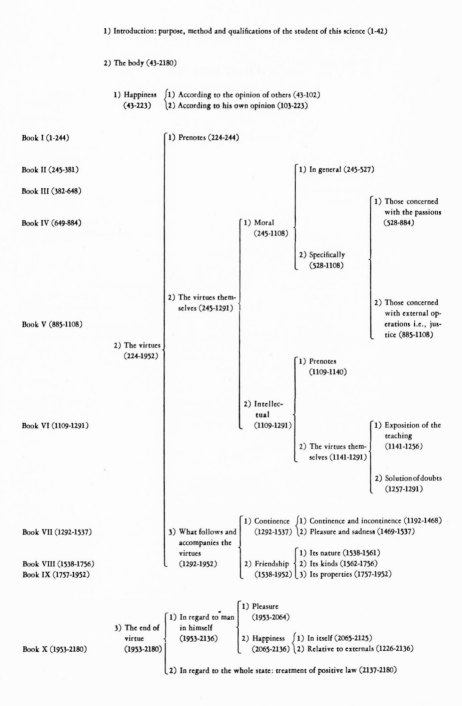

1) Introduction: purpose, method and qualifications of the student of this science (1-42)

2) The body (43-2180)

1) Happiness (43-223)
  1) According to the opinion of others (43-102)
  2) According to his own opinion (103-223)

Book I (1-244)
  1) Prenotes (224-244)

Book II (245-381)
Book III (382-648)

Book IV (649-884)

2) The virtues (224-1952)

  2) The virtues themselves (245-1291)
    1) Moral (245-1108)
      1) In general (245-527)
      2) Specifically (528-1108)
        1) Those concerned with the passions (528-884)

Book V (885-1108)
        2) Those concerned with external operations i.e., justice (885-1108)

Book VI (1109-1291)
    2) Intellectual (1109-1291)
      1) Prenotes (1109-1140)
      2) The virtues themselves (1141-1291)
        1) Exposition of the teaching (1141-1256)
        2) Solution of doubts (1257-1291)

Book VII (1292-1537)
  3) What follows and accompanies the virtues (1292-1952)
    1) Continence (1292-1537)
      1) Continence and incontinence (1192-1468)
      2) Pleasure and sadness (1469-1537)

Book VIII (1538-1756)
Book IX (1757-1952)
    2) Friendship (1538-1952)
      1) Its nature (1538-1561)
      2) Its kinds (1562-1756)
      3) Its properties (1757-1952)

3) The end of virtue (1953-2180)
  1) In regard to man in himself (1953-2136)
    1) Pleasure (1953-2064)
    2) Happiness (2065-2136)
      1) In itself (2065-2125)
      2) Relative to externals (1226-2136)

Book X (1953-2180)
  2) In regard to the whole state: treatment of positive law (2137-2180)

BOOKS OF THE ETHICS (Nos. 1-2180)

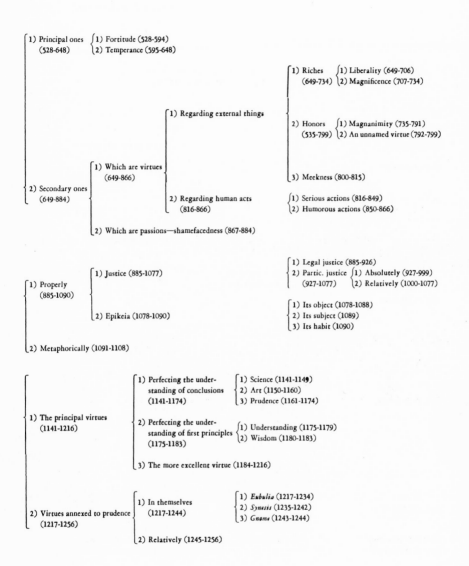

1) Principal ones (528-648)
  1) Fortitude (528-594)
  2) Temperance (595-648)

2) Secondary ones (649-884)
  1) Which are virtues (649-866)
    1) Regarding external things
      1) Riches (649-734)
        1) Liberality (649-706)
        2) Magnificence (707-734)
      2) Honors (535-799)
        1) Magnanimity (735-791)
        2) An unnamed virtue (792-799)
      3) Meekness (800-815)
    2) Regarding human acts (816-866)
      1) Serious actions (816-849)
      2) Humorous actions (850-866)
  2) Which are passions—shamefacedness (867-884)

1) Properly (885-1090)
  1) Justice (885-1077)
    1) Legal justice (885-926)
    2) Partic. justice (927-1077)
      1) Absolutely (927-999)
      2) Relatively (1000-1077)
  2) Epikeia (1078-1090)
    1) Its object (1078-1088)
    2) Its subject (1089)
    3) Its habit (1090)

2) Metaphorically (1091-1108)

1) The principal virtues (1141-1216)
  1) Perfecting the understanding of conclusions (1141-1174)
    1) Science (1141-1149)
    2) Art (1150-1160)
    3) Prudence (1161-1174)
  2) Perfecting the understanding of first principles (1175-1183)
    1) Understanding (1175-1179)
    2) Wisdom (1180-1183)
  3) The more excellent virtue (1184-1216)

2) Virtues annexed to prudence (1217-1256)
  1) In themselves (1217-1244)
    1) *Eubulia* (1217-1234)
    2) *Synesis* (1235-1242)
    3) *Gnome* (1243-1244)
  2) Relatively (1245-1256)

CONTENTS

INTRODUCTION

Many good English translations of Aristotle's *Nicomachean Ethics* are in circulation; but so far as we know, no complete translation of St. Thomas' *Commentary* on this work exists. Since all are not as gifted as St. Augustine, who read and understood the *Categories* unaided,[1] some clarification is almost imperative because of Aristotle's depth of thought and conciseness of style. To fill this need J. A. Stewart (1892) and J. Burnet (1900) have written excellent commentaries; H. H. Joachim's commentary,[2] first published in 1951, was reprinted in 1962. Frequent notes in H. Rackham's translation is further evidence of the necessity for an explanation of the text.

Our age is not alone in its inability to understand Aristotle fully without the aid of a commentator. The thirteenth century, too, looked for similar help during the revival of interest in the Greek philosophers; and St. Thomas wrote his commentary to furnish such assistance to his contemporaries. In the centuries following, this has been the classical explanation of Aristotle's *Nicomachean Ethics* for the Western World; that it can be helpful also to the student today is recognized by such scholars as Paul Shorey, who says: ". . . if I had the choice of putting into the hands of a student of Aristotle the commentary of Thomas or the book of some recent interpreter of Aristotle, I would choose the medieval schoolman as more educative in sensible methods and less likely to mislead and confuse the student." [3]

St. Thomas' unique qualifications as an interpreter of Aristotle is attested by Professor Harry V. Jaffa who maintains that the teaching of Aristotle can be discovered more readily in St. Thomas than in Aristotle himself; that St. Thomas is unequaled in his mastery of the whole of Aristotelian doctrine and in his ability to co-ordinate its parts.[4] The Professor goes on to note this significant fact about St. Thomas' interpretation of the *Ethics:* "Thomas rarely, if ever, attempts to explain any statement of Aristotle except in terms of other of his statements. Nothing extraneous to the *Ethics* itself is, apparently, permitted to serve as the basis for the interpretation of the *Ethics*." [5]

Unfortunately this font of thomistic ethical doctrine has not been available to English readers. At the present time there is keen interest in Aristotle's approach to moral problems and in his theories on politics.[6] Some of this interest we trust extends also to St. Thomas' interpretation of that teaching. In this expectation we thought it opportune to offer an English translation of St. Thomas' *Commentary on the Nicomachean Ethics* together with a new rendition of Aristotle's text.

But why, it may be asked, add another translation of Aristotle's text when we already have such readable and scholarly translations as those of Ross and Rackham? In the beginning it was intended to use one of the existing texts in English, but as the work progressed it became evident that St. Thomas' understanding of

[1] *Confessions*, Bk. IV, 28.
[2] *Aristotle: The Nicomachean Ethics*, Clarendon Press, Oxford 1962.
[3] *Platonism Ancient and Modern* (p. 90), University of California Press: 1938.
[4] *Thomism and Aristotelianism* by Harry V. Jaffa. University of Chicago Press: 1952, p. 6-7.
[5] Ibid., p. 19.
[6] *The Politics of Aristotle* by Ernest Barker. Oxford University Press, New York: 1961, p. iv sq.

Aristotle occasionally differs from the current translations. Since our primary purpose is to put into English St. Thomas' understanding, it was decided to attempt a translation that would be more conformable to his Commentary.

The present translation of the text of Aristotle has been made from the Latin version, generally attributed to William of Moerbeke, as found in the Cathala-Spiazzi edition. This *versio antiqua* was used because it has great authority among scholars,[7] and because it was the basis for the Commentary, although St. Thomas at times varies from this rendition.

In general, Spiazzi's divisions of the text and the Commentary have been followed. Bekker's enumeration of the text has been included to facilitate reference to other translations; it appears in italicized numbers in the text itself. Chapter numbers have been made to correspond with those now in common use. The format, suggested by Father Anthony D. Lee, O.P., Managing Editor of The Thomist, has been devised to make references to the text easy to follow. It consists of two parallel columns entitled *Analytical Outline of St. Thomas* and *Text of Aristotle*. In the first column are given explanatory sentences, and sometimes phrases, taken verbatim from the Commentary. These sentences are placed above and to the left of the text, and have been numbered and lettered to correspond with bracketed marks found in the Commentary. A number appears at the end of each section of the text to indicate the paragraph or paragraphs of St. Thomas' Commentary on the text.

The purpose of a translator is to present the author's ideas, to convey these thoughts through the medium of another language, and to express their meaning intelligibly in that language. It goes without saying that the translator must first of all thoroughly understand the ideas. Hence an adequate knowledge of the author's language is indispensable. To this must be added a competence in the language of the translation to insure the incorporation of the author's thought into the new medium. Moreover, the translator must formulate and express that thought in words understandable to his prospective readers.

How these ends can best be achieved is a problem the translator must solve. Should he translate word for word, phrase for phrase, construction for construction? Evidently William of Moerbeke did this in translating the *Nicomachean Ethics* into Latin. Such a method has the advantage of excluding interpretation that has no place in a translation. But literalness can be self-defeating, since a simple rendering of a text may not serve to make the meaning clear. On the other hand, the translator certainly cannot ignore the author's words, phrasing, and sentence construction; to do so would be to assume the role of interpreter.

Evidently a middle course must be followed, for the translator is under obligation to present as clearly as possible the meaning of the author. When a literal translation best serves this purpose it should be used; when a freer rendition is necessary to bring out the thought, he should not hesitate to adopt this more suitable means. Thus he will make a faithful reproduction of the original, an essential quality of any translation.

St. Thomas confirms this procedure in the *Contra Errores Graecorum:*[8] ". . . There are many expressions that sound well in Greek which would perhaps be awkward in Latin. . . . Consequently the skillful translator in the exercise of his work . . . will retain the meaning and fashion his manner of expression in accordance with the peculiar genius of the language into which he is translating.

[7] Cf. H. Rackham, *Aristotle: The Nicomachean Ethics,* Introduction p. xxvi.
[8] *Opuscula Theologica,* Vol. I, p. 315 sq., Marietti 1954.

Obviously, if what is said literally in Latin is expressed in the vernacular, the exposition of the material will be awkward when the rendition is simply word for word. What is more, obscurity is not surprising when a slavish literal translation is made." How successfully these norms have been observed must be left to the judgment of others.

A special debt of gratitude is due Father Urban Voll, O.P., of Catholic University of America for his invaluable assistance in the production of this work. He generously devoted his free time, apart from the demands of a busy schedule, to reading the entire manuscript. His corrections eliminated imperfections that would have marred the translation. His suggestions and advice have helped to clarify the ideas expressed and make them acceptable to the reader. It is no exaggeration to say that without his aid the translation would not have been published.

Father Francis Conway, O.P., former professor of Ethics at St. John's University, Brooklyn, N.Y., and now at Emmanuel College, Boston, Massachusetts, gave unstintingly of his time and talent to make the translation accurate. His comments have been most helpful in determining the meaning of the text, especially where St. Thomas apparently differs from modern translations of Aristotle. He kindly pointed out latinisms, circumlocutions, and unevenness in expression and suggested appropriate ways to avoid these defects. His resourcefulness in recommending alternatives for monotonous repetitions has contributed to a smoother reading.

I am indebted to Father Anthony D. Lee, O.P., who, besides arranging the details of publication, read part of the manuscript and offered constructive criticisms of the contents. He has given helpful suggestions to insure agreement between the outlines and the body of the Commentary.

The students of St. Stephen's House of Studies, Dover, Massachusetts, made important contributions to these volumes. They used the first draft of the translation as a help to the Latin text studied in class, and their questions were the occasion of changes that clarified the meaning of passages difficult to render into English. They also assisted in looking up references and checking footnotes to guarantee accuracy.

It should be added that any merit the present work may possess is due in no small measure to the generous co-operation of my fellow professors at St. Stephen's. Their continued interest in the progress of the translation was a constant source of encouragement. Their patience in listening to my difficulties was matched by their promptness in proposing and finding correct solutions. Their readiness in assuming extra professorial duties made possible the leisure requisite for translation.

Finally, I should like to express my gratitude to Father Ferrer Smith, O.P., Regent of Studies for St. Joseph's Province, for his advice and good offices in promoting publication; to Father W. D. Marrin, O.P., Provincial, for his help and fatherly interest; to Father Aniceto Fernandez, O.P., Master General, with whose paternal blessing the translation is appearing.

Commentary on the
NICOMACHEAN ETHICS

Library of Living Catholic Thought

VOLUME I

BOOK I

THE GOOD FOR MAN

CONTENTS

BOOK I

---

[1] Numeration according to Bekker.

CONTENTS

BOOK I

LECTURE I

Subject Matter and End of Moral Philosophy: Diversity of Ends

ANALYTICAL OUTLINE
OF ST. THOMAS

TEXT OF ARISTOTLE
(B.1094)
Chapter 1

PRELIMINARY NOTIONS   1 to 7

I. FIRST (ARISTOTLE) SHOWS WHAT HE INTENDS TO DO.

A. He presents in advance certain things necessary to explain his intention.

I. HE SHOWS HOW IT IS NECESSARY TO START WITH THE END.

a. He states . . . that all human things are ordered to an end.

i. He states his intention.

All arts and all teaching, and similarly every act and every choice seem to have the attainment of some good as their object.   8

ii. He explains his purpose.

For this reason it has correctly been proclaimed that good is what all desire.   9-11

b. He shows that there can be a number of ends.

Now a certain diversity of ends is apparent, for some are operations while others are works outside the operations.   12-13

c. He makes a comparison among ends.

If the ends are works then the works are better than the operations.   14

2. HE COMPARES HABITS AND ACTS WITH THE END.

a. He shows that different things are ordered to different ends.

Since there are many operations and arts and sciences there must also be different ends for each of them. Thus the end of medical art is health; of ship-building, navigation; of strategy, victory; of domestic economy, riches.   15

b. He arranges the order of habits among themselves.

In all such skills a subordination of one to another is found. For in-   10 stance, the art of bridle-making is subordinated to the art of riding as also are the arts which make riding equipment. The art of riding in turn, and all military operations, come under strategy. In a similar way other arts are subordinated to still others.   16

5

c. He lays down the order of ends . . .

It follows then that in all these, architectonic ends are more desirable than the ends subordinated to them. The reason is that men seek the latter for the sake of the former.   17

d. He shows that it makes no difference . . . whether the end is a product or an operation.

It does not matter whether the ends are operations themselves or something other than the operations as in the skills mentioned above.   18

COMMENTARY OF ST. THOMAS

1. As the Philosopher says in the beginning of the *Metaphysics* (Bk. I, Ch. 2, 982 a 18; St. Th. II, 41-42) [1], it is the business of the wise man to order. The reason for this is that wisdom is the most powerful perfection of reason whose characteristic is to know order. Even if the sensitive powers know some things absolutely, nevertheless to know the order of one thing to another is exclusively the work of intellect or reason. Now a twofold order is found in things. One kind is that of parts of a totality, that is, a group, among themselves, as the parts of a house are mutually ordered to each other. The second order is that of things to an end. This order is of greater importance than the first. For, as the Philosopher says in the eleventh book of the *Metaphysics* (Bk. XII, Ch. 10, 1075 a 15; St. Th. Bk. XII, Lect. XII, 2629-2631), the order of the parts of an army among themselves exists because of the order of the whole army to the commander. Now order is related to reason in a fourfold way. There is one order that reason does not establish but only beholds, such is the order of things in

nature. There is a second order that reason establishes in its own act of consideration, for example, when it arranges its concepts among themselves, and the signs of concepts as well, because words express the meanings of the concepts. There is a third order that reason in deliberating establishes in the operations of the will. There is a fourth order that reason in planning establishes in the external things which it causes, such as a chest and a house.

2. Because the operation of reason is perfected by habit, according to the different modes of order that reason considers in particular, a differentiation of sciences arises. The function of natural philosophy is to consider the order of things that human reason considers but does not establish—understand that with natural philosophy here we also include metaphysics. The order that reason makes in its own act of consideration pertains to rational philosophy (logic), which properly considers the order of the parts of verbal expression with one another and the order of principles to one another and to their conclusions. The order of voluntary actions pertains to the consideration of moral philosophy. The order that reason in planning establishes in external things arranged by human reason pertains to the mechanical arts.

[1] Reference to the text of Aristotle will be given according to Bekker. Reference to the Commentary of St. Thomas on the *Metaphysics* is based on *In Duodecim Libros Metaphysicorum Aristotelis Expositio.* Cathala-Spiazzi Edition, Turin: Marietti, 1950.

Accordingly it is proper to moral philosophy, to which our attention is at present directed, to consider human operations insofar as they are ordered to one another and to an end.

3. I am talking about human operations, those springing from man's will following the order of reason. But if some operations are found in man that are not subject to the will and reason, they are not properly called human but natural, as clearly appears in operations of the vegetative soul. These in no way fall under the consideration of moral philosophy. As the subject of natural philosophy is motion, or mobile being, so the subject of moral philosophy is human action ordered to an end, or even man, as he is an agent voluntarily acting for an end.

4. It must be understood that, because man is by nature a social animal, needing many things to live which he cannot get for himself if alone, he naturally is a part of a group that furnishes him help to live well. He needs this help for two reasons. First, to have what is necessary for life, without which he cannot live the present life; and for this, man is helped by the domestic group of which he is a part. For every man is indebted to his parents for his generation and his nourishment and instruction. Likewise individuals, who are members of the family, help one another to procure the necessities of life. In another way, man receives help from the group of which he is a part, to have a perfect sufficiency for life; namely, that man may not only live but live well, having everything sufficient for living; and in this way man is helped by the civic group, of which he is a member, not only in regard to bodily needs—as certainly in the state there are many crafts which a single household cannot provide—but also in regard to right conduct, inasmuch as public authority restrains with fear of punishment delinquent young men whom paternal admonition is not able to correct.

5. It must be known moreover that the whole which the political group or the family constitutes has only a unity of order, for it is not something absolutely one. A part of this whole, therefore, can have an operation that is not the operation of the whole, as a soldier in an army has an activity that does not belong to the whole army. However, this whole does have an operation that is not proper to its parts but to the whole—for example, an assault of the entire army. Likewise the movement of a boat is a combined operation of the crew rowing the boat. There is also a kind of whole that has not only a unity of order but of composition, or of conjunction, or even of continuity, and according to this unity a thing is one absolutely; and therefore there is no operation of the part that does not belong to the whole. For in things all of one piece the motion of the whole and of the part is the same. Similarly in composites and in conjoined things, the operation of a part is principally that of the whole. For this reason it is necessary that such a consideration of both the whole and its parts should belong to the same science. It does not, however, pertain to the same science to consider the whole, which has solely the unity of order, and the parts of this whole.

6. Thus it is that moral philosophy is divided into three parts. The first of these, which is called individual (monastic) ethics, considers an individual's operations as ordered to an end. The second, called domestic ethics, considers the operations of the domestic group. The third, called political science, considers the operations of the civic group.

7. Thus Aristotle as he begins the treatment of moral philosophy in the first part of this book called *Ethics,* or morals, first gives an introduction in

which he does three things. First [I] [1] he shows what he intends to do. Second [Lect. III, II], at "Our study will be etc." (B.1094 b 13), he determines the manner of treatment. Third [III] in the same lecture, at "Now every man etc." (B.1094 b 29), he explains what manner of person the student of this science ought to be. In regard to the initial point he does two things. First [A] he presents in advance certain things necessary to explain his intention. Second [Lect. II, B], at "If our actions etc." (B.1094 a 19), he manifests his intention. In regard to the first he does two things. Initially [1] he shows how it is necessary to start with the end. Then [2], at "Since there are many etc.," he compares habits and acts with the end. On the first point he does three things. He states initially [1, a] that all human beings are ordered to an end. Next [1, b], at "Now a certain diversity etc.," he shows that there can be a number of ends. Last [1, c], at "If the ends are works etc.," he makes a comparison among ends. In regard to the first point he does two things. He states his intention [i]; and then, at "For this reason etc." [ii], he explains his purpose.

8. In regard to the first we should consider that there are two principles of human acts, namely, the intellect or reason and the appetite, which are active principles as explained in the third book De Anima (Ch. XI, 434 a5-a22; St. Th. Lect. XVI, 840-846).[2] The intellect or reason considers both the speculative and the practical. The rational appetite is concerned with choice and execution. Now all these are ordered to some good as to their end; for truth is the end of speculation.

Therefore, in the speculative intellect he includes teaching by which science is conveyed from teacher to student, while in the practical intellect he locates art which is right reason applied to things to be made, as is stated in the sixth book of this work (1153).[1] He indicates that the act of the appetitive intellect is choice, and that execution is "actus." He does not mention prudence, which is in the practical reason together with art, because choice is properly directed by prudence. He says therefore that each of these faculties obviously seeks some good as an end.

9. Then [ii], at "For this reason," he manifests his intention by the effect of good. In regard to this we should bear in mind that good is enumerated among the primary entities to such a degree—according to the Platonists—that good is prior to being. But, in reality, good is convertible with being. Now primary things cannot be understood by anything anterior to them, but by something consequent, as causes are understood through their proper effects. But since good properly is the moving principle of the appetite, good is described as movement of the appetite, just as motive power is usually manifested through motion. For this reason he says that the philosophers have rightly declared that good is what all desire.

10. There is no problem from the fact that some men desire evil. For they desire evil only under the aspect of good, that is, insofar as they think it good. Hence their intention primarily aims at the good and only incidentally touches on the evil.

11. The saying ". . . what all desire" is to be understood not only of those who knowingly seek good but also of beings lacking knowledge.

[1] The marks enclosed in brackets refer to the divisions of Aristotle as given in St. Thomas' Commentary.
[2] Sancti Thomae Aquinatis In Aristotelis Librum De Anima Commentarium. Ed. Pirotta (Turin/Rome: Marietti, 1948).

[1] The Spiazzi Edition gives the reference in such cases to the Commentary and not to the text. We have done the same, since the translation is based on this edition.

These things by a natural desire tend to good, not as knowing the good, but because they are moved to it by something cognitive, that is, under the direction of the divine intellect in the way an arrow speeds towards a target by the aim of the archer. This very tendency to good is the desiring of good. Hence, he says, all beings desire good insofar as they tend to good. But there is not one good to which all tend; this will be explained later (58-59; 108-109). Therefore he does not single out here a particular good but rather discusses good in general. However, because nothing is good except insofar as it is a likeness and participation of the highest good, the highest good itself is in some way desired in every particular good. Thus it can be said that the true good is what all desire.

12. Then [1, b], at **"Now a certain diversity,"** he indicates that there is a diversity of ends. In this we must keep in mind that the final good, to which the inclination of each thing tends, is its ultimate perfection. Now the first perfection is possessed after the manner of a form, but the second perfection by way of an operation. Consequently, there must be this diversity of ends: some are operations and others are the objects achieved, that is, the products which exist apart from the operations.

13. For evidence of this we must consider that activity is of two kinds, as noted in the ninth book of the *Metaphysics* (Ch. 8, 1050 a 23; St. Th. Lect. VIII, 1862-1865). One, which remains in the agent himself, as seeing, wishing and understanding, is an operation of the type properly called "action." The other is an operation passing over into external matter and is properly called "making." Sometimes a person accepts external matter only for use, as a horse for riding and a zither for playing, and at other times he takes external matter to change it into some

other form, as when a carpenter constructs a house or a bed. Accordingly, the first and second of these operations do not have any product which is their term, but each of them is an end. The first, however, is more excellent than the second, inasmuch as it remains in the agent himself. But the third operation is a kind of generation whose term is a thing produced. So, in operations of the third type, the things done are the ends.

14. Then [1, c], at **"If the ends,"** he presents the third type, saying that whenever the products which are extrinsic to the activities are ends, the things produced necessarily are better than the operations that brought them to be, as the thing generated is better than the generative action. The end is more important than the means—in fact, the means have goodness from their relation to the end.

15. Then [2], at **"Since there are many operations,"** he compares habits and acts with the end. In this matter he does four things. First [2, a] he shows that different things are ordered to different ends. He says that, since there are many operations and arts and sciences, there must be different ends for each of them, for the ends and the means are proportional. This he shows by saying that the end of medical art is health; of shipbuilding, navigation; of strategy, victory; and of domestic economy or managing a household, riches. He accepts this last example on the opinion of the majority of men, for he himself proves in the first book of the *Politics* [1] (Ch. 3-4, 1253 b 12-1254 a; St. Th. Lect. II, 46-51; Ch. 9-11, 1256 b 40-1259 a 36; St. Th. Lect. VII-IX, 71-100) that riches are not the end of domestic economy but the instruments thereof.

16. Second [2, b], at **"In all such**

[1] Sancti Thomae Aquinatis, *In Libros Politicorum Aristotelis Expositio.* Ed. Spiazzi (Turin/Rome: Marietti, 1951), pp. 13 sq; pp. 34 sq.

9

skills," he arranges the order of habits among themselves. It happens that one operative habit, which he calls virtue (skill), is subordinated to another, as the art of bridle-making is subordinated to the art of riding because the rider tells the bridle-maker how he should make the bridle. In this way the rider is the designer, that is, the chief producer of the thing itself. The same arguments hold for the other arts making additional equipment needed for riding, such as saddles or the like. The equestrian art is again subordinated to the military, for in ancient times the army included not only mounted soldiers but everyone who fought for victory. Hence under military science there is not only the equestrian but every art or skill ordered to the prosecution of war—archery, ballistics and everything else of this kind. In this same way other arts are subordinated to still others.

17. Third [2, c], at "It follows then," he lays down the order of ends according to the order of habits. He says that in all arts or skills it is commonly true that the architectonic ends are absolutely more desirable to everyone than are the ends of the arts or skills that are subordinated to the chief ends. He proves this from the fact that men follow or seek the ends of the inferior arts or skills for the sake of the ends of the superior. The text, however, is suspensive, and should be read as follows: In all such skills a subordination of one to another is found . . . in all these the architectonic ends etc.

18. Fourth [2, d], at "It does not matter," he shows that it makes no difference in the order of ends, whether the end is a product or an activity. He says that it makes no difference in what pertains to this order that these ends be activities or some product other than the activities, as is evident from the explanation given above (16). The end of bridle-making is a finished bridle; but the end of horsemanship, which is of greater importance, is an operation, that is, riding. The contrary is true in medicine and gymnastics, for the end of medicine is something produced, namely, health. But of gymnastics which is comprised under it, the end is an activity, which is exercise.

LECTURE II

The Supreme End of Human Affairs; Political Science

ANALYTICAL OUTLINE
OF ST. THOMAS

TEXT OF ARISTOTLE
(*B.1094 a 19*)
Chapter 2

B. The philosopher now begins . . . to show what the principal purpose of this science is.

1. HE SHOWS . . . THERE IS SOME SUPREME END OF HUMAN AFFAIRS.

If our actions have an end that we wish for itself and if we wish other things for that end, and not each *20* thing on account of another (for this would involve us in an infinite process making our desire useless and in vain) then obviously that will be not only a good end but a supreme end. *19-22*

2. HE SHOWS THAT IT IS NECESSARY TO KNOW THIS END.

a. He shows that it is necessary for man to know such an end.

A knowledge of it, therefore, will be a great help in human living, for like archers keeping their eye on the target, we will more likely attain our objective. *23*

b. He manifests what man should know about it.

This being the case, we must try to determine the general characteristics of this end and to which of the sciences or skills its study pertains. *24*

3. HE SHOWS TO WHICH SCIENCE THIS KNOWLEDGE BELONGS.

a. He gives a reason in proof of his statement.

It seems undoubtedly to belong to the most truly architectonic science. This, to all appearances, is political science. *25*

b. He proves something that he had previously assumed.
   i. He proves that (political science) is most truly architectonic.
      x. HE ASCRIBES TO POLITICAL SCI-ENCE . . . THE THINGS BELONG-ING TO AN ARCHITECTONIC SCI-ENCE.

Now such a science ordains which studies are to be followed in a *b* state, and who are to pursue them and to what extent. Hence we see the noblest of the operative arts, for example, strategy, domestic economy, and rhetoric fall under political science. **26-28**

Y. FROM THIS HE DRAWS THE CONCLUSION HE INTENDED.

Political science in fact makes use of other practical sciences, even legislating what is to be done and what is not to be done. Its end, therefore, embraces the ends of the other practical sciences. For these reasons, then, this end will be the good of man. **29**

ii. (*He proves*) *that it is most important.*

Even though the good be the same for one man and for the whole state, it seems much better and more perfect to procure and preserve the good of **10** the whole state. It is admirable, indeed, to preserve the good of an individual but it is better still and more divine to do this for a nation and for cities. With such a good as the object of our inquiry we may call our study political science. **30-31**

COMMENTARY OF ST. THOMAS

19. After having stated premises on which his proposition must rest, the Philosopher now begins to manifest it, that is, to show what the principal purpose of this science is [B]. To achieve this he does three things. First [1] he shows from what he has already said, that there is some supreme end of human affairs. Second [2], at "A knowledge of it etc.," he shows that it is necessary to know this end. Third [3], at "It seems undoubtedly," he shows to which science this knowledge belongs. He gives three proofs for the first statement. The principal one is this. Whenever an end is such that we wish other things because of it, and we wish it for itself and not because of something else, then that end is not only a good end but a supreme one. This is obvious from the fact that

an end for the sake of which other ends are sought is of greater importance than they, as is evident from his earlier remarks (16). But it is necessary that there be some such end of human affairs. Therefore, human life or activity has some good end which is supreme.

20. He proves the minor premise by an argument leading to an impossible conclusion. Thus, it is evident from the premises (16) that one end is desired on account of another. Now, either we arrive at some end which is not desired on account of another, or we do not. If we do, the proposition is proved. If, however, we do not find some such end, it follows that every end will be desired on account of another end. In this case we must proceed to infinity. But it is impossible in

ends to proceed to infinity. Therefore, there must be some end that is not desired on account of another.

21. That it is impossible in ends to proceed to infinity is proved also by an argument having an impossible resolution. If we should proceed to infinity in our desire for ends so that one end should always be desired on account of another to infinity, we will never arrive at the point where a man may attain the ends desired. But a man desires fruitlessly what he cannot get; consequently, the end he desires would be useless and vain. But this desire is natural, for it was said above (9) that the good is what all beings naturally desire. Hence it follows that a natural desire would be useless and vain. But this is impossible. The reason is that a natural desire is nothing else but an inclination belonging to things by the disposition of the First Mover, and this cannot be frustrated. Therefore, it is impossible that we should proceed to an infinity of ends.

22. It follows that there must be some ultimate end on account of which all other things are desired, while this end itself is not desired on account of anything else. So there must be some supreme end of human affairs.

23. Then [2], at "A knowledge of it," he shows that the knowledge of this end is necessary for man. He proves this in two steps. First [2, a] he shows that it is necessary for man to know such an end. Second [2, b], at "This being the case etc.," he manifests what man should know about it. He concludes then from what has been said (19-22), that it is necessary for man to know that there is a supreme end of human affairs because this has great importance for life, that is, it is of great help in all phases of human living. This conclusion is apparent for the following reasons. Nothing that is directed to another can be immediately attained by man unless he knows that other to which it is to be directed. An obvious indication of this is found in the example of the archer who shoots straight because he keeps his eye on the target at which he is aiming. Now man's whole life ought to be ordered to the supreme and ultimate end of human life. It is necessary, therefore, to have a knowledge of this end of human life. The explanation is that the reason for the means must always be found in the end itself, as also is proved in the second book of the *Physics* (Ch. 9, 199 b 34-200 b 10; St. Th. Lect. XV, 184-188).[1]

24. Then [2, b], at "This being the case," he shows what ought to be known about that end. He states that inasmuch as the knowledge of the supreme end is necessary for human life, we must determine what is the supreme end, and to which speculative or practical science its study belongs. By sciences he understands the speculative sciences, and by skills the practical sciences since there are principles of some operations. According to him we must make this attempt, in order to suggest the difficulty there is in grasping the ultimate end of human life, as in considering all ultimate causes. He says then that we should understand it in its general outlines, that is, with only the evidence of probability because such a manner of understanding is largely what is available in human things, as he will explain later on (131-134). Now the first of these two belongs to the treatise on this science because such a consideration is about the matter of this science. But the second belongs to the introduction, where its purpose is explained.

25. Therefore when immediately after this material he says "It seems undoubtedly" [3], he shows to which science the consideration of this end should belong. In regard to this he

[1] Sancti Thomae Aquinatis *in Octo Libros Physicorum Aristotelis Expositio.* Ed. Maggiolo (Turin/Rome: Marietti, 1954), pp. 132 sq.

does two things. First [3, a] he gives a reason in proof of his statement. Second [3, b], at "Now such a science etc.," he proves something which he had previously presumed. First then, he states the reason for his proposal, which is this: the supreme end belongs to the most important and most truly architectonic science. This is clear from what was said above, for it was pointed out (16, 20) that the sciences or arts treating of the means to the end are contained under the science or art treating of the end. So it is necessary that the ultimate end should belong to the most important science concerned with the primary and most important end and to the truly architectonic science as directing the others in what they should do. But political science appears to be such, namely, the most important and the most truly architectonic. Therefore, it belongs to it to consider the supreme end.

26. Then [3, b], at **"Now such a science,"** he proves what he had taken for granted: that political science is such a science. First [b, i] he proves that it is most truly architectonic, and next [b, ii], at "For even though the good etc.," that it is most important. He handles the first statement in two ways. First [i, x] he ascribes to political science or politics the things which belong to an architectonic science. Second [i, y] from this he draws the conclusion he intended, at "Political science etc." There are two characteristics of architectonic knowledge. One is that it dictates what is to be done by the art · or science subject to it, as the equestrian art dictates the manner of bridle-making. The other is that it uses it for its own ends. Now the first of these is applicable to politics or political science both in regard to speculative and in regard to practical sciences—in different ways, however. Political science dictates to a practical science both in the matter of its activity, that is, whether or not it should

operate, and in regard to the objects to which its operation is to be directed. It dictates to the smith not only that he use his skill but also that he use it in such a fashion as to make knives of a particular kind. Both (characteristics of architectonic knowledge) are ordered to the end of human living.

27. But political science dictates to a speculative science only as to activity, but not concerning the specification of its proper activity. Political science orders that some teach or learn geometry, and actions of this kind insofar as they are voluntary belong to the matter of ethics and can be ordered to the goal of human living. But the political ruler does not dictate to geometry what conclusions it should draw about a triangle, for this is not subject to the human will nor can it be ordered to human living but it depends on the very nature of things. Therefore, he says that political science ordains which sciences, both practical and speculative, should be studied in a state, who should study them, and for how long.

28. The other characteristic of an architectonic science, the use of subordinate sciences, belongs to political science only in reference to the practical sciences. Hence he adds that we see the most highly esteemed, the noblest skills, i.e., the operative arts, fall under political science—for example strategy, domestic economy, and rhetoric. Political science uses such skills for its own end, that is, for the common good of the state.

29. Then [i, y], at **"Political science in fact,"** he draws a conclusion from two premises. He says that since political science uses the other practical sciences, as already noted (28), and since it legislates what is to be done and what omitted, as previously stated (27), it follows that the end of this science as architectonic embraces or contains under itself the ends of other practical sciences. Hence, he concludes, the end of political science is **the good**

of man, that is, the supreme end of human things.

30. Then [b, ii], at **"For even though the good be the same,"** he shows that political science is the most important science from the very nature of its special end. It is evident that insofar as a cause is prior and more powerful it extends to more effects. Hence, insofar as the good, which has the nature of a final cause, is more powerful, it extends to more effects. So, even though the good be the same objective for one man and for the whole state, it seems much better and more perfect to attain, that is, to procure and preserve the good of the whole state than the good of any one man. Certainly it is a part of that love which should exist among men that a man preserve the good even of a single human being. But it is much better and more divine that this be done for a whole people and for states. It is even sometimes desirable that this be done for one state only, but it is much more divine that it be done for a whole people that includes many states. This is said to be more divine because it shows greater likeness to God who is the ultimate cause of all good. But this good common to one or to several states is the object of our inquiry, that is, of the particular skill called political science. Hence to it, as the most important science, belongs in a most special way the consideration of the ultimate end of human life.

31. But we should note that he says political science is the most important, not simply, but in that division of practical sciences which are concerned with human things, the ultimate end of which political science considers. The ultimate end of the whole universe is considered in theology which is the most important without qualification. He says that it belongs to political science to treat the ultimate end of human life. This however he discusses here since the matter of this book covers the fundamental notions of political science.

LECTURE III

Qualities of the Student and Teacher

ANALYTICAL OUTLINE
OF ST. THOMAS

TEXT OF ARISTOTLE
(*B.1094 b 13*)
Chapter 3

II. HE NOW DETERMINES THE METHOD PROPER TO THIS SCIENCE.

a. On the part of the teacher.

Our study will be adequately treated if it is investigated according to the nature of the subject matter. The same certitude should not be sought in all discussions just as the same exactness should not be expected in all the productions of art. Now good and just deeds, with which political science is concerned, are differently and mistakenly judged to such a degree that none of them seems to be good and just by nature but merely by disposition of law. Because of bad judgment, many have been harmed even by good things: some men have lost their lives by reason of riches, others by reason of physical courage. It is desirable therefore when treating of these variable subjects and when arguing from them as premises, to bring out roughly *20* the outlines of the truth, and to conclude about those things which occur in the majority of cases.   **32-35**

b. On the part of the student.

In this same spirit the student ought to take whatever is taught, for it is proper to an educated man to look for as much certitude in each study as the nature of the subject admits. It approximates the same thing to allow a mathematician to use rhetorical arguments and to demand conclusive demonstrations from a rhetorician.   **36**

III. HE SHOWS WHAT SORT OF PERSON THE STUDENT . . . OUGHT TO BE.

a. Who is an incompetent student.

i. *He introduces certain things nec-*
   essary to explain his proposition.

Now every man is a good judge of the things he knows. Accord- B.1095 ingly, then, one educated in a particular subject judges well what belongs to that subject. But the man who is well educated in all subjects can judge well about all.   37

ii. *He proves his statement.*

In keeping with this a young man is not a good student of political science, for he is inexperienced in the ways of life that are the starting point and subject matter of this science.   38

b. Who is an unprofitable student.

Furthermore, because he is strongly influenced by his emotions, he will study political science without result and uselessly, for the end of this science is not knowledge but human action. Nor does it matter whether the student be immature in age or immature in character, for the deficiency is not due to time but to a life lived according to the passions and to the pursuit of each object of passion. Such men gain no profit from their knowledge; and the same is true of the inconti- 10 nent.   39-40

c. He explains the characteristics of the ideal student.

But it will certainly be very useful to have a knowledge of moral matters for those who desire and act according to the dictates of reason. To sum up what has been treated in the introduction: we have discussed the student, the method of demonstrating and the purpose of our science.   41-42

COMMENTARY OF ST. THOMAS

32. After the Philosopher has shown what is the good principally intended in this science, he now [II] determines the method proper to this science. He does this first on the part of the teacher [II, a]; and then, at "In the same spirit etc.," on the part of the student [II, b]. In regard to the first he lays down this reason. The method of manifesting truth in any science ought to be suit-

able to the subject matter of that science. He shows this from the fact that certitude cannot be found, nor should it be sought, in the same degree in all discussions where we reason about anything. Likewise, the same method is not used in all products made by art; but each workman works with the material in a way suited to that material, in one way with the soil, in another with clay, in still another with metal. Now the matter of moral study is of such a nature that perfect certitude is not suitable to it. He shows this from two classes of things which seem to belong to the material with which moral study is concerned.

33. In the matter of morals the first and foremost place is held by virtuous works. They are called just and are the chief concern of political science. Regarding them there are no agreed opinions, but rather a decided difference is found in what men judge about them. In this matter a variety of errors occur, for certain actions, considered just and good by some, are looked upon as unjust and bad by others according to different times and places and persons. Now a deed is considered vicious at one time and in one country, but at a different time and in a different country it is not considered to be so. Because of this disagreement, it happens that some are of the opinion that no action is just or good by nature but only by disposition of law. We shall treat more fully of this opinion in the second book of this work (245-254).

34. Second, external goods that are used purposively by men have a moral consideration. In regard to them it happens that we find the mistake just mentioned inasmuch as these material goods are not always used in the same way by everyone. Some men are helped by them, while others indeed are harmed by them. Many are ruined by having riches—for instance, those who are murdered by robbers. Some by reason of their physical courage on

which they rely have carelessly exposed themselves to dangers. Thus it is evident that moral matters are variable and divergent, not having the same certitude each time.

35. Because, in the art of demonstrative science, principles must conform to conclusions, it is desirable and preferable when treating subjects so variable, and when proceeding from premises likewise variable, to bring out the truth first in a rough outline by applying universal principles to singulars and by proceeding from the simple (universal) to the complex (particular) where acts are concerned. For it is necessary in every practical science to proceed in a composite (i.e., deductive) manner. On the contrary in speculative science, it is necessary to proceed in an analytical manner by breaking down the complex into elementary principles. Second, we should bring out the outlines of the truth, that is, an approximation to the truth. This is to proceed from the proper principles of this science. Moral science treats the acts of the will, and the thing moving the will is not only the good but even fictitious good. Third, we must speak of events as they happen in the majority of cases, that is, of voluntary acts that proceed from the will, inclined perhaps to one alternative rather than another but never operating under compulsion. In these, too, we must proceed in such a way that principles are conformable to conclusions.

36. Then [II, b], at **"In this same spirit,"** he shows that the student must accept this limitation in moral matters. He says that it is proper that each one should take whatever is said to him by another in the same spirit, that is, as the matter warrants. The reason is that a learned or well-instructed man should look for as much certitude in any matter as the nature of the subject admits. There cannot be as much certainty in variable and contingent

matter as in necessary matter which is always the same. Therefore, the educated man ought not to look for greater, nor be satisfied with less, certitude than is appropriate to the subject under discussion. It seems an equal fault to allow a mathematician to use rhetorical arguments and to demand from a rhetorician conclusive demonstrations such as a mathematician should give. But mistakes happen because the method appropriate to the matter is not considered. Mathematics is concerned with matter in which perfect certitude is found. Rhetoric, however, deals with political matter where a variety of views occurs.

37. Then [III], at **"Now every man,"** he shows what sort of person the student of this science ought to be. First [III, a] he shows who is an incompetent student; and second [III, b], at "Furthermore etc.," who is an unprofitable student. Third [III, c], at "But it will certainly etc.," he explains the characteristics of the ideal student. In respect to the first he does two things. First [a, i] he introduces certain things necessary to explain his proposition. He states that each man can judge well only the things he knows. Thus a man educated in one particular subject can judge well what belongs to that subject. But the man who is well educated in all subjects can judge well about all, without restriction to a particular subject.

38. Second [a, ii], at **"In keeping with this,"** he proves his statement, namely, that a young man is not a good student of political science nor of any part of moral science comprised under political science, because as was said (37) a man can judge well only the things he knows. Now every student should make good judgments about what he studies, so that he may accept what is true but not what is false. Therefore, no one can be a good student unless he has some knowledge of what he ought to study. But a young man does not have a knowledge of things belonging to moral science, which are known mostly by experience. A young man is inexperienced in the ways of life because of the very brevity of his life, while the principles of moral science proceed from what pertains to and also treats of the actions of human life. For instance, if it be said that the generous man keeps the cheaper things for himself and makes a present of the more expensive to others, a young man will perhaps judge this not to be true because of inexperience. It is the same with other social dealings. Hence it is evident that a young man is not a good student of political science.

39. Then [III, b], at **"Furthermore,"** he shows who is an unprofitable student of this science. Here we must consider that moral science teaches men to follow reason and to refrain from the things to which the passions incline, such as concupiscence, anger, and the like. Toward these, men are inclined in two ways. In one way by choice, for instance, when a man of set purpose intends to satisfy his concupiscence. Such a one he calls a slave of his emotions. In another way, when a man resolves to abstain from harmful pleasures but is sometimes overcome by the urge of passion, so that contrary to his resolution he follows the promptings of passion. A man of this type is said to be incontinent.

40. He affirms then that the one who is ruled by the emotions will study this science in vain, that is, without any result and uselessly without attaining its proper end. The end of this science is not knowledge alone, which those enslaved to passion can perhaps gain. But the end of this science, as of all practical sciences, is human action. Now those who follow the emotions do not attain virtuous acts. So in regard to this it makes no difference whether the student of this science is immature in age or immature in character, that

is, a slave of the emotions. The reason is that, as the person immature in age fails to achieve the end of this science that is knowledge, so the immature in character fails to achieve the end that is action. His deficiency is not due to time but to the fact that he lives according to his emotions, seeking everything to which the emotions incline. Now, for such men the knowledge of this science is useless; the same may be said of the incontinent who do not act in accord with their knowledge of moral matters.

41. Then [III, c], at **"But it will certainly,"** he indicates the good student of this science. He says that it is very useful to have a knowledge of moral matters for those who regulate their desires and act in externals according to the dictates of reason.

42. Last, in the conclusion he sums up what has been discussed in the introduction (1-41), stating that certain things have been said in a preliminary manner about the student—this was treated last; stating also what is the method of demonstrating—this was treated in the middle of the introduction; and last what is our purpose, namely, what is the principal aim of this science—this was treated first.

LECTURE IV

Opinions About Happiness

ANALYTICAL OUTLINE
OF ST. THOMAS

TEXT OF ARISTOTLE
(*B.1095 a 15*)
Chapter 4

I. FIRST HE EXPLAINS HIS INTENTION.

> Since all knowledge and choice have some good for their objective, let us ask on resuming our inquiry what it is that we call the objective of political science? What is the highest good of all human actions?　**43**

II. HE CARRIES IT OUT.

A. He investigates the opinions of others about happiness.

A' He gives the opinions of others.

I. HE PRESENTS OPINIONS ABOUT THE ULTIMATE END OF HUMAN ACTIONS.

a. He indicates the aspects of general agreement.

> As to the name nearly all agree, for both the common people and the educated say it is happiness. They *20* identify happiness with living well and acting well.　**44-45**

b. He shows in what way there is disagreement.

> But as to where happiness is to be found men are at variance. The multitude differs from the philosophers, for the people generally think that happiness consists in something apparent and obvious such as pleasure or riches or honors; some place it in one of these, others in another; and oftentimes even the same person shifts his position. For instance, the sick man thinks happiness is found in health, the poor man considers that it is found in riches, while men conscious of their own ignorance esteem those happy who give utterance to lofty ideas that are above their comprehension. Some philosophers [1] were

[1] The Platonists.

of the opinion that, over and above the many goods, there exists an absolute good which is the cause of goodness in all other things.   **46-49**

2. HE POINTS OUT HOW WE SHOULD EXAMINE OPINIONS OF THIS KIND.

a. He shows which of these opinions we ought to investigate.

It is perhaps vain to examine all these opinions, and it will be sufficient to give special attention to those appearing probable on the surface *30* or are thought by many to have some probability.   **50**

b. He shows in what order we should do this.

In this matter we should be aware of the difference in arguments, some of which proceed from principles and others to principles. Previously Plato had learnedly discussed the subject when he examined the question whether we proceed from or to principles like athletes in the race- *b* course running from or toward the judges. In either case we must start from things known. Now these are of two kinds, namely, things known to us and things known absolutely. Presumably then we should begin from what is known to us.   **51-52**

c. He shows how the student should be disposed.

One who is going to devote himself seriously to the study of good and just deeds and to political affairs in general ought to have been accustomed to a virtuous life. This will serve as a principle and if it be adequate he will have no need to know the reasons for virtuous conduct. A student with this upbringing will discover working principles within himself or readily acquire them from someone else. The man, however, who can do neither of these things should listen to the verdict of Hesiod.[1] That man, the poet says, is best who understands everything by himself; and that man good who takes what is well *10* said by another. But he who neither himself understands nor takes to heart what he hears from another is indeed a useless fellow.   **53-54**

---

[1] *Works and Days*, 293 sq.

COMMENTARY OF ST. THOMAS

43. Having finished the introduction, Aristotle here begins the treatise on the science itself. He divides the treatise into three parts. In the first part he investigates happiness, which is the supreme human good, and he comes to the conclusion from a study of the subject that happiness is activity flowing from virtue. In the second part [Lect. XIX] he discusses virtues at "If then happiness is a kind of operation according to perfect virtue etc." (B.1102 a 4). In the third part he completes his treatise on happiness, explaining which operation it is and of what nature. This he does in the tenth book (B.1172 a 19) at "After these matters we ought perhaps next to discuss pleasure." In regard to the first he does two things. First [I] he explains his intention. Second [II], at "As to the name etc.," he carries it out. He says first, resuming what he was investigating before (9-13), that since all knowledge and choice aim at some good, that is, are ordered to some desired good as an end, we must discuss the nature of that good to which political science is ordered. Such is the highest good of all actions, that is, the highest among those attainable by human operation. Moreover, it was said above (18) that these two notions must be studied about the ultimate end of human good; what it is—this is here proposed for consideration—and to what science it belongs and this was treated above in the introduction (25-30).

44. Next [II], at "As to the name," he treats happiness. He proceeds here in two steps. First [A] he investigates the opinions of others about happiness. Second [Lect. IX], at "Let us return again to a consideration etc." (B.1097 a 16), he states his own opinion. In regard to the initial point he does two things. First [A'] he gives the opinions of others about happiness. Second [Lect. V; I], at "Let us return to the subject etc." (B.1095 b 12), he examines these opinions. He handles the first point in two ways. Initially [1] he presents opinions about the ultimate end of human actions. Then [2], at "It is perhaps vain," he points out how we should examine opinions of this kind. In regard to the first he does two things. He indicates the aspects of general agreement [1, a]; and then [1, b], at "But as to where happiness etc.," he shows in what way there is disagreement.

45. In the beginning he presents two points on which there is general agreement about the ultimate end. First [1, a], at "As to the name," he asserts that both the many, that is, the common people and the cultured or philosophers, name happiness the highest human good. Second, they have a common understanding of the term because all consider that living well and acting well are identified with being happy.

46. Then [1, b], at "But as to where happiness," he shows in what respect the opinions of men differ about happiness. He affirms that especially about the nature of happiness men are at variance, i.e., hold different opinions. This difference is threefold. First of all the multitude does not think in this matter like the philosophers. People commonly consider that happiness consists in something apparent and obvious among the objects of sense,

which alone are evident to the multitude and, therefore, so obvious as not to need exhaustive search—such as pleasure, riches, honor, and the like. The views of the philosophers on this point are given later (49).

47. The second difference is found among the common people themselves. Some of them place happiness in one sensible good, others in another. The avaricious place it in riches, the self-indulgent in pleasures, the ambitious in honors.

48. The third difference arises from the end in itself. Since it is characteristic of the ultimate end that it be greatly desired, people consider that to be happiness which is desired most of all. Now, need of a good increases the desire for it, and so the sick man who lacks health judges the supreme good to be health; the beggar looks upon riches in the same way. Likewise those who are conscious of their own ignorance esteem as happy others who give utterance to lofty ideas which are above the comprehension of the ignorant. All this pertains to the opinion of the multitude.

49. But some among the philosophers, the Platonists, were of the opinion that, over and above the many different sensible goods, there exists one which is absolute good and which is the separated essence of goodness itself. As the separated form of man was called by them "man in himself" so the separated good was "good in itself," and this is the cause of the goodness of all other things as they partake of that highest good.

50. Then [2], at "It is perhaps vain," he shows how we should proceed in our investigation of the aforesaid opinions. He handles the discussion in three steps. First [2, a] he shows which of these opinions we ought to investigate. Second [2, b], at "In this matter we should etc.," he shows in what order we should do this. Third [2, c] he shows how the

student should be disposed so that he may properly understand what is taught. He says then that to examine all opinions men hold about happiness would be useless for a good philosopher, inasmuch as some of them are altogether unreasonable. But it suffices to examine at most the opinions that on the surface are probable either because they give that appearance or at least are considered to have weight by many.

51. Then [2, b], at "In this matter we should be aware," he shows in what order we must discuss opinions of this sort and in general all moral matters. He points out a difference in the manner of reasoning. There are some argumentations proceeding from principles, that is, from causes to effects, such as demonstrations of the reasoned fact (*propter quid*). On the contrary, there are other argumentations proceeding from effects to causes or principles. These do not produce a demonstration of the reasoned fact but only of the fact (*quia*). This distinction was previously made by Plato when he inquired whether we should proceed from or to principles. Then he offers this example from the racecourse. In order to judge athletes running in a race certain agonothetes or judges were stationed at the beginning of the course. Sometimes the athletes started from the judges and ran to the finishing line, and sometimes they started from the end and ran toward the judges. Likewise there is a twofold order in the process of reasoning.

52. In order to know the order of procedure in any subject we should reflect that it is necessary to begin from what is better understood. Through things better known we arrive at a knowledge of things unknown. Now things are said to be better known in two ways. Some are better known in regard to us such as the composite and the sensible; oth-

ers are better known absolutely and in themselves, as the simple and the intelligible. Because we acquire knowledge by reasoning, we must proceed from what is better known to us. Now if the better known absolutely are the same as the better known to us, the reason proceeds from principles as in mathematics. If, however, the better known absolutely are different from the better known to us, then we must use the effect-to-cause procedure as in the natural and moral sciences.

53. Then [2, c], at "One who is going," he shows how a student of such subjects should be disposed. He says that since in moral matters we ought to begin from what is better known to us, that is, from certain effects noted about human acts, a man who wishes to be a competent student of moral science must be well-informed and experienced in the ways of human living, that is about external good and just actions or works of virtue, and in general about all civil matters like laws and political affairs and other things of this sort. The reason for this is that in moral matters we must take as a principle that a thing is so. For example, we accept from experience and custom that concupiscence is restrained by fasting.

54. If this is obvious to someone it is not so necessary for him in acting to understand the total explanation. Thus to effect a cure a physician need know only that this medicine cures a particular malady. But to know the reason, we must have a scientific knowledge that is sought chiefly in speculative sciences. Now one who is skilled in human affairs either discovers working principles for himself and sees them as self-evident, or he readily acquires them from someone else. But a man about whom neither of these things can be correctly said should listen to the verdict of the poet Hesiod. He calls that man best who can understand by himself, and that man good who takes what is said by another. But the man who is capable neither of understanding by himself nor of bearing in mind what he hears from another is useless as far as acquiring a science is concerned.

LECTURE V

Examination of the Opinions

ANALYTICAL OUTLINE   TEXT OF ARISTOTLE
OF ST. THOMAS   (*B.1095 b 12*)
                       Chapter 5

I. HE EXAMINES THE OPINION OF THOSE DISCUSSING HAPPINESS FROM THE MORAL POINT OF VIEW . . .

A. He lays down a notion that opinions on the subject have in common.

> Let us return to the subject from which we have disgressed. Some seem to think, not without reason, that the supreme good called happiness is a good belonging to this life. **55**

B. He begins to investigate the variety of opinions.

A' He examines the opinions that seem more likely to be true.

I. HE EXAMINES THE OPINION THAT PLACES HAPPINESS IN . . . A LIFE OF PLEASURE.

a. He presents the opinion.

> Now, most men, including some very eminent persons, place happiness in pleasure and so logically prefer a sensual life. **56-57**

b. He distinguishes three types of life.

> There are indeed three very prominent types of life: that just mentioned, another called public life, and last the contemplative life. **58-59**

c. He examines the truth of the opinion presented.
   i. He disproves it.

> The majority of men seem quite *20* bestial in choosing to live a life of pleasure. **60**

   ii. He advances a reason why some are drawn to this life.

> They justify their choice on the plea that many in high places share the tastes of Sardanapalus. **61**

2. HE EXAMINES THE OPINION THAT PLACES HAPPINESS IN THE THINGS PERTAINING TO PUBLIC LIFE.

a. In regard to honor.

  i. Presenting the opinion, he notes . . .

Men of superior refinement, however, and those occupied in the active life, place happiness in honor, **62** for honor seems to be nearly the whole purpose of public life. **63**

  ii. He offers a reason for this.

  iii. He disproves this opinion.

    x. FIRST (REASON).

But this seems too superficial to be the good we are looking for. Honor consists in the action of those rendering it rather than anything in the power of the person honored; while happiness certainly should be a good proper to man and a thing not easily taken from him. **64**

    y. SECOND REASON.

Another reason is that men appear to seek honor to convince themselves of their own good qualities. They strive to be honored by the prudent, by those who know them best and for their virtue. Obviously then, in their opinion, virtue is a better thing than honor. **65**

b. In regard to virtue.

  i. The opinion.

From this someone may con- *30* clude that virtue rather than honor is the end of public life. **66**

  ii. He rejects this (first).

But apparently virtue too is lacking in perfection because a man may have a habit of virtue when he is asleep or when he has no opportunity to exercise its acts for a lifetime. **67**

  iii. He gives the second reason.

Moreover, he may be subject to evils and very often may be *B.1096* ill-favored by fortune. No one would call such a man happy, unless he were merely defending an argumentative position. Enough has now been said, for we treated the subject sufficiently in the *Encyclis*. **68**

3. HE MENTIONS THE CONTEMPLATIVE LIFE.

Later on we shall investigate the third type of life, the contemplative. **69**

B' He examines an opinion rather remote from the truth.

I. HE EXAMINES ANOTHER OPINION . . . WHICH PLACES HAPPINESS . . . IN MONEY.

a. He rejects it . . . first.

b. He gives the second reason.

As to the accumulator of riches, he lives a life of constraint;   **70-71**
and riches themselves are not the good we seek, for they are merely useful and sought for the sake of something else. Rather therefore the things previously treated are considered ends, since they are desired for them- *10* selves. Yet even these are not the supreme good and happiness, although many arguments have been marshalled to prove this. But these discussions must be terminated now.

72

COMMENTARY OF ST. THOMAS

55. After the Philosopher has recounted the different opinions about happiness, he begins to investigate the truth of these opinions. First [I] he examines the opinion of those discussing happiness from the moral point of view who place happiness in some good of this life. Second [Lect. VI], at "Perhaps it will be better" (B.1096 a 12), he examines the opinion of those who do not discuss happiness from the moral point of view but place it in some separated good. In regard to the first he does two things. He lays down a notion [A] that opinions on this subject have in common; and next [B], at "Now, most men," he begins to investigate the variety of opinions. Then, because the Philosopher seemed to have made a digression from his principal purpose while he was determining the mode of procedure, he returns to the point whence he had digressed, that is, to the opinions about happiness. He asserts that some seem

to think, not without reason, that the final good called happiness is a good belonging to this life on the purely human level. This is the goal of all the works of life. Now, means are proportionate to that end. Hence it is probable that happiness is among the number of goods belonging to this life. But what the truth may be in this matter will be indicated later (60, 64, 65, 70-72).

56. Next [B], at **"Now, most men,"** he searches for the truth about the things on which the opinions differ. In regard to this he does two things. First [A'] he examines the opinions that seem more likely to be true. Second [B'], at "As to the accumulator of riches etc.," he examines an opinion rather remote from the truth. In regard to the first he does three things. First [1] he examines the opinion placing happiness in the things that pertain to a life of pleasure. Second [2], at "Men of superior refinement etc.,"

he examines the opinion placing happiness in the things pertaining to public life. Third [3], at "Later on we shall investigate etc.," he mentions the contemplative life. In regard to the first he does three things. First [A', 1, a] he presents the opinion. Second [A', 1, b], at "There are indeed three etc.," he distinguishes three types of life without elaborating on them. Third [A', 1, c], at "The majority of men etc.," he examines the truth of the opinion presented.

57. He says then in the first place that some men, from the goods of this life, choose pleasure and place happiness in it. They include not only the majority or the common people who by and large favor pleasure, but also persons eminent either in knowledge and teaching or in uprightness of life. Even the Epicureans, who considered pleasure the highest good, carefully cultivated the virtues. They did so, however, on account of pleasure, that is, for fear their pleasure would be hindered by means of contrary vices. The vice of gluttony, for instance, causes bodily suffering through excessive eating; because of theft a man is thrown into prison. So different vices are an impediment to pleasure in different ways. Since then the ultimate end is exceedingly delectable, they who make pleasure the highest good intensely love the life of pleasure.

58. Then [A', 1, b], at "There are indeed three," he distinguishes three types of life: the sensual just mentioned, the public, and the contemplative. These he calls the most prominent types. For evidence of this we must now bear in mind what will later be discussed in the ninth book (1944-1949), that every man thinks his life to be that to which he is most strongly drawn, as the philosopher to philosophizing, the hunter to hunting, and so on. Because man is most strongly drawn to the last end, it is necessary that the types of life be distinguished according to the diversity of the ultimate end. Now the end has the nature of good, and good is threefold: the useful, the pleasurable, and the virtuous or honorable. Two of these, namely, the pleasurable and the virtuous or honorable, have the nature of end because both are desirable for their own sake. That indeed is called virtuous which is good according to reason, and this has pleasure attached to it. Hence the pleasurable, as distinguished from the virtuous, is so called in reference to the senses. Reason, we must remember, is both speculative and practical.

59. Therefore, that life is called sensual which fixes its end in the pleasures of the senses; and that public which fixes its end in the good of the practical reason, for example, in the exercise of virtuous deeds; and that contemplative which fixes its end in the good of the speculative reason or in the contemplation of truth.

60. Next [A', 1, c], at "The majority of men," he examines the opinion cited above. In regard to this he does two things. First [c, i] he disproves it. Second [c, ii], at "They justify their choice etc.," he advances a reason why some are drawn to this life. In regard to the first we must consider that the sensual life, which fixes its end in sense pleasure, necessarily has to place that end in those very intense pleasures following from the natural operations by which the individual is preserved by eating and drinking and the race by sexual intercourse. Now pleasures of this kind are found in both men and beasts. It follows then that the multitude of men who fix their end in such pleasures seem quite bestial in choosing a life which even the pigs enjoy. If the happiness of man would consist in this, dumb animals enjoying the pleasure of food and sexual intercourse would have to be called happy for the same reason. Assuming that happiness is

a characteristically human good, it cannot possibly consist in these things.

61. Then [c, ii], at **"They justify their choice,"** he gives the reason why some hold this opinion. He says that the reason they offer is that many in high places, like kings and princes who are considered very happy by the common people, share the tastes of a certain Assyrian king named Sardanapalus who was much given to sensuality. On this account it is thought that pleasure is something very good since it is a thing highly esteemed by the great.

62. At **"Men of superior refinement"** [2] he investigates opinions concerning the active or public life. First [2, a] he does this in regard to honor; and second [2, b], at "From this someone etc.," in regard to virtue. This is a reasonable procedure, for the active or public life aims at the honorable good. Now it is called honorable as pertaining to the state of honor. Hence both honor itself and virtue, which is the cause of honor, appear to belong to it. In regard to the first he does three things. First [2, a, i], in presenting the opinion, he notes that persons of superior refinement, namely, the virtuous and those occupied in the active life, place happiness in honor.

63. Second [2, a, ii], at **"for honor seems,"** he offers a reason for this: the sole purpose of public life appears to be honor which is rendered as a reward to the politically successful. Therefore, for those engaged in public life happiness probably seems to consist in honor.

64. Third [2, a, iii], at **"But this seems,"** he disproves this opinion by two reasons. In the first [iii, x] of these he says that in a way we divine the true nature of happiness, that is, we surmise happiness to be a good proper to the happy man, a thing belonging preeminently to him and taken from him with difficulty. But this is not true of honor which seems rather to consist in the action of the one rendering the honor, and to be in his power rather than in the power of the one honored. Therefore honor is something more extrinsic and superficial than the good we are seeking, which is happiness.

65. He gives the second reason at **"Another reason"** [iii, y]. Happiness is some very good thing which is not sought on account of another. But there is something better than honor, namely, that on account of which honor is sought. Men appear to seek honor in order to confirm the solid opinion they have formed of themselves that they are good men and that they may be assured of this by the judgment of others. They look, therefore, for honor from prudent men with correct judgment and from those who know them best and can be better judges. Hence they seek to be honored for their virtue, which is the source of man's good, as will be shown in the second book (307-308). So virtue, for whose sake honor is sought, is a better thing than honor. It follows then that happiness does not consist in honor.

66. Then [2, b], at **"From this someone,"** he investigates the opinion of those who place happiness in virtue. In regard to this he does two things. First [2, b, i] he states the opinion and says that perhaps someone will think, by reason of what was just said, that virtue rather than honor is the end of public life.

67. Second [2, b, ii], at **"But apparently,"** he rejects this for two reasons. The first is that happiness seems to be a most perfect good. But virtue is not of such a nature, for sometimes it is found without the perfection of activity, as we see in those who are asleep and yet have the habit of virtue. It is possible, too, that a man may have the habit of virtue, but for lack of opportunity not perform a single

act of a particular virtue during his whole life. This is particularly evident regarding magnanimity and magnificence, virtues perhaps possessed by a poverty-stricken person who is never able to perform great deeds. Therefore virtue is not the same as happiness.

68. He gives the second reason at "Moreover he may be" [2, b, iii]. It is this. It happens that one who has the habit of virtue may be ill-favored by fortune. Who will call such a man happy except someone obstinately defending a thesis against the plain truth? Therefore happiness is not the same as virtue. This, he says, is sufficient for his purpose. Enough has been said on the subject in his *Encyclis,* that is, in certain learned verses that Aristotle composed on happiness.

69. Then [3], at "Later on we shall investigate," he mentions the contemplative life, saying that it will be investigated later on in the tenth book (2086-2125).

70. At "As to the accumulator of riches" [B', 1], he examines another opinion, less probable, which places happiness in a thing which has the nature of a useful good, money. But this is incompatible with the nature of an ultimate end, for a thing is called useful because it is ordered to an end. However, since money has an over-all utility in respect of temporal goods, the opinion that places happiness in money has some probability.

71. But he rejects it for two reasons [B', 1, a]. The first is that money is acquired under coercion and is parted with under coercion. But this is not in keeping with happiness, which is the goal of voluntary operations. Consequently happiness does not consist in money.

72. He gives the second reason [B', 1, b] at "and riches themselves." It is this. We look for happiness as a good that is not sought for something else. But money is sought for something beyond itself since it is by its nature a useful good, as was just said (70). Therefore happiness does not consist in money.

73. A further conclusion notes that pleasure, honor, and virtue, all of which were treated above (57-72), can be considered ultimate ends at least in the sense that they are sought for themselves, as was said (57, 61, 63, 70). However, the ultimate end is not to be found in these, as has been shown (57-72), although many arguments have been marshalled by various philosophers to prove that happiness consists in these goods. But these discussions must be terminated.

LECTURE VI

Happiness and a Separated Good

ANALYTICAL OUTLINE   TEXT OF ARISTOTLE
OF ST. THOMAS   (*B.1096 a 12*)
                              Chapter 6

A. He disproves the opinion of those placing it in a separated good.

I. HE SHOWS THE NECESSITY OF DISCUSSING THIS OPINION.

a. He suggests the advantage of this inquiry.

Perhaps it will be better to investigate thoroughly the existence of the universal good and to inquire about its nature,   **74**

b. He points out . . . an unpleasant aspect of the investigation.

even if the investigation has become unpleasant owing to the fact that the doctrine of ideas was introduced by good friends.   **75**

c. He shows that this should not deter us from seeking the truth.

However, it seems indeed better, and in fact especially obligatory on philosophers, to sacrifice even the rights of friendship for the sake of truth. While it is commendable to have love for both, we ought to honor truth as sacred above friends.   **76-78**

2. HE BEGINS TO DISPROVE IT.

a. He shows there is no one common idea or form of good.
   i. *There cannot be one common idea of good.*
      X. THE FIRST . . . ARGUMENT.

Those who hold this opinion did not postulate ideas in which priority and posteriority were found. On this *20* account they made no provision for an idea of numbers. Now good is found in the category of substance and quality and relation. But being in itself, i.e., substance, is naturally prior to being in reference to something else, for the latter is likened to an offspring of being and an accident of it. Therefore there will not be any common idea for these.   **79-80**

Y. HE LAYS DOWN THE SECOND
REASON.

Z. HE GIVES THE THIRD REASON.

Furthermore, good is convertible with being. For good is predicated of substance such as God and intellect. It is predicated of quality such as virtues, of quantity such as the mean, of relation such as the useful, of time such as the opportune, of place such as a summerhouse, and so on. Hence it is obvious that one common idea of good that is universal does not exist. Otherwise good would not be found in every category but in one alone. **81**

Moreover, because a single sci- *30* ence treats things falling under one idea, there would have to be a single science of all good things. But we have many sciences, even of things contained in one category like time, for the opportune is studied in war by strategy, in disease by medicine, and in exercise by gymnastics. **82**

COMMENTARY OF ST. THOMAS

74. After the Philosopher has rejected the opinion of those who place happiness in one of the obvious goods, here [A] he disproves the opinion of those placing it in a separate good. In regard to this he does two things. First [1] he shows the necessity of discussing this opinion. Second [2] he begins to disprove it. In regard to the first he does three things. First [1, a] he suggests the advantage of this inquiry. Second [1, b], at "even if the investigation etc.," he points out what may seem an unpleasant aspect of the investigation. Third [1, c], at "However, it seems etc.," he shows that this should not deter us from seeking the truth. In regard to the first we must consider that the separated good, in which the Platonists asserted that man's happiness consists, was called a universal good. By participation in it all

things are said to be good. Hence he says that perhaps it is better to investigate thoroughly the existence of this universal good and to inquire what its nature is than to discuss the opinions mentioned before. The investigation of the good is more philosophical and more properly belongs to the discussion of the true good and the ultimate end than do the opinions considered in themselves. If, however, they be considered according to our stated intention of inquiring about the opinions mentioned above, it would seem to be more in agreement with our plan. On this account he uses "perhaps," an adverb indicating doubt.

75. Then [1, b], at **"even if the investigation,"** he states what might deter him from an investigation of this opinion. He says that the investigation is made reluctantly because the opin-

ion was introduced by friends of his, the Platonists. He himself was a disciple of Plato, and by rejecting this opinion he might seem to disparage his teacher. He raises the point here rather than in his other works where he likewise rejects the opinion of Plato because the repudiation of the opinion of a friend is not contrary to truth, which is the principal object in speculative sciences. It is, however, contrary to good morals, the subject discussed in this book.

76. Then [1, c], at **"However, it seems indeed better,"** he shows that this consideration ought not to deter him. The reason is that it seems to be better, meaning more honorable and in agreement with good morals, and indeed obligatory, that a man should not hesitate to oppose his friends for the sake of truth. It is so necessary for good morals that without it virtue cannot be preserved. Unless a man prefer truth to his friends, it follows that he will make false judgment and bear false witness in their defense. This is contrary to virtue. While reason prescribes that all men should prefer truth to their friends, this holds in a special way for the philosophers whose calling is to study wisdom, which is knowledge of the truth.

77. That truth should be preferred to friends he proves in this way. He is the greater friend for whom we ought to have the greater consideration. Although we should have friendship for both truth and our fellow man, we ought rather to love truth because we should love our fellow man especially on account of truth and virtue, as will be shown in the eighth book (1575-1577). Now truth is a most excellent friend of the sort to whom the homage of honor is due. Besides, truth is a divine thing, for it is found first and chiefly in God. He concludes, therefore, that it is virtuous to honor truth above friends.

78. Andronicus, the peripatetic, says that piety makes men faithful to and observant of the things of God. Along the same line is the judgment of Plato who, in rejecting the opinion of his teacher Socrates, says a man ought to care more for truth than anything else. Somewhere else too he affirms that while Socrates is certainly his friend, truth is still more so. In yet another place he says that we should have some care for the views of Socrates but more for truth.

79. Then [2], at **"Those who hold his opinion,"** he rejects the position of Plato who maintains that the happiness of man consists in a common idea or form of good. In regard to this he does two things. First [2, a] he shows there is no one common idea or form of good. Second [Lect. VIII; 2, b], at "But perhaps we should etc." (B.1096 b 29), he shows that even if there were, human happiness would not consist in it. In regard to the first he does two things. First [2, a, i] he shows that there cannot be one common idea of good. Second [Lect. VII; 2, a, ii], at "Someone will rightly etc." (B.1096 a 34), he examines the manner of speaking used by the Platonists when they talk about this idea. In regard to the first we must consider that Aristotle does not intend to reject the opinion insofar as Plato maintained a separated good on which all good would depend. In the twelfth book of the *Metaphysics* (Ch. 10, 1075 a 11 sq.; St. Th. Lect. XII, 2627-2663), Aristotle expressly mentions a good, separated from the universe, to which the whole universe is ordered as an army is ordered to the good of the general. He does reject the opinion insofar as Plato held that the separated good is an idea common to all goods. He uses three reasons to disprove the opinion.

80. The first [i, x] of these is taken from the argument of the Platonists themselves who did not postulate an idea for these classes of things in which priority and posteriority are found, as

is the case with numbers, for two is naturally prior to three. So the Platonists did not hold that number in general would have a separated idea. They did, though, place separated ideas for individual numbers, for example, two, three and so on. The reason for this is that the things in which priority and posteriority are found do not seem to be of one order and consequently do not partake of one idea. But among good things there is priority and posteriority. This is clear from the fact that good is found in the *quodquidest* or substance, and likewise in quality and also in other genera. Now it is evident that what is being in itself, such as substance, is naturally prior to all those things that have being only in relation to substance—as quantity, which is the measure of substance; quality, which is the disposition of substance; and relation, which is the reference of substance. The same is true in other categories that are all, as it were, the offspring of being or substance. This is being in the full sense, and from it are engendered and derived all other genera, which are called being to the extent that they are accidents of a substance. From this he concludes that there cannot be a common idea of good.

81. He lays down the second reason [i, y] at **"Furthermore, good etc."** To understand this we must know that Plato held the "idea" to be the "ratio" or nature and essence of all things that partake of the idea. It follows from this that there cannot be one idea of things not having a common nature. But the various categories do not have one common nature, for nothing is predicated of them univocally. Now good, like being with which it is convertible, is found in every category. Thus the *quodquidest* or substance, God, in whom there is no evil, is called good; the intellect, which is always true, is called good. In quality good is predicated of virtue, which makes its possessor good; in quantity, of the mean, which is the good in everything subject to measure. In relation, good is predicated of the useful which is good relative to a proper end. In time, it is predicated of the opportune; and in place, of a location suitable for walking as a summerhouse. The same may be said of other categories. It is clear, therefore, that there is not some one good that is the idea or the common "ratio" of all goods. Otherwise good would not be found in every category but in one alone.

82. He gives the third reason at **"Moreover, because etc."** [i, z]. To understand this we must know the following. Things existing outside the mind, according to Plato, acquire the form of genus or species by participating in the "idea" so that the mind does not know a stone except by participating in the "idea" of stone. The mind in this way partakes of science and knowledge of those things when the "forms" or "ideas" of them are impressed in it. It follows that there is a single science of all the things that partake of one "idea." If, therefore, there be one "idea" of all goods, it will belong to the study of one science. But we see that this is false even in regard to the goods belonging to a single category. He adds this for fear that someone may specify sciences according to the diversity of categories. We see, however, that strategy studies the opportune in war, medicine studies it in disease, and gymnastics in exercise. It remains then that there is not one common "idea" of all goods.

LECTURE VII

The Separated Good and an Absolute Good

ANALYTICAL OUTLINE
OF ST. THOMAS

TEXT OF ARISTOTLE
(*B.1096 a 34*)
Chapter 6

(2,a) ii. . . . Whether it is properly called by this name.
    X. . . . IS NOT PROPERLY
    NAMED ABSOLUTE GOOD.

      aa. . . . Not properly
      called absolute good.

Someone will rightly ask what they mean in calling anything "absolute" *b* if in both absolute man and this particular man there exists one and the same nature, that of man. This is the truth for they differ in no way as man. On the same supposition an absolute good or a good in itself and a particular good do not differ as good.   **83-84**

      bb. He rules out a . . . re-
      joinder.

It may not be countered that the good in itself is better because eternal, since what endures a long time is not necessarily better by nature than a thing that lasts a day.   **85-86**

      cc. . . . The Pythagorean
      view.

A more likely explanation seems to have been given by the Pythagoreans who place unity in their list of goods. In this apparently Speusippus followed them. But further discussion of the point will have to wait.   **87-88**

    Y. (THIS) IS INCONSISTENT
    WITH . . . THE COMMON
    IDEA . . . OF ALL GOODS.

      aa. . . . An absolute good
      cannot be an idea com-
      mon to all goods.

Contrary to what they have as- *10* serted, some doubt arises because their words are not said of every good and yet they do so apply. Now things are said to be good according to one species of good which are sought and desired for their own sake, and things productive or in some way preservative of these or prohibitive of their contraries are said to be good according to another species. It is obvious then that good is predicated in two ways, for some things are sought for their own sake and some for the sake of others. **89-90**

bb. (No) common idea of . . . things . . . good in themselves.
    a′. He declares his intention.

    b′. He investigates . . . by proposing a question.

Let us separate from the useful good things good in themselves and examine whether they can be called good according to one idea. **91**

But what would you have enumerated among goods in themselves? Would you include even all the goods sought for themselves alone, as intelligence, sight, and some types of pleasure and honor? These are sometimes sought for the sake of another, but they always have an intrinsic value. Otherwise nothing else seems an absolute good except the "idea" or "form." **92**

    c′. He resolves the second part.
    d′. He resolves the first part.

Wherefore the idea will be empty. **20** **93**

If things in themselves are demonstrated as absolute good, then the same nature of goodness will have to appear in all of them as the nature of whiteness in snow and in white lead. But just as we find different natures in honor, prudence, and pleasure, so too we find differences in goodness. The absolute good is not, therefore, something common according to one idea. **94**

cc. He handles a pertinent query.

In what way then are they to be called good? Not as things purely equivocal. Are they at least to be compared as things referring to one principle or as all tending to one end? Or still better, should we say according to analogy? Indeed, as sight is the good of the body so intellect is the good of the soul and so of other things. **95-96**

COMMENTARY OF ST. THOMAS

83. The Philosopher has shown above that there is no common idea of all goods. But because the separated good is called by the Platonists not only the "idea" or "form" of good but also absolute good, Aristotle here intends to inquire whether it is properly called by this name [(2, a) ii]. In regard to to this he does two things. First [ii, x] he shows that the separated good is not properly named absolute good. Second [ii, y], at "Contrary to what etc.," he shows that to postulate a separated good as absolute is inconsistent with saying that it is the common idea or form of all goods. In regard to the first he does three things. First [x, aa] he shows that the separated good is not properly called absolute (*per se*) good. Second [x, bb], at "It may not be countered etc.," he rules out a particular rejoinder. Third [x, cc], at "A more likely explanation etc.," he compares this doctrine with the Pythagorean view.

84. In regard to the first we must consider that the separated good, which is the cause of all goods, ought to be placed in a higher degree of goodness than the good things about us because the separated good is the ultimate end of all. But it seems that, according to this doctrine, it is not a higher degree in goodness than other goods. This is apparent because the Platonists called each of the separated things absolute or in itself, as man in himself and even horse in itself. Now it is clear that one and the same nature belongs to man who lives among us and to man in himself, that is, ideal man. He proves this by the fact that ideal man and man clothed with matter do not differ as man, but they do differ in certain other respects—for example, this particular man has matter. Thus the notions of animal and man do not differ in animality but rather in man's rational principle that he has over and above animality. So too it seems that the ideal man does not differ from this particular man in the nature of man but because this particular man has matter in addition to being man. For the same reason the good that is called absolute will not have goodness different in nature from this particular good, although there can be a difference in other respects than the nature of good.

85. Then [x, bb], at "It may not," he rules out a particular answer. Someone could say that the good in itself is better because eternal while the goods here are perishable. Indeed, a thing that lasts longer does seem better and more desirable. To exclude this he points out that the good in itself is eternal does not mean that it is better. The eternal differs from the non-eternal by reason of duration, and the difference of duration of a thing is outside the nature of the species, as life that lasts only a day and life more enduring are not different by reason of life but only by duration. So then if good be understood as one species, its duration will be outside the nature of good. The longer duration of a thing then does not make that thing any better.

86. If we do not hold that there is one species or idea of good as the Platonists did, but that good, like being, is predicated in every genus, duration itself will be a good of time. It would, in that case, add something to goodness. Hence what is more last-

ing will be better. But this cannot be said if the good is one species in itself. It follows then that it is not better because eternal.

87. Then [x, cc], at **"A more likely explanation,"** he compares this opinion with that of the Pythagoreans. We must consider that according to the Platonists the nature of the one and the good is the same, and so they identified one in itself and good in itself. Hence they were obliged to postulate one first good. The Pythagoreans did not do this, however, but they put one among the things contained in the list of the good under which they placed:

Light (The contrary evil of which they declared to
be:) . . . . *Darkness*
Unity . . . . *Multitude*
Knowledge . . . . *Opinion*
Rest . . . . *Motion*
Straight . . . . *Curved*
Masculine . . . . *Feminine*
Right . . . . *Left*
Finite . . . . *Infinite*
Equal . . . . *Unequal*
Square . . . . *Rectangular*

88. He says, therefore, that on this point the Pythagoreans gave a more likely explanation than the Platonists because the Pythagoreans were not compelled to hold one nature for the good. Even Speusippus, who was a son of Plato's sister and his successor in the Academy, did not follow Plato but Pythagoras on this point. He adds that further discussion of the subject will be taken up in the *Metaphysics*. (Cf. Bk. I, Ch. 5, 986 a 13-986 b 9; St. Th. Lect. VIII, 124-133. Cf. Bk. XI, Ch. 9, 1066 a 13-17; St. Th. Lect. IX, 2303.)

89. Then [ii, y], at **"Contrary to what,"** he shows that the assertion that the separated good is an absolute good or a good in itself is inconsistent with their view that there is one idea or form of all goods. He does three things on this point. First [y, aa] he shows

that an absolute good cannot be an idea common to all goods. Second [y, bb], at "Let us separate etc.," he shows that there cannot be a common idea of all things called good in themselves. Third [y, cc], at "In what way etc.," he handles a pertinent query. He says then in the first place that contrary to what the Platonists assert, there seems to be a subtle hesitation here. When they speak about the good in itself, it does not seem from the obvious meaning of their words that the discussion concerns every good, but as much can be gathered from the context because there are various species or forms of goods.

90. Those things sought, pursued, chosen, or desired for themselves are good according to one species or form of goodness. Those desired insofar as they are good in some way for the sake of others, which in their turn are really good, are called good for another reason. In a third way, some things are called good because they prevent the contrary evil. It is clear, therefore, that good is predicated in two ways. Primary goods are good in themselves. As we have already remarked (9-13, 58) they are sought for themselves. Both of the other things called good— the productive or preservative of good and the restrictive of contrary evil— are called good in reference to things good in themselves. It is obvious then that the "ratio" of absolute good is not suited to all goods.

91. Then [y, bb], at **"Let us separate,"** he shows that the "ratio" of absolute good cannot belong to all goods in themselves. First [bb, a'] he declares his intention. We must consider that those things that are productive or preservative of goods in themselves, or restrictive of contraries, are called good because they are useful, and the nature of absolute good does not belong to the merely useful. Let us then separate from these useful things the things that are in themselves good and

see whether they can be designated good according to one form, which is called absolute good.

92. Second [bb, b'], at **"But what would you,"** he investigates this last point by proposing a question: what kinds of things should be considered goods in themselves? He presents this question in two parts. In the first he asks whether we are to call absolute whatever goods are sought for themselves alone to the exclusion of all others, so that they are not ordered to any further use. Such would be, for example, sight, and certain kinds of pleasure and honors. These things are sometimes sought for the sake of something else to which they are useful, but even if they have no use beyond themselves they are good and desirable in themselves. The second part of the question asks whether there is any other absolute good besides the idea or form itself.

93. Third [bb, c'], at **"Wherefore the idea,"** he resolves the second part just mentioned. He concludes that if nothing else be a good in itself except the idea, then the idea will be a kind of exemplar whose likeness will be impressed on others. An exemplar is useless if it has no likeness to something else. Hence it follows that the idea is useless if there is no other good in itself.

94. Fourth [bb, d'], at **"Things in themselves,"** he resolves the first part in this way. If all the aforementioned things are good in themselves by partaking of the idea which is itself good, the same nature of goodness must appear in all of them, as we find the same nature of whiteness in snow and in white lead from the fact that they share in the one form. But this apparently is not true of the things mentioned above. Honor, prudence, and pleasure differ in their natures, that is, the nature of honor precisely as honor differs from the nature of prudence as prudence. Moreover, the nature of honor as a good differs from the nature of prudence as it is a good. There is not, then, one nature of goodness in all good things nor are they all desirable under the same aspect. Hence it remains that what is called absolute good is not something common as one idea or form common to all goods.

95. Then [y, cc], at **"In what way,"** he handles a pertinent query. This inquiry belongs here since predication according to different reasons is made in the first of two ways according to meanings that are without any relation to any one thing. These are purely equivocal because it happens by chance that the same word has been used by one person for one thing and then by someone else for an entirely different thing, as is plainly evident in the case of different men having the same name. In another way, one word is used of several things with meanings not entirely different but having some sort of common likeness. Sometimes they agree in referring to one principle, as a thing is called military because it is a soldier's weapon (like a sword), or his clothing (like a uniform), or his transportation (like a horse). Sometimes they agree in referring to one end. Thus medicine is called healthy because it produces health, diet is called healthy because it preserves health, and urine in its turn is called healthy because it is a sign of health. Sometimes the agreement is according to a different proportion to the same subject, as quality is called being because it is a disposition of a being in itself, i.e., a substance, and quantity because it is a measure of substance, and so on. Or the agreement is according to one proportion to different subjects. For instance, sight has the same proportion to the body as intellect to the soul. Hence as sight is a power of a physical organ so also is the intellect a power of the soul without the participation of the body.

96. In this fashion, therefore, he affirms that "good" is predicated of many things not with meanings entirely different, as happens with things completely equivocal, but according to analogy or the same proportion, inasmuch as all goods depend on the first principle of goodness, that is, as they are ordered to one end. Aristotle indeed did not intend that the separated good be the idea and "ratio" of all goods but their principle and end. Likewise, all things are called good by an analogy or the same proportion just as sight is the good of the body and intellect is the good of the soul. He prefers this third way because it is understood according to goodness inherent in things. The first two ways, however, are ascribed to a separated goodness from which a thing is not so properly denominated.

LECTURE VIII

This Matter Really Belongs to Another Science

ANALYTICAL OUTLINE
OF ST. THOMAS

TEXT OF ARISTOTLE
(*B.1096 b 29*)
Chapter 6

(2, b). (Supposing a common idea of good) it would not follow that happiness would have to be sought according to it.

    i. He presents a proof of his position.

But perhaps we should now leave these subjects, for a precise deter- *30* mination of them properly belongs to another branch of philosophy.[1] The same too may be said about the idea. **97**

Even if there is some one good univocally predicated or if a separated good in itself does exist, it is obvious that it is not a thing produced or possessed by man. Now it is a good of this kind that we are looking for. **98**

    ii. He gives an apparent rejoinder.

Perhaps some will think it *B.1097* better for the sake of the goods produced or possessed to obtain a knowledge of the separated good. Using this as a guide we will have a more thorough understanding of the objects that are good for us, and thus enlightened, we may acquire them. **99**

    iii. He refutes it.

        X. BY TWO REASONS.
        THE FIRST.

This reasoning certainly has some probability, although it does not seem to square with what we observed in the sciences. While sciences tend to some good and seek the necessary, they all neglect to use a knowledge of the separated good. But it is not reasonable to suppose that all artists and scientists would be ignorant of and would fail to seek a thing so advantageous to themselves. **100**

Indeed the separated good would be

[1] I.e., Metaphysics.

useless. What help does a knowl- *10* edge of it afford a weaver and a carpenter in the practice of their trades? Or how is a man a better doctor or a better soldier by studying the idea itself? A doctor surely is not intent on health so understood but on the health of man in the concrete, or even better perhaps, on the health of this man. It is the individual man whom a doctor intends to cure. Enough has now been said on these topics.   **101-102**

COMMENTARY OF ST. THOMAS

97. After the Philosopher has explained that there is no common idea of good, now [(2, b)] he shows that even if there were, it would not follow that happiness would have to be sought according to it. In regard to this he does three things. First [i] he presents a proof of his position. Second [ii], at "Perhaps some will think etc.," he gives an apparent rejoinder. Third [iii], at "This reasoning certainly etc.," he refutes it. He says first that the manner of predicating good according to one or different reasons must now be put aside because more accurate study of the matter properly belongs to another branch of philosophy, metaphysics. Likewise, the consideration of the idea of good is not pertinent to our purpose. As reason for these statements he maintains that if there were one good univocally predicated of all, or even if a separated good did exist in itself, it would obviously not be a thing produced or possessed by man. Now it is precisely such a thing we are seeking.

98. We are looking for the happiness that is the end of human acts. The end, however, of man is either some thing he does or some external

thing. This can be the end of man because either it is produced, as a house is the end of building or it is possessed as a thing that is used. Now it is clear that the common or separated good cannot be the operation itself of man, nor is it something produced by man. Moreover, it does not seem to be something possessed by man as he possesses things used in this life. Obviously, then, the common or separated good is not the good of man that is the object of our present search.

99. Then [ii], at **"Perhaps,"** he gives an apparent rejoinder. Someone might say that the separated good, although not produced or possessed by man, nevertheless is the pattern of all the good produced and possessed. Now one who wishes to understand the copies ought to know the pattern. So it would seem that one should know the separated good itself for the sake of the goods produced and possessed. The reason is that, having the separated good as a guide, we will be better able to know and consequently better able to acquire the things that are good for us, as an artist looking at a model is better able to paint a likeness.

100. Then [iii], at **"This reasoning**

certainly," he refutes this response by two reasons. The first [iii, x] he takes from ordinary observation. While the reason given seems probable, he says that it does not appear to be in agreement with what we observe in other sciences. All sciences and arts tend to some good, as we said above (8), and to attain the end aimed at, each uses what is necessary for itself. None of them, though, uses the knowledge of this separated good. This would not be reasonable if some advantage could be derived from it. Therefore, the knowledge of this separated good contributes nothing to the goods produced and possessed.

101. He offers a second reason [iii, y] at "Indeed the separated good would be useless." This is taken from the very nature of the thing. He states that the good under consideration is altogether useless for the sciences and the arts, both in regard to their exercise, since a weaver or a carpenter is in no way aided in the practice of his art by a knowledge of that separated good, and in regard to the acquisition of a science or an art. No one becomes a better physician or a better soldier because he has studied the separated form of good. The reason he assigns is that an exemplar, at which it is necessary to gaze, must be in conformity with the work produced. Art, however, does not produce some good in common or an abstract good but a good that is concrete and individual. A physician does not intend health in the abstract but in the concrete, the health of this particular man. He does not give medicine to mankind in general but to this individual man. We must conclude then that the knowledge of a universal and separated good is not needed either for the acquisition or for the exercise of the sciences.

102. On this note he concludes his discussion of the opinions offered about happiness.

LECTURE IX

The Nature of Happiness

ANALYTICAL OUTLINE
OF ST. THOMAS

TEXT OF ARISTOTLE
(*B.1097 a 16*)
Chapter 7

I. HE SHOWS WHAT HAPPINESS IS.

A. He shows what happiness is.

A' He shows what happiness is.

1. HE PROPOSES SOME GENERAL NOTIONS AND CONDITIONS.

a. He states that happiness is the ultimate end.

Let us return again to a consideration of the good we are seeking in order to find out what it is. It seems that the good differs in different operations and arts. In medicine it is one good, in war it is another, and in other arts, still other goods. As the thing sought in every activity, the good is the end for the sake of which other things are *20* done. This will be health in medicine, victory in war, a building in architecture, something else in some other art. In every activity and choice there is an end, the agent doing everything he does for the sake of that end. Therefore, if there is an end for all that we do, this will be the good intended. If there are many ends, there will be many goods, and in this case our discussion will go beyond the many until it arrives at that supreme good.   **103-106**

b. He lays down the conditions belonging to the ultimate end.
i. *The first is that it be a perfect thing.*

We must make a considerable effort to give this a fuller explanation. Apparently there are many ends, some of which we choose for the sake of something else like riches, flutes, and in general all instruments. It is obvious then that not all ends are perfect. But the ultimate end appears to be perfect. Wherefore, if there be only one *30*

45

of this kind, it will be what we are looking for. If there are a number of goods, then it is the most perfect of these. Now we call that object which is desired for its own sake more perfect than one that is desired for some further purpose. That which is never desired for any further utility is more perfect than the things desirable in themselves and for the sake of this further purpose. In the event that the object is perfect without qualification it will always be desirable for itself and never for anything beyond itself. Happiness in fact seems especially to be *b* of this nature, for we choose it in every case for itself and never for something else. Honor and pleasure and knowledge and every virtue we do indeed choose for themselves, for we would choose every one of them even if no advantage accrued to us. But we choose them also on account of happiness because we hope to become happy. On the other hand, no one chooses happiness for the sake of these goods or for any other good whatsoever.   **107-111**

ii. The second, that it be self-sufficient.

X. FIRST IN REGARD TO . . . THE
   NATURE OF SUFFICIENCY.

The same seems to follow from the viewpoint of self-sufficiency, for the perfect good apparently is self-sufficient. We call it self-sufficient not only as adequate for a man living a solitary life by himself but also for his parents, children, wife, friends in general, and *10* fellow citizens because this good naturally will include man's social life. But some limitation must be placed on the number provided for, since the extension to relatives, neighbors and friends might go on without limit. We must return to examine this question later. Now we call that self-sufficient which, taken alone, makes life desirable and lacking nothing. In our opinion happiness is of this nature.   **112-114**

Y. AS REGARDS THE PREFIX "SELF."

Moreover, happiness without further addition will be the most desirable of all things. With any addition it will certainly be more desirable even though the addition be ever so slight. The reason is that the addition has increased the good, and a greater good is al- *20* ways more desirable. Therefore, happiness as the end of all human actions is the perfect self-sufficient good.

115-117

COMMENTARY OF ST. THOMAS

103. After the Philosopher has thoroughly discussed the opinions of others about happiness, he now gives his own opinion on the subject. He divides this treatment into two parts. In the first [I] he shows what happiness is. In the second [Lect. XVIII; II], at "Having settled these matters etc." (B.1101 b 10), he treats a particular property of happiness. He makes a twofold division of the first part. In the first division [A] he shows what happiness is. In the second [Lect. XV], at "Many changes take place etc." (B.1100 a 5), he solves a particular problem. In regard to the first he does two things. First [A'] he shows what happiness is. Second [Lect. XII], at "In our study of the principles etc." (B.1098 b 8), he shows that everything said about happiness is in agreement with this doctrine. In regard to the first he does two things. First [1] he proposes some general notions and conditions of happiness that are obvious to nearly everyone. Second [Lect. X; 2], at "But to say that happiness etc." (B.1097 b 22), he inquires into the nature of happiness. In regard to the first he does two things. First [a] he states that happiness is the ultimate end. Second [b], at "We must make etc.," he lays down the conditions belonging to the ultimate end.

104. Therefore, he says first that, after completing the treatise (43-102)

on the opinions of others, we must again return to a consideration of the good that is the subject of our inquiry —happiness—to find out what it is. Our first consideration about it must be that in different activities and arts the good sought differs. In the medical art the good sought is health, and in the military art victory, and in other arts some other good.

105. If it be asked what good is sought in every art and in every activity, we must know that it is the object for the sake of which all other things are done. In medicine everything is done on account of health, in war everything is done on account of victory, and in architecture everything is done for the sake of the building to be constructed. Likewise, in every other activity the good sought is some one thing for the sake of which all other things are done. This good, the object of every activity or choice, is called the end, for the end is nothing else than that for the sake of which other things are done.

106. If, therefore, there should be some end immediately apparent to which all the products of all arts and human activities are directed, such an end will be the good unqualifiedly sought, that is, the thing intended in all human operations. But if at this point many goods arise to which the different ends of different arts are or-

dered, our reason will have to inquire beyond this number until it arrives at this one thing, that is, some obvious good. There must be, indeed, one ultimate end for man precisely as man because of the unity of human nature, just as there is one end for a physician as physician because of the unity of the art of medicine. This ultimate end of man is called that human good which is happiness.

107. Then [b], at **"We must make,"** he lays down two conditions of the ultimate end. The first [b, i] is that it be a perfect thing; the second [b, ii], that it be self-sufficient, at "The same seems to follow etc." The ultimate end is the ultimate term of desire's natural inclination. But in order that something be the ultimate term of natural inclination, two things are required. First that it be a thing actually having a species and not on the way to have a species. The generation of fire, for instance, is not terminated at the disposition to the form but at the form itself. Now a thing that has form is perfect, but a thing that is merely disposed to a form is imperfect. Therefore, the good that is the ultimate end must be a perfect good. Second, the term of the natural inclination must be integral since nature is not deficient in necessary things. Hence the end of human generation is not a deformed man but a perfect man. Likewise the ultimate end that is the term of desire must be self-sufficient as an integral good.

108. In regard to the perfection of a final good we must consider that, as an agent moves towards the end, so the end moves the desire of the agent. Hence the gradations of the ends must be in proportion to the gradations of the agent. Now an agent may be of three kinds. One, the most imperfect, does not operate by its own form but only insofar as moved by another, as a hammer forges a blade. Hence, the effect in the acquired form is not like this agent but like the one who moves

the agent. Another, a perfect agent, operates indeed according to its form so that the effect is like it, as fire gives off heat, but nevertheless it must be moved by some prior principal agent. In this respect it partakes imperfectly of the nature of an instrument. A third agent, the most perfect, operates according to its own form and is not moved by any other.

109. The same is true in the order of ends. There we find an object desired not on account of some formal goodness existing in itself but only as useful for something else like bitter medicine. We find also an object is indeed desirable on account of what it is, but besides, it is desired for something else like sweet-tasting medicine. This is better than the first. But the most perfect good is that which is so desired for its own sake that it is never desired for the sake of anything else. Here then the Philosopher distinguishes three degrees of good. He says, as we have just stated (107-109), that we must give a more complete explanation of the ultimate end by examining the conditions required for it.

110. There are also, it seems, many degrees of ends. Some of these we choose purely for the sake of something else, riches, for instance, which are sought for their utility in human living. Flutes on which music is made is another example. All such instruments are ends sought merely because of their usefulness. It is obvious that such ends are imperfect. The best end, namely the ultimate end, must be perfect. Therefore, if there is only one such end, it must be the ultimate end we are looking for. If, however, there are many perfect ends, the most perfect of these should be the best and the ultimate. What is desirable in itself is more perfect than what is desirable because of another. It clearly follows then that what is never desired for some thing beyond itself is more perfect than the

things which, although sought for themselves, are also sought as a means.

111. Therefore, that is absolutely perfect which is always desirable for itself and never for another. But happiness appears to be of this nature, for we never seek it for something else but always for itself. We do choose honor, pleasure, knowledge, and virtue for themselves. We would choose them or have a desire for them even if no other good would come to us through them. In fact we choose them for happiness precisely because we think we will be happy in having them. But no one chooses happiness for them or for anything else. We conclude then that happiness is the most perfect good, and consequently the ultimate and best end.

112. Then [b, ii], at "The same seems," he treats the self-sufficiency of happiness—first [ii, x] in regard to that which pertains to the nature of sufficiency, and second [ii, y], at "Moreover, happiness etc.," as regards the prefix "self." He says first that the same conclusion seems to follow from self-sufficiency as well as from perfection: happiness is the best and the ultimate end. Indeed, the latter two follow one another, for the perfect good seems to be self-sufficient. If it is not sufficient in some particular, it does not perfectly satisfy desire, and so it will not be the perfect good. It is called a self-sufficient good not because it suffices merely for one man living a solitary life but also for his parents, children, wife, friends, and fellow citizens as well, so that it will adequately provide the necessaries in temporal matters, instruction and counsel in spiritual matters for them too. Such extension is required because man is a social animal, and his desire is not satisfied in providing for himself but he wants to be in a position to take care of others. This, however, must be understood within limits.

113. If someone should want to extend such care not only to his own relatives and friends but even to the friends of his friends this would go on indefinitely so that no one could have a sufficiency and therefore no one could be happy, if happiness would require such infinite sufficiency. In this work the Philosopher speaks of happiness as it is attainable in this life, for happiness in a future life is entirely beyond the investigation of reason. To what extent a man needs a sufficiency to be happy will have to be investigated again elsewhere, namely, in domestic ethics or in political science.

114. Because he has already shown (112-113) that the perfect good called happiness ought to be sufficient not for one man alone but for all whose care is incumbent upon him, next he explains the nature of what is called self-sufficient. He says that the self-sufficient is that which, even when had by itself, makes life desirable and free from want. Happiness does this eminently, otherwise it would not terminate the inclination of desire if something that man needed remained outside it. Certainly everyone in need desires to have what he lacks. Hence it is clear that happiness is a self-sufficient good.

115. Then [ii, y], at "Moreover," he explains the nature of self-sufficiency as regards the expression "self." A thing is said to be self-sufficient when, taken apart from other things, it is sufficient. This can happen in two ways. First in such a manner that the perfect good, which is called self-sufficient, would be incapable of receiving an increase of goodness from another—a condition of the being that is totally good, God. As an additional part is not greater than the whole since the part itself is included in the whole, so too any good whatsoever added to God does not increase His goodness because the addition is good only by participating in the divine goodness. Likewise, a thing taken alone, no addition being made, is said to be sufficient in that it

49

has everything a man absolutely needs.

116. In this sense happiness, the subject of our present discussion, has self-sufficiency because of itself it furnishes everything that is absolutely necessary, but it does not supply everything that can come to a man. Man can be made better by an additional good. But a man's desire for this does not remain unsatisfied because a desire controlled by reason, such as a truly happy man should have, is undisturbed by the things that are unnecessary even though attainable. Happiness, therefore, has this quality above everything else; it is desirable even when not augmented by other goods. However, if it does receive an addition, be it ever so small, surely that is even more desirable. The reason is that by the accession, a superabundance or an increase of good is effected, and because something is a greater good, it is more desirable.

117. Last, he repeats in the epilogue the conclusion of what has been established (104-116), namely, that since happiness is the ultimate end of all our activities, it is the perfect good and self-sufficient.

LECTURE X

The Definition of Happiness

ANALYTICAL OUTLINE
OF ST. THOMAS

TEXT OF ARISTOTLE
(*B.1097 b 22*)
Chapter 7

2. HE . . . EXAMINES ITS DEFINITION.

a. He shows the necessity of this inquiry.

But to say that happiness is the best of goods seems merely to state something already perfectly obvious. However, since we wish to bring out more clearly what it is, we must investigate the matter further. **118**

b. He searches for the definition of happiness.

    i. First he inquires into its genus.
      x. HE SHOWS THAT HAPPINESS CONSISTS IN AN ACTIVITY OF MAN.

Perhaps this can be done by considering the activity of man. As the good of a flute player or sculptor or any artist, or of anyone who has some special activity, seems to consist in that activity and its skillful performance, so also the good of man who has an activity characteristic of himself precisely as man. **119-120**

      y. HE SHOWS THAT THERE IS AN ACTIVITY PROPER TO MAN.
        aa. First by activities . . . incidental to man.

Have a weaver and a tanner a special work and activity while man pre- *30* cisely as man has none? Is he left by nature without a purpose? **121**

        bb. Second, . . . by means of of the human members.

If the eye, hand, foot, and each member have a proper operation, surely we will not refuse to concede an activity proper to man as man. **122**

      z. HE SHOWS WHICH IS MAN'S PROPER ACTIVITY.

What therefore will it be? Life belongs even to plants and we *B.1098* are in search of something characteristic of man. The life of nutrition and growth must then be ruled out. Even the life of sense experience, which is a step higher, is shared with the horse, cow, and other animals. The remaining type of life belongs to the rational part of man and finds its expression in actions. This rational part either follows the dictates of reason, or it possesses and exercises the power of understanding. Of the two functions, the latter seems the more correct, for when we speak of reasoning, we signify the exercise of our rational powers. **123-126**

ii. (He inquires) into its differences.
x. HE DIVIDES THE INQUIRY INTO TWO PARTS (FIRST)

The function of man, therefore, is activity of the soul according to reason or at least not independent of reason. Now as a rule we classify in the same way the function of an artist and of a skillful artist, of a flute player and of a good flute player. This applies generally where skill is an addition to the function, for a flute player is *10* one who plays the flute and a good flute player one who plays the flute well. If then we place the function of man in a certain kind of life, that is, of an activity of the soul according to reason, it will be proper to a good man to act well and to the best of his ability according to reason. In every case the good of man will consist in action conformable to virtue, and if there are a number of virtues, action conformable to the best and most perfect of them. **127-128**

y. HE BEGINS THE SECOND PART.

Further, it must extend to a complete life. A single swallow or one good day does not mean that spring has come. So one day (of goodness) or a short practice of virtue does not make a man blessed and happy. **129-130**

COMMENTARY OF ST. THOMAS

118. After the Philosopher has laid down certain conditions of happiness, he here [2] examines its definition.

Concerning this he does three things. First [2, a] he shows the necessity of this inquiry. Second [2, b], at "Perhaps this can be done etc.," he searches for the definition of happiness. Third [Lect. XI], at "In this way, therefore etc." (B.1098 a 20), he shows that the definition given is insufficient and further inquiry must be made. He says first that all admit that happiness is the very best of things including the belief that it is the ultimate end and the perfect self-sufficient good. But it is rather obvious that some clarification must be made about happiness to give us a knowledge of its specific nature.

119. Then [2, b], at "Perhaps this," he investigates the definition of happiness in a twofold manner. First [b, i] he inquires into its genus, and second [b, ii], at "The function of man," into its differences. The first point requires a threefold procedure. First [i, x] he shows that happiness consists in an activity of man. Second [i, y], at "Have a weaver etc.," he shows that there is an activity proper to man. Third [i, z], at "What therefore etc.," he shows which is man's proper activity. He says first that the nature of happiness can be made evident by consideration of human activity. When a thing has a proper operation, the good of the thing and its well-being consist in that operation. Thus the good of a flute player consists in his playing, and similarly the good of the sculptor and of every artist in their respective activity. The reason is that the final good of everything is its ultimate perfection, and the form is its first perfection while its operation is the second. If some exterior thing be called an end, this will be only because of an operation by which a man comes in contact with that thing, either by making it as a builder makes a house, or by using or enjoying it. Accordingly, the final good of everything must be found in its operation. If then man has some characteristic activity, his final good which is happiness must consist in this. Consequently, happiness is the proper operation of man.

120. But if happiness is said to consist in something else, either this will be a thing fitting man for an operation of this kind, or it will be something he attains by his operation, as God is said to be the beatitude of man.

121. Then [i, y], at "Have a weaver," he proves in two ways that there is an operation proper to man. He does this first [y, aa] by activities that are incidental to man. It may happen that a man is a weaver, tanner, grammarian, musician, or anything else of the kind. In none of these capacities does he lack a proper operation, for otherwise he would possess them as empty and useless things. Now it is far more unfitting that a thing ordained by divine reason, as is the naturally existent, should be unprofitable and useless than a thing arranged by human reason. Since, therefore, man is a being possessing a natural existence, it is impossible that he should be by nature without a purpose, or a proper operation. There is then a proper operation of man no less than of the abilities that are incidental to him. The reason is that everything, either natural or acquired by art, exists by means of its form which is a principle of some operation. Hence as each thing has a proper existence by its form so also does it have a proper operation.

122. Second [y, bb], at "If the eye," he proves the same truth by means of the human members. We must consider that the same mode of operation is found in the whole and in the parts of man, because, as the soul is the act of the whole body, so certain powers of the soul are acts of certain parts of the body, as sight is of the eye. But each part of man has a proper operation; for example, the operation of the eye is seeing; and of the hand, touching; and of the feet, walking; and so of the other parts. We conclude, therefore, that some operation proper to man as a whole exists.

53

123. Then [i, z], at **"What therefore,"** he explores the nature of the operation proper to man. Now it is evident that each thing has an operation which belongs to it according to its form. But the form of man is his soul, whose act is life, not indeed life as the mere existence of a living thing, but a special vital operation, for example, understanding or feeling. Hence happiness obviously consists in some vital operation.

124. It cannot be said that man's happiness should arise from any kind of life, for even plants have life. But happiness is sought as a good characteristic of man since it is called a human good. Likewise, happiness must be different from the life of nutrition or growth, which even vegetables possess. From this we take it that happiness does not consist in health, beauty, strength, or great stature, for all these things result from activities of vegetative life.

125. On the step above the life of mere nutrition and growth is the life of sense experience. Again, this is not proper to man but is possessed by horses, oxen, and other animals. In this kind of life, then, happiness does not consist. So we conclude that human happiness is not found in any form of sense perception or pleasure.

126. Beyond the life of assimilation and of sense experience there remains only the life that functions according to reason. This life is proper to man, for he receives his specific classification from the fact that he is rational. Now the rational has two parts. One is rational by participation insofar as it is obedient to and is regulated by reason. The other is rational by nature as it can of itself reason and understand. The rational by nature is more properly called rational because a thing possessed intrinsically is always more proper than a thing received from another. Since, therefore, happiness is the most proper good of man, it more

likely consists in the rational by nature than in the rational by participation. From this we can see that happiness will more properly be found in the life of thought than in a life of activity, and in an act of reason or intellect than in an act of the appetitive power controlled by reason.

127. Then [b, ii], at **"The function of man,"** he inquires into the specific differences of happiness. He divides the inquiry into two parts [ii, x] according to the two specific differences investigated, and he begins the second part [ii, y] at "Further, it must extend etc." First then we know from the premises (126) that the proper function of a man is a psychic activity in accord with reason itself or at least not independent of reason. The latter is mentioned because of the activity of the appetite controlled by reason. Now as a rule we find that the function of a thing generally and the efficient activity of that thing are of the same nature, except that allowance must be made for the part played by skill. For example, the function of a harpist is to play the harp, and the function of a good harpist is to play the harp well. The same is true of all other functions.

128. If, therefore, man's proper role consists in living a certain kind of life, namely, according to the activity of reason, it follows that it is proper to a good man to act well according to reason, and to the very good man or the happy man to do this in superlative fashion. But this belongs to the nature of virtue that everyone who has virtue should act well according to it, as a horse with good training or "virtue" should run well. If, then, the activity of the very good man or the happy man is to act well, in fact to act to the best of his ability according to reason, it follows that the good of man, which is happiness, is activity according to virtue. If there is only one

virtue for man, his activity according to that virtue will be happiness. If there are a number of such virtues for man, happiness will be the activity according to the best of them. The reason is that happiness is not only the good of man but the best good.

129. Then [ii, y], at "**Further, it must extend,**" he inquires into the other specific difference of happiness. Continuity and perpetuity, to some extent, are also required for happiness. These qualities are naturally desired by the appetite of a person endowed with reason, who apprehends not a particular being, as our senses do, but also being in itself. Now being is of itself desirable. It follows then that, as an animal which apprehends a particular being by its senses desires that particular being, so also man appre-hending being in itself desires it as always existing and not this particular being alone. So continuity and perpetuity, which are not found in the present life, belong to the nature of perfect happiness. Hence perfect happiness cannot be had in this life. However, the happiness attainable here must extend to a complete life, that is through the whole life of man. As the sight of a single swallow or one clear day does not prove that spring is here, so a single good deed is not enough to make a man happy. It arises rather from the continued performance of good deeds throughout his whole life.

130. From this discussion, therefore, it is clear that happiness is a virtue-oriented activity proper to man in a complete life.

LECTURE XI

The Task Before Us

ANALYTICAL OUTLINE OF ST. THOMAS	TEXT OF ARISTOTLE (*B.1098 a 20*) Chapter 7

3. HE NOW SHOWS . . . WHAT MAY STILL REMAIN TO BE DONE.

a. He indicates first what remains to be done.

    i. He manifests what has been done and what remains to be be done.

In this way, therefore, the good of happiness has been sketched, for the proper procedure is first to study a subject according to its general notions and afterwards to explain it more fully. **131**

    ii. He assigns the reason for the statement just made.

It would indeed seem a reasonable mode of procedure to make a sketch of the matter and then to investigate its features one by one. **132**

    iii. He shows how a man may be helped in this procedure.

In this matter time seems to be, as it were, a good discoverer and a special assistant. Thus improvements in the arts have been due to successive artists, each making his own contribution. **133-134**

b. (He indicates) how this should be done.

    i. He presents this in general.

We must recall what was said before,[1] that the same certitude is not to be expected in all sciences but in each according to the subject matter, and that the degree of certitude should be suited to the subject taught. **135**

    ii. He makes specific what he has said.

        X. HE TAKES UP WHAT MUST BE HANDLED DIFFERENTLY FOR DIFFERENT SUBJECTS.

            aa. The first . . . is the difference between a practical and a speculative science.

For a carpenter and a geometrician both study a straight line, but for *30* different reasons. The carpenter does so to the extent that this is useful in

[1] Ch. 3, 1094 b 11-27.

bb. He treats a second
difference.

y. (HE TAKES UP) WHAT MUST
BE OBSERVED GENERALLY IN
ALL SUBJECTS.

his work; the geometrician as a student
of truth wants to learn what a line is
and how it differs from other figures.
This distinction must be observed in
other practical sciences lest they be
burdened with discussions that are out
of place.   **136**

Likewise, we must not seek *b*
causes equally in all matters but in
some it suffices to establish a fact. This
is the case with the first principles of
a science since a principle is a starting
point. Now, we understand some principles by induction, some by observation, some by custom and others in
other ways.   **137**

In all cases we must strive for a
thorough knowledge of each set of
principles according to their nature and
must study how to define them properly.

Principles are a great help in understanding what follows. Indeed a single
principle seems to be more than half
of the whole, for it furnishes answers
to many of our questions.   **138**

COMMENTARY OF ST. THOMAS

131. After the Philosopher has investigated the definition of happiness
itself, he now [3] shows in a twofold
fashion what may still remain to be
done. He indicates first [3, a] what
remains to be done, and second [3, b],
at "We must recall etc.," how this
should be done. In regard to the initial point he does three things. First
[a, i] he manifests what has been done
and what remains to be done. He says
that the final good of man which is
happiness has been previously sketched
(103-130). By a sketch he understands
that knowledge through some common principles which indeed give a
picture of the matter but not in such

a way that the nature of that thing
in particular is manifested. The reason
for this is, as he himself says, that a
thing should first be studied according
to its general characteristics, i.e., by a
general description which is like it
and in a way extrinsic to it. Then
with other matters clarified, we must
take up what was previously sketched
roughly and etch in the lines more
sharply. For this reason he himself will
take up in greater detail the treatise
on happiness toward the end of this
work (Bk. X, Ch. 6-8, 1176 a 30-1179
a 33; St. Th. Lect. IX-XIII, 2065-2136).

132. Second [a, ii], at **"It would
indeed seem,"** he assigns the reason

for the statement just made (131) saying that it seems natural for man to advance from the imperfect knowledge which covers a good description of things to a perfect knowledge of them by filling in the details. This he does by investigating first one part and then another, for it is according to man's nature to proceed by the steps of reason to a knowledge of the truth. Reason has this peculiar characteristic that it grasps the truth gradually, and as a consequence man properly perfects himself in knowledge little by little. On the contrary, separated or intellectual substances attain at once to the knowledge of the truth without any such investigation.

133. Third [a, iii], at "In this matter time," he shows how a man may be helped in this procedure. He says that time seems to be, as it were, a discoverer of things well suited to sketch a subject and to be of special assistance in the work. The meaning is not that time itself contributes anything but that this help comes with time. If someone should busy himself investigating the truth for a period, he will be aided in the discovery of the truth by the passage of time. This is true in the case of the same person who will understand subsequently what he had not understood before, and also for different persons, as in the case of a man who learns the things discovered by his predecessors and adds something himself. In this way improvements have been made in the arts, in which a small discovery was made first and afterwards notable advances were made by the efforts of various men, each looking upon it as a duty to supply what is lacking in the knowledge of his predecessors.

134. But if, on the contrary, application to study be neglected, time is rather a cause of forgetfulness, as is said in the fourth book of the *Physics* (Ch. 12, 221 a 32; St. Th. Lect. XX, 604). We see indeed that the negligent individual forgets what he knows, and in human history we observe that many sciences which flourished among the ancients gradually have been lost when interest in them ceased.

135. Then [3, b], at "We must recall," he shows how we must follow up the remainder of our task. First [b, i] he presents this in general by recalling to mind what was said in the introduction (32, 36), that we must not look for the same certitude in all subjects but in each according to the matter, namely, that which is proper to the subject taught.

136. Second [b, ii], at "For a carpenter," he makes specific what he has said. First [ii, x] he takes up what must be handled differently for different subjects, and second [ii, y], at "In all cases we must etc.," what must be observed generally in all subjects. In regard to the first he gives a threefold difference. The first of these [x, aa] is the difference between a practical and a speculative science. He says therefore that a carpenter, who is a practical man, and a geometrician, who is a theorist, study a straight line for different reasons. A practical man—a carpenter—studies a line insofar as it is useful for his work, in sawing wood or in doing anything else of this nature. But the geometrician investigates what a line is—its qualities and its nature by considering the properties and potentialities. He is interested only in the study of truth. We must proceed in the first way to avoid many discussions that are out of place in the practical sciences. For instance, in moral matters we must steer clear of an exhaustive treatment of the intellect and the other powers of the soul to the neglect of the study of human acts themselves. It is a serious defect in any science to squander time on matter outside the science.

137. He treats a second difference at "Likewise, we must not" [x, bb].

Here he considers the difference between principles and deductions made from them. He says that the cause is not to be sought equally in all matters, otherwise we would proceed to infinity in demonstrating. But in some cases it is sufficient to show clearly that a thing is so. This is true of principles that are taken for granted in a science, since they are the beginning and cannot be reduced to anything previous. Now principles themselves are not manifested in the same way. But some are understood by induction from particular examples, for instance, that every number is even or odd. Some are taken from observation, as in nature, that every living thing needs nourishment. Some are taken from custom, as in morals, that sensual desires are diminished if we do not give in to them. Still other principles are manifested in still other ways, as in the practical arts principles are learned by a sort of experience.

138. Then [ii, y], at "In all cases we must," he sets down the procedure to be followed generally in all such matters. He says that a person ought to persist in going over thoroughly each set of principles, both speculatively and practically, in the way a knowledge of their nature demands and in studying how men understand them. Thus a man will learn how to distinguish one principle from another, and one set of principles from another set. A knowledge of principles is a great help in understanding the conclusions that flow from them. Indeed a single principle seems to be more than half of the whole, since the content of a science is contained in the principles. He adds that many answers we look for in a science are clear from one principle well understood and completely thought out.

LECTURE XII

Confirmation of the Definition

ANALYTICAL OUTLINE   TEXT OF ARISTOTLE
OF ST. THOMAS   (*B.1098 b 8*)
                            Chapter 8

I. HE PROPOSES HERE TO CONFIRM THE VIEW HE HAS JUST GIVEN.

A. He indicates his intention.

> In our study of the principles we must carefully examine not only the conclusions and the premises from which the argument proceeds but also the considered views of others. Everything indeed will fall into agreement with what is true, and the truth *10* will be quickly seen to be at variance with the false.   **139-140**

B. He begins to carry it out.

A' He shows . . . the consensus of others is in agreement with his view.

I. HE SHOWS THAT WHAT IS COMMONLY SAID BY PHILOSOPHERS IS IN HARMONY WITH THE GIVEN DESCRIPTION OF HAPPINESS.

a. He proves (this) . . . by dividing human goods into three classes.

> Goods have been classified as (a) external, (b) of the soul, and (c) of the body. Among these we hold that the goods of the soul are the best and most properly called goods. We attribute vital actions and operations to the soul. Therefore, our opinion must be sound for it is in agreement with that ancient one held by the philosophers.   **141-143**

b. He proves the same thing in a different way.

> It was stated accurately then that we identify the end with certain acts and operations. Thus happiness will be accounted one of the goods of the soul and not an external good.   **144**

2. HE SHOWS THAT THE SAME IS TRUE FROM WHAT IS GENERALLY AFFIRMED BY EVERYONE.

This coincides with the common notion that one who lives well and does well is a happy man. As a matter of fact, a good life appears to be nothing else but good activity. *20* **145**

B' He shows that the points on which others disagree substantiate his view.

I. HE BRINGS FORWARD THE POINTS ON WHICH MEN DIFFER ABOUT HAPPINESS.

a. He states what he wishes to show.

Everything that philosophers have looked for in happiness seems to be found in our notion of it. **146**

b. He gives different views on happiness.
  i. The first.

  ii. The second opinion.

  iii. A third opinion.

Some have taught that happiness consists in virtue either generally, or specifically in prudence or in wisdom. Others say it consists in all or one of these virtues accompanied by pleasure, or at least not without pleasure. Still others would include a goodly share of external goods. **147-149**

c. He indicates the difference in the persons holding the foregoing views.

The rank and file together with some ancient philosophers held this last opinion, while a distinguished minority chose virtue. It is likely *30* that no one was entirely wrong but each was right on one or more points. **150**

2. HE SHOWS THAT EACH OF THESE IS IN AGREEMENT WITH THE ABOVE VIEW.

a. He shows that this is true of the first opinion . . . that virtue is happiness.
  i. He shows that the first opinion . . . is in agreement with his.

Our definition of happiness is acceptable to those who hold that happiness consists in all or in one of the virtues, for virtuous activity clearly is something belonging to it. **151**

  ii. He shows how his opinion is better.
  X. FROM REASON.

But besides, it makes a *B.1099* great difference whether the chief good be placed in possession or use, in habit or activity because a habit may exist in a person not actually performing any good, for instance, in

Y. FROM A CUSTOM AMONG MEN.

one who is asleep or otherwise not engaged in any way whatsoever. This is not possible with an activity, for a man having it necessarily is active, and if the activity be virtuous he will act virtuously.   152

At the Olympic games the best looking and strongest athletes do not receive the crown but the victorious competitors. So, too, among those who are good and best in virtuous living, those who perform righteous deeds become illustrious.   153

COMMENTARY OF ST. THOMAS

139. After the Philosopher has shown in general what happiness is, he proposes here [I] to confirm the view he has just given, by what is said by others on happiness. Concerning this he does two things. First [I, A] he indicates his intention. Then [I, B], at "Goods have been etc.," he begins to carry it out. He says first that it is most important to have a principle thoroughly understood. The principle in practical matters is the ultimate end. To insure a more careful study of it, we must examine not only the conclusions and the premises from which the discussion of the reasoner proceeds, but also the observations of others concerning the principle itself, namely, the ultimate end or happiness. He then assigns the reason for this procedure, that everything harmonizes with the truth. This is so because, as will be said in the sixth book (1143), truth is the good of the intellect. Good, as explained later (320), is achieved only in the concurrence of all the factors pertaining to the perfection of the thing.

140. Evil, on the contrary, comes about in a variety of ways by the de-

fect of any single necessary qualification. No evil, however, can be found in which the good is completely corrupted, as will be shown in the fourth book (808). So not only all good things are in agreement with the good but even evil things in that they retain something of good. In a similar way all false things are in agreement with the truth insofar as they retain some likeness of truth. It is not possible that the mind holding a false opinion is completely deprived of the knowledge of the truth, because by means of the true it immediately judges something false as lacking in the truth. This is what he understands by saying that the true is at variance with the false, somewhat like a right angle with an oblique angle.

141. Then [I, B], at "Goods have been classified," he begins to carry out his intention, first in respect to what he has affirmed about happiness. In regard to this he does two things. First [B, A'] he shows that what is the consensus of others is in agreement with his view (touching on the things said above by him at ". . . our opinion is in agreement"). Second

[B, B'], at "Everything that philosophers etc.," he shows that the points on which others disagree substantiate his view. In regard to the initial point he does two things. First [A', 1] he shows that what is commonly said by philosophers is in harmony with the given description of happiness. Second [A', 2], at "This coincides with etc.," he shows that the same is true from what is generally affirmed by everyone. He proves the first observation in two ways, and

142. initially [A', 1, a] by dividing human goods into three classes. Of these some (a) are external, as riches, honors, friends, and such like. (b) Others are internal, and these again are of two kinds: (1) some concern the body, as physical strength, beauty, and health. (2) Others concern the soul, as knowledge, virtue, and the like. These are the chief goods, for external things are for the sake of the body, and the body for the sake of the soul, as matter for form and as an instrument for a principal agent. Now the common view of all philosophers is that the goods of the soul are the most important.

143. The Stoics and the Peripatetics held divergent views about some goods. The Stoics were of the opinion that some goods are not human goods because they do not make man better. The Peripatetics, that is, the followers of Aristotle, asserted indeed that external goods are the least of goods— the goods of the body being, as it were, means—but the chief goods in their judgment were the goods of the soul, by which man is made good. Other goods, however, according to them are called good insofar as they serve as means toward the principal goods. Thus happiness, since it is the chief good, must be numbered among the goods of the soul. Hence it is evident that the placing of happiness in an operation of the rational soul, as we said above (119-126), is in agreement with this ancient opinion common to all philosophers, that the most important goods are those belonging to the soul.

144. Second [A', 1, b], at "It was stated accurately," he proves the same thing in a different way. The soul, he says, has two kinds of operations. Some of these pass into external matter, as weaving and building. Operations of this sort are not ends but things done for ends, that is, woven cloth and a completed house. Other operations of the soul, however, remain in the agent himself, as understanding and willing. Operations of this kind are ends. It was correctly stated (119-120), when we said that happiness is an operation and not a product, that acts and operations themselves are ends. Thus happiness is classified as one of the goods belonging to the soul and not an external good. Now in an immanent action the operation itself is a perfection and a good of the agent, but in a transient action the perfection and the good is found in the external effect. Hence not only is the aforesaid view in agreement with the position of the philosophers who hold that goods of the soul are the chief goods—and we said happiness was concerned with the operation of the soul—but also in this, that we place happiness in the operation itself.

145. Then [A', 2], at "This coincides," he shows that the things generally agreed on about happiness fit in with our view, for it was said above (45, 128) that everyone identifies living a good life and doing well with being happy. What we said is in agreement with this notion or understanding of happiness because a good life appears to be good activity and happiness seems to be of this nature. Those things truly are said to live which of themselves are moved to activity.

146. Then [B, B'], at "Everything that philosophers," he shows that even

the things in which others differ are in agreement with the aforesaid view. On this point he does three things. First [B', 1] he brings forward the points on which men differ about happiness. Second [B', 2], at "Our definition of happiness etc.," he shows that each of these is in agreement with the above view. Finally [Lect. XIV; 3], at "Next we investigate etc." (B.1099 b 9), he asks and answers a certain question concerning the premises. In regard to the first he does three things. First [B', 1, a] he states what he wishes to show, that everything that was looked for in happiness by various philosophers in various ways seems "to be found in our notion," that is, to be preserved in his view.

147. Second [B', 1, b], at "Some have taught," he gives different views on happiness. (1) The first [b, i] of these is that happiness consists in virtue. This has three variations. Some taught that (a) any virtue, but especially moral virtue which perfects the appetite under the control of the reason, constitutes happiness. To others it seemed that (b) happiness consists in prudence which perfects the practical reason. Still others think that (c) happiness is found in wisdom which is the ultimate perfection of the speculative reason.

148. (2) The second opinion [b, ii] holds that all or any of these may constitute happiness provided that pleasure be added. This is understood in two senses. Some maintained that (a) virtue and pleasure almost in equal measure constitute happiness. Others (b), while placing happiness in virtue primarily, assign a secondary role to pleasure.

149. (3) A third opinion [b, iii] adds to these elements of happiness a full measure of external goods, like riches and other material goods.

150. Third [B', 1, c], at "The rank and file," he indicates the difference

in the persons holding the foregoing views. He says that the majority, that is, the common people and some men of antiquity who were not well-grounded in such matters, held some of these opinions such as pleasure and riches being necessary for happiness. But others, the minority but distinguished and famous men, held that happiness consisted rather in goods of the soul. It is likely that none of these was entirely wrong but that each of them was right on some points.

151. Then [B', 2], at "Our definition of happiness," he shows that these views are in agreement with what he previously assigned to happiness. First [2, a] he shows that this is true of the first opinion which held that virtue is happiness. Second [Lect. XIII; 2, b], at "The life of those etc." (B.1099 a 9), he shows that it is true of the second opinion which adds pleasure. Finally [Lect. XIII; c, i], at "It seems, however etc." (B.1099 a 32), that it is true of the third opinion which adds external goods. In regard to the first assertion he does two things. First [2, a, i] he shows that the first opinion given is in agreement with his. Second [2, a, ii], he shows how his opinion is better. He affirms, therefore, that the definition of happiness given above (130) as an activity according to virtue is acceptable to those who held that all virtue or one virtue constitutes happiness. It is evident that virtuous activity is something belonging to virtue.

152. Then [a, ii], at "But besides, it makes a great difference," he shows that his own view is better: first [ii, x], from reason; second [ii, y], from a custom among men by the words "At the Olympic games." He says first that it makes a great deal of difference in external goods whether the most important good is in the possession of a thing or in its use—which is obviously better than possession. It is

the same, too, with a habit of virtue and its operation or use which is of greater value than the habit. A habit can exist in a person who is not actually doing any good act, as in one who is asleep or not engaged in any way whatsoever. But this is not possible with an operation. It necessarily follows that that man should operate in whom there is an operation, and that he should produce a good effect if there be in him a virtuous operation. Consequently, a virtuous operation is more perfect than virtue itself.

153. Then [ii, y] when he says "At the Olympic games," he proves the same thing by a custom among men. Concerning this we must know that in Macedonia there is a very high mountain called Olympus where certain competitive sports, called Olympic games, were held. In these, not the strongest and best looking athletes but only the winning contestants received the crown, for those who did not compete were ineligible for the prize. So also, of those who are good and best in virtuous living, only those are illustrious and happy who actually perform good deeds. Hence it is better to say that happiness is a virtuous operation than virtue itself.

LECTURE XIII

Some Place Happiness in Virtue with Pleasure; Others Say External Goods Are Necessary for Happiness

<table>
<tr><td>

ANALYTICAL OUTLINE
OF ST. THOMAS

</td><td>

TEXT OF ARISTOTLE
(*B.1099 a 9*)
Chapter 8

</td></tr>
</table>

b. (He shows that) the second opinion, which holds that happiness consists in virtue together with pleasure, (is in agreement with the definition given above).

    i. He shows how this position harmonizes with his own opinion.

        X. FIRST HE STATES HIS PROPOSITION.

        Y. HE GIVES EVIDENCE FOR HIS STATEMENT.

           aa. By showing first that virtuous action should be pleasurable.

The life of those who act in accord with virtue is itself pleasurable. **154**

Now pleasure is an activity *10* proper to a living being. And everyone finds pleasure in what he is fond of, as a lover of horses finds pleasure in horses and a lover of shows in shows. In the same way a man who loves justice finds pleasure in just deeds, and in general one who loves virtue finds pleasure in virtuous activity. **155**

           bb. This pleasure is preferable to others.

Many experience pleasure in things that are in opposition to one another because the pleasure is not in accord with human nature. Men, however, who love the good find pleasure in the things which are inherently pleasurable. Of this kind are virtuous operations that therefore are pleasurable not only to virtuous men but also by their very natures. **156**

    ii. He shows how it differs (from his own opinion).

        X. HE STATES A PROPOSITION.

This type of life then has no need of pleasure as an accessory but is pleasurable in itself. **157**

Y. HE GIVES EVIDENCE FOR HIS
STATEMENT.
    aa. Virtuous life is pleasurable
        in itself.

It should be added that every virtuous person rejoices in virtuous acts, for no one will call a man just who does not enjoy doing just deeds; no one will call a man generous who does not *20* enjoy giving generously. Similarly we speak of men in other virtuous activities. From this it is clear that actions in accord with virtue are pleasurable in themselves.   **158**

    bb. It has nobility and good-
        ness in a high degree.

Granting this, such actions are noble and good. In fact they have each of these qualities in the highest degree, if a good man judge truly in this matter as we have said he does. Happiness is the best, therefore, the noblest and most pleasurable of all things.
    159-160

    cc. He excludes a false opin-
        ion.

These qualities do not belong to different things as the inscription at Delos has it: "The best is the just thing, the most desired is health, and the sweetest to obtain is the heart's desire." But they are all found together in the most virtuous actions. In all these or in the best of these we say happiness con- *30* sists.   **161**

c. He comes to the third opinion . . .
that external goods are necessary to
happiness.
    i. . . . This opinion may conform
    to the truth.

    ii. . . . Evidence for his statement.

It seems, however, that happiness stands in need of external goods, as we have said,   **162**

for it is impossible, or at least difficult, for an indigent man to perform certain virtuous actions. Many good *b* deeds become feasible, as we have pointed out, by the aid of friends and money and political influence. Then, too, the lack of other blessings, like noble birth, good children, and physical beauty spoil a man's happiness. One who is extremely ugly, lowborn, or alone in the world and without children cannot be entirely happy. Much less is he happy who is cursed with wayward children or evil associates or who has lost friends by death. In our opinion then it seems that happiness has need of external prosperity to a degree.   **163**

For this reason some have identified good fortune with happiness. Others, however, prefer to place happiness in virtue.   **164**

COMMENTARY OF ST. THOMAS

154. After the Philosopher has shown how the first opinion, which places happiness in virtue, is in agreement with the definition given above, and how it differs from it, he now does the same [b] regarding the second opinion, which holds that happiness consists in virtue together with pleasure. On this point he does two things. First [b, i], he shows how this position harmonizes with his own opinion. Second [b, ii], at "This type of life etc.," he shows how it differs. On the initial point he does two things. First [i, x] he states his proposition; and then [i, y] gives evidence for his statement at "Now pleasure is etc." He says, therefore, first that the life of those who act virtuously is itself pleasurable. Happiness then which we place in an operation of virtue does not lack pleasure which, in their judgment, happiness requires.

155. Then [i, y], at **"Now pleasure is,"** he proves his statement by showing first that virtuous actions should be pleasurable [i, y, aa] and second [i, y, bb], at "Many experience etc.," that this pleasure is preferable to others. He says first that pleasure is an activity proper to animals. Although we may attribute a natural appetite to inanimate things, we attribute pleasure only to a being having perception. From this we see that pleasure properly belongs to the activities of a soul, one of which

is happiness. Now in activities of this kind, everyone finds pleasure in what he is fond of. As a lover desires the thing which is absent, so he takes pleasure in it when it is present. In this way a lover of horses finds pleasure in a horse; and a lover of shows, in a show. Hence it is evident that every virtuous person loves the activities of his own virtue as something agreeable to him. To the extent that the just man loves justice he will take pleasure in doing just deeds. It is universally true that virtuous operations are pleasurable to virtuous persons who love virtue.

156. Then [i, y, bb], at **"Many experience,"** he shows that this pleasure is preferable to others. He explains that the things pleasurable to the majority of men are contrary to one another. Prodigality, for instance, is a source of pleasure to the spendthrift, while hoarding delights the miser. This happens because these pleasures are not in accord with human nature common to all men, in other words with reason, but rather with the corruption of an appetite departing from reason. But to men loving the good of virtue, these things are pleasurable that are inherently so, that is, that are agreeable to man according to reason, the perfection of his nature. Because of this, all virtuous men take pleasure in the same things—virtuous operations—which are naturally pleasurable to men according

to right reason. These are pleasurable not only to men but also in their very nature. But evil actions give pleasure to men who get used to them by corrupt habits. Since then what is of itself and by nature such is preferable, pleasure arising from virtuous operation will be more delightful than other pleasures.

157. Then [b, ii], at "This type of life," he shows in what respect this opinion may not be true. In regard to this he does two things. First [ii, x] he states a proposition. Second [ii, y], at "It should be added etc.," he gives evidence for his statement. We must, therefore, consider in regard to the first that those who hold that happiness consists in virtue together with pleasure seemed to intimate that virtue may have need of some extrinsic pleasure for the perfection of happiness. Aristotle disagrees here saying that the life of those who act in accord with virtue does not need pleasure as an extrinsic addition. That life is pleasurable in itself.

158. Then [ii, y], at "It should be added," he gives evidence for what he has affirmed. In regard to this he does three things. First [ii, y, aa] he proves that virtuous life is pleasurable in itself. Second [ii, y, bb], at "Granting this, such actions etc.," he proves that it has nobility and goodness in a high degree. Third [ii, y, cc], at "These qualities do not etc.," he excludes a false opinion. He says first that to the reasons proving (154-156) that virtuous actions are naturally pleasurable, we must add that pleasure necessarily belongs to virtue and pertains to its very nature. There is no virtuous person who does not enjoy the good deeds he does. He proves this inductively by saying that no one will call that man just who does not rejoice in doing just deeds. A similar observation may be made of the generous man and of a man practicing any virtue. The reason is that the act of a virtuous man is agreeable to him according to a proper habit, and as a

consequence he derives pleasure from it. From this it is clear that virtuous actions are pleasurable in themselves and do not require pleasure external to them.

159. Then [ii, y, bb], at "Granting this," he shows that actions in accord with virtue are not only pleasurable but also noble and good. Actions indeed are pleasurable to an agent when they are agreeable to him by reason of a proper habit. They are noble or beautiful because of a right order of circumstances as of parts, for beauty consists in a fitting arrangement of parts. They are good because ordered to the end.

160. He adds that each of these three qualities belongs to virtuous actions in a high degree. He proves this by the judgment of a good man. Such a man, since he has the right feeling for human works, judges them correctly. In another field the man with a healthy sense of taste will make correct judgment on flavors. But a good man judges that actions in accord with virtue are eminently pleasurable, noble, and good, so much so that he puts them before any other pleasures, beauties, or goods. Since, therefore, happiness consists in virtuous actions, it follows that happiness is the best, most beautiful, and most pleasant.

161. Then [ii, y, cc], at "These qualities do not belong," he excludes from his doctrine a certain opinion. To understand this we must recall the inscription in Apollo's temple at Delos: "The best is what is most just. The most desired is to be healthy. The most delightful is that which one desires to enjoy." But the Philosopher says that these three qualities do not belong to different things, but all three belong to virtuous actions in all of which or in the best of which happiness consists. Therefore there is one—happiness—which is the best, most beautiful, and most desired or most delightful.

162. Then [c], at "It seems, however," he comes to the third opinion

which held that external goods are necessary to happiness. In regard to this he does three things. First [c, i] he brings out in what way this opinion may conform to the truth. Second [c, ii], at "for it is impossible etc.," he gives evidence for his statement. Third [c, iii], at "For this reason some etc.," he draws a conclusion from the premises. He says first that the third opinion given above (149) seems true in this that happiness has need of external goods, as was indicated previously (111).

163. Then [c, ii], at **"for it is impossible,"** he gives evidence for his statement. In this matter we must consider that happiness needs certain external goods as instruments to perform the good deeds in which happiness consists. Touching on this he says that it is impossible or difficult for a man, who does not possess the means for gifts and expenditures, to practice certain virtuous acts. In many works of virtue we we make use of friends, wealth, and political power, as in the case of someone who is a ruler or an official. There are some external goods which lend a beauty to happiness insofar as they make a man pleasing in the eyes of others giving him a kind of splendor. At this point he adds that a lack of certain externals clouds a man's happiness making him as it were contemptible in the eyes of others, as is evident in a man who lacks noble birth, good children or even physical beauty. A man is not entirely happy when he is ugly since this makes him contemptible and despised. The same is true of one who is lowborn or who does not have good children. Much less is he happy who has wicked sons or friends, for this limits his virtuous activity. Likewise, it is incompatible with happiness to have lost good friends by death, for such a loss means grief of heart. So it seems then that happiness has some need of goods of fortune.

164. Then [c, iii], at **"For this reason,"** he comes to the conclusion that although happiness consists in virtuous actions, nevertheless it needs external goods to some extent. Such externals are called goods of fortune because they often fall into a man's lap, or, in bad luck, desert him. For this reason some have held that good fortune and happiness are identical. But others have identified happiness with virtue, as was said above (66-68).

LECTURE XIV

The Cause of Happiness

ANALYTICAL OUTLINE
OF ST. THOMAS

TEXT OF ARISTOTLE
(*B.1099 b 9*)
Chapter 9

3. HE . . . INVESTIGATES THE CAUSE OF HAPPINESS.

a. He states the question.

Next we investigate whether happiness is something which can be learned or acquired by habit or attained in some way by training. Does it come to us by divine providence or by *10* chance?   165-166

b. He explains it.
  i. *First . . . in parts.*
    X. IT IS EMINENTLY REASONABLE FOR HAPPINESS TO HAVE A DIVINE CAUSE.

If anything is the gift of the gods to men it is reasonable to think that happiness, the best by far of all human goods, is the gift of God. But this subject is perhaps more properly treated in another science.   167-168

    Y. IT IS ACCEPTABLE FOR IT TO HAVE A HUMAN CAUSE.
      aa. (This) does not do away with . . . (it being) most excellent and divine.

On the other hand, if happiness is not sent directly by God, but comes to men by virtue and study and exercise, it would still be judged most divine. As the reward and end of virtue it is apparently most excellent and divine and blessed.   169

      bb. He proves the same point in this way.

It will also be common to human nature because, supposing it be the result of discipline and study, happiness can be had by all who are not impeded from virtuous action.   170

    Z. HE SHOWS IT IS NOT FITTING FOR (HAPPINESS) TO BE AN EFFECT OF CHANCE.
      aa. First.

If such is the case, it is better that happiness be attained in this way *20* than by chance, and it is reasonable to have it so. The things that are in accord with nature are as good as they can

71

bb. He offers a second reason.

ii. Then (he explains) by offering a common reason.

c. He shows that the previously discussed definition . . . is in agreement . . . with his opinion.

i. He shows what concurs with his earlier remarks.

ii. He concludes what is the correct view in accord with this opinion.

    x. NO DUMB ANIMAL IS CALLED HAPPY.

    y. HE ALSO EXCLUDES CHILDREN FROM HAPPINESS.

be by their very make-up. The same too can be said of what is produced by art or by any cause especially the highest.   171

Besides, to abandon the greatest and the best good to the vagaries of chance is most pernicious.   172

What we seek is evident from the definition of happiness as a certain kind of activity of the soul in accord with virtue. Of the remaining goods some are necessary to enrich happiness and others work instrumentally for its attainment.   173

This—that happiness is a virtuous activity—is apparent in the light of what was laid down in the beginning.[1] There we stated that the end of political *30* science is the best of human goods, for the principal aim of this science is the formation of men in such a way that they will become upright citizens and doers of good works.   174

That is why we do not say properly that a cow or a horse or any other animal is happy, for it is not pos- *B.1100* sible for any of them to participate in moral activity.   175

For the same reason children are not really happy, in that they have not yet attained sufficient age for the performance of virtuous deeds. Children are called happy because they give promise of happiness, while real happiness needs perfect virtue and a complete life as we have already pointed out.[2]   176

[1] Ch. 2, 1094 a 27.
[2] Ch. 7, 1098 a 16-18.

COMMENTARY OF ST. THOMAS

165. After the Philosopher has shown how different opinions are in agreement with the definition of happiness presented above, here [3] he naturally investigates the cause of happiness. First [3, a] he states the question, and second [3, b], at "If anything etc.," he explains it. In regard to the first we must consider that happiness must proceed from either a *per se* and determined cause, or an incidental and indetermined cause, that is, chance. If from a *per se* and determined cause, this will be either human or divine. In the case of a human cause, the effect is produced in us in three ways: first by learning, as a science; second by practice, as a moral virtue; third by exercise, as a military drill and other things of this kind.

166. Accordingly he proposes the question in three parts. The first concerns a human cause. He asks whether happiness is something that can be learned as a science, or that can be acquired by habit as a moral virtue, or that can to some extent be had by training, like setting-up exercises. The second part concerns a divine cause. He asks whether happiness is something divine in us and a sharing in some way of godlike qualities which are above men. The third part concerns an incidental and indetermined cause. In other words he asks whether happiness occurs to man by chance.

167. Then [3, b], at "If anything," he explains the question first [b, i] as it were in parts by considering the individual sections of the question; and then [b, ii], by offering a common reason taken from the definition of happiness at "What we seek is evident etc." In regard to the first he does three

things. First [i, x] he shows it is eminently reasonable for happiness to have a divine cause. Second [i, y], at "On the other hand etc.," he shows that it is acceptable for it to have a human cause. Third [i, z], at "If such is the case etc.," he shows it is not fitting for it to be an effect of chance. He says first that if the gods (i.e., beings called gods by the ancients) make gifts to men, it is reasonable that happiness be the gift of the supreme God because it is the most excellent of human goods. It is obvious that a thing is led to a higher end by a higher virtue or power, for instance, man is led to a higher end by military art than by bridle-making. Hence it is reasonable that the ultimate end, happiness, should come to man from the highest power of all, that of the supreme God.

168. That separated substances may bestow something on men becomes evident from the fact that men and separated substances are alike in the power of intelligence. As the lower bodies are brought to perfection by the higher bodies so the lower intellectual beings by the superior intellectual beings. But there is no reason to delay any longer on this matter for it belongs rather to another science, metaphysics.

169. Then [i, y], at "On the other hand," he shows it is acceptable to say that happiness has a human cause. Although God is the principal cause, man does contribute something to happiness. Aristotle shows this in two ways. First [y, aa], the fact that happiness has a human cause does not do away with its chief characteristic, that it is most excellent and divine. He says that if happiness is not a gift sent directly by God but comes to men by virtue as a thing

acquired by habit, or by study as a thing to be learned, or by exercise as a thing to be had by training, nevertheless it seems to be something especially divine. The reason is that since happiness is the reward and end of virtue, it follows that it is something most excellent and divine and blessed. A thing is not called divine only because it comes from God but also because it makes us like God in goodness.

170. Second [y, bb], at "It will also," he proves the same point in this way. Applicable to happiness is the idea that what belongs to the purpose of a nature should be something common to the things having that nature, for nature does not fail in what it intends except in the minority of cases. So if happiness is the end of human nature, it must be common to all or many having human nature. This principle remains intact if the cause be a human one. If happiness be had through discipline and study it could come to everyone who is not impeded in the performance of virtuous works either by defect of nature as those who are naturally stupid, or by an evil habit which imitates nature. From this it is clear that the happiness spoken of by the Philosopher, does not consist in that contact with separated intelligence by which man can understand all things, as certain people have maintained. Such experience does not happen to very many, in fact, to no one in this life.

171. Then [i, z], at "If such is the case," he rejects chance as the cause of happiness for two reasons. First [z, aa], things that are in accord with nature are very good, since nature produces what is suitable. The same is true also of everything made by art or by any cause whatsoever. This is especially the case with the principal cause from which happiness, as the most excellent good, seems to depend. The reason is that art and all efficient causes operate for the sake of good. It fol-

lows, then, that every agent should most aptly arrange, as far as possible, what he does. This particularly applies to God who is the cause of all nature. The things which are in accord with nature seem to be better from their very make-up. But it is better that happiness springs from a *per se* cause, either divine or human, than from chance which is an incidental cause, for what is *per se* is preferable to what is incidental. Consequently, chance is not the cause of happiness.

172. He offers a second reason [z, bb] at "Besides, to abandon." Happiness is the most perfect of all human goods because all others are ordered to it as to an end. Now it would be very harmful if this good were to depend on chance, for other goods would be much more subject to chance. As a result man's zeal in pursuing these goods would vanish, a most perilous situation. Chance, therefore is not the cause of happiness.

173. Then [b, ii], at "What we seek," he settles the question we are considering. He says it is evident, from the definition already given (130), where the truth lies in our investigation of the present question. As was previously indicated (127-128), happiness is an activity of the rational soul in accord with virtue. Now what is in accord with virtue is according to reason influenced by some divine cause. But what is according to chance is contrary to reason. It follows that happiness does not spring from chance but from some human cause immediately and from a divine cause principally and ultimately. Certain other goods, however, in which chance plays a part, do conduce to happiness, but happiness does not chiefly consist in them. Some, though, are necessary for a certain enrichment of happiness, and others work instrumentally to attain it, as we have said (169). But we must

not attribute happiness to chance because of these secondary goods.

174. Then [c], at "**This—that happiness,**" he shows that the previously discussed definition of happiness is in agreement not only with the opinions of others on happiness but also with observations made in keeping with his own opinion. In regard to this he does two things. First [c, i] he shows what concurs with his earlier remarks about happiness (19-42). Second [c, ii], at "This is why etc.," he concludes what is the correct view in accord with this opinion. He says first "this"—that happiness is an activity in accord with virtue—"is apparent," that is, in harmony with the words of the introduction (19-42). We said there that the best human good, happiness, is the end of political science whose goal manifestly is activity in accord with virtue. Political science is especially concerned with framing laws and apportioning rewards and punishments in order to develop good citizens and doers of good works. This is to operate in accord with virtue.

175. Then [c, ii], at "**That is why,**" he concludes from the reason assigned that happiness cannot be attributed to certain beings according to what has been correctly laid down. First [ii, x] he says that no dumb animal is called happy, and rightly so because none of them can share in the activity of virtue which is in accord with reason and which constitutes happiness.

176. Second [ii, y], at "**For the same reason,**" he also excludes children from happiness saying that for a similar reason they cannot be called happy. Lacking sufficient age they have not attained that full use of reason requisite for the performance of virtuous actions. If children are sometimes called happy, this is because we see in them signs that give promise of future excellence. At present, therefore, they are not happy, for happiness as we have indicated (127-129) needs perfect virtue to be not only a good but the best operation and a life perfected by good activity which is continuous and permanent.

LECTURE XV

A Problem About Happiness

ANALYTICAL OUTLINE
OF ST. THOMAS

TEXT OF ARISTOTLE
(*B.1100 a 5*)
Chapter 9

A. Whether anyone can be called happy in this life.

A' He gives the reason for the problem.

> Many changes take place in life and all kinds of fortune are met with in the course of a lifetime. Sometimes a very prosperous man falls into great misfortune in old age as we read of Priam in the epic poems. Certainly no one calls a man happy who has enjoyed such goods of fortune and then ends his days in misery.   **177-178**

Chapter 10

B' He presents the problem.

1. FIRST HE ASKS A QUESTION.

> Is no man then to be called *10* happy so long as he lives, but must we consider the end of life, as Solon believed?   **179**

2. HE BRINGS UP AN OBJECTION.

> If we hold this to be so, it follows that a man will be happy only when he dies. But such an opinion is altogether unreasonable especially for us who maintain that happiness is a kind of activity.   **180**

3. HE REJECTS A PARTICULAR ANSWER (FOR TWO REASONS).

a. In regard to the first.
  i. *He proposes an answer and rejects it.*

> We may say that a dead man is not happy and that Solon did not wish to assert that he is. We may say Solon meant that a man will safely be called

happy at death because he is then beyond the reach of evils and misfortune. This meaning, though, gives rise to a problem. It seems that the dead no less than the living, even though unaware of it, are influenced by good and evil, for instance, by honors *20* and dishonors, by the prosperity and misfortune of children and of descendants in general. **181-182**

ii. He brings up a problem.

A difficulty, however, here presents itself. It may happen that a man lived happily to a ripe old age and has died a worthy death, and afterwards many changes take place in regard to his children. Some of them are good and have gained a position in life they well deserve, while others are just the opposite. Indeed, it does happen that children are quite different from their parents. Now it is incongruous that a dead man should suffer these same changes so that he at one time becomes happy and then again unhappy. On the other hand, it seems unfitting that the affairs of the children should in no way affect the parents, at *30* least for a certain length of time.

183-184

b. He gives the second reason.

But we must return to our first problem. Perhaps from its solution light will be shed on our present difficulty. Let us suppose that we must look at the end and then declare each man happy, not because he is happy but because he formerly was happy. How nonsensical, if when a man is happy we may not affirm it of him since we are unwilling to call the *b* living happy on account of the changes in the present life, because we think happiness permanent and not easily changeable, and because fortune often goes in cycles for the same persons. Obviously, if we use fortune as our norm we will very often call the same person happy and again unhappy as though he were a chameleon, and declare him happy and yet insecure in his happiness. **185-186**

COMMENTARY OF ST. THOMAS

177. After the Philosopher has shown what happiness is, he here raises a problem about happiness, namely [A], whether anyone can be called happy in this life. On this point he proceeds in three steps. First [A'] he gives the reason for the problem. Second [B'], at "Is no man then etc.," he presents the problem. Third [Lect. XVI, C'], at "We ought not to make etc." (B.1100 b 7), he gives the solution. He says first that many changes take place in life; for life rarely remains the same either good or bad. It is stable in few things, changing from good fortune to bad and from bad to good. Sometimes, indeed, the changes occur in small matters and sometimes in great, and sometimes in matters of medium importance. Changes of this sort occur at any age, in adolescence, maturity, or old age.

178. Sometimes it happens that a man has had an abundance of external goods all his life, and in old age falls into great misfortune as Priam did, according to the epic poem of Homer. No one will call that man happy who has enjoyed such goods of fortune and ends his life in misery. The fact that one has been reduced from great prosperity to extreme wretchedness seems to add to his misery.

179. Then [B'], at **"Is no man then,"** he proposes the difficulty. But first [B', 1] he asks a question. Second [B', 2], at "If we hold this etc.," he brings up an objection. Third [B', 3], at "We may say etc.," he rejects a particular answer. First then he asks the question about the view of Solon, one of the seven wise men, who framed the laws of the Athenians. Considering man's life as subject to the changes of fortune, Solon said that no one ought to be called happy so long as he lives, but only at the end of his life. In light of what happened to Priam, the question arises whether any man is to be called happy so long as he lives. Is it best, as Solon holds, to consider the end of life if happiness continues that long, in order that a man may be called happy? Or should this be disregarded?

180. Then [B', 2], at **"If we hold,"** he brings up an objection to the question that was asked, and disproves the saying of Solon. If we hold as true what Solon said, it follows that man will be happy only when he dies. But this seems unreasonable on other grounds, for example, because death is the worst of evils and happiness the greatest of perfections. Besides, happiness is a kind of activity, as we indicated above (119-126). But a dead man does not seem to have an activity. The dead, therefore, cannot be called happy. It should be noted that the Philosopher is not here speaking of happiness in a future life, but of happiness in the present life. Can we attribute happiness to man while he lives or only at death?

181. Then [B', 3], at **"We may say,"** he rejects an answer, and this for two reasons. He gives the second reason [3, b] at "But we must return to our first problem etc." In regard to the first [3, a] he does two things. Initially [a, i] he proposes an answer and rejects it. Second [a, ii] by reason of this he brings up a problem at "A difficulty, however, here presents itself etc." In regard to the first point we must consider that the previous argument of Aristotle showed that a

man is not happy in death. Now this will be granted by anyone who says that a dead man is not happy: Solon did not mean that a man is happy when he dies. But he did mean that when a man is dead, a valid argument can be made about his happiness, because the dead man is now beyond the danger of evils and misfortune so that there is no longer any doubt about it. But he rejects this answer saying it contains an uncertainty.

182. A dead man differs from a living man in the loss of consciousness. A good thing or a bad thing—such as defamation of character, the murder of his children, or the loss of riches—could conceivably happen to someone still living, and he might not feel it precisely because he does not know about it. By the same argument, it seems, some good or evil could happen to a dead man who is unaware of it. Here Aristotle is talking about good and evil in public life as his examples —"honor and dishonor"—show. Sometimes certain honors are given to the dead when they are praised and their memory celebrated. Likewise certain dishonors are heaped upon them, for example, when their bodies are exhumed and their remains burned. Also something good or bad can happen to them by reason of the prosperity or misfortune of their children and their grandchildren. Then it would seem that not even the dead are entirely beyond evils and misfortunes. Consequently, even in death men cannot be called happy.

183. Then [a, ii], at "A difficulty, however," he interposes a difficulty arising from the premises. Such things as the prosperity and misfortunes of children and grandchildren present a problem for him. It happens sometimes that a man lives happily—in the way we have described happiness—to old age and dies a worthy death but afterwards many changes take place in regard to his children, some of whom

are good after the example of a worthy father, but others just the opposite. Indeed it does happen that children are quite different from their parents: good parents have wicked children and wealthy parents, needy children. From this statement something unfitting seems to follow for both parents and children.

184. It is inappropriate that a dead man should suffer change because of misfortunes of this sort, so that he who at one time is happy now becomes unhappy. On the other hand it seems improper if, at least for a short time after death, the lot of children should in no way affect the happiness of deceased parents.

185. Then [3, b], at "But we must return," he gives a second reason for rejecting the previous answer. He says that, passing over the second problem, we must return to the first, the solution of which will shed light on the truth of the second. Now it seems that the answer given is not consistent. If we must look to the end of life and then call a man happy, not because he is then truly happy but because he was previously happy, there seems to be this inconsistency: that when a man is happy, we may not say of him that he is happy, since the truth of a statement in the past is founded on the statement being true at the time it actually occurred. Therefore "fuisse" is true of a thing because "esse" was true of it.

186. But some were unwilling to call a man happy because of the changes in the present life inasmuch as they were under the impression that happiness was something permanent and not easily changeable; otherwise it would not satisfy the natural desire. For everyone naturally desires to remain secure in the good he possesses. But the wheel of fortune very often turns for the same persons, so that they change from good fortune to bad and conversely. Thus it is evident that

if in judging about happiness we should follow the consideration of fortune and should say of someone that he is happy in this life, very often we will say of one and the same person that he is happy and again that he is unhappy. In this way we will be saying that a person is happy after the manner of a chameleon, an animal which changes color in keeping with different surroundings. We will be declaring that the happy are insecure in their happiness which is contrary to the nature of happiness.

LECTURE XVI

Happiness and Changes of Fortune

ANALYTICAL OUTLINE
OF ST. THOMAS

TEXT OF ARISTOTLE
(*B.1100 b 7*)
Chapter 10

I. HE SOLVES THE PRINCIPAL PROBLEM.

C' The philosopher here solves (his problem).

a. He introduces a point necessary for the solution of the problem.

We ought not to make changes of fortune our norm because good and evil do not consist in these, although human living does stand in need of external goods, as we have indicated. But virtuous action is the dominant factor in human happiness just as *10* vicious action is the dominant factor in man's unhappiness. **187**

b. He applies it to the solution of the present problem.

   i. First he shows that deeds of virtue are especially long-lasting compared to other human things.

This contention is strengthened by what we have just learned, for virtuous actions are more uniformly constant than other human activities. They are more abiding apparently than the speculative sciences. Among the virtues the most noble seem to be more lasting both because the happy man is quite intent on them and because he lives according to them at all times. For this reason man does not forget about the virtues. **188-190**

   ii. He shows that . . . happiness can endure all during life.
     X. FROM THE ACTIONS THEMSELVES.

The happy man will have what we had inquired about,[1] for he will be happy all his life. He will always, or nearly always, perform virtuous *20* actions and be contemplating the life of virtue. **191-192**

[1] I.e., stability.

Y. FROM THE GOODS OF FORTUNE.
aa. (In general).

Because he is really good and four-square without reproach, he will bear all changes of fortune most admirably and will be eminently prudent in all matters.[1]   193

bb. In detail.

Many events differing in importance happen by the change of fortune. A short run of good luck or of bad luck clearly does not notably affect life. But great and frequent good fortune will be an occasion of a happier life, for external goods were made to enrich human life and their use is becoming and a means of virtue. On the contrary, great and frequent evils cause the happy man external annoyance and internal affliction bringing about sadness and hindering many good *30* works. However, even here the good of virtue shines forth when a man gracefully endures frequent and major misfortunes not because he is insensible to the sorrow but because he is courageous and magnanimous.
                                    194-197

iii. He shows that all inconveniences are avoided if we follow this teaching.

If virtuous actions play the dominant role in a happy life that we have indicated, a happy person will not become unhappy nor will he *B.1101* sometimes perform hateful and evil actions. As a truly good and wise man in the estimation of all, he will bear the changes of fortune in a becoming manner. He will always make the best of the existing circumstances like a general who employs his present forces to the best advantage in battle or like the cobbler who makes the best shoe possible from the leather at hand or like other artisans in similar circumstances. This being the case, then the unhappy man will certainly not become happy. We can say too that the happy man will not fall into the misfortunes of Priam. He will not *10* easily be moved. He will not be changed from happiness by minor misfortunes but only by great and fre-

[1] Cf. Plato's *Protagoras,* 339.

c. He brings to an end his own
thoughts on happiness.

quent ones. After such catastrophies
he will not become happy again soon
but, if indeed he does, it will take an
abundance of good and noble deeds
during a long period.   **198-199**
    What therefore hinders us from call-
ing that man happy who acts in accord with perfect virtue and has sufficient external goods not for a short
time but all during life? We must also
add that he will live his whole life in
this way and will die in a manner
befitting reason because the future is
not clear to us; and we understand
happiness as an end altogether perfect
in every respect. If this be so, we shall
call those happy in this life— *20
happy we must remember as men—
who have now and will have the conditions we presented. Now we have
said enough on these points. **200-202**

COMMENTARY OF ST. THOMAS

187. After explaining his problem,
the Philosopher here [C'] solves it.
First [C', 1] he solves the principal
problem. Second [Lect. XVII; 2], at
"It seems quite foreign etc." (B.1101
a 22), he solves the lesser one. In regard to the first he does two things.
First [1, a] he introduces a point necessary for the solution of the problem.
Second [1, b], at "This contention is
strengthened," he applies it to the solution of the present problem. In regard
to the initial point we should consider
that while happiness consists essentially in the performance of virtuous
actions, external goods that are subject to fortune are in a way tools of
happiness. Hence he says we ought
not to make changes of luck the norm
for reckoning a man happy or unhappy, because man's good or evil,
which is judged by reason, does not

consist principally in such changes of
luck. Human living however does
stand in need of external goods as
means, as has been indicated (163).
But virtuous actions are the principal
and predominant factor in a man's
happiness so that he can be called
happy principally because he acts virtuously. On the contrary, vicious actions are powerful and dominant in
the opposite state, which is misery, so
that he is truly miserable who is occupied with evil deeds.
    188. Then [1, b], at "**This conten-
tion is strengthened,**" he applies what
was said just now (187) to the solution of the problem. First [b, i] he
shows that deeds of virtue are especially long-lasting compared to other
human things. Second [b, ii], at "The
happy man will have etc.," he shows
that in keeping with what was said,

happiness can endure all during life. Third [b, iii], at "If virtuous actions play etc.," he shows that all inconveniences are avoided if we follow this teaching. He says first that what we have now learned (186) about the permanence of happiness confirms our contention that virtuous actions are of foremost importance in happiness. The reason is that no human activity is found so uniformly constant as these. It is clear that external goods, and even internal bodily goods, because material and corporeal, are subject to change by their nature. But the goods that belong to the soul are changeable only indirectly, and so less liable to change. Of the goods pertaining to a man's soul, some belong to the intellect as the sciences, and some to the activities of living as the virtues. These virtues are indeed more lasting than the disciplines, i.e., the demonstrative sciences.

189. However, this must not be understood as referring to the matter, for demonstrative sciences have as their object necessary things which cannot be otherwise. It is to be understood rather as referring to the exercise of the act. Now we do not have the same opportunity to cultivate the study of the sciences continually as we do to practice virtue, for situations are constantly arising where we must act according to virtue or contrary to virtue as in the use of food, association with women, conversations with other men, and similar actions with which human life is continuously concerned. Hence it is reasonable that the habit of virtue be more firmly fixed in man because it is used more than the habit of science.

190. Among the virtues themselves, the most noble seem to be more lasting both because they are more intense and because men work more constantly to live according to them. Such are the virtuous operations in which happiness consists, because they are most

perfect as has been proved (128, 130, 150, 160, 164). This is naturally the reason why man does not forget to be virtuous because he continually has the occasion to exercise the virtues. Another reason too is that virtue consists chiefly in the inclination of the appetite which is not destroyed by forgetfulness.

191. Then [b, ii], at "The happy man will have," he shows that according to this doctrine happiness can last a lifetime. He says that virtuous actions are most lasting, as was pointed out (188-190). If then happiness be placed principally in them as we have said (153-190), it would follow that the happy man will have what was inquired about in a previous question, that is, he will be happy all his life. He proves this first [ii, x] from the actions themselves at "He will always."

192. One who has a habit perfectly can act always or almost continually according to that habit in everything he does. The happy man possesses perfect virtue, as was explained above (187, 188). Consequently, he can always or nearly always perform virtuous actions in a life of activity and can attentively consider in a life of contemplation.

193. Second [ii, y], at "Because he is really good," he shows the same thing from the goods of fortune, an object of lesser importance in happiness. He says [y, aa] that the happy man will bear all changes of fortune most admirably and will be eminently prudent in all matters, since he is really a good man and not superficially so. He is "foursquare" without reproach, or, as some have explained, perfect in the four cardinal virtues. But this interpretation does not seem to be according to the mind of Aristotle who has never been found making such an enumeration. The tetragon does however indicate something perfect in virtue after the manner of a cube, which has six squared surfaces and so lies

evenly on any surface. Similarly the virtuous person is of an even temperament in any fortune. Since, therefore, it pertains to virtue to bear all fortune becomingly, obviously the happy man will not cease to act virtuously because of any change of fortune. He shows this then in detail [y, bb], as it were by way of division, when he adds "Many events."

194. He says that since many good and bad things differing in importance may happen by changes of fortune, it is evident that a short run of good luck and likewise a short run of bad luck do not change life from happiness to misery or conversely. If, however, they are great and frequent they will be either good or bad. If good, they will make a man's life happier. The reason is that, as was indicated above (169, 173), happiness has need of external goods either as adornments or as means of virtuous actions. In regard to adornments he says that they were made to enrich the life of man. As to the means of virtuous actions, he says that the use of external goods is becoming and virtuous insofar as virtues make use of them to perform worthy deeds.

195. If on the contrary the evils should be frequent and great, they will cause the happy man external annoyance and internal affliction, because internally they bring about sadness and externally they hinder good works. However they do not eliminate virtuous action entirely, because virtue makes good use even of misfortunes themselves. In this way the good of virtue shines forth insofar as a man gracefully endures frequent and great misfortunes, not because he may not feel the sorrow or sadness as the Stoics held but, being courageous and magnanimous, his reason does not succumb to such afflictions.

196. This, in fact, was the difference between the Stoics and the Peripatetics, whose leader was Aristotle.

The Stoics held that sorrow in no way afflicts a virtuous man, because, in their view, corporeal or external things are not in any sense a good of man. The Peripatetics, on the contrary, said that a virtuous man is affected by sadness, yet this does not overwhelm reason but is moderated by it. In their opinion corporeal and external things do not constitute the greatest but the least good of man and this in the degree that they help him.

197. But it should be observed that some change could happen that would entirely take away a man's happiness by hindering virtuous action altogether. For example, some sickness could cause madness or insanity or any other mental breakdown. Since happiness may not be attained except by living humanly or in accord with reason, when the use of reason is gone, human living is not possible. Consequently, in what concerns living humanly, the condition of madness must be equated with the condition of death. So seemingly we must say the same of him who continues in virtuous action until loss of mind as if he had continued until death.

198. Then [b, iii], at "If virtuous actions play," he excludes the unsuitable things that seemed to follow from the premises. He says that if virtuous actions play the dominant role in happiness, as we have asserted (188), it will not follow that the happy man becomes unhappy on account of misfortunes, or that because of misfortune he will perform actions contrary to virtue. But by reason of his perfect virtue the happy man—it can be predicted—will bear all changes of fortune becomingly like a truly good and wise man. In other words he will act according to virtue under every condition. Even if he does not perform the same actions in every contingency, he will always act most nobly according as the circumstances are favorable or unfavorable. He will use the ma-

terial that fortune provides in the way that a good general with an awareness of the condition of his army ought to dispose his existing forces to the best advantage in battle. A commander will do one thing if he has seasoned troops and another if he has an army of raw recruits. Likewise, a cobbler ought to make the best shoes possible from the leather at hand. He will of course make better shoes from one piece of leather than from another. The same may be said of all other craftsmen.

199. If this is so, the unhappy man will not be made happy by any additional good fortune. The reason is that he will use that good fortune badly and the evildoer will always remain unhappy. Likewise the happy man will not fall into the misfortune of Priam. First because he will prudently guard against it. Second, because if he should be stricken unexpectedly, he will bear it most gracefully, as we have pointed out (198). He will not, therefore, be changed easily from happiness to unhappiness by any misfortune whatsoever except by frequent and great changes that deprive him of the use of reason. If he has been made unhappy, he will not readily become happy again but he will need an abundance of great and noble things acquired after a long time by the exercise of virtuous action and by the restoration of external fortune.

200. Then [1, c], when he says **"What therefore,"** he brings to an end his own thoughts on happiness. He says that nothing hinders us from calling that man happy who acts in accord with perfect virtue and has sufficient external goods for virtuous activity, not just for a short time but all during life or at least for a long period. This is enough for a man to be called happy in this life.

201. If we wish to understand happiness in the most perfect sense possible, we must add to the definition of happiness that the happy man will live his whole life as we have indicated (129) and will complete it by dying in a manner befitting reason. It appears that this condition must be added because the future is unknown to us. Now all that is perfect and best seems to belong to the definition of happiness, since it is the ultimate end. In this second way Solon was speaking of happiness. If the case be as just described (200) we shall call those men happy in this life who have now and will have in the future the conditions we have laid down (177-186).

202. But because these things seem not to measure up in all respects to the conditions required for happiness above (104-117), he adds that those we call happy are men, subject to change in this life, who cannot attain perfect beatitude. Since a natural desire is not in vain, we can correctly judge that perfect beatitude is reserved for man after this life. He concludes with the remark that we have said enough on these points.

LECTURE XVII

The Fortune of Friends and Happiness of the Dead

ANALYTICAL OUTLINE
OF ST. THOMAS

TEXT OF ARISTOTLE
(*B.1101 a 22*)
Chapter 11

2. HE SETTLES A DOUBT . . . ABOUT THE CHANGE OF FORTUNE IN REGARD TO FRIENDS.

a. He compares the good fortunes and misfortunes happening to friends with those which happen to man himself.

   i. He proposes that the things happening to one's friends affect the man himself.

It seems quite foreign to the nature of friendship and contrary to the common opinion to say that changes in the fortunes of descendants and of friends have no influence on man's happiness.   **203**

   ii. He shows what the things are and their nature.

Many and vastly different things happen in fortune. Since some of these touch us closely and others remotely, it would be a long, even an endless, task to determine the extent of each. It will be enough to discuss the subject in broad and general terms. Some of the fortunes affecting a man himself are of sufficient importance to better the conditions of life while *30* others are of lesser moment. We can affirm the same of the events which happen to friends generally.   **204-205**

b. He compares the events that happen to the dead with what happens to the living.

   i. He shows . . . there is a difference in regard to . . . the living and dead.

It makes much more difference that an experience should happen to the living or the dead than that certain injustices and evils should be indicated as happening before the action of the drama or should be committed in the course of the drama. We must take this difference into consideration.   **206-208**

ii. He inquires whether the lot of friends affect the dead.

X. FIRST HE EXAMINES THE PROPOSITION.

Perhaps we should rather in- *b* quire whether the dead share in any prosperity or adversity. It seems from what has been said that if any event either good or bad affects the dead, it will be fleeting and insignificant in itself or in its effect upon them. If this be the case, then the event will not be so great or of such a nature as to make happy those who are not happy, or to take away happiness from those who have it. **209**

Y. HE BRINGS TO A CONCLUSION HIS CHIEF PROPOSAL.

The good actions done by friends, therefore, do have some influence on the dead. Misfortunes too seem to affect them. But all these take place in such a way and to such an extent that they do not make the happy un- happy nor produce any other like changes. **210-212**

COMMENTARY OF ST. THOMAS

203. After the Philosopher has solved the principal doubt concerning the change of fortune for the happy man, here [2] he settles a doubt raised above (183) about the change of fortune in regard to friends. On this point he does two things. First [2, a] he compares the good fortunes and misfortunes happening to friends with those which happen to man himself. Second [2, b], at "It makes much more etc.," he compares the events that happen to the dead with what happens to the living. In regard to the first he does two things. Initially [a, i] he proposes that the things that happen to one's friends affect the man himself. Second [a, ii], at "Many and vastly different etc.," he shows what the things are and what their nature is. He affirms, first, that to say that the

prosperity or adversity of great grand- children or of descendants in general and of all friends would have no effect on the happiness of a man, liv- ing or dead, seems to be incongruous for two reasons. Primarily indeed, be- cause it would be contrary to the na- ture of friendship that is a union among friends to such an extent that one considers as his own what belongs to the other. Then too, because this would be contrary to the common opinion which cannot be entirely false.

204. Then [a, ii], at **"Many vastly different things,"** he shows what events may affect the happiness of a friend and the nature of these events. He says that many and vastly different things happen in prosperity or adversity, in kind, in quantity, in time, and in other respects. Some of them touch us closely

and others remotely. If then we should wish to determine in every case which of them affect the man himself and which do not, the task would be a long one, in fact almost endless, because differences happen in an infinite variety of ways.

205. With regard to the fortunes affecting a man himself it is sufficient to note in general, and so to speak, typically, by way of distinctive qualities or superficial likeness, that some acts of fortune are of sufficient importance and influence to change the condition of human life and do contribute to happiness. Others, however, are of lesser moment and help man's life but little. The same thing takes place in the events that happen to any of our friends except that things even of lesser moment happening to blood-relatives affect us more.

206. Then [2, b], at "It makes much more difference," he shows in what manner the changing fortunes of friends affect a person—it is rather evident how this touches a man while he lives, even how this may affect the dead. On this point he does two things. First [b, i] he shows in what way there is a difference in regard to this about the living and the dead. Second [b, ii] he inquires whether the lot of friends affect the dead, since it is clear they do affect the living. This he does at "Perhaps we should rather inquire." On the first point we must consider that the dead are outside the present life, the happiness of which Aristotle here intends to inquire about, as appears from what has been previously said (180). They have contact with this life only as they remain in the memories of the living. The dead, therefore, may be compared in this way to the living—when we consider this life—as the events actually happening now are compared to those that took place long ago and are now recounted—for example, the Trojan war or any incident of this kind.

207. He then remarks that it makes a great difference whether a particular misfortune befalls men while they are living or after they are dead—a far greater difference than it makes in a tragedy whether certain evil deeds like murder, robbery, or any other kind of misfortune be recounted by the playwrights as preceding the action of the drama or are performed in the course of it. The reason is that in the first case (the living and the dead) the same misfortunes affect them but in a different way because of their different states, for some are actually engaged in human affairs, while the others exist only in memory. But in the second case (in tragedies) the converse is true, for the "dramatis personae" are all engaged in human affairs, but some of the trials befalling them are recounted as here and now taking place, while others are simply indicated as having previously occurred. Because happiness refers rather to persons than to things happening externally, the Philosopher says that the first difference (which refers to the living and the dead)—precisely as it pertains to the point at issue, namely, a change of happiness—is of more importance than the second (which refers to actions in tragedies). And by reason of a similar inference concerning the difference of events, he says that we must consider the difference in our question.

208. Now it is clear that even though a recitation of past evils in a way influences the hearer who is in some measure affected by them, it does not do so to the extent of changing his condition. Consequently, much less do fortunes change the condition of the dead. This is brought out by the Philosopher to clear up, as it were, the statement made above (184), which concluded that if something affects men who are not conscious, it affects also the dead.

209. Then [b, ii], at "Perhaps we should rather inquire," he inquires last

whether things happening to friends affect the dead in some way. First [ii, x] he examines the proposition; and second [ii, y], he brings to a conclusion his chief proposal at "Therefore the good actions." He says first that we should rather inquire whether the dead in any way share in the prosperity and adversity that take place in this life. That a man is not changed from happiness to unhappiness or the other way round seems sufficiently established. The reason is that if an event taking place here, either good or bad, affects the dead, it will be fleeting and insignificant in itself or in its effect on them. But if this is the case, it will not be so great or of such a nature as to make them happy who are not happy, nor to take away happiness from them who have it. It has been said already (194) that trifling happenings do not cause a change in life. If then an insignificant event, among the things that happen, affects the dead, it follows that their condition of happiness will not be changed.

210. Then [ii, y], at **"Therefore the good actions,"** he concludes his opinion. He says that the good actions done by friends or the evil befalling them seem to have some influence on the dead, and misfortunes too seem to affect them. But these take place in such a manner and to such an extent that they do not make the happy unhappy or the unhappy happy, nor do they change the dead in such things as wisdom or virtue or the like. However, the construction can be conditioned by the words "If this be the case." Then the statement "do have some influence" will be properly conditional, and the conjunctive particle will be superfluous.

211. It seems that Aristotle intends that the things said here are to be understood of the dead not as they are in themselves but as they live in the memory of men. In this way what happens to their friends after death seems to affect the dead so that their memory and glory become more distinct and more obscure. But this, he says, is indeed a fleeting thing because nothing is more fleeting than what exists only in the opinion of men. He says also that it is an insignificant thing especially for the dead themselves because it belongs to them only to the extent they are remembered by men.

212. The questions, however, whether the souls of men survive in some fashion after death and whether they are aware of or are changed in any way by what occurs in this life do not pertain to our purpose since the Philosopher here is treating of the happiness of the present life, as is evident from what was said above (206). Consequently inquiries of this kind, which need to be considered at some length, must be omitted at this point lest in this science which is practical many discussions outside its scope be carried on—a procedure that the Philosopher condemned (136). Elsewhere we have treated these subjects more fully.

LECTURE XVIII

Happiness, A Good Deserving Honor

ANALYTICAL OUTLINE
OF ST. THOMAS

TEXT OF ARISTOTLE
(B.*1101 b 10*)
Chapter 12

II. HE INQUIRES ABOUT A CERTAIN PROPERTY OF HAPPINESS.

A. He asks a question.

Having settled these matters we *10* must investigate whether happiness is one of the goods to be praised or, more properly, to be honored. It is obviously not in the genus of potentiality.
213-214

B. He ascertains the truth.

A' He shows that happiness is of the number of goods to be honored.

1. HE SHOWS TO WHOM PRAISE IS GIVEN.

a. He presents his proposition.

Now a thing that is praiseworthy has a certain proportion in itself and some sort of relation to another. **215**

b. He proves his proposition.
   i. From human praises.

Thus we generally praise the just, the brave, and the good man and even virtue itself because of the works and actions. We praise also the physically strong, the swift, and the like as possessing a certain natural ability, and as ordered in some way to a thing good in itself and desirable. **216-217**

   ii. From divine praises.

Our point is obvious too from the praises of the gods, for such praises *20* would be ridiculous if judged by our standard. This happens because praises are given by reason of relation to another, as we have indicated. **218**

2. HE CONCLUDES THAT SOMETHING BETTER THAN PRAISE IS GIVEN TO THE BEST.

a. He puts the conclusion this way.

If praise belongs to things of this kind, clearly something greater and better than praise is given to the best.
219

b. He proves the previous conclusion from what is commonly held.

   i. In regard to the things of which there is something better than praise.

     X. HE FIRST PRESENTS WHAT SEEMS TO BE COMMONLY HELD.

This seems to be true, for we call gods blessed and happy as we do the most godlike among men. We speak in a similar way of goods, for no one praises happiness as he praises a just man, but he ascribes to happiness something better and more divine, namely, blessedness. 220

     Y. SECOND, WHAT SEEMED SO TO EUDOXUS.

Apparently Eudoxus put pleasure in the first place for a good reason. He thought that this is intimated from *30* the fact that pleasure is a good not praised but is better than things praised, such as God and any good in itself. To things of this kind, other things are referred. 221

   ii. In regard to the things of which there is praise.

Praise surely belongs to virtue since doers of good works are praised for activity of body and of soul in accord with virtue. But perhaps a consideration of this subject more properly belongs to those who labor over the study of laudatory statements. It is *B.1102* obvious now to us from our discussion that happiness is a perfect good and one to be honored. 222

  B' He shows the same thing from the fact that happiness has the nature of a principle.

This appears to be true also from the nature of a principle. Now men do all that they do for the sake of happiness. But we look upon such a principle and cause of good as something divine and a thing to be honored. 223

COMMENTARY OF ST. THOMAS

213. After the Philosopher has shown what happiness is, here [II] he inquires about a certain property of happiness. First [II, A] he asks a question, and second [II, B], he ascertains the truth, at "Now a thing that is

praiseworthy etc." He says that after determining the preceding matters, it is necessary to examine whether happiness is of the number of goods to be honored or to be praised. He proves that happiness must be contained under the one or the other kind of good by the fact that happiness is not in the genus of potentiality. A man is not praised or honored because he has the potentiality to good but because he is somehow disposed to good.

214. To have an understanding of this question, we must consider that honor and praise differ in a twofold manner. First on the part of that in which honor or praise consists. In this respect honor is more extensive than praise. Honor signifies testimony manifesting a person's excellence either by word or by deed, as when one genuflects to another or rises for him. But praise consists only in words. Second, praise and honor differ in regard to that for which they are given, for both are given on account of some excellence. Now there are two kinds of excellence. One is absolute and in this sense honor is due to it. But the other is an excellence in relation to some end, and in this sense praise is due.

215. Then [II, B], at **"Now a thing that is,"** he answers the question. First [B, A'] he shows that happiness is of the number of goods to be honored, because it is a thing perfect and best. In the second place [B, B'] he shows the same thing from the fact that happiness has the nature of a principle, at "This appears to be true also etc." On the first point he does two things. Initially [A', 1] he shows to whom praise is given. Second [A', 2] he concludes that something better than praise is given to the best, at "If praise belongs etc." In regard to the initial point he does two things. First [1, a] he presents his proposition. Second [1, b] he proves the proposition at "Thus we generally praise the just etc." He says first that everything that is praised

seems to be praiseworthy for two reasons simultaneously: (1) because it has a certain kind of disposition in itself and (2) because it has a relation of some sort to another.

216. Then [1, b], at **"Thus we generally praise,"** he proves the proposition first [1, b, i] from human praises and second [1, b, ii] from divine praises at "Our point is obvious too from the praises of the gods." In regard to the first we must consider that a man is praised both because of virtue of mind and because of power or strength of body. By reason of virtue of mind, a man (for instance, one who is just or brave or virtuous in any way) is praised for having virtue. The virtue also is praised, and this because of something else, namely, virtuous works and actions. The virtuous man and virtue itself then are praised insofar as they are ordered to do the work of virtue. Second, a man is praised by reason of power or strength of body because he is strong in fighting, swift in running, and so forth. This happens because the athlete is in a way ordered to something good in itself and desirable as worthy of achievement.

217. We must pay attention to the difference between virtues or powers of mind and body. It is sufficient in the praise of virtue of soul that a man be well disposed to the proper act of the virtue. The reason is that the good of man consists in the very act of virtue. But in the virtue or strength of body it is not sufficient that a man be well disposed to the act of virtue, for instance, for running or for wrestling. Human goodness does not consist in such things, since a man can run, wrestle, or fight for both a good and an evil purpose. Consequently, when speaking of the praises of the virtues of the soul he said they are praised because of works and actions (that flow from them). But in speaking of the powers of the body he indicated that

93

they are praised in relation to something else.

218. Then [1, b, ii], at **"Our point is obvious too,"** he explains what is meant by divine praises. If something be praiseworthy absolutely and not as related to some other thing, it follows that the thing is praiseworthy in all circumstances. But this is clearly false in the case of praises given to separated substances that he calls gods. It would seem ridiculous to praise them for things that are praised in men, for instance, because they are not overcome by concupiscence or fear. This is so because praises are given by reason of a relation to something else, as has been pointed out (214).

219. Then [A', 2], at **"If praise,"** he concludes his proposition from what has been said. First [2, a] he puts the conclusion this way. Praise is given to the things whose goodness is considered in relation to something else. But the best things are not ordered to anything else but rather other things are ordered to them. Therefore, something better than praise is given to the best. In a somewhat similar way, there is no science for the study of speculative principles, but something higher than science, understanding. Science is concerned with conclusions which are known by means of principles. Likewise, praise is concerned with things whose goodness is for the sake of others. But honor, a thing better than praise, is concerned with things to which other things are ordered.

220. Second [2, b], at **"This seems to be true,"** he proves the previous conclusion from what is commonly held. First [2, b, i] in regard to the things of which there is something better than praise; and second [2, b, ii] in regard to the things of which there is praise at "Praise surely belongs etc." In regard to the first he does two things. To prove his proposition he first [i, x] presents what seems to be commonly held and second [i, y] what seemed so

to Eudoxus at "Apparently Eudoxus." He says first that it seems commonly held that there is something better than praise for the best. This is made clear from the fact that those ascribing to the gods as it were something better than praise call them blessed and happy. They say the same, too, of the best among men who have a certain likeness to the gods by reason of excellence. As we ascribe something better than praise to the best among men, so also to the best of goods like happiness. No one praises happiness in the way he praises a just or virtuous man. Something better is ascribed to happiness when we call it blessedness.

221. Then [i, y], at **"Apparently Eudoxus,"** he reduces the saying of Eudoxus to the same argument. Now Eudoxus called pleasure the first fruits of good, saying that pleasure is the supreme good. He thinks this is intimated from the following. Pleasure is a good that is not praised because in itself it is something better than the things that are praised. No one indeed is praised on account of pleasure, for instance, God and any other good in itself. The reason is that things whose goodness is praised are referred to things good in themselves. Things that are praised are praised precisely because they are somehow related to the things that are good in themselves.

222. Then [2, b, ii], at **"Praise surely,"** he proves what he said in respect of the things to which praise is given. He says that praise belongs to virtue which makes us doers of good works, for a person is praised because of activity of body or soul as was just mentioned (216-217). But a consideration of the words used by men in bestowing compliments pertains more properly to rhetoricians who labor over the study of laudatory statements. It belongs to the kind of subject that deals with praise or dispraise (*demonstrativum genus*)—one of the three

falling under the study of rhetoric, as is clear from the Philosopher in the first book of the *Rhetoric* (Ch. 3, 1358 b 21-1359 a 5) and from Tully (Cicero) in his *Rhetoric* (*De Oratore,* Bk. II, Ch. x, xi). So far as we are concerned it is obvious from the above (220) that happiness is of the number of goods to be honored because it is a perfect good.

223. Then [B, B'], at **"This appears to be true also,"** he proves his proposition from the nature of a principle. We look upon the principle and the cause of goods as a thing to be honored, for it is as it were something divine, since God is the first principle of all good. But happiness is the principle of all human good because men do all that they do by reason of happiness. Now the end in things to be done and things to be desired has the nature of a principle because the nature of the means is understood from the end. Hence it follows that happiness is a good to be honored.

LECTURE XIX

Happiness and Virtue

ANALYTICAL OUTLINE   TEXT OF ARISTOTLE
OF ST. THOMAS   (*B.1102 a 4*)
                              Chapter 13

I. HE PREMISES CERTAIN THINGS NECESSARY FOR THE STUDY OF VIRTUE.

A. He shows that it pertains to this science to study virtue.

A' First by a reason taken from the doctrine on happiness.

> If then happiness is a kind of operation according to perfect virtue, we must investigate the question of virtue. In this way we shall perhaps make a more profound study of happiness. **224**

B' Second . . . from the particular nature of this science.

> Now political science really seems to be concerned especially with the attainment of virtue. Its object is to produce good citizens obedient to the laws, as is exemplified by the lawmakers of the Cretes and the *10* Spartans, and others like them. If this investigation belongs to political science, the study will be obviously conducted according to the disposition we made in the beginning. **225**

B. He assumes certain things we must know about the parts of the soul.

A' He shows it is necessary that such things be discussed in this science.

I. HE SHOWS THAT IT IS NECESSARY . . . TO CONSIDER CERTAIN QUESTIONS ABOUT THE PARTS OF THE SOUL.

> The virtue we are investigating then will be human virtue, for we were seeking human good and human happiness. Now we call that virtue human which is proper not to the body but to the soul. Besides, we say that happiness is an activity of the soul. *20* Since this is so, obviously the statesman

must know to some extent the things pertaining to the soul, as he who is to heal the eyes or the whole body should know something about physiology. In fact the knowledge of the statesman should be greater insofar as political science is nobler and more important than medicine. But skillful physicians make it their business to know much about the body. Therefore, the statesman must study the soul.   226-227

2. HE SHOWS HOW WE MUST CONSIDER THESE QUESTIONS.

The soul must be studied for the sake of the objects investigated and to the extent that suffices for them. To make a more exhaustive study would be a greater task than the subject requires.   228

B' He takes them up.

I. HE DIVIDES THE PARTS OF THE SOUL.

a. He gives the division.

Certain things about the soul are adequately treated in extraneous discourses. We should use these, for instance, this distinction of the soul into irrational and rational.   229

b. He says that a certain question must be left unanswered.

But whether the parts are distinct as particles of a body or anything *30* physically divisible, or whether the parts are indivisible in nature and distinguishable according to reason alone, as the convex and concave of the circumference of a circle, is irrelevant to the present question.   230

COMMENTARY OF ST. THOMAS

224. After the Philosopher has finished the treatise on happiness, he begins the consideration of virtue. First [I] he premises certain things necessary for the study of virtue. Second (B.1103 a 14) he begins to define virtue in the beginning of the second book at "Virtue is of two kinds etc." [Lect. I]. In regard to the first he does three things. First [I, A] he shows that it pertains to this science to study virtue. Second [I, B], at "The virtues we are etc.," he assumes certain things we must know about the parts of the

97

soul. Third [Lect. XX; C], at "Virtue is divided etc." (B.1103 a 4), he divides virtue according to the division of the parts of the soul. He proves the initial point in two ways. First [A, A'] by a reason taken from the doctrine on happiness. It was pointed out previously (128, 130, 150, 160, 164, 175, 187, 190) that happiness is an action according to perfect virtue. Hence we can study happiness better by means of knowledge of virtue. In keeping with this, he completes the treatise on happiness when he finishes the study of all the virtues in the tenth book (1953-2180). Since then the principal object of this science is the good of man, which is happiness, an inquiry into virtue fittingly comes within the scope of this science.

225. Second [A, B'], at **"Now political science,"** he proves the proposition from the particular nature of this science. Political science seems really to make a special study of virtue and its attainment. Indeed the object of political science is to produce good citizens obedient to the laws (as is evident from the lawmakers of the Cretes and the Spartans who had model states, and from others framing similar laws to make men virtuous). But the study of the present science is connected with political science because its principles are given here. Obviously then a consideration of virtue will be suitable to this science. Accordingly in the introduction (25-31) we placed political science, which investigates the ultimate end of human actions, above all other sciences.

226. Then [I, B], at **"The virtue,"** he takes up certain questions pertaining to the parts of the soul, which are necessary for the knowledge of virtues. On this point he does two things. First [B, A'] he shows it is necessary that such things be discussed in this science. Second [B, B'] he takes them up at "Certain things about the soul etc." In regard to the first he does

two things. First [A', 1] he shows that it is necessary in this science to consider certain questions about the parts of the soul. Second [A', 2], at "The soul must be studied etc.," he shows how we must consider these questions. First, since it is our intention to investigate virtue, we understand that we are speaking of human virtue. We have just now noted (224) that we are looking for human good and human happiness in this science. If, therefore, we seek virtue for the sake of happiness, we necessarily seek human virtue. But that virtue is peculiarly human which is proper to the soul, for it does not belong to the body nor is it shared in common with other beings. Pertinent here is what we said before (123-126), that happiness is an activity of the soul.

227. In the study of the soul whose virtue he seeks, the statesman is compared to the physician who studies the body seeking its health. Obviously then the statesman must know to some extent the things belonging to the soul, as the physician who treats the eyes and the whole body must study something about the eyes and the whole body. The obligation of the statesman to study the soul whose virtue he seeks is greater because political science is more important than the science of medicine—a fact we know from what was said previously (25-31). Consequently, the study of political science must be more thorough. We see that skillful physicians study many things which will give them a knowledge of the body and not merely what concerns cures. Hence a statesman gives some thought to the soul.

228. Then [A', 2], at **"The soul must be studied,"** he shows in what way the statesman ought to investigate these things. In this science, he says, the soul must be studied for the sake of the virtues and human actions that are the principal objects here investigated. Therefore, the study of the

soul must be such as suffices for the things chiefly sought. If a man should wish to make a more exhaustive study, he will be imposing a greater task than the object of our investigation requires. So too in all other things sought for the sake of an end, the extent of them must be measured according to the end itself.

229. Then [B, B′], at **"Certain things about the soul,"** he takes up the things we must consider here about the parts of the soul. First [B′, 1] he divides the parts of the soul into rational and irrational. Second [Lect. XX; 2], at "One part of the irrational soul etc." (B.1102 a 33), he subdivides the irrational. Third [Lect. XX; 3], at "If however we must etc." (B.1103 a 2), he subdivides the other member of the first division, that is, the rational part of the soul. In regard to the first he does two things. First [1, a] he gives the division. Second [1, b], at "But whether the parts etc.," he says that a certain question must be left unanswered. He says first that certain things about the soul have been adequately treated in the book *De Anima,* which he calls extraneous discussions because he wrote the book as an epistle to persons living at a considerable distance. The books that he was accustomed to teach his students (auditors) were called reports or notes

(auditions), as the books of the *Physics* are entitled on the audition of classes about Nature; or they are called extraneous for the better reason that they are outside the scope of the immediate science. However, here we must use the things discussed in that book, for instance, one part of the soul is rational, another part irrational as is asserted in the third book *De Anima* (Ch. 9, 432 a 27; St. Th. Lect. XIV, 797).

230. Then [1, b], at **"But whether the parts,"** he asks a certain question which is to be left unanswered intentionally. Are the two parts of the soul, rational and irrational, distinct from one another in their subject according to location and position, as particles of a body or of some other divisible continuum? Plato located the rational part or power of the soul in the brain, the emotional part in the heart, and the assimilative part in the liver. Or perhaps these two parts are not divided according to subject but only in concept as in the circumference of a circle the convex and concave are not distinguished by subject but in concept alone. He says that so far as it concerns us at present, it does not matter which opinion is held. Hence he leaves the question unanswered because it does not pertain to our present purpose.

LECTURE XX

Subdivisions of the Irrational Soul

ANALYTICAL OUTLINE
OF ST. THOMAS

TEXT OF ARISTOTLE
(*B.1102 a 33*)
Chapter 13

2. HE SUBDIVIDES THE IRRATIONAL PART.

a. He presents one member of the subdivision.

   i. He mentions an irrational part of the soul.

One part of the irrational soul is like the vegetative soul common to all living things. By vegetative I understand that part which is the cause of nutrition and growth. Such a power of the soul is found in all things *b* that assimilate food. It is found even in embryos and in the lowest forms of animal life. To these it is more reasonable to assign the vegetative part than some other.   231-232

   ii. He shows that this part is not properly human.
     X. FIRST HE CONCLUDES THIS FROM THE PREMISES.

Because this power is common, it follows that it is not human.   233

     Y. HE ADDS A PROOF FROM A PARTICULAR EVIDENT SIGN.

It seems that the vegetative part and potency of the soul are most active during sleep. Now good and evil persons are hardly distinguishable in their sleep. Hence the saying that the happy are no better off than the miserable for half their lives. This is a reasonable doctrine, for sleep is a cessation from the operation according to *10* which the soul is called good and evil. Yet perhaps certain activities do penetrate the soul of the sleeper gradually. In this way the dreams of the virtuous become better than the dreams of other persons. But what we have now said on this subject will suffice. Therefore, discussion of the nutritive part must come to an end because it has no part in human virtue.   234-235

b. He presents the other (member of the subdivision).

   i. He indicates what he intends.

Seemingly there is another part of the soul, irrational also but participating in reason to some extent.   236

   ii. He proves his proposition.
      x. THERE IS ANOTHER PART OF THE IRRATIONAL SOUL.

We praise the rational principle in the incontinent and continent man, for reason rightly induces to what is best. But something besides reason seems to be innate in them, which conflicts with reason and resists reason. As paralyzed members of the body are said to *20* move wrongly to the left contrary to the will choosing the right, so also in the soul, for the movement of the incontinent are to things contrary to reason. While the uncontrolled movement can be seen in bodies, it is invisible in the soul. Nevertheless we must judge that there is something in the soul besides reason which is contrary and resistant to reason. But how this differs from reason does not matter at present.   237-238

   Y. THIS PART PARTICIPATES IN REASON.
     aa. His first argument is based on acts taking place within man.
       a' He shows that this irrational part participates in reason.

Now this part seems to share in reason, as we have said. Therefore, as found in the continent man, it is obedient to reason. But it is even more fully subject in the sober and courageous man whose every act harmonizes with reason.   239

       b' He finishes . . . the difference of this irrational part from the part presented above.

Apparently the irrational part is *30* twofold. The vegetative power does not partake of reason at all. But the concupiscible power and every appetitive power participate to some extent because they heed and are obedient to reason. Therefore, we say that reason holds the place of a father and friends but not of mathematicians.   240

    bb. His second (argument) is based on acts external to man.

Persuasion, reproach, and entreaty in all cases indicate that the *B.1103* irrational principle is somewhat influenced by reason.   241

3. HE SUBDIVIDES THE OTHER MEMBER OF THE FIRST DIVISION, THE RATIONAL
PART OF THE SOUL.

> If, however, we must say that this
> part shares in reason, then the ra-
> tional will be of two kinds: one having
> reason principally and of itself, the
> other obedient to the reason as to a
> father.   242

C. He divides virtue according to this difference in the parts of the soul.

> Virtue is divided according to this
> difference, for we call some virtues
> intellectual, others moral. Wisdom,
> understanding, and prudence are said
> to be intellectual virtues, while liberal-
> ity and sobriety are called moral. When
> speaking of man's good morals we do
> not describe him as wise or intelligent
> but as mild-tempered or sober. We do
> praise a person for acquiring the   10
> habit of wisdom since praiseworthy
> habits are called virtues.   243-244

COMMENTARY OF ST. THOMAS

231. After the Philosopher has divided the parts of the soul into rational and irrational, here [2] he subdivides the irrational part. First [2, a]
he presents one member of the subdivision; and then [2, b], he presents
the other at "Seemingly there is another part etc." In regard to the initial point he does two things. First
[a, i] he mentions an irrational part
of the soul. Then [a, ii] he shows that
this part is not properly human, at
"Because this power etc." He says first
that one of the parts of the irrational
soul is like the plant soul and is common to all things living here below.
It is that part which is the cause of
assimilation and growth. Such a part
of the soul is found in every being
that assimilates food not only in creatures after birth but even before birth,

as in embryos that are obviously nour-
ished and grow.

232. Likewise this part of the soul
is discovered not only in the highly
organized animals having all the senses
and endowed with local motion but
also in the lowest animals, like oysters
having only the sense of touch and
rooted to one place. Evidently all these
creatures live and have some kind of
soul. But this vegetative type of soul
rather than some other part is more
reasonably assigned to these lowest animals because the effects of this part are
more evident in them.

233. Then [a, ii], at "Because this
power," he shows that the aforementioned part of the soul is not human.
First [a, ii, x] he concludes this from
the premises. We call human that
which is distinctive of man. If then

a part of the soul is altogether common, it will not be human.

234. Secondly [a, ii, y], at **"It seems that,"** he adds a proof from a particular evident sign. This part of the soul is found to be especially active during sleep, for when the natural heat has returned to the internal organs and the animal is asleep, digestion works better. But what is proper to man precisely as he is said to be good or evil operates only slightly during sleep. Good and evil persons are hardly distinguishable in their sleep. Hence the saying that the happy do not differ from the unhappy for half their life which is spent in sleep. The reason is that judgment of the intellect is bound during sleep, and the external senses do not function, although the imagination and the power of nutrition are active.

235. It is reasonable that the good and evil, the happy and the unhappy are indistinguishable while asleep because that part of man by which he is called good ceases to function during sleep. Good and evil men differ while asleep not on account of a difference occurring during their slumbers but because of what happened in their waking moments. Conscious activity gradually penetrates to the soul of the sleeper so that the things a man has seen or heard or thought while awake, present themselves to his imagination in sleep. In this way the virtuous who spend their wakeful hours in good works, have more edifying dreams than other persons who occupy their conscious moments with idle and evil works. What we have now said on this subject will suffice (234-235). We conclude then from the premises (233-235), that the nutritive part of the soul is not adapted by nature to participate in human virtue.

236. Then [2, b], at **"Seemingly there is,"** he presents the other member of the division. First [b, i] he indicates what he intends; and second

[b, ii] he proves his proposition at "We praise the rational etc." He says first that besides the vegetative part of the soul, there seems to be another part, irrational like the vegetative, but participating in reason to some extent. In this it differs from the vegetative part that has nothing whatsoever to do with human virtue as was just said (235).

237. Then [b, ii], at **"We praise the rational,"** he proves his proposition: first [b, ii, x] that there is another part of the irrational soul; second [b, ii, y] that this part participates in reason at "Now this part seems to share in reason." He proves the first by an argument taken from continent and incontinent men. In this matter we praise the part of the soul having reason because it rightly deliberates and induces to what is best, as if by entreaty and persuasion. Both—continent and incontinent—choose to abstain from unlawful pleasures. But seemingly in both there is something innate in them other than reason, and this something conflicts with reason and resists or hinders reason in the execution of its choice. Obviously it is something irrational, since it is contrary to reason. The sensitive appetite, which desires what is pleasant to sense and at times opposes what reason judges absolutely good, would be such a thing. This appetite in the continent man is restrained by reason, for he certainly has evil desires but his reason does not follow them. On the other hand the appetite in the incontinent man overcomes reason, which is seduced by evil desires.

238. Then he adds an illustration. The members of the body are incapacitated when they cannot be controlled by the regulative power of the soul, as happens to paralytics and the intoxicated who move to the left side when they wish to move to the right. This is true also of the souls of incontinent persons who are moved to the opposite of what the reason chooses.

But the process is not so apparent in the parts of the soul as in the parts of the body. We see clearly in what way a bodily member moves unnaturally, but the movement of the parts of the soul is not so obvious to us. Despite this, we must judge there is something in man that is contrary to reason and resists it. But how this may differ from reason—whether by subject or by concept alone—does not matter at present.

239. Then [b, ii, y], at **"Now this part,"** he shows that an irrational part of this kind participates in reason. His first argument [y, aa] is based on acts taking place within man; his second [y, bb], at "Persuasion, reproach," is based on acts external to man. With the first he does two things. First [aa, a'] he shows that this irrational part participates in reason. Second [aa, b'] he finishes the treatment of the difference of this irrational part from the part presented above, at "Apparently the irrational part." He says first that the irrational part, of which we have now spoken (233-235), seems in some way to participate in reason, as was just said (236). This is obvious in the continent man whose sensitive appetite obeys reason. Although he may have evil desires, nevertheless he does not act according to them but according to reason. In the sober or temperate man this part of the soul is even more fully subject to reason. Such a man has so subdued his sensitive appetite that evil desires in him are not vehement. We may say the same of the courageous man and of anyone endowed with the habit of moral virtue. The reason is that in these men nearly everything—both external actions and internal desires—harmonize with reason.

240. Then [aa, b'], at **"Apparently the irrational,"** he concludes the difference between the two irrational parts from the premises. He says that according to the premises the irra-

tional part is apparently twofold. Now the vegetative part, found in plants, does not partake of reason in any way, for it is not obedient to the direction of reason. But the concupiscible power and every appetitive power like the irascible emotion and the will participate in reason in some measure because they heed the movement of the reason and are obedient to its regulations. Hence we say reason holds the place of a father giving guidance and of friends offering advice. But reason here does not play the role of a mere theorist like the reason of a mathematician, for the irrational part of the soul does not partake in any way of reason understood in this sense.

241. Then [y, bb], at **"Persuasion, reproach,"** he shows through the things externally done that the irrational part participates in reason. In his opinion this is indicated from the fact that the persuasion of friends, the reproach of superiors and the entreaties of inferiors aim to keep a man from following his desires. But all these would be useless unless this part of the irrational soul could share in reason. From this too it is apparent that reason is not controlled by the movements of the passions of the sensitive appetite but quite the contrary—reason can restrain such movements. Therefore, reason is not governed by the motions of the heavenly bodies, which can effect some change in the sensitive appetite of the soul through a change in the human body. Since the intellect or reason is not a faculty of any bodily organ, it is not directly subject to the action of any bodily power. The same is true of the will that is in the reason, as was said in the third book *De Anima* (Ch. 3, 427 a 21; St. Th. Lect. IV, 617-621).

242. Then [3], at **"If however,"** he subdivides the other member of the first division, the rational part of the soul. According to him (if we must say that that part of the soul that par-

ticipates in reason is rational in some way) the rational part will be of two kinds: one, having reason principally and in itself, is rational by nature. But the other is inherently adapted to obey reason as a father, and is called rational by participation. In accord with this, one member is contained under both rational and irrational. Now, one part of the soul, the vegetative, is irrational alone; another part is rational alone, the intellect and reason. Still another part is of itself irrational but rational by participation, like the sensitive appetite and the will.

243. Then [C], at **"Virtue is divided,"** he divides virtue according to this difference in the parts of the soul. He says that virtue is designated or divided according to the above-mentioned difference in the parts of the soul. Since human virtue perfects the work of man which is done according to reason, human virtue must consist in something reasonable. Since the reasonable is of two kinds, by nature and

by participation, it follows that there are two kinds of human virtue. One of these is placed in what is rational by nature and is called intellectual. The other is placed in what is rational by participation, that is, in the appetitive part of the soul, and is called moral. Therefore, he says, we call some of the virtues intellectual and some moral. Wisdom, understanding, and prudence are said to be intellectual virtues while liberality and sobriety are called moral.

244. He proves this point from human praises. When we wish to praise someone for good morals, we do not describe him as wise and intelligent, but as sober and mild-tempered. We do not praise a man for good morals alone but also for the habit of wisdom. Praiseworthy habits are called virtues. Therefore, besides the moral virtues, there are also intellectual virtues like wisdom, understanding, and some others of this kind. Thus ends the first book.

BOOK II

MORAL VIRTUE IN GENERAL

CONTENTS

CONTENTS

LECTURE I

Moral Virtue Is Caused by Habit

ANALYTICAL OUTLINE
OF ST. THOMAS

TEXT OF ARISTOTLE
(*B.1103 a 11*)
Chapter 1

I. HE TREATS THE VIRTUES THEMSELVES.

A. He studies the moral virtues.

A' He investigates the matter of the moral virtues in general.

    1. HE TREATS MORAL VIRTUE IN GENERAL.

a. He is looking for the cause of moral virtue.

  i. He shows that moral virtue is caused in us by actions.

    x. HE SHOWS THE CAUSE OF THE FORMATION OF VIRTUE.

      aa. He proposes that moral virtue originates in us from the habit of acting.

Virtue is of two kinds, intellectual and moral. The intellectual is generated and fostered for the most part by teaching, and so requires time and experience. Moral virtue however is derived from customary action (*mos*). Hence by a slight variation of the original term we have this name "moral."
245-247

      bb. He shows that moral virtue is not in us by nature.

        a' The first (reason) is this.

From this it is clear that moral virtue is not instilled in us by nature, 20 for nothing natural is changed by habit. Thus a stone that naturally gravitates downward will never become accustomed to moving upward, not even if someone should continue to throw it into the air ten thousand times. Neither will fire become accustomed to tend downward, nor will anything else that naturally tends one way acquire the contrary custom. Therefore, the moral virtues are not in us by nature nor are they in us contrary

to nature. We do have a natural aptitude to acquire them, but we are perfected in these virtues by use.

248-249

b′ The second reason.

Again in the things that come to
us from nature, we first receive the
potentialities and afterwards we put
them into operation. This is obvious
in the case of the senses, for we did
not acquire our senses from seeing and
hearing repeatedly but on the contrary
we made use of the senses after we
have them—we did not come into *30*
possession of them after we used them.
Virtues however we acquire by previous activity as happens in different
arts, for the things we must learn how
to make, we learn by making. Thus
men become builders by building and
harpists by playing the harp. Likewise
we become just by doing just ac- *b*
tions, we become temperate by doing
temperate actions, and we become
courageous by doing courageous ac-
tions.   **250**

cc. He explains by a sign what
he had said.

Our contention is verified by what
is done in the state, for legislators
make men good in accordance with
political norms. Such is the aim of
every legislator. In fact he who does
not succeed in this fails in lawmaking.
It is precisely in this way that a good
constitution differs from a bad one.

251

y. (HE SHOWS) WHAT THE CAUSE
OF ITS DESTRUCTION IS.

aa. He explains his proposition.

Again, every virtue has both its
origin and its deterioration from the
same principles. A similar situation is
found in any art, for it is from playing
the harp that both good and bad *10*
harpists are made. Proportionately this
can be said of builders and of all the
rest. Men become good builders from
building well, but they become poor
builders from building poorly. If this
were not so, there would be no need
of a teacher but all would be born
good or bad workmen. This is the
case also with virtue. Of those who

engage in transactions with their fellowmen, some become just and others unjust. Of those exposed to dangers who habitually experience fear or confidence, some become brave and some cowardly. We may say the same of men in reference to concupiscence and anger, for some become temperate and mild, others self-indulgent and *20* irascible; some conduct themselves well in these matters, others badly. We may then universally state in one sentence: like actions produce like habits.

252-253

bb. He infers a corollary.

Therefore, we must cultivate actions of the right sort because differences in actions are followed by differences in habits. It is not of small moment but it matters a great deal—more than anything else—whether one becomes promptly accustomed to good or bad habits from youth.   *254*

COMMENTARY OF ST. THOMAS

245. After the Philosopher has treated the questions introductory to virtue, he now begins the study of the virtues. He divides the treatise into two parts. In the first part [I] he treats the virtues themselves. In the second he examines certain things that follow or accompany the virtues. He does this in the seventh book (B.1145 a 15) at "Now, making a new start, we must say etc." [Lect. I; I]. The first part is subdivided into two sections. In the first [I, A] he studies the moral virtues; in the second the intellectual virtues, in the sixth book (B.1138 b 18) at "But since we previously said etc." [Lect. I]. The reason for this order is that the moral virtues are more known, and through them we are prepared for a study of the intellectual virtues. In the first [A, A'],

which is divided into two parts, he investigates the matter of the moral virtues in general. In the second [Bk. III, Lect. XIV] he examines the moral virtues specifically, at "We stated previously . . . is a mean etc." (B.1115 a 7). This first is again subdivided into two parts. In the first of these [A', 1] he treats moral virtue in general. In the second he examines certain principles of moral actions. This is in the third book [Lect. I] beginning at "Since virtue is concerned with passions etc." (B.1109 b 30). This first has a threefold division. In the first part [1, a] he is looking for the cause of moral virtue. In the second [Lect. V] he seeks to find out what moral virtue is, at "Now we must search out the definition of virtue" (B.1105 b 20). In the third part [Lect. XI] he shows how a man may become virtuous, at "A sufficient explanation has been given etc." (B.1109 a 19). On the initial point he does three things. First [a, i] he shows that moral virtue is caused in us by actions. Second [Lect. II; a, ii] he shows by what actions it may be caused in us, at "The present study etc." (B.1103 b 27). In the third part [Lect. IV] he finds a particular problem in what was previously said, at "Someone may rightly ask etc." (B.1105 a 18). In regard to the first he does two things. Initially [i, x] he shows the cause of the formation of virtue; and second [i, y] what the cause of its destruction is, at "Again, every virtue etc." On the initial point he does three things. First [x, aa] he proposes that moral virtue originates in us from the habit of acting. Second [x, bb] he shows that moral virtue is not in us by nature, at "From this it is clear etc." Third [x, cc] he explains by a sign what he had said, at "Our contention is verified by what is done etc."

246. He says first that virtue is of two kinds, intellectual and moral, and that the intellectual is both generated and increased for the most part by teaching. The reason is that intellectual virtue is ordered to knowledge which we acquire more readily from teaching than by discovery. More people can know the truth by learning from others than by ascertaining it themselves. Everyone indeed who finds out from others will learn more than he can discover by himself. But because we cannot proceed to infinity in the process of learning, men must learn many truths by discovery. Besides, since all our knowledge is derived from the senses, and the senses in turn very often beget experience, it follows that intellectual virtue may need long experience.

247. But moral virtue is derived from customary activity. Now moral virtue, found in the appetitive part, implies a certain inclination to something desirable. This inclination is either from nature, which tends to what is agreeable to itself, or from custom, which is transformed into nature. Hence the name "moral" differing somewhat from custom is taken from it. In Greek *ethos* spelled with epsilon—a short e—means habit or moral virtue, while *ithos* spelled with eta—a long e—signifies custom. With us also, the name "moral" means custom sometimes and other times it is used in relation to vice or virtue.

248. Then [x, bb], at **"From this it is clearly,"** he proves from the premises that moral virtue is not produced by nature for two reasons. The first [bb, a'] is that none of the things from nature are changed by use. He illustrates this point by the example of a stone that naturally tending downward will never become accustomed to moving upward, no matter how often it is thrown into the air. The reason is that the things which naturally operate either merely operate or they operate and are operated upon. If they merely operate, their principle of action is not changed. So long as the cause remains the same, the inclination to the same effect remains. If, however, they so operate as also to be operated upon—unless the passivity be such that it removes the principle of action—the natural tendency in them will not be destroyed. But if the passivity be such as to take away the principle of action, then it will not belong to the same nature. Thus what was previously natural will cease to be natural. When a thing operates naturally, therefore, no change is effected regarding its action. The same is also true if the operation is contrary to nature unless perhaps the motion be such that it destroys nature. But if the natural principle of the operation remains, there will always be the same action. Therefore, in the things that are according to na-

ture and in the things that are contrary to nature habit plays no part.

249. The reason for this is that moral virtue pertains to the appetite that operates according as it is moved by the good apprehended. When the appetite operates often, therefore, it must be often moved by its object. In this the appetite follows a certain tendency in accordance with the mode of nature, as many drops of water falling on a rock hollow it out. Thus it is obvious that the moral virtues are not in us by nature, nor are they in us contrary to nature. We do have a natural aptitude to acquire them inasmuch as the appetitive potency is naturally adapted to obey reason. But we are perfected in these virtues by use, for when we act repeatedly according to reason, a modification is impressed in the appetite by the power of reason. This impression is nothing else but moral virtue.

250. He presents the second reason [bb, b'] at **"Again in the things."** In all the things with which nature has endowed us, potency is previous to operation. This is obvious in the senses. We did not receive the sense of sight and hearing from seeing and hearing repeatedly. On the contrary, from the fact that we had these senses, we began to use them. It did not happen that we came into possession of the senses from the fact that we used them. But we have acquired the virtues by acting according to virtue, as happens in the operative arts in which men learn by making the things that are to be made after they have mastered the skill. In this way men become builders by building, and harpists by playing the harp. Likewise men become just or temperate or courageous by doing just actions or temperate actions or courageous actions. Therefore, virtues of this kind are not in us by nature.

251. Then [x, cc], at **"Our contention is verified,"** he makes known what

he had said, by a sign. He says the statement just made (250) that by performing actions we become virtuous is verified by what is done in the state. Legislators make men virtuous by habituating them to virtuous works by means of statutes, rewards, and punishments. Such ought to be the aim of every legislator—in fact he who does not succeed in this fails in lawmaking. It is precisely in this way that a good constitution differs from a bad one.

252. Then [i, y], at **"Again, every virtue,"** he shows that virtue is produced and destroyed by identical works. First [y, aa] he explains his proposition, and second [y, bb] he infers a corollary from what has been said, at "Therefore, we must etc." He says first that the production and the destruction of virtue have their source in the same principles taken in a different way. The same is true in any art. He shows this first from activities, because men become both good and bad harpists—understanding this proportionately—from the way they play the harp. A similar reason holds for builders and all other workmen. Men become good builders by building well repeatedly, they become poor builders by building poorly. If this were not so, men would not need to learn arts of this kind from some master workman who would direct their actions, but there would be good and bad workmen in all the arts no matter how they would be practiced. As it is in the arts, so also in the virtues.

253. Those who act well in their dealings with their fellowmen become just, and those who act in an evil way become unjust. Likewise those faced with danger who accustom themselves to fear and confidence in the right way become courageous; in the wrong way, cowardly. This is true also of temperance and meekness in the matter of concupiscence and anger.

115

We may then universally sum up in one sentence: like actions produce like habits.

254. Then [y, bb], at **"Therefore, we must,"** he affirms that a person must give careful attention to the performance of such actions because differences in actions are followed by differences in habits. He concludes, therefore, it is not of small moment but it makes a great difference—indeed everything depends on it—that one becomes accustomed to perform either good or evil actions from earliest youth, for we retain longer the things impressed on us as children.

LECTURE II

Virtue and Action

ANALYTICAL OUTLINE
OF ST. THOMAS

TEXT OF ARISTOTLE
(*B.1103 b 27*)
Chapter 2

ii. He now inquires how (virtues are caused in us by actions).

X. HE SHOWS WHAT ARE THE ACTIONS WHICH CAUSE VIRTUE IN US.

aa. He shows the necessity of the present investigation.

a' He presents the necessity itself.

The present study is not pursued for the sake of contemplation like other studies. We seek the definition of virtue not in order to know but in order to become virtuous; otherwise it would have no utility. *30* We must then thoroughly investigate what concerns actions and how they are to be performed, for actions control the formation of habits, as we have pointed out.   **255-256**

b' He shows what we must suppose.

To be in accord with right reason is a quality common to these actions and should be taken for granted. Later we will discuss the question both as to the definition of right reason and as to how right reason is related to the other virtues.   **257**

bb. He treats the method of investigation.

It must be presupposed that *B.1104* any discussion concerning actions to be performed ought to be given in a general way and not definitively. We remarked in the beginning [1] that discussions must be pursued according to the nature of the subject matter. Now things pertaining to actions, and relevant considerations, do not have anything fixed about them any more than the things that concern health. If this be true in the general treatment, still

---

[1] Bk. 1, Ch. 3, 1094 b 13–27.

cc. He shows actions as causes
of virtue.
   *d' He shows by what actions
   virtue is caused.*

*b' He shows that virtue
   already formed pro-
   duces in turn like
   actions.*

more uncertainty will be found in the
consideration of particular cases. Indeed this study does not fall under
either art or tradition. But those who
perform moral actions must always
pay attention to what is appropriate
to the occasion as is done in medicine
and navigation. Although this is *10*
the situation, we ought to try to be
of assistance to others in the present
study.   **258-259**

We must then first consider that
moral matters are of such a nature
as to be destroyed by defect and excess. To prove such notions that are
not readily manifest we must use obvious signs and evidence such as we
have in the case of bodily strength and
health. An excessive amount of exercise no less than a lack of it impairs
health. Likewise eating and drinking
too much or too little causes damage
to health. But health is produced, increased, and preserved by eating and
drinking in moderation. It is the same
then with temperance and fortitude *20*
and the other virtues. The man who is
afraid of everything, who runs away
and will endure nothing becomes a
coward. On the other hand, the man
who fears absolutely nothing and wades
into every danger becomes reckless.
Likewise a man who tastes every pleasure and passes up none, becomes intemperate while he who seeks to avoid
all pleasures like a boor becomes as it
were insensible. Temperance and fortitude are destroyed by excess and defect but are preserved by the golden
mean.   **260-263**

Not only the production, increase,
and destruction of virtues have identical sources and causes but the actions
themselves also have the same *30*
sources and causes. We see this in the
more obvious actions like bodily
strength. A man becomes strong from
taking abundant nourishment and

from hard work. Then when he is strong, he will be more able to do these things. We find the same thing in the virtues since we become temperate by giving up pleasures, and having become temperate we can *b* very easily give up pleasures. The same is true of the virtue of fortitude. We become brave by accustoming ourselves to despise and endure terrors, and having become brave we are very capable of enduring terrors.   264

COMMENTARY OF ST. THOMAS

255. After the Philosopher has shown that virtues are caused in us by actions, he now inquires how this is done [ii]. On this point he does two things. First [ii, x] he shows what are the actions that cause virtue in us. Second [Lect. III; y], at "We may understand etc." (B.1104 b 4), he shows what is the sign of virtue already produced in us. On the initial point he does three things. First [x, aa] he shows the necessity of the present investigation. Second [x, bb], at "It must be presupposed etc.," he treats the method of investigation. Third [x, cc] he shows actions as causes of virtue. In regard to the first he does two things. Initially [aa, a'] he presents the necessity itself. Second [aa, b'], at "To be in accord with right reason etc.," he shows what we must suppose here. Regarding the first we must consider that in the speculative sciences where we seek only the knowledge of the truth, it is sufficient to know what is the cause of a determined effect. But in the practical sciences whose end is action, we must know by what activities or operations a determined effect follows from a determined cause.

256. He says then that the present study, moral philosophy, is not pursued for the sake of the contemplation of truth like the other studies of the speculative sciences, but for the sake of action. In this science we seek a definition of virtue not only to know its truth but to become good by acquiring virtue. The reason he assigns is that if the investigation of this science were for the knowledge of truth alone, it would have little utility. It is not of great importance nor does it contribute much to the perfection of the intellect that a man should know the changeable truth about contingent actions with which virtue is concerned. This being the case, he concludes that we must thoroughly inquire about the actions we ought to perform because, as we have already observed (248-253), actions have influence and control over the formation of good and bad habits in us.

257. Then [aa, b'], at **"To be in accord with right,"** he shows it should be taken for granted that actions causing virtue possess the common quality of being in accord with right reason. This happens because the good of everything consists in the fact that its

operation is suited to its form. Now the distinctive form of man is that which makes him a rational animal. Hence man's action must be good precisely because it harmonizes with right reason, for perversity of reason is repugnant to its nature. Later in the sixth book (1109) we shall ascertain what is right reason, which belongs to the intellectual virtues, and how it pertains to the other virtues, which are the moral.

258. Then [x, bb], at "It must be," he explains the method of investigating matters of this kind. We must presume, he says, that any discussion concerned like this with actions to be performed ought to be given in a general way, that is, as a precedent or as likely, but not definitively. This was pointed out in the introduction to the whole work (24). The reason is that the discussions are to be carried on according to the nature of the subject matter, as was noted in the same place (32). We see that things pertaining to moral actions and materials useful to them, like external goods, do not have in themselves anything fixed by way of necessity, but everything is contingent and changeable. The same occurs in works relating to medicine, which are concerned with health, because the disposition of the body to be cured and the remedies used to effect a cure are changeable in many ways.

259. The teaching on matters of morals even in their general aspects is uncertain and variable. But still more uncertainty is found when we come down to the solution of particular cases. This study does not fall under either art or tradition because the causes of individual actions are infinitely diversified. Hence judgment of particular cases is left to the prudence of each one. He who acts prudently must attentively consider the things to be done at the present time after all the particular circumstances

have been taken into consideration. In this way a doctor must act in bringing about a cure and a captain in steering a ship. Although this doctrine is such as to be uncertain in its general aspects and incapable of precision in particular cases, we ought to study it so that in these matters we may be of some assistance to men in directing their actions.

260. Then [x, cc], at "We must then first," he shows what are the operations that may cause virtue. On this point he does two things. First [cc, a'] he shows by what actions virtue is caused. Second [cc, b'], at "Not only the production etc.," he shows that virtue already formed produces in turn like actions. He says first we must consider before anything else that virtues or operations causing virtues are of such a nature as to be destroyed by excess and defect. To prove this we must use certain more obvious signs and evidence, that is, the things happening in regard to the powers of the body that are more manifest than the capacities of the soul.

261. We see that bodily strength is impaired by immoderate games, that is, certain bodily exercises in which the contestants do battle naked, because the natural power of the body is weakened by excessive exertion. Likewise the lack of exercise destroys bodily strength because, when not exercised, the members remain flabby and incapable of work. A similar comment may be made about health. If someone takes either too much food or drink, or less than he needs, his health is impaired. But if a man uses exercise, food, and drink in moderation, he will become physically strong and his health will be improved and preserved.

262. It is the same with the virtues of the soul, for instance, fortitude, temperance, and the other virtues. A person who fears everything, takes to flight, and never faces anything terri-

fying becomes a coward. Likewise he who fears nothing and wades into every danger thoughtlessly becomes rash. The same is true of temperance. He who tastes every pleasure and avoids none becomes intemperate. But he who avoids all pleasures as a boor does, without any reason, becomes as it were insensible.

263. However we are not to conclude from this that virginity, which abstains from all venereal pleasure, is a vice. The reason is that virginity does not abstain from all pleasures, and that it abstains from particular pleasures according to right reason. Similarly, it is not a vice for some soldiers to refrain from all venereal pleasure in order to devote themselves more fully to fighting. Now these things have been said because temperance and fortitude are destroyed by excess and defect but are preserved by the golden mean, which is understood not according to quantity but according to right reason.

264. Then [cc, b'], at **"Not only,"**

he shows that virtue produces actions similar to the actions that caused it. He says that the same kinds of activity cause the production and increase of virtue, and also its destruction if they are taken in a contrary way. Likewise the operations of the virtues already produced consist in these same works. This is obvious in bodily actions which are more manifest. As bodily strength is caused from the fact that a man can take abundant nourishment and can work hard, and when he has become strong he will be more able to do these things, so also it is with the virtues of the soul. From the fact that we give up pleasures, we become temperate; and when we have become temperate, we can very easily give up pleasures. It is the same with the virtue of fortitude. We become brave by accustoming ourselves to despise and endure terrors, and having become brave we are very capable of enduring terrors. So also, fire once kindled from generated heat can give off intense heat.

LECTURE III

Signs of Virtue

ANALYTICAL OUTLINE OF ST. THOMAS	TEXT OF ARISTOTLE (*B.1104 b 4*) Chapter 3

Y. HE NOW EXPLAINS HOW WE MAY RECOGNIZE VIRTUE ALREADY PRODUCED.

  aa. He presents what he intends to do.

We may understand pleasure or sorrow that follows activity as an indication of the habits that are present. Indeed the man who avoids bodily pleasures is temperate if he is glad about it; intemperate, if sad about it. Likewise, the man who encounters dangers is brave if he rejoices or is not sad, but cowardly if he is saddened. Moral virtue then is concerned with pleasure and sorrows. **265-267**

  bb. He proves his proposition.
  a' By reasons . . . belonging to virtue.
      A. FIRST REASON.

We perform evil actions for the *10* sake of pleasure and avoid good actions because of sadness. Therefore, as Plato says,[1] we need some sort of training from our earliest years so that we may rejoice and be sorrowful about the right things, for proper instruction consists in this. **268**

      B. SECOND REASON.

Besides, if virtues are concerned with activities and passions, and pleasure and sorrow follow every act and passion, then certainly virtue will deal with pleasures and sorrows. **269**

      C. THIRD REASON.

Penalties inflicted because of pleasure and sorrow also prove our point, for penalties are, as it were, remedies. Remedies by their very nature work through contraries. **270**

      D. FOURTH REASON.

Furthermore, as we said pre- *20* viously, every habit of the soul has

[1] *Laws*, 653 sq.

a natural disposition to do and to be busied with those things by which it is made better and worse. Men become wicked by pursuing the pleasures and avoiding the sorrows that are wrong, or by doing this at the wrong time or in the wrong manner or in some other way that one may deviate from reason. Consequently, some define virtues as certain quiescent and emotionless dispositions. But they err in speaking absolutely and in not qualifying the passions as to manner, time, and so forth. We must suppose therefore that virtue is such that it works what is best regarding pleasures and sorrows, and vice does the contrary.   271-272

b' *By reasons on the part of the virtuous man himself.*

A. FIRST REASON.

Our contention will become *30* evident from the following consideration. Three things fall under our choice: the good, the useful, the pleasurable; and three contrary things we avoid: the evil, the harmful, the sorrowful. In regard to all these, the virtuous man disposes himself rightly and the vicious man badly. This is especially true in the matter of pleasure that is common to animals and is found in all things obtained *B.1105* by choice, for the good and the useful seem also to be pleasurable.   273-275

B. SECOND REASON.

Pleasure, too, has grown up with all of us from childhood. Therefore, it is difficult to curb this passion which is acquired with life itself.   *276*

C. THIRD REASON.

Some regulate their activities to a greater degree and others to a lesser degree by pleasure and sorrow. About these, then, our whole study must be concerned, for it is not a thing of small importance in human actions to take pleasure or sorrow in the right or wrong way.   277

D. FOURTH REASON.

As Heraclitus says, it is even more difficult to fight against pleasure than anger. Now the more difficult is *10* always treated by art and virtue, which operate well and more efficiently in the face of difficulty. Hence the whole business of virtue and of political science is occupied with pleasures and sorrows. Assuredly he who uses these well will be virtuous, and he who uses them badly will be evil.   278

cc. He sums up . . . what has been said.

It has been said that (1) virtue treats of pleasures and sorrows, (2) virtue is produced and increased by the same actions that, when done in a different way, destroy virtue, (3) the same actions that produce virtue are in turn produced by virtue.   279

COMMENTARY OF ST. THOMAS

265. After the Philosopher has shown what kind of activity produces virtue, he now [y] explains how we may recognize virtue already produced. On this point he does two things. First [y, aa] he presents what he intends to do; and second [y, bb], at "We perform evil actions etc.," he proves his proposition. Regarding the first we must consider that when virtue produces actions similar to the actions that formed it, as was just noted (264), the performance of this action differs before and after virtue. Before virtue man does a kind of violence to himself in operating this way. Such actions, therefore, have some admixture of sorrow. But after the habit of virtue has been formed, these actions are done with pleasure. The explanation is that a habit exists as a sort of nature, and that is pleasurable which agrees with a thing according to nature.

266. He says that an indication that habits, good or bad, have already been formed is given by the pleasure or sorrow that follows the operations. He illustrates this by examples. The man who is glad that he has avoided bodily

pleasures is temperate because he performs an action in keeping with the habit. Likewise, he who encounters dangers with pleasure, or at least without sorrow, is brave. Particularly in the act of fortitude it is enough not to have sorrow, as will be explained in the third book (584-585). One who faces dangers with sorrow is cowardly. He then assigns the reason for what he has said from the fact that every moral virtue is concerned with pleasures and sorrows.

267. From this we must not conclude that every moral virtue is concerned with pleasures and sorrows as its proper matter. The matter indeed of every moral virtue is that on which reason imposes a norm. Thus justice treats of dealing with others, fortitude treats of fears and aggressiveness, temperance of certain pleasures. But pleasure is the principal end of all the moral virtues, as will be said in the seventh book of the present work (1504-1515). In every moral virtue it is requisite that a person have joy and sorrow in the things he ought. In keeping with this, he says that moral virtue is concerned with pleasures and sorrows be-

cause the purpose of any moral virtue is that a man be rightly ordered in his pleasures and in his sorrows.

268. Then [y, bb], at **"We perform evil actions,"** he proves his proposition: first [bb, a'] by reasons taken from things belonging to virtue, and second [bb, b'], at "Our contention will etc.," by reasons on the part of the virtuous man himself. He presents four reasons pertaining to the first point. The first reason [a', A] is taken from the inclination of men intent on virtue. It was shown previously (264-265) that virtue is produced and destroyed by deeds of the same person done in a contrary way. Indeed, we see that virtue is destroyed by pleasure and sadness; we perform evil actions out of a desire for pleasure, we avoid good or virtuous works because of the sadness we fear in honest labor. Hence, as Plato said,[1] one who is intent on virtue should have some sort of moral training from his earliest years that he may rejoice and be sorrowful about the right things. This is proper instruction for youths so that they become accustomed to take pleasure in good works and be grieved in evil works. Therefore, teachers of youth compliment those who do good deeds and reprove those who do evil.

269. At **"Besides, if"** [a', B] he presents the second reason based on the matter of the moral virtue in the following way. Every moral virtue deals with actions (as justice which treats of buying, selling, and other things of this kind), or with passions (as mildness which treats of anger), and so with the other virtues. But pleasure or sorrow follows every passion that is nothing else but the motion of the appetitive power in pursuit of good or in flight from evil. When the good to which the appetite tends is forthcoming, therefore, or when the evil which it flees is avoided, pleasure follows.

[1] *Laws*, 653 sq.

But when the contrary happens, sorrow follows. Thus the angered man rejoices in getting revenge and likewise the cowardly man in avoiding dangers. But when the opposite is true, these persons are sorrowful. It remains, therefore, that every moral virtue regards pleasures and sorrows as having the aspect of ends.

270. The third reason presented at **"Penalties inflicted"** [a', C] is taken from the idea of a remedy for the soul. As a medicine used for the restoration of health is a kind of disagreeable potion from which the sweetness has been removed, so a penalty used for the restoration of virtue is a kind of medicine, for a penalty consists in taking away certain pleasures or applying certain disagreeable things. The reason for this is that a medicine is naturally to be used as a contrary thing. Thus in the case of fever doctors apply cooling remedies. Hence moral virtue also is concerned with certain pleasures and sorrows.

271. At **"Furthermore, as"** [a', D] he presents the fourth reason, which is taken from what is contrary to and destructive of virtue. Every habit, he says, has a disposition to do and to be busied with the things by which it is made worse and better, that is, by which the goodness of a good habit and the evil of a bad habit is increased. This can be understood likewise of the things by which the habit naturally becomes worse or better, that is, by which it naturally is formed or increased (which is to be made better), or destroyed or diminished (which is to be made worse). We see that men become evil through the deterioration of virtue from the fact that they pursue the pleasures and steer clear of the sorrows which they ought not, or when they ought not, or in some other way by which one may deviate from right reason.

272. The Stoics took occasion of this to say that virtues are certain

quiescent and passionless dispositions. The reason was that they saw men become evil through pleasures and sorrows, and consequently they thought that virtue consists in the total cessation of the changes of the passions. But in this they erred wishing to exclude entirely the passions of the soul from a virtuous man. It belongs, of course, to the good of reason to regulate the sensitive appetite—and the passions are movements of this appetite. Hence it is not the business of virtue to exclude all but only the inordinate passions, that is, those which are not as they ought to be and are not at the time they ought to be (he adds also all the other things belonging to the remaining circumstances). From this he then concludes that we must suppose that virtue should work what is best regarding pleasures and sorrows but vice, which is the habit opposed to virtue, should work what is evil.

273. Then [bb, b′], at "Our contention will," he introduces to his proposition four other reasons taken on the part of men in whom virtue, pleasure, and sorrow are found. The first reason [b′, A] is derived from pleasures in general. He says that three things fall under human choice: the good or virtuous, the helpful or useful, and the pleasurable. Contrary to these are also three things: evil or vice as opposed to the virtuous, the harmful as opposed to the useful, the sorrowful as opposed to the pleasurable. In regard to all these, the virtuous man disposes himself rightly but the vicious man badly, especially in the matter of pleasure, which is more common among the things mentioned since it belongs to two of them.

274. First in regard to the things partaking of pleasure. Pleasure is found in all animals since it is not only in the intellectual power but also in the sensitive power. The useful and the virtuous, however, pertain to the

intellectual power alone. This is so because the virtuous act is performed in accord with reason while the useful implies an order of one to another, and "to order" is proper to reason.

275. Another common feature is on the part of the things themselves in which pleasure is gained. Pleasure, in fact, follows everything that falls under choice. Now the virtuous is pleasurable to man because it is agreeable to reason, and the useful also gives pleasure by reason of the expected benefit. But, on the other hand, not every pleasurable action is useful or virtuous, as is obvious in the pleasures of sense.

276. At "Pleasure, too" [b′, B] he presents the second reason, which is taken from an inherent characteristic of pleasure. Pleasure has grown up with us all alike from childhood, since a newborn child delights in his milk. Therefore, it is difficult for man to curb this passion acquired with life because it starts in man at the beginning of life. Hence moral virtue is especially concerned with pleasure.

277. He assigns the third reason at "Some regulate" [b′, C]. This reason is derived from man's inclination. All men regulate their activities by pleasure and sorrow. They are intent on activities they find pleasant and they avoid activities they find distressing. Hence the whole business of a moral virtue, which is ordered to good activity, must concern pleasure and sorrow. It is quite important to note what activities one finds pleasant or painful, and whether rightly or wrongly so. The reason is that he who rejoices in good performs good actions, but he who rejoices in evil performs evil actions.

278. He assigns the fourth reason at "As Heraclitus says" [b′, D]. This is taken from a comparison with anger. It is more difficult, as Heraclitus said, to fight against pleasure than against anger, even though it seems most difficult to fight against anger because of

its vehemence. But the desire of pleasure is both more common and more natural, and besides, it lasts longer. Art and virtue however always treat of the more difficult, for anyone can operate well in the easier things. But it takes one skilled in virtue and art to operate well in difficult things. Thus it is obvious, from what has been said, that the whole business of virtue and of political science or of public affairs is concerned with pleasures and sorrows. If a man uses these well he will be virtuous, but if he uses them badly he will be evil.

279. Then [y, cc], at "It has been said that," he sums up in conclusion the points that have been made: virtue is concerned with pleasures and sorrows; virtue is produced and increased by the same actions that, when done in the opposite way, destroy virtue; the same actions producing virtue are in turn produced by virtue once formed.

LECTURE IV

Comparison between Virtue and Art

ANALYTICAL OUTLINE
OF ST. THOMAS

A. He presents a problem.

B. He solves it.

I. FIRST BY REJECTING WHAT WAS ASSUMED ABOUT ART.

2. SECOND BY DISPROVING THE LIKENESS SAID TO EXIST BETWEEN VIRTUE AND ART.

a. He eliminates the likeness between
art and virtue.

TEXT OF ARISTOTLE
(*B.1105 a 18*)
Chapter 4

Someone may rightly ask how we can say that man must become just by doing just actions, and temperate 20 by doing temperate actions. If people perform just and temperate works they are already just and temperate, as those who produce grammatical or musical works are already grammarians or musicians.   **280**

But this is not true in the arts. A man may at times produce something grammatical by chance or with the help of another. He will therefore be a grammarian only if he produces a grammatical work in a grammatical way, that is, in accordance with the science of grammar that he possesses.   **281**

Another dissimilarity between the arts and virtues is that works of art have their perfection in themselves. It is enough then that these be made with certain qualities. Yet works of virtue are not justly and temperately performed if they have certain qualities; but the agent performing them must fulfill the following conditions. (1) He must know what he is doing. (2) He must choose the virtuous works for 20 their own sakes. (3) He must possess the disposition and operate according to it resolutely and with stability. *b* Except for knowledge, these conditions are not required in the other arts. Mere knowledge, however, has little or no importance to the virtues but what occurs from the frequent performance of just and temperate actions is all important. **282-284**

b. He concludes the solution.

Works then are called just and temperate when they are such as a just and temperate man will do. Now a just and temperate man is not one who performs these actions but who performs them as the just and temperate perform them. **285-286**

C. He comes to the conclusion principally intended.

I. FIRST HE BRINGS HIS PROPOSITION TO AN END.

It has been well said, therefore, that a man becomes just by doing just actions and temperate by doing tem- *10* perate actions. Anyone who does not perform these actions has not the slightest interest in becoming virtuous. **287**

2. HE DISCREDITS A FALSE OPINION.

Many, however, fail to do good actions but, taking refuge in theory, think that by philosophizing they will become virtuous. They act like the sick who listen carefully to the doctor but do nothing he prescribes. Hence, just as those who take care of themselves in this way will never have a healthy body, so those who merely philosophize will not have a healthy soul. **288**

COMMENTARY OF ST. THOMAS

280. After the Philosopher has shown that virtues are caused by actions, he now raises a doubt about this assertion. Regarding it he does three things. First [A] he presents a problem. Second [B], at "But this is not true etc.," he solves it. Third [C], from

the discussion of the question he comes to the conclusion principally intended, at "It has been well said, therefore, etc." The doubt that he first raises is this. What is true of virtue is true of art. But in art it is true that no one produces a work of art except one who possesses the art, as no one produces anything grammatical unless he is a grammarian, nor anything musical unless he be a musician. It will be true in virtue, therefore, that whoever performs just works is already just and whoever performs temperate works is already temperate. Hence our previous contention (164) does not seem to be true, that men become just by doing just actions and temperate by doing temperate actions.

281. Then [B, 1], at **"But this is not,"** he solves this doubt first by rejecting what was assumed about art and second [B, 2] by disproving the likeness said to exist between virtue and art, at "Another dissimilarity etc." He says first that it is not true in art, as was assumed, that whoever produces a grammatical work is already a grammarian. It happens sometimes that an ignoramus by chance pronounces a word correctly. Sometimes this happens with the help of another whose example is followed, for instance, a mimic imitates the correct pronunciation given by a grammarian. But a man is to be judged a grammarian only when he produces a grammatical work and in a grammatical way, that is, in accord with the science of grammar that he possesses.

282. Then [B, 2], at **"Another dissimilarity,"** he gives the second solution, in two steps. First [2, a] he eliminates the likeness between art and virtue. Second [2, b] he concludes the solution at "Works then are called just etc." He says first that there is no similarity in art and virtue since works of art have in themselves what belongs to the perfection of the art. The explanation is that art is the right plan of making things, as will be said in the sixth book of the present work (1153, 1160, 1166). "Making" is an operation that passes to external matter, and an operation of this kind is a perfection of the thing made. Hence in such actions the good consists in the object

made. It is enough for the good of art, therefore, that the things made be good. But virtues are principles of actions that do not go out into external matter but remain in the agents. Hence actions of this kind are perfections of the agents. So the good of these actions is identical with the agents themselves.

283. He says, therefore, in order that actions be justly and temperately performed, it is not enough that the things done be good but the agent must work in a proper manner. Regarding this manner, he says we must pay attention to three things. (1) The first, pertaining to the intellect or reason, is that one who performs a virtuous action should not act in ignorance or by chance but should know what he is doing. (2) The second is taken on the part of the appetitive power. Here two things are noted. One is that the action be not done out of passion, as happens when a person performs a virtuous deed because of fear. But the action should be done by a choice that is not made for the sake of something else, as happens when a person performs a good action for money or vainglory. The actions should be done for the sake of the virtuous work itself which, as something agreeable, is inherently pleasing to him who has the habit of virtue. (3) The third, taken from the nature of a habit, is that a person should possess a virtuous choice and operate according to it resolutely—that is, consistently on his part—and with stability so as not to be moved by any external thing.

284. Only the first of these, knowledge, is required in the arts. A man can be a good artist even if he never chooses to work according to art and does not persevere in his work. But knowledge has little or no importance in a person being virtuous, but his goodness consists entirely in other things that take place within him by frequent actions, and thus he becomes stable.

285. Then [2, b], at **"Works then,"** he concludes the solution of the above-mentioned doubt. He states that things done are called just and temperate because they are similar to the things that a just and temperate man does. Whoever performs these actions need not necessarily be just and temperate, but he who performs them as just and temperate men perform them according to the three conditions just laid down is said to be just and temperate. Men, therefore, first perform just and temperate actions—not in the same way as the just and temperate do—and such actions in their turn produce the habit.

286. If it should be asked how this is possible, since nothing can move itself from potency to act, we must answer that the perfection of moral virtue, which we are treating, consists in reason's control of the appetite. Now, the first principles of reason, no less in moral than in speculative matters, have been given by nature. Therefore, just as by means of previously known principles a man makes himself actually understand by personal effort of discovery, so also by acting according to the principles of practical reason a man makes himself actually virtuous.

287. Then [C], at **"It has been well said, therefore,"** he comes to the conclusion principally intended. First [C, 1] he brings his proposition to an end; and second [C, 2], at "Many, however, fail etc.," he discredits a false opinion of certain persons. He concludes that it has been well said above (264, 280) that a man becomes just by doing just actions and temperate by doing temperate actions. But he who does not perform actions nor develop his disposition will never become virtuous.

288. Then [C, 2], at **"Many, however"** he discredits the false opinion of certain persons who do not perform works of virtues but, by taking refuge in the discussion of virtues, think they can become virtuous by philosophizing. Such people, he says, are like the sick who carefully listen to what the doctor has to say but do nothing about carrying out his prescriptions. Thus philosophy is to the cure of the soul what medicine is to the cure of the body. Hence, as those who listen to the advice of doctors and disregard it will never have a well regulated body, so those who listen to the warnings of moral philosophers and do not heed them will never have a well regulated soul.

LECTURE V

The Definition of Virtue

ANALYTICAL OUTLINE
OF ST. THOMAS

TEXT OF ARISTOTLE
(*B.1105 b 20*)
Chapter 5

I. FIRST HE SHOWS WHAT VIRTUE IS.

A. He determines what virtue is in general.

A' He investigates the definition of virtue.

I. HE INVESTIGATES THE GENUS OF VIRTUE.

a. He offers the division.

Now we must determine the *20* definition of virtue. Since there are three principles occurring in the soul: passions, powers, and habits, virtue will be one of these three. **289-290**

b. He explains its parts.
  i. He makes known those which are passions.

By passions I mean: concupiscence, anger, aggressiveness, envy, joy, love, hatred, desire, jealousy, pity, and all the movements followed by pleasure and sorrow. **291-296**

  ii. . . . Those which are powers.

I call those principles powers in respect of which we are said to be capable of experiencing passions, for example, of becoming angry or being sad or having pity. **297**

  iii. . . . Those which are habits.

I call those principles habits in respect of which we are well or badly disposed towards the passions. Thus we are badly disposed in becoming angry in a violent or feeble way, but we are well disposed in doing so with moderation. The same applies to all habits and passions. **298**

c. He argues from the accepted definition.
  i. He shows that virtues are not passions . . . he assigns four reasons.
    W. THE FIRST (REASON).

Neither virtues nor vices, there- *30* fore, are passions because: (1) We are not called good or evil by reason of the

X. THE SECOND REASON.

Y. THE THIRD REASON.

Z. THE FOURTH REASON.

ii. *He shows that (virtues) are not powers (for two reasons).*
    X. THE FIRST.

Y. THE SECOND.

iii. *He concludes (virtues) are habits.*

passions but by reason of virtue or vice.   299

(2) We are neither praised nor reproached for the passions. Now a man is not praised or blamed for *B.1106* being afraid or angry simply but in a particular way. We are, though, praised or blamed for virtues or vices.   300

(3) We become angry and are afraid without willing it, but the virtues are certain choices or at least not without choice.   301

(4) We are said to be moved by the passions. However we are not moved but disposed in a certain way by the virtues and vices.   302

For this reason also the virtues are not powers, for we are not called good or evil, we are not praised or blamed because we are simply capable of being affected by the passions.   303

Furthermore, the powers are in us by nature, but we are not good or *10* evil by nature, as we said above.[1] 304

If then virtues are neither passions nor powers, it remains that they are habits. We say, therefore, that habit is the genus of virtue.   305

[1] Ch. 1, 1103 a 18 sq.

COMMENTARY OF ST. THOMAS

289. After the Philosopher has treated the cause of virtue, he now begins to investigate the definition of virtue. He divides the investigation into two parts. In the first [I] he shows what virtue is, and in the second [Lect. X] he ascertains the opposition of virtue to vice at "There are three etc." (B.1108 b 11). The first part is treated under two headings. In the first [I, A] he determines what virtue is in gen-

eral. In the second [Lect. VIII] he applies the adopted definition to particular virtues, at "We must speak of virtue not only under its universal aspect" (B.1107 a 28). This first section is also twofold, and in the first of these [A, A'] he investigates the definition of virtue. In the second [Lect. VII; 1] he concludes the definition, at "Virtue then is a habit etc." (B.1107). On the first point he first

[A', 1] investigates the genus of virtue and second [Lect. VI] its specific difference, at "We must consider not only etc." (B.1106 a 16). He investigates the genus by parts. Hence, regarding the first he does three things. First [1, a] he offers the division. Second [1, b], at "By passions I mean etc.," he explains its parts. Third [1, c], at "Neither virtues nor vices," he argues from the accepted definition.

290. He says first that to establish the definition of virtue we have to take for granted three principles in the soul: passions, powers, and habits. Virtue must come under one of these, for he just said (282) that virtue is a principle of certain operations of the soul. Now no principle of operation is found in the soul outside these three. Sometimes a man seems to act from passion, for example, anger; sometimes from habit, as when he works by art; sometimes from mere potentiality, as when he begins a new activity. It is obvious that not absolutely everything in the soul is included under this division—the essence of the soul and the operation of the intellect do not belong here—but only the things that are principles of some operation are considered.

291. Then [1, b], at "By passions I mean," he indicates the members of the division just mentioned. First [b, i] he makes known those that are passions; second [b, ii], those that are powers, at "I call those principles powers etc."; third [b, iii], those that are habits, at "I call those principles habits etc." Regarding the first we must consider that passions are not attributed to the vegetative soul because the powers of this part of the soul are not passive, as they are in both the sensitive part and the intellective part, but active. The perceptive and appetitive powers, except the active intellect, are passive. Although feeling and understanding are in a way passions (i.e., they "suffer" change), passions are

properly denominated not because of the apprehension of sense or intellect but only because of the appetite. The reason is that the operation of the perceptive power takes place according as the thing perceived is in the knower according to the state of the knower. Now the object perceived is, so to speak, drawn to the knower. But the operation of the appetitive power takes place according as the one desiring is inclined to the thing desired. Because it is characteristic of the recipient (*patientis*) that he be drawn by the agent, and not the converse, it follows that only the operations of the appetitive powers, but not the operations of the perceptive powers, are called passions.

292. Even among the appetitive powers the operation of the intellective appetite is not properly called passion. It does not take place with a change of a bodily organ, which is necessary to the nature of a passion properly speaking. Also in the operation of the intellective appetite, which is the will, man is not the passive recipient, but rather he directs himself as the master of his action. It remains, therefore, that operations of the sensitive appetite, which are accompanied by a change of a bodily organ and which in a way draw man, should be called passions in a strict sense.

293. The sensitive appetite is divided into two powers: (1) the concupiscible, which concerns sensible good absolutely (this is pleasurable to sense) and evil contrary to it; (2) the irascible, which concerns good under the aspect of a certain eminence. For example, victory is said to be a kind of good, although it is not accompanied by pleasure of sense. Whatever passions concern good or evil absolutely, therefore, are found in the concupiscible appetite. Certain of these—three in number—regard the good: love (which implies a certain connaturality of the appetite with the good loved), desire

(which implies a movement of the appetite towards the good loved), and delight (which implies a repose of the appetite in the good loved). Opposed to these in respect to evil are: hatred to love, aversion or flight to desire, sadness to delight. But those passions that concern good or evil under the aspect of difficulty belong to the irascible, as fear and boldness in regard to evil, hope and despair in regard to good. A fifth is anger, which is a composite passion and so has no opposite.

294. In enumerating the passions, therefore, he says they are: concupiscence (which we call desire), anger, fear, boldness, envy (which is contained under sadness), and joy (which is contained under pleasure) for this is a non-corporeal pleasure that consists in an interior perception of the good, and likewise a love, hatred, and desire of the same interior kind. Desire differs from concupiscence in that concupiscence pertains to bodily pleasure while desire concerns every pleasure without distinction.

295. He adds jealousy and pity, which are species of sadness. Pity is sadness at another's misfortune, and jealousy is sadness because one lacks what others have.

296. He also adds that pleasure and sorrow universally follow the above-mentioned passions, because all others imply certain movements to good and evil, and these movements are accompanied by pleasure or sorrow. Hence all other passions are terminated at pleasure and sorrow.

297. Then [b, ii], at "I call those principles powers," he identifies the powers not in general but those pertaining to moral study precisely as they differ from the passions. He affirms that powers are said to exist according as we are considered capable of experiencing these passions, that is, the powers are said to "suffer" or to receive these passions. Thus the irascible power exists according as we are ca-

pable of becoming angry and the concupiscible power according as we are capable of becoming sad or showing pity.

298. Then [b, iii], at "I call those principles habits," he identifies the habits. Likewise this is not done in general but in regard to those pertaining to moral study by comparison with the passions. Habits, he states, are said to exist according as we consistently use the passions well or badly. Now a habit is a disposition determining a power in reference to something. When the determination is made conformable to the nature of the thing, there will be a good habit which disposes that a thing be done well. Otherwise there will be a bad habit according to which a thing will be done badly. He illustrates what we do according to habit, how we may be angry either wrongly—when this is done in a violent or weak manner, that is, according to excess or defect—or well if done with moderation.

299. Then [1, c], at "Therefore neither virtues," he argues from the division previously given. First [c, i] he shows that virtues are not passions. Second [c, ii], at "For this reason also etc.," he shows that they are not powers. Third [c, iii], at "If then virtues etc.," he concludes they are habits. For the first statement he assigns four reasons. The first is this [i, w]. We are called good according to virtues and evil according to the opposite vices. But we are not called good or evil according to passions taken absolutely. Passions, therefore, are neither virtues nor vices.

300. He presents the second reason at "We are neither" [i, x]. It is taken from praise and reproach, which are kinds of attestation of goodness and evil. He says that we are praised for virtues and reproached for the opposite vices. But we are neither praised nor reproached for the passions taken absolutely. A man is not praised or blamed

because he is simply afraid or angry but only because he is afraid or angry in a particular way, that is, according to reason or contrary to reason. The same must be understood of the other passions of the soul. The passions of the soul, therefore, are neither virtues nor vices.

301. At **"We become angry"** [i, y] he presents the third reason, which is taken from a virtuous manner of acting. Virtues are either choices or not without choice, for the very act of virtue can be called virtue. If we consider the principal acts of virtues, which are interior, virtue is choice; but if we consider the exterior acts, virtue is not without choice because the exterior acts of virtue proceed from interior choice. If virtue be taken as the very habit of virtue, even in this sense it does not lack choice, as a cause is not without its proper effect. The passions, however, come to us without choice because they precede the deliberations of the reason necessary for choice. This is what he means saying that we are angry and are afraid without willing it, that is, not by choice of the reason. The passions, therefore, are not virtues.

302. He presents the fourth reason at **"We are said"** [i, z]. This is taken from the very nature of virtue. The passions are movements according to which we are said to be moved. The virtues and vices are qualities according to which we are said not to be moved but to be disposed in some way, whether well or badly that our movement may ensue. The passions, therefore, are neither virtues nor vices.

303. Then [c, ii], at **"For this reason,"** he shows that virtues are not powers for two reasons. The first of these [ii, x] is taken from the nature of good and evil, as has just been proved (299-300) about the passions. The reason is this. No one is called good or evil, no one is praised or reproached, because he is capable of being affected by some passion—for instance, that he is capable of becoming angry or being afraid. But we are called good or evil and are praised or reproached because of virtues and vices. Virtues and vices, therefore, are not powers.

304. He gives the second reason at **"Furthermore, the powers"** [ii, y]. It is taken on the part of the cause and is this. Powers are in us by nature because they are natural characteristics of the soul. But virtues and vices by which we are called good or evil are not in us by nature, as was proved above (248-251). Virtues and vices, therefore, are not powers.

305. Then [c, iii], at **"If then,"** he concludes his proposition. If virtues are neither passions nor powers, it remains that they are habits according to the previously given division. Thus he concludes that virtue with regard to its generic definition obviously is a habit.

LECTURE VI

Virtue, a Kind of Habit

ANALYTICAL OUTLINE OF ST. THOMAS	TEXT OF ARISTOTLE (*B.1106 a 16*) Chapter 6

I. HE PRESENTS HIS PROPOSITION.

We must consider not only that virtue is a habit but also what kind of habit. **306**

II. HE MAKES KNOWN THE PROPOSITION.

  A. He manifests a certain common quality of virtue.

We must explain, therefore, that virtue perfects everything of which it is the virtue, rendering both the possessor good and his work good. Thus the virtue or power of the eye makes good both the eye and its operation, for it is by the power of the eye that we see well. Likewise the virtue or excellence of a horse makes the horse *20* good and also makes him good for running, riding and awaiting the enemy. If this be true in all other things, then human virtue will be a habit making man good and rendering his work good. **307-308**

  B. From this quality he explains its specific difference.

  A' First according to the property of the operations.

How this takes place has already been described,[1] **309**

  B' Second according to the nature of virtue.

    I. HE INTRODUCES CERTAIN PRELIMINARIES.

a. He proposes the things necessary to elucidate the proposition.

but it will become still clearer if we study the nature of virtue. In all continuous and divisible matter, we can take the more, the less, and the

---

[1] Ch. 2, 1104 a 27 sq.

equal amount. These are understood either in regard to the thing or in regard to us. But the equal is a mean between excess and defect.   **310**

b. He clarifies what he has said.
   i. *First by means of reason.*

By the mean on the part of the thing, I understand that which is equally distant from both extremes and which is one and the same for everybody. *30* By the mean in regard to us, I understand that which is neither in excess nor in defect. This, however, is not one and the same for everybody. **311**

ii. *By way of example.*
   x. FIRST REGARDING THE OBJECTIVE MEAN.

For example, if ten be taken as many and two as few, then six will be the mean on part of the thing because six both exceeds and is exceeded by an equal amount. This mean is according to arithmetic proportion. **312**

y. HE GIVES EXAMPLES OF THE MEAN . . . IN COMPARISON WITH US.

But the mean in regard to us is not to be taken in this way. A trainer will not order six pounds of food for *b* someone simply because eating ten pounds is a great deal and eating two pounds is a small amount. This may be much or little for the person eating. For Milo it would certainly be little, but it would be much for a champion [1] in gymnastics; and the same holds true in running and wrestling. Thus everyone who is wise avoids excess and wants to find the mean, not on the part of the thing but in regard to us.   **313-314**

2. HE CONCLUDES HIS PROPOSITION.

Every practical science then perfects its work by keeping in view the mean and executing the work according to the mean. Hence it is customary to tell a man who has done a good piece of work that nothing is to be added or taken away, meaning that ex- *10* cess and defect disfigure a work but the mean preserves it. As we have said, good workmen work with an eye on the mean. But virtue like na-

[1] "Dominatori" in the text.

ture is more certain and better than
art. Virtue then will aim at the mean.
315-316

3. HE EXPLAINS AN INFERENCE.

I am speaking of moral virtue, for
it treats of passions and operations in
which we find excess, defect, and the
mean. Thus aggressiveness, fear, concupiscence, aversion, anger, pity, and,
in general, pleasure and sorrow take
place with excess and defect. Both *20*
of these are evil; but to experience
these passions at the right time, for
the right objects, toward the right
persons, with the right motive, and in
the right way is the mean and the
highest good of virtue. Similarly, excess, defect, and the mean are to be
be found in actions. Now moral virtue
is concerned with passions and operations in which excess is vicious, defect is reproachable, and the mean receives praise and shows the right path.
These two (praise and righteousness)
pertain to virtue. Moral virtue, therefore, is a kind of middle course and
aims at the mean. **317-318**

COMMENTARY OF ST. THOMAS

306. After the Philosopher has explained the genus of virtue, he now
begins an inquiry into the specific
difference of virtue. First [I] he presents his proposition. He says that in
order to know what virtue is we must
consider not only that it is a habit—
thus the genus is understood, but
what kind of habit—thus the specific
difference is indicated.

307. Second [II], at **"We must explain, therefore,"** he makes known the
proposition. On this point he does two
things. First [II, A] he manifests a
certain common quality of virtue. Sec-

ond [II, B], from this quality of virtue he explains its specific difference,
at "How this etc." He says first that
every virtue makes its possessor good
and his work good. Thus the virtue or
power of the eye makes the eye good
and gives us good sight, which is the
proper function of the eye. Likewise
the virtue or excellence of a horse
makes a horse good and makes it
perform well, that is, run fast, ride
easily, and fearlessly await the enemy.

308. The reason is that the virtue or
power of a thing is judged by the best
it can do. For example, the power of

one who can carry a hundred pounds is determined by his actual carrying of this weight, as is said in the first book *De Coelo* (Ch. 11, 281 a 8; St. Th. Lect. XXV, 249),[1] and not by the fact that he carries fifty pounds. Now the utmost or best to which the power of anything extends is called its excellent performance. It belongs to the virtue of every thing, therefore, to render an excellent performance. Because a perfect operation proceeds only from a perfect agent, it follows that everything is both good and operates well according to its own virtue. If this be true in all other things—and such was already apparent from our examples—human virtue must be a kind of habit, as was mentioned above (305). From this habit man becomes good formally speaking (as one becomes white by whiteness) and operates well.

309. Then [II, B], at **"How this,"** he investigates the specific difference of virtue according to the quality of virtue previously indicated. He does this under three headings: first [B, A′] according to the property of the operations; second [B, B′], according to the nature of virtue, at "but it will become still clearer etc."; third [Lect. VII; C′] according to the special character of good or evil, at "Moreover, there are many etc." (B.1106 b 29). He says first that the way in which a man may become good and do good has been treated already (257). It was noted also (260-264) that we are made good in every virtue by operations according to the mean. Then having become good we perform good actions. It remains, therefore, that if virtue makes a man good and his work good, it will consist in the mean.

310. Then [B, B′], at **"but it will become etc.,"** he proves the same by

[1] Sancti Thomae Aquinatis *in Aristotelis Libros de Coelo et Mundo Expositio.* Ed. Spiazzi, Turin/Rome: Marietti, 1952.

the nature of virtue. Regarding this he does three things. First [B′, 1] he introduces certain preliminaries necessary to explain his proposition. Second [B′, 2], he concludes his proposition at "Every practical science then etc." Third [B′, 3], he explains an inference at "I am speaking of moral virtue etc." On the first point he does two things. First [1, a] he proposes the things necessary to elucidate the proposition. Second [1, b] he clarifies what he has said, at "By the mean on the part etc." He says first that the manner in which we become good and perform good acts will be clearer still if we consider the nature of virtue. For an understanding of this, we must take for granted beforehand that virtue treats three things: the more, the less, and the equal. Virtue treats these both in continuous, contingent matters, and even in any other divisible matter, whether it be numerically divided as all discrete things, or whether it be divided incidentally—for example, by intensity and indistinctness of a quality in a subject. These three are so arranged that the equal holds a middle place between the more, which pertains to excess, and the less, which pertains to defect. This can be understood in two ways: one according to absolute quantity in some thing and the other in relation to us.

311. Then [1, b], at **"By the mean on the part of the thing,"** he clarifies what he said about the difference on the part of the thing (objective) and in regard to us (relative): first [b, i] by means of reason, and second [b, ii] by way of example at "For example, if etc." He says first that the objective mean is the point equidistant from both extremes. It is the same for all because it is understood according to the absolute quantity of the thing. But the mean is relative in regard to us inasmuch as it neither exceeds nor falls short of a proportion suitable to us. Hence this mean is not the same

for all. If we apply the relative mean to a shoe, it will not be more than the length of the foot nor less. It will not be the same for all because not all have the same size foot.

312. Then [b, ii], at **"For example, if,"** he clarifies what he has said, by way of example: first [ii, x] regarding the objective mean which is equally distant from the extremes. Thus six is the mean between ten (which is the more) and two (which is the less) because six is less than ten and more than two by the same amount, four. The mean, which is taken in numbers from the equal distance between two extremes, is said to be according to arithmetic proportion which considers numerical quantity. But the mean, which is taken from the equality of proportion in regard to us, is said to be according to the geometric proportion as will be made clear afterwards in the fifth book (944, 949, 950, 972).

313. Second [ii, y], at **"But the mean in regard to us,"** he gives examples of the mean. He says that the mean, which is understood in comparison with us, is not to be taken according to equal distance between extremes. This is sufficiently clear in the previous example of the shoe. If a shoe twenty fingers' breadth is long and a shoe four fingers' breadth is short it does not necessarily follow that one twelve fingers' breadth will be the right fit. Perhaps it will be large compared to the foot of one person and small compared to the foot of another. He also exemplifies this mean in food. If eating ten pounds or ten portions is much and eating two pounds is little, a trainer—whose duty it is to make out someone's diet —should not for this reason prescribe six pounds, since even this is much for one person and little for another.

314. This would indeed be little for a man called Milo who, according to Solinus, ate a whole beef in a day.

But it would be much for a champion in gymnastics, for one who has to excel in sports—in which men used to contend naked—and must eat lightly to be in better condition. The same is true of those who run at the stadium and of those who take up wrestling— a sport engaged in by the Greeks for exercise. So it is also in every operative science. The wise man avoids excess and defect, and wants to find the mean not objectively but relative to us.

315. Then [B', 2], at **"Every practical science,"** he argues from the premises in this way. Every operative science perfects its work in this: that in planning it aims for the mean, and in execution it carries out its work in accord with the mean. Indications of this can be had from the fact that men are in the habit of saying, when a work is well done, that not a thing is to be added nor taken away. Thus they give us to understand that excess and defect spoil a work which is preserved by the mean. Hence good workmen, as has been pointed out (313-314), work with an eye on the mean. But virtue like nature is more certain and even better than any art. Moral virtue operates by inclining in a determined way to one thing as nature does. Indeed custom becomes nature. But art, which operates according to reason, is indifferent to various objects. Hence like nature it is more certain than art.

316. Likewise virtue is better than art because by art a man is capable of doing a good work, but art does not cause him to do the good work. He can do a bad work because art does not incline to the good use of art; a grammarian for example can speak incorrectly. But by virtue a man not only is capable of operating but actually performs the action because virtue like nature inclines to a good operation. Art alone gives only the knowledge of the operation. Conse-

quently even for this secondary reason virtue, which is better than art, aims at the mean.

317. Then [B', 3], at **"I am speaking,"** he explains a further conclusion. He affirms that what has been said (256-263) ought to be understood of moral virtue that concerns passions and operations to which belong excess, defect and mean. He gives an example first from the passions saying that fear, aggressiveness, concupiscence, aversion (which is a fleeing from something), anger, pity, and any pleasure and sorrow may happen in greater and less degree than they ought. Both the excess and the defect are evil. But if a man should fear and dare (so of the other passions) what he ought, in the things he ought, in regard to the persons he ought, for

the motive he ought, and in the way he ought, this will be a mean for the passions. It will be also the highest good of virtue. Similarly excess, defect, and mean are found in actions. Moral virtue treats of passions and actions as its proper matter so that in them excess is vicious and defect worthy of reproach, but the mean receives praise and shows the right path. These two pertain to virtue: righteousness (which is opposed to vicious perverseness) and praise (which is opposed to reproach). This and vicious perverseness follow from the first two (excess and defect).

318. Thus he concludes that moral virtue considered in itself is a kind of middle course and is an indicator of the mean inasmuch as it aims at the mean and accomplishes it.

LECTURE VII

Conclusion of the Definition

ANALYTICAL OUTLINE
OF ST. THOMAS

TEXT OF ARISTOTLE
(*B.1106 b 29*)
Chapter 6

C' The philosopher now adds a third (reason) based upon the nature of good and evil.

Moreover, there are many ways of sinning (for evil partakes of the 30 unlimited in the opinion of the Pythagoreans, and good partakes of the limited). However, there is only one way of doing what is right. It is easy to sin, therefore, but difficult to do what is right. It is easy indeed to miss a bull's eye but difficult to hit it. For this reason then defect and excess pertain to vice but the mean to virtue. Men are good in but one way but evil in many ways.   **319-321**

D' He infers the definition of virtue from the premises.

I. HE PRESENTS THE DEFINITION.

Virtue then is a habit that *B.1107* chooses the mean in regard to us, as that mean is determined by reason and understood by a wise man.   **322-323**

2. HE EXPLAINS IT.

a. First he shows between what things there is a mean.

Virtue is a mean between two vices: of that which is according to excess and of that which is according to defect.   **324**

b. Second in reference to what thing this mean may be considered.

In regard to this mean, some vices fall short but others exceed what is right both in the passions and in actions. Virtue, however, discovers and chooses the mean.   **325**

c. Third he deduces a corollary.

For this reason, virtue according to its essence and definition is a mean.

But it is also an extreme as having
the nature of what is best and right.
326-327

3. HE REJECTS AN ERROR.

a. He explains this first from reason.

Not every action or passion of the
soul admits a mean. Certain ones *10*
imply vice by their very name: passions such as ill-will, shamelessness,
envy and actions such as adultery,
theft, murder. All these and their ilk
are said to be evil in themselves and
not only in their excess or defect.
Neither do we have the option of acting well or badly in an action like
adultery, as though it could be considered proper in itself, or done in a
fitting manner, or at a right time, or
in due circumstances, but to do any
of them is sinful without any qualification.   328-329

b. He gives some examples by way of
proof in the matter of vice.

To seek a mean in these matters
would be like assigning a mean to
excess and defect in unjust, or in
cowardly or lustful actions. Thus there
would be a mean of an excess and *20*
of a defect, and an excess of an excess
and a defect of a defect.   330

c. He explains the same thing by
example in the matter of virtue.

An excess and defect are not found
in temperance and fortitude because
a mean is in no way an extreme, so
excess or defect cannot be the mean
of vice but what is done is vicious.
As a consequence there cannot be a
mean in any excess or defect, nor can
there be excess or defect in any mean.
331-332

COMMENTARY OF ST. THOMAS

319. After giving the two previous
reasons, the Philosopher now [C']
adds a third based upon the nature
of good and evil. Accepting the Pythagorean view, he says that there are
many ways of sinning because evil,
which is included in the nature of
sin, partakes of the unlimited, but
good partakes of the limited. We must
understand then, on the contrary, that
there is only one way of doing what
is right.

320. The reason for this can be found in the statement of Dionysius in the book *De Divinis Nominibus*,[1] that good results from a united and complete cause but evil from any single defect, as is evident in physical goodness and badness. Ugliness, which is a defect of physical beauty, results from any member being unsightly. But beauty arises only when all the members are well proportioned and of a healthy hue. Likewise sickness, a defect in the constitution of the body, happens from a single disorder of any humor. But health is dependent on the proper proportion of all the humors. Likewise sin is committed in human action from any circumstance being inordinate in any way either by excess or defect. But goodness will be present only when all the circumstances are rightly ordered. As health or beauty comes about in a single way but sickness and ugliness in many, even in an unlimited number of ways, so also moral goodness results in only one way but the act of sin takes place in countless ways. Hence it is easy to sin because sin can happen in a variety of modes, but it is difficult to do what is right because rectitude happens only in one way.

321. He gives as an example that it is easy to miss the center of the target, because a miss can happen in numerous ways. But to hit the center spot is difficult because a hit happens in only one way. Now it is obvious that excess and defect take place in various ways but the mean in a single way. Hence excess and defect manifestly pertain to vice but the mean to virtue because men are good simply, that is, in one way, but evil at sundry times, i.e., in many ways as has just been stated (320).

322. Then [D'], at **"Virtue then is,"**

[1] Sancti Thomae Aquinatis *in Librum Beati Dionysii De Divinis Nominibus Expositio*, C. IV, 237; Lect. XXII, 572. Ed. Pera, Turin/Rome: Marietti, 1950.

he infers the definition of virtue from the premises. First [D', 1] he presents the definition, and second [D', 2] he explains it, at "Virtue is a mean between two etc." Third [D', 3] he rejects an error, at "Not every action etc." In the definition of virtue he treats four points. The first of these is the genus, which he touches on when he says that virtue is a habit (305). The second is the act of the moral virtue, for the habit must be defined by the act. This he mentions by the word "chooses," that is, acts according to choice, for the principal act of virtue is choice—he will discuss this later (432). Since the act must be determined by the object, he refers then, third, to the object or the term of the action when he says "the mean in regard to us." It was shown above (314) that virtue seeks out and uses the mean not of the thing but in regard to us. Similarly it has been said (257) that moral virtue is in the appetite, which participates in reason. He had to add, therefore, a fourth notion, which refers to the cause of goodness in virtue, by the words "determined by reason." It is good to seek the mean only insofar as it is determined by reason, but because reason can be right or erring, we must perform virtue according to right reason, as was ascertained previously (257).

323. To explain this he adds "as understood by a wise man." "Wise" here does not refer to one who is wise simply, knowing the ultimate causes of the whole universe, but rather to one who is prudent, that is, wise in human affairs, but this he will discuss in the sixth book (1163). Certainly the making of what is good in the art of building is determined by the judgment of one wise in that art, and the same is true in all the other arts.

324. Then [D', 2], at **"Virtue is a mean,"** he explains the previously given definition in regard to his say-

ing that virtue consists in the mean. On this point he does three things. First [2, a] he shows between what things there is a mean and, second [2, b], in reference to what thing this mean may be considered, at "In regard to this etc." Third [2, c] he deduces a corollary at "For this reason virtue etc." He says first that virtue itself is a kind of middle course between two vices and between two vicious habits: one by way of excess and the other by way of defect. Thus liberality is the middle course between extravagance tending toward excess and miserliness tending toward avarice.

325. Then [2, b], at **"In regard to this,"** he shows in reference to what norm we are to judge excess, defect, and mean. He says we must further consider that some vices fall short of but others exceed, both in the passions and in actions, what is right. In regard to this some are deficient and others are in excess. But virtue, precisely as it observes what it ought, is said to discover the mean by reason and to choose it by the will. Thus it is evident that virtue itself is a middle course and, on the other hand, it employs the mean. It is indeed the middle course between two habits, but it uses the mean in actions and passions.

326. Then [2, c], at **"For this reason,"** he draws a further conclusion from his remarks: that virtue in its essence and definition is a mean. But precisely as it possesses the character of the best and as it acts or guides well in a determined genus it is an extreme. For an understanding of this, we must consider (as has been pointed out in 322), that the entire goodness of moral virtue depends on the rectitude of the reason. Hence good is in harmony with moral virtue according as it follows right reason, but evil has a reference to each vice, viz.: excess and defect inasmuch as both depart from right reason. Therefore, accord-

ing to the nature of goodness and evil both vices are in one extreme, that is, in evil which is thus shown to be a deviation from reason. Virtue however is in the other extreme, that is, in good which is characterized as a following of reason.

327. By reason of this, virtue and the contrary vices do not follow the species indicated by the definition, because right reason is the motive and the extrinsic norm for the right appetite. But an evil appetite does not intend by vice to deviate from right reason—this is contrary to its intention—for it directly intends that object in which excess or defect is present. What is contrary to its intention is incidental. Now the incidental and the extrinsic do not constitute a species but the species of a habit is taken from the object to which the habit tends. But according to objects the mean belongs to virtue, and the extremes to vices. He says, therefore, that according to the nature of good, virtue lies in the extreme but according to the essential species, in the mean.

328. Then [D', 3], at **"Not every action,"** he rejects an erroneous view. Because virtue can occupy the middle course and vice the extremes in actions and in passions, someone might think that this would happen in all actions and passions. But he rejects this by saying that not every action or passion of the soul admits a mean in the context of virtue.

329. He explains this first from reason [3, a], at **"Certain ones etc."** Certain actions and passions by their very name imply vice: passions such as illwill, shamelessness, envy and actions such as adultery, theft, murder. All of these and their like are evil in themselves and not only in their excess or defect. Hence in such things a person cannot be virtuous no matter how he acts, but he always sins in doing them. In explaining this he adds that right

or wrong in actions like adultery does not arise from the fact that a person does the act as he ought or when he ought, so that then the act becomes good, but on the other hand evil when not done as it ought. Without qualification sin is present whenever any of these is present, for each of them implies an act opposed to what is right.

330. Second [3, b], he gives some examples by way of proof in the matter of vice, at **"To seek a mean."** He says that because such things imply evil in themselves, seeking a mean and extremes in them is like attributing a mean to excess and defect, whether it be in acting unjustly, or cowardly or lewdly—this would certainly be unfitting. Since these actions imply excess and defect, it follows that excess and defect would be a mean

(which is a contradiction) and that we would have to find the excess of the excess and the defect of the defect, which could go on forever.

331. Third [3, c], he explains the same thing by example in the matter of virtue at **"An excess."** Because temperance and fortitude imply a mean of themselves, they do not admit excess and defect in the sense that a man can be temperate or courageous in an excessive or defective manner. Likewise the mean of those things, which of themselves imply extremes, cannot be excess and defect. But no matter how any one of them is done, it is vicious.

332. Last he concludes that there cannot be a mean of any excess or defect, nor can there be an excess or defect of any mean.

LECTURE VIII

Explanation of the Definition in Detail

ANALYTICAL OUTLINE
OF ST. THOMAS

TEXT OF ARISTOTLE
(*B.1107 a 28*)
Chapter 7

I. HE SHOWS THE NECESSITY OF THIS PROCEDURE.

> We must speak of virtue not only under its universal aspect but we must apply the doctrine to individual *30* cases. In discussions which treat of actions, universals are not of much utility and particulars are more accurate, for actions are concerned with singulars. It is fitting then that discussions be in harmony with particulars. Therefore our teaching must be based on the explanation of individual virtues.   **333-334**

II. HE CARRIES OUT HIS PROPOSAL.

A. He shows (by particular cases that the mean is good . . . but the extreme is evil) first in the virtues.

A' Virtues which . . . pertain to bodily life.

1. FIRST HE SPEAKS OF FORTITUDE.

> In actions concerned with fear and daring, the mean is fortitude. Here an excess in fearlessness lacks an *b* applicable name (many things indeed are unnamed). But the man who is extreme in daring is called foolhardy, while the man who fears excessively and lacks daring is a coward. **335-341**

2. SECOND HE SPEAKS OF TEMPERANCE.

> With regard to pleasures and pains— but not all of them—the mean is temperance (which is less concerned with pains). Excess in these things is called intemperance, but the defect does not often occur. Hence persons lacking a

sense of pleasure are unnamed, although they may be called insensible. 342

B' (*Virtues*) *which pertain to external goods.*

I. HE TREATS THOSE VIRTUES . . . CONCERNED WITH THE DESIRE OF EXTERNAL GOODS.

a. First . . . he presents the virtues regulating riches.

i. *First he treats liberality.*

In respect to the giving and re- *10* ceiving of money, the mean is liberality. The excess and defect are found in extravagance and stinginess, which in opposite ways do too much and too little. The spendthrift overdoes the giving and falls short in the acquisition, but the miser on the contrary is excessive in acquiring and deficient in giving. For the present we are content to discuss these matters in outline and as contained under headings, later we shall treat them more in detail. 343

ii. *Then* (*he treats*) *magnificence.*

Having to do with the use of money are other habits, the mean of which is magnificence. The magnificent or princely person, as concerned with bestowing great sums, differs from the liberal person who gives small amounts. Excess in magnificence is called *apyrocalia* (vulgar display) and *banausia,* but the defect, meanness. These extremes differ from the extremes opposed to liberality, the *20* manner however of the difference will be treated later. **344**

COMMENTARY OF ST. THOMAS

333. After the Philosopher has explained what virtue is in a general way, he now applies the definition in a special way to each virtue. On this point he does two things. First [I] he shows the necessity of this procedure. Second [II] he carries out his proposal at "In actions concerned with fear etc." He says first that we must speak of the essence of virtue not only in its universal aspect but the general doctrine must be applied to each case in a special way. The reason he gives is that in discussions concerned with

actions, universals are not of much utility and particulars are more accurate because actions pertain to singulars. Fittingly then discussions about actions should be in harmony with particulars.

334. If then our study be about actions considered only universally, it will be futile both because it does not accomplish its purpose, which is the direction of individual actions, and because a study from a universal viewpoint—where deficiencies in particulars may not occur—cannot be made in these things by reason of the changeableness of the matter, as was said before (32-36). But the study of particulars is more effective, being suitable to control actions, and also more accurate because particulars are understood to the extent that the universal is verified in them. What was said (289-332), therefore, about virtue in general must have been based upon the explanation of individual virtues.

335. Then [II], at **"In actions concerned with,"** he carries out his proposal, showing by particular cases that the mean is good and praiseworthy but the extreme is evil and blameworthy. He shows this first in the virtues [II, A]; and second [Lect. IX; B], in the passions at "Also in the passions etc." (B.1108 a 31). Regarding the first point we must consider that virtues have been distinguished in two ways. Some observe the distinction of virtues according to certain general modes which are four in number. The root of virtue consists in the rectitude of reason according to which we must direct our actions and passions. Actions however are to be directed in a way different from the passions, for actions in themselves do not resist reason, as buying, selling, and so forth. Consequently, for such things reason need only establish a certain equality of rectitude. But the passions indicate a kind of inclination that can be contrary to reason in a twofold way.

336. In one way it draws reason to something else, as is evident in all passions that deal with following the appetite—for example, concupiscence, hope, anger, and others of this kind. For these passions reason must establish a rectitude in suppressing and restraining them. In another way passion shrinks from what is according to reason, as in all passions that denote flight of the appetite—for example, fear, hatred, and the like. In passions of this kind reason must establish a rectitude by stabilizing the soul in what is conformable to reason. According to this we designate four virtues, which some men call principal. Rectitude of reason itself pertains to prudence, equality established in operations to justice, constancy of soul to fortitude, and moderation of the passions—as the words indicate—to temperance.

337. Some, therefore, have understood these virtues in a general way, thinking that all knowledge of truth belongs to prudence, the equality of all actions to justice, all constancy of soul to fortitude, and all curbing and moderation of the passions to temperance. Cicero, Seneca, and others spoke of these virtues in this way. They considered such to be general virtues and called all other virtues species of these.

338. But this distinction does not seem to be appropriate. First because the above-mentioned virtues are of such a nature that without them there can be no virtue. Hence the species of virtue cannot be differentiated by this. Second, virtues and vices are not specified by reason but by their object (322).

339. Aristotle then distinguishes virtues more fittingly according to their objects or matter. Thus the previously mentioned four virtues are not called principal because they are general but because their species are taken according to certain important notions, as prudence is not concerned with all knowledge of the truth but especially with the act of reason that is command.

Justice is not concerned with equality of all actions but only of those referring to another, where the better thing is the establishment of equality. Fortitude is not concerned with every kind of constancy but only that which arises at the fear of the danger of death. Temperance is not concerned with all restraint but only with that of the desires and pleasures of touch. The other virtues, however, are as it were secondary. They can be reduced, therefore, to the previously mentioned virtues not as species to general but as secondary to principal virtues.

340. Since then these things have been taken for granted, we must know that the Philosopher does not treat justice and prudence here but later on in the fifth book (885-1108) and the sixth book (1161-1173). He does treat here, however, temperance, fortitude, and certain other secondary virtues, all of which are concerned with some of the passions. But all passions regard some object that pertains either to the bodily life of man or external goods or human acts. Therefore, he first [A, A'] mentions the virtues touching on the passions, the objects of which pertain to bodily life. Second [A, B'] he mentions those pertaining to external goods at "In respect to the giving and receiving of money etc."; and third [Lect. IX, C'] those regarding exterior acts at "There are three other means etc." (B.1108 a 9). On the first point he does two things. First [A', 1] he speaks of fortitude, which regards dangers destructive of life. Second [A', 2] he speaks of temperance, which regards things useful for the preservation of life, such as food by which life is preserved in the individual and sex by which life is preserved in the species, at "With regard to pleasures and pains etc."

341. He says first that fortitude is a mean concerned with fear and daring precisely as they regard the danger of death. But of those sinning by ex-

cess, the state of the man who is excessive in being fearless and also deficient in fearing is not given any special name because this rarely happens. Likewise many things are without a name because men do not advert to them ordinarily so that they would give them a name. But he who is extreme in daring is called rash. Such a one differs from the fearless man who is so-called from the lack of fear, but the rash man is so-called from an excess of daring. He who fears excessively and lacks daring is called a coward.

342. Then [A', 2], at "With regard to pleasures," he discusses temperance. He says that temperance is a mean not for all pleasures and pains but for those of touch, pertaining to food and sex. It is less concerned with pains than with pleasures, for pains of this kind are caused only from the absence of pleasures. Excess in such things is called intemperance, but the defect does not often occur because everyone naturally desires pleasure. Hence this defect is unnamed. He himself, however, invents a name and calls insensible those who do not feel pleasures of this kind. One who, contrary to right reason, avoids such pleasures is appropriately called insensible.

343. Then [A, B'], at "In respect to the giving," he introduces the virtues that regard external things. First [B', 1] he treats those virtues concerned with the desire of external goods and second [Lect. IX; B', 2] those that regard external evils, at "With respect to anger etc." (B.1108 a 3). External goods are riches and honors. First [1, a] then he presents the virtues regulating riches; second [Lect. IX; b] those referring to honors at "The mean in regard to honor etc." (B.1107 b 23). Regarding the first he does two things. First [a, i] he treats liberality, which is concerned with moderate riches; then [a, ii] magnificence, which is concerned with great riches, at "Hav-

ing to do with the use of money etc."
He says first that liberality is a mean
between the giving and receiving of
money. But extravagance and stinginess
constitute, in an opposite way, excess
and defect. The spendthrift overdoes
the giving and falls short in the acquisition, but the miser on the contrary
is excessive in acquiring and deficient
in giving. These matters are here discussed in outline or as conforming to
a pattern, and as falling under headings
or summarily. Later (528-594; 595-648;
658-706) he will treat more accurately
both these and other matters.

344. Then [a, ii], at **"Having to do
with the use of money,"** he introduces
magnificence. He says that besides the
above-mentioned habits, liberality and
the opposed vices, there are also other
virtues concerned with money, for
which even magnificence is a kind of
mean. The princely or munificent person, as engaged in expending great
sums, differs from the generous person
who gives small amounts. Excess in respect to magnificence is called *apyrocalia: a* meaning "without," *pyros*
meaning "practice," *kalos* meaning
"good," that is, without the practice
of what is good. Thus those who spend
a great deal care little about how they
bestow their goods. This excess is also
called *banausia* from *banos* meaning
"furnace" because, like a furnace, the
squanderer consumes everything. The
defect however is called meanness.
These extremes in fact differ from
those that are opposed to liberality, but
the way they differ will be treated
subsequently in the fourth book (707-
734).

LECTURE IX

Virtues Dealing with Honors

ANALYTICAL OUTLINE
OF ST. THOMAS

TEXT OF ARISTOTLE
(*B.1107 b 23*)
Chapter 7

b. He now treats those (virtues) dealing with honors.
   i. He deals with the virtue referring to great honors.

   ii. (He deals) with the virtue referring to ordinary honors.

The mean in regard to honor and dishonor is magnanimity. But the excess is *chapnotes* (i.e., presumption); and the defect, smallness of soul.   **345**

As we pointed out, liberality that bestows small amounts differs from magnificence. So also there is a virtue concerned with ordinary honors that differs from magnanimity whose province is great honors. A man can desire ordinary honors in the right way, more than he ought, and less than he ought. If he is excessive in the desire of honors, he is called ambitious; if deficient, he is said to be unambitious. But *30* he who strikes a mean has no special name. Likewise the habits are without names except for ambition, which we call the excessive love of honors. Hence persons who are in the extremes argue about the location of the mean. Even we sometimes call the man   *B.1108* possessing the mean ambitious, and sometimes we call him unambitious. Why we do this will be explained afterwards, but for the present we should refer to the remaining states in the way indicated.   **346-348**

2. HE PROPOSES THE VIRTUE CONCERNING EXTERNAL EVILS.

With respect to anger we find an excess, a defect, and a mean. Although these are for the most part without names, we call the man following the mean "mild" and the mean "mildness." In regard to the extremes, he who is excessive is called irascible and his vice irascibility. But he who is deficient is said to be apathetic and to have the defect of apathy.   349

C' He proposes the virtues which concern human actions.

1. HE SHOWS THEIR VARIETY.

There are three other means which are alike in one respect and different in another. They are all concerned   10 with communicating what we say and do, but they differ because one of them refers to the truth, and the others to the pleasantness found in this communication. One of these latter concerns pleasantness in the things said and done in jest, the others regard the things that belong to the usual manner of living. We must speak of these things so that we may better understand that the mean is always praiseworthy but that the extremes are neither right nor to be praised but rather to be condemned. Many of these also are without special names, but as we have done with the others, we shall try to invent names for them for the sake of the clarity and the good that results.   350-351

2. HE GIVES EXAMPLES OF THESE.

a. First of that which concerns truth.

In regard to truth the mean is possessed by the man who is truthful   20 and is called truthfulness. But pretension, which is the excess, is called boasting, and the pretender is known as a braggart. The defect, however, may be named dissimulation or irony and the pretender a dissembler.   352

b. He gives an example of the virtue concerned with amusement.

In respect to pleasantness concerned with amusement, the man who observes the mean is called witty and the disposition itself wit. But the excess is designated as buffoonery and the person who is excessive a buffoon. If one falls short in this matter he is said to be boorish and to have the quality of boorishness.   353

c. He exemplifies the third of these virtues.

In the remaining kind of pleasantness, that is, in life generally, the man who is pleasant as he should be is called affable, and the mean he attains is affability. But he who carries this too far merely for the sake of pleasing is called obsequious. If however he acts for his own utility he is called a flatterer. One who falls short in this matter and is always difficult is termed contentious and perverse.   *30*   **354**

B. He gives an example of certain laudable passions.

a. First of modesty.

Also in the passions and the things regarding the passions a mean exists. Modesty, for example, is not a virtue, but it is praised as is the modest person, for in this question a mean is attainable. The person who exceeds the mean and is embarrassed at everything is bashful. But one who falls short, that is, blushes at nothing, is shameless, while the person who strikes a happy mean is called modest.   *b*   **355**

b. Second he discusses . . . *nemesis*.

Righteous indignation may be assigned as the mean between envy and *epicacotharchia* or rejoicing in evil. These are concerned with pleasure and sorrow over what happens to our neighbors. The righteously indignant person is saddened at the unmerited prosperity of the wicked. But the envious person goes far beyond this and eats his heart out over the success of everyone. The man called *epicacotharchos* is so deficient in sadness that he actually rejoices. However, there will be time to treat of these matters elsewhere. Because justice is understood in various ways, we shall later treat its parts showing how the mean is constituted in them.[1] Likewise we shall discuss the intellectual virtues.[2]   *10*   **356-357**

[1] Bk. V, Cha. 1–7.
[2] Bk. VI.

COMMENTARY OF ST. THOMAS

345. Having completed the virtues that concern riches, he now [b] treats those dealing with honors. First [b, i] he deals with the virtue referring to great honors, and second [b, ii] with the virtue referring to ordinary honors, at "As we pointed out etc." He says first that magnanimity is the mean between honor and dishonor. But the excess in following after the things belonging to great honors is a certain disposition that is called *chaumotes* because it blazes forth in things pertaining to the desire of honor. In Greek *cauma* is fire, and *capnos* means smoke. If the word be written *chapnotes* it can be translated "exhalation" or presumption. We are accustomed to say that they who breathe with great difficulty on climbing high altitudes are wheezing or puffing. But the defect opposed to magnanimity is faintheartedness.

346. Then [b, ii], at **"As we pointed out,"** he proposes another virtue referring to ordinary honors. He says, as has been indicated (344), that liberality differs from magnificence because liberality bestows small amounts while magnificence bestows great sums. So too there is a virtue concerned with ordinary honors which differs from magnanimity which is concerned with great honors. That in this question there should be some virtue consisting in a mean is made clear by his adding that ordinary honors are desired as they ought (this belongs to the mean of virtue), more than they ought (this belongs to excess), and less than they ought (this belongs to the defect). He who excessively desires honor is ambitious or a lover of honor. He who is deficient in the desire of honor is unambitious or without the desire of honor. But he who strikes a happy mean has no special name.

347. Likewise the dispositions, i.e., the habits of vice or of the mean-virtue are unnamed. However, we can invent names: calling the habit by which a person excessively loves honor, ambition; and the habit by which a person is deficient in the love of honor, "unambitiousness." But because the mean has not been named, the persons who are in the extremes argue about the location of the mean. Both maintain that they possess the mean. He explains this by drawing a comparison with two states that are in the habit of bickering over their common border when the boundary has not been fixed. Both claim the intervening territory as their own. But this is fairly common to all the vices for each of the extremes to think they possess the mean and that the virtuous are in the other extreme, e.g., the coward considers the brave man reckless; the reckless man says the brave man is a coward. Hence Aristotle states what is proper to this matter, that not only do the vicious appropriate the name of virtue to themselves, but even the virtuous use the name of the vice as if it were a virtue because the mean has not been named.

348. This is what he refers to when he adds that even we (speaking correctly too) sometimes call a man who possesses the mean ambitious, and other times unambitious. Also at times we praise a person because he is ambitious. We are accustomed to say in commending a person that he is solicitous about his honor, and thus we call the man who loves honor, virtuous. On the other hand we sometimes praise an

unambitious man, saying in his praise that he does not care about the esteem of men, but about the truth. So we call the unambitious man virtuous. Why we do this will be explained afterwards in the fourth book (794-795). But for the present we should continue with the remaining mediums in the way designated, that is, as conforming to a pattern.

349. Then [2], at **"With respect to anger,"** he proposes the virtue concerning external evils by which man is provoked to anger. He says that in regard to anger there is an excess, a defect, and a mean. Although all these for the most part are without names, we are accustomed to call the man following the mean mild, and the mean itself mildness. But he who is excessive in this passion we call irascible and we say he has the quality of irascibility. The man however who is deficient we call apathetic and say he has the defect of apathy.

350. Then [C'], at **"There are,"** he proposes the virtues that concern human actions. First [C', 1] he shows their variety, and second [C', 2] he gives examples of these at "In regard to truth etc." He says first that three means are alike in one respect and different in another. They are alike in that all refer to words and deeds in which men communicate among themselves. They are different in that one of them refers to the truth of such words and deeds. The others, however, refer to pleasantness in these words and deeds, so that one of them regards pleasantness in the things that are said or done in jest, the others regard what belongs to the usual manner of living, i.e., serious matters.

351. We must speak of these things so it will become more apparent that the mean is always praiseworthy and the extremes are not to be praised but rather condemned. Many of these are without special names, but, as we have done with the others, we shall try to

invent names to clarify what is said for the sake of the good that will ensue. The reason is that the purpose of this science is not the manifestation of truth but virtuous activity.

352. Then [C', 2], at **"In regard to truth,"** he gives examples of these virtues and first [2, a] of that which concerns truth. He says that in regard to truth the mean is had by the man who is called truthful, and the mean itself is called truthfulness. But pretension, which is the excess (when a person pretends greater things about himself than are true), is called boasting, and the pretender is called a braggart. But dissembling, which is the defect (when a person makes pretense of certain contemptible things about himself), is called dissimulation or irony. Such a pretender is called a dissembler.

353. Second [2, b], at **"In respect to,"** he gives an example of the virtue concerned with amusement. He says, regarding pleasantness in amusement, that the man who observes the mean is called witty (*eutrapelos*) giving as it were a pleasant turn to every incident. The disposition itself is called wit (*eutrapelia*). But the man who is guilty of excess is called a buffoon or *bomolochus,* from *bomo* meaning "altar" and *lochos* meaning "plundering." He is said to be like the bird of prey which always flew near the sacrificial altars to snatch some food. In a similar way the man who is excessive in amusement always insists on snatching a word or action of someone to give it a comic turn. The disposition however is called buffoonery. But the man who is deficient is said to be boorish and to have the quality of boorishness.

354. Third [2, c], at **"In the remaining,"** he exemplifies the third of these virtues saying that in the remaining pleasantness, which is in life, touching on our serious actions, the mean is struck by the friendly person—not so designated from the effect of friendship but from amicable conversation. Such a

one we term affable. The mean itself is called friendliness or affability. But one who overdoes this merely for the purpose of pleasing is called obsequious. If he acts for his own utility, for example, his profit, he is called a sycophant or a flatterer. One who falls short in this matter and does not fear to sadden those he lives with is called contentious and perverse.

355. Then [B], at **"Also in the passions,"** he gives an example of certain laudable passions—first [B, a], of modesty. He says that a mean is found even in the passions and their phases, modesty, for instance, is not a virtue, as will be explained in the fourth book (867-882). The modest person is praised because a mean can be taken in such matters. One who goes to excess so that he blushes at everything is called *cataplex,* a bashful person. But he who falls short, blushing at nothing is called shameless, while he who strikes the mean is called modest.

356. Second [B, b], at **"Righteous indignation,"** he discusses another passion called *nemesis* or righteous indignation, which is a mean between envy and *epicacotharchia* (*tharcus* meaning "rejoicing," *kakos* meaning "evil," *epi* meaning "over") or rejoicing in evil. These are dispositions concerned with pleasure and sorrow over what happens to our neighbors. The righteously indignant person or the fair critic is saddened at the prosperity of the wicked. But the envious person goes to excess in grieving over all—both good and bad—who prosper. The person however called *epicacotharchos* is so deficient in sadness that he actually rejoices over the wicked who are successful in their wickedness. But these topics are treated elsewhere, in the second book of the *Rhetoric* (Ch. 10).

357. Last, because justice has various parts in which the mean is differently understood, justice will be treated in the fifth book (885-1108) together with the manner in which the parts consist in the mean. Likewise, the rational or intellectual virtues will be discussed later in the sixth book (1109-1291).

LECTURE X

Opposition Among the Virtues and Vices

ANALYTICAL OUTLINE
OF ST. THOMAS

TEXT OF ARISTOTLE
(*B.1108 b 11*)
Chapter 8

1. HE SHOWS THERE IS A TWOFOLD OPPOSITION AMONG THESE HABITS.

a. He states his proposal.

There are three dispositions, of which two are vices: one by excess, the other by defect. The third is virtue and consists in the mean. Everyone of these is opposed in some way to every other one because not only are the extremes opposed to one another and to the mean, but the mean is opposed to the extremes.   358

b. He proves the proposition.

As the average is greater compared to the less and less compared to the greater, so mean habits are in excess compared to the defect and in defect compared to excess. This is true both in the passions and in actions. The brave man seems reckless compared to the coward, and cowardly com- 20 pared to the reckless. Likewise the moderate man seems self-indulgent compared to the insensible man, and insensible compared to the self-indulgent. Also the generous person is a spendthrift in comparison with the miser but a miser in comparison with the spendthrift.   359-361

c. He deduces a corollary.

For this reason the extremes tend to throw the mean toward one another. The coward calls the brave man reckless, and the reckless man calls him a coward. A similar tendency is found in other extremes.   362

2. HE SHOWS THAT THE OPPOSITION AMONG THE VICES THEMSELVES IS THE GREATER.

a. First reason.

These things are mutually opposed in such a way that there is a greater opposition of the extremes among themselves than to the mean. The reason is that the extremes are more removed from one another than from the mean, as great is more re- *30* moved from small and small from great than either from the average. **363**

b. He states the second reason.

Moreover there seems to be a similarity between some extremes and the mean, for example, between rashness and fortitude, between extravagance and generosity. But between the extremes themselves a complete dissimilarity exists. Now the things that are farthest removed from one another are said to be contraries. Therefore the things most removed from one another are more contrary. **364**

3. HE SHOWS HOW ONE OF THE EXTREMES IS MORE OPPOSED TO VIRTUE THAN THE OTHER.

a. He states his proposal.

In some cases it is the de- *B.1109* fect that is more opposed to the mean but in other cases it is the excess. Thus it is not rashness but cowardice, the defect, that is more opposed to fortitude. On the contrary, however, it is not insensibility (the defect) but self-indulgence (the excess) that is more opposed to temperance. **365**

b. He assigns the reasons.
  i. *One is taken from the thing itself.*

This happens for two reasons, one of which is drawn from the very thing itself. It is not the extreme that is nearer and more like the mean but its contrary that is more opposed to the mean. Thus, since rashness seems nearer and more like fortitude, it *10* is cowardice having less likeness that is more opposed to fortitude. Things that are more removed from the mean seem to be more opposed to it. This first reason then comes from the thing itself. **366-367**

  ii. *He assigns another reason.*

But the other reason arises on our part. Those vices which are somewhat innate in us seem in a way to be more opposed to the mean. For example, we more naturally follow pleasure and so we are more easily moved to self-indulgence than to temperance. Therefore, we say that the vices that more readily increase are more opposed to virtue. For this reason self-indulgence (which is an excess) is more opposed to temperance.   368

COMMENTARY OF ST. THOMAS

358. After the Philosopher has shown in general what virtue is, and has applied the definition to particular virtues, he treats the opposition of virtues and vices. Regarding this question he does three things. First [1] he shows that there is a twofold opposition among these habits: one, of the vices among themselves, the other, of the vices to the virtue. Then [2] he shows that the opposition among the vices themselves is the greater, at "These things are mutually opposed etc." Last [3] he shows how one of the extremes is more opposed to virtue than the other, at "In some cases etc." On the first point he does three things. First [1, a] he states his proposal. Second [1, b] he proves the proposition, at "As the average etc." Third [1, c] he deduces a corollary from what has been said, at "For this reason the extremes tend to throw etc." He says first that there are three dispositions of which two are vices: one by excess, and the other by defect. The third is according to virtue which consists in a mean. Everyone of these is opposed in some way to every other one, because not only are the extremes opposed to one another but also the mean to the extremes.

359. Then [1, b], at "As the average," he proves what he had said. It was unnecessary to prove that two vices, which are compared to one an-

other as excess and defect, are opposed since they are far removed from one another. But it will seem doubtful that virtue is opposed to vices, as was just said (358). Since virtue holds a middle place between the vices, virtue is not very far removed from either of them, while opposition is farthest apart, as stated in the tenth book of the *Metaphysics* (Ch. 4, 1055, a 4-32; St. Th. Lect. V, 2023-2035). Therefore, the Philosopher here makes a special point that virtue is opposed to both extremes.

360. On this subject we must consider that the mean partakes to some extent of both extremes. Precisely as it partakes of one of them it is contrary to the other, as the average—a mean between the great and small—is small compared to the great and great compared to the small. Therefore, the average is opposed both to the great by reason of the small and to the small by reason of the great. Because of this there is a motion of the contrary against the mean as against a contrary, as is explained in the fifth book of the *Physics* (Ch. 1, 224 b 30-35; St. Th. Lect. I, 476).

361. Therefore, the habits of the mean both in regard to passions and actions appear excessive to one who is in defect and deficient to one who is in excess. Thus a brave man compared to a coward is reckless, but com-

pared to a reckless man, a brave man is a coward. Likewise a moderate man compared to an insensible man is self-indulgent, but compared to the self-indulgent the moderate man is insensible. The same may be said of the generous man who is a spendthrift in comparison with the miser, but a miser in comparison with the spendthrift. It is evident then that virtue is opposed to the extremes.

362. Then [1, c], at **"For this reason,"** he deduces a corollary from what was said. Because the mean habit is constituted by comparison of one extreme with the nature of the other, the extremes tend to throw the mean toward one another. In other words, both extremes consider the mean as it were an extreme opposed to them. Thus the coward calls the brave man reckless and the reckless man calls him a coward. This is an indication of what we just stated (359, 361), that virtue is opposed to both extremes.

363. Then [2], at **"These things are mutually opposed,"** he shows there is greater opposition of the vices among themselves than to virtue for two reasons. The first reason [2, a] is that the more removed things are from one another, the more opposed they are because opposition is a kind of distance. But the extremes are more removed from one another than from the mean, as great and small are more removed from one another than from the average, which is a mean between them. Therefore, vices are more opposed to one another than to virtue. We must consider that Aristotle speaks here about the opposition of virtue to vices, not according to good and evil—in this way both vices come under one extreme—but according as virtue by reason of its own species is a mean between two vices.

364. He states the second reason [2, b] at **"Moreover there seems."** It is this. There is some similarity between virtue and one extreme, for instance,

between fortitude and rashness, between generosity and prodigality. But there is complete dissimilarity between the two extremes or vices. Therefore, they are opposed to one another in the greatest degree because their opposition denotes the greatest distance, as was indicated (359).

365. Then [3], at **"In some cases,"** he shows that one extreme is more opposed to virtue than the other. On this point he does two things. First [3, a] he states his proposal. Second [3, b] he assigns the reasons at "This happens for two reasons." He says first that in some cases it is the defect that is more opposed to the mean of the virtue, but in other cases it is the excess. Thus not rashness, which certainly pertains to the excess, but cowardice, which pertains to the defect, is most opposed to fortitude. On the contrary, however, it is not insensibility (to which lack and defect belong) but self-indulgence (to which excess pertains) that is most opposed to temperance.

366. Then [3, b], at **"This happens for two reasons,"** he assigns two reasons for what he said. One [b, i] is taken from the thing itself, that is, from the very nature of the virtues and vices. It was just stated (364) that one extreme has a similarity to the mean of virtue. From the very fact that one extreme is nearer and more like the mean of virtue than the other, it follows that not the one more similar to the mean but the one contrary to it is more opposed to the virtue. Thus if rashness is nearer and more like fortitude, it follows that cowardice is more unlike and consequently more opposed to fortitude. The reason is that the habits more removed from the mean seem to be more opposed to it. But the explanation of these things must be taken from the nature of the passions.

367. What Aristotle says here touches on the moral virtues concerned with

the passions. To these virtues it belongs to preserve the good of reason against the movement of the passions. Now passion can destroy the good of reason in two ways. First, its vehemence can incite to greater activity than reason prescribes, especially in the desire of pleasure and in the other passions pertaining to the following of the appetite. Hence the virtue, which touches the passions of this kind, aims principally at restraining these passions. For this reason the vice referring to the defect is more like the virtue, and the vice referring to the excess is more opposed to it, as is evident in temperance. But other passions destroy the good by withdrawing to something less than what is according to reason, as is evident in the case of fear and other passions having to do with flight. Hence the virtue concerned with such passions strives as much as possible to strengthen man against defect in the good of reason. On this account the vice of defect is more opposed to the virtue.

368. Then [b, ii], at "But the other," he assigns another reason on our part. Since virtue ought to restrain vices, the aim of virtue is to curb more effectively those vices to which we have a stronger inclination. For this reason those vices, which are in any way somewhat innate in us, are more opposed to virtue. As from birth we more readily follow pleasures than flee from them, we are very early moved to self-indulgence which implies an excess of pleasure. Therefore, we say that those vices, which rather naturally tend to increase in us because we are by nature inclined to them, are more opposed to virtue. For this reason self-indulgence, to which excess of pleasure pertains, is more opposed to temperance than insensibility is, as has been observed (365).

LECTURE XI

The Ways of Becoming Virtuous

ANALYTICAL OUTLINE
OF ST. THOMAS

TEXT OF ARISTOTLE
(*B.1109 a 19*)
Chapter 9

I. FIRST HE SHOWS THAT IT IS DIFFICULT FOR MAN TO BECOME VIRTUOUS.

a. He reviews what has been said.

A sufficient explanation has been given to show that moral virtue *20* is a mean, how it is a mean, that it is a mean between two vices—one by excess and the other by defect—and that it aims at the mean both in the passions and operations.   **369**

b. He concludes from the premises.

It is not easy to be virtuous because in every case it is difficult to discover the mean. Thus, not everyone can locate the center of a circle—it takes a person who knows. Likewise it is easy for anyone to become angry, or to hand out money and waste it. But not everyone (for it is not easy) can give to the right person, the right amount, at the right time, for the right purpose, in the right manner. All this pertains to virtuous giving, which *30* is rare, praiseworthy, and good.   **370**

2. HE SHOWS HOW MAN MAY ATTAIN THIS.

a. He shows how a person can discover the mean . . . he gives three admonitions.
  i. One of these is taken from the nature of the thing.

For this reason he who aims at the mean must first avoid the extreme which is more opposed to the mean. (Circe used to give this warning: keep your ship beyond spray and rolling billow.[1]) One of the extremes indeed is a greater sin and the other a lesser sin. Therefore, since it is exceedingly difficult to reach the mean, we must *b*

[1] Cf. *Odyssey* xii, 219 sq.

choose the lesser of the evils, as they
say in navigation. This will be done
best in the way we are going to point
out.   371-373

ii. He gives the second admonition.

We must take into account the
things to which we are easily inclined.
Some of us are more prone by nature
to one thing than another. Our natural inclination will be made known
from the pleasure or sorrow we experience. We must then draw ourselves
to the opposite, for by leading ourselves far away from sin we shall arrive at the mean. A similar thing is
done by nurserymen who straighten
crooked saplings.   374-376

*iii. He lays down the third ad-
monition.*

Everyone ought to be on guard especially against the pleasurable thing
and pleasure, for we cannot judge them
without being unduly influenced by
them. What the elders of the people
felt toward Helen, we ought to *10*
feel toward pleasure, and in all that
concerns pleasure repeat their words.[1]
Rejecting pleasure in this way we will
fall into sin less frequently. Those who
do as we have suggested under this
heading will be quite able to acquire
the mean.   377-378

b. He treats the discovery of the mean.
   i. He indicates the difficulty of this.

This is perhaps difficult in individual cases. It is not easy to determine
in what manner we should be angry,
in regard to what persons we should
be angry, in what type of things we
should be angry, and for how long a
time we should be angry. Sometimes
we praise those who are deficient in
becoming angry and call them mild;
sometimes we praise the irascible and
call them manly.   379

*ii. He shows what suffices to de-
termine the mean.*

One who deviates a little from what
is virtuous is not censured whether
it be in excess or defect. But one *20*
who deviates much is blameworthy,
for his deviation is not hidden. **380**

iii. He answers a latent question.

It cannot easily be determined, in
so many words, at what point and
how much a person is censurable.

[1] Cf. *Iliad* iii. 156-160.

Neither is any other thing perceived by the senses determined in this way, for these are particular things and judgment of them is in the sensitive part of the soul. This much, then, shows that the mean habit is praiseworthy in all instances. However, sometimes we must incline towards excess and sometimes towards defect. Thus we shall easily reach the mean and what is virtuous.   381

COMMENTARY OF ST. THOMAS

369. After the Philosopher has treated the nature of virtue, he shows here how a person can acquire virtue. He does this because, as was indicated before (351), the purpose of this teaching is not that men may know the truth but that they may become good. On this point he does two things. First [1] he shows that it is difficult for man to become virtuous. Second [2] he shows how man may attain this, at "For this reason he who aims etc." The first notion calls for a twofold procedure. First [1, a] he reviews what has been said. It has been sufficiently explained before (310, 316), he states, that moral virtue is a mean, how it is a mean (not objectively but relative to us), and between what things it is the mean, i.e., between two vices—one by excess, the other by defect. It has also been explained (317-318) why virtue is a middle course, namely, because it aims at the mean; virtue searches out and chooses the mean both in the passions and actions.

370. Second [1, b], at "It is not easy," he concludes from the premises that it is difficult to be good or virtuous because we see that in every case it is difficult to discover the mean but easy to deviate from the mean. Thus, not

everyone—only an informed person who is a geometrician—can find the center of a circle. On the other hand, anyone can easily deviate from the center. Likewise, anyone can hand out money and waste it. But not everyone (for it is not easy) can give to the right person, the right amount, at the right time, for the right purpose, in the right manner—all of which belongs to virtuous giving. Indeed, because of the difficulty it is a rare and difficult thing, but praiseworthy and virtuous precisely as conforming to reason.

371. Then [2], at "For this reason," he shows the ways in which a person may become virtuous. On this point he does two things. First [2, a] he shows how a person can discover the mean. Second [2, b] he treats the discovery of the mean at "This is perhaps difficult etc." In regard to the first he gives three admonitions. One of these [a, i] is taken from the nature of the thing. He states that it is difficult to become virtuous and to discover the mean. Therefore, one who aims at the mean (i.e., he who intends to attain the mean) must strive principally to avoid the extreme more opposed to the virtue. Thus if someone

wishes to arrive at the mean of fortitude he ought to direct his principal efforts to avoiding cowardice, which is more opposed to fortitude than rashness is, as has been explained (365).

372. He gives an example of a certain Circe who used to warn sailors to beware chiefly of the greatest dangers from the sea, which are waves sinking the ship and mist obscuring the vision of the sailors. This was the warning: "Clear of the smoke take care and clear of the rollers to keep her," [1] as if to say: so guard your ship that you may escape spray and waves.

373. He gives the reason for this admonition, saying that one of the extremes—that which is more opposed to the virtue—is a greater sin; but that the extreme, which is less opposed to the virtue, is a lesser sin. Therefore, since it is exceedingly difficult to reach the mean of virtue, a man ought to try to avoid at least the greater dangers that are more opposed to virtue. Thus sailors say that after the best voyage on which a man is exposed to no dangers, the next best is to choose the least of the dangers. A similar thing happens to a man's life in the way that was explained (371), that he may chiefly avoid the vices that are opposed to virtue.

374. He gives the second admonition [a, ii] at "We must take into account." It is understood on our part, as far as concerns the things proper to each of us. One who wishes to be virtuous, he says, must take into account that to which his appetite is naturally inclined. Different people are by nature more inclined to one thing than another. Each one can know what he is naturally inclined to from the pleasure and sorrow he experiences, because what is agreeable to each according to his nature is pleasurable.

375. Hence, if someone takes pleas-

[1] *Odyssey* xii. 219 sq. (H. B. Cotterill's Trans.)

ure in a particular action or passion, this is a sign that he is naturally inclined to it. But men vehemently tend to the things to which they are naturally inclined, and so, easily exceed the mean in this matter. We, therefore, must draw ourselves as much as possible to the opposite. The reason is that when we make an effort to recede from sin, to which we are prone, we will finally with difficulty arrive at the mean. He makes a comparison with nurserymen who straighten crooked saplings. These men wishing to make trees straight force them the opposite way and so bring them to the mean, an upright position.

376. Here we must consider that this way of acquiring virtues is most effective: that a man should strive for the opposite of that to which he is inclined either by nature or habit. However, the way advocated by the Stoics is easier: that a man little by little withdraw from those things to which he is inclined, as Cicero relates in his work *Questiones Tusculanae* (Bk. IV, C. 31-35, n. 65-76). The way that Aristotle lays down is suitable for those who strongly desire to withdraw from vice and to attain virtue. But the way of the Stoics is more appropriate to those who have weak and half-hearted wills.

377. He lays down the third admonition [a, iii] at "Everyone." This is also understood on our part, not in the sense that it is proper to every individual, as has been said (374-376) of the second admonition, but precisely as it is common to all. All are naturally inclined to pleasure. Therefore, he says that everyone without exception who aims at virtue ought to be on his guard especially against pleasures. Because men are very inclined to pleasure, pleasurable objects apprehended easily move their appetite. Hence, he notes that we cannot easily judge pleasure by dwelling on its consideration without the appetite

accepting it and bursting forth in desire for it. What the Trojan elders felt toward Helen when they decided that she must depart, we ought to feel toward pleasure; in all that concerns pleasure we ought to reecho their words [1] in order that we may reject bodily pleasures. Rejecting pleasures in this way, we will fall into sin less frequently since the desire of pleasure leads men to many sins.

378. He concludes then that those who do what has been suggested under this heading, i.e., summarily, will be quite able to acquire the mean of virtue.

379. Then [2, b], at **"This is perhaps difficult,"** he shows how the mean of virtue must be determined. On this point he does three things. First [b, i] he indicates the difficulty of this. Next [b, ii] he shows what suffices to determine the mean, at "One who deviates a little etc." Last [b, iii] he answers a latent question at "It cannot be determined etc." He says first that it is difficult to discover the mean especially when we consider the particular circumstances in individual actions. The reason is that it is not easy to determine how a thing is to be done and in regard to what persons, and in what type of things, and how long a time one should be angry. He gives a sign of this difficulty: that those, who are deficient in getting angry for instance, are sometimes praised by us and called mild, while those who are rather irascible in inflicting punishment or making resistance are sometimes praised by us and called manly.

380. Then [b, ii], at **"One who,"** he

¹ Cf. *Iliad* iii. 156–160.

indicates what suffices for the mean of virtue. He says that one who deviates a little from what is done well according to virtue is not censured, whether he inclines to excess or defect. The reason is that a slight departure from the mean of virtue is hidden on account of the difficulty with the mean. But one who deviates greatly is censured because the deviation is not hidden.

381. Then [b, iii], at **"It cannot easily,"** he answers a latent question. Someone could ask how much departure from the mean should be censured and how much should not. He himself answers that it cannot easily be determined, in so many words, at what point and how much a person departing from the mean should be blamed. Likewise no other sensible thing, which is judged rather by sense than reason, can easily be determined. Things of this kind, belonging to the operations of the virtues, are individual cases. For this reason judgment about them exists in the sensitive part of the soul, even if not in the external, at least in the internal sense by which a person judges well about singulars, and to which belongs the judgment of prudence, as will be said in the sixth book (1215, 1249). But this much suffices here to show that the mean habit in all cases is rather praiseworthy. However, sometimes we must incline toward excess and sometimes toward defect either on account of the nature of virtue or on account of our inclination, as is clear from what was explained above (369-378). Thus the mean according to which a thing is done well will be easily discovered. So ends the second book.

BOOK III

THE VOLUNTARY. FORTITUDE AND TEMPERANCE

CONTENTS

BOOK III

CONTENTS

BOOK III

LECTURE I

Spontaneous Action and the Involuntary

ANALYTICAL OUTLINE
OF ST. THOMAS

TEXT OF ARISTOTLE
(B.1109 b 30)
Chapter 1

I. HE DEALS WITH . . . THREE . . . PRINCIPLES OF VIRTUOUS ACTIONS.

A. He determines the voluntary and the involuntary.

A' He shows that it pertains to the present discussion to consider the voluntary and the involuntary.

I. THE FIRST (REASON).

> Since virtue is concerned with passions and actions, and since praise and censures are apportioned for what is voluntary, but pardon—or at times even pity—for what is involuntary, the study of the voluntary and the involuntary is required of those who intend to treat of virtue. **382-384**

2. HE GIVES THE SECOND REASON.

> It is useful also for legislators in decreeing honors and punishments. **385**

B' He actually treats them.

I. HE TREATS THE INVOLUNTARY.

a. He divides the involuntary.

> Involuntary actions seem to be those that arise either from violence *B.1110* or from ignorance. **386**

b. He treats one member of the division.
   i. *He discloses what the "compulsory action" . . . is.*
      X. HE MAKES KNOWN WHAT THE "PHYSICALLY FORCED ACTION" . . . IS.

> The "compulsory action" (*violentum*) is one whose principle is from outside and to which the person involved or the recipient contributes nothing, for example, if he is driven somewhere by the wind, or if he is in the power of other men. **387**

Y. . . . WHAT THE "MORALLY
FORCED" ACTION . . . IS.

aa. He raises a doubt.

Some things are done because of the fear of greater evils or because of the hope of some good. Thus a tyrant, having in his power the parents or children of a certain man, commands him to do a disgraceful deed on condition that they will be spared if he does it but killed if he does not do it. Here a doubt arises whether his actions are voluntary or involuntary. A similar case is found in the decision to throw goods overboard during storms at sea. Absolutely speak- *10* ing, no man would do so voluntarily, but if it means that his life and that of others are saved as a result, a sensible man will do it. **388-389**

bb. He solves the doubt.

Operations of this kind are mixed. However, they approach more closely to voluntary actions for they are voluntary at the time they are done, and the end of the action conforms to this particular time. An action then must be called voluntary or involuntary by reference to the time at which it was done. In our case he acts voluntarily because the principle moving his bodily members in these operations is within the man himself. Actions whose source is within man are in his power to do or not to do, and this belongs to the nature of the voluntary. But the actions may be called involuntary in the abstract (*simpliciter*), for no one would choose to do such a thing in itself. **390-391**

COMMENTARY OF ST. THOMAS

382. After the Philosopher has treated virtue in general, he treats here certain principles of virtuous acts. In defining virtue, he said (305) that virtue is a habit of correct choosing be- cause virtue works by means of choice. Now he logically discusses choice together with the voluntary and "willing." The voluntary is common to these three: for the voluntary is any-

thing that is freely done, choice however concerns the things that are for the end, and willing considers the end itself. Hence this section falls into two parts. In the first part [I] he deals with the three previously mentioned principles of virtuous actions. In the second part, at "Since willing regards the end etc." (B.1113 b 3), he compares these principles with the acts of the virtues [Lect. XI]. His initial point calls for a threefold procedure. First [A] he determines the voluntary and the involuntary. Next [Lect. V; B], at "After the treatise etc." (B.1111 b 4), he deals with choice. Last [Lect. X; C], at "As was stated before etc." (B.1113 a 15), he treats the act of willing. In regard to the first of these he does two things. Initially [A'] he shows that it pertains to the present discussion to consider the voluntary and the involuntary. Then [B'], at "Involuntary actions seem etc.," he actually treats them. Two reasons are advanced in proof of the first point.

383. The first of these reasons [1] is taken from what is peculiar to our present study which concerns the virtues. He concludes from his previous remarks that moral virtue, our present concern, deals with passions and actions in such a way that in the things which are voluntary in regard to actions and passions, praise is due anyone acting virtuously and blame for anyone acting viciously. But when someone involuntarily performs an action in accordance with virtue, he does not merit praise. On the other hand, if his action is contrary to virtue he deserves pardon because he acted involuntarily, and so is less blameworthy. Sometimes he even deserves pity, and should be entirely freed from blame.

384. Pardon can also be distinguished from pity in this way: we speak of pardon when censure, i.e., a penalty is lessened or entirely absolved as a consequence of the judgment of reason. Pity, on the other hand, arises as a consequence of an emotion. But praise and blame are peculiarly due to virtue and vice. Therefore, the voluntary and the involuntary, according to which the reason for praise and blame is diversified, ought to be treated by those who intend to study virtue.

385. At "It is useful" [2] he gives the second reason. This is taken from the viewpoint of political science to which the present study is ordered. It is useful for legislators, he says, to consider the voluntary and the involuntary that they may decree honors for the law-abiding and punishments for the law-breakers, for in regard to these the distinction of voluntary and involuntary is of importance.

386. Then [B'], at "Involuntary actions seem," he deals with the voluntary and the involuntary. First [B', 1] he treats the involuntary, and second [Lect. IV], at "Since the involuntary etc." (B.1111 a 22), he treats the voluntary. The reason for this order is that the involuntary proceeds from a simple cause, as ignorance alone, or violence alone, but the voluntary has to take place by the concurrence of many factors. The explanation of the involuntary [B', 1] is achieved in three stages. First [a] he divides the involuntary. Second [b], at "The 'compulsory action' is etc.," he treats one member of the division. Third [Lect. III; c], at "Every action done etc." (B.1110 b 18), he treats the other member. He says first that some involuntary actions seem to be of two kinds: those arising from violence, or those arising from ignorance. This division is made in order to indicate that the involuntary is a privation of the voluntary. But the voluntary implies a movement of the appetitive power presupposing a knowledge via sense or reason because a good perceived moves the appetitive power. A thing is involuntary on two accounts: one, because the movement of the appetitive power is excluded— this is the involuntary resulting from

175

violence—the other, because a mental awareness is excluded—this is the involuntary resulting from ignorance.

387. Next [b], at **"The 'compulsory action,'"** he deals with the involuntary resulting from violence. Here he proceeds in two ways: first [i] he discloses what the "compulsory action" (*violentum*) is. Next [Lect. II; ii], at "If someone should say etc." (B.1110 b 9), he rejects an error about this. His initial point requires a triple consideration. First [i, x] he makes known what the "physically forced action" (*simpliciter violentum*) is, and second [i, y], at "Some things are done because of the fear," what the "morally forced action" (*violentum secundum quid*) is. Third [Lect. II; z], at "What sort of actions etc." (B.1110 b), he concludes with a summary. He says first that the forced action is one whose principle is from outside. It was just noted (385) that violence excludes the appetitive movement. Hence, since the appetitive faculty is an intrinsic principle, it is appropriate that the forced action arise from an extrinsic principle. However, not every action whose principle is from the outside is a forced action but only that action which is derived from an extrinsic principle in such a way that the interior appetitive faculty does not concur in it. This is what he means by his statement that a forced action must be such that a man contributes nothing to it by means of his own appetitive faculty. A man is here said to be an agent (*operans*) inasmuch as he does something because of violence and a patient inasmuch as he suffers something because of violence. Aristotle gives an example: if the air or wind drives a thing to some place by its violence, or if rulers having dominion and power exile someone against his will.

388. At **"Some things"** [i, y], he explains what a morally forced action is. Three steps clarify this conclusion. First [aa] he raises a doubt. Next

[bb], at "Operations of this kind etc.," he solves the doubt. Third [Lect. II; cc], at "People doing such actions etc." (B.1110 a 19), he clarifies the solution. He says first that a man sometimes performs an action because he fears to incur greater evils or because he is afraid to lose some good. A tyrant, for instance, has under his dominion and power the parents or children of a certain man. This tyrant commands the man to do a disgraceful deed on condition that if he does it his relatives will be spared; if he refuses they will be killed.

389. There is then a doubt whether things done because of such fear should be called voluntary or involuntary. He gives another example of sailors who during storms at sea throw merchandise overboard. Absolutely speaking, no man does this voluntarily but what he and his shipmates do in order to save their lives, any sensible man in a similar situation does.

390. Then [bb], at **"Operations of this kind,"** he solves this doubt by concluding from his previous remarks (387) that the afore-mentioned actions done out of fear are mixed, i.e., have something both of the involuntary (inasmuch as no one absolutely wishes to throw his goods overboard) and of the voluntary (inasmuch as a sensible man wishes this for the safety of himself and others). However, these actions approach more closely to the voluntary than to the involuntary. The reason is that throwing merchandise overboard, or any action of this kind, can be considered in two ways: one, absolutely and in general (involuntary); the other, in the particular circumstances occurring at the time the action is to be done (voluntary). But, since actions are concerned with particulars, the nature of the action must be judged rather according to the considerations of particulars than according to the consideration of what is general. This is what he means in his statement that

these actions were done voluntarily at the time they were performed (i.e., after having considered all the particular circumstances then occurring), and the end and completion of the action conform to this particular time.

391. Therefore, an action must be properly called voluntary or involuntary in view of the time at which the agent performed it. It is obvious that he acts voluntarily at the time. This is evident because in these actions the principle moving the bodily members to act is within the man himself. It would be different, however, if his members were not moved by himself but by a more powerful agent. The things done by an intrinsic principle are in the power of man to do or not to do, and this belongs to the nature of the voluntary. Obviously then actions of this kind are properly and truly voluntary. They are, however, involuntary simply, that is considering them in general, because no one as far as in him lies would choose to do a thing of this kind except out of fear, as was just stated (390).

LECTURE II

What Voluntary Actions Merit

ANALYTICAL OUTLINE
OF ST. THOMAS

TEXT OF ARISTOTLE
(*B.1110 a 19*)
Chapter 1

cc. He now clarifies the solution.
  d' He discloses in what way these actions merit praise and blame . . .
   A. HE DISTINGUISHES THREE GRADES . . . FIRST.

People doing such actions are at times praised for enduring some- 20 thing dishonorable or painful to achieve great and good results. But when they do the opposite of this they are blamed, for only a perverse man suffers very dishonorable things in exchange for little or no good. 392-393

   B. HE SETS DOWN THE SECOND GRADE.

Some actions do not deserve praise but only pardon, for example, if a person does things that are wrong because he fears evils beyond human endurance which no one would undergo in any case. 394

   C. HE TREATS THE THIRD GRADE.

Yet it is probable that there are some actions that a man cannot be forced to do and he ought to undergo death of the cruelest kind rather than do them. (The reasons that constrained Euripides' Alcmaeon to kill his mother seem to be ridiculous.) 395

b' He makes known the pending difficulties.
   A. THE FIRST.

Sometimes it is difficult to judge 30 what is to be chosen for the price and what is to be endured for the gain. 396

   B. THE SECOND DIFFICULTY.

It is still more difficult to abide by our decisions. As often happens, the expected results are painful but the compulsory acts are disgraceful. Hence we receive praise and blame according as we yield or stand firm against the constraint. 397

z. HE CONCLUDES WITH A SUMMARY.

What sort of actions then are to *b* be called compulsory? Those actions are entirely (*simpliciter*) compulsory that have their cause from the outside, the person involved contributing nothing. Some actions that in themselves are involuntary become voluntary in particular circumstances. Although of themselves involuntary, if their principle is in the agent who seeks them at this time and in these circumstances, they are voluntary. They are then more like the voluntary because actions take place in particular cases that are voluntary. It is not easy to assign the sort of things we must choose in such circumstances, for particular cases admit of many differences.   398-399

ii. He rejects an error . . . for five reasons.

v. THE FIRST REASON.

If someone should say that pleasurable and good things are the cause of violence (they are external to us *10* and influence us), all our actions will then be compulsory because men perform all their actions for the sake of something pleasing and good.   400-401

w. THE SECOND REASON.

Those who act by violence act involuntarily and with sadness, but those who act to attain something enjoyable act with pleasure.   402

x. THE THIRD REASON.

It is ridiculous that a man blame external goods, and not accuse himself for being snared by such pleasures; 403

y. THE FOURTH REASON.

while he takes to himself the credit for virtuous deeds, and lays the blame for his shameful deeds upon pleasure. 404

z. THE FIFTH REASON.

It seems that the compulsory action is one whose origin is external in such a way that one who suffers violence contributes nothing to the action.   405

COMMENTARY OF ST. THOMAS

392. After the Philosopher has solved the doubt raised about the actions done because of fear, showing that such actions are voluntary, he now clarifies the solution [cc] by explaining that praise and blame, honor and punishment are due to voluntary actions of this kind. On this point he does two things. First [a'] he discloses in what way these actions merit praise and blame, honor and punishment. Next [b'], at "Sometimes it is difficult etc.," he makes known the pending difficulties about this. In regard to the first he distinguishes three grades of these actions performed by reason of fear, as far as they merit praise or blame.

393. Considering now the first grade [a', A], he shows that regarding such actions, which he says are a mixture of the voluntary and the involuntary, some persons are praised for suffering something dishonorable—not indeed of a sinful nature but a kind of ignominy —or even saddening or grievous in order to persevere in certain great and good things, for example, virtuous actions. When the opposite happens they are blamed since it seems that only a perverse man suffers very dishonorable things, i.e., great disorders in exchange for little or no good. No one suffers any evil to preserve a good unless that good is of greater value in his estimation than the other goods to which the evil he suffers are opposed. It belongs to a disordered desire to prefer small goods to great ones that are destroyed by greater evils. Therefore, he says this pertains to a perverse man, i.e., one who has a disordered desire.

394. At "Some actions" [a', B], he sets down the second grade, stating that some actions performed because

of fear do not deserve praise but only pardon. A person should not be blamed very much for doing certain things he ought not do, such as actions unbefitting his state. These actions should not be considered seriously binding on account of the fear of evils beyond human endurance. No one would undergo such evils especially for the reason alleged, for example, if someone is threatened with punishment by fire unless he tells a jocose lie, or unless he performs some lowly menial tasks unbecoming his dignity.

395. At "Yet it is probable" [a', c], he treats the third grade. He states that other actions are so evil that no amount of force can compel them to be done but a man ought to undergo death of the cruelest kind rather than do such things, as St. Lawrence endured the roasting on the gridiron to avoid sacrificing to idols. The Philosopher affirms this either because glory remains after death for one dying for the sake of virtue or because courageous perseverance in virtue is so great a good that continuance of life —which a man loses by death—cannot equal it. He says, therefore, that *Alcmaeona* or the poems about Alcmaeon written by Euripides seem to be satirical. These poems narrate the story of Alcmaeon who was forced to kill his mother by the command of his father. The father had ordered this when dying in the Theban war to which he had gone by the advice of his wife.

396. Then [b'], at "Sometimes it is," he brings forward two difficulties which threaten the above-mentioned activities. The first of these pertains to the judgment of reason [b', A]. Sometimes it is difficult, he says, to

judge what is to be chosen so that one may avoid evil and what evil is to be endured so that one may not be lacking in some good.

397. The second difficulty [b', в], which he gives at "It is still more," pertains to the stability of the affection. He says that it is even more difficult to be steadfast in a reasonable decision that has been made than to make a right judgment. He assigns the reason for the difficulty saying that—as often happens—the things that are expected are painful, i.e., afflicting or sorrowful, but those to which men are forced because of fear are disgraceful. It is difficult, however, for a man's affections not to be moved by fear of pain. Since those actions to which one is forced by a motive of this kind are disgraceful, it is fitting that for those who are forced to do such things by fear of painful effects, blame should be forthcoming. But those who cannot be forced to do them are worthy of praise.

398. Next [z], at "What sort of actions then," he sums up in conclusion the things that have been said and assigns a reason for them. First he reviews the principal question, what sort of actions are to be called compulsory (*violenta*). Then, he sums up the answer so far as concerns the entirely (*absolute*) compulsory actions, the cause of which is from the outside so that the person involved contributes nothing because of violence. Third he gives a resumé of mixed actions. He says that those actions that in themselves, i.e., abstractly (*absolute*) and universally considered, are involuntary become voluntary at a definite time and by reason of certain events. Although they are involuntary in themselves, their principle is in the agent.[1] Therefore, they should be called voluntary at this time and for these reasons. Thus it is evident that these

[1] "Operatione" in the Commentary should be "operante."

actions are more like the voluntary than the involuntary because they are voluntary when we consider the particular circumstances in which the actions are performed.

399. Last, he recapitulates what he had stated about the difficulty occurring in things of this kind. He says that it is not easy to assign the sort of thing we must choose in such circumstances. He assigns as the reason that many differences are found in singulars. Hence the judgment of them cannot be comprised under an exact rule but they are to be left to the evaluation of a prudent man.

400. At "If someone" [ii], he rejects an error of certain philosophers concerning actions done as a result of violence. Because man is what he is by reason, it seemed to some that man of himself, and as it were voluntarily, does only that which he performs according to reason. But when it happens that man acts contrary to reason either on account of the desire of some pleasure or greed for some external good, he acts in a violent manner. They say, therefore, that pleasurable and external goods like riches cause forced actions inasmuch as being external things they force man to act against his reason. But Aristotle shows this to be false for five reasons.

401. The first reason is this [ii, v]. If external things, precisely as they are pleasurable and seemingly good, cause violence, it would follow that all actions we perform in human affairs are forced actions and none is voluntary. (All men do what they do for the sake of these things, i.e., for something that is pleasurable or good under a certain aspect.) But this is unreasonable. Therefore, the first (that these external things cause violence) is also untenable.

402. He sets down the second reason at "Those who act" [ii, w]. All who act as a result of violence, act

involuntarily and with sadness. Hence in the fifth book of the *Metaphysics* (Ch. 5, 1015 a 26 sq.; St. Th. Lect. VI, 829-831), it is well said that necessitation is saddening because it is opposed to the will. But those who act to acquire something enjoyable act with pleasure. They do not then act by violence and involuntarily.

403. He gives the third reason at "It is ridiculous" [ii, x]. He says it is ridiculous that a man plead as an excuse or blame external goods and not accuse himself that he was snared, i.e., permitted himself to be overcome by such pleasures. Our will is not of necessity moved by these desirable things but it can cling to them or desert them. None possesses the nature of a universal and perfect good, as happiness (which everyone necessarily wishes) does.

404. He assigns the fourth reason at "while he takes" [ii, y]. It is ridiculous, he says, that a person should call himself the cause of his good and virtuous works, and pleasurable things the cause of his shameful deeds inasmuch

as they induce desire. Aristotle says it is ridiculous because directly opposed operations are referred back to the same power as a cause. Consequently it is necessary that as reason operating according to itself is the cause of virtuous action so also in following the passions it should be the cause of vicious action.

405. He gives the fifth reason at "It seems that" [ii, z], saying that the forced action is one whose source is from the outside in such a way that he who suffers by reason of it contributes nothing to the action. But the man who acts on account of external goods does contribute something to the action. Accordingly, although the principle inclining his will is from outside, his action is forced neither wholly (*simpliciter*) because he contributes something to the action, nor by some mixture because in mixed actions a thing is not rendered simply voluntary, as happens here. Therefore, a man acts in that case with sadness but here with pleasure, as has been stated (402).

LECTURE III

The Involuntary Resulting from Ignorance

ANALYTICAL OUTLINE
OF ST. THOMAS

TEXT OF ARISTOTLE
(*1110 b 18*)
Chapter 1

c. He now turns his attention to the involuntary resulting from ignorance.
  i. *He shows how there is an involuntary resulting from ignorance.*
    X. HE SETS DOWN THREE DIFFERENCES CONCERNING IGNORANCE. THE FIRST.

Every action done because of ignorance is not voluntary; it is in- 20 voluntary if sorrow and repentance follow. One who does something on account of ignorance and is not sorry about what he did, cannot be said to have acted voluntarily, for he was unaware of his action. But neither can he be said to have acted involuntarily if he is not sorry. A man who has acted from ignorance and regrets his action seems to have acted involuntarily. But if he does not regret it, his case is different; let us call him nonvoluntary. Because of his differing, it is better that he have a distinctive name. **406-408**

Y. HE SETS DOWN THE SECOND DIFFERENCE.

There seems to be a difference between acting on account of ignorance and acting in ignorance. A drunken or angry person does not act because of ignorance but because of one of the things mentioned (drunkenness or anger). Such a one however does not act knowingly but in ignorance. Therefore, every wicked person acts in ignorance of the things he ought to do and avoid. Men acting on account 30 of an error of this kind become unjust and wicked generally. **409-410**

Z. HE ASSIGNS THE THIRD DIFFERENCE.

When we speak of an action as involuntary we do not mean that a man is ignorant of what he ought to do.

183

The ignorance that accompanies choice is not the cause of an involuntary but of sin. The same may be said of ignorance that is of a general nature because a person is blamed for such ignorance. But a person who *B.1111* is ignorant of particular conditions about which and on which human activity is exercised deserves mercy and pardon because he who is ignorant of any of these circumstances acts involuntarily.   **411-413**

ii. He explains some of his statements. (Circumstances the ignorance of which is a cause of an involuntary.)

    X. HE POINTS OUT WHAT THESE CIRCUMSTANCES ARE.

Perhaps it is not out of place to determine the nature and number of these circumstances: who, what, concerning what or in what one operates; sometimes, too, by what, for example, a tool; for the sake of which, for instance, safety; and in what manner, for example, quietly or violently.

414-416

    Y. . . . IN WHAT WAY IGNORANCE OF THEM MAY BE PRESENT.

No one but a madman will be ignorant of all these circumstances. It is obvious that no one can be ignorant of the agent. How can he be ignorant about himself? But someone can be ignorant of what he does, for instance, those speaking out of turn say it escaped them unawares or they did not know that certain things were not to be disclosed, like Aeschylus when he revealed the sacred mysteries; or *10* someone wishing to show the working of a weapon discharges an arrow; or a man mistakes his son for an assailant, as Merope did; or he thinks a piked lance blunted, or a rock merely pumice; or he may kill someone by a blow meant to save him; or a trainer sparring with a boxer to teach him takes his life.   **417-421**

    Z. HE EXPLAINS HOW IGNORANCE OF THESE CIRCUMSTANCES IS THE CAUSE OF AN INVOLUNTARY.

      aa. First . . . man seems to act unwillingly . . . who

Since ignorance can be concerned with every one of the circumstances is ignorant of one (circumstance).

bb. . . . The most important circumstances.

cc. . . . Ignorance of these very things is not enough for an involuntary.

occurring with the action, that man seems to act involuntarily who is ignorant of one of them. This applies especially to ignorance of the most important circumstances.   422

These seem to be the circum- 20 stances of the action and its motives.
                                                      423

For an action to be called involuntary in respect of such ignorance it must be painful to the agent and cause repentance.   424

COMMENTARY OF ST. THOMAS

406. After the Philosopher has determined the involuntary resulting from violence, he now turns his attention to the involuntary resulting from ignorance [c]. Concerning it he does two things. First [i] he shows how there is an involuntary resulting from ignorance. Second [ii], at "Perhaps it is etc.," he explains some of his statements. In regard to the initial point he sets down three differences concerning ignorance. The first of these [i, x] is considered insofar as what is done on account of ignorance is related to the will in different ways. Sometimes it is opposed to the will, and then it is properly called an involuntary. But other times it is not opposed to the will but is over and above the will precisely as it is unknown. In this sense it is not called involuntary but non-voluntary.

407. He says then that what is done on account of ignorance in such a way that ignorance is the cause, is not voluntary in any case because the act of the will is not moved to it. The act of the will cannot be moved to what is entirely unknown since the will's object is the known good. But only then is that which is done out of ig-

norance called involuntary—as it were opposed to the will—when on becoming known, sorrow and repentance (which is sorrow over one's past actions) follow. A thing is sorrowful because it is opposed to the will, as is stated in the fifth book of the *Metaphysics* (Ch. 5, 1015 a 26 sq.; St. Th. Lect. VI, 829-831).

408. One who does something on account of ignorance and is not sorry about what he did after he knows it, for instance, if he takes silver thinking he took tin, cannot be said to have voluntarily (willingly) taken silver since he did not know that it was silver. It cannot be said that he involuntarily (unwillingly), i.e., against his will, took silver since he is not sorry that he did take silver by reason of ignorance. He seems to have acted involuntarily who has sorrow or repents for the fact that he took silver by reason of ignorance, just as if someone had, on the contrary, taken tin thinking he has taken silver. But because he who does not repent is different from the man who does repent (he is said to be unwilling) let the first be called non-willing. Since he really differs from the one who is un-

willing, it is better that he have a proper and separate name.

409. He sets down the second difference at **"There seems to be"** [i, y]. This is taken according to the difference of what is done in ignorance; for ignorance sometimes is the cause of an action, but sometimes the act proceeds from another cause. He says that a person acting on account of ignorance seems to be different from a person acting in ignorance. Sometimes one acts in ignorance but not on account of ignorance. A drunken or angry person does not act on account of ignorance but on account of drunkenness or anger. Neither of these, however, acts knowingly because ignorance is caused at the same time as the action by drunkenness and anger. Thus ignorance is concomitant with the action and is not its cause.

410. From this he concludes that as an angry person acts in ignorance and not on account of ignorance but on account of anger, so every wicked person acts not indeed on account of ignorance but partly in ignorance of the good he ought to do and of the evil he ought to avoid, inasmuch as he thinks that at this moment he should do this evil and refrain from this good. For this reason he sins because he does what he ought not to do. Men who act in ignorance universally become unjust with respect to others and wicked with respect to themselves. From this it is evident that when someone acts in ignorance, and not on account of ignorance, he does not cause an involuntary. The reason is that no one, by reason of what he does involuntarily, is unjust or wicked.

411. He assigns the third difference at **"When we speak"** [i, z]. This is taken from the object of the person's ignorance. Here we must consider that ignorance can be of two kinds. According to one, a person is ignorant of what he ought to do or avoid. He says this is ignorance of what is fitting—of what

he ought to be doing. This ignorance does not cause an involuntary because ignorance of this kind cannot happen to a man with the use of reason except from negligence. The reason is that everyone is bound to be solicitous about knowing what he is obliged to do and to avoid. Hence if a man does not wish to avoid (as he is bound) ignorance that is considered voluntary, it follows that what is done through this ignorance should not be judged involuntary. This is the meaning of the saying that one does not wish an involuntary (i.e., what is by nature an involuntary) if he is ignorant of what he does, that is, of what is suitable under the circumstances. Of this someone can be ignorant in two ways:

412. One is in a particular choice. For instance, because of sensual desire a person thinks he should commit fornication at this time. The other way is in general, as is evident in one who is of the opinion that fornication is always lawful. Both kinds of ignorance concern what is done. Hence neither causes an involuntary. This is what is meant by saying that that ignorance accompanying choice (by which a person thinks he should do this evil at this time) is not the cause of an involuntary but is rather the cause of vice or sin. Neither is the ignorance that is of a general nature the cause of an involuntary since a person is blamed on account of ignorance of this kind. But no one is censured because of an involuntary, as was said previously (410).

413. The other ignorance (the first is in 411) is of singular conditions, for instance, that this woman is married, that this man is a parent, that this place is holy. It is about these conditions and on them that human activity is exercised; by reason of a justifiable ignorance of such conditions that a person deserves mercy and pardon because he who is ignorant

of one of these conditions acts involuntarily. Therefore, it is obvious that ignorance of particular circumstances of this kind—not however ignorance of what one should do—is the cause of an involuntary.

414. Then [ii], at **"Perhaps it is not,"** he explains what he had referred to: those circumstances the ignorance of which is a cause of an involuntary. In regard to this he does three things. First [ii, x] he points out what these circumstances are. Next [ii, y], at "No one but etc.," he shows in what way ignorance of them may be present. Last [ii, z], at "Since ignorance can be etc.," he explains how ignorance of these circumstances is the cause of an involuntary. On the first point we must consider that circumstances are nothing else but certain particular conditions of a human act. These can be taken either on the part of the causes of the act or on the part of the act itself. The cause of the act is efficient or final. The efficient cause is either the principal or the instrumental agent. On the part of the act three things can be understood: the genus of the act, the matter or the object itself, and the mode of acting. In agreement with this the Philosopher here places six circumstances. He says that it is not out of place—indeed it is very appropriate—to determine what and how many are these particular circumstances, the ignorance of which is the cause of an involuntary. He uses an adverb (*forsitan*) indicating doubt, as in many other places of this book because of the uncertainty in moral matters.

415. Enumerating then these particular things he names "who," which refers to the person of the principal agent; "what is done," which refers to the genus of the act; and "concerning what," which refers to the matter or the object. But he adds also "concerning this"—which refers to the measure of the act—as belonging to the agent, i.e., place or time, since he says "or in what he operates." The reason is that all external things seem to have relation to the human act. Cicero includes what we call "concerning what" under "what." What is here called "in what" he divides into two circumstances: time and place.

416. So far as concerns the instrumental agent Aristotle adds: sometimes also "by what" (*quo*), for instance an instrument, since not every action is performed through an instrument, for example, understanding and willing. In place of this some put "by what means" (helps), for one to whom help is given uses help as an instrument. Referring to the end he says "for the sake of which," for instance, a doctor cuts for the sake of health. Referring to the mode of acting he says "and in what manner," for example, quietly, or violently, that is, strongly.

417. Next [ii, y], at **"No one but,"** he shows in what way there may be ignorance about the preceding circumstances. He says that only a totally insane person is ignorant of all these circumstances. Among the other circumstances it is obvious that a man cannot be ignorant of what is meant by the one acting, because in this case he would be ignorant about himself (which is impossible). But someone can be ignorant of what he does, as those who disclose things that should not be disclosed say in excusing themselves that it slipped their mind or they never knew that such things were secret, i.e., were not to be spoken. Thus were revealed the sacred mysteries or secrets by Aeschylus, a certain poet. He who speaks such things is ignorant of what he does because he does not know this is a revelation of secrets.

418. He gives another example so far as concerns what is done, for instance, an archer wishing to teach a pupil how archery is practised shoots

an arrow into something. Such a one does not know what he does because he does not know he is shooting an arrow. Then he exemplifies ignorance "concerning what" (*circa quid*), thus if a man should mistake his son for an enemy besieging his home, and kill him, just as a certain woman named Merope killed her son. So it is obvious that in a case of this kind a man knows what he does because he knows he kills, but he does not know the "concerning what" of his act because he does not know he kills his son.

419. Then he gives an example of ignorance of the instrument, thus if a lancer should use a piked lance that he thought was blunted or if a thrower of rocks thinks what he throws are pumice stones.

420. Farther on he gives an example of ignorance of the end. He says that a doctor or a blood-letter lancing a patient to make him better, or a teacher striking a pupil to correct him, may take a life. These have ignorance of the end, not indeed of what they intended but of what followed from their action. They were ignorant that their action would lead to such an end.

421. Last, he illustrates ignorance of the manner of the action, for instance, a man thinks he is tapping with his fist to show how to hit like boxers do but he strikes with force. Such a man strikes with force in ignorance or unknowingly.

422. At **"Since ignorance can be"** [ii, z], he shows how ignorance of the previously named things is a cause of the voluntary. First [aa] he says that since ignorance can be concerned with any one of the five afore-mentioned that concur with the action, that man seems to act unwillingly or involuntarily who is ignorant of one of the preceding. This does not apply in equal measure to all but it does apply especially if the ignorance concerns the most important circumstances.

423. Next [bb], at **"These seem to be,"** he shows what he considers the most important circumstances. He says that the principal circumstances seem to be those on which the act takes place, i.e., the object or the matter of the act, and that "for the sake of which" or the end, because acts are specified by their objects. Just as the matter is the object of the external act so the end is the object of the internal act of the will.

424. Last [cc], at **"For an action,"** he says that ignorance of these very things is not enough for an involuntary. He states that although an action may be called involuntary according to the preceding ignorance, a further requirement is that the action be connected with sadness and repentance, as was pointed out before (408).

LECTURE IV

Definition of the Voluntary

ANALYTICAL OUTLINE
OF ST. THOMAS

TEXT OF ARISTOTLE
(*B.IIII a 22*)
Chapter 1

I. HE SHOWS WHAT THE VOLUNTARY IS.

Since the involuntary comes about on account of force and ignorance, the voluntary seems to originate within the agent who has knowledge of the circumstances of the action.   **425**

II. HE DISMISSES AN ERRONEOUS VIEW OF IT.

A. First he explains (the error).

Perhaps it is not accurate to call involuntary the things that are done on account of anger or sensual desire.   **426**

B. Second he rejects this opinion for five reasons.

a. The first.

(1) The main reason is that neither animals nor children would then act voluntarily.   **427**

b. The second.

(2) Are none of the things done by reason of sensual desire or anger done voluntarily? Are the noble actions done voluntarily but the evil involuntarily? The latter views seems ridiculous since there is one cause of all our actions. Likewise it seems unreasonable to *30* call involuntary the things we ought to seek. We ought to be angry under certain circumstances, and we ought to desire certain things, for example, health and learning.   **428**

c. The third reason.

(3) Involuntary things seemingly are accompanied by sadness. But what is done in agreement with sensual desire seems to be done with pleasure.   **429**

d. The fourth reason.

(4) Further what difference is there from the viewpoint of involuntariness

189

between sins committed after reflection and sins committed on account *b* of anger? It is our duty to avoid both.   **430**

e. The fifth reason.

(5) The irrational passions seem to be truly human. So too then are the actions of man proceeding from anger and sensual desire. It is unreasonable, therefore, to regard these as involuntary.   **431**

COMMENTARY OF ST. THOMAS

425. After the Philosopher has considered the involuntary, he next turns his attention to the voluntary. First [I] he shows what the voluntary is. Then [II], at "Perhaps it is not accurate etc.," he dismisses an erroneous view of it. On the first point we must consider that although the term involuntary seems to indicate the removal of the voluntary, nevertheless the causes lead us to understand that a thing is called voluntary by reason of the removal of the things causing an involuntary, such as violence and ignorance. Because every single thing is known through its cause, he gives the definition of the voluntary by taking away the cause of the involuntary. He says that since the involuntary comes about through physical compulsion and ignorance, as has been determined previously (386), the voluntary seems to be: that which the agent himself originates (thus violence is excluded) in such a way that the agent knows the individual circumstances that concur with the action. Thus ignorance as the cause of the involuntary is excluded.

426. Then [II], at "Perhaps it is," he rejects an error. First [A] he explains it. Certain people were of the opinion that not everything, which the agent originates through a knowledge

of circumstances, is a voluntary. It can happen that that principle which is from within is not the rational appetitive faculty called the will (*voluntas*), whence the voluntary receives its name, but a passion of the sensitive appetitive faculty, for instance, anger, sensual desire, or something else of this kind. This, the Philosopher says, is not an accurate statement. It should be noted that because the passions of the sensitive appetitive faculty are aroused by external things grasped by means of an external sense, this error seems to be of the same nature as the one he discarded previously (400-405), according to which it was indicated that external things bring about violence. It was imperative to state that in that context it was a question of violence, whose origin is external. But this must be treated here where it is a question of the voluntary, the principle of which is intrinsic, for the passions are within us.

427. Second [B], at "The main reason is," he rejects this opinion for five reasons. Here is his primary reason [a]. Whatever irrational animals and children do, they do in conformity with the affections of the sensitive faculty, and not in conformity with the rational faculty because they lack the use of reason. If then the things that are done

through anger, sensual desire, and the other affections of the sensitive faculty were involuntary it would follow that neither animals nor children would act voluntarily. But agents are said to act voluntarily, not because they operate under the impulse of the will, but because they operate of their own accord by their proper movement in such a way that they are not moved by any external thing. It follows then that things done by reason of anger or sensual desire are voluntary.

428. He gives the second reason at "Are none" [b]. If the things that are done because of anger or sensual desire are not voluntary, either this is universally true or it is true of evil actions, not of good actions, so that the good actions that a person does by reason of passion he does voluntarily but the evil actions involuntarily. The proponents of this view were probably influenced by the fact that good actions conform to and evil actions are opposed to reason. But this second supposition seems unacceptable since the one cause of all human actions, both good and bad, is the will. A man does not rush to do whatsoever is rendered desirable by anger or sensual desire without the consent of the rational appetitive faculty. Likewise, the first supposition seems unreasonable, namely, that someone should call not-voluntary the good things that he ought to seek even according to passion, for the reason by means of the will incites to the things we ought to seek. We ought to be angry under certain conditions, for instance, to curb sin. Likewise we ought to desire certain things, for example, health and learning. It remains false

then to hold that the things done on account of passion are not voluntary.

429. He assigns the third reason at "Involuntary things" [c]. It is this. Actions resulting from violence are accompanied by sadness, but those which are done in agreement with sensual desire are done with pleasure. Consequently they are not involuntary.

430. The fourth reason, given at "Further, what" [d], is this. As has been pointed out before (383, 393), voluntary faults are to be censured and avoided. This cannot be said of the involuntary because a man is neither able to avoid these nor is he censured on account of them. But as sins that are committed after reflection, that is, with deliberation, are to be avoided and are blameworthy so also sins that are committed on account of anger or another passion. A man can, by means of his will, resist passion. Hence if he does a disgraceful act because of passion he is blamed. Therefore, they do not differ from things done by deliberation so far as they are voluntary.

431. He assigns the fifth reason at "The irrational passions" [e]. Irrational passions, i.e., of the sensitive appetitive faculty, seem to be human insofar as the sensitive appetitive faculty can obey reason, as was stated before (272). Therefore, the actions proceeding from anger, sensual desire, and the other passions are human. But no involuntary operation is human, for neither praise nor blame are imputed to a man who acts involuntarily. Therefore, it is unreasonable to say that things done out of passion are involuntary.

LECTURE V

Choice

ANALYTICAL OUTLINE   TEXT OF ARISTOTLE
OF ST. THOMAS   (B.*IIII b 4*)
                               Chapter 2

I. HE GIVES AN EXPLANATION OF CHOICE ITSELF.

A. He shows that it belongs to our present study to consider choice.

> After the treatise on the voluntary and the involuntary, we naturally proceed to a consideration of choice. Such a study is especially proper to virtue, for moral practices are judged by choice rather than by actions.   **432-433**

B. He investigates the nature of choice.

A' He investigates its genus.

> Choice certainly is something voluntary, but choice and voluntary are not identical, for the voluntary is more extensive in range. Children and all the brutes participate in voluntariety but not in choice. Then too the things done on the spur of the moment *10* are called voluntary but they are not said to be done by choice.   **434-436**

B' (He investigates) its different aspects.

   1. HE EXPLAINS HIS INTENT.

> Those who say that choice is sensual desire, or anger, or wish, or opinion of some sort do not speak accurately.   **437**

   2. HE PROVES IT.

a. He shows first that choice is not sensual desire.

   i. He gives four reasons. The first.

> Choice does not belong to the brutes while sensual desire and anger are common both to men and brutes.   **438**

   ii. Second reason.

> The incontinent man acts in conformity with sensual desire but not in conformity with choice. But the conti-

nent man on the contrary acts from choice and not from sensual desire. **439**

iii. Third reason.

Sensual desire is opposed to choice, but one desire is not contrary to another. **440**

iv. Fourth reason.

Sensual desire is accompanied by pleasure or sorrow, but choice is not necessarily associated with sorrow or pleasure. **441**

b. (He shows) that . . . (choice) is not anger.

There is less argument in favor of choice being anger, for the things done on account of anger do not seem to be done by choice. **442**

c. (He shows) that . . . (choice) is not wishing.
  i. First he sets forth his proposition.

Choice is not identical with *20* wishing although it is closely connected with it. **443**

  ii. Then he proves it.
    x. . . . BY THREE REASONS, OF WHICH THE FIRST IS THIS.

Choice is not concerned with impossibles, and if a person should say that he does choose the impossible, he will appear foolish. Wishing on the other hand can be directed to the impossible, for instance, to live forever. **444**

    Y. SECOND REASON.

Wishing can be concerned with things not done by oneself, for instance, that a man pretending to be an athlete may win, or even that a man who is really an athlete may win. No one, however, chooses these things but only those that he thinks he can do himself. **445**

    z. THIRD REASON.

Moreover, wishing is directed rather to the end, and choice to the means. Thus we wish health but we choose the remedies that restore us to health. Likewise, we wish to be happy and we do say this. Yet it is not suitable to say that we elect or choose to be happy. **446**

  iii. He deduces the origin of the difference between choice and wishing.

In general, choice seems to be directed to the things which are within our power. **447**

COMMENTARY OF ST. THOMAS

432. After the Philosopher has treated the voluntary and the involuntary, he here makes a study of choice. First he gives an explanation of choice itself [I], and then [Lect. VII, II] of counsel (which is placed in the definition of choice) at "Should men take counsel about all things etc." (B.1112 a 19). Regarding the initial point he does two things. First [A] he shows that it belongs to our present study to consider choice. Next [B], at "Choice certainly is something," he investigates the nature of choice. He says first that, after the treatise (382-431) on the voluntary and the involuntary, he will undertake a passing consideration of choice. Here then he proposes briefly the things necessary to study choice. He proves here that it belongs to our science to consider choice because choice seems especially proper to virtue, which is our principal concern at present.

433. Its appropriateness is clearly shown by the fact that although both inner choice and outward action flow from the habit of virtue, virtuous or vicious practices are judged rather by choice than by outward works. Every virtuous man chooses good but sometimes he does not do it because of some external hindrances. On the other hand the vicious man sometimes performs a virtuous deed not out of virtuous choice but out of fear or for some unbecoming motive, for instance, vainglory or something else of this kind. Hence it obviously pertains to our present purpose to consider choice.

434. Then [B], at "Choice certainly," he shows what choice is. First [A'] he investigates its genus, and next [B'] its different aspects, at "Those

who say that choice etc." Last [Lect. VI, C'], at "What, then, is its genus etc." (B.1112 a 13), he concludes the definition. The voluntary is the genus of choice because it is universally predicated of choice and of other things besides. Hence first he says that every choice is voluntary, but choice and the voluntary are not identical, for the voluntary is more extensive. He proves this in twofold fashion:

435. The first proof he gives by the words ". . . participate in voluntariety etc." It is this. Children and the various brutes participate in voluntariety inasmuch as of their own accord they do things by their own movement, as has been noted above (427). But they do not communicate in choice because they do not act with deliberation, which is required for choice. Therefore, the voluntary is more extensive than choice.

436. He assigns a second reason by the words "Then too the things done on the spur of the moment etc." It is this. The things we do on the spur of the moment are called voluntary because their origin is within us. However, they are not said to be according to choice because they are not done with deliberation. Therefore, the voluntary is more extensive than choice.

437. Next [B'], at "Those who say," he investigates the different aspects of choice, proving that choice differs from things with which it appears to agree. On this question he does two things. First [1] he explains his intent. Then [2], at "Choice does not belong etc.," he proves it. He says first that some philosophers have held that choice is sensual desire because both imply a movement of the appetitive faculty

toward good. Others maintained that
choice is anger, perhaps because in
both there is a certain use of reason.
The angry person uses reason inasmuch
as he judges that an injury received
deserves punishment. Still others who
consider that choice is without passion
ascribe choice to the rational part,
either so far as concerns the appetitive
faculty (saying it is wishing) or so far
as it concerns perception (saying it is
opinion). In these four states all the
principles of human actions are included in a simple way: reason to
which opinion belongs; the rational
appetitive faculty that is the will; the
sensitive appetitive faculty divided into
irascible to which belong anger, and
concupiscible to which belong sensual
desire. The Philosopher says, however,
that those who hold that choice is one
of these do not speak accurately.

438. At "Choice does not" [2], he
proves his proposition. He shows first
[a] that choice is not sensual desire;
next [b], at "There is less argument
etc.," that it is not anger; third [c], at
"Choice is not identical etc.," that it
is not wishing; last [Lect. VI, d], that
it is not opinion, at "Choice is not opinion etc." (B.1111 b 31). Regarding the
first he gives four reasons. The first of
these [a, i], common to sensual desire
and anger, is this. Sensual desire and
anger are found both among men and
brutes. But choice is not met with
among the brutes as has been said
(435). Therefore, choice is neither
sensual desire nor anger.

439. He gives the second reason at
"The incontinent man" [a, ii]. It is
this. If choice were sensual desire, whoever acts with choice would act with
sensual desire. This, however, is false
because the incontinent man acts in
conformity with sensual desire but not
in conformity with choice, for he does
not reasonably direct his choice because
of his sensual desire. But the continent
man on the contrary acts from choice
and not from sensual desire, which he

resists by choice, as will be made evident in the seventh book (1143).
Therefore, choice is not the same as
sensual desire.

440. He assigns the third reason at
"Sensual desire is opposed" [a, iii]. It
is this. Sensual desire is opposed to
choice in one who is continent or incontinent. One chooses according to
reason the opposite of that which the
other desires according to the sensitive
appetitive faculty. But the sensual desire in the one is not opposed to the
sensual desire in the other, because the
whole sensual desire of each one tends
to the same thing, the pleasure of the
senses. But this must not be understood
in the sense that one desire may not be
opposed to another. We do find desires
of contraries, for instance, one man desires to move and another to remain
in repose. Therefore it is evident that
choice is not identical with sensual desire.

441. The fourth reason, given at
"Sensual desire is accompanied" [a,
iv], is this. Sensual desire is always accompanied by pleasure because of the
presence of the thing desired, or by
sorrow because of the absence of that
thing. Every passion is followed by
pleasure or sorrow, as has been pointed
out in the second book (296). But
choice is not necessarily associated with
pleasure or sorrow, for it can occur
without any passion by the judgment
of reason alone. Therefore, choice is
not sensual desire.

442. Then [b], at "There is less
argument," he shows that choice is not
the same as anger. As to this, he says
that there is less argument in favor of
choice being anger than sensual desire.
The reason is that even according to
appearances the things done from anger
do not seem to be done by choice because, by reason of the swiftness of the
movement of wrath, the actions done
through anger are very sudden. Although in anger there is some use of
reason, insofar as the angry person

begins to attend to his reason as it judges that an injury ought to be avenged, nevertheless he does not perfectly heed reason in determining the manner and the order of the vengeance. Hence anger especially excludes deliberation, which is necessary for choice. But sensual desire does not act so suddenly. Hence things done in conformity with sensual desire do not seem to be remote from choice as the things done out of anger.

443. Next [c], at **"Choice is not identical,"** he explains the difference between choice and wish. First [c, i] he sets forth his proposition. Then [c, ii], at "Choice is not concerned etc.," he proves it. Last [c, iii], at "In general, choice," he deduces the origin of the difference between choice and wishing. He says first that choice is not even wishing although it seems to be closely connected with wishing. Both belong to the one power, the rational appetitive faculty or the will. Wishing designates an act of this power related to good absolutely. But choice designates an act of the same power related to good according as it belongs to an act by which we are ordered to some good.

444. At **"Choice is not concerned"** [c, ii], he proves the statement by three reasons, of which the first is this [x]. Because choice refers to our activity, it is said that choice is not concerned with impossible things. If a person should say that he chooses something impossible he will appear foolish. But wishing can be directed to any good even the impossible because it regards good absolutely. Thus a man can wish to be immortal, an impossible thing according to the condition of this perishable life. Therefore, choice and wish are not the same.

445. He gives the second reason at **"Wishing can be"** [y]. The wishing of someone can be concerned with things not done by himself. Thus he who is a spectator at a duel can wish that a pretender playing an assumed role may win (for example, a man who comes into the ring as a boxer when he is not a boxer) or even that one who is really an athlete may win. No one, however, chooses these things that are done by another but only those that he thinks he can do himself. Therefore, choice differs from wishing.

446. He assigns the third reason at **"Moreover, wishing."** He says that wishing is directed rather to the end than to the means because we wish the means on account of the end. But that for the sake of which something exists is itself greater. But choice concerns only the means and not the end itself because the end as already predetermined is presupposed. The means, however, are sought by us as things to be ordered to the end. Thus we wish health principally since it is the end of healing. But we choose the remedies by which we are restored to health. Likewise we wish to be happy—happiness is our ultimate end—and we say we wish this. Yet it is not suitable to say that we elect or choose to be happy. Therefore, choice is not the same as wish.

447. Then [c, iii], at **"In general, choice,"** he gives the root of the whole difference to which all the previous differences in general are referred. He says that choice seems to be directed to the things that are within our power. This is the reason why it does not concern impossibles, things done by others, nor the end that, for the most part, is prearranged for us by nature.

LECTURE VI

Choice and Opinion

ANALYTICAL OUTLINE
OF ST. THOMAS

TEXT OF ARISTOTLE
(*B.IIII b 31*)
Chapter 2

d. He shows that choice is not the same as opinion.
    i. . . . Choice is not the same as opinion in general.
        Y. HE PROVES THE STATEMENT BY TWO REASONS, . . . FIRST.
        Z. SECOND REASON.

Choice is not opinion, for opinion can concern everything—no less eternal and impossible things than things lying within our power. Then, too, opinion is divided into false *B.1112* and true but not into good and bad, as is the case with choice. Perhaps there is no one who maintains that choice is generally identical with opinion. **448-449**

    ii. Choice is not the same as . . . particular opinion.
        V. HE PROVES THIS BY (FIVE) REASONS. THE FIRST.

Nor is choice identical with a particular opinion. In choosing good or bad things we are said to be good or bad but this is not the case in forming opinions about them. **450-451**

        W. SECOND REASON.

We choose to accept or reject this or anything pertaining to our actions. But we have an opinion as to what a thing is or what effect it has or how it is to be used. However, accepting or rejecting something is hardly a matter of opinion. **452**

        X. THIRD REASON.

Choice is rather praised because it chooses what it ought—as it were—in the right way, while opinion is praised because it has the truth about something. **453**

        Y. FOURTH REASON.

We choose those things that we especially know are good. But we have an opinion about things we are not sure of. **454**

z. FIFTH REASON.

iii. He raises a doubt.

C' He concludes the definition.

And it is not necessarily the same people who make the best choices **10** and form true opinions. Some men form a true opinion of what is better but on account of bad will they do not make the right choice.   **455**

Whether opinion should be said to precede choice or follow it, does not matter, for we do not intend to determine this but whether choice is identical with a particular opinion.   **456**

What then is its genus, what its specific difference, since it is none of the things previously mentioned? Seemingly it is a voluntary. However, not every voluntary—but certainly the deliberately intentional voluntary—is a thing chosen, for choice must be accompanied by reason and intellect. Even the name seems to imply that one thing be preferred to others.   **457**

COMMENTARY OF ST. THOMAS

448. After the Philosopher has shown that choice is not the same as sensual desire; nor anger, which belongs to the sensitive appetitive faculty; nor wishing, which belongs to the rational appetitive faculty, he here shows [d] that choice is not the same as opinion, which pertains to reason itself. He illustrates this point by a threefold consideration. First [i] he shows that choice is not the same as opinion in general. Next [ii], at "Nor is choice etc.," he shows that choice is not the same as that particular opinion that concerns itself with the things we do. Last [iii], at "Whether opinion should be," he raises a doubt (which he leaves unsolved). He says first— this is apparent from the premises— that choice is not the same as opinion in general. He proves the statement

by two reasons, the first of which is this [i, y]. Opinion can concern everything—no less eternal and impossible things than things lying within our power. But choice concerns these things only within our capacity, as was just noted (447). Therefore, choice is not the same as opinion.

449. He gives the second reason at **"Then, too, opinion is divided etc."** [i, z]. It is this. The things that are distinguished by various reasons are said to differ and not to be the same. Opinion, however, is divided into true and false since it pertains to the faculty of knowledge, the object of which is the truth. Opinion is not divided into good and bad as is the case with choice which belongs to the appetitive faculty, the object of which is the good. He concludes from this that choice is not the

same as opinion in general. This is so obvious that no one affirms the contrary.

450. Then [ii], at **"Nor is choice,"** he shows that choice is not identical with that opinion which deals with the things we do. He proves this by (five) reasons, the first of which is this [ii, v]. From the fact that we choose good or bad things we are said to be such, that is, good or bad. But from the fact that we have an opinion about good or bad things, or about true or false things, we are not said to be good or bad. Therefore choice is not identical with opinion, which refers to eligible things.

451. The reason for this difference is that a man is not called good or bad on account of his capabilities but on account of his actions (as noted in the ninth book of the *Metaphysics:* Ch. 9, 1051 a 4-15; St. Th. Lect. X, 1883-1885), that is, not because he is able to act well but because he does in fact act well. When a man understands perfectly he becomes able to act well but he does not yet act well. Thus one who has the habit of grammar is able by that very fact to speak correctly, but that he actually speak correctly he must will it. The reason is that a habit is that quality by which a person acts when he wishes, as the Commentator says on the third book *De Anima.*[1] It is obvious then that good will makes a man act well according to every capability or habit obedient to reason. Therefore a man is called good simply because he has a good will. However, from the fact that he has a good intellect he is not called good simply but relatively good, for example, a good grammarian or a good musician. Therefore, since choice pertains to the will but opinion to the intellect, we are called good or bad by

[1] Averroes, *In Tertio De Anima* (Comment. XVIII).

reason of choice but not by reason of opinion.

452. He gives the second reason at **"We choose to accept"** [ii, w]. Choice has to do especially with our actions. We choose to accept or reject this thing, or whatever else there is that pertains to our actions. But opinion principally refers to things. We have an opinion as to what this thing is (for instance, what bread is) or what effect it has or how one must use it. Opinion, however, does not principally concern our actions, for example, that we are of an opinion about accepting or rejecting something. The reason is that our actions are particular contingent things and quickly passing. Hence a knowledge or opinion of them is not often sought for the sake of the truth in them but only because of something done. Therefore choice is not identical with opinion.

453. He assigns a third reason at **"Choice is"** [ii, x]. It is this. The good of choice consists in a kind of rectitude, that is, the appetitive faculty rightly orders something to an end. This is what he means saying that choice is rather praised because it chooses what it ought, as it were in the right way, while opinion is praised because it has the truth about something. Thus the good and perfection of choice is rectitude but the perfection of opinion consists in truth. Things which have different perfections are themselves different. Therefore choice is not opinion.

454. The fourth reason, given at **"We choose those things"** [ii, y], is this. Choice is accompanied by certitude, for we choose those things which we especially know are good. But opinion lacks certitude, for we have an opinion about the things we are not sure are true. Therefore choice and opinion are not identical.

455. He assigns the fifth reason at **"And it is not necessarily"** [ii, z]. If opinion and choice were identical,

those who make the best choices and those who have true opinions about them would necessarily be identified. This is obviously false, however, for some men form a true opinion in general of what is better but on account of bad will they do not choose what is better but what is worse. Therefore choice and opinion are not identical.

456. At "Whether opinion" [iii] he raises a doubt whether opinion should be said to precede choice or follow it. He states that it does not matter for the present because we do not intend to determine the order of these things but only whether choice is identical with a particular opinion. Nevertheless, we must know that opinion, since it pertains to the faculty of knowledge, strictly speaking, precedes choice pertaining to the appetitive faculty, which is moved by the cognoscitive power. However, it sometimes happens accidentally that opinion follows choice, for instance, when a person on account of the affection for things he loves changes the opinion he formerly held.

457. Then [C'], at "What then," he shows what choice is. He says that, since it is none of the four things previously mentioned, we must consider what it is according to its genus and what according to its specific difference. As to its genus, seemingly it is a voluntary. However, not every voluntary is a thing chosen (as has been pointed out before, 434-436), but only the deliberately intentional voluntary. That this difference should be given attention is clear from the fact that counsel is an act of the reason, and choice itself must be accompanied by an act of reason and intellect. The very name—meaning that one be accepted rather than another—seems to imply or signify this in a hidden way. It pertains to deliberative reason to prefer one to others.

LECTURE VII

Counsel

ANALYTICAL OUTLINE
OF ST. THOMAS

TEXT OF ARISTOTLE
(*B.1112 a 19*)
Chapter 3

II. HE TAKES UP THE QUESTION OF COUNSEL.

A. He treats counsel in itself.

A' *He shows the things about which counsel ought to be taken.*

I. HE PUTS FORWARD HIS PROPOSITION.

a. He proposes the question he intends to treat.

Do men take counsel about all things in such a way that everything is worthy of deliberation, or are some things not objects of counsel?   **458**

b. He explains the proposed question.

A thing must not be called worthy of deliberation because some fool- *20* ish or insane person takes counsel about it but because men of good sense do so.   **459**

2. HE EXECUTES IT.

a. He shows where counsel should function, first by distinguishing things according to their own causes.

   i. He shows where counsel is unnecessary.

      V. HE SAYS THAT NO ONE SHOULD TAKE COUNSEL ABOUT ETERNAL THINGS.

No one takes counsel about:

(1) eternal things, for instance, about the whole universe or the incommensurability of the diagonal and the side of a square;   **460**

      W. . . . NO ONE TAKES COUNSEL ABOUT THINGS IN MOTION . . . UNIFORM.

(2) things that are in motion provided their motion is always uniform either by necessity or from nature or on account of some other cause, for instance, the solstices and the risings of the sun;   **461**

      X. DELIBERATION IS UNNECESSARY ABOUT THINGS IN MOTION FOLLOWING THE SAME PATTERN.

(3) things that sometimes happen otherwise, for instance, droughts and rains;   **462**

Y. COUNSEL IS NOT TAKEN ABOUT
THINGS THAT HAPPEN BY
CHANCE.

Z. MEN DO NOT TAKE COUNSEL
. . . ABOUT ALL HUMAN
THINGS.

*ii. He infers the areas with which
counsel does deal.*

*iii. He shows that the conclusion
follows from the premises.*

b. (He shows where counsel should
function) by distinguishing things
according to every cause.

  *i. He shows in the arts where
counsel is taken.*

  *ii. . . . In these matters counsel is
not taken in the same way.*

  *iii. He shows the difference relative
to the necessity of counsel.*

c. (He shows where counsel should
function) by distinguishing things
according to the qualities of the
things themselves.

  *i. Counsel has to do with things
that occur more frequently.*

  *ii. Counsel must attend to those
situations in which no determination has been made.*

  *iii. We take others into our con-
fidence for advice in things of
importance.*

(4) things that happen by chance,
for example, the finding of a treasure;
463

(5) all human things, for instance,
the Spartans do not take counsel *30*
about how the Scythians ought best
to live their lives. None of these things
will take place by our efforts. **464**

We do take counsel about practicable
things within our power. **465**

There is actually no other class of
things left. Seemingly the causes are
nature, necessity, and chance, to which
must be added the intellect and anything else causing what is done by
man. Each man takes counsel about
those practicable matters which can be
done by him. **466**

About certain self-sufficient *b*
branches of instruction counsel is not
taken, for instance, about writing the
letters of the alphabet, for there is
no doubt about how the letters must
be formed. But counsel is taken about
whatever is determined by us. **467**

In these matters counsel is not always taken in the same way, for instance, in regard to things pertaining
to the art of medicine, to business and
to navigation. In all these—inasmuch
as they are less certain—we take more
counsel than in gymnastics. The same
is to be understood of other arts. **468**

It is more necessary to take counsel
in the arts than in the sciences, for
more doubts arise in the arts. **469**

Counsel has to concern things occurring more frequently. **470**

It must concern uncertain things *10*
where it has not been determined in
what way they will come to pass. **471**

We invite counsellors in matters of
importance not trusting ourselves as
capable of coming to a decision. **472**

COMMENTARY OF ST. THOMAS

458. After the Philosopher has finished the treatise on choice, he here [II] takes up the question of counsel. First [A] he treats counsel in itself; and then [Lect. IX; B], at "The objects of counsel etc." (B.1113 a 3), he treats it in comparison with choice. On the initial point he does two things. First [A'] he shows the things about which counsel ought to be taken. Next [Lect. VIII; B'], at "We do not take counsel about ends etc." (B.1112 b 13), he treats the method and order of taking counsel. He handles the first consideration in two steps. First [1] he puts forward his proposition; and then [2], he executes it at ". . . about: (1) eternal things etc." In regard to this first he also does two things. Initially [1, a] he proposes the question he intends to treat. The question is: should men take counsel about all things in such a way that everything is worthy of deliberation, or are some things not objects of counsel?

459. Next [1, b], at **"A thing must not,"** he explains the proposed question with the observation that a thing is not said to be worthy of deliberation from the fact that sometimes counsel is taken in the matter by some foolish person who perversely uses his reason, or by an insane person entirely lacking the use of reason. But something is deemed worthy of deliberation inasmuch as men with good sense do deliberate about it. Men of this type take counsel only about things that of their nature require careful consideration and that are properly said to be worthy of deliberation. Foolish people sometimes deliberate even about things wherein no counsel is required.

460. Then [2], at ". . . **about: (1)**

eternal things,"** he shows where counsel should function, first [2, a] by distinguishing things according to their own causes; next [2, b], at "About certain etc.," by distinguishing things according to every cause; and last [2, c], at "Counsel has to concern etc.," by distinguishing things according to the qualities of the things themselves. On the first point he does (three) things. First [a, i] he shows where counsel is unnecessary. Then [a, ii], at "But we do take counsel etc.," he infers the areas with which counsel does deal. Last [a, iii], at "There is actually etc.," he shows that the conclusion follows from the premises. In regard to the first, five considerations require his attention. First [i, v] he says that no one takes counsel about eternal things, that is, about things existing always and without motion. Examples of this sort are either those, the substances of which are not subject to motion (as separated substances and the whole universe itself), or those which, even though they exist in movable matter, nevertheless according to reason are separated from such matter, as mathematical entities. Hence he gives the example of the diagonal of a square and its rib or side—no one takes counsel about the commensurability of such things.

461. Next [i, w], at **"things that are in motion,"** he says that no one takes counsel even about things that are in action provided their motion is always uniform. This uniformity of motion may be either of necessity and not by reason of any other cause (as are those things which are of themselves necessary) or from the nature of movable bodies or through the agency of some

separated cause as immaterial substances, movers of the heavenly bodies,
about which he speaks here. Hence he
takes an example from the revolutions
or circular motions of the sun and its
risings, and so forth.

462. Third [i, x], at "things that
sometimes," he says that deliberation
is unnecessary about things in motion
and usually following the same pattern, even though sometimes in a
minor number of cases they happen
otherwise. Such are the droughts that
generally occur in summer and the
rains that commonly fall in winter;
although this may at times vary.

463. Fourth [i, y], at "things that
happen," he says that counsel is not
taken about things that happen by
chance as the finding of a treasure.
Just as the things spoken of above
(461-462) do not depend on our action, so things happening by chance
cannot depend upon our forethought
because they are unforeseen and beyond our control.

464. Fifth [i, z], at "all human
things," he says, as men do not take
counsel about necessary, natural, and
fortuitous things, so neither do they
take counsel about all human things.
Thus the Spartans do not take counsel about how the Scythians—who
dwell a long way from them—ought
best to live their lives. He then sub-
joins a common reason valid in all
the afore-mentioned cases when he says
"None of these things will take place
etc.," because none of these things that
are necessary or natural or fortuitous
or done by other men take place by
reason of our efforts.

465. Then [a, ii], at "But we do
take counsel," he concludes as it were
from the premises about the proper
field for counsel. He says that we take
counsel about practicable things within
us, that is, in our power. Counsel is
ordered to action.

466. Next [a, iii], at "There is actually," he shows that this follows

from the premises because, besides the
things just mentioned about which it
has been indicated that counsel does
not apply, there remain these situations within us on whose behalf counsel is required. He proves his contention by separating the causes. Seemingly there are four causes of things:
nature, which is the principle of motion either in the case of things always moved in the same way or of
things for the most part preserving
uniform motion; necessity, which is
the cause of things existing always in
the same way without motion; fortune,
an accidental cause outside the intention of the agent, under which is also
included chance. Besides these causes
there is the intellect and whatever else
is man's agent, as the will, the senses,
and other principles of this kind. This
cause is different in different men so
that each takes counsel about those
practicable matters which can be done
by him. From this it follows that counsel is not taken about things done by
other causes, as already noted (464).

467. At "About certain" [2, b] he
shows about what subjects counsel can
be taken in the creative arts according
to which we do what is within our
power. On this point he does (three)
things. First [b, i] he shows in the
arts where counsel is taken and where
it is unnecessary. He says that those
creative arts which have a fixed mode
of procedure and are self-sufficient to
the extent that what is done rests on
nothing extrinsic do not require counsel, as writing the letters of the alphabet. The reason for this is that we deliberate only about doubtful matters.
And there is no doubt about how a
letter should be formed because there
is a fixed method of writing which is
not doubtful and the written work depends only on the art and hand of the
scribe. But counsel is taken about those
situations in which we must fix for
ourselves in advance how to proceed

since they are not certain and determined in themselves.

468. Next [b, ii], at **"In these matters,"** he shows that in these matters counsel is not taken in the same way but that some cases require more deliberation and others less. First he explains this difference among the creative arts themselves. He states that in those cases in which we have the final say, we do not always take counsel in the same way, that is, with equal deliberation. We deliberate more about some things which are less certain and in which we must take into consideration more external things: in the art of medicine we must be mindful of the natural strength of the sick person; in business we must assess the needs of men and the supply of goods; and in navigation we must take into account the winds. In all these, we take more counsel than in gymnastics, i.e., the arts of wrestling and exercising that have more fixed and determined methods. According as the previously mentioned arts are less settled, by so much must we take more counsel in them. The same must be understood of other arts.

469. Last [b, iii], at **"It is more necessary,"** he shows the difference relative to the necessity of counsel in the creative arts and in the speculative sciences. He indicates that counsel is more necessary in the arts (the practicable) than in the sciences (the speculative). In the latter, deliberation occurs not in regard to their subject matter, for these exist necesarily or by nature, but as regards the use of these things, for example, how and in what order we are to proceed in the sciences. In this, however, counsel is less mandatory than in the practical sciences about which we have more doubts because of the great variety occurring in these skills.

470. Then [2, c], at **"Counsel has to,"** he shows about which things counsel ought to be taken, by considering the qualities of the things themselves. On this point he puts forward three qualities of things with which counsel deals. First [c, i] he says that counsel has to do with things which occur more frequently. However, because they can happen otherwise it is uncertain in what way they may take place. If a man should wish to deliberate about things that rarely happen, for instance, about the possible collapse of a stone bridge over which he must pass, he will never get anything done.

471. Second [c, ii], at **"It must concern,"** he says that counsel must attend to those situations in which no determination has yet been made of their outcome. A judge does not take counsel about how he ought to pass sentence on the cases stated in the law but rather about cases in which something is not determined in the law.

472. Third [c, iii], at **"We invite counsellors,"** he says that we take others into our confidence for advice in things of importance, as if we did not acknowledge our own capability of deciding what we ought to do. Thus it is obvious that counsel ought not to be taken about trifling things of every kind but only about things of importance.

LECTURE VIII

Method and Order of Taking Counsel

ANALYTICAL OUTLINE
OF ST. THOMAS

TEXT OF ARISTOTLE
(*B.1112 b 13*)
Chapter 3

B' He treats the method and order of taking counsel.

I. HE SHOWS THE METHOD OF DELIBERATIVE INQUIRY.

a. He proposes a method of deliberation.

    i. He shows what is taken for granted.

We do not take counsel about ends, only about means. A doctor does not deliberate whether he will cure a patient; an orator does not deliberate whether he will persuade people; a statesman does not deliberate whether he will achieve peace. Neither does any other agent take counsel about his end.
473-474

    ii. He shows what is the objective.

But having taken the end for granted, they will deliberate how and by what means it may be achieved; when the end is attainable in several ways, by which of these it can be most effectively and most easily attained; when the end is attainable by one means only, how it will be attained through this means; and how this means itself will be attained until they arrive at the first cause, which will be the last in the order of discovery.
475

b. He explains his statement.

One who takes counsel seems *20* to inquire and to resolve by the method mentioned, as by a diagram. It seems that not every inquiry is a taking of counsel, for instance, a mathematical (in the text: "metaphysicae") inquiry, but every taking of counsel is a kind of inquiry. What is last in resolution or analysis is first in the order of production.
476

2. HE SHOWS (THE METHOD'S) EFFECT.

a. He exposes his proposition.

If those taking counsel find the thing to be done is impossible, they give up the project, for instance, if they need money which cannot be provided. But if the thing to be done seems practicable, they begin to act. Things are called possible that can be done by us; what our friends do is done in some way by us, for the origin of their action lies in ourselves. **477**

b. He explains certain things that were said.

At times we inquire about what instruments may be used, and at times about the way we ought to use *30* them. It is the same in the other cases, for sometimes we investigate the means of doing a thing, sometimes we inquire how or why it is to be done. **478**

3. HE DETERMINES THE LIMIT OF THIS INQUIRY.

a. . . . on the part of the agent himself.

As has been previously stated, it would seem that man originates his own actions, and counsel is taken about the things which can be done by him. **479**

b. . . . on the part of the end.

Actions are performed for the sake of other things. Counsel, *B.1113* therefore, is not taken about the end but the means to the end. **480**

c. . . . on the part of particular instruments.

We do not deliberate about particular things, for instance, whether this thing is bread, or whether the bread is properly prepared or properly baked. This belongs to sense perception. If a man goes on deliberating forever he will never come to an end. **481-482**

COMMENTARY OF ST. THOMAS

473. After the Philosopher has shown about what things counsel is taken, he here [B'] treats the method and order of taking counsel. Because counsel is a kind of inquiry, he does three things concerning it. First [1]

he shows the method of deliberative inquiry; next [2], at "If those taking counsel etc.," he shows its effect; last [3], at "As has been previously stated etc.," he determines the limit of this inquiry. On the initial point he does two things. First [1, a] he proposes a method of deliberation. Second [1, b], at "One who takes counsel etc.," he explains his statement. Counsel is a practical deliberation about things to be done. Hence as in a speculative inquiry, where principles are necessarily taken for granted and certain other things are sought, so also should it be with counsel. Therefore, he shows first [a, i] what is taken for granted regarding counsel. Second [a, ii], at "But having taken etc.," he shows what is the objective in taking counsel.

474. We must consider that in practicable things the end holds the place of the principle because the necessity of practicable things depends on the end, as has been mentioned in the second book of the *Physics* (Ch. 9, 200 a 15 sq.; St. Th. Lect. XV, 273-274). On this account we must take the end for granted. This is what he means when he says that we do not take counsel about ends but about the means to the end. Thus in speculative matters we do not inquire about the principles but about the conclusions. He clarifies what he has said by examples: a doctor does not deliberate whether he ought to cure a patient but this is taken for granted as an end; an orator does not deliberate whether he ought to persuade people, for he intends this as an end; a statesman or a ruler of the state does not deliberate whether he ought to achieve peace which is compared to the state as health to the human body (health consists in the harmony of the humors as peace consists in the harmony of wills). Neither does any other agent take counsel about the end in this way.

475. Then [a, ii], at "But having taken the end for granted," he shows

about what and how deliberative inquiry should be made. He introduces three things concerning this. The first of these is that, having taken the end for granted, the primary intention of the one taking counsel is how (i.e., by what motion or action) he can attain that end, and by what means he must move or work toward the end, as by horse or ship. His next intention is—when he can attain some end by several things, either instruments or actions—to know by which of these he can better and more easily achieve his goal. This pertains to judgment in finding ways to the end in which some men are at times deficient. His last intention is—if it should happen that the end can be attained by one means or motion alone, or most aptly by a particular means—that the end be procured in such a way that it is reached through this means. For this, perseverance and care are necessary. If the means for attaining the end should not be at hand, we must inquire how it can be gained and so on until we arrive at a cause which holds first place in operating (this will be last in the order of discovery).

476. Next [1, b], at "One who," he further clarifies his statement by its likeness to speculative inquiry. He says that the cause that is first in operation is the last in the order of discovery because one who deliberates seems to inquire (as was just pointed out in 473) by some analytic method, just as he who wishes to prove a conclusion by a diagram or a geometrical explanation must resolve the conclusion into principles until he reaches the first indemonstrable principles. All counsel is an investigation, i.e., a kind of inquiry, although not every investigation or inquiry is counsel, for example, an inquiry in mathematics. Only an inquiry about practicable things is counsel. Because the man who takes counsel inquires in an analytic manner, his inquiry must lead

to that which is the principle in operation. The reason is that what is last in analysis is first in production or activity.

477. At "If those taking counsel" [2] he shows the effect of counsel. First [2, a] he exposes his proposition. Second [2, b] he explains certain things that were said by the words "At times we inquire etc." He says first that if those taking counsel, on reaching the point in the deliberative inquiry where the first operation must be done, find this impossible they give up, i.e., dismiss the whole matter as if without hope of success. For example, if in order to carry out a business venture, a man needs money to pay certain persons and he cannot pay it, he must abandon the project. But if it is apparent that what was discovered by means of counsel is possible, operation begins immediately because, as was just mentioned (476), the point at which the analytic inquiry of counsel ends must be the beginning of operation. A thing is said to be possible to an agent not only through his own power but also through the power of others. Hence things done by friends are enumerated by him among possibles because what our friends do is done in some way by us, inasmuch as the principle of the work is found in us, for they themselves do this in consideration of us.

478. Then [2, b], when he says "At times we inquire," he explains his previous statement, namely, the kinds of things that upon investigation we sometimes find possible and sometimes impossible. At times, he says, by counsel we inquire about instruments, for instance, a horse or a sword, and at times we inquire about the need or suitability of the instruments, that is, how we ought to use them. It is the same in the other arts: sometimes we seek the means of doing a thing, sometimes we inquire how or

why (these belong to the end just mentioned).

479. Next [3], at "As has been previously stated," he determines the limit or status of the deliberative inquiry. He does this under three headings. First [3, a] on the part of the agent himself. Hence he says, as has been previously stated (292), that man is the principle of his activity. Every individual takes counsel about the things which can be done by him. For this reason when he arrives, in the deliberative inquiry, at what he himself can achieve, at that point counsel ceases.

480. Second [3, b], at "Actions are," he shows that counsel has a limit or condition on the part of the end. All operations, he says, are performed for the sake of other things, that is, ends. Hence counsel is not taken about the end but about the means to the end. Evidently then there is a limit in deliberative inquiry (both on the part of the end and on the part of the agent) as in demonstrations (both from above and below) as it were on the part of either extreme.

481. Third [3, c], at "We do not," he shows the status of deliberative inquiry on the part of particular instruments which we use in our operations as available means for arriving at the end. He says that we do not deliberate about particular things, such as whether what is set before us is bread, whether it is properly prepared, i.e., baked or made as it should be. This belongs to sense perception.

482. That the status of counsel—as also of demonstration—is according to these three considerations is proved by an argument leading to an impossible conclusion. If a man would always be taking counsel, he would be reaching to infinity, which does not fall under the consideration of the reason and consequently not under counsel, which is a kind of inquiry belonging to reason, as has been pointed out (476).

LECTURE IX

A Comparison Between Counsel and Choice

ANALYTICAL OUTLINE
OF ST. THOMAS

TEXT OF ARISTOTLE
(*B.1113 a 3*)
Chapter 3

B. He now treats counsel in comparison with choice.

I. HE COMPARES COUNSEL WITH CHOICE.

a. He introduces his proposition.

The objects of counsel and of choice are the same, but the object of choice has already been determined by counsel.   483

b. He proves it.
  i. *He explains what he has said, by a reason.*

What was previously judged by means of counsel is an object of choice. Every individual inquiring how he is going to act ceases from counsel when he reduces the principle back to himself and this into what is to be done first. It is this which is chosen.   484

ii. . . . *By example.*

Our point is also brought out by the ancient political procedure delineated by Homer who presents the Greek kings as proclaiming their decisions to the people.   485

2. HE CONCLUDES FROM THIS WHAT CHOICE IS.

Since the object of choice is one   10 of the things considered by counsel as desirable and within our power, choice will be a desire (arising by reason of counsel) for the things which are in our power. When we have formed a judgment by taking counsel we desire a thing in accordance with our deliberation.   486

Choice has now been defined according to type and in a general way and not as is customary according to a full explanation. It has been stated of what nature the things are with which choice deals and that choice is

concerned with things which are ordered to ends.   487

COMMENTARY OF ST. THOMAS

483. After the Philosopher has considered counsel in itself, he now [B]
treats counsel in comparison with
choice. A twofold procedure clarifies
this point. First [1] he compares counsel with choice. Second [2], at "Since
the object of choice" [2], he concludes
from this what choice is. In regard to
the initial point he does two things.
First [a] he introduces his proposition;
second [b], at "What was previously
judged etc.," he proves it. First he
compares counsel with choice in two
ways. In one way relative to the object or matter of each where they are
in agreement. Touching on this he
says that an object of counsel and an
object of choice are the same because
both counsel and choice deal with
things that act for an end. The other
way is relative to the order of each.
Touching on this he says that when
something has already been decided
by means of counsel then it is first
chosen, counsel preceding choice as it
were.

484. Then [b], at "What was," he
explains what he has said, by a reason
[b, i] taken from his previous observations (473-484) about counsel.
The decision of counsel, he says, precedes choice because after the inquiry
of counsel a judgment concerning the
things discovered must follow. Then
what was previously judged is first
chosen. He shows clearly that the judgment of the reason should follow the investigation of counsel, by the fact that
every individual who inquires by taking counsel how he ought to act ceases
from deliberation when, by analysing

his investigation, he is led to what he
himself can do. If he can do several
things, then, when he reduces them to
the preceding, that is, to what he considers should be done first, this is what
is chosen, namely, what presents itself
to be done first. Hence it remains that
choice presupposes the decision of
counsel.

485. Second [b, ii], at "Our point is
also brought out," he proves his view
by an example. That choice ought to
follow the decision of counsel is
brought out by the regal procedure of
old, i.e., by the custom of ancient states
according to which kings did not possess dictatorial power over the multitude so that they could do whatever
they wished but were guides of the
citizens to whom it belonged to choose
the things decided by the kings in
counsel. For that reason he says that
the kings of old declared to the people
the things they themselves had chosen
by the decision of their counsel so that
the people might choose what had been
determined. Homer followed this by
presenting the Greek rulers as proclaiming to the people what they had
decided in counsel.

486. Next [2], at "Since the object,"
he shows from the premises what
choice is. He says that, since an object
of choice is simply one of the number
of the things within our power and
which is considered by means of counsel, it follows that choice is only a
desire (arising by reason of counsel)
for things in our power. Choice is an
act of the rational appetitive faculty

called the will. On this account he said that choice is a deliberating desire inasmuch as, via counsel, a man arrives at a judgment regarding the things which were discovered by means of counsel. This desire is choice.

487. Last [2], at **"Choice has now,"** he shows of what nature this definition of choice is. He says that choice has now been defined by type, that is, in outline, and not as he customarily determines a thing through a full explanation, i.e., giving a definition and then investigating each element of it. But the definition of choice has been given in a general way. It has been stated (486) of what nature the things are with which choice deals, i.e., things in our power. Also it has been said that choice is concerned with things that are ordered to ends—about these, too, counsel treats.

LECTURE X

The Object of Willing

ANALYTICAL OUTLINE
OF ST. THOMAS

TEXT OF ARISTOTLE
(*B.1113 a 15*)
Chapter 4

C. He begins the study of willing.

I. HE TAKES NOTE OF WHAT IS OBVIOUS ABOUT WILLING.

As was stated before, willing is concerned with the end.   488

2. HE RAISES A DOUBT.

a. He sets forth contrary opinions.

To some it seems that willing has for its object what is of itself good, but to others what is apparently good.   489

b. He disproves the first opinion.

For those who say the object of willing is what is good of itself, it follows that that thing is not an object of willing which a person does not rightly *20* will. If something were an object of willing, it would be good but what is to prevent a man from wishing something evil.   490

c. He disproves the second opinion.

On the other hand, for those who say the object of willing is apparent good, there is no such thing as a natural object of willing but only what appears so to each man. But different and sometimes contrary things seem to be objects of willing for different men.   491

3. HE SOLVES THE DOUBT.

a. First he gives a solution according to a certain distinction.

If these conclusions are not acceptable, it must be said, therefore, that in an absolute or true sense it is the good that is the object of willing, but for each man it is the apparent good.   492

b. He shows with whom both parts of this distinction agree.

For the good man that thing is an object of willing which is truly good; for the vicious man that thing is an object of willing which seems pleasing to him. Thus when men are in good bodily health those things are healthful which are such in reality, but for men who are ill, it is otherwise. The same applies to bitter, sweet, warm, and heavy things and to others of this kind.   493

c. He explains what he said.

    i. First as it affects virtuous men.

The virtuous person correctly passes judgment on each individual thing   *30* and in each case what appears to him is truly good. Those things which are proper to each habit seem pleasurable to it. The good man perhaps is much different in his capacity to see what is truly good in individual matters, being as it were a norm and measure of these things.   494

    ii. Next . . . as it affects vicious men.

Many men are apparently de-   *b* ceived because of pleasure. What is not good seems good, so they desire as good the pleasurable and seek to avoid the painful as evil.   495

COMMENTARY OF ST. THOMAS

488. After the Philosopher has finished the treatise on the voluntary and on choice, he here begins the study of willing [C]. He initiates his discussion by three stages. First [1] he takes notes of what is obvious about willing. Next [2], at "To some it seems etc.," he raises a doubt. Last [3], at "If these conclusions etc.," he solves the doubt. First he restates what he has previously insisted on (466) that willing is concerned with the end itself. He speaks here of willing (*voluntas*) as it denotes the act of the faculty of the will. The act of any faculty is named from the faculty itself and regards that to which the faculty primarily and of itself tends. Thus the act of the visive faculty is called vision

in relation to visible things. In this manner understanding (*intellectus*) is named in relation to first principles that of themselves are referred primarily to the intellective faculty. Hence also willing is properly said to concern ends themselves which, as certain principles, the faculty of the will primarily and of itself regards.

489. Then [2], at "To some it seems," he raises a doubt. Regarding it he does three things. First [2, a] he sets forth contrary opinions about willing. He says that to some it seems that willing has for its object what is of itself good, but to others what is apparently good.

490. Next [2, b], at "For those who say," he disproves the first opinion stat-

ing that for those who say that only
the good in itself is the object of willing
(i.e., to which the will tends), it follows
that that thing which a person does
not rightly will is not an object of willing. The reason is that, according to
their opinion, it would follow that if
something were an object of willing,
it would be good, but it happens sometimes that it is evil. Therefore willing
does not always have real good as its
object.

491. Last [2, c], at "On the other
hand," he disproves the second opinion,
stating that for those who say the object of willing is apparent good, it follows that there is no natural object of
willing but for each one the object of
willing is what seems so to him. But
for different men different and sometimes contrary things seem to be the
object of willing. Thus if color were
not visible but only what seemed to
be color were visible, it would follow
that nothing would be by nature visible.
This, however, would not be fitting for
every natural faculty has some object
determined by its nature. Therefore it
is not true that the object of willing is
apparent good.

492. At "If these conclusions" [3],
he solves the afore-mentioned doubt.
First [3, a] he gives a solution according to a certain distinction. He says
that if these disagreeable conclusions
following from both these opinions are
unacceptable, we must answer with a
distinction that what seems good to a
man is desirable either without qualification or under some aspect, i.e., in
relation to this or that.

493. Second [3, b], at "For the good
man," he shows with whom both
parts of this distinction agree. He says
that for the good man that thing is an
object of willing which is truly worthy
of being willed, i.e., good in itself. But
for the wicked or vicious man that
thing is the object of willing which
attracts him, i.e., whatever seems pleasing to himself. He exemplifies this in

things of the body. We see that for men
whose bodies are in good health those
things are healthful that are really so.
But for the sick, certain other things
are healthful, namely, those that moderate their diseased condition. Likewise
things really bitter and sweet seem bitter and sweet to those who have a
healthy taste, things really warm seem
warm to those who have a normal
sense of touch. Those who have normal
bodily strength properly estimate the
weight of objects; those who are weak
think light objects heavy.

494. Third [3, c], at "The virtuous
person," he explains what he said, first
[c, i] as it affects virtuous men. He says
that the virtuous person correctly
passes judgment on individual things
that pertain to human activity. In each
case that which is really good seems to
him to be good. This happens because
things seem naturally pleasurable to
each habit that are proper to it, that is,
agree with it. Those things are agreeable to the habit of virtue that are in
fact good because the habit of moral
virtue is defined by what is in accord
with right reason. Thus the things in
accord with right reason, things of
themselves good, seem good to it.
Here the good man differs very much
indeed from others, for he sees what
is truly good in individual practicable
matters, being as it were the norm and
measure of all that is to be done because in these cases a thing must be
judged good or bad according as it
seems to him.

495. Next [c, ii], at "Many men,"
he explains what he said as it affects
vicious men. He says that for many, the
vicious, deception in the distinction between good and evil occurs especially
because of pleasure. As a consequence
of this it happens that they desire as
good the pleasurable, which is not
good, and seek to avoid as evil what is
for them painful but in itself good.
The explanation is that they do not
follow reason but the senses.

LECTURE XI

Virtue and Vice Are Within Our Power

ANALYTICAL OUTLINE   TEXT OF ARISTOTLE
OF ST. THOMAS   (*B.1113 b 3*)
                                    Chapter 5

I. HE DETERMINES THE TRUTH.

   A. He shows that virtue is within us.

> Since willing regards the end but counsel and choice the means to the end, the actions concerning these means will be in accordance with choice and voluntary. But virtuous actions deal with the means. Virtue then is within our power. **496**

   B. He shows the same about vice.

> For a similar reason vice is voluntary. If it is in our power to act, it is also in our power not to act; and contrariwise. Therefore if to do good is in our power, then not to do evil will also be in our power. If not to do good is in our power, then to do evil will also be in our power. **497-498**

   C. He shows the reason for this necessary consequence.

> If it is in our power to do and *10* likewise not to do good or evil actions (by reason of this men become good or evil), it will be within our power to be virtuous or vicious. **499**

II. HE REJECTS AN ERROR.

   A. First he removes the error itself.

   A' He explains his rejection of the error.

> It is said that no one is voluntarily evil and that no one is unwillingly happy. The first statement is really false and the second true. In fact no person

will be happy unwillingly. Vice, on the other hand, is a voluntary thing. **500**

B' He raises a doubt over this.

Must we dispute even about what has now been said and hold that man is not the principle and begetter of his actions as he is father of his children? **501**

C' He determines the truth.

1. HE CONFIRMS THE TRUTH FIRST BY REASON.

If these things (counsel, choice and willing) seem to be principles of our actions and we cannot reduce them *20* into principles other than those within our power, then also our actions the principles of which are under our control will themselves be in our power and voluntary. **502**

2. (HE CONFIRMS THE TRUTH) BY SIGNS.

a. He explains his proposition . . . first in the things that are clearly voluntary.

This view seems to be supported by the testimony of private individuals and of legislators themselves for legislators punish and chastise evildoers, unless these do evil by compulsion or on account of ignorance of which they themselves were not the cause. Likewise legislators decree honors for those who do good, thus encouraging them as it were but restraining the others. No one persuades a man to do whatever things are not in his power and not voluntary because before it takes place it is of no use to persuade a man not to become hot, or afflicted, or hungry, or anything whatsoever of this kind. We will suffer these things nonetheless. **503-504**

b. . . . In the things that seem to have something of the involuntary.

A man who is ignorant will be *30* punished if he is the cause of his ignorance. A drunken man, for instance, is worthy of double punishment. The beginning is within him because he has it in his power not to get drunk. And his intoxication is the cause of his ignorance. Legislators punish those who are ignorant of things stated in the law that they should have known, but not those who are ignorant of the difficult things. Likewise in other cases we punish people whenever it seems that their ignorance was due to negligence because it is in their power not to be ignorant. They have it in their power to inform themselves.   **505-506**

COMMENTARY OF ST. THOMAS

496. After the Philosopher has treated the voluntary, choice, counsel, and willing that are principles of human acts, he here applies what has been said to vices and virtues. Concerning this question he does three things. First [I] he determines the truth. Then [II], at "It is said that no one etc.," he rejects an error. Last [Lect. XIII; III], at "We have discussed virtues etc." (B.1114 b 26), he concludes with a summary of what has been said about virtue. On the first point he does three things. First [I, A], on the basis of his previous discussion, he shows that virtue is within us, i.e., in our power. Next [I, B], at "For a similar reason etc.," he shows the same about vice. Last [I, C], at "If it is in our power etc.," he shows the reason for this necessary consequence. He says first that since willing regards the end but counsel and choice the means to the end, it follows that actions concerning this (i.e., the means to the end) are in accordance with choice and are consequently voluntary. The reason is that choice is a voluntary as was indicated before (434-436, 457). But virtuous actions deal with the afore-mentioned (means) and are voluntary. Consequently, virtue itself must be voluntary and within us, that is, in our power.

497. Then [I, B], at **"For a similar reason,"** he shows the same thing about

badness, i.e., about vice as opposed to virtue. He says that badness is likewise voluntary and within us because its operations are of this kind. He proves this in the following way: if the capacity to act is within us, the capacity not to act must also be in our power. If the capacity not to act were not in our power, it would be impossible that we would not act. Therefore, it would be necessary that we act, and so the capacity to act would not come from us but from necessity.

498. As a consequence we must conclude that wherever affirmation is within our power, negation is also; and conversely. Virtuous and vicious actions differ according to affirmation and negation. For instance, if honoring parents is good and an act of virtue, then not to honor one's parents is evil and pertains to vice. If not to steal pertains to virtue, to steal pertains to vice. Hence it follows that if the operation of virtue is within us, as has been proved (496), then the operation of vice also is within us. So consequently vice itself is within us, that is, in our power.

499. Next [I, C], at **"If it is,"** he assigns the reason for this necessary inference: if the operations are within us, the habits too are within us. He says that if it is in our power to do or not to do good or evil actions, as has now

been shown (497-498), while by reason of the fact that man works or does not work good or evil he becomes good or evil as was pointed out in the second book (250-253), it follows that it is within our power to be virtuous, i.e., good in conformity with the habit of virtue, and vicious in conformity with the habit of vice.

500. At **"It is said"** [II], he rejects an error about the afore-mentioned teaching. First [II, A] he removes the error itself. Second [Lect. XII; II, B], at "Perhaps such a person etc." (B.1114 a 3], he removes its roots. On the first point his division is threefold. First [A′] he explains his rejection of the error. Next [B′], at "Must we dispute even about what etc.," he raises a doubt over this. Last [C′], at "If these things etc.," he determines the truth. In regard to the first we must consider that some have held that no one is voluntarily evil, nor is anyone unwillingly happy or good. They say this because the will of itself tends to good. Good is what all desire and consequently the will of itself seeks to avoid evil. He says, therefore, that one of these statements is in all likelihood false, namely, that no one is willingly evil since vice is something voluntary. The other seems to be true, that no one is unwillingly good and happy.

501. Then [B′], at **"Must we dispute,"** he raises a doubt about things said before. If it is true that virtuous and vicious actions (and consequently virtue and vice) are voluntary, obviously what has presently been said is true. But is there anyone who believes there should be a doubt about what has been said, so that he might say that a man is not the principle and begetter of his actions as a father is the principle of his children? He as much as says: that anyone would say this, is to be wondered at.

502. Next [C′], at **"If these things,"** he confirms the truth first [1] by reason; and then [2], at "This view seems

etc.," by signs. He says first that if counsel, choice, and willing—which are in our power—are seen as principles of our actions and we cannot reduce our actions to principles other than those that are in our power (i.e., counsel and choice) it follows that our good and bad actions are within our power. Because their principles are in our power, they themselves are in our power and hence are voluntary.

503. At **"This view seems"** [2], he explains his proposition by means of signs: first [2, a] in the things that are clearly voluntary; and then [2, b], at "A man who is ignorant etc.," in the things that seem to have something of the involuntary. He says first that the particular things that are done by individual private persons seem to bear witness to what has been said, i.e., that virtuous and vicious actions are within our power. Any father of a family punishes a child or a servant who does wrong. Likewise the things that are done by legislators, who care for the welfare of the state, bear witness. They give sometimes a light, other times a heavy sentence to criminals, provided however the wrongdoers do not act under coercion or through ignorance (of which they are not the cause); if they acted by compulsion or ignorance, their acts would not be voluntary, as is evident from what was said before (400-405). Hence it is clear that they were punished as acting voluntarily.

504. Likewise legislators decree honors for those who voluntarily do good: as it were encouraging the virtuous to good deeds by means of honors, and restraining the vicious from evil by means of punishments. No one encourages a man to do the things that are not in his power and not voluntary because in such matters encouragement before the act is entirely useless. It is useless, for instance, to urge a man in summer not to be hot, or in sickness not to be afflicted or not to be hungry when there is no food, or to do any-

thing beyond his power. The reason is that he would suffer these things notwithstanding encouragement. If, therefore, we are not urged to do the things that are not within our power, but are urged to do good and avoid evil, such things are in our power.

505. Then [2, b], at **"A man who is,"** he manifests the same truth in those things which seem to have something of the involuntary. Ignorance causes an involuntary, as was explained before (406-424). If, however, we are the cause of the ignorance, the ignorance will be voluntary and we will be punished for it. A man can be the cause of his own ignorance in two ways. In one way directly, by doing something, as is evident in those who get drunk and for this reason are rendered ignorant. These should be doubly blamed. First because they drank too much, and next because they committed a sinful deed in their drunkenness. The principle of drunkenness is in the man himself because he has the power to remain sober and his drunkenness is the cause of his ignorance. Accordingly in this way a man is the cause of ignorance.

506. In the other way a man is the cause of ignorance indirectly by reason of the fact that he does not do what he ought to do. On account of this, ignorance of the things a man can and is bound to know is considered voluntary and therefore he is punished for it. This is why he says that legislators punish those who are ignorant of laws everyone ought to know (as that which forbids stealing), but not those who are ignorant of laws which are difficult to know and which not all are bound to know (because it is not possible). The same is true of those things which men do not know apparently by reason of negligence, because they could have learned. They are masters of themselves and they can be diligent and not negligent.

LECTURE XII

Refutation of the Opinion: No One Is Voluntarily Evil

ANALYTICAL OUTLINE
OF ST. THOMAS

TEXT OF ARISTOTLE
(*B.1114 a 3*)
Chapter 5

(II)B. He removes the root of this error.

    A' . . . In regard to the internal disposition.

        I. HE PROPOSES THAT WHICH ONE CAN DEPEND ON IN SUPPORT OF THE
        PRECEDING ERROR.

Perhaps such a person is naturally not diligent. **507**

        2. HE DISPROVES THIS.

a. He shows that habits of the soul . . . are voluntary.

    i. . . . *With respect to their formation.*

        x. HE BRINGS FORWARD HIS PROPOSITION.

But men make themselves negligent by living carelessly, and unjust and incontinent by doing evil to others and spending their time in drinking and such things. **508-510**

        y. HE PROVES IT.

        aa. . . . By means of a likeness.

A man's outlook depends on the way he exercises his powers. This is clearly manifest in the case of those who devote their attention to some exercise or activity. They perfect themselves *10* by constant practice. It seems then that only a man lacking understanding would be ignorant that habits are produced by individual actions. **511**

        bb. . . . By a reason taken from the relation of an act to a habit.

Moreover, it is unreasonable to assert that a man who does unjust actions does not wish to be unjust, or who perpetrates seductions does not wish to be incontinent. If one knowingly does those things from which it follows that he is unjust, he will be voluntarily unjust. **512**

ii. He shows they (i.e., habits) are not voluntary after their formation.

Because a person becomes unjust voluntarily, it does not follow that he will cease to be unjust and become just whenever he wishes. One who is sick does not become well in this way. So too it is with a man who voluntarily becomes sick by living immoderately and disregarding the doctor's advice. Before, it was within his power not to become sick, but having placed the cause the effect is no longer within his power, just as one who throws a stone has not the power to take back the throwing. Nevertheless it is within a man's power to cast or throw a stone because the original act was under his control. So it is also with the *20* unjust and the incontinent who in the beginning had the power not to become like this. For this reason they are voluntarily unjust and incontinent although after they have become such it is no longer within their power not to be such.   513

b. He indicates that even bodily defects . . . are voluntary.

Not only vices of the soul are voluntary but also defects of the body in certain men whom we justly reproach. No one reproaches those who are born ugly but only those who are so because of slothfulness and carelessness. The same is true with weakness, disgrace, and blindness. No one justly taunts a man who is blind from birth or disease or a wound but he is rather shown sympathy. But everyone does reproach a man blind because of excessive drinking of wine or other incontinence. Men are reproached for those vices and bodily defects that are within our power; but not for those beyond our con- *30* trol. This being so, in other things (pertaining to the soul) the vices we are blamed for must be within our power.   514

COMMENTARY OF ST. THOMAS

507. After the Philosopher has rejected the error of those who hold that no one is voluntarily evil, he now [B] removes the roots of this error: first [A'] in regard to the internal disposition by reason of which (contrary to his own will) someone can tend to evil. Then [Lect. XIII; B'], at "Someone may say" (B.1114 a 32), in the matter of the faculty of knowledge by which a thing is judged good or bad. He handles the first point in two steps. First [1] he proposes that which one can depend on in support of the preceding error. Then [2], at "But men make themselves," he disproves this. The Philosopher has stated (506) that it is in the power of man to be diligent or negligent about something. But someone could deny this, saying that some person is naturally not diligent. Thus we see that men with phlegmatic temperaments are naturally lazy, men with choleric temperaments are naturally irascible, men with melancholic temperaments are naturally sad and men with sanguine temperaments are naturally joyful. According to this, it is not within man's power to be diligent.

508. Then [2], at **"But men make,"** he rules out what was just said. To understand this we must consider that a man can be said to be of a particular bent in two ways. In one way according to bodily disposition following either the temperament of the body or the influence of the heavenly bodies. By reason of this disposition there can be no direct change of the intellect or will, which are faculties altogether incorporeal not using a bodily organ, as is made clear by the Philosopher in the third book *De Anima* (Ch. 4, 429 a 29-429 b 4; St. Th. Lect. VII, 687-699).

But by this type of disposition some change can follow in the sensitive appetitive faculty, which does use a bodily organ, the movements of which are the passions of the soul. Accordingly, from such a disposition there is no more movement of the reason and will (which are principles of human acts) than is had from the passions of the soul, and concerning these it was likewise pointed out in the first book (241) that they are susceptible of persuasion by the reason. The other disposition is on the part of the soul. This is a habit by means of which the will or reason is inclined in operation.

509. On this account the Philosopher, having passed over the dispositions or qualities of the body, treats only the disposition of habits. On this point he does two things. First [2, a] he shows that habits of the soul according to which a man is negligent or unjust are voluntary from the fact that he is censured on account of them. Second [2, b], at "Not only vices of the soul etc.," he indicates that even bodily defects which are blameworthy are voluntary. Regarding the first he does two things. First [a, i] he indicates that habits of the soul are voluntary with respect to their formation. Then [a, ii] he shows that they are not voluntary after their formation has already been completed. Touching on the first he does two things. First [i, x] he brings forward his proposition; and next [i, y], at "A man's outlook etc.," he proves it.

510. We must consider that evil habits differ as evil acts do. Some habits are evil from the fact that they withdraw a man from doing good. With respect to habits of this kind he says

that men are the cause of their own evil lives for they are not diligent in doing good; they live carelessly without attempting good works. Other habits are evil because through them a man is inclined to do evil, whether this brings about the injury of others or one's own disordered condition. With respect to these he says men by their own volition are the reason why they are unjust inasmuch as they do evil to others, and incontinent inasmuch as they live their lives in unnecessary drinking and in other things of this kind which pertain to the pleasures of touch.

511. Next [i, y], at **"A man's outlook,"** he proves the proposition first [y, aa] by means of a likeness in other things. We see that things done in individual actions make men of that particular stamp, i.e., disposed to do similar things. This is clearly manifest in the case of those who are diligent in and take pains with an exercise (like wrestling or soldiering) or any activity whatsoever. Everyone, from the fact that he does the action many times, becomes so adept that he can do similar things perfectly. Since then we see this happen in all cases, it seems that only a man lacking understanding would be ignorant that habits are produced by operations.

512. Then [y, bb], at **"Moreover, it is,"** he shows the same thing by a reason taken from the relation of an act to a habit. If a man wills some cause from which he knows a particular effect results, it follows that he wills that effect. Although perhaps he does not intend that effect in itself, nevertheless he rather wishes that the effect exist than that the cause not exist. Thus if someone wishes to walk when it is hot, knowing beforehand he will work up a sweat, it follows that he wishes to perspire. Although he does not wish this in itself, nevertheless he wishes rather to perspire than to forego the walk. Nothing hinders a thing from

being non-voluntary in itself, although it may be voluntary on account of something else, as a bitter potion taken for health. It would be otherwise if a man were ignorant that such an effect would follow from such a cause, e.g., a voluntary is not effected when a man who walks along the road falls among robbers because he did not know this beforehand. Obviously then men who do unjust actions become unjust and those committing seduction become incontinent. Therefore, it is unreasonable for a man to will to do unjust actions and nevertheless not intend to be unjust or to will to perpetrate seductions and not will to be incontinent. Thus obviously if a man who is aware of his action does voluntarily those things which make him unjust, he will be voluntarily unjust.

513. At **"Because a person becomes unjust"** [a, ii], he shows that evil habits are not subject to the will after they have been formed. He says that because a person becomes unjust voluntarily, it does not follow that he ceases to be unjust and becomes just whenever he may will. He proves this by means of a likeness in the dispositions of the body. A man who in good health willingly falls into sickness by living incontinently i.e., by eating and drinking to excess and not following the doctor's advice, had it in his power in the beginning not to become sick. But after he has performed the act, having eaten unnecessary or harmful food, it is no longer in his power not to be sick. Thus he who throws a stone is able not to throw it; however once he has thrown the stone he has not the power to take back the throwing. Nevertheless we do say that it is within a man's power to cast or throw a stone because it was from a principle under his control. So it is also with the habits of vice; that a man not become unjust or incontinent arises from a principle under his control.

Hence we say that men are voluntarily unjust and incontinent, although, after they have become such, it is no longer within their power to cease being unjust or incontinent immediately, but great effort and practice are required.

514. Then [2, b], at **"Not only,"** he shows by means of a likeness to bodily defects that vicious habits are voluntary. He says that not only vices of the soul are voluntary but also defects of the body in certain men. Such men we justly reproach. No one reproaches those who are born ugly but only those who are ugly by reason of some negligence in proper care. The same is true with weaknesses and blindness. No one justly taunts a man who is blind from birth or disease or a wound which is not voluntary. But on account of those things sympathy rather is shown to the victim. Thus it is evident that we are reproached for those vices and bodily defects which are within our power. Hence obviously in other things, i.e., those things which pertain to the soul, the vices or vicious habits are in our power.

LECTURE XIII

Refutation of the Opinion: We Have No Faculty Cognoscitive of Good

ANALYTICAL OUTLINE
OF ST. THOMAS

TEXT OF ARISTOTLE
(*B.1114 a 32*)
Chapter 5

B' *He excludes another fundamental principle on the part of the cognoscitive power.*

1. HE EXPLAINS THIS FUNDAMENTAL PRINCIPLE.

Someone may say that every man desires what appears good to him for we are not in command of our im- *b* agination, but according to the character of each man, so does the end seem to him. **515-516**

2. HE REJECTS IT.

a. He gives the reason repudiating these allegations.

Since, therefore, everyone is in some measure the cause of his habits, he is to some extent the cause of the manner in which his imagination reacts. **517-520**

b. He adds an answer that seems to counter this.

Perhaps no one is himself the cause of the evil he does, but each acts because of ignorance of the end under the impression that something very good will follow by means of his action. It ensues then that the end is not an object desired by a man's free will but must be innate as though a man had some (moral) sight to judge correctly and to desire what is really good. He is well-born who has this good judgment from birth. For he will possess the greatest and best of gifts, one which can never be received or learned from others, but kept *10* just as nature gave it, and to be well and nobly endowed with this will be

c. He disproves the counterargument.

a perfect and true and propitious heritage.   521-523

If this is true how is virtue more voluntary than vice? For both alike, i.e., the good and the wicked, the end appears and is fixed by nature or howsoever it may be. In referring everything else to this end, men do whatever they do. Whether the end then, whatever it may be, does not so present itself by nature, but also depends on him, or whether the end is natural, and the good man using the means is voluntarily virtuous, in either case virtue as well as vice will be vol- *20* untary. For voluntariety exists in the evil man also since it influences him both in his actions and in his view of the end. If then, as is affirmed, virtues are voluntary (for indeed we ourselves are partly responsible for the way our habits dispose us and by living in a certain way we fix our end accordingly) it follows that vices also are voluntary because a similar reason is present.   524-525

III. HE SUMS UP IN CONCLUSION THE MATERIAL PREVIOUSLY DISCUSSED.

A. He shows what has already been said about virtues.

We have discussed virtues in general and the outline of their genus. We have shown that each is a mean and a habit. We have explained that habits produce the same actions by which the habits themselves are caused. We have said that habits are in our power and voluntary, that they follow right reason and that voluntary *30* operations are otherwise than habits because we have control over our operations from the beginning to the end when we know the par- *B.1115* ticular circumstances. We are masters only of the beginning of our habits, but the individual steps by which they grow are not known to us, as in sicknesses. But because it was in our power to act or not to act in this way, the habits are called voluntary.   526

B. He shows what remains to be treated.

> Taking up again the consideration of virtues, we will discuss what each virtue is, with what matter it deals and in what way it operates. At the same time we will clearly see also how many virtues there are. First we will treat the virtue of fortitude. **527**

COMMENTARY OF ST. THOMAS

515. After the Philosopher has overthrown the fundamental principle of those who hold that vice is not voluntary on the part of the disposition inclining the appetitive faculty, he here [B'] excludes another fundamental principle on the part of the cognoscitive power. On this point he does two things. First [1] he explains this fundamental principle; and second [2], at "Since, therefore, etc.," he rejects it. In regard to the first we must consider that good precisely as it is perceived moves the desire. As the natural desire or inclination follows the form naturally inherent, so the animal desire follows the perceived form. In order then that a thing be desired, it is first required that it be perceived as good. Hence everyone desires what appears good to him.

516. Therefore someone can say it is not in our power that this thing should seem or appear good to us. The reason is that we are not in command of our imagination, i.e., over the way things appear or seem to us. But in accord with the disposition of a man, so does his end seem to him, that is, such as a thing seems to a person, it must be desired as good and an end. A thing is agreeable to each according to its proper form: as fire tends upward, and things of earth tend to the center. So also we see that among the animals each one strives after something as good and an end according to its own natural disposition. Hence different animals have different activities and operations, although all animals of one species have similar movements and operations. But in the human species individuals are found having different movements and operations. Hence some were of the opinion that this arose from a natural disposition on account of which this thing seems good to one person and that to another in such a way that the procedure was not subject to a man's control.

517. Then [2], at "Since, therefore," he excludes the afore-mentioned principle, and concerning it he does three things. First [a] he gives the reason repudiating these allegations (516). Next [b], at "Perhaps no one etc.," he adds an answer which seems to counter this. Last [c], at "If this is true," he disproves the counterargument. On the first point we must consider that a thing can appear good to someone in two ways.

518. In one way in general, it is so by a kind of speculative consideration. Such a judgment about good follows not any particular disposition but the universal power of reason syllogizing about actions, as it does in the case of natural things. Since practicable

things are contingent, reason is not forced to assent to this or that as it does when demonstration occurs. But man has the power to give assent to one or the other part of a contradiction, as happens in all practicable things especially when we have under consideration many objects, any one of which can be judged good.

519. In the other way a thing can appear good to someone, as it were by a practical knowledge, by reason of a comparison with what is to be done. The Philosopher here speaks of this type of judgment that can be made in two ways about some good. In one way, a thing may appear good to someone absolutely and in itself. This seems to be a good in conformity with the nature of the end. In the other way, a thing may appear to someone not absolutely in itself but judged by present considerations.

520. The appetitive faculty is inclined to an object on two accounts: one, by reason of a passion of the soul, the other by reason of habit. Under the impulse of passion it happens that a thing is judged good as it is at present. Thus to one who is afraid of drowning it appears good at the moment to throw his merchandise overboard; as does fornication to one filled with lust. But the judgment, by which a man accounts a thing good in itself and absolutely, arises from the inclination of habit. This we will discuss now. He, therefore, says that since a man in some measure is the cause of his own evil habit by reason of his continual sinning—as has been pointed out (509-512)—it follows that he himself is also the cause of the imaginative reaction that follows such a habit, i.e., of the appearance by which this thing seems to be good in itself.

521. Next [b], at "Perhaps no one," he gives the counterargument of the adversary against the point that has just been made (518-520). He says that perhaps someone will maintain that

nobody is himself the cause of his own evil acts but each individual does evil because of ignorance of the end, inasmuch as he thinks that something very good is to follow from what he does wrongly. That a person desires a proper end does not arise from his own free will but must belong to him from birth. As from birth a man has external sight by which he correctly distinguishes colors, so also from birth he should have a well-disposed internal vision by which he may judge well and desire what is really good. Thus he must be said to be of good birth in whom the previously mentioned judgment has been implanted from birth. When a man innately has in good and perfect fashion what is greatest and best for him, this is a perfect and truly good birth. For man cannot gain this through the help or guidance of another; rather it is proper for him to possess it in the manner that nature has endowed him with it. Therefore, that a man should have this from birth renders his birth doubly praiseworthy: in one way through the excellence of the good, in the other because of the impossibility of otherwise acquiring it.

522. We must consider that this seems to be the opinion of certain mathematicians who hold that man is disposed at his birth by the power of the heavenly bodies to do this or that. This opinion is attributed by Aristotle in his work *De Anima* (Bk. III, Ch. 3, 426 a 21 sq.; St. Th. Lect. IV, 616-623) to those who did not hold the distinction between sense and intellect. If anyone should say, as in fact it is said in that place (*ibid.*), that the human will is impelled by the father of men and gods, i.e., the heavens or the sun, it will follow that the will (and the reason in which the will resides) is something corporeal as the senses are. It is not possible that what is in itself incorporeal should be moved by a body. Thus the will and

intellect will contain a bodily organ and they will differ in no way from the senses and the sensitive appetitive faculty. Wherefore he draws a comparison between the sense of sight and intellectual vision by which we judge a thing.

523. It must be said then that the heavenly bodies can cause in the human body a disposition inclining the sensitive appetitive faculty, the motion of which is a passion of the soul. Hence by reason of the influence of the heavenly bodies, a man does not have the inclination to judge that a thing is good absolutely and in itself (as through the habit of choice in virtue and vice) but to judge that a thing is good as it is at the moment, for example, in accordance with passion. The same observation must be made about the inclination that occurs from bodily temperament. In the present context, however, there is no question of a judgment by which we judge something good in accordance with passion, for the will is able to reject this—as was stated in (516)—but of a judgment by which we judge that something is good by means of habit. Therefore, this answer does not destroy the reason of Aristotle.

524. At "If this is" [c] he rejects this answer on the basis of the presuppositions of the adversary who took for granted that virtue is a voluntary but denied this of vice. Then returning to his earlier discussion (516)—which he had interrupted—he says that if this is true, namely, that the desire of the end exists in man by nature, there is no greater reason why virtue more than vice is voluntary. Reasoning in a similar fashion we say that, for both the virtuous and the vicious man, the goal must be innate no matter in what way it may seem to be perceived and actually desired. Although virtuous and vicious operation is concerned not only with the end but also with the means to the end, nevertheless men act by referring the remaining things (i.e., means to the end) to an end not from nature but howsoever it seems to them.

525. Therefore either it should be said that the end for every man does not seem to be such by nature but that it is relative to each man as it is in his power to cling to such or such an end, or even that the end is natural and by working on the means, man becomes voluntarily virtuous. Then virtue nonetheless will be voluntary. The same is true about vice because what is for the sake of the end in operations is attributable to the vicious man not less than to the virtuous, just as they are alike in regard to the end—as has been pointed out before (358-362). Therefore, if virtues are voluntary because of the fact that we are the causes of the habits by which we are disposed to fix an end of such a kind, it follows that vices also are voluntary because a similar reason holds for one as well as the other.

526. Then [III], at "We have discussed," he sums up in conclusion the material previously discussed (224-525). First [A] he shows what has already been said about virtues, and then [B] what remains to be treated. He states first that virtues in general have been treated (*ibid.*) and their genus has been clearly manifested in type, i.e., according to their general characteristics. Then it has been said (324-331) what the mean is (this belongs to the proximate genus) and what the habits are (this belongs to the remote genus under which the vices are also contained). It has been affirmed also (255-279) that habits produce the same actions by which the habits themselves were caused. It has been stated too (496-525) that habits are in our power, that they follow right reason and that voluntary operations are otherwise than habits because we have control over operations from the beginning to the end, provided we know the particular

circumstances. Although we do have control of habits from the beginning, afterwards, when we are inattentive, something is added in the generation of habits by means of particular operations. Thus it happens in sicknesses brought on by voluntary actions, as has been noted (513). But because it was in our power from the beginning to act or not to act in this way, the habits themselves are called voluntary.

527. Next [B], at **"Taking up again,"** he shows what remains to be treated. He says we must take up again the consideration of the virtues in order to determine what each virtue is, its subject matter, and its mode of operation. Thus we will clearly see also how many virtues there are. First we will treat the virtue of fortitude.

LECTURE XIV

Fortitude

ANALYTICAL OUTLINE
OF ST. THOMAS

TEXT OF ARISTOTLE
(*B.1115 a 7*)
Chapter 6

I. HE TREATS THE MORAL VIRTUES THAT DEAL WITH THE PRINCIPAL PASSIONS TOUCH-
ING THE VERY LIFE OF MAN.

A. He studies fortitude.

A'. He investigates the matter of fortitude.

I. HE REVIEWS WHAT WAS CLEARLY EVIDENT FROM THE PREMISES ABOUT
THE MATTER OF FORTITUDE.

We stated previously that fortitude is
a mean dealing with fear and rashness.
528-529

2. HE INVESTIGATES THE OBJECTS OF THESE PASSIONS AS FORTITUDE IS
CONCERNED WITH THEM.

a. He shows what the objects of fear
are.

Terrifying things are what we fear.
They are the things which we universally call evil. For this reason *10*
philosophers define fear as the expectation of evil. We all fear certain evils,
e.g., a bad reputation, poverty, sickness,
enmity, and death.   **530-531**

b. He explains with what class of these
objects fortitude deals.

i. *He shows about what evils it is
not concerned.*

X. HE SETS FORTH HIS PROPOSI-
TION.

But fortitude does not seem to deal
with all evils.   **532**

Y. HE PROVES HIS PROPOSITION.

aa. Fortitude does not deal
with the fear of a bad
reputation.

For, to fear some things is both
proper and good, and not to fear others
is base. For instance, in the matter of
a bad reputation, he who fears this is
said to be decent and modest; one who
does not have this fear is called shameless. Such a person is said by some to
be brave in a metaphorical sense, because he is like a brave man inasmuch
as he is without fear.   **533**

bb. Fortitude does not deal with the fear of poverty.

Poverty is not to be feared; neither is sickness, nor any of those things which are not caused by wickedness or man himself. But one who has no fear of these things is not called brave, except perhaps by way of similarity. *20* Some are cowardly in the dangers of war, but generous, and courageous in the face of the loss of their fortune. **534**

cc. Fortitude does not deal with . . . personal evils.

No one is called cowardly because he fears injury to his children or his wife, or because he fears envy or any other thing of this kind. No one is called brave because he does not fear a flogging. **535**

ii. He concludes about what evils it is concerned.

About what kind of terrifying things is a brave man concerned? Is he concerned with the most terrifying? No one can sustain such perils more than he. Now the most frightening of all is death, for it is the end, and nothing either good or bad seems to exist any longer for the dead. **536**

c. He shows in particular what kind of death fortitude envisages.
  i. He shows with what kind of death fortitude deals.
    X. HE SETS FORTH HIS PROPOSITION.

It does not seem that fortitude is concerned with death, which occurs in every case, for instance, at sea or in sickness. In what circumstances then? In the most suitable, as when men die fighting for their country. **537**

    Y. HE PROVES HIS PROPOSITION.
      aa. . . . By two reasons. The first.
      bb. Next.

Such men lose their lives in the greatest and noblest dangers. **538**
Honors are given to them both in the city-states and in the monarchies. **539**

  ii. He explains the relation of fortitude to all the kinds of death.
    X. . . . TO THE FEAR OF DEATH.
      aa. He explains the death about which fortitude is principally concerned.

A man is called brave principally because he is not afraid of death for a good cause nor of all emergencies that involve death. Such emergencies are to be met with most often in battle. **540**

      bb. . . . Fear of other kinds of death.

Moreover, brave men are un- *b* afraid both in shipwreck and in sickness. They differ from sailors, for these

233

brave men despise this sort of death when there is no hope of rescue, while sailors may well hope to be saved by reason of their experience.　　**541**

Likewise, brave men act manfully in danger where it is praiseworthy to be courageous and to give one's life. But neither of these conditions exist in these other forms of death.　　**542**

COMMENTARY OF ST. THOMAS

528. After Aristotle has finished the treatise on virtues in general, he begins here a particularized study of the individual virtues. First he treats the virtues concerned with the interior passions. Next, he treats justice and injustice (concerned with external actions) in the fifth book (Lect. I) at "We must give our attention to justice and injustice etc." (B.1129). The first section falls into two parts. In the first part [I] he treats the moral virtues dealing with the principal passions touching the very life of man. Next, he treats the moral virtues that are concerned with the secondary passions touching the external goods of man, in the fourth book (Lect. I) at "Let us next discuss etc." (1119 b 21). Concerning the first part he does two things. First [A] he studies fortitude, which deals with the passions touching things destructive of human life. Then [Lect. XIX] he studies temperance, which deals with the passions touching things preservative of human life, i.e., food and sex, at "Following this treatise (on fortitude) we must etc." (B.1117 b 22). On the first point he does three things. First [A'] he investigates the matter of fortitude. Next, "The same thing is not terrifying etc." [Lect. XV], he treats the method of its operation (B.1115 b 7). Last, at "Although fortitude is con-

cerned etc." [Lect. XVIII], he determines certain properties of the virtue (B.1117 a 29). In regard to the first he does two things. First [I] he reviews what was clearly evident from the premises about the matter of fortitude, i.e., with what passions it deals. Next [2], at "Terrifying things are what etc.," he investigates the objects of these passions as fortitude is concerned with them.

529. He says, as has already been explained in the second book (267, 341), that fortitude is a kind of mean dealing with fear and rashness. Fortitude denotes a firmness of soul by which it remains unmoved by the fear of dangers.

530. Then [2], at **"Terrifying things,"** he investigates the objects of the previously mentioned passions according as fortitude treats them, especially on the part of fear about which fortitude is principally concerned, as will be pointed out later (536). The objects of fear and rashness are identical, for what one man flees because of fear, another attacks in his rashness. On this point three considerations demand his attention. First [2, a] he shows what the objects of fear are. Next [2, b], at "But fortitude does not etc.," he explains with what class of these objects fortitude deals, since it is con-

cerned with fear of death. Finally [2, c], at "It does not seem etc.," he shows in particular what kind of death fortitude envisages.

531. He says first that terrifying things are those we are afraid of, objects of fear so to speak. All evil things are universally of this kind. Hence philosophers in giving a definition of fear say that it is the expectation of evil. Expectation is here taken generally for any movement of the appetitive faculty toward some future things, although expectation properly speaking is directed only to good, as is hope. It is evident then that we all fear some evils, like a bad reputation and disgrace (which are contrary to respectability), destitution and poverty (which are contrary to the goods of external fortune), sickness, enmity, and death (which are contrary to personal goods).

532. Next [2, b], at "But fortitude does not," he shows that fortitude deals with the fear of some particular evils. First [b, i] he shows about what evils it is not concerned. Second [b, ii], at "About what kind of terrifying things etc.," he concludes about what evils it is concerned. On the first point he does two things. First [b, i, x] he sets forth his proposition that fortitude does not seem to deal with the fear of all evils.

533. Second [b, i, y], at "For, to fear some things," he proves his proposition, the first part of which is that fortitude does not deal with the fear of a bad reputation [b, i, y, aa]. The brave man is praised because he does not fear. But there are certain things which we ought to fear in order to live a good life. It is good to fear these things inasmuch as fear is not only necessary for the preservation of respectability, but even fear itself is something honorable. There is a kind of disgrace attached to the person who does not fear evils of this sort. This is obvious from the fact that one who fears a bad reputation is praised as

decent, i.e., morally good and modest. But one who does not fear evil of this kind is blamed as shameless. It is evident, therefore, that fortitude is not concerned with fear of these evils. Sometimes, it is true, a man who does not fear a bad reputation is called by some brave, in a metaphorical sense, because he has a likeness to a brave man inasmuch as he is without fear.

534. In the second part (of his proposition) at "Poverty is not to be feared" [b, i, y, bb], he shows that fortitude does not deal with the fear of poverty. He says that poverty is not to be feared in the way that a bad reputation is to be feared (533). Neither is sickness to be feared, nor indeed any of those things that do not pertain to wickedness of which man himself is the cause. It is useless for man to fear what he is unable to avoid. In regard to such things, therefore, a man ought to fear lest he fall into any of them by his own wickedness. The reason is that fear is useful to avoid these very things, but not otherwise. Although it is not necessary to fear things of this sort, nevertheless one who has no fear of them is not called brave except perhaps in a metaphorical sense. The reason is that not to fear poverty seems to belong to another virtue, liberality. Some are praised for the act of this virtue, inasmuch as they spend money freely. Yet they are called complete cowards in the greater dangers of war. Therefore, fortitude is not concerned with the fear of poverty.

535. In the third part, at "No one is" [b, i, y, cc], he shows that fortitude does not deal with any fear whatsoever of personal evils. He says that a man is not called cowardly because he fears injury or envy of himself, his children or his wife, or any other thing of this kind. A person is not said to be brave because he does not fear the lash but boldly endures it, since these things are not especially terrifying. But a person is brave without qualification from

the fact that he is brave in the face of the most terrifying dangers. One who is undaunted in some other circumstances is not called absolutely brave, but brave in that particular category.

536. At "About what kind of" [b, ii] he shows that fortitude is concerned with the fear of certain evils, saying that man is called absolutely brave from the fact that he is fearless in the face of dangers which are most terrifying. Virtue is determined according to the maximum of the faculty, as is pointed out in the first book of *De Coelo* (Ch. 11, 281 a 8; St. Th. Lect. XXV, 249). Therefore, the virtue of fortitude must deal with the things that are most terrifying, so that no one endures greater dangers than the brave man. Among all dangers the most frightening is death. The reason is that death is the end of all present life, and after death there does not seem to be any good or evil equal to those things of this life that inflict death on us. Things belonging to the state of the soul after death are not visible to us, but that by which a man loses all his goods is appallingly frightening. Hence it seems that fortitude is properly concerned with fear of the dangers of death.

537. Then [2, c], at "It does not seem," he shows that fortitude is concerned with the fear of a particular kind of death. On this point he does two things. First [c, i] he shows with what kind of death fortitude deals. Next [c, ii], at "A man is called brave etc.," he explains the relation of fortitude to all the kinds of death. In regard to the first he does two things. First [c, i, x] he sets forth his proposition. Then [c, i, y], at "Such men lose their lives etc.," he proves his proposition. He says first that fortitude is not even concerned with death that a man suffers in some kind of accident or employment, as at sea or in sickness, but with death that he suffers from the best of causes, as happens when a man dies fighting in defense of his coun-

try. The same reason holds in the case of any other death that a person undergoes for the good of virtue. But he makes a special mention of death in battle because in that undertaking men more frequently suffer death for the sake of good.

538. Then [c, i, y], at "Such men lose," he proves his proposition by two reasons. The first [c, i, y, aa] is that death in battle happens in the greatest danger since a man easily loses his life there. It happens also in the most noble of dangers since a man undergoes the danger in that case on account of the common good that is the greatest good, as has been noted in the beginning (30). But virtue is concerned with what is greatest and best. Therefore, the virtue of fortitude especially deals with death that takes place in battle.

539. Next [c, i, y, bb], at "Honors are given," he proves the same thing from the fact that honors are given to those who die such a death or bravely expose themselves to the danger of a death of this kind. (This is the practice both in city-states that exist by association and in monarchies where kings alone rule.) The reason is that those who fight bravely in battle are honored both while they live and after death. But honor is the reward of virtue. Therefore, the virtue of fortitude is considered as dealing with death of this kind.

540. At "A man is called brave" [c, ii] he shows how fortitude has a relation to all the kinds of death. First [c, ii, x] he shows the way fortitude is related to the fear of death. Next [c, ii, y], at "Likewise, brave men etc.," he shows its relation to boldness which is a reaction to dangers of this kind. On the first point he does two things. First [c, ii, x, aa] he explains the death about which fortitude is principally concerned. A man is called brave, he says, mainly because he is not afraid of death for a good cause, nor is he afraid of the threats—especially sudden threats

—of death. The reason is that every virtue is ordered to good. Actions that must be done on the spur of the moment show in a special way that a person acts from habit. In other situations a man after careful deliberations can perform actions like those that proceed from the habit. Actions pertaining to good and the unexpected dangers in battle are especially of this kind. Hence the brave man who is not afraid is concerned principally with these actions.

541. Next [c, ii, x, bb], at **"Moreover, brave men,"** he shows how the brave man himself is without fear of other kinds of death. He says that as a consequence brave men are unafraid both in storms at sea and in sickness because they do not lose their heads and become upset because of fear of such dangers. In storms, however, they differ from sailors. Even if the brave have no hope of rescue, they nevertheless despise death and are without fear. But sailors are unafraid of dangers from the sea by reason of their experience, for they have hope of being easily able to escape them.

542. Then [c, ii, y], at **"Likewise, brave men,"** he shows that fortitude is principally concerned not only with fear of death but also with boldness in dangers of this kind. He says that brave men likewise act manfully by meeting dangers in those circumstances where fortitude is praiseworthy and where it is noble to die, as in battle. It is good that a man endanger his life for the common welfare. But in the aforesaid modes of death, by shipwreck or by sickness, fortitude is not honorable nor does any good follow from death. Hence it does not belong to the virtue of fortitude to meet such dangers boldly.

LECTURE XV

The Act of Fortitude

ANALYTICAL OUTLINE   TEXT OF ARISTOTLE
OF ST. THOMAS   (*B.1115 b 7*)
                                  Chapter 7

I. HE DISTINGUISHES THE ACT OF FORTITUDE FROM THE ACTS OF THE OPPOSITE VICES.

  A. He determines how acts can be differentiated in the matter presently investigated.

    A'. He assigns the reason for differentiating acts in this matter.

> The same thing is not terrifying to all, but we do call that terrifying which is above the power of man to resist. The superhuman is frightening to every sensible person. However, what is within the power of man differs according to magnitude and degree. It is the same with daring undertak- *10* ings.   **543-544**

    B'. He shows how they are differentiated.

> The brave man does not lose his head but acts like a man. He will, therefore, fear such things, and he will undergo them as he ought, and as reason will judge, for the sake of good which is the end of virtue. But man sometimes fears dangers more or less; he fears things that are not terrifying as if they were terrifying. Man is at fault because he fears at times the wrong things, at other times in the wrong way or at the wrong time and so forth. The same observation may be made about what inspires confidence.   **545-546**

  B. He shows what the proper act of fortitude is by comparison with the acts of the opposite vices.

    I. HE EXPLAINS THE ACT OF VIRTUE AND OF THE VICES.

a. He defines the acts of the virtue and the vices relating to fear and rashness.

i. He defines the act of the virtuous man.

X. HE EXPOUNDS HIS PROPOSITION.

One who endures and fears the right things, for the right motive, in the right manner, and at the right time is brave. Likewise the brave man acts daringly, for he endures and acts *20* in conformity with what is worthy and according to reason.   **547-548**

Y. HE MAKES CLEAR SOMETHING HE HAD SAID.

The end of every action is conformity with its own habit. The good intended by the brave man is fortitude and this is also an end since every means is determined by its end. The brave man endures and works, for the sake of good, the things which are in conformity with fortitude.   **549-550**

ii. (He defines) the acts of the vicious man.

X. . . . OF THE MAN DEFICIENT IN FEAR.

Of those who go to excess, that man who fears nothing is unnamed. We mentioned before that many vices are unnamed but a person is a madman or insensible who fears nothing, neither earthquakes nor floods, as it is said of the Celts.   **551**

Y. . . . OF THE MAN EXCESSIVE IN DARING.

He who is excessive in daring when dealing with frightening things is called reckless. The reckless man *30* is thought to be vain but only feigns courage. As the brave man really is in face of danger, so the vain man wishes to appear (even imitating the actions of the brave man). Hence many who seem brave, are in fact cowards. They are daring in these circumstances (of little danger) but do not stand up when fearful things occur.   **552**

Z. . . . OF THE MAN EXCESSIVE IN FEARING.

One who is excessive in fearing is a coward; he fears the things he ought not to fear, as he ought not *B.1116* (and similarly in the other circumstances). He is also deficient in daring but he is more conspicious from the fact that he fears painful situations too much.   **553**

b. (He defines) those relating to hope and despair.

The coward is a despairing man inasmuch as he fears everything. The brave man, on the contrary, has great hope inasmuch as he is courageous.

554

c. He concludes with a summary.

The cowardly, the reckless, and the brave are all concerned with these passions but are disposed towards them in a different way. The reckless and the cowardly have excess and defect but the brave man holds a middle course as he ought.　　　**555**

2. HE COMPARES THE VIRTUE WITH CERTAIN THINGS THAT SEEM SIMILAR TO IT.

a. He shows the difference between the brave and the reckless man.

The reckless are precipitate and rush to meet danger, but, when actually in it, they fall down. The brave however are vigorous while in action and calm beforehand.　　　**556**

b. . . . Between the brave man and the man who undergoes death to escape misfortunes.

As has been pointed out, fortitude is a mean concerned with situations that inspire confidence or terror about　*10* which we have spoken; it desires or endures things because it is good to do so, or because it is base not to do so. But to suffer death in order to avoid poverty or a disappointed love or something painful is not characteristic of a brave man but rather of a coward. It is a kind of effeminacy not to endure these misfortunes, and besides, such a one suffers a death not for an honorable good but to escape evil. Such then is the nature of fortitude.　　**557-558**

COMMENTARY OF ST. THOMAS

543. After the Philosopher has investigated the matter of fortitude, he now treats its act. First [I] he distinguishes the act of fortitude from the acts of the opposite vices. Next [Lect. XVI; II], at "Other kinds of fortitude are enumerated etc.," he treats certain things that have an act similar to fortitude (B.1116 a 16). He discusses the first point under two aspects. First [A] he determines how acts can be differentiated in the matter presently investigated. Then [B], at "One who endures etc.," he shows what the proper

act of fortitude is by comparison with the acts of the opposite vices. He handles the first point in a twofold manner. First [A, A'] he assigns the reason for differentiating acts in this matter. Second [A, B'], at "The brave man does not lose etc.," he shows how they are differentiated. He observes first that the same thing is not terrifying to all.

544. Since fear is in the irascible part—the object of which is the difficult—fear is concerned only with an evil which is in some way above the power of the one fearing. Hence a

thing is terrifying to a child which is not terrifying to a mature man. There are evils that exceed human power to overcome, such as earthquakes, tidal waves, and other disasters of this sort. Hence evils of this kind are terrifying to every sensible man endowed with good judgment. But that terrifying thing which does not seem to exceed man's power to resist may be viewed in a twofold way. One, according to the different magnitude of the thing, for example, it is more terrifying to have many enemies come together than to have only a few. The other, according to degree, for instance, that enemies have greater or less hatred, or that they are closer or farther away. What has been said about terrifying things must be said likewise about things inspiring courage because fear and boldness have the same object, as has been said previously (530).

545. Then [A, B′], at **"The brave man,"** he shows by the reason just given how acts are differentiated in this matter. When it is affirmed that the brave man does not lose his head because of fear, this must be understood as referring to a man of sound judgment. Such a one will fear the things which are above man. Hence the brave man too will fear them. However, in case of necessity or utility, he will undergo such things as he ought and as right reason, which is proper to man, will judge. In this way he will not forsake the judgment of reason on account of the fear of such things, but will endure terrifying things of this kind, no matter how great, on account of the good which is the end of virtue.

546. It happens at times that a man fears terrifying things that are above his power, or within his power more or less than reason judges. What is more, it happens that he fears the things which are not terrifying as if they were terrifying. Man's sin consists principally in what is contrary to right reason. As sickness takes place in the body by reason of a disorder of some humor, so too sin against reason takes place in the soul by reason of a disorder of some circumstance. Hence sometimes a person sins in the matter of fear from the fact that he fears what he ought not to fear, but other times from the fact that he fears when he ought not to fear. The same must be said about the other circumstances enumerated above (544). What has been affirmed about terrifying things is to be understood about things inspiring boldness where a similar reason is found, as has been said (544).

547. Next [B], at **"One who,"** he shows what the act of fortitude is by means of a comparison with the opposite vices. He treats this under two headings. First [1] he explains the act of the virtue and of the vices. Next [2], at "The reckless are etc.," he compares the virtue with certain things that seem similar to it. He discusses the first point in a threefold manner. First [1, a] he defines the acts of the virtue and the vices relating to fear and rashness; and then [1, b], at "The coward is etc.," those relating to hope and despair. Finally [1, c], at "The coward, the reckless etc.," he concludes with a summary. He handles the first point from two aspects. First [a, i] he defines the act of the virtuous man; and then [a, ii], at "Of those who go etc.," the acts of the vicious man. He considers the first point in a twofold way. First [i, x] he expounds his proposition. Next [i, y], at "The end etc.," he makes clear something he had said.

548. He says first that one who endures the things he ought to endure and flees through fear the things he ought to avoid with the right motivation, in the right manner, and at the right time is called brave. Likewise, he who dares in the things he ought for the right motive and so forth is also brave. He assigns the reason for this when he says that a brave and virtuous man endures on account of fear and he

241

acts by means of daring in conformity with what is fitting and as right reason indicates. Every moral virtue is in accord with right reason, as was stated previously (323, 326).

549. At "The end" [i, y] he makes clear something he had said, namely, the right motive for operating. He remarks that the end of every virtuous operation is in conformity with the nature of its own habit. A habit—caused by custom—operates after the manner of a nature because custom is a kind of nature, as is noted in the book *De Memoria et Reminiscentia* (Ch. 2, 452 a 28; St. Th. Lect. VI, 383).[1] The ultimate end of an agent naturally operating is the good of the universe, a perfect good; but the proximate end is to imprint its likeness in another. Thus the end of a warm object is to make things warm by means of its activity. Likewise the ultimate end of operative virtue is happiness, a perfect good, as was said in the first book (45, 111, 112, 117, 118, 201, 222). But the proximate and proper end is to impress a likeness of the habit on the act.

550. This is what he means in his statement that the good, which the brave man intends, is fortitude—not the habit of fortitude, for this already exists, but the likeness of it in the act. This also is the end since every means is determined by its proper end because the character of means to the end is derived from the end. For this reason the end of fortitude is something pertaining to the nature of fortitude. In this way the brave man endures and works for the sake of good, that is, inasmuch as he intends to perform the actions which are in conformity with fortitude.

551. Then [ii], at "Of those who go to excess," he defines the acts of vicious

[1] Sancti Thomae Aquinatis *in Aristotelis Libros de Sensu et Sensato, de Memoria et Reminiscentia Commentarium*. Ed. Pirotta, Turin/Rome: Marietti, 1928.

men: first [ii, x] of the man deficient in fear; next [ii, y], of the man excessive in daring, at "He who is excessive in daring etc." Last [ii, z], at "One who is excessive in fearing etc.," he defines the acts of the man excessive in fearing. He says first that there is no special term for the man who abounds—speaking of the vices pertaining to excess—in fearlessness, i.e. who fears nothing. It was said before (341) that many vices have no names. This particularly happens in things that rarely occur. And fearlessness of this sort rarely happens. It occurs only in the case of madmen and insensible persons who fear nothing—not even earthquakes, floods, or anything of this kind. This is said to happen among certain people called Celts (the name of a race). He speaks here of one who is insensible or without a sense of pain because the future things we fear and the things that cause us pain when present are the same.

552. Next [ii, y], at "He who," he treats those who are excessive in daring. He says that the man who, dealing with terrifying things, abounds in daring by boldly attacking them beyond what reason suggests is called reckless. But there is also one who is apparently but not really reckless, the vain man who pretends to be brave. Hence as the brave or reckless man really is in regard to terrifying things, so the vain man seeks to appear. Because of this the vain man imitates the works of the brave or reckless man when he can do so without danger. Hence many of those who seem brave or reckless are cowardly. Many of those who are reckless in circumstances having little danger do not endure when truly frightening things occur.

553. At "One who" [ii, z], he treats of one who is excessive in fearing. The Philosopher says a man is a coward when he fears what he should not fear, in the way he should not fear, and so on. The man inordinate in fear

is lacking in daring. The only reason why a person does not attack to destroy frightening things is fear. But the lack of fear can exist without the recklessness of attack. It does not follow then that everyone, who does not flee as he ought, attacks more than he ought. But whoever is deficient in attacking the right things is motivated only by fear. For this reason Aristotle separates the defect of fear from the excess of recklessness, but joins the excess of fear with the defect of recklessness. Although the coward is extreme in fearing and deficient in daring, nevertheless he is more conspicuous from the fact that he abounds in the fear of painful situations than from the fact that he is lacking in daring, because the defect is not so easily seen as the excess.

554. Then [1, b], at "The coward is," he shows how the previously named things are related to hope and despair. For an understanding of this we must consider that the object of recklessness and fear is evil. But the object of hope and despair is good. The appetitive faculty of itself tends towards the good, but incidentally flees the good by reason of some evil attached. Likewise, the appetitive faculty of itself flees the evil. But what is essential causes that which is incidental. For this reason, hope—whose characteristic is to tend towards good—causes recklessness that tends towards the evil it attacks. For the same reason fear, which flees evil, is the cause of despair, which withdraws from good. He says, therefore, that the coward is a despairing man inasmuch as he fears his deficiency in everything. On the contrary the brave man has great hope because he is courageous.

555. Next [1, c], at "The cowardly, the reckless," he sums up what has been said, concluding from the premises that the cowardly, the reckless, and the brave man all are concerned with

these passions but related to them in a different way. The reckless man exceeds in daring and is lacking in fear; the cowardly man exceeds in fear and is lacking in daring. But the brave man follows a middle course in these matters as he ought according to right reason.

556. At "The reckless" [2] he compares fortitude with things similar to it. First [2, a] he shows the difference between the brave and the reckless man. Next [2, b], at "As has been pointed out etc.," he shows the difference between the brave man and the man who undergoes death to escape misfortunes. The coward seems to have nothing in common with the brave man, and for this reason Aristotle does not care to assign the difference between them. He remarks that the reckless are impetuous, rushing into danger, i.e., swiftly and spiritedly going out to meet it, because they are moved by a surge of passion beyond reason. When they are actually in the danger they are checked, for the movement of the preceding passion is overcome by the threatening danger. But when the brave are in the very midst of the dangers, they are vigorous because the judgment according to which they act is not overcome by any danger. But before they meet the difficulties, they are calm because they do not act from violence of passion but from deliberate reason.

557. Then [2, b], at "As has been pointed out," he shows the difference between a brave man and the man who undergoes death to escape misfortune. He says, as has been noted (535-540), that fortitude is a mean in terrifying things, which are evils concerned with the dangers of death spoken of before (535-540); that fortitude tends to operate virtuously and sustains sufferings of this kind in order to bring about something good and honorable, or in order to flee something disgraceful and dishonorable. However, that one should

die by laying hands on himself or by voluntarily suffering death inflicted by another (in order to escape poverty or a longing for a thing which he cannot possess or whatever else there is that causes sorrow) does not belong to a brave man but rather to a coward. This happens for two reasons. First, because a certain effeminacy of soul, contrary to fortitude, seems to exist when a person is unable to undergo hardships and sorrows. Second, because such a one does not suffer death for an honorable good, as the brave man does, but to escape a painful evil.

558. Finally, he concludes that we can know, from what was said, the nature of fortitude.

LECTURE XVI

Acts of Civic and Military Fortitude

ANALYTICAL OUTLINE
OF ST. THOMAS

TEXT OF ARISTOTLE
(*B.1116 a 16*)
Chapter 8

II. HE TREATS CERTAIN DISPOSITIONS HAVING AN ACT SIMILAR TO BUT LACKING REAL FORTITUDE.

(PRENOTES)   559-560

A. He treats civic fortitude (three kinds).

    I. THE FIRST BELONGS TO THOSE WHO UNDERGO DANGERS FOR THE SAKE OF HONOR.

a. He brings out this kind of fortitude.

Other kinds of fortitude are enumerated according to five types. Among these, fortitude of the citizen holds first place, for it is most like real fortitude. Citizens apparently undergo dangers because of legal penalties and the disgrace of cowardice, and also for *20* the sake of honor. For this reason men are found to be very brave in those states where the cowardly are censured and the brave accorded honors.

561-562

b. He gives examples taken from Homer.

Homer mentions men of this kind, Diomede and Hector, for instance. Polydamas (says Hector) would be the first to reproach me.[1] And Diomede: "Hector at some time or other when boasting to the Trojans will say: Tydides has fled from me."[2]   563

c. He clarifies what he has said.

This fortitude is most like that we just discussed as being exercised on account of virtue. It is indeed practiced on account of shame and the desire of the honorable, for fortitude of this sort is for the sake of honor and the avoidance of the disgrace of opprobrium.   564

[1] Cf. *Iliad* xxii. 100.
[2] Cf. *Iliad* viii. 148.

2. THE SECOND (BELONGS) TO THOSE WHO UNDERGO DANGERS BECAUSE OF FEAR OF PUNISHMENTS.

Those who are under compul- *30* sion from their rulers will be included in the same type of fortitude. They are less worthy of the title, however, insofar as they do not act bravely because of shame but rather out of fear, for they flee not what is disgraceful, but what is painful. Masters coerce their subjects by threats as Hector did: "Anyone I find giving way to fear and not doing battle will not have a chance to escape the dogs." [1] *565*

3. THE THIRD (BELONGS) TO THOSE WHO ATTACK AND EXPOSE THEMSELVES TO DANGEROUS SITUATIONS.

Rulers do the same thing when they command their subjects not to give *b* ground, and beat those who do. A similar judgment is to be passed on those who before battle construct walls, trenches, and other such obstacles to retreat. All such have coerced their subjects. But the virtuous man must be brave not because of constraint but because of the good of virtue. *566*

B. (He treats) the fortitude of the soldier.

I. HE SHOWS WHAT LEADS SOLDIERS TO FIGHT BRAVELY.

In particular cases experience seems to be a kind of fortitude. For this reason Socrates thought that fortitude was knowledge. As others are brave in other things from experience, so soldiers are brave in warfare. In war there are many operations without danger which soldiers know very well. Those engaged in these exercises seem brave to others who are ignorant of the nature of such things. Hence professional soldiers are especially able *10* by reason of experience to attack their adversaries without harm to themselves: skilled in the use of arms, they are able to guard themselves from

[1] Cf. *Iliad* ii. 391.

blows and to strike back. They possess other skills like those that enable them to inflict injury while they themselves are not injured. They fight against others like the armed against the un-armed, like well-trained athletes against inexperienced rustics. In athletic contests of this kind it is not the brave who can fight the most but rather those who are physically powerful and well-conditioned. **567-569**

2. HE COMPARES THE FORTITUDE OF THE SOLDIER AND THE CITIZEN.

Soldiers turn cowards when they see that the danger exceeds their skill and that they are inferior in numbers and military preparations. They are the first to run away, while those possessing the fortitude of the citizen, refusing to leave, give up their lives. This actually happened in the battle at the temple of Hermes.[1] Citizens think it disgraceful to flee, and choose to die rather than to be saved under such 20 circumstances. But soldiers expose themselves to danger because from the beginning they think themselves more powerful. When the truth dawns on them they take flight fearing death more than disgrace. Not so the brave man. **570**

[1] In a battle at Coronea, 353 B.C.

COMMENTARY OF ST. THOMAS

559. After the Philosopher has ascertained how the act of real fortitude and of the opposite vices is constituted, he treats here certain dispositions having an act similar to but lacking real fortitude (II). This happens in five ways. Since real fortitude is a moral virtue (for which knowledge is required and because of this, choice), a person exercising an act of fortitude can fall short of real virtue in three ways. In one way because he does not operate with knowledge. This is the fifth type of counterfeit fortitude, according to which a person is said to be brave through ignorance. In another way because a person does not operate by choice but by passion (whether it is a passion urging one to undergo dangers as anger does, or a passion quieting fear of the mind as hope does). According to this consideration,

there are two kinds of counterfeit fortitude.

560. The third way a person falls short of real fortitude is that he operates by choice, but he does not choose what the brave man chooses. In undergoing dangers he does not think it hazardous, because of his skill, to fight in battle, as is evident among soldiers; or he chooses to undergo the dangers not on account of the end that a brave man chooses but on account of honors or punishments decreed by rulers of states.

561. Accordingly, this portion falls into five parts. In the first part [A] he treats civic fortitude or fortitude of the citizen; in the second [B], the fortitude of the soldier at "In particular cases etc."; in the third part [Lect. XVII, C], fortitude that operates through anger, at "People confuse rage etc." (B.1116 b 23); in the fourth part [Lect. XVII, D], fortitude that operates through hope, at "Likewise the confident etc." (B.1117 a 11); in the fifth part [Lect. XVII, E], fortitude that operates through ignorance, at "Those who operate in ignorance etc." (B.1117 a 23). In regard to the first he indicates three kinds of civic fortitude. The first kind [A, 1] belongs to those who undergo dangers for the sake of honor. The second [A, 2], to those who undergo dangers because of the fear of punishments, at "Those who are under compulsion etc." The third [A, 3], at "Rulers do the same etc.," to those who attack and expose themselves to dangerous situations because of pressing compulsion. He discusses the first point under three headings.

562. First [1, a] he brings out this kind of fortitude. He says that over and above real fortitude, certain other kinds of fortitude are enumerated according to five types. Among these, civic fortitude or fortitude of the citizen holds first place because this type is very similar to real fortitude. Citizens undergo dangers to avoid penalties and disgrace which, according to the civil laws, are inflicted on the cowardly, and to acquire honors which by the same laws are bestowed on the brave. So in those states where blame is heaped on the cowardly and honors on the brave, men are found most brave according to this type of fortitude, and perhaps even according to the real virtue by reason of habit.

563. Second [1, b], at "Homer mentions," he gives examples taken from Homer who, describing the Trojan War, introduces men brave for honor or fear of blame: Diomede among the Greeks and Hector for the Trojan side. He represents Hector as saying these words: "Polydamas, the Trojan leader, will be the first to reproach me (i.e., he will find fault first of all with me) if I do not fight manfully." [1] And Diomede exhorting himself to act bravely said: "Hector haranguing the Trojans will say in praise of himself and in vituperation of me that Tydides (a name given him from his father's), alias Diomede, has fled from me and has been beaten." [2]

564. Third [1, c], at "This fortitude," he clarifies what he has said: that this kind of fortitude is very similar to the genuine virtue. He says that the citizen's fortitude is much like the one of which we have spoken (562), since it is for the sake of virtue. This fortitude of the citizen is practiced through shame or fear of the disgraceful, inasmuch as someone flees disgrace, and through a desire of the good or honorable insofar as this fortitude seeks honor, which is the testimony of goodness. For this reason he adds in explanation that fortitude of this sort is motivated by honor and avoidance of opprobrium, which is the disgraceful. Since then honor is a thing near to an honorable good, and blame to

[1] Cf. *Iliad* xxii. 100.
[2] Cf. *Iliad* viii. 148.

the disgraceful, it follows that this fortitude is close to real fortitude, which seeks what is honorable and flees from what is shameful.

565. Then [A, 2], at **"Those who,"** he indicates the second kind of civic fortitude that is practiced on account of punishment. He says that those who are brave, because compelled by the fear of punishments inflicted by rulers of the state, can be assigned the same type of civic fortitude. They are, however, inferior to the previously mentioned insofar as they do not act bravely on account of the shame of disgrace but on account of fear of punishment. This is why he adds that they do not flee what is disgraceful or dishonorable but what is sorrowful, i.e., painful or injurious, from the fact that someone is made sad. In this way the masters compel their subjects to fight bravely. According to Homer, Hector threatened the Trojans in these words: "Anyone running away and not doing battle, i.e., without fighting bravely, I will handle so roughly that he will not have a chance to escape the dogs." [1]

566. Next [A, 3], at **"Rulers do the same,"** he presents the third kind of civic fortitude according as some are compelled by their rulers then and there and not only by fear of future punishment. This is why he says that rulers do the same thing by their actions when they command their subjects not to run away from battle, and beat those who do. A similar judgment is to be passed on those who, before battle, construct walls and trenches and other such obstacles to retreat so that their subjects cannot take to flight. All rulers who do things of this kind coerce their subjects to fight. And those who act under compulsion in this way are not really brave, because the virtuous man must be brave not on ac-

count of the constraint he suffers but because of the good of virtue.

567. At **"In particular cases"** [B] he treats the fortitude of the soldier. He explains this question in a twofold manner. First [B, 1] he shows what leads soldiers to fight bravely. Next [B, 2] he compares the fortitude of the soldier and the citizen, at "Soldiers turn cowards." He says first that in individual cases experience seems to be a kind of fortitude. In any undertaking one who has knowledge from experience works boldly and without fear, as Vegetius says in his book on military affairs: "No one fears to do what he believes he has learned to do well." [1] For this reason Socrates thought fortitude was knowledge which is acquired by experience. He even thought all the virtues are kinds of knowledge. But this question will be studied later in the sixth book (1286). Therefore, since certain others are brave by experience in particular affairs, so soldiers are brave in warfare by reason of experience.

568. Two things follow from this. The first is that in war there are many great things like the clash of arms, the charge of the cavalry, and so on that strike the inexperienced with terror, although there is little or no danger in them. These things, as the professional soldiers know, are not really to be dreaded. Hence men seem brave when engaging, without fear, in exercises that appear dangerous to others who are inexperienced and ignorant of the nature of what is taking place. Second, it follows that by reason of experience professional soldiers in fighting can do hurt to their adversaries, and not suffer or be harmed in turn. They can guard themselves from blows and can strike back, for they are clever in the use of weapons,

[1] Cf. *Iliad* ii. 391.

[1] *Epitoma Rei Militaris*, Liber I, I, 6, ll. 4-5.

and they possess other skills effective in enabling them to inflict injury while they themselves are not injured. Hence it is obvious they fight against others as the armed against the unarmed. A man is in effect unarmed if he does not know how or is unable to use arms.

569. The same can be said of athletes, i.e., strong and well-trained boxers compared to simple and inexperienced farm boys. In such athletic contests it is not the brave who can fight the most but those who are physically powerful and well-conditioned.

570. Then [B, 2] at **"Soldiers turn,"** he compares the fortitude of the soldier and the citizen. He says that soldiers fight bravely so long as they do not see danger threatening. But when the danger exceeds the skill they have in arms and when they lack numbers and adequate military preparations, they become cowardly. Then they are the first to run away; they were daring for no other reason than that they thought the danger was not imminent. Therefore, when they first see the danger, they take to their heels. But those who possess the fortitude of the citizen—refusing to leave the danger—lose their lives, as happened in a certain place where the citizens remained after the soldiers had fled. The reason is that citizens think it disgraceful to run away, and choose to die rather than save themselves by flight. But soldiers expose themselves to dangers because, from the beginning, they think themselves more powerful. But after they have recognized that the enemy is more powerful, they take to flight fearing death more than ignominious escape. It is not so with the brave man who fears disgrace more than death.

LECTURE XVII

Counterfeit Fortitude

ANALYTICAL OUTLINE
OF ST. THOMAS

TEXT OF ARISTOTLE
(B.1116 b 23)
Chapter 8

C. He proposes . . . a third kind operating by means of rage.

I. HE SHOWS HOW RAGE INCLINES TO THE ACT OF FORTITUDE.

People confuse rage or wrath with fortitude. Indeed the enraged appear brave in the way that wild animals turn on those who have wounded them. The brave man does give the appearance of rage which acts most impetuously against danger. Hence Homer warns: "Put strength into thy wrath," [1] and "arouse thy might and wrath"; [2] and (in reference to a certain man) "he panted harsh courage through both nostrils," [3] and "his blood boiled." [4] All such expressions *30* seem to signify the stirring up and the impulse of rage.   **571-572**

2. HE SHOWS HOW THIS FORTITUDE DIFFERS FROM REAL FORTITUDE.

a. He shows what pertains to true fortitude.

b. (He shows) what pertains to the rage of beasts.

The brave are incited to valorous deeds by reason of honor with rage co-operating.   **573**

Wild animals attack danger because of pain from a wound or from fear; undisturbed in the woods and swamps they do not come out to attack. They are not truly brave because, aroused against danger by pain and rage, they do not foresee the risks involved. Otherwise hungry jackasses would *B.1117* be brave since they do not stop eating when beaten. (Adulterers too under-

[1] Cf. *Iliad* xiv. 151.
[2] Cf. *Iliad* v. 470.
[3] Cf. *Odyssey* xxiv. 318.
[4] This occurs in Theocritus xx. 15.

take many risks for their sensual desire.) Animals, therefore, who are incited against danger by pain and rage are not truly brave. That reaction which is prompted by passion seems to be a most natural one, and, if to it be added choice and a proper end it is fortitude. **574-575**

c. (He shows) what pertains to human rage.

Angry men are grieved (because of injury suffered) but delighted when taking vengeance. Those who act in this way perhaps are fighters, but hardly brave men, for they do not do what is honorable, nor are they led by reason but rather by passion. *10* They do though possess something similar to real fortitude. **576**

D. He mentions a fourth kind of fortitude.

1. HE EXPLAINS THIS TYPE OF FORTITUDE.

Likewise the confident are not truly brave; they are hopeful because they have often conquered many enemies in the midst of dangers. **577**

2. HE COMPARES THIS TYPE WITH TRUE FORTITUDE.

However, such confident people are like the truly brave because both are daring. But the truly brave are daring in the fashion already indicated,[1] while the confident dare because they think themselves better fighters and expect to suffer nothing. The intoxicated too act in this way, becoming abundantly hopeful, but when they fail to get what was expected, they give up. The brave man though will suffer evils that seem, and really are, terrifying to men—and this for the sake of what is honorable and to avoid disgrace. **578**

3. HE DEDUCES A COROLLARY.

Therefore, that man seems to be braver who does not fear more, *20* and is not more disturbed by unexpected terrors than by those that were foreseen. He seems to act more by

[1] Ch. 7, 1115 b 11-24.

habit since he acts less from preparation. Someone can choose by reason and deliberation things that are foreseen, but in unexpected events habit asserts itself. **579**

E. He introduces the fifth kind of counterfeit fortitude.

Those who operate in ignorance of dangers seem to be brave. They do not differ greatly from people who are brave by reason of great hope. They are, however, inferior since they have no self-reliance unlike the confident who remain in the fight for some time. Those who are bold through ignorance take flight as soon as they know the situation is different from what they suspect. This happened to the Argives when they fell on the Spartans whom they thought Sicyonians.[1] We have now discussed both the brave and those thought to be brave. **580-582**

[1] In the battle at the Long Walls of Corinth: (Xenophon, *Hellenica*, iv. 4, 10).

COMMENTARY OF ST. THOMAS

571. After having disposed of two types of counterfeit fortitude, he proposes here [C] to treat a third kind operating by means of rage which urges to the act of fortitude. He treats this point in a twofold manner. First [C, 1] he shows how rage inclines to the act of fortitude. Next [C, 2], at "The brave are etc.," he shows how this fortitude differs from real fortitude. He observes first that men in common usage of speech confuse rage with fortitude when they attribute to fortitude things that enraged or angry people do. Indeed the enraged and angry do seem to be brave. So too do beasts who, when aroused to rage, attack men beating them. Fortitude has some likeness to rage inasmuch as rage incites against danger with a very strong impulse. But the brave man strives against danger with great strength of soul.

572. As an example he quotes the verses of Homer who warned someone in these words: "Put strength into your wrath"[1] so that wrath may be directed by the virtue of the soul; "Arouse your might and wrath"[2] that the virtue of your soul may be rendered more prompt by anger. Elsewhere he remarks that certain people "pant harsh courage through both

[1] Cf. *Iliad* xiv. 151.
[2] Cf. *Iliad* v. 470.

nostrils"; [1] in other words, wrath, because of the beating of the heart, makes breathing so heavy that sometimes "the blood boils up" [2] through the nostrils from the force of rage. And the Philosopher observes that Homer's statements here seem to indicate that anger is aroused and gives impetus to fortitude's act.

573. Then [C, 2], at "The brave," he explains the difference between this and genuine fortitude. He discusses this point from three aspects. First [2, a] he shows what pertains to true fortitude; next [2, b], at "Wild animals attack etc.," what pertains to the rage of beasts; and finally [2, c], at "Angry men," what pertains to human rage. He says that the brave are not incited to perform works of fortitude by the impulse of rage but by the intention of good. Rage, however, does operate secondarily in these acts in the manner of a co-operator.

574. Next [2, b], at "Wild animals," he shows how the anger of beasts compares with the act of fortitude. He remarks that wild animals attack dangers out of pain from harmful things —which they are actually suffering when wounded, for instance—or because of the dread of the things they fear they are about to suffer, e.g., when incited to anger by fear of being wounded, they attack men. The reason is that if they were in the woods or swamps they would not be wounded nor fear to be wounded, so would not come out to attack men. Hence it is clear that real fortitude is not found in these animals because they are aroused against the dangers only by pain and rage, since they do not foresee dangers, as those who act bravely by choice. If beasts who act by passion were brave, then by the same argument hungry jackasses (who, because of the

desire for food do not stop eating even when beaten) would be brave. Adulterers too undertake many risks for the sake of lust, but real fortitude is not found in them because they do not act by choice of good, but by reason of passion. So it is clear that animals who are incited against danger on account of pain do not have true fortitude.

575. However much is the likeness between desire and rage, nevertheless among all the passions fortitude out of rage seems to be more connatural to genuine fortitude, so that if rage be antecedently directed by choice and the motivation of a fitting end, real fortitude will be present. He expressly says "antecedently directed" because in true fortitude rage ought to follow rather than precede choice.

576. At "Angry men" [2, c] he shows what belongs to fortitude that operates by the anger of men who seem to act by choice and to intend some purpose—the punishment of the person with whom they are angry. For this reason he says that angry men are grieved over an injury received and as yet unavenged. But when they are taking vengeance they are delighted in the satisfaction of their desire. Those who work vigorously at this may perhaps be called pugnacious but hardly brave because they are not doing the right thing, nor are they led by reason but rather by passion for the sake of which they desire vengeance. However, they do possess something similar to genuine fortitude as is evident from the premises (571-572).

577. Then [D], at "Likewise the confident," he mentions a fourth kind of fortitude according to which some are called brave by reason of hope. He develops this idea in a threefold fashion. First [D, 1] he explains this type of fortitude. Next [D, 2], he compares this type with true fortitude at "However, such confident people etc."

---

[1] Cf. *Odyssey* xxiv. 318.
[2] This occurs in Theocritus xx. 15.

Finally [D, 3], he deduces a corollary from what has been said, at "Therefore, that man etc." He says first that, as those who act bravely on account of anger are not truly brave, so neither are they who act bravely for the sole reason of their hope for victory. But they have a certain preeminence by which they differ from others. From the fact that they have very often conquered in the midst of danger, they are now confident of obtaining victory not by reason of any skill acquired through experience—this belongs to the second type of fortitude—but solely by reason of a confidence derived from their frequent victories in the past.

578. Next [D, 2], at **"However, such confident people,"** he compares this fortitude to real fortitude. He notes that those who have abundant confidence in this manner are like the truly brave because both are daring—resolute in meeting dangers—but not in the way that a reckless person is at fault. They differ however since the brave boldly attack in the fashion already indicated, i.e., by choice and on account of good. But those who have high hopes attack boldly because they think themselves more able fighters and are not going to suffer any reverse from others. They resemble drunkards who also become confident when their spirits are reinforced by wine. But when such persons fail to get what they expect, they do not persist; they run away. It is a mark of the brave man, however, to suffer—for the sake of what is honorable and to avoid disgrace—evils that are terrifying to men, real evils and not merely apparent ones.

579. At **"Therefore, that man"** [D, 3] he deduces a corollary from what has been said. Because the brave man characteristically endures terrifying things according to the inclination of a proper habit, that person seems to be braver who is not more afraid or disturbed by unexpected terrors than by those which were apparent beforehand. Such a one seems to act more from habit inasmuch as he apparently has had less opportunity to prepare himself to endure these evils. A man can choose by reason and deliberation (even contrary to the inclination of habit and passion) the things that are foreseen. In no case is the inclination of habit or passion so vehement that reason is unable to resist provided that the use of reason—which of itself has a relation to contraries—remains with man. But in unexpected events a man cannot deliberate. Hence he seems to operate by an interior inclination according to habit.

580. Then [E], at **"Those who operate,"** he introduces the fifth kind of counterfeit fortitude. He says that those who are ignorant of dangers seem to be brave when they resolutely attack things equally dangerous, but which do not seem so dangerous to them. They do not differ much from people who are brave by reason of great confidence. Each thinks that dangers do not threaten him.

581. They differ, however, in that the ignorant do not consider the evils they attack to be dangers in themselves and without qualification. On the other hand those who have high hopes know the nature of the evils they assail but do not think that these constitute dangers for them. Those who are ignorant are the more inferior to those who have high hopes inasmuch as the ignorant have no self-reliance at all, but go out to meet dangers only because of the lack of knowledge. But those who have great hopes remain for some time—even after they recognize the dangers—until the greatness of the danger overwhelms their hope. Those who are brave through ignorance, however, take flight as soon as they know the situation is different from what they

suspected. The Argives, Greek citizens, reacted in this way when thinking they were fighting against Sicyonians—citizens weaker than themselves—they in fact fell upon other stronger soldiers.

582. He concludes that those we have discussed (571-581) are called brave inasmuch as they are considered brave by a similitude and not because they are truly brave.

LECTURE XVIII

The Properties of Fortitude

ANALYTICAL OUTLINE
OF ST. THOMAS

TEXT OF ARISTOTLE
(*B.1117 a 29*)
Chapter 9

I. HE DETAILS THE PROPERTIES OF FORTITUDE.

a. He shows how fortitude is related to fear and daring.

Although fortitude is concerned with both daring and fear, it is not concerned with each in the same way. *30* Its task rather is to manage terrifying things, for one who is not disturbed by these things, but conducts himself as he ought in regard to them, is braver than the man who behaves well in regard to daring. **583**

b. (He shows) how fortitude is related to pain.

As has been said, men are called brave because they endure distressing things.[1] Consequently, fortitude is justly praised because it does not withdraw on account of pain. It is more difficult to endure afflictions, as we have indicated, than to abstain from what is pleasant. **584-585**

c. (He shows) how fortitude is related to pleasure.
   i. *He submits his proposition.*

Still the brave man seems to take *b* pleasure in attaining the end for the sake of fortitude but this pleasure vanishes on account of the accompanying discomforts, as we see happen in athletic contests. Boxers take pleasure in the end they strive for, the laurel wreath and the honors. But being flesh and blood they suffer pain from blows, and all the labor they undergo is disagreeable. Because these distressing things are many and the end insignificant, they do not seem to feel any pleasure. Such also is it with the act of fortitude, for death and wounds

[1] Ch. 7, 1115 b 7-13.

257

ii. *He rejects an error.*

    x. HE PROVES THAT VERY INTENSE
    PAIN BEFALLS THE BRAVE MAN.

    y. BECAUSE OF THIS, HIS FORTI-
    TUDE IS NOT LESSENED BUT IN-
    CREASED.

iii. *He deduces a corollary.*

2. HE EXCLUDES (THESE PROPERTIES) FROM FORTITUDE OF THE SOLDIER.

3. HE SUMS UP . . . WHAT HAS BEEN SAID.

are painful to the brave man who endures them to attain the good of virtue
and to avoid disgrace.   **586-587**

  As a man is more perfect in virtue
and happier, so much the more is   *10*
he saddened by death. The virtuous
man most of all deserves to live and
he is knowingly deprived of the most
excellent goods.   **588-590**
This is saddening but it does not
lessen the virtue of the brave man.
Rather a man is said to be brave because he prefers the good of fortitude
in battle to those goods.   **591**
The pleasurable operation is not
found in all virtues except as it attains
to the end.   **592**

Nothing hinders men, who are not
such as we have described, from being
very good soldiers. But perhaps even
those who are less brave and have no
other good in view are good sol-   *20*
diers. They are prepared for dangers
and barter their life for trifling gains.
     593

So much then have we discussed the
question of fortitude. From what has
been said we can, without difficulty,
understand the outline of the definition of fortitude.   **594**

COMMENTARY OF ST. THOMAS

583. After the Philosopher has
treated the matter and the act of fortitude, he considers here certain properties according as it is related to pleasure
and pain. On this point he does two
things. First [1] he details the properties of fortitude. Then [2] he excludes
them from fortitude of the soldier, at

"Nothing hinders etc." He develops
the first consideration in three ways.
First [a] he shows how fortitude is
related to fear and daring; next [b],
how fortitude is related to pain, at
"As has been said etc."; last [c], how
fortitude is related to pleasure, at "Still
the brave man seems etc." He says first

that although fortitude is concerned with both daring and fear, it is not concerned with each in the same manner. But praise of this virtue consists rather in this, that a person behaves well with respect to terrifying things. One who is not disturbed by frightening evils but conducts himself as he ought in regard to them is more commended for bravery than one who conducts himself well in regard to daring. The reason is that fear is a threat to a man from someone stronger rising up against him. But daring originates from the fact that a man thinks that the one he attacks is not too powerful to overcome. It is more difficult to stand against a stronger man than to rise up against an equal or weaker one.

584. Then [b], at "As has been said," he shows in what manner fortitude is concerned with pain. To understand this we must consider that the object of fear and pain is the same, evil. But they differ according to past and future. Future evil is something terrifying while evil threatening in the present is something afflicting. It pertains to the brave man not only to stand against the fear of future dangers but also to continue steadfastly in the midst of these very dangers, as was noted previously (548). For this reason he says that men are called brave particularly because they stout-heartedly endure distressing things, i.e., immediately threatening things like blows and wounds. So it is that fortitude has pain connected with it.

585. Consequently, fortitude is justly praised because it does not withdraw from the good of virtue to escape pain. On this account it is reasonable that fortitude is most praiseworthy, since the praise of virtue consists especially in the fact that a person deals courageously with troublesome matters. It is more difficult to endure distressing things (which pertains to fortitude) than to abstain from pleasurable things (which pertains to temperance). There-

fore fortitude is more praiseworthy than temperance.

586. Next [c], at "Still the brave man," he shows in what manner fortitude is related to pleasure. He discusses this point from three aspects. First [i] he submits his proposition. Next [ii], he rejects an error, at "As a man is more perfect etc." Last [iii], he deduces a corollary from what has been said, at "The pleasurable operation etc." He says first that since fortitude consists in enduring distressing things, the brave man seems to take some pleasure in attaining the end for which he bravely struggles. But this pleasure is vapid, i.e., feebly felt on account of the accompanying griefs, as happens in athletic contests in which boxers fight with no protection.

587. Boxers take pleasure in the end they strive for, i.e., that they may receive the crown and be honored. But to take a beating is painful to them. To deny this is to deny that they have flesh and blood, because if they have sensitive flesh, hurtful things must cause them pain. Likewise, all the drudgery they suffer in fighting is disagreeable to them. Since there are many disagreeable and painful experiences they undergo, and since the good they possess as an end is something insignificant, they do not seem to be sensible of any pleasure because the pleasure is absorbed by the stronger pain. So it occurs too in the act of fortitude, for death and wounds are painful to the brave man, although he endures them to attain the good of virtue and to avoid disgrace—an end more important than that of boxers. Hence some pleasure abides rather by reason of the end.

588. At "As a man is more" [ii] he rejects the error of the Stoics who held that virtuous men feel no pain. He considers this point in a twofold manner. First [x] he proves that very intense pain befalls the brave man; and next [y] that, because of this, his forti-

tude is not lessened but increased, at "This is saddening etc." He argues in the first part from what the Stoics took for granted, that there was no human good except virtue. Therefore, they said that the virtuous man is not subject to grief because, by reason of his own good, he suffers no harm. On the contrary, the Philosopher says that as a man is more perfect in virtue and happier according to the happiness of the present life, so much more he is saddened (according to the consideration of the goods of this life) by the imminence of death.

589. A man's sadness at the loss of any good can be increased by two circumstances. First if the loss is of a deserved good, and second if the loss is of something great. Both things are present in our case because the virtuous man most of all deserves to live. Likewise he is knowingly deprived of the most excellent good, i.e., the best life and the virtues which he loses so far as the use in the present life is concerned. This causes him distress, even granted that sorrow does not befall him in respect of any other evils whatsoever that are suffered without the loss of life.

590. We must consider, however, that to some virtuous men death is desirable on account of the hope of a future life. But the Stoics did not discuss this, nor did it pertain to the Philosopher in this work to speak of those things that belong to the condition of another life.

591. Then [y], at "This is saddening," he says that this sorrow, of which we were speaking, does not lessen fortitude. Rather someone is said to be brave from the fact that he chooses the good of fortitude—which is sought in battle—in preference to those goods that he loses by death, desiring more to do one great good than to preserve many lesser goods, as will be explained later in the ninth book of this work (1879-1880).

592. Next [iii], at "The pleasurable operation," he concludes from the premises that, although it was stated in the first and second books (154-160, 267, 275-279) that virtuous operations are pleasurable, the pleasurable operation is not found in all virtues, except as it attains to the end. This is noted on account of fortitude, as is evident from what was just said (586-587).

593. At "Nothing hinders" [2] he excludes the previously mentioned properties from the fortitude of the soldier. He says that nothing hinders some men from being very good soldiers, who are not such as we have described the brave man to be. But perhaps those who are less brave and attend to no other good, not even the good of fortitude, are better soldiers. They are prepared for danger not by reason of any good of virtue, but in a measure they barter their life, which they expose to risk, for trifling gains of money and booty for instance.

594. Then [3], at "So much then," he sums up in conclusion what has been said. He states that the definition of fortitude can be understood according to its general outlines, so that we may say that it is a virtue consisting in a mean according to right reason dealing with fear and daring on account of the good.

LECTURE XIX

Temperance

<table>
<tr><td>ANALYTICAL OUTLINE
OF ST. THOMAS</td><td>TEXT OF ARISTOTLE
(*B.1117 b 22*)
Chapter 10</td></tr>
</table>

I. HE INDICATES WHAT HE INTENDS TO DO.

Following this treatise (on fortitude) we must discuss temperance, for these virtues seem to pertain to the irrational parts of the soul. **595-597**

II. HE CARRIES OUT HIS INTENTION.

A. He inquires what the matter of temperance is.

A'. He proposes the matter of temperance in general.

Temperance is a mean dealing with pleasures, as we have said before. It is less concerned, and not in the same way, with sorrows. Intemperance too seems to deal with these things. **598**

B'. He inquires about its special matter.

    I. HE SAYS WHAT HE INTENDS TO DO.

We must now determine with what kind of pleasures temperance has to do. **599**

    2. HE DISTINGUISHES THE KINDS OF PLEASURES.

There are pleasures of the body and pleasures of the soul, such as the love of honor and learning. The lovers of each of these latter (i.e., of honor *30* and learning) rejoice not as a result of any bodily passion but more as a result of mental activity. **600**

    3. HE SHOWS WITH WHAT KIND OF PLEASURES TEMPERANCE DEALS.

a. He shows that temperance is not concerned with pleasures of the soul.
    i. . . . That have an appearance of propriety.

Men are not called temperate or intemperate on account of pleasures of the soul. **601**

ii. . . . With other pleasures that are not of the body.

Likewise, temperance is not concerned with any other pleasures that are not of the body. Those who love to listen to and tell stories, and who waste the day making small talk are not called intemperate but garrulous. **602**

iii. . . . (With) a third class of pleasures of the soul that refer to external things.

Those who are inordinately saddened by the loss of friends and *B.1118* money are not called intemperate. Therefore, temperance will be concerned with the pleasures of the body, **603**

b. He shows that temperance is not concerned with all but with some bodily pleasures.
  i. . . . Does not regard the pleasures of the three senses which perceive through a separate medium.
    x. . . . DOES NOT DEAL WITH THE PLEASURES OF THE THREE . . . SENSES.
      aa. . . . Does not concern pleasures of sight.

but not with all of them. Those who take delight in things seen: colors, figures and writing for instance, are not called temperate or intemperate, although it happens that men take pleasure in such things as they ought, and according to excess and defect. **604-606**

      bb. . . . Does not have to do with pleasures proper to hearing.

Temperance is related in a similar way to pleasures concerned with hearing. No one, who delights excessively or as he ought in songs or instrumental music will be called intemperate or temperate on this account. **607**

      cc. . . . Does not have to do with the pleasures of smell.

The same is to be said in respect *10* to those who take pleasures, except incidentally, in odors. We do not call intemperate people who delight in the fragrance of apples or roses or incense, but rather those who take pleasure in the perfume of cosmetics or the aroma of tasty dishes. The intemperate enjoy these pleasures because in this way things they desire are recalled. One may see others too taking delight in the aroma of food when hungry. But it pertains to the intemperate man to

Y. . . . SUCH PLEASURES DO NOT
BELONG TO THE BRUTES.

rejoice in this aroma as representing
what is desirable.   **608-609**

Other animals do not take pleasure
according to these senses except incidentally. Hounds do not delight in the
scent of rabbits for itself but in the
prospect of food, the sense of *20*
which they get through smell. The
lion does not rejoice in the lowing of
the ox, but in the meal that he senses
is at hand because of the sound he apparently enjoys. Likewise, he does not
take pleasure in the sight of the stag
or the wild she-goat which he discovers,
but in the hope of possessing food.
                                      610-611

Z. HE DRAWS A CONCLUSION.

Temperance and intemperance then
have to do with such pleasures as the
other animals have in common with
man. Hence gratifications of touch and
taste seem to be servile and brutish.
                                          612

COMMENTARY OF ST. THOMAS

595. After the Philosopher has
treated fortitude concerned with terrifying things which are destructive of
man's life, he now takes up the question of temperance concerned with
pleasurable things which preserve
human life, i.e., food and sex. On this
point he does two things. First [I] he
indicates what he intends to do. Next
[II] he carries out his intention, at
"Temperance is a mean etc." He says
first that, after the treatise on fortitude,
we must speak about temperance. He
finds the reason for this succession in
the fact that these two virtues agree
in subject. Both pertain to the irrational part, according as that part of
the soul is called irrational which is designed by nature both to conform to,
and to obey reason, as was stated in the
beginning (239). Such is the sensitive

appetite to which the passions of the
soul belong.

596. Hence all the virtues dealing
with the passions must be placed in the
sensitive appetite. Fortitude is concerned with the passions of fear and
daring, which reside in the irascible
part, but temperance is concerned with
pleasures and pains, which reside in
the concupiscible part. Consequently,
fortitude is placed in the irascible part,
but temperance in the concupiscible
part.

597. We must consider that the
pleasures of food and sex, with which
temperance deals, are common to us
and the brutes. Likewise, the fear of
death, with which fortitude is concerned, is common to us and them. For
this reason he notes particularly that
these two virtues are of the irrational

parts, because they belong to the irrational parts of the soul not only on account of the passions themselves but also because of the objects of the passions. There are some passions whose objects do not concern the brutes, like riches, honors and so on.

598. Then [II], at **"Temperance is a mean,"** he begins to define temperance. First [A] he inquires what the matter of temperance is. Second [Lect. XX, B], at "Some desires are," he defines the act of temperance and of the opposite vices (B.1118 b 8). He considers the first point under two aspects. First [A'] he proposes the matter of temperance in general. Next [B'], at "We must now determine etc.," he inquires about its special matter. In regard to the first point he reviews three considerations which were discussed in the second book (342). The first is that temperance keeps a mean concerning pleasures. The second is that temperance deals also with sorrows that arise from the absence of pleasures. Temperance is less concerned, however, with sorrows than with pleasures because a thing acts more efficaciously by its presence than by its absence. The third is that intemperance likewise deals with pleasures and sorrows because contraries are concerned about the same thing.

599. Next [B'], at **"We must now determine,"** he inquires about the special matter of temperance. Three aspects claim his attention. First [1] he says what he intends to do. Then [2], at "There are," he distinguishes the kinds of pleasures. Last [3], at "Men are not called etc.," he shows with what kind of pleasures temperance deals. He says first that, since temperance deals with pleasures, we must now determine with what kind of pleasures it deals, so that the nature of temperance in particular may be known.

600. At **"There are"** [2] he distinguishes the kinds of pleasure. He says that some of them are of the

soul, others of the body. Pleasures of the body are those that are completed in some bodily affection of an external sense. Pleasures of the soul are those that are completed by interior apprehension alone. He gives an example of pleasures of the soul, beginning with the cause of pleasure—which is love. Every one takes pleasure from the fact that he possesses what he loves. In some men we find the love of honor; in others, the love of learning. This love is not perceived by an external sense but by an apprehension of the soul, which is interior. Therefore each of these, i.e., the man who loves honor or learning, rejoices on account of what he loves while he has it. This joy does not arise as the result of any bodily passion, but as a result of the mind's awareness alone.

601. Then [a], at **"Men are not called,"** he shows that temperance is not concerned with pleasures of the soul. He indicates three classes of these pleasures. Some [a, i] that have an appearance of propriety like honor and learning, as we have just noted (600), are pleasurable to the soul. For this reason he says that men are not called temperate or intemperate on account of such pleasures, since temperance seems to refer to pleasures which have something of shame about them. Concerned with the pleasures of honor and learning there are, however, certain other means and extremes pertaining to other virtues, as will be clearly shown in the fourth book (792-799).

602. Second [a, ii], at **"Likewise, temperance,"** he now recalls other pleasures of the soul which consist in the sayings and deeds of men. He says that, as temperance is not concerned with pleasures of honor or learning, so also it is not concerned with other pleasures which are not of the body. Those who love to listen to and tell stories, and who waste the whole day talking about all kinds of contingent

remarks and deeds (unnecessary and useless affairs) are said to be garrulous but we do not call them intemperate. The reason is that intemperance has not only a futility about it, but also a certain baseness.

603. Third [a, iii], at **"Those who are,"** he introduces a third class of pleasures of the soul which refer to external things, as money and friends. Hence he says that those, who are inordinately saddened by the loss of money and friends, are not called intemperate. But they can be called vicious from one aspect, because such sorrows do not show turpitude but only a disordered condition of the appetite. From this, that temperance is not concerned with any class of pleasures of the soul, he concludes that it does concern pleasures of the body.

604. Then [b], at **"but not with all,"** he shows that temperance is not concerned with all but with some bodily pleasures. First [b, i] he discloses that temperance does not regard the pleasures of the three senses which perceive through a separate (from the sense organ) medium. Next [Lect. XX; b, ii], at "Any use of taste etc.," he explains in what manner temperance regards the pleasures of the other two senses which perceive through a contiguous (with the sense organ) medium (B.1118 a 26). He develops the first point [b, i] in three steps. First [i, x] he shows that temperance does not deal with the pleasures of the three previously mentioned senses. Next [i, y], at "Other animals do not etc.," he shows that such pleasures do not belong to brutes. Last [i, z], at "Temperance and intemperance etc.," he draws a conclusion from what has been said. Regarding the first he excludes the three senses. First [x, aa] he proves that temperance does not concern pleasures of sight.

605. He says that temperance is not concerned with all bodily pleasures which arise by means of the external

senses. Those who take delight in things seen are not on that account called temperate or intemperate. He gives examples of three classes of visible objects. Some are the proper sensibles of sight, as colors. Others are common sensibles, which however are known most particularly through sight, as figures. Still others are sensible incidentally, as writing, by reason of what is signified through the writing.

606. This does not mean that virtue and vice are not to be encountered here. It happens in such matters that a person may take pleasure as he ought—this is the mean, or according to excess and defect, but this pertains to curiosity and not to intemperance which regards the more vehement pleasures.

607. Next [x, bb], at **"Temperance is related,"** he proves that temperance does not have to do with the pleasures proper to hearing. He says that temperance is related in a similar way to the pleasures concerned with hearing; neither it nor intemperance is involved. If someone delights too much, or as he ought, in melodies (i.e., harmonies of human voices) and symphony (that is, the imitation of the human voice achieved through instruments) he will not be called temperate or intemperate on this account because these are not very vehement pleasures either. But this matter can belong to another virtue or vice.

608. Third [x, cc], at **"The same is to be said,"** he proves that temperance does not have to do with the pleasures of smell. Regarding this we must consider that, as stated in the work *De Sensu et Sensato* (Ch. 5, 443 b 17 sq.; St. Th. Lect. XIII, 177-186), the kinds of scents are distinguished in two ways. In one way in themselves. In the other way by a comparison with the species of savors. He says then that they are not called temperate and intemperate who take reasonable or excessive pleasure in odors considered in themselves but only when they take pleasure in

odors incidentally, i.e., according as these odors coincide with the pleasures of taste and touch.

609. We do not call intemperate those who take pleasure in the fragrance of apples or roses or incense, which are species of odor in itself, but those who take pleasure in the aroma of foods or the perfume of cosmetics used by women. The intemperate delight in these pleasures on account of memory of certain things they long for. He clearly shows this by the example of the hungry who take pleasure in odors that do not interest them when they have eaten. So it is evident that these men do not take pleasure in odors as such but incidentally. In this way it pertains to the intemperate man —to whom the things represented by the odors are desirable—to take pleasure in those odors.

610. At "Other animals do not take" [i, y] he proves that pleasures arising from these senses belong only indirectly to other animals. He says that the brutes find pleasure via these three senses indirectly, i.e., by reference to taste and touch. He clearly shows this first in regard to the sense of smell. Hounds do not take pleasure in the scent of rabbits on account of the scent itself but on account of the expected food, the sensation of which they receive through smell. Second, he makes the same point in regard to the sense of hearing. He says that the lion takes pleasure in the lowing of an ox because the lion knows from the sound that a meal is near. Hence he seems to de-

light in the bellow of the bull, but this is incidental. Third, Aristotle manifests the same thing in regard to seeing. He says that the lion does not take pleasure even at the sight of the stag or roe (which he calls a wild she-goat) when he finds something of this kind, but he is delighted by the hope of getting a meal.

611. The reason for these things is that the appetite of the other animals is moved by the instinct of nature alone. On this account animals take pleasure only in the things referring to the preservation of nature; that is why senses of this kind were given them. But senses have been given to men for the perception of sensible things leading in turn to a knowledge of reason which moves the appetite of man. So it is that man takes pleasure in the very appropriateness of sensible things considered in themselves, even if they are not ordered to the conservation of nature.

612. Then [i, z], at "Temperance and intemperance," he concludes from the premises that temperance has to do with such operations or pleasures as the other animals have in common with man. The same is true of intemperance. Hence pleasures of this kind seem to be servile and brutish because what we have in common with irrational animals is slavish and naturally subject to reason in us. Such are the pleasures of touch and taste which are the two senses besides the three mentioned before.

LECTURE XX

Temperance in Relation to Touch and Taste

ANALYTICAL OUTLINE
OF ST. THOMAS

TEXT OF ARISTOTLE
(*B.1118 a 26*)
Chapter 10

ii. He shows what concerns the pleasures of taste and touch.

    X. . . . DOES NOT DEAL DIRECTLY
    WITH THE PLEASURES OF TASTE
    BUT . . . TOUCH.

Any use of taste made by temperance, or intemperance for that matter, is small or even non-existent. Taste here means the discernment of flavors, the occupation of wine-tasters and cooks sampling their own food. The intemperate do not take delight *30* in these things or at least not much, but in the enjoyment by touch in the taking of food and drink and in the gratification of sex.   613-614

    Y. HE CLARIFIES . . . WHAT HE HAS
    AFFIRMED.

On this account a certain man by the name of Philoxenus Erichius—a voracious eater—prayed for a gullet longer than a crane's, so he could take more pleasure in the contact with *b* his food.   615

    Z. HE DRAWS A CONCLUSION.

Touch, with which intemperance deals, is the most widely shared of all the senses. Rightly then intemperance seems worthy of reproach, since it does not exist in man as belonging to what is proper to him, but to what he has in common with the animals. To take pleasure in things of this sort and to love them above everything else is brutish. We exclude those pleasures of touch which are especially liberal, for instance, those taken in gymnasia by massages and heat-treatment. But the pleasure of touch, which the intemperate man seeks, is not that of the whole body but of certain parts of the body.   616-617

B. He shows how the act of temperance and of the opposite vices is constituted.
A' He explains his proposition.

    I. HE TREATS INTEMPERANCE.

Chapter 11

a. He shows how temperance is related to pleasures.
  *i. He makes a certain division of
desires.*
  ii. He explains the division.
    X. HE POINTS OUT WHAT THE
    COMMON DESIRES ARE.

Some desires are common, and others are proper and acquired. **618-619**

The desire for food is natural, *10*
for everyone—when he is without it
—desires food and drink (and sometimes both) just as, according to
Homer,[1] the young and growing man
longs for a bed. **620**

    Y. HE POINTS OUT WHAT THE
    PROPER DESIRES ARE.

Not all men, however, do want such
and such a bed, or the same kinds of
food. For this reason such desires
seem to be peculiar to each of us, although they still have something of
the natural. Different people enjoy different pleasures, and some persons take
more pleasure in certain kinds of things
than in chance objects. **621**

*iii. He shows in what manner in-
temperance deals with both
desires.*
    X. . . . IN THE NATURAL DESIRES
    WHICH ARE COMMON.

In natural desires few men go
astray and then only in one way, by
excess. This happens when men eat
or drink even to an immoderate full-
ness, which is an excess in the quantity of food nature requires. (Nature
desires that its need be supplied.)
These people are called "belly-mad"
because they stuff their stomachs *20*
beyond need. Such persons become
very brutish. **622-623**

    Y. . . . WITH PROPER DESIRES.

But in regard to proper desires,
many sin in numerous ways. Those
who love such pleasures sin in de-
lighting in things they ought not, or
more than they ought, or as many of
the foolish do, or not according to
measure. The intemperate are excessive in all these ways because they
enjoy certain odious things they ought

[1] Cf. *Iliad* xxiv. 130.

not to enjoy. If pleasure may be taken, they delight in such things (as many do) more than they ought. Therefore, since intemperance is excess in regard to pleasures, it is despicable. **624-625**

COMMENTARY OF ST. THOMAS

613. After the Philosopher has proved that temperance and intemperance do not deal with the pleasures of three senses but with the pleasures of two, i.e., taste and touch, he shows now [b, ii] what concerns the pleasures of taste and touch. He treats this from three aspects. First [ii, x] he shows that temperance does not deal directly with the pleasures of taste but with the pleasures of touch. Next [ii, y], at "On this account etc.," he clarifies by an example what he has affirmed. Finally [ii, z], at "Touch, with which etc.," he draws a conclusion from what has been said. He says first that temperance and intemperance seem to make little use of what is proper to taste, namely, the discernment of flavors. Those who test wine use taste in this way; likewise, those who season food and sample to see whether their dishes have a delicious taste.

614. The intemperate do not take much delight in this, and they are not deprived of much pleasure when they do not perfectly discern the flavors of food. But all their delight consists in the enjoyment of certain pleasurable things, for instance, in eating, drinking, and sex—all of which occur through touch. It is obvious, therefore, that the pleasure of the intemperate has to do directly with the sense of touch, and with taste only because flavors make the enjoyment of food delectable. For this reason he

previously said (608-611, 613) that intemperance has little use for taste, i.e., as it is ordered to touch, or no use, i.e., in respect to what belongs to taste in itself.

615. Then [ii, y], at "On this account," he clarifies by an example what he had said. A certain man named Philoxenus Erichius who, since he ate his meals greedily, desired to have a throat longer than a crane's so the food would remain a long while in his throat. From this it is evident that he did not take pleasure in taste (which is active in the tongue and not in the throat) but in touch alone.

616. Next [ii, z], at "Touch, with which," he draws a corollary from what has been said. The sense of touch, which temperance deals with, is the most common of all the senses because all the animals share in it. On this account intemperance seems to be really despicable since it does not exist in man as belonging to what is proper to him, but to what he has in common with other animals. But to take pleasure in things of this sort and to love them as the highest goods seems to be especially animal–like. So it is that vices of intemperance possess the most disgusting shamefulness because they make man like the brutes. Therefore, by reason of such vices, man is rendered notoriously evil and blameworthy.

617. Someone might say that even in things pertaining to touch there is

some properly human good that is not bestial. In order to answer this objection, he adds that we exclude from temperance those pleasures of touch that are especially liberal—appropriate for humans—and used according to reason. Such pleasures are found in gymnasia by massage and heat-treatment in view of the games (since some are going to wrestle or indulge in other sports). These pleasures of touch are not ordered to the desire of food or sex. The pleasure of touch which the intemperate man seeks is not that of the whole body but of certain parts of the body.

618. At "Some desires" [B] he shows how the act of temperance (in the previously mentioned matter) and of the opposite vices is constituted. Here he proceeds in twofold fashion. First [A'] he explains his proposition. Next [Lect. XXII, B'], at "Intemperance is more etc." (B.1119 a 21), he compares the vices of intemperance with certain other vices. Regarding the first he has three considerations. First [1] he treats intemperance, showing in what manner it operates in the previously investigated matter. Next [Lect. XXI, 2], at "It does not happen etc.," he treats insensibility (B.1119 a 5). Last [Lect. XXI, 3], at "The temperate man etc.," he treats temperance (B.1119 a 12). In regard to the first he does two things. First [a] he shows how temperance is related to pleasures. Then [Lect. XXI, b], at "With regard to sorrows etc.," how it is related to sorrow (B.1118 b 29). Fear and sorrow are ordered to the same thing—we noted this before (584)—because sorrow has to do with present evils, as fear with future ones. So also desire (which concerns future goods) and pleasure (which concerns present goods) are ordered to the same thing. Temperance is in the reason concerned with sensual desires and pleasures. First [a, i] he makes a certain division of desires. Next [a, ii], at "The de-

sire for food etc.," he explains the division. Last [a, iii], at "In natural desires etc.," he shows in what manner intemperance deals with both desires.

619. He says first that some desires are common and others are proper, being in addition to the common.

620. Then [a, ii], at "The desire for food," he explains this division. First [a, ii, x] he points out what the common desires are, saying that the desire for food in general is natural, as following the whole nature of the species and genus. Hence every man desires dry nourishment called food or moist nourishment called drink—and sometimes both—in order to succor a natural need, just as according to Homer[1] every man (the young as well as the growing, i.e., the adolescent) longs for a bed to rest in.

621. Next [a, ii, y], at "Not all men however," he points out what the proper desires are, saying that not all men want this particular bed—say a couch strewn with feathers and costly covering. Likewise, not everyone craves such and such a food, an expensive dish for example, or one daintily prepared. All do not yearn for the same gratification, but in such matters some desire one thing, others another. Hence desires of this kind seem to be our very own because we are not inclined to them by nature but by our own devising. Here nothing hinders a thing from being natural as belonging to the nature of the individual, although it may not belong to the nature of the genus or species. We see that different people enjoy different pleasures according to their different temperaments. And, because of natural temperament, some persons take more pleasure in certain kinds of things than in other commonplace objects.

622. At "In natural desires" [a, iii] he explains in what manner intem-

[1] Cf. Iliad xxiv. 130.

perance has to do with the desires just mentioned. He says that in the natural desires that are common [a, iii, x] few men go astray. Here transgression occurs only in one way, according as someone takes more than nature requires. This happens when someone eats or drinks what is given him in an immoderate amount, in which there is an excess in regard to the quantity of food nature needs. Nature desires only that the need be supplied. Therefore, that someone should take more than he needs is an excess above nature.

623. People of this type are called "belly-mad" (*gastrimargoi:* from *gastir* meaning belly and *marges* meaning a raving or madness) as if they had a raving or mad stomach, because they stuff nature beyond requirement. Such persons are very brutish because their only concern is to fill their bellies without discrimination like animals.

624. Next [a, iii, y], at "**But in regard to proper desires,**" he explains in what manner intemperance has to do with proper desires or pleasures. He says that in regard to them, many sin in numerous ways, i.e., according to all the circumstances. Those who love such pleasures sin because they enjoy things they should not (like eating food which does not agree with them) or they sin by taking more enjoyment than they should (for instance, someone takes too much pleasure in eating agreeable dishes). Others sin by taking pleasure in foods without discernment —like most fools do—or finally they do not observe due measure in enjoyment, as they should. The intemperate are excessive in all these ways because they enjoy objects highly indecorous and blameworthy by nature, which they ought not to enjoy. Even when pleasure in certain things may be lawful, they commonly take more enjoyment than they ought without discrimination.

625. So he concludes that, since intemperance is excess in regard to pleasures of this kind, it is blameworthy like other excesses, as was explained in the second book (333-334).

LECTURE XXI

How Sorrows, Pleasures, and Desires Affect the Temperate Man

<table>
<tr><td>ANALYTICAL OUTLINE
OF ST. THOMAS</td><td>TEXT OF ARISTOTLE
(B.1118 b 29)
Chapter 11</td></tr>
<tr><td>b. He shows that the brave, the temperate . . . are affected in different ways by sorrow.</td><td>With regard to sorrows, one is not —as in fortitude—called temperate because he faces them, nor intem- 30 perate because he does not undergo them. But the intemperate man grieves more than he ought because he does not attain the pleasures he desires. But his pleasure is what causes him grief. On the contrary, the temperate man does not grieve for absent things, and in abstention from pleasure.
 626-627 </td></tr>
<tr><td>c. He makes clear his assertion.</td><td>The intemperate man then desires all pleasures and he especially B.1119 desires exquisite pleasures. He is led by sensual desire to choose pleasurable things in preference to all others. For this reason the intemperate man is saddened when he does not get the pleasure he wants; his desire in fact brings sorrow. He is like the incontinent person who is also saddened by pleasure.   628-629</td></tr>
</table>

2. HE CONSIDERS THE VICE OPPOSITE TO TEMPERANCE WHICH FALLS SHORT IN REGARD TO PLEASURES.

It does not happen too often that men become deficient in pleasure, taking less enjoyment than they ought. Insensibility of this kind is not in keeping with human nature because the other animals differentiate foods in this, that they take pleasure in some things, and in others they do not. If someone finds no joy in anything <i>10</i> and does not prefer one thing to another, he is a long way from being

human. As this rarely happens, there
is no special name for it.   **630-631**

3. HE EXPLAINS IN WHAT WAY THE TEMPERATE MAN SHOULD CONDUCT HIMSELF IN
REGARD TO THE MATTER PREVIOUSLY MENTIONED.

a. He shows from what things the
temperate man should abstain.

The temperate man follows the
golden mean in these matters. He does
not delight in those shameful things
in which the intemperate man takes
the keenest pleasure, but rather he is
saddened if they occur. In no way does
he rejoice in things more ardently than
he ought. He is not unnecessarily saddened by the absence of pleasurable
things. If he desires them, he does so
in the right measure. He does not
crave pleasures more than he ought,
nor when he ought not, nor according
to any other unreasonable circumstance.   **632**

b. He shows what things the temperate man should enjoy and in what
manner.

The temperate man desires whatever pleasures are useful to the health
and well-being of the body, and he
wants them according to right measure and as he ought. He desires other
pleasures only if they are not a hin-
drance to health, nor opposed to what
is honorable, nor beyond his means.
One who is otherwise disposed takes
more enjoyment than is reasonable.
The temperate man is not of this
nature but he acts according to *20*
right reason.   **633-634**

COMMENTARY OF ST. THOMAS

626. After the Philosopher has defined in what way temperance is concerned with pleasures, he now explains
how it is concerned with sorrows. On
this point he does two things. First
[(1) b] he shows that the brave, the
temperate, and the intemperate are
affected in different ways by sorrow.
Then [(1) c], at "The intemperate
man then etc.," he makes clear his as-

sertion. He says first that the brave,
the temperate, and the intemperate are
not disposed toward sorrow in the same
way. The brave man indeed suffers
many sorrows, but he is praised for
this very endurance which is done
nobly. This has already been remarked
(584, 596). The temperate man however is not praised because he undergoes sorrows. Nor is the intemperate

man blamed for not undergoing them, although the cowardly man is blamed. But the intemperate man is censured for the fact that he grieves more than he should. His sorrow does not arise from any harmful thing threatening him—which is the cause of the coward's sorrow—but he is sorry because he does not get the pleasures he wants. Thus it is by its very absence that pleasure causes him grief. On the contrary the temperate man is praised for not grieving and for undertaking to abstain from pleasures that he does not desire very much. An effect that follows from the presence of a cause is more important than an effect that follows from its absence.

627. For this very reason fortitude is primarily concerned with sorrows which follow from the presence of harmful things. Temperance, however, is secondarily concerned with sorrows that follow from the absence of pleasures but primarily with pleasures following from the presence of pleasurable things.

628. Then [(1) c], at "The intemperate man then," he makes evident his assertion, that pleasure is the occasion of sorrow for the intemperate man. This happens because the intemperate man desires all pleasurable things. He strives after pleasure itself. On this account he strives after everything giving pleasure and he strives after the thing pleasurable in the highest degree in comparison with which he cares less for other delightful things. Therefore his pleasure is not guided by reason, but led by sensual desire to choose pleasurable things—especially those which are most abundantly so—in preference to all other useful and honorable goods. The intemperate put aside what is useful and decent in order that they may obtain pleasure. For this reason the intemperate man is saddened when he does not get the pleasure he wants. Sensual desire brings

sorrow when it does not gain the thing coveted.

629. Although, according to a superficial likelihood, it seems incongruous that anyone should be saddened by reason of pleasure, nevertheless it is true that the intemperate man is distressed by pleasure. He is saddened only by its absence, like a ship lost by the absence of its pilot.

630. Next [2], at "It does not happen," he considers the vice opposite to temperance which falls short in regard to pleasures. He says it does not happen very often that men become deficient in pleasures (so that they take less enjoyment than they ought, i.e., than is required for the health and well-being of the body and for decent living with others) in which this vice consists and which we have called insensibility in the second book (262, 342). This defect is not in keeping with human nature because the other animals differentiate foods in this, that they take pleasure in some, and in others not. So it seems to belong to the common nature of the genus to take some pleasure.

631. Therefore, if there is anyone, who does not take pleasure in anything, he seems to be a long way from being human. Because this rarely happens, he who falls short in this manner does not have a special name, except that before (262, 342) we called him insensible. When men abstain from pleasures for a useful or honorable reason, as merchants for gain and soldiers for victory, we do not have instances of insensibility. This is not beyond what is reasonable, as is the case with the vice.

632. At "The temperate man follows" [3], he explains in what way the temperate man should conduct himself in regard to the matter previously mentioned. He clarifies this point in two stages. First [3, a] he shows from what things the temperate man should abstain. Next [3, b], at

"The temperate man desires etc.," he shows what things the temperate man should enjoy and in what manner. He says first that the temperate man follows the golden mean regarding the preceding, i.e., pleasure, sorrow, and desire. First in regard to pleasure, he does not delight in those shameful things in which the intemperate take pleasure but rather is saddened if any such thing should occur. In general he does not rejoice in things he ought not, nor does he rejoice more ardently than he ought. Likewise he is not excessive according to any other circumstance. Next, in respect to sorrow he is not saddened beyond measure by the absence of pleasurable things. Third, in respect to desire he does not long for absent pleasures, because he cares little for them, or he longs for them in the right measure which is not excessive; he does not crave pleasure more than he ought, nor when he ought not, nor according to any other circumstance exceeding the norm of reason.

633. Then [3, b], at **"The temperate man desires,"** he shows which pleasures the temperate man enjoys and in what way. He says that the temperate man desires whatever pleasures are useful to the health of the body or its well-being so that he may be prompt and unimpeded for the things of this kind which he has to do. He desires these pleasures, however, according to the right measure and as he ought. If there are other pleasures not necessary for the two reasons previously named, the temperate man desires them under the three following conditions.

634. First, that they are not hindrances to health and well-being, like superfluous food or drink. Second, that they are not contrary to good, i.e., opposed to decency, like the pleasure of fornication. Third, that they are not beyond his means, i.e., they do not exceed a man's power to possess, as would be the case if a poor man desired to enjoy foods which are too costly. One who is so disposed that he longs for pleasures harmful to health and well-being, and contrary to decency, or exceeding his means takes more enjoyment than is reasonable. This does not pertain to the temperate man who loves these pleasures in conformity with right reason.

LECTURE XXII

Intemperance Compared with Cowardice and the Sins of Children

ANALYTICAL OUTLINE
OF ST. THOMAS

TEXT OF ARISTOTLE
(B.*1119 a 21*)
Chapter 12

B' He compares the sin of intemperance with other sins.

I. HE COMPARES INTEMPERANCE WITH THE VICE OF COWARDICE.

a. He shows that intemperance has more of the voluntary than cowardice has.
  i. He explains . . . (by two reasons).
      X. FIRST.

Intemperance is more like the voluntary than fear is, because the former is motivated by pleasure, and the latter by pain. One of these (pleasure) is to be chosen, the other (pain) is to be avoided.   635-636

      Y. SECOND.

Pain stupefies and corrupts the nature of its possessor but pleasure does no such thing, and so is more voluntary.   637

  ii. He infers a corollary from his discussion.

For this reason intemperance is also more despicable; it is easy to become accustomed to the objects of temperance, for many occasions occur in a man's life and the habits can be practiced without danger. With terrifying objects, however, the reverse is the case.   638-639

b. He shows that the voluntary in each vice is found in a different order.
  i. He shows in what order the voluntary is found in cowardice.

There does not appear to be a likeness in voluntariety between fear itself and individual cases of it. Fear itself seems to be painless, but particular cases stupefy men by reason of pain, so that they throw away their arms and do other disgraceful actions. On this account these things seem to *30* be done under compulsion.   640

ii. . . . In intemperance.

In regard to intemperance the order is reversed. Particulars are voluntary because they are in accord with what a man strives for and desires, but the condition (intemperance) as a whole is less voluntary, for no one wants to be intemperate.   **641-642**

2. (HE COMPARES INTEMPERANCE) WITH THE SINS OF CHILDREN.

a. He states the agreement as to the name.

We transfer the name intemperance to the sins of children, for they do *b* have a certain resemblance. But which one is named from the other does not concern us now. It is clear, however, that the later is derived from the earlier.   **643**

b. He assigns the reason for the agreement.
   i. . . . In respect to the necessity of chastising or restraining.

This transference does not seem to be unsuitable. He who strives after what is base and increases greatly in evil must be punished. In this, sensual desire and the child are alike. Children live in accord with sensual desire and they strive most of all after pleasure. Therefore, if it will not be properly obedient, sensual desire will come to rule and increase considerably. To a stupid person the desire for pleasure is insatiable and omnipresent; and the exercise of desire increases its natural power. For the appetites are strong and violent, going even to the extent of interrupting *10* the act of reasoning.   **644-646**

ii. . . . In respect to the manner of chastising and restraining.

For this reason sensual desire and pleasure must be moderated, that is, sense pleasures must be few in number and in no way contrary to reason. Such a state is what we call obedient and disciplined. As a child must live according to the instructions of his tutor, so the concupiscent part must conform to reason; each, i.e., the tutor and reason aspires to the good. And the temperate man desires the right things at the right time as reason disposes. These then are the things we have to say about temperance.   **647-648**

COMMENTARY OF ST. THOMAS

635. After the Philosopher has treated the act of temperance and the opposite vices, he now compares the sin of intemperance with other sins [B′]. He makes two points here. First [1] he compares intemperance with the vice of cowardice; and then, with the sins of children, at "We transfer the name" [2]. He clarifies the first point by a twofold distinction. First [1, a] he shows that intemperance has more of the voluntary than cowardice has. Next [1, b], at "There does not appear etc.," he shows that the voluntary in each vice is found in a different order. In regard to the first he does two things. First [a, i] he explains that intemperance has more of the voluntary than cowardice has. Next [a, ii], at "For this reason intemperance etc.," he infers a corollary from his discussion. He says first that intemperance is more like the voluntary than fear is, because intemperance has more of the voluntary. He proves this by two reasons.

636. The first of these is taken from what follows the voluntary and the involuntary as a property [i, x]. Everyone delights in what he does voluntarily, but is sad over what is contrary to his will. It is obvious that the intemperate man acts for the pleasure he desires. The coward, on the other hand, acts because of the pain which he flees. (Of course the operation of both is pleasing because not only is actual pleasure a matter for joy but even the hope of future pleasure.) But pain is a thing to be avoided and consequently is contrary to the will. So it is evident that intemperance is caused by what is of itself voluntary. Cowardice, however, is caused by something involun-

tary and repugnant. Therefore intemperance comes closer to the voluntary than cowardice.

637. He gives the second reason at "Pain stupefies" [i, y]. This is taken from the fact that ignorance causes an involuntary. Because pain follows from the presence of some contrary and harmful principle, it stupefies and corrupts the nature of its possessor. So it is that the mind of man is impeded by pain from proper knowledge. But pleasure is caused by the presence of an agreeable object that does not corrupt the nature. Hence pleasure does not stupefy nor corrupt the mind of the one who takes pleasure. From this it follows that intemperance, which operates on account of pleasure, has more of the voluntary than fear does —which is caused by pain.

638. Then [a, ii], at "For this reason intemperance," he concludes that, since in voluntary acts praise is due to the good and blame to the evil, the vice of intemperance is more disgraceful than the vice of cowardice which has less of the voluntary. To this he adds also another reason taken from the fact that a vice is more worthy of reproach insofar as it is more easily avoidable.

639. Each vice can be avoided by the contrary habit. For two reasons it is easy to become accustomed to good actions in matters of temperance. First, because pleasures in food, drink, and so forth take place very often in man's life. Hence there is no lack of opportunity to get used to virtuous actions in such matters. Second, becoming accustomed to good deeds of temperance does not constitute a danger. A person does not run any great risk in ab-

staining at times from some pleasure of touch. But quite the reverse is true in the vice of cowardice because the dangers from war happen rarely. Besides it is dangerous to get mixed up in wars. It follows then that the vice of intemperance is more worthy of reproach than the vice of cowardice.

640. Next [1, b], at **"There does not appear,"** he shows that the voluntary in each vice is not found in the same order. First [1, b, i] he shows in what order the voluntary is found in cowardice; and second in intemperance, at "In regard to intemperance etc." [1, b, ii]. He says first that fear does not seem to be voluntary in the same way for the universal and for particular cases. Universals seem to be without pain, for example, anyone may go into battle and attack the enemy. But particular happenings, for instance, that a man is wounded or routed or suffers other misfortune, bring such great pain that men are stupefied on account of these things—so much so that they throw away their arms and do other disgraceful actions. Hence, since in reference to the universal these acts are voluntary, and in reference to the particular they become involuntary, they seem to be done under compulsion (inasmuch as a man is induced by an external principle to give up what he had previously wished).

641. At **"In regard to intemperance"** [1, b, ii], he shows what the order is in regard to intemperance. He says that in this case the order is reversed, for singular things are voluntary in the highest degree because they occur in accordance with what a man strives for and desires. But the whole, considered in the abstract, is less voluntary—for instance, that anyone should commit adultery. No one desires to be intemperate in general. However particular things, by which a man becomes intemperate, are delightful.

642. The reason for this difference is taken from this: pain that causes fear pertains to the involuntary, as pleasure that causes intemperance pertains to the voluntary. Every inclination of the soul towards particular things is rather vehement. For this reason cowardice regarding particular things has more of the involuntary but intemperance more of the voluntary. Therefore in sins of intemperance it is exceedingly harmful to dwell upon the thought by which a man comes down to the particular that entices the will.

643. Then [2], at **"We transfer the name,"** he compares the vice of intemperance with the sins of children. First [2, a] he states the agreement as to the name. Next [2, b], at "This transference etc.," he assigns the reason for the agreement. He says first that the name intemperance is transferred to the sins of children. This is more apparent in our language on the part of the virtue than on the part of the vice. We call chastity a species of temperance, as we say that disciplined children are chastened. And those who are not disciplined can be called unchastised. So too one who is not chaste is said to be "incestuosus" (in–castus). The reason for this transference is that sins of this kind have a certain likeness, as will be shown later (647). But which of these is named from the other does not concern us now. It is clear, however, that the thing given the name later was called after that which had the name earlier.

644. Next [2, b], at **"This transference,"** he assigns the reason for the previous transference in accordance with the likeness of the sin of intemperance to the sins of children. First [2, b, i] in respect to the necessity of chastising or restraining; and second [2, b, ii] in respect to the manner of chastising and restraining, at "For this reason sensual desire etc." He says first that the transference of this name from one sin to another does not seem to be unsuitable because of the likeness

according to which the transferences are made. It is necessary to punish, i.e., chastise and discipline, one who strives after improper things and whose evil inclination is greatly increased—points on which sensual desire and the child are in agreement.

645. This agreement seems to be reasonable because children live especially in accord with sensual desire, since they strive most of all after pleasure, which belongs to the nature of sensual desire. The reason why they strive after pleasure will be given in the seventh book (1531). Therefore, if the child and sensual desire are not rightly restrained by reason, they come to rule and increase so that the appetite for pleasure, i.e., sensual desire, will be lord and master.

646. The reason for this is that the desire of pleasure is insatiable; indeed the more pleasure is enjoyed, the more it is desired in that pleasure itself is desirable. Hence, just as with a child and a simpleton so with sensual desire—the proper operation increases what is innate, i.e., that which is like them. If a child and a simpleton should be allowed to work according to their folly, the folly increases more in them. When a man satisfies sensual desire, it increases more in him and becomes master. This is especially true if sensual desire or pleasure is great by reason of the object, that is, things very delightful and also vehement for the man

who desires and takes pleasure. This man is so influenced by pleasures that they may impede his knowledge or reasoning. The power of thought remains more efficient, the less sensual desire can dominate.

647. Then [2, b, ii], at "For this reason sensual desire," he shows the likeness between the two sins in respect to the manner of chastising or restraining. He says that, since sensual desire and pleasure are vehement, they grow by themselves. For this reason they must be moderated, i.e., not excessive in extent or in vehemence of inclination or in number. They must not be contrary to reason in any way, especially in regard to the species of sensual desire or pleasure taken on the part of the object. That which is so disposed in the matter of sensual desires and pleasures is said to be readily obedient and chastised, i.e., corrected by reason. As a child must live according to the instructions of his tutor, so the faculty of sensual desire must be in conformity with reason. Each, i.e., reason and the tutor, aspires to the good. The concupiscent part in the temperate man is so disposed that he desires the right things, in the right way, and at the right time—as reason directs.

648. He says in conclusion that these are the things we have discussed about temperance. With this the third book ends.

BOOK IV

OTHER MORAL VIRTUES

CONTENTS

CONTENTS

LECTURE I

Liberality

ANALYTICAL OUTLINE   TEXT OF ARISTOTLE
OF ST. THOMAS   (*B.1119 b 21*)
                                         Chapter 1

I. HE EXAMINES THE MATTER OF LIBERALITY AND THE OPPOSITE VICES.

  A. He shows that liberality has to do with wealth.

    A'. He says what his intention is.   Let us next discuss liberality,

                                                           649-650

    B'. He shows the matter of liberality.

which seems to be a mean in regard to wealth. No one is praised as liberal for exploits in war, or for conduct in matters with which the temperate man is concerned, or again for pronouncing judgments. But a man is praised as liberal for his giving and taking of wealth.

    C'. He explains what he had said.

(Wealth here means whatever can be evaluated in terms of money.)
651-653

  B. He shows that there are opposite vices dealing with this matter.
    A'. He states his general intention.

Extravagance is the excess and miserliness, the defect in the use of wealth.
654

    B'. He mentions . . . we always . . . charge with miserliness people who are more diligent . . . about . . . wealth than they ought to be.

Miserliness is always attributed *30* to people who are more careful about money than they should be.   **655**

    C'. He explains in what manner extravagance may be concerned with wealth.

But the intemperate are sometimes accused of extravagance by inference,

285

for the incontinent and the intemperate are notorious as extravagant wasters. For this reason, too, they seem to be very depraved; indeed they have many vices. However, they are not properly called prodigal, for a spendthrift is a man who has acquired one *B.1120* vice, that of wasting his substance (he is ruined by his own fault). The dissipation of one's substance seems to be a kind of ruin of one's being, since a man lives by means of riches. It is in this sense that extravagance is treated here.　　**656-657**

II. HE DEFINES THEIR ACTS CONCERNED WITH THE PROPER MATTER (I.E., OF LIBERALITY AND OPPOSITE VICES).

A. . . . considering first the liberal man.

A'. He examines the act of liberality.

I. HE SHOWS WHAT THE PRINCIPAL ACT OF LIBERALITY IS.

a. He makes clear that the act of liberality is the proper use of wealth.

Things that have utility—among which are riches—can be used well or badly. And the man who possesses the virtue concerned with particular objects uses each one best. Therefore he who has the virtue dealing with wealth will use riches to the best advantage. This man is the liberal man.　　**658**

b. He explains what the use of wealth is.

The spending and distribution　*10* of wealth seem to be the use of it; the acceptance and saving of wealth more properly are the possession.　　**659**

c. He draws a conclusion.
　i. He states it.

For this reason liberality is rather the bestowal of wealth on the right persons than the acceptance of wealth from proper sources or the refusal from improper sources.　　**660**

　ii. He substantiates the conclusion by five reasons.
　　v. FIRST.

Virtue consists more in bestowing than in receiving benefits, more in performing good actions than in refraining from disgraceful ones. But it is obvious that the conferring of benefits and the performance of good deeds accompany disbursements.　　**661**

W. SECOND.

X. THIRD.

Y. FOURTH.

Z. FIFTH.

Thanks and, in a special way, praise are due the giver and not the recipient. **662**

Likewise, it is easier (not) to take from another than to give, for people prefer not to accept what belongs to others rather than give what is theirs. **663**

People who give donations are called liberal, but not so those who receive gifts even honorably—such persons are praised for justice rather than liberality; those who simply accept gifts, however, are praised very little. **664**

Of all virtuous men the liberal person is particularly loved, since he is useful because of his benefactions. **665**

COMMENTARY OF ST. THOMAS

649. Having completed the study of fortitude and temperance which deals with means preservative of human life itself, he now begins to examine other mediums which concern certain subsidiary goods and evils. First he defines the laudable mediums which are the virtues. Then [Lect. XVII], at "Shame is not properly spoken of etc." (B.1128 b 10), he defines the mediums that are not virtues but passions. On the first point he does two things. Initially, he considers the virtues that regard external things. Next [Lect. XIV], at "Some men seem to be etc." (B.1126 b 10), he considers the virtues pertaining to human actions. In regard to the first point he considers the virtues relating to riches. Second [Lect. VIII], at "Judging by the name etc." (B.1123 a 33), he considers the virtues having to do with honors. He handles the initial point in two ways. First he considers liberality. Then [Lect. VI], at "It

seems logical etc." (B.1122 a 18), he investigates magnificence.

The first point he subdivides in a twofold manner. Initially [I] he examines the matter of liberality and the opposite vices. Next [II], at "Things that have utility etc.," he defines their acts concerned with the proper matter. He discusses the initial point from two aspects. First [I, A] he shows that liberality has to do with wealth. Then [I, B], at "Extravagance is the excess etc.," he shows that there are opposite vices dealing with this matter. The first point is developed in three ways. Initially [I, A, A'] he says what his intention is. Next [A, B'], at "which seems to be a mean etc.," he shows the matter of liberality. Last [A, C'], at "Wealth here etc.," he explains what he had said.

650. After the treatise on temperance, he says first that we must take up the study of liberality because of the likeness between liberality and tem-

perance. As temperance moderates the desires of tactile pleasures, so liberality moderates the desire of acquiring or possessing external goods.

651. At "which seems" [A, B'] he defines the matter of liberality, saying that it is a certain mean in regard to wealth. This is obvious from the fact that a man is praised as liberal not in military affairs (with which fortitude is concerned), nor in tactile pleasures (temperance has to do with these), nor in judgments (which are matters for justice). But he is praised for the giving and taking, i.e., the acceptance of wealth—more in giving than in taking, as will be shown afterwards (660, 661, 665, 666, 683).

652. We must consider that something can be called the matter of moral virtue in two ways: in one way as the proximate matter (thus the passions are the matter of many moral virtues); in the other way, as the remote matter (thus the objects of the passions are called their matter). Accordingly the proximate matter of fortitude is fear and recklessness; the remote matter, the fear of death; the proximate matter of temperance is desires and pleasures but the remote matter is food, drink, and sexual acts. Hence we find that the proximate matter of liberality is desire or love of wealth, and the remote matter is wealth itself.

653. Then [A, C'], at "Wealth here," he explains what is understood by the name "wealth," saying that the term signifies everything the value of which can be computed in dollars and cents, like a horse, a coat, a house, or whatever can be evaluated in cash. The reason is that to give or take these objects is the same as to give or take wealth.

654. At "Extravagance is" [I, B] he shows in what manner there are vices contrary to liberality. Here he makes the following points. First [B, A'] he states his general intention, saying that extravagance and miserliness in the use

of wealth are denominated such by excess and defect.

655. Next [B, B'], at "Miserliness is always," he mentions particularly that we always connect or charge with miserliness people who are more diligent, i.e., solicitous, about making or keeping wealth than they ought to be.

656. Finally [B, C'], at "But the intemperate," he explains in what manner extravagance may be concerned with wealth. By extension the term "extravagance" is applied occasionally to the intemperate, for men who live riotously and dissipate their riches by overindulgence in food and sex are sometimes called spendthrifts. Hence they seem very depraved in the sense that they also possess many vices, like intemperance and extravagance. Although such men at times may be called extravagant, nevertheless they do not strictly deserve the name that is used to signify a vice consisting in inordinate waste or consumption of one's substance or riches. He proves the statement by the name "extravagance." The extravagant person is spoken of as ruined inasmuch as dissipation of his own riches, by which he ought to live, seems to destroy his existence—a thing sustained by riches.

657. This name should be predicated of a man in relation to himself because each thing receives its species and name from what pertains to it essentially. Therefore a man is truly called extravagant who dissipates his riches precisely because he does not have proper care of them. On the other hand, he who wastes his substance for some other reason, for example, intemperance, is not essentially a spendthrift but an intemperate person. It happens now and then that even the covetous and grasping waste their goods because of the influence of concupiscence. For the present then we are treating extravagance according as some squander riches themselves and do not waste them in some other way.

658. Then [II], at **"Things that have,"** he explains in what way liberality and the opposite vices function in this matter. Here he takes up two (three) points, considering first [II, A] the liberal man; next [Lect. III; II, B] the spendthrift, at "But the spendthrift etc." (B.1120 b 25); and finally [Lect. V; II, C], the miser, at "Illiberality etc." (B.1121 b 13). He treats the first point from two aspects. First [II, A, A'] he examines the act of liberality; then [Lect. II; II, A, B'], he states certain characteristics of it at "The liberal person however" (B.1120 b 5). He discusses the first point in a twofold manner. First [A', 1] he shows what the principal act of liberality is; and next [Lect. II; A', 2], what qualities this act should have, at "Since virtuous actions" (B.1120 a 23). He handles the initial point under two headings. First [1, a] he makes clear that the act of liberality is the proper use of wealth, by the following argument. Whatever has any utility can be used well or badly. But riches are sought because they have some utility. Therefore they can be used well or badly. Now the proper use of things pertains to that virtue which deals with those things. Consequently, the proper use of wealth belongs to liberality, which is concerned with wealth, as we proved before (651-653).

659. Next [1, b], at **"The spending,"** he explains what the use of wealth is, indicating that it consists in spending which takes place by disbursements and gifts. To accept or save wealth is not to use it, for acceptance brings about possession, and saving is the preservation of wealth; acceptance is a kind of production, and saving is an habitual retention. Use, however, does not signify production or habit but act.

660. Finally [1, c], at **"For this reason,"** he draws a conclusion from what has been said. First [c, i] he states it, inferring from the premises that it is more characteristic of a liberal man to distribute wealth to the right persons than to accept wealth from the proper sources (this pertains to a lawful increase of wealth), and to refuse wealth from improper sources (this pertains to removal of the contrary).

661. Then [c, ii], at **"Virtue consists,"** he substantiates the conclusion by five reasons. The first reason [ii, v] is that it is more characteristic of virtue to bestow than to receive benefits because the act of benefitting is better and more difficult. Likewise, it is more characteristic of virtue to perform a good action than to refrain from an evil one, because departure from a terminus is the principle of motion to which the avoidance of an evil action is likened. But the performance of a good action is likened to the arrival at the goal which perfects motion. It is obvious when someone gives gifts that he bestows a benefit and performs a good action. On the other hand, it pertains to taking or acceptance to receive benefits worthily (inasmuch as a man acquires them from proper sources), and not to act unworthily (inasmuch as a man refuses them from improper sources). Consequently, it belongs to the virtue of liberality to give well rather than to receive worthily or refrain from reprehensible acceptance of gifts.

662. The second reason [ii, w], at **"Thanks and,"** follows. Praise and thanks are due in return for a good act. But each one of these is ascribed with better reason to the giver than the receiver, worthy or unworthy. Therefore, the virtue of liberality consists rather in giving than receiving.

663. The third reason is presented at **"Likewise it is easier"** [ii, x]. Virtue is concerned with the difficult. But it is easier not to receive what belongs to others than to give what is one's own because a person giving what is his

cuts himself away, so to speak, from what was a part of him. Therefore, the virtue of liberality more properly has to do with giving than receiving.

664. The fourth reason, beginning at "People who" [ii, y], is taken from common usage. Men who give gifts are said to be liberal in a marked degree; those who do not accept dishonest gifts are commended not so much for liberality as justice, and those who simply accept presents are praised very little. Therefore, the virtue of liberality seems to be concerned in a special way with giving gifts.

665. The fifth reason is given at "Of all virtuous men" [ii, z]. Among all virtuous men the liberal person is especially loved not by an honorable friendship—as if liberality was a most excellent virtue—but by a friendship of utility precisely as he is useful to others. The liberal are indeed useful in this that they make disbursements. Therefore, liberality deals especially with giving gifts.

LECTURE II

The Act of Liberality

ANALYTICAL OUTLINE
OF ST. THOMAS

TEXT OF ARISTOTLE
(*B.1120 a 23*)
Chapter 1

(II, A, A')2. HE SHOWS WHAT ITS QUALITIES (OF THE PRINCIPAL ACT OF LIBER-
ALITY) SHOULD BE.

a. He explains the quality of the principal act.
  *i. What should be the quality of
giving . . .*
    X. THE GIVING OF THE LIBERAL
    MAN SHOULD BE ENDOWED WITH
    CIRCUMSTANCES . . .

Since virtuous actions are good both
in themselves and in their intent, the
liberal man will give with a good intention and in the right circumstances.
He will make gifts to the proper persons, at the opportune time, of whatever gifts are fitting and with all the
requisites of reasonable giving.   **666**

    Y. THE GIVING OF A LIBERAL PER-
    SON SHOULD BE ENJOYABLE.

Besides, he will give with pleasure
and without sadness, for a virtuous
action is pleasurable and either not sad
at all or in a very slight degree.   **667**

  *ii. The other kinds of donations do
not pertain to liberality.*
    X. ONE WHO GIVES TO THE WRONG
    PERSONS . . . IS NOT CALLED
    LIBERAL.

The man, however, who gives to
the wrong persons, or not with the
right intention, but for some other
cause will be called not liberal but by
some other name.   **668**

    Y. A MAN WHO GIVES WITH SAD-
    NESS IS NOT LIBERAL.

Nor will anyone be called liberal *30*
who gives with sadness, for he would
choose money rather than the generous
deed. Such a one surely is not liberal.
  669

b. (He explains) the qualities of the
secondary acts.
  *i. What the liberal person avoids in
accepting.*

Nor will a liberal man accept a gift
from an improper source, since an accepting of this sort is not characteristic
of one who does not pay homage to
wealth. And certainly he will not be

inclined to seek favors, for it is not the usual thing that a man who bestows benefactions readily accepts them.   670

ii. What (the liberal man) should observe.

He will take from the proper *b* sources, i.e., from his own possessions, for money is not good itself but necessary that he may have something to give. He will not give to everyone so that he can give to the right persons when and where it is fitting.   671

B'. He states four properties of liberality.

I. IT PERTAINS TO THE LIBERAL PERSON TO GIVE EAGERLY AND GENEROUSLY.

The liberal person, however, is characteristically eager to be generous, keeping things of lesser value for his own use, for he is not solicitous about himself.   672

2. LIBERALITY IS ATTRIBUTED ACCORDING TO THE . . . QUANTITY OF A MAN'S SUBSTANCE.

Liberality makes allowance for the amount of one's wealth, since the liberal deed does not lie in the number of gifts but in the condition of the *10* giver who gives according to his means. Nothing hinders the smaller donor from being more liberal, if he contributes from more limited resources.   673

3. PEOPLE WHO INHERIT RICHES . . . ARE MORE LIBERAL THAN THOSE WHO ACQUIRE THEM BY THEIR OWN LABOR.

People who inherit wealth—not having any experience of need—are more liberal than those who earn their money. All men esteem more highly what they themselves have produced, like parents and poets.   674

4. THE FOURTH PROPERTY.

a. He indicates the property.

It is not easy to increase the wealth of the liberal man who is inclined neither to accept nor keep riches but rather to distribute them, placing value not on riches themselves but on the bestowal of them.   675

b. He makes clear . . . what he had said.

Men bring the accusation against fortune that those who deserve wealth

most do not become rich—a fact that
has a reasonable explanation. Here
(and the same is true in other matters)
it is not possible for a person to possess
money who does not trouble himself
about it.   676

c. He excludes a false opinion.

The liberal man, however, will 20
not give to the wrong persons, nor at
the wrong time, nor in any other
wrong manner, for he would not be
directed to these things according to
liberality. Besides, by this squandering
he would be without the resources on
which to draw. As has been explained,
the liberal man then spends according
to his means and in the way he ought.
                                              677

COMMENTARY OF ST. THOMAS

666. After the Philosopher has made
clear what the principal act of liberality
is, he now [(II, A, A′)2] shows what
its qualities should be. First [2, a] he
explains the quality of the principal act;
and next [2, b] the qualities of the
secondary acts, at "Nor will a liberal
man accept." In regard to the initial
point he does two things. First [a, i]
he shows what should be the quality
of giving which is the principal act of
liberality. Then [a, ii] he shows that
other kinds of donations do not pertain to liberality, at "The man, however, etc." He treats the first point in
a twofold manner. First [i, x] he explains that the giving of the liberal
man should be endowed with circumstances because all virtuous operations
ought to be good, directed by reason
according to the required circumstances
and ordered to a good end. Since, then,
giving is the principal act of liberality,
it follows that the liberal man should
give with rectitude of intention and of
deed, i.e., in conformity with the norm

of reason. This means that he bestows
on the proper person, in a fitting manner and according to all other requisite
circumstances called for by right reason.

667. Next [i, y], at "Besides, he will
give with pleasure," he shows that the
giving of a liberal person should be
enjoyable. This is what he means saying that the liberal man gives cheerfully, or at least without sadness. It
is true of any virtue, as evident in
previous discussions (265-279, 371-
378), that virtuous action is either
pleasurable or at least without sadness. If the virtuous man has some
sadness mingled with his activity, it
will be very slight compared with what
other men suffer. This was said before
in regard to the brave man who, even
if he does not take much pleasure in
his operation, nevertheless is not made
sad or at least has less sadness than
anyone who undergoes trials of this
kind in his activities.

668. Then [a, ii], at "The man,

however," he brings out that other donations do not pertain to the liberal man. First [ii, x] he says—speaking of disbursements that lack the proper circumstances—that one who gives to the wrong persons, or not for an honorable motive but for some other reason, good or bad, is not called liberal. But he is given a different name according to the difference of the end for which he gives, since moral matters take their species and name from the end.

669. Second [ii, y], at "Nor will anyone," he affirms that a man who gives with sadness is not liberal. The reason is that the cheerless giver seems to prefer wealth to the virtuous action of honorable giving—which is not the case with a liberal person.

670. Next [2, b], at "Nor will a liberal man accept," he explains the nature of the secondary acts of liberality like receiving and so on. Here he makes two points, showing first [b, i] what the liberal person avoids in accepting; and then [b, ii] what he should observe, at "He will take etc." On the first point he makes two comments. The first is that the liberal man does not take from improper sources, for to take in this way does not seem becoming to a man who does not highly prize wealth. The second is that the liberal man is not quick to make requests. As in the natural order, what is greatly active has little receptivity, for example, fire, so in the moral order the liberal person, who is prompt in making benefactions, is not eager to accept benefits from others, i.e., to be easily receptive.

671. Then [b, ii], at "He will take," Aristotle shows what the liberal man should observe in taking and retaining. He makes three observations, of which the first is that the liberal man takes from the proper sources, i.e., from his own possessions and not from others, since he seeks wealth not as a good itself but as something necessary for making gifts. The second is that he

does not neglect the care of his own goods because he wants to have enough to bestow on others. The third is that he does not give to everyone but holds back so he can give to the right persons at a fitting place and time.

672. Then [B'], at "The liberal person," he states four properties of liberality. The first [B', 1] is that it pertains to the liberal person to give eagerly and generously, not however without right reason but in such a way that what he gives is more than what he retains, because he keeps less for himself than he gives to others. He is indeed content with a few things for himself but if he wants to care for many people, he must distribute much more. It is not a mark of the generous man to have himself alone in mind.

673. At "Liberality makes allowance," he gives the second property [B', 2], saying that liberality is attributed according to the relative quantity of a man's substance or riches. Hence there is no reason why someone who bestows smaller gifts may not be judged more liberal, if he gives from more moderate means.

674. He presents the third property at "People who inherit" [B', 3], affirming that persons who inherit riches from their parents are more liberal than those who acquire them by their own labor. He assigns two reasons for this. The first is that people who are given wealth by their parents have never felt the pinch of need. Consequently, they are not afraid to spend, as those are who have experienced poverty at one time. The second reason is that all men naturally love their own works; parents love their children, and poets, their poems. Likewise, those who acquire riches by their labor look upon them as their own works and rather desire to keep them.

675. He presents the fourth property at "It is not easy" [B', 4]. He considers this point under three aspects.

First [4, a] he indicates the property, saying that the liberal man is not easily made rich, since he is not disposed to accept or keep riches but rather to distribute them in gifts and disbursements. Nor does he value riches for themselves but for their distribution.

676. Next [4, b], at "Men bring the accusation," he makes clear by a certain sign what he had said. Since the liberal do not readily become wealthy, the common people blame fortune—to which they attribute riches—because those who would be especially deserving (i.e., the liberal who give generously to others) are not rich. But Aristotle says that this is not an unreasonable occurrence, for it is not possible that a person should possess wealth who troubles himself very little about it, just as it is not possible that

anything else which a man does not care for should be retained.

677. Finally [4, c] he excludes a false opinion at "The liberal man, however, will not." It was not said that the liberal man does not care about riches because he gives to the wrong person, or at the wrong time, or in the wrong manner according to some other circumstance. The reason is both that such an operation would not be liberal and that the liberal person would be hindered in this way from truly generous action, for by reason of useless waste he would lack the means to make the most worthy disbursements. As has been explained (658-659), he is called liberal, then, who gives donations in the proper manner and according to the condition of his own resources.

LECTURE III

Extravagance

ANALYTICAL OUTLINE
OF ST. THOMAS

TEXT OF ARISTOTLE
(*B.1120 b 25*)
Chapter 1

(II)B. He begins the consideration of the spendthrift.

A'. He treats the person who is altogether extravagant.

1. HE CONSIDERS THE SPENDTHRIFT AS SUCH.

a. In what respect the spendthrift is excessive.

But the spendthrift is a man who squanders. Hence we do not call tyrants spendthrifts, for it is not easy to be excessive in gifts and expenditures with a vast sum of money in their possession.   678

b. Of what nature (the spendthrift's) act is.
   i. He . . . resumes what was said about the act of the liberal man.
   X. HOW THE LIBERAL MAN SHOULD CONDUCT HIMSELF IN MATTERS PRINCIPALLY PERTAINING TO HIM.

Since liberality is the mean concerned with the giving and taking of wealth, the liberal man will both give and expend whatever he ought *30* and in the way he ought, whether the sum be large or small. He will also do this gladly.   679

   Y. IN MATTERS SECONDARILY PERTAINING TO HIM.
   aa. The liberal man's reaction to taking.

Likewise he will accept both large and small amounts from the proper sources and under the proper conditions. Since virtue consists in the mean regarding both (taking and giving), he will do both as he ought because virtuous taking goes hand in hand with virtuous giving, while improper taking is contrary to virtuous giving. Accordingly, the operations that go hand in hand exist at the same time in the liberal man, but contrary operations obviously cannot.   680

bb. (The liberal man's reaction) to sadness.

    a'. . . . Saddened by disordered giving.

If it should happen that he **B.1121** spends inopportunely and unsuccessfully, he will be sad but in a moderate and fitting manner, for it is characteristic of virtue to be pleased and saddened at the proper things and in the proper circumstances. **681**

    b'. . . . By the privation of wealth.

But the liberal man is disposed to share his wealth with others. He is even willing to suffer loss by not valuing money highly. **682**

    c'. . . . Is grieved at inappropriate retention of money.

He is more grieved over failure to make an appropriate outlay than over an inopportune expenditure—a thing displeasing to Simonides. **683**

ii. How the act of the spendthrift is constituted.

The spendthrift, however, sins in these matters too. Besides, he neither takes pleasure in the right things, nor is saddened when he should be. This will be clarified by what follows. **684**

2. HE MAKES A COMPARISON BETWEEN THE SPENDTHRIFT AND THE MISER.

a. . . . In regard, first to opposition.

We have seen that extravagance and miserliness pertain to excess and defect, and occur in two actions, **10** namely, giving and taking. Extravagance then abounds in giving and falls short in taking. On the other hand, miserliness falls short in giving and abounds in taking, except in trifling things. **685**

COMMENTARY OF ST. THOMAS

678. After the Philosopher has finished the study of the liberal man, he now [(II)B] begins the consideration of the spendthrift. First [A'] he treats the person who is altogether extravagant; and next [Lect. IV, B'] the person who is partly extravagant and partly liberal at "But, as we have noted etc." (B.1121 a 30). In regard to the first, he does two things. Initially [1]

he considers the spendthrift as such. Then [2] he makes a comparison between the spendthrift and the miser, at "We have seen etc." He clarifies the initial point by a twofold distinction. First [1, a] he shows in what respect the spendthrift is excessive; and next [1, b], of what nature his act is, at "Since liberality is the mean etc." Although a man may be called liberal when he spends according to his means, he is called extravagant when he spends or gives beyond his means. From this he concludes that tyrants, who have an inexhaustible supply of wealth—usurping as they do public goods for themselves—are not called extravagant. The reason is that it is not easy for tyrants to exceed the amount of their riches by donations and expenditures because of the great amount of their possessions.

679. Then [1, b], at **"Since liberality,"** he discloses what the act of the spendthrift is. Because opposites are mutually revealing, he first [b, i] resumes what was said about the act of the liberal man. Next [b, ii], he shows how the act of the spendthrift is constituted, at "The spendthrift, however, etc." On the first point he proceeds in two ways. First [i, x] he reviews how the liberal man should conduct himself in the matters principally pertaining to him, i.e., in giving and in the pleasure of giving; and next [i, y] in matters secondarily pertaining to him, at "Likewise he will accept." He says first that, since liberality is a certain dealing with giving and taking of wealth, the liberal person disposes of his funds by making gifts and disbursements—and this in agreement with right reason—in the proper way, of the proper things, and according to other appropriate circumstances. By this the liberal man is distinguished from the spendthrift; by the fact that he gives both in large and small amounts he is distinguished from the munificent man, who is concerned only with great donations; by the fact that he gives with pleasure he differs from the miser who is saddened by the giving away of his wealth.

680. Next [i, y], at **"Likewise he will accept,"** Aristotle reviews the way the liberal man should act in matters which secondarily pertain to liberality. He touches first [y, aa] on the liberal man's reaction to taking; and next

[y, bb], to sadness at "If it should etc." He says first that the liberal person accepts from the proper sources and observes all proper conditions. Since the virtue of liberality abides by the golden mean in regard to both, i.e., taking and giving, the liberal man will perform both as he ought—worthy acceptance going hand in hand with worthy giving. But acceptance that is not virtuous is contrary to virtuous giving because the two proceed from contrary causes. Virtuous giving proceeds from the fact that a man prefers the reasonable good to the desire for wealth. But dishonorable taking arises from placing the desire of wealth before the reasonable good. Things that go hand in hand exist at the same time in the same subject, but not things that are contrary. Hence virtuous giving and taking that accompany one another are united in the liberal person, but dishonorable taking is not found in him together with virtuous taking, its contrary.

681. Then [y, bb], at **"If it should,"** he explains how the liberal man reacts to sadness arising from the loss of wealth. He develops this point in three steps. First [bb, a'] he shows in what manner the liberal person is saddened by disordered giving, affirming that if some of his own money be lost by reason of foolish spending and unfortunate conditions, he becomes sad as any virtuous man is saddened by doing something contrary to virtue. In this sorrow, however, he observes the rule of reason with moderation and as he should. The reason is that it is characteristic of the virtuous person to be delighted and to be saddened by the right thing and in the right manner.

682. Next [bb, b'], at **"But the liberal man,"** he shows how the generous person is saddened by the privation of wealth, saying that he is disposed to share his wealth, i.e., is inclined to

possess it in common, as it were, with others. He can, without grief, permit someone to injure him in money matters because he does not attach great importance to wealth.

683. Third [bb, c'], at **"He is more grieved,"** he discloses in what manner the liberal man is grieved at inappropriate retention of money, explaining that he is more grieved or saddened over not using his wealth in gifts or expenditures than over spending something which he should not have spent. The reason is that he is more concerned with giving than taking and keeping, although this would not please Simonides, a certain poet, who said we ought to do the opposite.

684. Then [b, ii], at **"The spendthrift, however,"** he explains by the premises how the act of the spendthrift is constituted, saying that the spendthrift sins in all the preceding matters, i.e., not only in giving and accepting but also in taking pleasure and grieving because he is neither delighted nor saddened by the right things and in the right way. This will be made clearer by what follows.

685. Next [2], at **"We have seen,"** he compares extravagance to miserliness in regard, first [2, a] to opposition; and second [Lect. IV, (A', 2), b] to the gravity of the sin, at "The things that" (B.1121 a 16). He affirms, as was noted before (654), that extravagance and miserliness are constituted by excess and defect in two things, viz., taking and giving. He says this because expenditures, which pertain to liberality, are included under giving. And it is precisely in expenditures that the spendthrift and the miser exceed and fall short in opposite things. The spendthrift is excessive in giving and in not taking. But the miser, on the contrary, is deficient in giving and excessive in taking, except perhaps in trifling things that he gives and does not care to take.

LECTURE IV

The Gravity of Extravagance

ANALYTICAL OUTLINE OF ST. THOMAS	TEXT OF ARISTOTLE (*B.1121 a 16*) Chapter 1
b. He shows that miserliness is the more serious fault for three reasons. *i. The first reason is taken from the mutability of extravagance.*	The things that are proper to extravagance are not increased very much at the same time, because a man cannot easily take nothing and at the same time give with an open hand to everyone. A generous simpleton—such the spendthrift seems to be—is soon separated from his money. A person of this sort, though, is somewhat *20* better than the miser, for he is quickly set right both by age and want. **686-687**
ii. The second reason . . . based on the likeness of extravagance to liberality.	He can attain the mean of virtue, for he possesses qualities of the liberal person. He gives and does not take, although he does neither of these things properly and as he ought. If indeed he performs them out of custom or by reason of some change, he will become liberal, for he will then give to the right persons and not take from the wrong sources. For this reason he does not seem to be entirely evil in the moral sense, for it is not characteristic of an evil or vicious person, but of a foolish one, to give excessively and not to take. **688-689**
iii. The third reason taken from a defect in extravagance.	In this way the spendthrift seems to be much better than the miser because of what has been said and because he benefits many people while the miser benefits no one, not even himself. **690**

(II)B'. He considers the man who is a blend of spendthrift and miser.

1. HE SHOWS IN WHAT MANNER SOME SPENDTHRIFTS HAVE A BIT OF ILLIBERALITY.

a. He . . . explains how some spend-thrifts sin in taking.

i. He presents his proposition.

But, as we have noted, many 30 spendthrifts take from tainted sources and in this way they are ungenerous. **691**

ii. He assigns two reasons.

They are inclined to take because they want to spend. But they cannot readily take enough, for their resources quickly vanish forcing them to acquire from others. Likewise they care *b* nothing about what is right, and take from any quarter whatsoever. They want to give presents, so the how and the whence make no immediate difference to them. **692-693**

b. How (spendthrifts) conduct themselves in giving.

For these reasons their donations are not liberal, being good neither in motive nor mode. But they make rich those who would better remain poor. They would give nothing to good men, yet are generous with flatterers and others who provide them with other pleasures. **694**

2. HE DRAWS SOME CONCLUSIONS.

a. The first is . . . many spendthrifts are intemperate.

Therefore, many of them are intemperate, for being inclined to spend, they waste their resources by in- 10 temperance. Moreover, since they do not order their life to good, they turn aside to sensual pleasures. **695**

b. He draws the second conclusion.

The spendthrift then who will not learn (the way of virtue) suffers consequences. But with effort he may attain the mean and adopt the right attitude. **696**

COMMENTARY OF ST. THOMAS

686. After the Philosopher has explained the opposition between extravagance and miserliness, he now

shows [b] that miserliness is the more serious fault for three reasons. The first reason [b, i] is taken from the mutability of extravagance: although not readily increased it is easily eliminated. Hence he says that the things belonging to extravagance cannot at the same time be increased very much, so that a person takes nothing and gives to everyone because resources or riches are quickly exhausted for those who spend recklessly, like the simple and senseless. And spendthrifts seem to be of this type. Since then a vice, which is not increased very much but easily remedied, is not so serious, it follows that the spendthrift is somewhat better, i.e., less evil than the miser.

687. The spendthrift is easily cured of his vice in two ways. In the first way by age because the older a man grows the more inclined he is to keep things and not give them away. The reason is that riches are desired to supply the needs of man, and as these needs become greater so a man is more prone to husband and not hand out his wealth. Second, the spendthrift is cured by poverty resulting from excessive giving, for poverty prevents extravagant spending both by reason of the impossibility of further giving and the experience of need.

688. At "He can attain" [b, ii] he gives the second reason, which is based on the likeness of extravagance to liberality. Hence he says that the spendthrift can easily be directed to the mean of virtue on account of the similarity he has with the liberal man. Since the spendthrift generously gives and does not readily take, he has qualities possessed by the liberal person. But he differs from the liberal man in not doing either of these actions properly and as he ought, i.e., according to right reason. Therefore, if he is induced to perform these things as he ought, either by custom or by some change in age or fortune he will become liberal so that he will give to the right persons and not take from the wrong sources.

689. He concludes from this that the spendthrift does not seem to be evil precisely as it pertains to moral virtue, which directly regards the power of the appetite. It is not characteristic of an evil or perverted appetite or of an effeminate mind to give excessively and not to take. This belongs rather to a kind of stupidity. Thus it seems that extravagance does not belong so much to moral depravity, which regards the inclination of the appetite to evil, as to a lack of common sense.

690. At "In this way" [b, iii] he presents the third reason taken from a defect in extravagance. That the spendthrift is much better than the miser is apparent not only from the two reasons already stated but also from a third, namely, the spendthrift helps many by his giving, although he may hurt himself by giving extravagantly. The miser, on the other hand, benefits no one for he fails in giving; he does not benefit even himself, for he fails in spending.

691. Then [II, B'], at "But, as we have noted," he considers the man who is a blend of spendthrift and miser. First [1] he shows in what manner some spendthrifts have a bit of illiberality. Next [2] he draws some conclusions from what has been said, at "Therefore." On the initial point he first [1, a] explains how some spendthrifts sin in taking; and then [1, b] how they conduct themselves in giving, at "For these reasons." In regard to this first, he presents his proposition [a, i], saying that many who are extravagant in unnecessary donations are also ungenerous in some way, taking as they do from the wrong sources.

692. Next [a, ii], at "They are inclined," he assigns two reasons. The first is that spendthrifts are disposed to take because they want to spend their goods in superfluous gifts and expenditures. They readily succeed in this, for their resources are quickly

depleted. Hence, in order that they may satisfy their desire regarding unnecessary gifts and disbursements, they are forced to acquire dishonestly from some other place the means they do not possess.

693. The second reason is that they give rather out of a desire of giving than according to right reason, tending, as it were, to some good. They want to give presents but it makes no difference to them how or whence these come. Consequently, they do not concern themselves about what is right and so take from any source without distinction.

694. Then [1, b], at "For these reasons," he explains how spendthrifts may be at fault in making donations. He declares that, because they do not care about what is right, their gifts are neither liberal nor good, either in motive or circumstance. But sometimes they make rich evil men who would be better off poor—men who abuse their riches and thereby cause harm both to themselves and others. Yet they would give nothing to men who regulate their lives according to virtue. Thus they are deficient in giving. They are, however, generous with sycophants or others who give them

pleasure in any way whatsoever, e.g., buffoons or panderers. In this way they go to excess in giving.

695. Next [2], at "Therefore," he draws two conclusions from the premises. The first [2, a] is that many spendthrifts are intemperate. This is evident first, because (being inclined to spend), they readily waste their substance by intemperance in food and sex, from which many people are restrained by fear of the cost. Second, because they do not order their life to an honorable good, consequently they turn aside to the pleasures of sense. These two (the honorable and the pleasurable) are desirable in themselves—the honorable according to rational desire, the pleasurable according to sensual desire. The useful refers to both.

696. He draws the second conclusion [2, b], at "The spendthrift," pointing out what is clear from the premises: that if the spendthrift cannot be attracted to virtue, he falls into the previously mentioned vices. But if he possesses zeal for virtue, he will easily attain the mean so that he will give and refrain from taking according to what he ought, as was stated before (688).

LECTURE V

The Incurableness of Illiberality

ANALYTICAL OUTLINE
OF ST. THOMAS

TEXT OF ARISTOTLE
(*B.1121 b 13*)
Chapter 1

(II)C. He treats illiberality.

A'. He states a quality of illiberality.

> Illiberality, however, is incurable for it seems that old age and every other disability make men miserly. Besides, it is more innate to men than extravagance because more men are lovers of wealth than donors of it.   **697-698**

B'. He distinguishes the . . . species of illiberality.

I. HE SHOWS THAT ILLIBERALITY IS CONSIDERED FROM TWO ASPECTS.

> Likewise illiberality can greatly increase, and is very diversified since many species of it seem to exist. It is made up of two elements, namely, deficient giving and needless grasping, which are sometimes found separately and not always together in all *20* subjects. Some indeed are always getting and others never giving.   **699**

2. HE GIVES THE SPECIES . . . ACCORDING TO DEFICIENCY IN GIVING.

> All those who are given names like stingy, grasping, close, fall short in giving. But they do not covet the goods of others, nor do they want to acquire them. With some this is due to a kind of moderation and fear of disgrace. They seem to be, or say that they are, careful about this in order not to be forced at times to do anything dishonorable. Among these are the cumin-splitter and anyone of the type designated before by reason of an excessive desire of not giving to anyone. Some

again refrain from what is not theirs
for fear that their taking of what   *30*
belongs to others should make it easy
for others to take what is theirs. Therefore, they are content neither to give
nor to take.   **700-702**

3. HE GIVES THE SPECIES . . . ACCORDING TO UNNECESSARY TAKING.

a. Those who take in a disgraceful
way.

Others again are immoderate in their
taking by accepting anything and from
any quarter, for example, those who
engage in disreputable enterprises,
those who live from the proceeds of
prostitution, and such like, and usurers
who lend small sums and at *B.1122*
high rates. All of these receive more
than they should and from reprehensible sources. Common to them is sordid
gain because they all become infamous
for the sake of a little money. People
who wrongly take great sums from
wrong sources are not called illiberal,
for instance, usurpers who plunder
cities and despoil sacred places but
rather wicked, impious, and unjust.
                                    703

b. . . . Who take in an unjust way.

Among the illiberal, however, we
count the gambler, the despoiler of
the dead and the robber—shameful
profit-makers. For the sake of evil
gain, these engage in occupations   *10*
having the stamp of infamy. Some run
the risk of very great danger for gain,
while others would take from friends
to whom they should give. In both
cases, those wishing to enrich themselves are makers of shameful profit.
It is clear then that all taking of this
kind is opposed to liberality.   **704**

C'. He makes a comparison of illiberality with its opposite.

Appropriately then illiberality is said
to be the vice opposed to liberality, for
it is a graver evil than extravagance.
Likewise men sin more by illiberality
than by extravagance. So far, therefore, we have discussed liberality and
the opposite vices.   **705-706**

COMMENTARY OF ST. THOMAS

697. After the Philosopher has finished the treatise on extravagance, he now [(II)C] treats illiberality, examining it under three headings. First [A'] he states a quality of illiberality. Next [B'], he distinguishes the modes, i.e., the species of illiberality, at "Likewise etc." Last [C'], he makes a comparison of illiberality with its opposite at "Appropriately then etc." He says first that illiberality is incurable, and assigns two reasons for this. The first reason is that human life, and even earthly things, tend to be defective for the most part. It is obvious from experience that old age and every other disability or defect make a man parsimonious, because it seems to him that he is very much in need. Therefore, he has a great desire for external things that supply the wants of man.

698. The second reason is this. That to which man is naturally inclined cannot easily be removed from him. But man is more inclined to illiberality than extravagance. A sign of this is that more lovers and custodians of money exist than donors. What is natural is found in the majority of cases. And nature inclines to the love of riches to the extent that man's life is preserved by them.

699. Then [B'], at "Likewise," he distinguishes the modes or species of illiberality. On this point he does three things. First [1] he shows that illiberality is considered from two aspects, viz., excess in getting and defect in giving. Next [2], at "All those who," he gives the species which are understood according to deficiency in giving. Last [3], at "Others again," he gives the species that are able to be distinguished according to unnecessary tak-

ing. He says first that illiberality is increased greatly; it extends to a multitude of things and is diversified inasmuch as there are many kinds of illiberality. Although illiberality may exist in two forms, defect of giving and excess of taking, not all illiberal people sin in both ways as though they possessed the whole nature of illiberality. But it is found separately in various persons so that some abound in taking who nevertheless do not fall short in dispensing, like the spendthrift previously considered (678). Others, however, fall short in dispensing and, notwithstanding, do not abound in taking.

700. Next [2], at "All those who," he sets down the types of persons who are deficient in giving. He says that some are called stingy who spend very little; others are called grasping who retain nearly everything from a defect in giving. Still others are called closefisted, or cumin-splitters from an excessive tenacity they manifest in refusing to give the smallest thing without a return. However, these are not excessive in taking because they do not covet the goods of others, nor do they care much about accepting gifts. This happens for two reasons.

701. The first reason is that they pass up these opportunities out of moral consideration and fear of turpitude. They seem to keep what is theirs—they even say so expressly—lest, if they give what they have, they may be forced sometimes to a shameful act because of need. Likewise, they are unwilling to accept the goods of others since they think it dishonorable. They even hesitate lest they be induced to something unseemly by those who gave to them.

Among these seem to be the skinflint or the cumin-splitter, so named because he has an aversion to giving anyone even a tiny seed. The same reason holds in all similar cases.

702. The second reason is that some refrain from taking other people's goods because they fear they may have to give, as if it were not easy for men to take the things that belong to others and others not to take the things which are theirs. On this account they are content neither to give nor to take.

703. Then [3], at "Others again," he mentions the species of illiberality in regard first [3, a], to those who take in a disgraceful way; and next [3, b], who take in an unjust way, at "Among the illiberal." He says first that certain illiberal persons are immoderate in taking, not caring what or whence they take or profit. Some benefit from cheap and servile operations. Others, like pimps, make profit from sordid and unlawful dealing, e.g., prostitution and the like. Still others enrich themselves by unjust exaction, for instance, usurers and those who want at least a little gain from a large gift or loan. All these receive from reprehensible sources, i.e., mean or shameful works, or they receive more than they should, like usurers who take more than the interest. All have profit, and this paltry, in common. Those who make enormous profits, and make them by shameful means—they are considered disgraceful for this reason —are not called illiberal but rather wicked, unjust, and impious against God, as if they were criminals. Men of this caliber are not so designated even though they take when they ought not and what they ought not, for example, usurpers who despoil cities and temples.

704. Next [3, b], at "Among the illiberal," he mentions those who take

unjustly, like the gambler who makes money by throwing dice, the fellow who steals from the dead (formerly buried in rich apparel), and the robber who plunders the living. All these are enriched by shameful means, inasmuch as, for the sake of gain, they engage in certain occupations considered disgraceful. This agrees with what was said about those persons just mentioned (703). But in these there is a special reason for turpitude. Some, for example, the despoiler of the dead and the robber expose themselves to great danger in doing things punishable by law. Others, namely, gamblers want to take something from their friends with whom they play, although it is more appropriate to liberality to give something to friends. It is obvious then that both types, by wanting to enrich themselves from improper sources, are makers of shameful profits. It is necessary, therefore, to say that all the previously mentioned taking or accepting is opposed to liberality.

705. Then [C'], at "Appropriately then," he explains illiberality by comparison with the opposite vice, saying that illiberality is fittingly named from the contrast with liberality. It always happens that the worse vice is more opposed to the virtue. But illiberality is worse than extravagance, as was shown before (686-690). Consequently, it remains that illiberality is more opposed to liberality. The second reason is that men commit graver sins by the vice of illiberality than by the vice of extravagance. Therefore, illiberality gets its name from the privation of liberality because liberality is frequently destroyed by this vice.

706. Lastly, he sums up what has been said, stating that so far we have discussed liberality and the opposite vices.

LECTURE VI

Magnificence

ANALYTICAL OUTLINE   TEXT OF ARISTOTLE
OF ST. THOMAS   (*B.1122 a 19*)
                                       Chapter 2

I. HE TREATS THE MATTER OF MAGNIFICENCE AND THE OPPOSITE VICES.

   A. He shows what the matter of magnificence is.

   A'. He proposes the matter common to magnificence and liberality.

> It seems logical to pass now to the consideration of magnificence which apparently is a certain virtue con- *20* cerned with wealth. **707**

   B'. He explains the difference between the two.

      I. HE PROPOSES THE DIFFERENCE.

> Unlike liberality it does not embrace all but only lavish expenditures of money; it is in wealth's magnitude (as the name itself indicates) that magnificence exceeds liberality, although the amount expended is not out of proportion. **708**

      2. HE MAKES CLEAR WHAT HE SAID.

> But magnitude is a relative term, for the same expenditure is not fit for a captain of a trireme and a leader of a solemn mission to Delphi; it is fitting according to the spender, the thing, and the purpose. **709**

   C'. He proves his proposition.

> The man, however, who spends small or moderate sums in a becoming manner is not called munificent, for instance, if he makes frequent donations **that in the aggregate** are large; only he who gives on a grand scale. The munificent man is indeed liberal, but *30*

> one who is liberal and nothing more
> is not munificent.   **710**

B. (He shows) what the vices opposed to it are.

> In this matter the habit of defect is
> called meanness, and of excess *banausia*
> (ostentation); the name *apirocalia*
> (lack of taste) is given to all other
> such defects that are not excessive in
> the sums expended on the right projects
> but in the wrong circumstances and
> with a certain vulgar display. We shall
> discuss these vices afterwards.   **711**

II. HE EXPLAINS IN WHAT MANNER MAGNIFICENCE AND THE OPPOSITE VICES OPERATE.

A. . . . Magnificence.

A'. He assigns to the munificent man certain qualities pertaining to the manner of spending.

1. HE ATTRIBUTES . . . SIX QUALITIES: THE FIRST . . .

> A munificent person is like a wise
> man, for he can judge rightly and *b*
> spend great sums prudently. (As we
> said in the beginning,[1] habit is deter-
> mined by operations and is a product
> of them.) He makes great and digni-
> fied expenditures, and the effects are of
> a like nature. Thus his expenses will
> be great and also suited to the work.
> Therefore, the work must be worth
> the cost, and the cost equal to or in
> excess of the work.   **712-713**

2. THE SECOND QUALITY . . . ON THE PART OF THE END.

> Things of this kind he spends for
> the sake of good, and this is common
> to virtues.   **714**

3. THE THIRD . . . TO SPEND GREAT SUMS CHEERFULLY.

> Furthermore, he acts cheerfully and
> open-handedly, for closeness in reckon-
> ing is niggardly.   **715**

4. THE FOURTH QUALITY.

> He plans how the best and most *10*
> splendid work may be achieved rather
> than how he may acquire as much for
> a minimum cost.   **716**

[1] Bk. II, Ch. 1, 1103 b 22 sq.

5. THE FIFTH . . . ONE WHO IS MUNIFICENT SHOULD BE LIBERAL.

Likewise the munificent man is necessarily liberal, since the liberal person makes the right expenditures in the right manner; and it is in this that the greatness of the munificent person lies—a greatness in these matters being a kind of grand liberality. 717

6. THE SIXTH QUALITY.

Besides, for the same cost he will produce a more magnificent work, for the perfection of possession and work does not reside in the same thing. But the perfect possession consists of what is most valued and honored, for example, gold. On the other hand, the perfect work consists of what is great and good, for consideration of it brings about admiration. And truly a magnificent work is a cause of admiration, and the perfection of the work, magnificence, resides in its magnitude.
718

COMMENTARY OF ST. THOMAS

707. After the Philosopher has finished the study of liberality, he now begins to consider magnificence, the treatment of which he divides into two parts. In the first part [I] he treats the matter of magnificence and the opposite vices. In the second [II] he explains in what manner magnificence and the opposite vices operate in their respective matter, at "A munificent person is like a wise man etc." On the first point he does two things. First [I, A] he shows what the matter of magnificence is; and second [I, B] what the vices opposed to it are, at "In this matter etc." To clarify the first division he does three things. First [I, A, A'] he proposes the matter common to magnificence and liberality. Next [I, A, B'] he explains the difference be-

tween the two, at "Unlike liberality etc." Last [I, A, C'], he proves his proposition, at "The man, however etc." He says first it seems appropriate that the treatise on magnificence should follow that on liberality. The reason is that magnificence, like liberality, is apparently a virtue concerned with wealth.

708. Then [I, A, B'], at "Unlike liberality," he explains the difference between the matter of magnificence and liberality. He explains this point in a twofold manner. First [I, A, B', 1] he proposes the difference. Next [I, A, B', 2] he makes clear what he said, at "But magnitude etc." Regarding the first he mentions two differences. The first is that liberality refers to all transactions concerned with money, viz.,

expenditures, receipts and donations. But magnificence refers only to disbursements or expenditures. The second difference is that in disbursements or expenditures magnificence exceeds liberality in the magnitude of the amount expended. Magnificence deals only in princely outlays, as the name implies, while liberality can be concerned also with moderate or excessive expenditures. Although magnitude indicates a kind of excess, we are not to understand that the munificent person spends on such a grand scale that he exceeds the bounds of reason, but his expenditures are made in amounts that are also in keeping with what is becoming. It is in keeping with both the one who spends and the projects on which the money is spent, as will be pointed out later (721-724).

709. Next [I, A, B′, 2], at "But magnitude," he explains what he said, i.e., the manner in which the greatness of the expense is becoming to a munificent person. Because the word "great" is predicated relatively, as stated in the *Categories* (Ch. 6, 5 b 15),[1] it is said here that the greatness of the expenditure is judged in reference to something else, for instance, the thing for which the expenditures are made or the person spending. The reason is that not the same outlay is considered large for a triarch (a commander of galleys having three rows of oars and called a trireme) and for a leader of a solemn enterprise, i.e., the chief superintendent,[1] like a master of a temple or a school. The expenditure must be suitable in comparison with the dispenser and the thing for which the money is spent. Likewise the purpose for which

the thing is used must be taken into consideration. Thus if expenses are incurred for the building of a house, we must consider further for whom the house is intended, whether for a public official or a private person, because different expenditures are demanded for different purposes.

710. Then [I, A, C′], at "The man, however," he proves his statement, i.e., that great expenditure pertains to magnificence. The reason is that one who spends small or even moderate sums in a proper manner is not called munificent, for instance, if he frequently makes many separate disbursements for trifling things, so that all his expenditures taken together would make as great an amount as that which the munificent man spends, nevertheless he would not be called munificent even though he disbursed these small sums promptly and generously. Because every munificent person is liberal, it does not follow that every liberal person is munificent.

711. At "In this matter" [I, B] he shows what vices are contrary to magnificence. He says that the vice opposed to the habit of magnificence by defect is called meanness; but the vice by excess, *banausia* (ostentation) from *baunos* meaning furnace,[1] because such as have the vice consume all their goods as in a furnace. If other terms of this kind exist, they come under the name *apirocalia* (lack of taste): offenders being, as it were, without experience of what is suitable because they do not know how to do the proper thing. Such names signify excess not because they surpass the munificent person in the amount of disbursements on the right projects, but they are excessive in going beyond right reason, spending, with a certain display, great sums on the wrong things. It is obvious from this

---

[1] *The Works of Aristotle.* Ed. by W. D. Ross, Vol. I, London: Oxford University Press, 1928.

[1] "Principem speculationis" is translated "chief superintendent." Cf. *Medieval Latin Word List,* by Charles Johnson and J. H. Baxter, London: Oxford University Press, 1934: "speculatio" is defined as "superintendence over."

[1] *Banausia* means handicraft, the work of a mechanic—from *baunos,* forge or furnace; by extension it signifies vulgarity, ostentation: makeshift work by a poor artisan.

that the mean and the extremes in moral virtues are not taken according to absolute quantity but in relation to right reason. He adds that he will discuss these vices afterwards in this book (784-791).

712. Next [II], at **"A munificent person,"** he explains in what manner magnificence and the opposite vices are concerned with the previously mentioned matter. First [II, A] he treats magnificence, and then [Lect. VII (II) B] the opposite vices, at "One who sins etc." (B.1123 a 19). On the initial point he does two things. First [II, A, A'] he assigns to the munificent man certain qualities pertaining to the manner of spending. Then [Lect. VI, (II, A), B'] he shows on what objects the munificent person makes expenditures, at "Magnificence belongs etc." (B.1122 b 19). In regard to the first he attributes to the munificent person six qualities, the first [II, A, A', 1] of which is that he is like a wise man. The reason is that, as it belongs to a wise craftsman to know the proportion of one thing to another, so also it belongs to the munificent man to know the proportion between expenditures and that for which the expenditures are made. In virtue of his habit the munificent man is able to judge what may be proper to spend. Thus he will make grand disbursements in a prudent way because prudent operation is required for every moral virtue.

713. The Philosopher clarifies the statement by what was said in the second book (322), that every habit is determined by operations and objects of which it is the habit, because determined habits have their own proper operations and objects. Since the operations of magnificence are expenditures, and the objects of the operations are the things for which the expenditures are made, it is therefore the duty of the munificent man to consider and expend large and handsome sums, which cannot be done without pru-

dence. In this way the vast outlay will be in keeping with the operation, for instance, the construction of a house or something of this sort. So then the project on which the money is spent must be such that it is worthy of the cost or expense and this ought to be worthy of the work, or in excess of it. It is very difficult to attain the mean; hence if a departure from the mean should occur, virtue always inclines to what has less evil, as the brave man to less fear, the liberal man to giving and so the munificent man to more spending.

714. He gives the second quality [II, A, A', 2], at **"Things of this kind,"** which is understood on the part of the end. The munificent person, he says, consumes grand and proper amounts for an honorable good as for an end. Now, to work for a good is common to all the virtues.

715. At **"Furthermore"** [II, A, A', 3] he presents the third consideration, saying that it is characteristic of the munificent man to spend great sums cheerfully and with an open hand, dispensing them promptly and readily. The reason is that great caution in accounting or computing expenses pertains to illiberality.

716. He introduces the fourth quality at **"He plans"** [II, A, A', 4], affirming that the munificent person plans how he may accomplish the best and most splendid work rather than how he can spend the least in doing the desired work.

717. He enumerates the fifth quality, at **"Likewise the munificent"** [II, A, A', 5] when he says that one who is munificent should be liberal. The reason is that the liberal person should make the right expenditures in the right manner. The munificent man, too, acts in this way, for he makes outlays for great and noble achievements, as was just said (708); and he does this cheerfully, generously, and

for a good purpose. But it is characteristic of the munificent person to do something on a grand scale touching this matter. In fact magnificence is nothing other than a kind of magnified liberality concerning these things.

718. At "Besides, for the same cost" [II, A, A', 6] he gives the sixth quality. He says that, although the munificent person incurs great expense for some noble work, he produces a more magnificent work with equal expenditure. This is so because excellence (what is ultimate and best) is not the same in possession of money and in a work for which money is spent. Excellence (what is greatest and best) in possessions is found in the most valued object, viz., gold, which men highly honor and prize. But excellence in a work is found in this that a work is great and good; for the contemplation of such a work gives rise to admiration—and this is what magnificence does. So it is evident that the "virtue" of a work, i.e., its greatest excellence corresponds to magnificence involving expenditures on a large scale.

LECTURE VII

The Objects of Magnificence

ANALYTICAL OUTLINE
OF ST. THOMAS

TEXT OF ARISTOTLE
(*B.1122 b 19*)
Chapter 2

B'. *He shows the principal object on which the munificent person should spend money.*

I. FOR WHAT THINGS THE MUNIFICENT MAN SHOULD MAKE EXPENDITURES.

a. The principal objects for which the munificent should spend money.

 i. The principal objects . . . for which the munificent person disburses funds.

Magnificence belongs to those princely outlays we call most honorable, like votive offerings to the 20 gods, preparations, sacrifices and other things pertaining to divine worship. It belongs, also, to any lavish gifts made for the common good, such as a splendid donation for the benefit of all, or the fitting out of a trireme, or the giving of a banquet to the whole community.   **719-720**

 ii. Who should make such expenditures.

  x. FOR WHOM, IN GENERAL, SUCH EXPENDITURES ARE APPROPRIATE.

But in all these things, as was just stated, reference is made to the agent —who he is and what possessions he has, for the disbursements must be commensurate with these circumstances and appropriate not only to the work but also to the spender. **721**

  y. FOR WHOM, IN PARTICULAR, THEY ARE INAPPROPRIATE.

For this reason the poor man will not be munificent, since he has not the resources from which he may spend large sums becomingly. If he tries to do so, he is unwise for this would be improper and inopportune. And what is according to virtue is done rightly.   **722**

  z. FOR WHOM, IN PARTICULAR, THEY ARE APPROPRIATE.

A great expenditure is suitable for those who have wealth themselves, 30 from their parents, or from others transferring it to them; likewise for the noble and those renowned for fame or other similar public acclaim, since all these things have a certain greatness and distinction.   **723-724**

iii. He sums up his views.

Such then, especially, is the munificent person, and as we have said, by such expenditures magnificence is exercised in the greatest and most honorable works;   **725**

b. The secondary objects (for which the munificent person should spend money).
   i. The first.

or even in any private affair that happens once, for example, a   *B.1123* wedding and the like;   **726**

ii. The second kind.

or in any event of great interest to the whole city and the dignitaries; or in the reception and departure of foreign guests, in the presentation of gifts and in the repayment of favors. Yet the munificent man does not spend lavishly on himself but donates for the public welfare gifts that have a likeness to those consecrated to God.   **727**

iii. The third kind.

It is the privilege of the munificent man to use his riches to build a home which is indeed an ornament, and to spend larger sums on whatever portions are of a permanent nature, for these are best.   **728-729**

2. HE PRESERVES PROPORTION BETWEEN THE COST AND THE OBJECTS PAID FOR.

He will spend in a manner proper to each thing. The same expendi-   *10* ture is not appropriate to gods and men, nor in building a temple and a tomb. He will make an outlay for each thing according to the kind, being most munificent in spending a great amount on a great work. But the expense will be great in comparison with the things. What is great in regard to the work differs from what is great in cost considered in itself. A very pretty ball or jar takes on magnificence when presented as a gift to a child, although the price is trivial and not in the category of liberal. Hence the munificent person has the advantage of performing a great work in any category. And a work, great in its class and reasonable in its cost, can hardly be surpassed. This, then, is a description of the munificent person.　　　　730-731

B. He treats the opposite vices.

A'. First, considering excess.

One who sins by excess, i.e., the vulgarian, is immoderate in spending contrary to what he ought, as has　20 been pointed out. He expends great sums on paltry things, and his lavishness is out of harmony, figuratively speaking. He banquets buffoons with dishes fit for a marriage feast, gives presents to comedians, and rolls out a red carpet for their entry like the Megarians. In all such affairs he does not act to attain the good but to show off his wealth, hoping in this way for admiration. Where grand outlays are called for, he spends little; where small expenditures are in order, he lays out much.　　　　732

B'. Next (considering) defect.

But the petty person falls short in everything; and after spending very much he will spoil the whole good effect for the sake of a trifle. Whatever expenditures he makes, he makes tardily and he takes care to spend　30 as little as he can. Moreover, he does this glumly and is of the opinion that he has done more than he should.　733

C'. Finally (considering) what is common to both.

These, then, are habits of vice; yet they do not bring shame because they do not injure our neighbor and are not very disgraceful.　　　　734

COMMENTARY OF ST. THOMAS

719. After the Philosopher has shown in what manner the munificent person should be concerned with spending, he now [II, B'] shows the principal object on which the munificent person should spend money. He gives two explanations of this point. First [B', 1] he explains for what things the munificent man should make expenditures; and next [B', 2], how he preserves proportion between the cost and the objects paid for, at "He will spend in a manner proper to each etc." He manifests the initial point in a twofold manner. First [1, a] he sets forth the principal objects for which the munificent should spend money; and then [1, b], the secondary objects, at "or even in any private etc." On this first point he does three things. First [a, i] he discloses what the principal objects are for which the munificent person disburses funds. Next [a, ii], he indicates who should make such expenditures, at "But in all these things etc." Last [a, iii], he sums up his views, at "Such then, especially etc." He says first that the munificent man lays out large amounts for things that are honorable in the highest degree. These sums are of two kinds. The first of them pertains to divine things (for example, the placing of votive offerings in the temples of the gods) and preparations (the building of the temple or some other things of this kind). Even sacrifices come under this heading. The gentiles, however, worshipped not only gods, i.e., certain separated substances, but also demons whom they held to be intermediaries between gods and men. Therefore, he adds that everything expended on the worship of any demon

whatsoever belongs to this same classification. The Philosopher speaks here of a heathen custom that has been abrogated by the plain truth. Hence if someone now spent any money on the worship of a demon he would not be munificent but sacrilegious.

720. The second kind of honorable expenditures are those made for the common good in a sumptuous manner: a person nobly and lavishly gives a becoming donation of something useful to the community; a man, charged with an office by the state like the captaincy of a trireme (a fleet of ships or galleys), makes great expenditures in the execution of that office; or someone gives a banquet for the whole community according to a custom, as is said in the second book of the *Politics* (Ch. 9, 1271 a 33; St. Th. Lect. XIV, 317).

721. Next [a, ii], at "But in all these," he shows for whom such expenditures are appropriate. Regarding this he does three things. First [ii, x] he explains for whom, in general, such expenditures are appropriate. Then [ii, y], at "For this reason the poor man," he infers for whom, in particular, they are inappropriate. Finally [ii, z], at "A great expenditure etc.," he shows for whom, in particular, they are appropriate. He says first that in all these things that are expended—as was just mentioned (712-713)—we must have regard not only for the objects for which a person spends money (so that we should consider whether the spender is a prince or a private person, a noble or a commoner) but also what possessions, large or small, he may have. Expenditures must be proper, i.e., well proportioned to

the wealth and station of the person, so that the expenses may be suited not only to the work for which they are incurred but also to the spender.

722. Then [ii, y], at **"For this reason,"** he infers that such expenditures may not be appropriate. Because of what was just said, the poor man who has little wealth cannot be munificent, for he does not have so great an amount that he can rightly afford to spend much. If he attempts to spend more, he is foolish since it is contrary to good taste and beyond what is proper. So it does not pertain to the virtue of magnificence because, by means of virtue, all things are done correctly, i.e., properly.

723. Next [ii, z], at **"A great expenditure,"** he discloses who may make these expenditures fittingly, understanding this in regard to two things. First he takes it according to the amount of riches. He says that great expenditures should be made by men who are wealthy, i.e., who possess great riches, much of which can be expended becomingly. It makes no difference whether they possess this abundant wealth of themselves, i.e., by acquiring it through their own industry, or have it from their parents (whose heirs they are), or even from any others through whom riches come to them, for example, when they become heirs of those outside the family.

724. Second, he considers the proposition according to the condition of persons. It is becoming that great sums be disbursed by the highborn and the renowned, i.e., those established in honor and other similar things. Everything of this nature has about it a certain greatness and decorum, so that such splendid donations may be made appropriately.

725. Then [a, iii], at **"Such, then,"** he sums up his views, affirming that the munificent person is of the sort described above, and that magnificence consists in expenditures of this kind—

as was stated in 719-720—viz., on things for divine worship and the public welfare, for such are the greatest and most honorable among all human goods.

726. Next [1, b], at **"or even,"** he shows on what secondary objects the munificent person spends money. He mentions three kinds of objects, the first [b, i] of which consists in the munificent man spending great sums on affairs pertaining properly to himself and happening only once, like marriage, military service, and so on.

727. He gives the second kind [b, ii], at **"or in any event."** If the whole city or the rulers are anxious to do something and a man makes great expenditures on this he will be munificent, for instance, if he should honorably receive some guests such as princes or kings, if he should give them great banquets, or even personally offer presents to them, or if he should repay certain favors received; in all these situations, the munificent person will spend large sums. He is not lavish with himself so that he spends much for his own use, but he makes great expenditures for the common good. The splendid gifts bestowed on some resemble those given to God. The reason is that, as offerings are consecrated to God not because He needs them but out of reverence and honor, so also presents are made to distinguished men more on account of honor than any need.

728. Then [b, iii], at **"It is the privilege,"** he mentions the third kind, stating that it pertains to magnificence to build a home in the proper manner with one's own riches, for a decent home adds to a man's distinction. And in constructing buildings the munificent man desires to spend money rather on lasting and permanent parts than on fragile decorations, for instance, on marble columns in the house rather than on glass windows. Things that are more permanent are best.

729. Hence, it is clear from what has been said that the munificent man spends money principally on the things destined for divine worship and the public welfare, but secondarily on things pertaining to private persons under three conditions: first that the things happen once, second that in addition the common good is pursued, third that they are of a permanent nature. These are the requisites making for greatness in private matters.

730. Next [B', 2], at **"He will spend,"** he explains in what way the munificent person maintains the proportion of costs appropriate to the things for which the expenditure is made, spending on each object what is fitting both in kind and quantity. It is obvious that not the same kind and quantity of outlay is suitably offered to gods and men, nor used in the construction of a temple and a tomb. He will see to it that he spends a sum large according to the kind of thing. Hence he will be very munificent when he makes a great expenditure on a great work. But in this work he will make what is great in this class. So, sometimes what is great in regard to the work differs from what is absolutely great in expense. From the fact that someone makes a very pretty globe, i.e., a ball, or a vase (a small vessel) as a gift to a boy, he is said to possess magnificence in the genus of children's gifts, although the price of the beautiful globe in itself is small, not belonging to the class of generous donations. Obviously, therefore, the munificent person has the advantage of performing a great work in any genus, making expenditures commensurate with the merit of the work. A production of this sort, which is great according to its kind and reasonable in its cost, can hardly be surpassed.

731. Last, he succinctly states the conclusion that the munificent man is such as has been described.

732. Then [(II) B], at **"One who sins by excess,"** he treats the opposite vices: first [B, A'], considering excess; next [B, B'] defect, at "But the petty person etc."; and last [B, C'] what is common to both, at "These, then, are." He says that the man who is immoderate in grand outlays—called *banausos* [1] because he consumes his goods as in a furnace—exceeds the munificent person not in the absolute amount spent but in spending in a way contrary to what he should. The reason is that he uses much money in superfluous expenses, and wants to make lavish expenditures contrary to harmony, i.e., against the right proportion—which is said by way of metaphor—for instance, he entertains buffoons and comedians with nuptial banquets, contributes much to actors, even rolling out the red carpet for their entry, as the Megarians (certain Greek citizens) are in the habit of doing. He does all these and similar things not for some good but for making a show of his riches, thinking that he will be admired for this reason. However, he does not always spend lavishly but sometimes he falls short. Where he ought to spend much, he spends little; but where little, much. The reason is that he does not keep his eye on the good but on vanity.

733. Next [B, B'], at **"But the petty person,"** he considers the vice of defect and states that the petty person falls short in everything, assigning him five traits. The first is that when the petty person does make great expenditures he fails to do well because of a trifle. The second, what sums he expends he expends tardily. The third, he always keeps his mind on how he may spend the least. The fourth, he is a gloomy spender. The fifth, when

[1] Cf. Note on 711.

he lays out everything, he thinks he has done more than he should, for it seems to him that he ought to spend less.

734. Then [B, C'], at **"These, then,"** he considers what is common to either vice. He comes to the conclusion that the two previously mentioned habits are certain vices because they are opposed to virtue by a departure from the mean. However, they are not opprobrious since they do not injure our neighbor in any way, and are not very disgraceful because it is difficult in disbursing large amounts not to depart from the mean.

LECTURE VIII

Magnanimity

ANALYTICAL OUTLINE OF ST. THOMAS	TEXT OF ARISTOTLE (*B.1123 a 33*) Chapter 3

I. HE INVESTIGATES THE MATTER OF MAGNANIMITY AND THE OPPOSITE VICES.

A. He sets forth his proposition.

> Judging by the name, magnanimity seems to be concerned with great things the nature of which we should first *b* understand. However, it does not matter whether we consider the habit or the man who operates according to the habit. **735**

B. He explains it.

A'. He exposes the matter of magnanimity generally.

1. MAGNANIMITY REFERS TO GREAT THINGS.

a. He exposes his viewpoint.

> A person seems to be magnanimous in thinking himself worthy of great things when he is worthy. **736**

b. The magnanimous person must be worthy of great things.

> But he who presumes this when it is not really so is foolish; yet the man who operates according to virtue in these matters is not unwise or foolish. Consequently, the magnanimous person is such as we have described. **737**

c. The magnanimous man should think himself worthy of great things.

> He who is worthy of small things and considers himself so is temperate, although he is not magnanimous. Magnanimity consists in greatness, as beauty consists in a good build. Short-statured people may be fair and well-proportioned but hardly handsome. **738**

2. HOW THE OPPOSITE VICES OCCUR IN REGARD TO THE SAME MATTER.

a. First regarding the vice of excess.

> The person who judges himself worthy of great things and is in fact unworthy is conceited. But one who judges himself worthy of greater things

b. Then (regarding) the vice of defect.

than he merits is not always said to be conceited.   **739**

On the other hand, the man *10* who thinks he deserves lesser things than he deserves—whether the things be great, ordinary, or little—is pusillanimous. This will be especially evident in one capable of splendid achievements. What would he have done if he had not this capability?   **740**

3. HOW THE VIRTUE CONSISTS IN THE MEAN.

However, the magnanimous man holds an extreme in extension but a mean in appropriateness, for he thinks himself deserving in accord with his worth. Others exceed and fall short of this mean.   **741**

B'. He exposes (the matter of magnanimity) specifically.

1. MAGNANIMITY IS CONCERNED WITH HONOR.

a. (The magnanimous man) should deem himself deserving of the greatest things.

If a man deems himself deserving of great things and especially of the greatest things when he deserves them, then he will be concerned with one particular object. He is said to be deserving in reference to external goods. But we place that external good highest which we attribute to the gods, which is desired most of all by *20* prominent men and is the reward for virtuous action. Such a good is honor, for it is the best of all external goods. Therefore, the magnanimous man will manage honors and dishonors in a manner which is fitting.   **742**

b. He manifests his proposition by experience.

Even independent of reasoning, the magnanimous seem to be concerned about honors, for the great exalt themselves in dignity principally by honor.   **743**

2. HOW THE OPPOSITE VICES SHOULD DEAL WITH THIS MATTER.

The pusillanimous person is deficient in regard both to his own merit and the worthiness of the magnanimous man. But one who is presumptuous is excessive respecting his own merit al-

though he does not exceed the merit
of the magnanimous person.   **744**

3. IN WHAT MANNER MAGNANIMITY IS RELATED TO OTHER VIRTUES.

a. Magnanimity is related to the other
virtues.
  i. . . . First by a general argument.

But the magnanimous man as worthy of the greatest goods will be best. Since the better person is worthy of greater things, the best will be *30* worthy of the greatest. Therefore, the magnanimous person must be truly good.   **745**

X. WHAT MAKES MAGNANIMITY A
    SPECIAL VIRTUE.
Y. HE REJECTS AN ERROR.

What is great in every virtue pertains to magnanimity.   **746**

It is never becoming for a magnanimous man to flee one about to give unsought advice, nor to practice injustice. Will not the man who considers nothing great be the one to do disgraceful deeds for gain?   **747**

  *ii. . . . By the things appearing in
individual cases.*

To an observer of what happens in individual cases, that person will seem altogether ludicrous who thinks himself magnanimous when he is not really virtuous. One who is in fact evil will not be magnanimous nor deserving of honor, for honor is a reward of virtue and is attributed to the virtuous.   **748**

b. Next drawing certain conclusions
from what has been said.

Therefore, it seems that magnanimity is an embellishment of *B.1124* the virtues, since it makes virtue more excellent and does not exist without them. It is difficult to be truly magnanimous because this is not possible without goodness.   **749**

COMMENTARY OF ST. THOMAS

735. After the Philosopher has finished the treatise on the virtues concerning money, he treats here the virtues having to do with honors. First he considers magnanimity, which regards great honors [Lects. VIII, IX, X, XI]; and then a nameless virtue concerned with ordinary honors [Lect. XII], at "As we remarked in the beginning etc." (B.1125 b). In the first consideration he does two things. First [I] he investigates the matter of magnanimity and the opposite vices; and second [Lect. IX; II] their acts and

properties, at "For the most part etc."
(B.1124 a 4). On the first point he
does two things. First [A] he sets
forth his proposition; and next [B] he
explains it, at "A person seems to be
etc." He says first: from its name,
magnanimity apparently is concerned
with great things. But at the beginning we must understand the nature
of the things with which it deals. Then
he designates the manner of consideration, viz., it does not matter whether
we speak of the habit of magnanimity
or of the man who is disposed by the
habit, i.e., the magnanimous person.

736. Next [B], at **"A person seems,"**
he explains his proposition by doing
two things. First [A'] he exposes the
matter of magnanimity generally; and
then [B'] specifically, at "If a man
etc." On the first point he does two
(three) things. First [A', 1] he shows
that magnanimity refers to great
things; and then [A', 2], at "The
person who judges etc.," how the opposite vices occur in regard to the
same matter. Last [A', 3] he explains
how the virtue consists in the mean,
at "However, the magnanimous etc."
He treats the first point under three
aspects. First [A', 1, a] he exposes his
viewpoint, saying that a person seems
to be magnanimous who thinks himself worthy of great things, viz., that
he may perform great deeds and that
great things should happen to him
when in fact he is worthy.

737. Then [A', 1, b], at **"But he
who presumes,"** he teaches that the
magnanimous person must be worthy
of great things. One who thinks himself worthy of great things contrary to
truth, i.e., of which he is not really
worthy, is foolish. It is characteristic
of a wise man to keep everything in
proper order. But the virtuous man
is neither unwise nor foolish because
virtue operates according to right reason, as was affirmed in the second book
(257, 322, 335). Consequently, it is
clear that the magnanimous man is

the person just described, i.e., one worthy of great things who thinks himself worthy.

738. Finally [A', 1, c], at **"He who
is worthy,"** he shows that the magnanimous man should think himself
worthy of great things. One who is
worthy of small things and considers
himself so, can be called temperate in
the sense that temperance is taken for
any moderation whatsoever. However,
he cannot be called magnanimous because magnanimity consists in a certain size, just as beauty properly consists in a good build. Hence those who
are short can be called fair by reason
of complexion or well-proportioned
members but not handsome because
they lack size.

739. Next [A', 2], at **"The person
who judges,"** he shows in what manner the opposite vices should be concerned with great things, first [A', 2,
a] regarding the vice of excess; and
then [A', 2, b] the vice of defect, at
"On the other hand etc." Aristotle says
first that the man who thinks himself
worthy of great things when he is
really unworthy is called conceited, i.e.,
puffed up—we can call him inflated
or presumptuous. But the person who
is really worthy of great things and
thinks himself worthy of still greater
things is not always called conceited,
because it is difficult to find an exact
norm so that someone may judge himself not worthy of great things.

740. Then [A', 2, b], at **"On the
other hand,"** he explains how the vice
of defect is concerned with great
things, saying that the man who thinks
himself worthy of lesser things than
he is worthy is called pusillanimous.
This is so, whether in fact he is worthy of great, mediocre, or small things.
However, the small-souled person is
one who refuses to strive after great
accomplishments and aims at certain
petty undertakings when he is truly
capable of what is great. He would
bring himself down to affairs more

trifling still, except for the fact that he is capable of great things.

741. Next [A', 3], at **"However, the magnanimous man,"** he shows how magnanimity is in the mean, for, treating as it does of great things, magnanimity seems to consist in the extreme. Since the average is the mean between the large and the small, the great has the nature of an extreme. Hence he says that the magnanimous person holds an extreme in reference to great things of which he deems himself worthy. But he holds the mean inasmuch as he does this in an appropriate manner in considering himself deserving according to his worth. The mean of virtue is not judged according to the quantity of the thing but according to right reason. Hence a man is not placed outside the mean of virtue by a work no matter what its size, provided he does not depart from reason. But the opposite vices exceed and fall short of what should be.

742. Then [B'], at **"If a man deems,"** he explains the matter of magnanimity specifically, taking up three points. He shows first [B', 1] that magnanimity is concerned with honor; second [B', 2] how the opposite vices should deal with this matter, at "The pusillanimous person etc."; and third [B', 3] in what manner magnanimity is related to other virtues at "But the magnanimous man etc." He explains the first point in two ways. First he reasons that if the magnanimous man deems himself worthy of great things when he is worthy of them, consequently [B', 1, a] he should deem himself deserving of the greatest things when he is deserving of the greatest. He says further that magnanimity is concerned with one object in particular, for what is predicated by excellence is attributed to one. When someone is said to be worthy of certain things, the worthiness refers to external goods which come to a man as a reward. But that must be placed highest which is

attributed to God, which is desired especially by those in eminent positions, and which is the reward of the most noble deeds. Such is honor, for honor is shown to God, is sought by the prominent and is the reward of virtuous action. Obviously then honor is the best of all external goods. Consequently, magnanimity should give the greatest consideration to honors and dishonors, inasmuch as the magnanimous person manages things of this kind in the proper manner.

743. Second [B', 1, b], at **"Even independent of reasoning,"** he manifests his proposition by experience, saying that, even without discussion, it is clear that magnanimity has to do with honor for the most part because experience shows the magnanimous deem themselves worthy of honor but not above their deserts.

744. Next [B', 2], at **"The pusillanimous,"** he explains in what manner the opposite vices should be concerned with the previously mentioned matter. He says that the small-souled person is deficient in regard to himself because he considers himself deserving of lesser things than he deserves, and also in regard to the worthiness of the magnanimous man because he considers himself deserving of lesser things than a magnanimous man deserves. But the conceited or presumptuous person is excessive in regard to himself because he makes himself greater than his worth, however, not in regard to the magnanimous man because he does not consider himself deserving of greater things than the magnanimous man deserves.

745. Then [B', 3], at **"But the magnanimous,"** he compares magnanimity with other virtues: first [B', 3, a] showing that magnanimity is related to the other virtues; and next [B', 3, b] drawing certain conclusions from what has been said, at "Therefore it seems." On the first point he does two things: he shows that magnanimity is related to

the other virtues, first [i] by a general argument; and then [ii] by the things appearing in individual cases, at "To an observer etc." Regarding the first he does two things. First [x] he explains what makes magnanimity a special virtue, at "What is great etc."; and next [y] he rejects an error, at "It is never becoming etc." Aristotle says first that when the magnanimous person deems himself worthy of the greatest goods and is really worthy of them, it follows that he is best. The better man is always deserving of greater things, and consequently he who is deserving of the greatest must be best. Therefore, the magnanimous man must be truly good, otherwise he would not be deserving of the highest honors.

746. Then [x], at **"What is great,"** he shows how magnanimity is a special virtue when it accompanies other virtues. He says that what is great in any virtue seems to pertain to magnanimity because one who does not perform a great act of virtue is not worthy of great honor. So, when that virtue strives for what is proper to itself, it performs an act of another virtue, for example, fortitude intends a courageous action, magnanimity strives for a great deed in the courageous action. Since moral acts take their species from the end to which they tend, it is clear that magnanimity and fortitude differ in species (although they operate in the same matter) because neither virtue follows the same motive.

747. Next [y], at **"It is never becoming,"** he rejects an error. Some seem to think that the magnanimous man should rely upon his own opinion and follow the advice of no one. Like-

wise, that he should not hesitate to do injustice to anyone. The Philosopher, however, says this is false because no one does a shameful deed except for the desire of something. But the magnanimous person does not place so great a value on any external thing that he would wish to do a shameful action for it.

748. Then [ii], at **"To the observer,"** he explains the clause: "of what happens in individual cases." [1] He says that to someone willing to observe individual cases, that man will seem altogether ridiculous who judges himself magnanimous without being virtuous. The reason is that if a man is evil he is not deserving of honor, for honor is the reward of virtue. Hence the magnanimous man thinks himself worthy of great honors. Consequently, no evil person is able to be magnanimous.

749. Last [B', 3, b], at **"Therefore it seems,"** he draws two conclusions from the premises. The first is that magnanimity seems to be an ornament of all the virtues because they are made more excellent by magnanimity, which seeks to perform a great work in all the virtues. In this way the virtues increase. Likewise, magnanimity accompanies the other virtues and so seems to be added to them as their ornament. The second conclusion is that it is difficult to be magnanimous because magnanimity cannot exist without the goodness of virtue, and even without great virtue to which honor is due. But it is difficult to attain this. Consequently, it is difficult for a man to be magnanimous.

[1] In the Commentary the words are *per ea quae in singulis apparent.* The text of Aristotle used here has *secundum singula.*

LECTURE IX

The Acts of Magnanimity

ANALYTICAL OUTLINE
OF ST. THOMAS

TEXT OF ARISTOTLE
(*B.1124 a 4*)
Chapter 3

II. HE . . . STUDIES . . . ACTS AND PROPERTIES (OF MAGNANIMITY AND THE OPPO-
SITE VICES).
A. First as touching magnanimity.
  A'. How the magnanimous person should work on matter proper to him.
    I. HOW THE MAGNANIMOUS MAN SHOULD CONDUCT HIMSELF TOWARD
       HONORS.

a. The matter of magnanimity.

For the most part the magnanimous
man deals with honors and dishonors.
750

b. How the magnanimous man deals
with matter of this kind.
  *i. The nature and mode of this
  man's reaction to great honors.*

He takes moderate delight in great
and desirable honors, receiving good
things as his own or less than his due.
In his opinion, honor is not an appropriate tribute to perfect virtue, but still
he accepts it from men who have
nothing greater to bestow on him.
751

  *ii. The way . . . the magnani-
  mous person should regard trifling honors.*

Honors given him by transitory   *10*
things and for insufficient reasons he
values very little as unworthy of him.
752

  *iii. In what manner the magnani-
  mous should deal with dishonor.*

He likewise counts of little value
any dishonor that will be imputed to
him unjustly. As we have said, then,
the magnanimous man for the most
part will be concerned with honors.
753

    2. (HE SHOWS HOW THE MAGNANIMOUS MAN SHOULD CONDUCT HIMSELF)
       TOWARD OTHER THINGS.

a. How the magnanimous man should
act in regard to such objects.

Moreover, he will observe moderation about wealth, power, good fortune, and adversity, no matter what

may happen. He will not be exalted by prosperity nor cast down by misfortune, nor does he even regard honor as if it were a very great thing. Power and wealth should be desirable for the sake of honor; and those who possess them seek to be honored by reason of them. But a man to whom honor is a trifle will place little value on the other things. For this reason the magnanimous seem to be disdainful. **754-755**

b. How the objects benefit magnanimity.
   i. They increase it.

The goods of fortune seem to   *20* contribute something to magnanimity, for the noble, the powerful, and the rich are thought to be worthy of honor as possessing goods of great excellence. But anything that excels in goodness is held in greater honor. For this reason such things make men more magnanimous, since they are honored by some people, but in fact the good or virtuous man alone is to be honored. However, he who possesses both (virtue and goods of fortune) becomes more worthy of honor.   **756**

ii. Without virtue they cannot make a man magnanimous.

Men who possess goods of this kind without virtue are not justified in thinking themselves worthy of great things, nor are they rightly called magnanimous, for this supposes perfect virtue. But those having such things become evil by disdaining and harming others, since it is not easy to bear   *30* the goods of fortune with moderation. They are not able to endure good   *b* fortune gracefully, but thinking themselves more excellent, they look down on others, and do as they please. Although not similar to the magnanimous man, they imitate him in the way they can, not by acting according to virtue, but in disdaining others. The magnanimous person justly disdains and properly glorifies others but many do not always act in this manner.   **757-758**

COMMENTARY OF ST. THOMAS

750. After the Philosopher has investigated the matter of magnanimity and the opposite vices, he now [II] studies their acts and properties, first [A] as touching magnanimity; and then [Lect. XI; B] the opposite vices, at "But the man who fails etc." (B.1125 a 16). On the initial point he does two things. First [A'] he shows how the magnanimous person should work on matter proper to him. Next [Lect. X; B'] he defines the traits of the magnanimous person, at "The magnanimous man does not run risks foolishly etc." (B.1124 b 6). He explains the first point by a twofold procedure. Initially [1] he shows how the magnanimous man should conduct himself toward honors, the matter of magnanimity; and then [2] toward other things, at "Moreover, he will etc." He treats the first in two ways. First [1, a] he resumes the previous discussion (735-749) about the matter of magnanimity, reaffirming what was clear from the premises, that someone is called magnanimous especially and principally from the fact that he conducts himself well in regard to honors and the opposites, viz., dishonors. The same virtue is concerned with opposites; fortitude, for instance, deals with fear and rashness.

751. Then [1, b], at "He takes moderate delight," he shows how the magnanimous man deals with matter of this kind. First [1, b, i] he shows the nature and mode of this man's reaction to great honors, saying that great and desirable honors bestowed on the magnanimous for virtuous activity are a source of moderate delight to them. A man might take inordinate pleasure in goods acquired because they

come to him unexpectedly, and value them far above their worth. But when the magnanimous person acquires things, he looks upon them as goods peculiarly suitable to him and, besides, less than his due. He judges that no honor outwardly shown to men is a sufficient reward of virtue. The reason is that the good of reason, for which virtue is praised, exceeds all external goods. Nevertheless, he is not displeased because lesser honors are bestowed on him than he deserves. But he accepts them with equanimity considering that men have nothing better to give him.

752. [1, b, ii], at "Honors given him," he sets forth the way in which the magnanimous person should regard trifling honors. If honors are given him by transitory things and for any other reason than virtue (for example, if he is extolled for riches or the like, or by some insignificant honors), he will despise such honors because he considers himself undeserving of this type of thing. It is not enough for the virtuous to be honored like the rich.

753. Last [1, b, iii], at "He likewise counts," he explains in what manner the magnanimous man should deal with dishonor, saying that here also he shows moderation. As his mind is not exalted by great honors, so it is not cast down by insults which he considers imputed to him unjustly. Hence it is obvious that the magnanimous person is especially praised in regard to honors.

754. Then [2], at "Moreover, he will observe," he shows in what way the magnanimous person should deal with secondary matters, for example,

riches and so forth. On this point he does two things. First [2, a] he explains how the magnanimous man should act in regard to such objects; and next [2, b] how the objects benefit magnanimity, at "The goods of fortune etc." He says first that, although the magnanimous person is concerned with honors principally, nevertheless secondarily he has to do with riches, power, and everything belonging to good fortune, inasmuch as someone is honored for these reasons. Likewise he will show moderation about such things and about misfortune, whatever may be the turn of events, so that he will not rejoice exceedingly in prosperity nor grieve unduly in adversity.

755. He proves the point by the argument given before (741-742) that the magnanimous man conducts himself with moderation in regard to honors that are the greatest of all external goods. This is clear from the fact that both power and riches are desired for the sake of honor according as men who have such things want to be honored for them. If then the magnanimous person thinks honor itself of little account so that he does not rejoice in it exceedingly, for a greater reason he will judge the other things of small moment, so that he will not rejoice in them immoderately. As a consequence, some judge the magnanimous to be disdainful because they despise external goods and value only the internal goods of virtue.

756. Next [2, b], at "The goods of fortune," he shows how external goods of fortune do confer something on magnanimity. He explains first [2, b, i] that they increase it when accompanying virtue; and second [2, b, ii] that without virtue they cannot make a man magnanimous, at "Men who possess." He says that all external goods of fortune seem to add something to magnanimity inasmuch as, for these very things, some are judged worthy

of honor, viz., the noble, the powerful, and the rich. All such goods consist of a certain great excellence, just as the noble surpass the baseborn in excellence, and so on. Everything that is surpassing in goodness is honorable in a high degree, for honor is a kind of reverence due to a very excellent good. Since the magnanimous person is worthy of honor, such goods consequently make men more magnanimous accordingly as they are honored by some people who recognize only these goods. But really only the good or virtuous man should be honored because honor is the proper reward for virtue. If someone should possess both at the same time, viz., virtue and the goods of fortune, he will become worthier of honor inasmuch as each matter is honorable. According to truth and opinion, even the goods of fortune are a help to virtuous operations after the manner of instruments.

757. Then [2, b, ii], at "Men who possess," he establishes that goods of fortune without virtue cannot make a man magnanimous. He says that those who have goods of this kind without virtue cannot rightly esteem themselves deserving of great honors. Hence they are not correctly called magnanimous because it cannot happen that a man deserves great things and is magnanimous without perfect virtue, as was pointed out before (749). But because of the excellence of external goods men who lack virtue look down on others, do them injury, and fall into similar evils, since without virtue it is not easy for someone reasonably to bear the goods of fortune. To conduct oneself with moderation among the goods of fortune is a great work of virtue. Those who lack virtue cannot bear good fortune gracefully. Consequently, thinking themselves better absolutely, they despise those whom they exceed in riches. Since they do not consider that any excellence is acquired by virtue,

they take no pains to do anything good but do whatever comes to mind.

758. They want to imitate the magnanimous person when in fact they are not like him. They imitate him in the way they can, not I grant in operating according to virtue—a thing the magnanimous man does especially— but in despising others although, not in the same way as he does. The magnanimous person justly despises the wicked, and properly glorifies the virtuous. But many, who are without virtue, manifest disdain and honor indiscriminately, i.e., sometimes despise the virtuous and honor the wicked.

LECTURE X

Properties of Magnanimity

ANALYTICAL OUTLINE
OF ST. THOMAS

TEXT OF ARISTOTLE
(*B.1124 b 6*)
Chapter 3

B'. He considers the traits of the magnanimous person.

I. THE TRAITS THAT ARE TAKEN BY COMPARISON WITH MATTERS OF THE VIRTUES.

a. The traits . . . understood in comparison with externally connected things.
   i. The traits . . . by a comparison with external dangers.

     X. FIRST.

The magnanimous man does not run risks foolishly, nor is he a lover of danger since he places a high value on few things. But he does undergo danger for things of great worth. **759-760**

     Y. SECOND.

When in danger, he exposes his life as if it were altogether unbecoming to continue living. **761**

   ii. (The traits) by a comparison with external benefits.

     V. FIRST.

He is good at helping others— **10** which is a mark of the man of excellence, but he shies away from taking favors—a thing characteristic of a man of lesser gifts. **762**

     W. SECOND.

He makes lavish recompense, so that the man who gave in the beginning will receive abundantly and become a debtor. **763**

     X. THIRD.

The magnanimous person likes to remember those he benefits but not those by whom he is or was treated generously. That man is less noble who gratefully receives benefits than he who bestows them. Hence it is in the bestowal that the magnanimous man wants to be eminent. **764**

     Y. FOURTH.

Likewise he gladly hears of the benefits he has bestowed but not of those he has received. For this reason Thetis did not recount to Jove,[1] nor the Spartans to the Athenians, the favors they had done but the benefits received. **765**

z. FIFTH.

The magnanimous person likes to show himself in need of nothing or hardly anything, but to minister to the needs of others promptly. **766**

iii. (*The trait*) *by a comparison with honors.*
x. THE TRAIT.

He acts with great dignity toward those in high places and the wealthy but with moderation toward the *20* middle class. **767**

y. TWO REASONS FOR WHAT HE SAID.

To attain excellence among the great is difficult and worthy of reverence, but among the mediocre it is easy. To seek respect from the great is not without nobility, but from the lowly is to make oneself irksome, **768-769**

z. AN ILLUSTRATION.

for instance, to display one's power against the weak, and to avoid tasks that are generally honorable or at which others excel. **770**

b. (The traits) in comparison with human acts.
 i. *Pertaining to himself.*

Leisure and slowness are marks of the magnanimous man, but where there is either great honor or great work he performs at least some great and noteworthy operations. **771**

ii. (*Pertaining*) *then to others.*
x. IN REGARD TO TRUTH.
 aa. First.

Of necessity he is an evident friend or enemy, for to be so in secret smacks of timidity. **772**

bb. Second.

He cares more for the truth than the opinion of men. **773**

cc. Third.

He speaks and works in the open, freely divulging things in public, since he pays little attention to others. **774**

dd. Fourth.

He is truthful in his speech, excepting what he says in irony, which *30* he uses with the common people. **775**

y. IN REGARD TO PLEASANTNESS.

He cannot conform his life *B.1125* to that of another, except perhaps a friend, since this is servile. Because of

---

[1] Cf. *Iliad* i. 503 sq., where Thetis did so.

servility all flatterers are obsequious and lowly people flatterers.   **776**

2. (THE TRAITS THAT ARE TAKEN) ACCORDING TO THE INCLINATION OF THE MAGNANIMOUS MAN.

a. Some that exist in the soul.
   i. First.

Nor is he given to admiration, for nothing seems great to him.   **777**

   ii. Next.

Nor is he mindful of injuries, since it is not becoming that a magnanimous person remembers evils at all, but rather despises them.   **778**

b. Others which exist in speech.
   i. First.

Neither is he a gossip, for he does not speak about himself or others. He is not anxious that he be praised, and he neither blames nor praises others. Therefore, he does not speak evil of his enemies except to ward off injuries.
                            779

   ii. Third (second).

In necessary or trival matters he does not lament or seek help, for this is characteristic of one who cares ex- **10** cessively about these things.   **780**

c. Traits that exist in communication with others.
   i. In regard to external possessions.

He is willing to possess unfruitful rather than fruitful and useful goods, for he is somewhat self-sufficient. **781**

   ii. In regard to bodily movements.

But the movements of the magnanimous man seem deliberate, his voice solemn and his speech measured. He is not hasty since he is concerned about few things. As he considers nothing too important, he is not given to contention from which sharpness of voice and hastiness of speech arise.

Such then is the magnanimous person.   **782-783**

COMMENTARY OF ST. THOMAS

759. After the Philosopher has explained how the magnanimous man should work on proper matter, he here [B'] considers the traits of the magnanimous person. First [1] he proposes the traits that are taken by comparison with matters of the virtues; and then [2] those according to the inclination

of the magnanimous man himself, at "Nor is he given to admiration etc." On the initial point he proceeds in a twofold manner. First [1, a] he sets forth the traits of the magnanimous person, which are understood in comparison with externally connected things; and next [1, b] in comparison with human acts, at "Leisure and slowness etc." In regard to the first he makes a triple enumeration. He enumerates the traits of the magnanimous person first [1, a, i] by a comparison with external dangers that are the matter of fortitude; then [1, a, ii] by a comparison with external benefits that properly pertain to liberality, at "He is good at helping others etc."; and last [1, a, iii] by a comparison with honors that properly pertain to magnanimity, at "He acts with great dignity etc." He passes over the matter of temperance, which does not have any greatness of itself but deals with material common to man and brute, as was stated in the third book (612). Nevertheless magnanimity tends to do what is great in all the virtues—this was pointed out before (746, 749).

760. Touching on the first point he sets forth two traits, the first [1, a, i, x] of which is that the magnanimous man is not *microcindinos,* does not expose himself to dangers for trifles, nor is he *philocindinos,* i.e., a lover of danger, as it were exposing himself to dangers hastily and lightly. This is so because no one lays himself open to danger except for something having considerable value. But it is characteristic of the magnanimous man that he values few things to such a degree that he is willing to expose himself to dangers for them. Hence he does not undergo danger readily nor for insignificant things. However, the magnanimous man is *megalocindinos,* i.e., braves great dangers for great things because he puts himself in all kinds of danger for great things, for instance,

the common welfare, justice, divine worship, and so forth.

761. He assigns the second trait [1, a, i, y] at "When in danger." He affirms that the magnanimous person in exposing himself to danger acts ardently, so that he does not spare his own life, as if it were unfitting for him to prefer to live rather than gain great good by his death.

762. Next [1, a, ii], at "He is good," he enumerates five traits of the magnanimous man, which are understood by comparison with benefits proper to liberality. The first [1, a, ii, v] is that the magnanimous person is proficient at doing good for others, i.e., prompt to bestow benefits, but is ashamed to accept favors from others. To receive favors pertains to one who has lesser gifts, while the magnanimous man tries to surpass others in virtue.

763. At "He makes lavish recompense," he indicates the second trait [1, a, ii, w], saying that if the magnanimous person does accept benefits he is anxious to return greater ones. In this way the man who bestowed benefits in the beginning will rather receive them, i.e., becomes the recipient of benefits inasmuch as he receives more than he gave.

764. At "The magnanimous person likes to remember," he gives the third trait [1, a, ii, x], which does not follow the choice but the disposition of the magnanimous man—he is so disposed that he cheerfully confers but unwillingly receives benefits. We think often about the things that delight us and consequently remember them. However, we rarely think of things which displease us and consequently hardly ever recall them. Accordingly it seems characteristic of the magnanimous person to remember those for whom he does favors but not those who do favors for him, since this is contrary to his desire of wanting to excel in goodness. That man who is properly receptive, i.e., accepts favors, is less

noble than he who grants favors. The magnanimous man does not choose to be unmindful of favors received but is anxious to bestow greater favors, as was just said (763).

765. At "Likewise," he places the fourth trait [1, a, ii, y], saying that the magnanimous person cheerfully listens to the benefits he has bestowed but does not enjoy hearing of the benefits he has accepted. He can take delight in the love of him on whom he has conferred benefits but does not find pleasure in the fact that he himself has accepted benefits. He gives two examples of this. The first is taken from the writings of Homer who represents Thetis (called the goddess of water) approaching Jove (called the king of all the gods). She does not recount the benefits she herself has conferred on Jove,[1] as if this would not be acceptable to him, but rather the benefits she has received from Jove. To this Jupiter listened more willingly. The other example is taken from Greek history in which it is narrated that certain Spartans, when seeking the help of the Athenians, did not recite the favors they had done for the Athenians but the favors received from them.

766. He assigns the fifth trait [1, a, ii, z], at "The magnanimous person likes to show," saying that it pertains to the magnanimous man not to show himself in need of anything at all or at least not readily, inasmuch as he does not ask for or take anything, but to be prompt to minister to the needs of others.

767. Then [1, a, iii], at "He acts with great dignity," he indicates a trait of the magnanimous person by a comparison with honors. He treats the first point in a threefold manner. First [1, a, iii, x] he names the trait, saying that it belongs to the magnanimous man to show himself noble and honorable to men of dignity and wealth, but to

[1] Cf. *Iliad* i. 503 sq., where Thetis did so.

display a certain moderation with the middle class, not using a grand manner toward them.

768. Second [1, a, iii, y], at "To attain excellence," he offers two reasons for what he said. The first is that every virtue strives for what is difficult and honorable. That someone should excel great men in virtue is difficult and worthy of honor, but to excel mediocre men is easy.

769. The second reason is that it is characteristic of a manly soul to show himself worthy of respect among the great. But to wish respect shown him by men of lowly rank is the attitude of a man who is a nuisance to others.

770. Finally [1, a, iii, z], at "for instance," he gives an illustration, stating that such a condition indicates lack of virtue, namely, that a man demonstrates his strength against the weak, and does not undertake difficult and honorable ventures in which others excel.

771. Next [1, b], at "Leisure and slowness," he distinguishes the traits of the magnanimous person by means of human acts pertaining first [1, b, i] to himself; and then [1, b, ii] to others, at "Of necessity etc." Aristotle says first that the magnanimous man is disposed to be leisurely, i.e., does not engage in many undertakings, and is disinclined, i.e., not readily occupied with business. He devotes himself only to those activities that are connected with some great honor or the accomplishment of some great work. Therefore, the magnanimous person performs at least some great operations that are worthy of the name.

772. Then [1, b, ii], at "Of necessity," he indicates the traits of the magnanimous person concerned with human acts that are related to another, first [1, b, ii, x] in regard to truth; and next [1, b, ii, y] in regard to pleasantness, at "He cannot conform." These things are required especially for social intercourse with others,

as will be explained later (816-849). To the first he ascribes four traits, the first [aa] of which regards internal inclination. The magnanimous man, he says, cannot make a secret of his friends and enemies. The reason is that a secret love or hatred of another arises from some fear, and fear is repugnant to a magnanimous person.

773. At **"He cares more"** [bb] he notes the second trait, saying that it is characteristic of the magnanimous man to be more solicitous about the truth than the opinion of man. He does not depart from what he ought to do according to virtue because of what men think.

774. At **"He speaks"** [cc] he gives the third trait, saying that it is a mark of the magnanimous person to speak and work openly because he pays little attention to others. Consequently, he publicly divulges his words and deeds. That a man hides what he does and says arises from the fear of others. But no one fears those he contemns. Therefore, these two things are interchangeable, viz., that a man freely divulge things and that he cares little for others. However, we do not say that the magnanimous man cares little for others in the sense that he despises them—as it were depriving them of proper respect—but because he does not value them above their worth.

775. At **"He is truthful"** [dd] he assigns the fourth trait, saying that the magnanimous man does not speak falsehood but the truth, except perhaps that he playfully utters certain things in irony. However, he does use irony in the company of the common people.

776. Next [1, b, ii, y], at **"He cannot conform,"** he indicates the trait concerned with pleasure that arises from companionship, saying that the magnanimous person does not easily associate with others; he finds company only with his friends. The servile soul has a tendency to occupy himself with the intimate affairs of everyone.

Consequently all flatterers, who want to please everybody without distinction are obsequious, i.e., prepared to be subservient. People of low station who lack greatness of soul are flatterers.

777. Then [2], at **"Nor is he given,"** he enumerates the traits of the magnanimous man which arise from his natural bent. Aristotle first [2, a] gives some that exist in the soul; then [2, b] others existing in speech, at "Neither is he a gossip etc." Last [2, c], he sets forth those traits that exist in communication with others, at "He is willing etc." In regard to the first he places two traits, the first [2, a, i] of which is that the magnanimous person is not quick to show admiration because this is prompted by great things. But there is nothing great for him among the things that can happen externally, because his whole life is busy with internal goods, which are truly great.

778. Next [2, a, ii], at **"Nor is he mindful,"** he says that the magnanimous person is not too mindful of the evils he has suffered, giving two reasons for this. The first is that the magnanimous man refuses to remember many things, just as he refuses to wonder at them. Another reason is that the magnanimous person deliberately determines to forget injuries he has suffered inasmuch as he despises the things by which he could not be disparaged. Hence Cicero said of Julius Caesar that he was in the habit of forgetting nothing but injuries.

779. Then [2, b], at **"Neither is he a gossip,"** he gives two traits of the magnanimous man concerned with speech. First [2, b, i] he seldom speaks about men because he does not value highly their particular affairs. But his whole attention is taken up with the goods of the community and God. Consequently, he says little either about himself or others. He is not solicitous that he be praised nor that others be blamed. Hence he does not have much praise for others nor does he speak

337

evil of others, even his enemies, except to ward off an injury inflicted on him by them.

780. At **"In necessary or trivial"** [2, b, ii] he assigns a third (second) trait, that the magnanimous person neither complains by lamenting and grumbling about his lack of the necessities of life and other things, nor asks that they be given to him. This is the characteristic of one who is anxious about the necessities of life, as if they were great things, and this view is contrary to magnanimity.

781. Next [2, c], at **"He is willing,"** he indicates the traits that have a relation to external things, and first [2, c, i] in regard to external possessions. He says that the magnanimous man is more ready to own certain honorable and unfruitful goods which are profitless than goods which are profitable and useful. The reason is that a self-sufficient man has no need of profit from other quarters.

782. Then [2, c, ii], at **"But the movements,"** he gives the trait of the magnanimous man referring to bodily movements, stating that his movements

seem deliberate, his voice solemn, his speech measured and slow. Assigning the reason for these things, Aristotle says that the movements of the magnanimous person cannot be hasty since he is intent on few things. Likewise, he is not contentious because he holds nothing external of value. Now, no one contends except for something of value. But sharpness of voice and hastiness of speech are resorted to because of contention. Therefore, the temperament of the magnanimous man obviously requires a solemn voice together with deliberate speech and movement. The Philosopher says in the *Categories* (Ch. 8, 9 b 12 sq.) that if someone is naturally inclined to a passion, for example, bashfulness, he must have by nature that complexion which corresponds to bashfulness. Hence if a man has a natural proneness toward magnanimity, consequently he should have a natural disposition to qualities of this kind.

783. He concludes with the summary observation that the magnanimous man is just as we have described him.

LECTURE XI

Vices Opposed to Magnanimity

ANALYTICAL OUTLINE OF ST. THOMAS	TEXT OF ARISTOTLE (*B.1125 a 16*) Chapter 3

B. He now begins to treat the opposite vices.

A'. What is common to each vice.

But the man who fails by defect is small-souled, and the man who fails by excess is conceited. These people, however, do not seem to be criminals although they do sin.   **784**

B'. Each (vice) in itself.

I. THAT WHICH IS ACCORDING TO DEFECT.

a. The act proper to the small-souled man.

The small-souled person, although indeed worthy of excellent things, deprives himself of them.   **785**

b. The cause of small-mindedness.

There seems something bad in *20* such a man because he does not consider himself deserving of good. Besides, he does not really know himself; otherwise he would want the goods of which he is worthy. However, men of this kind are more lazy than stupid.   **786**

c. The effect of small-mindedness.

This opinion (of themselves) seems to make them worse, for everybody strives after the things they deserve. But, thinking themselves unfitted, they forsake good works and undertakings, and even external goods.   **787**

2. THAT (WHICH IS) ACCORDING TO EXCESS.

a. The cause of this vice.

Conceited people are silly and obviously ignorant of their capability, for they set about those things to which honor is attached and thereupon they are discredited.   **788**

b. The act of this vice.

They adorn themselves with *30* clothing and outward show, and such

339

like. They want these goods of fortune to be indicative of themselves. They even talk about themselves in order to receive honor from their conversation.   789

C'. He compares one vice with the other.

But small-mindedness is more opposed to magnanimity than presumption is.

As more opposed, it is also worse. Magnanimity then is concerned with great honor, as was said.   790-791

COMMENTARY OF ST. THOMAS

784. After the Philosopher has finished the treatise on magnanimity, he now [B] begins to treat the opposite vices. Here he does two (three) things. First [A'] he determines what is common to each vice. Then [B'] he considers each in itself, at "The small-souled person etc." Last [C'] he compares the one vice with the other, at "But small-mindedness etc." He says first that the man who falls short of the mean of magnanimity is called small-souled. But he who exceeds the mean is said to be conceited, i.e., puffed up—what we call inflated or presumptuous. These persons are not said to be evil to the extent of being criminals, for they injure no one and do nothing disgraceful. However, they do sin in this: they depart from the mean of reason.

785. At "The small-souled person" [B'] he considers each vice: first [1] that which is according to defect; and next [2] that according to excess, at "Conceited people etc." He discusses the first point in a threefold manner. First [1, a] he states the act proper to the small-souled man, saying that although such a man is worthy of good

things, he deprives himself of those he deserves by not attempting to work or obtain things due to him.

786. Next [1, b], at "There seems," he shows the cause of small-mindedness, pointing out that in this cause three things must be taken by turns. That a man deprive himself of goods he is deserving of happens first from the fact that he does not think himself worthy of such goods when in fact he is worthy. This occurs because he is ignorant of his ability. If the small-souled man knew himself, he would strive for the things he deserves because they are good and desirable, since one's own good is desirable to everyone. Ignorance of this kind does not come from stupidity—for the stupid are not worthy of great things —but rather from a certain laziness by reason of which they are unwilling to engage in great things according to their dignity. This is the third source from which the other two arise.

787. Third [1, c], at "This opinion," he explains the effect of small-mindedness. A person's opinion that he is unworthy of the goods he really deserves appears to make him worse.

Individual men strive for the things befitting their own worth. Hence when they are ignorant of their worth, they suffer a twofold damage to their goodness. First, they abandon works of virtue and the pursuit of speculative truths, as if they were unfitted for and unequal to things of this kind. From this omission of great and good works, they become worse, since it is such actions that make men more virtuous. Second, by reason of this opinion they shirk certain external good works of which they are capable and which instrumentally serve for the performance of virtue.

788. Then [2], at "Conceited people," he discusses the vice of excess under two considerations. First [2, a], he gives the cause of this vice, saying that the conceited or presumptuous are both stupid and ignorant of their ability not because of laziness like the small-souled but because of stupidity. This is obvious because they attempt to do or attain certain honorable things utterly beyond their ability. So, when they fail in the action or accomplishment they manifestly appear to be discredited.

789. Next [2, b], at "They adorn themselves," he introduces the act of this vice, which consists in a kind of external glorification, inasmuch as the presumptuous greatly exalt themselves. First, they do this by certain external signs, that is, they wear elegant cloth-ing and set off their figure by walking pompously. Likewise they do other things to show their excellence in the external goods of fortune. Second, they manifest things of this sort by words, as if wishing to achieve honor in this way.

790. At "But small-mindedness" [C'] he compares these two vices with one another, stating that small-mindedness is more opposed to magnanimity than conceit is. He assigns two reasons for this. The first reason, given in the second book (368), is that the vice, which occurs more frequently because of a stronger inclination of human nature toward it, is more opposed to virtue whose chief purpose is to restrain man's inclination to evil. But some men are obviously more inclined to be small-souled (i.e., to omit the virtuous deeds possible to them) than to extend themselves in the performance of laudable feats beyond them. Hence small-mindedness is more opposed to virtue. The other reason is that small-mindedness is worse from the aspect of making men less virtuous, as was just stated (787). But what is worse is more opposed to virtue. Therefore, it is evident that small-mindedness is more opposed to virtue.

791. He summarily concludes that magnanimity is concerned with great honor, as has been pointed out (346, 742-744, 750, 754).

LECTURE XII

The Virtue Concerned with Ordinary Honors

ANALYTICAL OUTLINE
OF ST. THOMAS

TEXT OF ARISTOTLE
(*B.1125 b*)
Chapter 4

1. HE POINTS OUT THAT SUCH A VIRTUE EXISTS AT TIMES.

As we remarked in the beginning,[1] there appears to be a virtue that deals with honor and is compared to magnanimity as liberality is to magnificence. Neither of these virtues is in any way concerned with what is great, but both rightly dispose us in regard to mediocre and small things. **792**

2. HE PROVES HIS STATEMENT.

a. First by reasoning from similarity.

Just as one can take and give small sums of money according to a mean, and also according to excess and defect, so too one can desire honor more or less than he ought, and also from the source he ought and as he ought. **793**

b. By the general manner of speaking.
   i. The ordinary manner of usage.

We blame the ambitious man because he desires honor inordinately and from the wrong sources. Like- *10* wise we blame the unambitious man for not choosing to be honored even for the good that he does. On the other hand, it is a fact that we praise the ambitious person as noble and enamored of what is virtuous, but the unambitious person as moderate and temperate. We indicated this in our earlier discussion of the subject. **794**

ii. . . . Then (he) argues from this to the proposition.

Clearly, inasmuch as the term lover of honor (or ambitious man) has been used in different contexts, the expression does not always receive the same

[1] Bk. II, Ch. 7, 1107 b 26 sq.

meaning. But we praise him as more concerned about honor than most people and we blame him for desiring honor more than is right.   795

Since the mean lacks a name, being as it were abandoned, the extremes are not clearly distinguished.   796

Now, where there is an excess and defect, there also is a mean. But people strive for honor more than is be- 20 coming and less than is becoming, hence also becomingly.   797

Therefore, this unnamed habit as being a mean concerned with honor is praised. By comparison with ambition it seems to be contempt of honor, but by comparison with lack of ambition, love of honor. But by comparison with each, the habit seems to be one as well as the other. This seems to be true in regard to other virtues also.   798

However, here the extremes appear to be contradictory because the mean has no name.   799

COMMENTARY OF ST. THOMAS

792. After the Philosopher has concluded his study of magnanimity, which treats of honors on a grand scale, he now considers a certain unnamed virtue having to do with ordinary honors. To explain it he does three things. First [1] he points out that such a virtue exists at times. Next [2] he proves his statement, at "Just as one can etc." Last [3], he explains in what manner the mean and the extreme may be considered in this virtue, at "Since the mean lacks a name etc." He says first, as was stated in the second book (346-348), that there

appears to be a virtue concerned with honor. That virtue seems to be related to magnanimity as liberality is to magnificence. Both these virtues, i.e., liberality and the virtue under consideration, are separated from magnificence and magnanimity as from something great. The reason is that magnanimity deals with great honors and magnificence with great expenditures. But the two virtues, liberality and the virtue under consideration, dispose us in regard to small and mediocre things, either honors or riches.

793. Then [2], at **"Just as one can,"**

he proves his statement, first [2, a] by reasoning from similarity; and second [2, b] by the general manner of speaking, at "We blame the ambitious man etc." He says that in taking and giving of small or ordinary sums of money there is a mean—and also an excess and defect—as was said before (679, 710-711). Likewise in the desire of small or mediocre honors, it happens that a man strives more or less than he ought, or for improper reasons inasmuch as one desires to be honored for more or greater things than he ought and another for fewer and lesser things. Likewise it happens that a man strives to be honored rightly in all things. So, clearly there is reason to hold for a mean of virtue and extremes of vice in small or mediocre honors as in smaller sums of money.

794. Next [2, b], at **"We blame the ambitious man,"** he explains his proposition by an ordinary use of words. On this point he does two things. First [2, b, i] he indicates the ordinary manner of usage; and then [2, b, ii] he argues from this to the proposition, at "Clearly, inasmuch etc." He says first that sometimes we blame the ambitious man, i.e., the lover of honor, for desiring honor more than he ought and from an improper source. Likewise, we blame at times the unambitious person for not wanting to do those good actions by reason of which he would be honored. On the other hand, we praise at times one who is a lover of honor as being manly or having a noble soul, and as a lover of the good, i.e., virtuous action to which honor is due. Again we praise occasionally a man who does not love honor—as it were regulating and ruling himself—so that he does not exceed his ability, as was stated in the second book (345-348).

795. At **"Clearly, inasmuch"** [2, b, ii] he draws a conclusion from this manner of speaking, saying that at times we praise then again we blame the lover of honor. But it is obvious that one is called a lover of honor in various senses, and for this reason we do not praise and blame him for the same thing. But we praise the lover of honor according as he is more concerned than the general run of people for the things pertaining to honor. We blame him, however, inasmuch as he desires honors more than is proper. The same line of reasoning applies to one who does not love honor. Consequently, the mean in this matter is praiseworthy according as honor and desire for honor are valued at their true worth. However, the extremes are blameworthy insofar as one desires more than he ought or less than he ought.

796. Next [3], at **"Since the mean,"** he treats the mean and the extreme of this virtue. On this point he does two things. First [3, a] he shows the uncertainty occurring here; and then [3, b] the consequences of that uncertainty, at "However, here the extremes etc." He discusses the first point under three headings. First [3, a, i] he indicates the uncertainty with the observation that, since the mean concerned with desire for honor has no name—and so, because of this lack, appears as if passed over—the extremes do not seem consequently to be clearly drawn, inasmuch as they are sometimes praised, sometimes blamed.

797. Then [3, a, ii], at **"Now, where there is,"** he explains what the truth is concerning mean and extremes. He says that whenever we find an excess and defect, there also we must find a mean. Therefore, since some strive for honor both more and less than they ought, it follows that some strive as they ought—which belongs to the notion of a true mean.

798. Finally [3, a, iii], at **"Therefore, this unnamed habit etc.,"** he shows the

basis for this uncertainty. Because there is reason to accept a mean in regard to honors, the habit of the medium is praised. Likewise, because unnamed, it is designated by the names of extremes, as by a comparison with one of the extremes it seems to have a likeness to the other extreme. By comparison with excessive love of honor, the medium appears to have contempt of honor; but by comparison with contempt of honor, love of honor; by comparison with each it appears to be one as well as the other in some way. This is evident also in other virtues, for the brave man seems reckless by comparison with the timid man but timid by comparison with the reckless man. So, then, in our proposition the extremes considered in themselves are censured but as attributed to the mean they are praised.

799. Then [3, b], at **"However, here,"** he explains how it follows from this uncertainty that the extremes seem opposed only to one another but not to the mean of virtue because the mean has no name.

345

LECTURE XIII

Meekness and Its Opposed Vices

ANALYTICAL OUTLINE
OF ST. THOMAS

TEXT OF ARISTOTLE
(*B.1125 b 26*)
Chapter 5

I. HE TREATS MEEKNESS AND ITS OPPOSED VICES.

A. He shows how the mean and the extreme are discovered for anger.

Meekness is a kind of moderation concerned with anger. The mean in the strict sense being without a name (and the extremes nearly so), we *30* refer to meekness as the mean, although it inclines to the defect which is also nameless. However, the excess can be called irascibility.[1] **800**

B. Then he discusses them.

A'. He treats meekness.

I. WHAT BELONGS TO MEEKNESS AS . . . A VIRTUE.

Anger is a passion arising from many and various causes. Hence a man who is angry over the right things, with the right persons, and moreover in the right way, at the right time, and for the right interval is praised. He is a meek man. But if meekness is an object of praise, the meek man seeks to be undisturbed and not controlled by passion, but to be angry at the things and for the length of time that reason directs. **801**

2. WHAT BELONGS TO (MEEKNESS) ACCORDING TO THE REAL MEANING OF THE WORD.

However, he seems to sin more on the side of defect, for the *B.1126* meek person is not vindictive but rather forgiving. **802**

[1] The text has *verecundia* but the context requires *iracundia*.

B'. (He treats) the opposite vices.

I. FIRST THE VICES OF DEFECT.

a. The defect of anger . . . is censurable for three reasons . . . the first.

But the defect—either a certain apathy or something of the kind—is censured, for a man seems to be foolish who does not get angry at the things he should both in regard to the manner, the time, and the persons. Such a one appears not to feel things nor to be pained at them. **803-804**

b. Second.

Moreover, he who does not get angry will not stand up for himself; **805**

c. Third.

and it is considered slavish to endure insults to oneself and to suffer one's associates to be insulted. **806**

2. THEN THOSE OF EXCESS.

a. This vice takes place in many ways.

The excess can happen in all likely ways, for a man can be angry with the wrong people, at the wrong **10** things, more than he should, more readily than he should, and for a longer time than he should. However, all these excesses do not belong to the same man who certainly would not be able to survive, for evil which is complete destroys itself and would be unendurable. **807-808**

b. He considers its species.
   i. Three kinds of excess in anger. First.

Those persons are hot-tempered who become angry too readily, with the wrong people, at the wrong things, and more than they should. They do quiet down quickly—a very commendable trait which belongs to them because they do not retain anger, but in accord with their openness retaliate in a flare-up of temper, and then become tranquil. But the irascible (*acrocholi*) are intense in their excess, and get angry on every occasion and at every turn. It is from this that the name is derived. **809**

   ii. Second.

However, the sullen are angry **20** for a long time and are mollified with difficulty, for they do not relinquish their anger. But they are appeased when they have taken vengeance. The

347

infliction of punishment calms the surge of anger and brings delight in place of sadness. When this is not done they are glum because they do not externally express their anger, and no one can prevail upon them. In this case time is needed to absorb the anger. Such persons are burdensome to themselves and especially to their friends. **810**

iii. Third.

We call those persons ill-tempered who are angry at the wrong things, more than they should be, for too long a time, and who are not appeased until they inflict vengeance and punishment. **811**

3. HE COMPARES THESE TWO VICES WITH ONE ANOTHER.

Excess is more opposed to meekness, for it happens more frequently *30* since man is prone to take vengeance, and it makes the ill-tempered worse to live with. **812**

II. HE ANSWERS AN IMPLIED QUESTION.

A. This cannot be determined with certitude.

As was observed in previous discussions [1] and made plain, it is not easy to determine how, at what, and how long one ought to be angry, or when one acts rightly or makes a mistake. Persons, who transgress slightly, either in great or lesser things, are not blamed. In fact, sometimes we **b** praise men as meek who are wanting in anger, and as manly and competent to rule who abound in anger. However, it is not readily ascertainable by reason to what extent and in what manner a transgressor is blameworthy, for judgment is to be made according to sense perception in individual cases. **813**

B. What is clear in this matter.

But it is evident in these matters that the mean habit is praiseworthy according to which we are angry with

[1] Bk. II, Ch. 9, 1109 b 14 sq.

the right people, about the right things, in the right manner, and so on in other circumstances. Likewise, it is evident that excess and defect are blameworthy, in such a way however that if they are slight, they can be tolerated; if greater, then more blameworthy; and if very great, then very blameworthy. But obviously one must adhere to the mean habit. We have now discussed the habits concerned with anger.   **814-815**

COMMENTARY OF ST. THOMAS

800. After the Philosopher has finished the consideration of the virtues dealing with external goods, riches, and honors, he now considers meekness, which deals with the external evils which provoke people to anger. On this point he does two things. First [I] he treats meekness and its opposed vices; and then [II] he answers an implied question, at "As was observed." On the initial point he does two things. First [I, A] he shows how the mean and the extreme are discovered for anger; and then [I, B] he discusses them, at "Anger is a passion etc." He says first that meekness is a certain mean for anger. However, in this matter the mean taken in the proper sense has received no name. The same can almost be said about the extremes because they are not distinguished by explicit names. The name meekness is taken to signify a mean, although the word implies a lack of anger. People are called meek because they are not violent, as it were like domesticated animals who lose their irascibility. Even the disordered lack of anger has not been given a name. Someone is said to be meek who is not angry for any reason whatsoever,

either good or bad. However, the excess is called rage or irascibility.

801. Then [I, B], at "Anger is a passion," he first [A'] treats meekness; and then [B'], the opposite vices. He treats the first point from two aspects. Initially [A', 1] he explains what belongs to meekness as it is considered a virtue; and then [A', 2] what belongs to it according to the real meaning of the word, at "However, he seems to sin etc." He says first that irascibility is considered the vice of the extreme because it implies an excess of anger which is a passion arising from many and various causes. So, according to the diversity of these things, a mean and an extreme are found in anger. Consequently, the praiseworthy man is the one who is angry about the right things, at the right people, and in due moderation (since he is angry as he should be, when he should be, and as long as he should be). However, if the word meekness is used as a compliment, it would seem that the meek man is so disposed: first, that he is not disturbed internally in the judgment of reason by anger; second, he is not led by anger in external choice, for reason determines the ob-

jects of anger and the length of time within which anger should react.

802. Next [A', 2], at "**However, he seems to sin,**" he explains, in accord with the true meaning of the word, the character of the meek man who (he says) in this respect seems to err more in approaching the defect. When we call a person meek, we signify that he is not inclined to punish but to forgive and remit punishments. This is a thing belonging to a lack of anger which is a desire for vengeance achieved by punishment.

803. At "**But the defect**" [B'], he treats the opposite vices, taking up first [B', 1] the vices of defect; and then [B', 2] those of excess, at "The excess etc." Last [B', 3], he compares these two vices with one another, at "Excess is more opposed etc." He says that the defect of the mean in anger is censured whether we call it apathy or any other name whatsoever.

804. Since the Stoics were of the opinion that all anger is censurable, he consequently shows that the defect of anger sometimes is censurable for three reasons [B', 1, a]. He proposes the first reason at "**a man seems to be foolish etc.**" Whatever indicates a lack of wisdom is blameworthy because virtue is praised for working in accord with the right understanding of prudence. But for a man to fail to be angry at the things, in the manner, at the time, and with the persons he should be angry seems to denote a lack of wisdom. It is evident that anger is caused by sadness. But sadness is a feeling of injury. If then someone fails to be angry at the things he should, he does not grieve for them and so does not feel they are evil. This pertains to a lack of wisdom. Therefore it is clear that a defect of anger is blameworthy.

805. He gives the second reason [B', 1, b] at "**Moreover, he who does not get angry.**" Anger is a desire for vengeance. Hence one who is not angry at the things he should, accordingly does not punish the actions he ought to punish. This is blameworthy. However, this explanation is not to be understood as if another vengeance cannot be taken according to the judgment of the reason without anger, but as if the movement of anger stirred up by the judgment of the reason makes one more prompt to take vengeance in the right way. If the sensitive appetite did not help to carry out the judgment of the reason, it would be useless in human nature.

806. He introduces the third reason [B', 1, c] at "**and it is considered,**" saying only a cringing man suffers his household to be insulted and permits others to injure him without repelling the injury with due force. This follows from a defect of anger which renders a man slothful and remiss in warding off injury. Hence it is evident that the defect of anger is blameworthy.

807. Then [B', 2], at "**The excess can happen,**" he treats the excess of anger. First [B', 2, a] he shows that this vice takes place in many ways; and second [B', 2, b] he considers its species, at "These persons are hot-tempered etc." He says first that excess of anger can occur according to all the circumstances. It happens that someone is angry with the wrong people and in the wrong things, that he is provoked too much and too easily angered, that he is angry too long. However, all these excesses are not found in one man, both because of the trouble he himself would suffer from his own anger, and also because, being burdensome to all, he could not live with others.

808. This is universally true of evil —if it were complete, it would destroy itself. It could not continue to exist in taking away the subject by which it must be sustained if it is to continue to be. What does not exist can hardly be called evil, because evil is

a privation of good. But every being precisely as existing is good. Obviously then evil does not take away good entirely, but some particular good of which evil is a privation. In such a way blindness takes away sight but does not destroy the animal. If the animal were destroyed, blindness would cease to exist. Manifestly, then, evil cannot be complete because in so taking away the good entirely, it would destroy itself.

809. Next [B′, 2, b], at "Those persons," he presents three kinds of excess in anger. The first [2, b, i] is that of those called hot-tempered, those easily aroused to wrath, readily becoming angry both with the wrong persons, and at the wrong things, and too vehemently. However, their anger does not last long but quickly subsides. This is very fortunate in a way for them that anger is not retained internally in their heart, but immediately bursts forth externally because they either take vengeance at the time or show their anger in some other way by clear indications with a burst of temper. In this way, when their anger is expressed they quiet down. So, also, heat which is shut up is kept at a higher degree, but when dispersed in vapor it disappears rather quickly. To this kind of anger the choleric seem disposed most readily by reason of the subtlety or speed of the bile. It is from this speed that excess is acquired by the irascible or *acrocholi,* i.e., those excessive in anger, from *acros* meaning extreme and *cholos* meaning anger, because they are intense and quick in anger.

810. He presents the second kind (of anger) [2, b, ii], at "However, the sullen," saying that some are called sullen whose anger is dispelled with difficulty and lasts a long time because they keep it pent up in their hearts. But they cease to be angry only when they have satisfaction for the injury inflicted. Punishment calms the

surge of passion when the previous sadness is replaced by delight, inasmuch as a man takes pleasure in vengeance. But if this does not happen, that is, if punishment is not inflicted, they are sorely grieved inwardly, since they do not show their anger. No one can persuade them to moderate this wrath that is not indulged. But the dissolution of anger requires a long time in which the fire of wrath may cool off gradually and be extinguished. Such persons who retain anger for a long time are a trial to themselves and especially their friends with whom they cannot live pleasantly. For this reason they are called sullen. To this kind of excess, the melancholic seem particularly inclined because the influence received from the coarseness of the humor lasts a long time in them.

811. He introduces the third kind (of anger) [2, b, iii], at "We call those persons," saying that some are called ill-tempered or morose who are angry at improper things, in an improper degree and for an improper length of time, and do not leave anger until they wreak vengeance on or punish those with whom they are angry. Indeed their anger lasts long not because of a retention alone that can be dissolved in time but because of a firm resolve to inflict punishment.

812. Then [B′, 3], at "Excess is more opposed," he compares the things just treated with one another, stating that the excess of anger is more opposed to meekness than the defect is. He proves this by two arguments: first, it is the usual occurrence. Man is inclined more naturally to inflict punishment after suffering an injury to himself, while he is naturally inclined to meekness when he has not suffered any injury. The second reason is that the excessive in anger are more difficult to live with and to this extent are worse. Hence they are more in opposition to the good of virtue.

813. Next [II], at "As was ob-

served," he answers an implied question, namely, at what things and in what manner ought a man be angry. On this point he does two things. First [II, A] he affirms that this cannot be determined with certitude; and second [II, B] he states what is clear in this matter, at "But it is evident etc." He says first that, as was observed in the second book (379) and there made clear, it is not easy to determine in what manner one should be angry, i.e., at things of what nature, for how long a time, and up to what point one acts correctly or errs in becoming angry. One who departs a little from the mean, either in great or small matters, is not blamed. In fact, at times we praise those who are somewhat deficient in anger and call them meek, but those who are a little excessive we call manly, as if able and qualified to rule by reason of their promptness for vengeance, which is appropriate to rulers. It is not easy to determine by

reason the extent and kind of deviation from the mean for which a man should or should not be blamed. The reason is that judgment in this case depends on particulars and on sense perception which is more an interior than an exterior evaluation.

814. At **"But it is evident"** [II, B] he shows what is obvious in these matters, saying it is evident that the mean according to which we are angry with the right persons, at the right things, and so on with regard to the other circumstances, is praiseworthy. Likewise, it is evident that excess and defect are blameworthy, in such a way however that if they are slight they can be tolerated; if they are greater, they are more blameworthy; and if very great, they are blameworthy in the highest degree. Hence a man ought to draw himself towards the mean.

815. Last, he says in the epilogue that we have discussed the habits that deal with anger.

LECTURE XIV

Amiability

ANALYTICAL OUTLINE
OF ST. THOMAS

TEXT OF ARISTOTLE
(*B.1126 b 10*)
Chapter 6

I. HE TREATS THE SERIOUS (ACTIONS).

A. He investigates the virtue concerned with pleasantness and sadness arising from the serious actions of men.

A'. A mean and extremes are found.

I. THE VICE PERTAINING TO THE EXCESS OF PLEASANTNESS.

Some men seem to be obsequious in association with others and in interchange of words and deeds. They praise everything for the sake of pleasantness, and never contradict anyone, being of the opinion that unpleasantness ought to be avoided. **816**

2. THE VICE WHICH PERTAINS TO THE DEFECT.

Others, on the contrary, always find fault, taking care to emphasize anything unpleasant. They are called perverse and quarrelsome. **817**

3. THE CONCLUSION . . . THE MEAN IS PRAISEWORTHY.

These habits being reprehensible, obviously the mean habit is laudable —that habit according to which a person approves what he should and also disapproves what he should. **818**

B'. He examines (the mean and extremes).

I. FIRST THE MEAN.

a. The name of the mean habit.
  i. The mean habit has no name.

This mean habit has not been 20 given a name. **819**

  ii. He gives the habit a name . . . from friendship.

But it has a remarkable resemblance to friendship, for the man who is disposed according to the mean habit is

353

a man worthy of friendship, assuming
that he loves us.   820

However, since this virtue is without passion or affection for people with
whom we associate, it differs from
friendship. A man does not take particular things as becoming because he
is influenced by love or hatred but
because he is disposed in this way. He
will act similarly with strangers, intimates, and outsiders.   821

Nevertheless, in particular cases, he
does the proper thing; it is not becoming to treat intimates and strangers
in the same way, nor similarly to show
displeasure toward them.   822

Therefore, as has been pointed out,
he always communicates with others
in an amiable manner.   823

Considering it honorable and useful,
he aims to cause no offense, and even
to give pleasure, for he is con- *30*
cerned with pleasure and sadness
which occur in social intercourse. 824

Any virtuous man of this type will
refuse to give pleasure and will choose
to cause pain over what is dishonorable and harmful to himself or to the
person doing an injury or a great
wrong. Although his opposition brings
not a little offense, he will disregard
it.   825

He converses differently *B.1127*
with persons in high places and with
others, with friends, and with acquaintances. Likewise, according to
other differences he attributes what is
becoming to each.   826

He primarily strives to give pleasure and declines to inflict pain, considering that future events may be
of greater importance. (I speak of what
is honorable and useful.) But he will
cause grief especially in a slight degree for the sake of a pleasure in a
good that is to come. The mean then
is of this nature but is nameless. 827

2. (HE DEFINES) THE EXTREMES.

a. The vice that belongs to the excess of pleasantness.

Of those who are agreeable, the man who aims at being pleasant without personal profit is called affable, but he who does so for money and things valued in terms of money is called a flatterer.   828

b. He refers to the opposite vice.

But the individual who is a *10* trial to everyone is called quarrelsome and perverse, as has been stated.   829

c. He compares the two vices.

However, the extremes seem to be mutually opposed because the mean is nameless.   830

COMMENTARY OF ST. THOMAS

816. After the Philosopher has considered virtues relating to external things, now he considers the virtues that relate to human actions. First [I] he treats the serious; and then [Lect. XVI, II] the humorous actions, at "Since recreation should have a place etc." (B.1127 b 33). In the investigation of the serious actions, he examines pleasantness and veracity. First [A] he investigates the virtue concerned with pleasantness and sadness arising from the serious actions of men; and then [Lect. XV, B] the virtue concerned with veracity, at "Likewise, the mean opposed to boasting etc." (B.1127 a 13). He develops the first point in a twofold fashion. Initially [A'] he shows that a mean and extremes are found in regard to pleasantness and sadness in human acts; and then [B'] he examines these, at "This mean habit has not etc." He discusses the first from three aspects. First [A', 1] he presents the vice pertaining to the excess of pleasantness. He says that in human conversation (by which men especially associate with one another according to a natural tendency) and generally in all

human companionships (made possible by the fact that men communicate with one another in words and deeds) some seem to be obsequious, as it were straining to please men. Wherefore, they praise everything that others say and do for the purpose of making themselves agreeable. They never contradict people for fear of giving offense, thinking they must live without causing pain to anyone.

817. Second [A', 2], at "Others, on the contrary," he introduces the vice that pertains to the defect in such matters. He states that people who are cross-grained wish to be contrary to everything said or done as if trying to make others sad and taking care to emphasize anything that will make life unpleasant for others. These persons are called perverse or quarrelsome.

818. Last [A', 3], at "These habits," he draws the conclusion that the mean is praiseworthy, saying that these habits, which consist in an extreme, are unworthy of praise. Obviously, then, the mean habit is worthy of praise—that habit by which a man accepts what

355

others say or do, or rightly rejects and contradicts it.

819. Next [B'], at **"This mean habit,"** he defines the previous matter: first [B', 1] the mean; and then [B', 2] the extremes, at "Of those who are etc." He handles the initial point in a twofold manner. First [B', 1, a] he treats the name of the mean habit; and then [B', 1, b] its properties, at "Therefore, as has been pointed out." He considers the name under three headings. First [a, i] he states that the mean habit has no name.

820. Second [a, ii], at **"But it has,"** he gives the habit a name from a resemblance to friendship. This virtue, he says, is very much like friendship because there is agreement in the external act which is especially proper to friendship, viz., to live amicably with friends. That person, who is disposed according to the mean habit of this virtue, conducts himself in agreeable association with others in a manner becoming to a friend whose friendship is moderated by reason—a thing that pertains to honorable friendship. Not every friendship is virtuous, as will be pointed out later (1574-1577). If the man who has this virtue should love those with whom he lives, his friendship will be entirely virtuous.

821. Last [a, iii], at **"However, since,"** he shows how this virtue differs from friendship. He treats this point in a twofold manner. First [iii, x] he presents the difference; and then [iii, y] rejects a false understanding of it, at "Nevertheless, in particular cases etc." He says first that, since this virtue is without love (which is a passion of the sensitive appetite) and without affection (which pertains to the intellective appetite) for those with whom we associate, it differs from true friendship. A man does not take the particular things said or done by others as becoming, because he is influenced by hatred or love of them but because he is disposed in this way by

habit. This is proved by the fact that he observes the same not only with friends but generally with all acquaintances and strangers, intimates and outsiders. Liberality is like this. A friend gives gifts to his friends because he loves; the liberal man however gives not because he loves but because his nature is to be a free spender.

822. Then [iii, y], at **"Nevertheless,"** he rejects a false understanding of these things. Since he just stated (821) that this virtue is practiced alike toward strangers and acquaintances, a man might consider this likeness as extending to everything. But the previously mentioned likeness must be taken as referring to this common characteristic, which is to live agreeably with others. There is a difference in regard to the special ways of living with others. The reason is that the virtue affects the proper actions in particular cases, for a person should not delight or displease intimates and outsiders in the same way.

823. At **"Therefore, as has been"** [B', 1, b], he enumerates the five properties of this virtue; the first [b, i] of which is taken from the manner of communicating with others. As has been noted (821), one having this virtue always communicates with others in a becoming way.

824. At **"Considering,"** Aristotle gives the second property [b, ii], which is understood on the part of the end, saying that one having this virtue aims at living with others without offense or even with pleasure. This end pertains to a good that is honorable and advantageous, i.e., useful, because it is concerned with pleasure and sadness occurring in associations in which human companionship principally and fittingly consists. This is proper to men in contrast to animals who share food and the like in common.

825. At **"Any virtuous man,"** he introduces the third property [b, iii], which is understood by comparison

with pain, saying that the man who possesses this virtue sometimes refuses to give pleasure to another, in fact sometimes chooses to cause pain. This may take place in two ways. In one way it can happen on his part: if a thing is not honorable to him, for instance, another uses indecent language; or if a thing is harmful to him, for instance, another injures him in word. In the other way, it can happen on the part of the person he lives with. This person may say or do something pertaining to his own great disgrace, or he may be greatly harmed. By reason of the fact that he is contradicted he is grieved to some extent. So the virtuous man will not take what is said by others, or if he does he will nonetheless reprove them.

826. At **"He converses differently"** he introduces the fourth property [b, iv], which is understood by comparison with different persons. He says that a virtuous man speaks and converses in a different way with persons in high places and with private persons, with friends and with acquaintances, and so on according to other distinctions of persons, ascribing to each individual what is appropriate.

827. At **"He primarily strives,"** he presents the fifth property [b, v] which is taken by comparison of pleasure with pain. He affirms that the virtuous man

primarily strives to give pleasure and declines to inflict pain. However, at times he causes some grief considering that future events will outweigh the existing affliction in what concerns decency and utility or even a future important consideration, the evidence for which is provided by the present distress. He concludes that the mean habit is like this but is without a name, although we can call it affability.

828. Then [B′, 2], at **"Of those who,"** he defines the opposite vices, doing three things. First [B′, 2, a] he treats the vice belonging to the excess of pleasantness. He says that the man who is immoderate in being pleasant—if he does not act for something else—is called obsequious. But if he acts to acquire money or any other thing computable in money, he is called a sycophant or a flatterer.

829. Next [B′, 2, b], at **"But the individual,"** he refers to the opposite vice, saying that the individual who is a trial to everyone is called contentious and perverse, as has been stated previously (817).

830. Finally [B′, 2, c], at **"However, the extremes,"** he compares the two vices one with the other, saying that the extremes seem to be opposed to one another but not to the virtue because the mean of the virtue is nameless.

LECTURE XV

Veracity

<table>
<tr><td>ANALYTICAL OUTLINE
OF ST. THOMAS</td><td>TEXT OF ARISTOTLE
(B.1127 a 13)
Chapter 7</td></tr>
</table>

B. . . . A virtue . . . that possesses a mean in the same human actions.

A'. He explains his intention.

I. A CERTAIN VIRTUE IS A MEAN OPPOSED TO BOASTING.

> Likewise, the mean opposed to boasting treats of almost the same subject, and it too is nameless.   831

2. WE MUST TREAT THIS VIRTUE.

a. First (reason).

> It is not a loss to examine these matters, for in making the investigation we will learn more about particular habits.   832

b. Second.

> Observing what is so in all cases, we are assured that virtues are certain median states.   833

3. THE DIFFERENCE BETWEEN THIS AND THE PRECEDING VIRTUE.

> We have already discussed the people who cause pleasure or pain in their association with others. In like manner we will now investigate those persons who manifest truth and falsehood by words, operations, and pretense. *20*   834

B'. He defines his proposition.

I. HE PRESENTS THE VIRTUE AND THE OPPOSITE VICES.

a. What belongs to the mean and extremes in this matter.

> The boaster simulates non-existent qualities, or claims a greater distinction than he really has. On the contrary, the dissembler denies or minimizes the qualities he has. But the man who observes the mean is admirable, being truthful both in life and speech, acknowledging that his own qualities are

b. How the things . . . discussed pertain to the median habit and the extremes.

c. The median habit is praiseworthy.

neither more nor less excellent than they really are.   835

Each of these acts may be done both for the sake of something else and for nothing other than itself. As a man is, so he speaks, acts, and lives, unless some other cause affects him.   836

A lie is intrinsically evil and to be avoided but the truth is both good and to be praised. So, the man who *30* speaks the truth is worthy of praise as being better, while the above two who do not tell the truth are worthy of blame, more especially the boaster.
                                                 837

2. HE INVESTIGATES THEM.

a. First the virtue.
　i. *What truthful person we are discussing.*

We will discuss both, but first the truthful man. We are not going to investigate the person who speaks the truth in his agreements nor on any subject pertaining to right or its *b* violation, for this belongs to another virtue. But we do intend to study the person who manifests the truth by his conversation and way of living (insofar as he does this from habit) in matters not touching justice and injustice.
                                                 838

　ii. *What is especially characteristic of this person.*

Such a man seems to observe moderation, for he is a lover of the truth and, being truthful where it makes little difference, he will speak the truth all the more where it does matter. He will fear a lie as disgraceful because he feared it in itself. Such a man is worthy of praise.   839

　iii. *To what extreme the person is most inclined.*

He turns aside from the truth more by understatement, for this seems rather prudent since overstatements are irritating.   840

b. Then the opposite vices.
　i. *The vice pertaining to excess.*
　　x. IN HOW MANY WAYS WE MAY COMMIT . . . BOASTING.

The person who boasts more excellent talents than he possesses for *10* no ulterior motive has a semblance of evil; otherwise, he would not find pleasure in lying. He is really, though, more vain than evil. But one who

359

boasts for something else, like glory or honor, does not deserve great blame. However, the man who boasts for the sake of money or objects valued in money is more vicious.   **841-842**

A boaster is constituted not by capability but by choice. He is such in accordance with a habit, as is the case with the liar who finds pleasure in lying itself, or the one who lies because he desires glory or profit.   **843**

Therefore, people who boast for the sake of fame simulate qualities that win praise and admiration. Those who boast for the sake of gain pretend things more closely connected with profit and things whose absence is *20* not clearly apparent. For this reason many braggarts pretend to be doctors, soothsayers, or wise men, for the qualities mentioned are verified in them.   **844-845**

Dissemblers, however, who say less than what is true seem to be more gracious. For they apparently speak not to acquire gain but to avoid offense and vanity.   **846**

Some people especially deny qualities about themselves that bring renown, as Socrates did. Others, who disclaim insignificant and obvious things are called affected humbugs (*blato-panurgi*).[1] They are readily despised; and at times they seem guilty of ostentation, like the Spartans by their clothing. For this reason excess and immoderate deficiency seem characteristic of the boastful. Still others who moderately *30* employ dissimulation, even dissembling about things obvious and ready at hand, seem rather agreeable.   **847-848**

As being more vicious, the boaster seems more opposed to the truthful man.   **849**

[1] See note in the Commentary.

COMMENTARY OF ST. THOMAS

831. After the Philosopher has finished the treatise on the virtue possessing the mean in human actions in regard to amiability, he now [B] treats a virtue called veracity, which possesses a mean in the same human actions. First [A'] he explains his intention; and then [B'] he defines his proposition, at "The boaster simulates etc." He develops the first point in three ways. First [A', 1] he discloses that a certain virtue is a mean opposed to boasting. Next [A', 2], at "It is not a loss etc.," he shows that we must treat this virtue. Last [A', 3], at "We have already discussed etc.," he explains the difference between this and the preceding virtue. He says first that the mean opposed to boasting treats about nearly the same subject as the previous virtue. The reason is that it is concerned with human actions, but not in relation to the same thing, since it does not regard pleasantness but another topic to be discussed shortly (838). As in the case of the previous virtue, this mean too is nameless.

832. Then [A', 2], at "It is not a loss," he explains why it is necessary to investigate this virtue, giving two reasons. First [A', 2, a] he says that it is not profitless but in fact useful to moral science to treat the virtues as we go along. In this way we will learn better what pertains to morals if, as we proceed, we treat the material pertaining to individual habits. The reason is that the science of moral matters is completed by a knowledge of particulars.

833. At "Observing what," he presents the second reason [A', 2, b]. We shall be assured that the virtues are kinds of median states by seeing how this is the case in the individual virtues.

834. Next [A', 3], at "We have already," he defines the difference between this and the preceding virtue. He states that we have already considered (816-830) the people who in some way give pleasure or pain in their association and conversation with others. But we must still discuss those people who are truthful or deceitful in their words and actions or who simulate these qualities by their deeds.

835. Then [B'], at "The boaster simulates," he treats the virtues and vices. First [B', 1] he presents the virtue and the opposite vices; and then [B', 2], at "We will discuss both etc.," he investigates them. He handles the first point from three aspects. First [B', 1, a] he shows what belongs to the mean and extremes in this matter. Next [B', 1, b], at "Each of these etc.," he explains how the things which were discussed pertain to the median habit and the extremes. Third [B', 1, c], at "A lie is intrinsically etc.," he reveals that the mean habit is praiseworthy but the extremes, vicious. He says first that the boaster who sins by excess pretends certain praiseworthy qualities, and this in two ways. In one way he pretends to have some distinctions that he does not possess. In the other way, he claims distinctions greater than they really are. But the person who sins by defect is called a dissembler. However, the man who possesses the mean is said to be *autocastos,* i.e., admirable in himself, because he does not seek to be admired more than becomes him. He is also said to be *autophastos,* i.e., essentially sincere, manifesting himself to be what he is. He is truthful inasmuch as the things he divulges about himself are true. He does this not only by word

but also by his manner of living, according as his exterior conduct and his speech conform to his nature.

836. At "**Each of these**" [B′, 1, b], he explains how these things pertain to the three specified habits, saying that each of the above-mentioned acts may happen in two ways. In one way, it may be done for the sake of something else, for instance, a man denies that he is what he is because of fear; in the other way, not for the sake of something else but because he takes delight in the act itself. This property belongs to a habit, since everyone speaks, acts and lives according to the quality of his habit. Of course at times he may act differently because something else arises.

837. Then [B′, 1, c], at "**A lie is intrinsically etc.,**" he discloses what deserves praise and what blame in the habits mentioned, saying that a lie is essentially evil and to be avoided, but truth is good and to be praised. Signs were instituted to represent things as they are. Therefore, if a person represents a thing otherwise than it is by lying, he acts in an inordinate and vicious manner. But if he speaks the truth, he acts in an orderly and virtuous manner. Now, it is clear that the man who speaks the truth possesses the mean because he designates a thing as it is. The truth consists in an equality that is a mean between great and small. But the person who lies stands in an extreme either by excess because he affirms more than really is, or by defect because less than really is. Hence, it is evident that both are blameworthy. But the boaster who sins by excess deserves more blame since he departs farther from the truth; for the less, not the more, is found in the mean.

838. Next [B′, 2], at "**We will discuss both,**" he investigates the previously mentioned habits, treating first [B′, 2, a] the virtue and then [B′, 2, b] the opposite vices, at "The person who

boasts etc." He treats the first point in a threefold manner. First [a, i] he determines what truthful person we are discussing. Next [a, ii], at "Such a man etc.," he shows what is especially characteristic of this person. Third [a, iii], at "He turns aside etc.," he explains to what extreme the person is more inclined. He says first that we must talk about these habits, but first about the truthful man. However, we do not have in mind now the person who speaks the truth in judicial testimony, for example, a witness who reveals the truth when questioned by a judge; nor the person who speaks the truth in any matter touching right— this pertains to another virtue, viz., justice. But we are directing our attention to that truthful man who manifests the truth in his life and conversation in matter not having distinction of justice and injustice. However, he manifests the truth only by reason of the disposition of the habit, as was said before about a previous virtue (821) that it aims at living pleasantly with others, not by reason of love but by reason of its habit. So, too, this virtue shows the truth not on account of the observance of justice but on account of the inclination it has to manifest the truth.

839. At "**Such a man**" [a, ii], Aristotle explains what particularly pertains to the truthful man we have in mind, saying he is one who apparently observes moderation in his actions, avoiding excess and defect. He loves truthfulness and the truth even where damage or profit is of little importance. The reason is that he hates a lie as something shameful in itself, and not only because it injures another. A person of this kind is to be commended.

840. Then [a, iii], at "**He turns aside,**" he explains to what extreme the truthful man more inclines, affirming that since sometimes it is quite difficult to tell the exact truth, he wishes to lean towards understatement rather

than overstatement. This seems to pertain more to prudence since men tend to excess, and when speaking about themselves, they become tiresome to others. The reason for annoyance is that they seem in this to prefer themselves to others.

841. Next [B', 2, b], at **"The person who boasts,"** he examines the opposite vices. He considers this point under three aspects. First [b, i] he investigates the vice pertaining to excess; next [b, ii] the vice pertaining to defect, at "Dissemblers, however etc."; and last [b, iii] the opposition of vices among themselves, at "As being more vicious etc." He treats the first point in a threefold manner. First [i, x] he shows in how many ways we may commit the vice of boasting which is an extreme by excess. Second [i, y], at "A boaster is constituted etc.," he explains in what respect we may especially take into account the vice of boasting. Finally [i, z], at "Therefore, people who etc.," he shows in what things we may principally commit the vice of boasting.

842. He states first that sometimes a man says boastfully about himself things that are untrue or exaggerated, not for some other purpose but for the enjoyment he gets out of it. Such a man is said to have a semblance of evil, otherwise he would not find pleasure in lying, for this arises from a disordered soul. However, he is not at all evil since he does not intend any malice; he is only vain for taking pleasure in a thing which is really neither good nor useful. In another way, a person speaks boastfully about himself because he wants glory or honor. This person really ought not to be blamed since glory and honor have a certain relationship to honorable things for which people are praised and honored. In still another way, people brag about themselves for the sake of money or some other thing that can be valued in money. An individual be-

longing to this class is more vicious because he lies for an inferior good.

843. At **"A boaster is constituted"** [i, y], he explains in what respect we may take boasting into account, saying that a man is not considered a boaster from the fact that he has or has not the capability, but from the fact that he chooses to boast. He is called a boaster according to the habit that this choice follows. It is the same with any liar who is such in choosing to lie, or finding pleasure in lying, or lies out of his desire for fame or profit.

844. Then [i, z], at **"Therefore, people who,"** he explains the things that people usually boast about. Obviously, persons who find enjoyment in boasting boast indiscriminately. But those who boast for the sake of fame pretend things that seem worthy of praise, like virtuous works, or that have reference to good fortune, like the dignity of wealth and so on. Those, however, who boast for the sake of profit pretend things in which others find pleasure, otherwise it would profit them nothing. Again, when the things they boast about are not true, they take care that this fact can be hidden so their lie may not be discovered.

845. He takes an example from two fields: first, from things belonging to medicine, since everyone wants health and no one can find out whether the doctor makes a mistake; second, from divination, which naturally disturbs men and where they cannot easily discover a lie. For this reason people who boast for profit especially pretend to be doctors or men wise in foretelling the future. Perhaps his use of the word "wise" can be referred to this that these men boast that they have a knowledge of divine things that is desirable and hidden.

846. Next [b, ii], at **"Dissemblers, however,"** he considers the vice belonging to the defect. On this point he does two things. First [ii, x] he

compares this vice with boasting; and then [ii, y] points out its difference at "Some people especially etc." He says first that dissemblers who minimize the truth about themselves seem to have more pleasing ways than boasters, because they apparently do not speak this way for the sake of gain but as if fleeing from vanity.

847. At "Some people especially" [ii, y] he explains how this vice is practiced in different ways, saying there are some who especially deny about themselves things pertaining to great renown, for example, Socrates denied that he was wise. There are others who want to show by certain insignificant and obvious things that they do not pretend more excellent things about themselves than they possess. Such are called *blato-panurgi*, i.e., men who have their delight in a certain cunning pretense.[1] *Panurgi* is a Greek word for "cunning fellow," while *blaton* means something done amusingly.

[1] *Baukopanourgoi* appears in *Aristotle, the Nicomachean Ethics,* translated by R. Rackham (Harvard University Press, 1956).

These, he says, are readily despised because their pretense is too obvious. A defect of this nature in external things sometimes seems to pertain to boasting when in this way they want to appear better and more observant of moderation, like the Spartans who wore clothing humbler than became their state. For this reason an excess and an immoderate deficiency in externals seem to pertain to boasting precisely because a certain singularity in a man is displayed in case of each.

848. Still others exercise this vice in a mitigated form, since they neither altogether deny famous deeds done by themselves nor do they even attribute to themselves negligible qualities, practicing the vice in matter obvious and at hand. People like this seem to be pleasing, as was just said (846).

849. Then [b, iii], at "As being more vicious," he considers the opposition between the vice and the virtue, saying that the boaster is more in opposition to the truthful man because more vicious, as we have already noted (837). The worse vice is always more opposed to virtue.

LECTURE XVI

Amusement

ANALYTICAL OUTLINE OF ST. THOMAS	TEXT OF ARISTOTLE (*B.1127 b 33*) Chapter 8

II. HE CONSIDERS A CERTAIN VIRTUE THAT DEALS WITH AMUSEMENT.

A. There can be a virtue and vice having to do with amusement.

> Since recreation should have a place in our life and our social living by means of playful conversation, this would be a suitable time for *B.1128* a discussion of what things are proper to say and hear. In matters of this nature, speaking and listening are different, but it is clear that we have both excess and defect in respect to the mean. **850-851**

B. He treats the virtue and the opposite vices concerned with amusement.

A'. The nature of each habit.

I. WHAT THE MEAN AND THE EXTREMES IN AMUSEMENT ARE.

a. What belongs to excess.

> People who engage in too much derision are buffoons and nuisances wanting laughter at any cost. They try more to get a laugh than to converse politely and avoid offending the persons they mock. **852**

b. The nature of the vice by defect.

> On the other hand, persons who say nothing funny and are disagreeable to those who do, seem uncultured and rude. **853**

c. The nature of the mean in amusement.

> But men indulging in jest with good taste are called witty, like those *10* who give a humorous turn to things. **854**

2. (THE MEAN AND THE EXTREMES) BELONG TO A DIFFERENCE OF CHARACTER.

> Actions of this kind seem to belong to character, for as bodies are judged

from their movements, so too are characters.   **855**

Since laughter is quite popular,
most people take more pleasure in fun
and in joking reproach of others than
they should. Hence they are pleased
with buffoons who are called witty.
However, from what has been said it
is obvious that buffoons are quite different from persons of wit.   **856**

B'. What is proper to each habit.

I. WHAT IS PECULIAR TO THE MEAN OF THIS VIRTUE.

a. How the witty person conducts
himself in general.

   *i. That the use of clean fun per-
tains to the mean habit.*

Tact belongs to the mean habit of
this virtue. It is characteristic of a
tactful person to tell and listen to such
tales as become a decent and liberal
man.   **857**

   ii. Proof for what he has said.

Now, the witty person speaks and
listens to what is becoming in jest. *20*
But the jesting of the liberal man
differs from that of the servile man;
the jesting of the cultured man from
that of the uncultured.   **858**

   *iii. The jesting of the cultured and
the uncultured person differs.*

Anyone can see this in the comedies
of the ancient and modern authors. In
the earlier plays obscene language appears and is an object of laughter; in
the later it is rather implied. This difference towards obscenities is of no
small importance for decency.   **859**

b. How (the witty person) especially
acts in friendly banter.

   i. He asks (a) question.

We must determine, then, whether
a man is good at raillery because he
says what becomes a liberal man, or
because he does not offend his listener,
or because he even delights him. **860**

   ii. He answers the second part.

This norm is indefinite to the extent that what is hateful to one person
is pleasing to another. But each will
listen to the things which give him
pleasure, while he seems to encourage
the things which he permits.   **861**

iii. Something is settled as to the first part.

The virtuous person will not *30* employ every kind of jest, for some jokes are in fact an insult. But legislators forbid the making of some insulting remarks. Actually they should forbid all reviling. Here the pleasing and liberal man will be as it were a law unto himself. Therefore, either the witty or the tactful person possesses the mean in this matter.   **862-863**

2. WHAT IS PROPER TO THE EXTREME BY EXCESS.

However, the buffoon, less vi- *b* cious than the derider, spares neither himself nor others for the sake of a laugh. Likewise, he says such things as the polite person would never think of saying—would not in fact listen to.   **864**

3. WHAT PERTAINS TO THE EXTREME BY DEFECT.

But the lout is useless at these conversations, contributing nothing and making everyone uncomfortable. Nevertheless, recreation and jest seem to be necessary for human life. **865**

C. The difference between this and those virtues already considered.

In human living there are three median courses, all of which regard communication in speech and action. They differ, however, for one deals with truthfulness and the others with what is pleasing. Of this second class, one concerns pleasure taken in amusements, the other concerns pleasure in things according to another aspect of life, viz., conversations.   **866**

COMMENTARY OF ST. THOMAS

850. After the Philosopher has finished the consideration of the virtues dealing with human actions of a serious nature, he now considers a certain virtue which deals with amusement [II]. He develops this point in three ways. First [A] he shows there can be a virtue and vice having to do with

367

amusement. Next [B], at "People who engage in too much etc.," he treats the virtue and the opposite vices concerned with amusement. Third [C], at "In human living there are etc.," he explains the difference between this and those virtues already considered. In regard to the first we must consider that, as has been shown (329), there can be no corresponding virtue and vice concerned with what is intrinsically evil and incapable of having an aspect of good. Consequently, if no aspect of good can be found in amusement there will be no virtue connected with it.

851. But amusement does have an aspect of good inasmuch as it is useful for human living. As man sometimes needs to give his body rest from labors, so also he sometimes needs to rest his soul from mental strain that ensues from his application to serious affairs. This is done by amusement. For this reason Aristotle says that, since there should be some relaxation for man from the anxieties and cares of human living and social intercourse by means of amusement—thus amusement has the aspect of useful good—it follows that in amusement there can be a certain agreeable association of men with one another, so they may say and hear such things as are proper and in the proper way. Yet, in matters of this kind, talking and listening are very different, for a man properly listens to things he could not properly say. But wherever difference exists between the things that ought to be done and ought not to done, there is found not only a mean but also excess and defect in regard to this mean. Hence we have a virtuous mean and extremes concerned with amusement.

852. At "People who engage" [B] he considers the mean and the extremes. First [A'] he speaks about the nature of each habit; then [B'], at "Tact belongs etc.," he shows what is proper to each habit. He discusses the first point in a threefold manner: ini-

tially [A', 1] he explains what the mean and the extremes in amusement are; then [A', 2] at "Actions of this kind etc.," he shows that they belong to a difference of character; last [A', 3], at "Since laughter is quite etc.," he discloses that the extreme is sometimes taken for the mean. He treats this first point from three aspects. In the beginning [A', 1, a] he shows what belongs to excess, saying that those who indulge excessively in playful derision are *bomolochi* or temple plunderers because of a resemblance to birds of prey who used to fly over the temple to pounce upon the entrails of sacrificed animals. In that way these people lie in wait so they can pounce upon something to turn into a laugh. On this account persons of this kind are a nuisance because they want to make laughter out of everything. They make more effort to do this than to engage in becoming or polite conversation and avoid disturbing the man they heap with playful reproach. They would rather tell scandalous stories, even at the risk of offending others, than (not) cause men to laugh.

853. Second [A', 1, b], at **"On the other hand,"** he explains the nature of the vice by defect, stating that men who never want to say anything funny and are disagreeable to the people who do (these being reasonably disturbed) seem to be uncultured or boorish and coarse, like those who are not mellowed by amusing recreation.

854. Third [A', 1, c], at **"But men indulging,"** he explains the nature of the mean in amusement, saying that men who devote themselves to amusement in moderation are called witty (*eutrapeli*), as it were, good at turning because they becomingly give an amusing turn to what is said and done.

855. Then [A', 2], at **"Actions of this kind,"** he shows that the actions just mentioned belong to different habits. He says that these movements by which a person wishes to amuse

others too much, or too little, or in a moderate way are indications of internal dispositions of habit. As external movements of bodies clearly indicate their internal dispositions, so external actions manifest internal characters.

856. At "Since laughter is quite" [A', 3], he explains how the extreme sometimes is taken for the mean. He says that many people bubble over with laughter and take more pleasure than they should in jest and in joking reproach of others. Hence, they give the name witty to buffoons who please them by excessive indulgence in jest which the majority of men love immoderately. Nevertheless, as is clear from what was said before (852-854), buffoons are quite different from witty people.

857. Next [B'], at "Tact belongs," he shows what properly belongs to the preceding habits. First [B', 1] he explains what is peculiar to the mean of the virtue; and then [B', 2], at "However, the buffoon etc.," what is proper to the extreme by excess. Finally [B', 3], at "But the lout etc.," he discloses what pertains to the extreme by defect. He handles the initial point from two aspects. First [B', 1, a] he shows how the witty person conducts himself in general with reference to fun; and then [B', 1, b], at "We must determine etc.," how he acts especially in friendly banter. He considers this first in a threefold way. In the beginning [a, i] he brings out that the use of clean fun pertains to the mean habit. He affirms that what is characteristic of a tactful person (epydexiotis), i.e., of a man well-fitted and prepared to engage in conversation with others, belongs to the mean habit of this virtue. It is proper to men of this sort to narrate and listen to such amusing incidents as become a decent and liberal man who possesses a soul free from slavish passions.

858. Next [a, ii], at "Now, the witty

person," he gives a reason as proof for what he has said, viz., that wherever something is found that can be done in a becoming manner, there is a thing that belongs to virtue. But it happens that a witty person says and listens to what is becoming. This is obvious from the different kinds of jest. The jesting of the liberal man who spontaneously strives to act virtuously differs from the jesting of the servile man who is engaged in disreputable activities. The jesting of the cultured man who has been instructed how he should recreate differs from the jesting of the uncultured man who has not been trained by any instruction in jesting. Hence, it is clear that it pertains to the mean habit of virtue to speak and listen to what is becoming in jesting.

859. Last [a, iii], at "Anyone can see," he introduces a proof for the previous statement that the jesting of the cultured and the uncultured person differs. This, he says, is particularly evident in considering the conversation of the players with one another in the old and new comedies or plays. The evidence is that where these narratives in places contain obscene language, some create derision when they turn the obscene words into laughter; but others create a suspicion when they imply that those who were speaking in an obscene manner had evil in their hearts. However, obviously it is of great importance to human decency whether a man in playful conversation speaks obscenely or properly.

860. At "We must determine" [B', 1, b], he explains how the virtuous man conducts himself regarding jesting insults. On this point Aristotle does three things. First [b, i] he asks the question whether we must decide that a person does well at raillery by reason of the things which he says, i.e., because he says what is becomingly said by a liberal man who is virtuous and decent; or that he is not deter-

mined according to this but rather by reason of the end or effect, i.e., because he aims not to offend his listener; or, what is more, aims to give him pleasure.

861. Then [b, ii], at "This norm is indefinite," he answers the second part of the question, saying that it is indeterminate what may offend or please the listener because different things are odious and pleasant to different people. Everyone will gladly listen to what pleases him. And, as long as no offense is intended, a man seems to promote those things which he patiently hears by co-operating in them with others.

862. Third [b, iii], at "The virtuous person," he shows that something is settled as to the first part, viz., as to affronts that are offered. It is clear that the virtuous man does not make use of every reproach, since reproach is a kind of insult. Besides, legislators forbid the hurling of any insult that defames a man. They do not forbid reproachful remarks that are fittingly uttered for amusement or for a man's correction (a thing to be managed without loss of good name). That man who acts in a pleasing and polite manner in raillery seems to be a law unto himself, provided that by his own choice he avoids the things forbidden by the law and makes use of the things sanctioned by the law.

863. Finally, he comes to the conclusion that the man possessing the mean is such as was described, whether he is called *epidexios,* i.e., tactful, or *eutrapelos,* i.e., witty.

864. Next [B', 2], at "However, the buffoon," he explains the viciousness of the excess, saying that the buffoon is less vicious than the mocker because the mocker tries to put another to shame while the buffoon does not aim at this but only at getting a laugh. The latter spares neither himself nor others in attempting to create laughter, since he makes fun both of his own tales and of the sayings and deeds of others. Besides, he says things that a polite and virtuous person would not say, and some that he should not say and should not even listen to.

865. Then [B', 3], at "But the lout," he treats the vice by defect, saying that the man who is uncultured, i.e., boorish, is useless at these witty conversations. He contributes nothing to them but is disagreeable to everyone. He is vicious in that he completely abhors jest, which is necessary for human living as a kind of recreation.

866. Next [C], at "In human living there are," he deduces the difference between this virtue and the two previously discussed, stating that in human life there are the three median states mentioned, all of which regard communication in words and works. But they differ among themselves, since one of them deals with truthfulness in speech and action, while the others pertain to what is pleasing. One of these concerns pleasure taken in amusement; the other concerns pleasure taken in conversation according to our usual way of living, i.e., in serious matters.

LECTURE XVII

Shame

ANALYTICAL OUTLINE OF ST. THOMAS	TEXT OF ARISTOTLE *(B.1128 b 10)* Chapter 9

A. He shows that shame is not a virtue.

A'. He investigates the genus of shame.

    1. HE PRESENTS HIS PROPOSITION.

Shame is not properly spoken *10* of as a virtue because it is more like a passion than a habit.   **867**

    2. HE PROVES HIS PROPOSITION.

a. By means of a definition of shame.

In any case shame is defined as fear of disgrace.   **868**

b. By the effect of shame.

Like fear, shame is brought about by reason of danger, for people who feel ashamed blush, and those who fear death grow pale. Both qualities are in some measure modifications of the body, and so pertain rather to passion than habit.   **869-870**

B'. He examines its subject.

    1. AT WHAT AGE IT IS BECOMING.

a. He presents his proposition.

This passion is not becoming to persons of every age but only to the young.   **871**

b. Shame is becoming to adolescence.

We are of the opinion that it is well for the young to feel shame because, living according to their emotions, many of them would fall into sin but are restrained by shame. Moreover, we are in the habit of praising youngsters who have a sense of shame.   **872**

c. Shame is not becoming to . . . old age.

But no one praises an old man *20* because he is shamefaced, for we think it unbecoming of him to commit acts giving rise to shame.   **873**

2. FOR WHAT CONDITION (SHAME IS BECOMING).

a. It is not becoming to the virtuous person.

Likewise, shame is not characteristic of a virtuous person but follows evil actions such as must not be done.   874

b. He answers certain frivolous objections against his thesis.
   i. First.

If some actions are shameful in fact and others only considered such, this does not matter for neither kind should be done, and so should not be objects of shame. The wicked, however, perform disgraceful actions of this kind.
875-876

ii. Second. He proves in two ways that this (shame belongs to the virtuous person) is untenable.
   X. SHAME . . . REGARDS . . .
   FAILINGS FOR WHICH BLAME
   IS DUE.

It is unreasonable to hold that if a man is so constituted that he is ashamed if he does a disgraceful action, he is considered virtuous on this account. Shame is felt because of acts voluntarily done, and no virtuous man voluntarily does evil.   877-878

   Y. HE EXCLUDES THE PRECEDING
   OBJECTION.

Shame will be a virtue result- *30* ing from the supposition of something else, viz., if a man did such an act, he would be ashamed. But virtue does not work this way.   879

iii. Third.

But, if shamelessness and the absence of shame at doing dishonorable actions is evil, it is not on that account virtuous to be ashamed to do things of this kind.   880-882

B. He says a similar thing about continence which . . . is not a virtue.

Likewise, continence is not a virtue but has a mixture of virtue. Hence, we shall consider this in a later treatise,[1] but now we must treat justice.   883-884

[1] Bk. VII.

COMMENTARY OF ST. THOMAS

867. After the Philosopher has completed the treatise on the median qualities that are virtues, he now treats a median quality that is not a virtue, viz., shame. First [A] he shows that shame is not a virtue. Then [B], at "Likewise, continence is not etc.," he says a similar thing about continence, which, although laudable, is not a virtue. He discusses the first point from two aspects. First [A'] he investigates the genus of shame; and then [B'], at "This passion is not etc.," he examines its subject. He treats this first in a twofold manner. Initially [A', 1] he presents his proposition, saying that shame is not properly called a virtue. But shame is more like a passion than a habit which is the genus of virtue.

868. Next [A', 2], at "In any case," he proves his proposition in two ways: first [A', 2, a] by means of a definition of shame. Shame is said to be fear of disgrace or confusion which is the opposite of glory. But fear is a certain passion. Consequently, shame belongs to the genus of passion.

869. Then [A', 2, b], at "Like fear," he proves the same thing by the effect of shame. In this regard we must consider that passions are movements of the sensitive appetite that uses bodily organs. Hence all the passions are accompanied by some corporeal change. Shame and fear—which is concerned with the danger of death—have a general resemblance in that each passion is judged by a change in the color of the body.

870. But they have particular differences, since people who are ashamed blush, while those who fear death turn pale. The reason for this difference is that the spirit and the humors naturally rush to the place feeling the need. Now, the seat of life is the heart, and so when danger of death is feared, the spirit and the humors speed to the heart. Consequently, the surface of the body, being as it were deserted, grows pale. On the other hand, honor and confusion are numbered among external things. Therefore, since a man fears the loss of honor by shame, he blushes as the humors and spirits stream back to the surface. It is evident then that both shame and fear of death are certain alterations of the body inasmuch as they are accompanied by a change. Because this apparently belongs rather to passion than habit, it is obvious that shame is not a virtue.

871. At "This passion" [B'], he discloses what is the fitting subject of shame. First [B', 1] he shows at what age it is becoming; and then [B', 2], at "Likewise shame is not etc.," for what condition. He develops the first point in a threefold fashion. First [B', 1, a] he presents his proposition, viz., that it is not becoming to persons of every age but to the young.

872. Then [B', 1, b], at "We are of the opinion," he proves in two ways that shame is becoming to adolescence. In one way he shows this from the peculiar nature of youth, namely, that on account of the intense desires of their age they live according to their emotions. For that reason they are inclined to sin in various ways. But they are restrained from this because of shame by which they fear disgrace. Therefore, shame is becoming to youth. In the other way he gives evidence of the same thing from usage. We are accustomed to praise young people who have a sense of shame.

873. Third [B', 1, c], at **"But no one praises,"** he explains that shame is not becoming to another period of life, i.e., old age, saying that no one praises an old man for feeling shame. The reason is that we think it unbecoming of him to do any shameful deed from which shame usually arises. Besides, we think both that old men have been proved by their years and that they ought not to do any shameful act from passion after the fire of youth has subsided.

874. Next [B', 2], at **"Likewise, shame is not,"** he shows to what condition shame is or is not becoming. He handles this point under two headings. First [B', 2, a] he explains that it is not becoming to the virtuous person. Then [B', 2, b], at "If some actions etc.," he answers certain frivolous objections against his thesis. He says that shame does not belong to the man of virtue, for it occurs in regard to evil deeds. But the virtuous man does not do wicked actions because virtue is a quality which makes good both its possessor and his work. Therefore, shame is not becoming to a virtuous person.

875. Then [B', 2, b], at **"If some actions,"** he answers three objections dealing with what has just been said. The first [b, i] is that someone might say that shame arises not only from truly disgraceful acts, which are contrary to virtue, but also from actions believed to be disgraceful.

876. But Aristotle says that it does not make any difference for our thesis, since the morally good man must not do things shameful either according to truth or opinion, and so is not in danger of being ashamed of anything. But the wicked person characteristically is of the sort who perform acts certainly disgraceful or held to be such.

877. He introduces a second objection at **"It is unreasonable"** [b, ii]. A person could say that, although the man of virtue does not have anything

to be ashamed of, nevertheless he is so disposed that if he did something of the kind, he would be ashamed of it. Therefore, in case anyone should think on this account that shame belongs to the virtuous person, he proves in two ways that this is untenable.

878. First [ii, x] he says that shame, strictly speaking, regards only voluntary failings for which blame is due. But it is inconsistent with virtue that someone should voluntarily do evil. Therefore, shame does not belong to virtue for the reason just given. The case would be otherwise if shame were among the things which can happen involuntarily like sickness. Hence, it can be proper for the virtuous man even when well to be solicitous about a doctor on account of the sickness that can happen.

879. Second [ii, y], he excludes the preceding objection at **"Shame will be."** He says that if the objection were valid, shame would be a certain conditional virtuous state, for the virtuous man would be ashamed if he were to do wrong. But a conditional state (that a man would be ashamed) is not one of the qualities that properly belong to virtuous people. Rather, it belongs to them absolutely, as is the case of all the virtues. We must conclude then that shame is not a special quality in a virtuous person.

880. At **"But if shamelessness"** [b, iii] he gives a third objection. Someone could draw the conclusion that, because shamelessness and the absence of shame concerning a disreputable operation is an evil thing, for this reason shame is virtuous.

881. But Aristotle says that this is not a necessary inference because both shame and shamelessness suppose a dishonorable act which is not attributable to a morally good man. On this basis it is more reasonable that a man should reject the disgraceful operation by reason of shame than not care about it by reason of shamelessness. From

this it is clear also that shame is not a virtue, for if it were a virtue it would exist in a virtuous person.

882. We must take into account that the Philosopher previously (356) treated the praiseworthy passion of righteous indignation (*nemesis*), and that here he does not mention it because it is not his intention to treat these passions on this occasion. This matter pertains rather to rhetoric, as is clear from the second book of the *Rhetoric* (Ch. 9, 1386 b 9 sq.). Hence, neither does he here consider shame except to show that it is not a virtue. He leaves the same thing to be understood about righteous indignation.

883. Then [B], at "**Likewise, continence,**" he introduces something similar concerning continence which, although laudable, is not a virtue but has an admixture of virtue. Certainly, the continent man follows right reason, and this pertains to virtue. Nevertheless, he suffers vehement and evil desires, and this pertains to lack of virtue. We will discuss these subjects afterwards in the seventh book (1435-1454). It is enough that he brings out in a fitting manner shame's resemblance to continence because shame is especially necessary where evil passions abound, as they do in continent people. We have already remarked this (873).

884. Finally, he makes a connection with what follows, saying that we must next discuss justice. With this the teaching of the fourth book comes to an end.

BOOK V

JUSTICE

CONTENTS

CONTENTS

BOOK V

LECTURE I

Justice

ANALYTICAL OUTLINE OF ST. THOMAS	TEXT OF ARISTOTLE (*B.1129*) Chapter 1

I. HE EXAMINES JUSTICE IN THE PROPER SENSE.

A. He investigates the virtue of justice.

A'. He indicates what he intends to treat.

    1. WHAT SUBJECT HE INTENDS TO CONSIDER.

> We must give our attention to justice and injustice so as to determine what is the nature of the actions done, what is the mean of justice, and between what extremes the just action is a mean. **885-886**

    2. BY WHAT METHOD WE ARE TO EXAMINE THE DIFFERENCES.

> It is our intention to proceed according to the same method we used with the virtues just studied. **887**

B'. He carries out his intention.

    1. HE DISTINGUISHES PARTICULAR FROM LEGAL JUSTICE.

a. He divides justice into legal and particular.

  i. What the names . . . signify.

    X. HE EXPLAINS JUSTICE AND INJUSTICE.

> Apparently everyone wants to call justice that habit by which men are disposed to just works, and by which they actually perform and will just deeds. We must speak in a similar way about injustice, viz., that it is a habit by which men are disposed to unjust deeds and by which they do and will unjust actions. For that reason we *10* must presuppose what is said here in outline (*in typo*). **888-889**

    Y. THE EXPLANATION IS REASONABLE.

> Likewise, the same is not true in regard to sciences and potencies as in regard to habits, for contraries belong

381

to the same potency and the same science, but with a habit contrary things are not referred to it. We see, for example, that things contrary to health do not proceed from health, but only things in keeping with it. Thus we say that a man walks in a healthy way when he walks like a healthy man.

890-891

Z. HE INFERS A COROLLARY.

Oftentimes, then, one contrary habit is known by another, and oftentimes by its subject. If a healthy condition is known, then an unhealthy condition also becomes known. But from the things that make a man healthy a healthy condition is known, and the things themselves from the condition. If firmness of flesh is a sign of good condition, then flabbiness is neces- *20* sarily a sign of bad condition. Likewise, what makes a man healthy necessarily makes his flesh firm.

892

ii. He distinguishes the two concepts.
X. HE GIVES THE DIVISION.
　　aa. Various meanings of justice.

It follows in most instances that if one of opposites is spoken of in various ways then the other also can be, as is the case with what is just and unjust.

893

　　bb. He explains the . . . meanings.

Justice and injustice can be spoken of in various ways but the different meanings lending themselves to equivocation are not immediately apparent, and are not so evident as in the things which are widely separated. In these there is a great difference in concept, for instance, the name key is used equivocally both for the clavicle in the shoulder of animals and for the *30* instrument which locks doors.

894

　　cc. He explains . . . habits.

The unjust man should be understood in as many ways as he is designated. He is spoken of as lawbreaking, as covetous and as unfair. It is clear then that the just man will be taken as law-abiding and fair. Hence what is just is according to law and fair, but what is unjust is contrary to law *b* and unfair.

895-896

Y. THE PARTS OF THE DIVISION.
aa. He shows . . . the covetous . . . unjust.

Since the unjust man is covetous, he will be concerned not about all goods but about whatever pertains to fortune and misfortune. Goods of this kind are always good in themselves but not always for a particular man. They are objects of his prayers and pursuits. This ought not to be so, but a man should pray that the things that are good in themselves become good for him, and should choose such as are good for him. **897**

bb. He shows . . . the unjust person . . . unfair.

But the unjust man does not always choose too much, rather sometimes too little of the things burdensome in themselves. However, because a lesser evil apparently is in some way a good —covetousness is concerned with *10* a good—therefore it seems that this type of man is covetous. But he is unfair—a term which contains both and is common. **898**

cc. How the unjust man is . . . lawbreaking.

Besides, the unjust man is lawbreaking, but this lawlessness or inequality contains all injustice and is common in respect of all kinds of injustice. **899**

COMMENTARY OF ST. THOMAS

885. After the Philosopher has finished the consideration of the moral virtues dealing with the passions, he now begins to consider the virtue of justice dealing with actions. He divides the inquiry into two parts, in the first of which [I] he examines justice in the proper sense; and then [Lect. XVII], at "Whether or not it is possible etc." (B.1138 a 4), in the metaphorical sense. He discusses the first point under two headings. Initially [A] he investigates the virtue of justice; and then [Lect. XVI], at "Next we will treat equity etc." (B.1137 a 31), a certain virtue, namely, equity that

gives direction to ordinary justice. He handles the initial point in a twofold manner. First [A'] he indicates what he intends to treat; and next [B'], at "Apparently everyone wants to call etc.," he carries out his intention. He considers the first under two aspects. Initially [A', 1] he shows what subject he intends to consider, viz., justice and injustice. Concerning justice he proposes for consideration three differences existing between justice and the previously mentioned virtues.

886. The first difference is touched upon when he says that we must aim at such operations as are done by justice

and injustice. The virtues and vices discussed before (649-884) are concerned with the passions, for there we consider in what way a man may be internally influenced by reason of the passions; but we do not consider what is externally done, except as something secondary, inasmuch as external operations originate from internal passions. However, in treating justice and injustice we direct our principal attention to what a man does externally; how he is influenced internally we consider only as a by-product, namely, according as he is helped or hindered in the operation. The second difference is touched upon when he says "what is the mean of justice and the just action," i.e., the object of justice. In the virtues previously treated we took the mean of reason and not of the thing. But in justice the mean of the thing is used, as will be determined later (932-977). The third difference is touched upon when he says "and between what extremes the just action is the mean." Each of the afore-mentioned virtues is a mean between two vices, but justice is not a mean between two vices, as will be clear afterwards (993-994).

887. Then [A', 2], at **"It is our intention,"** he shows by what method we are to examine the differences just mentioned. He says that we intend to investigate justice in the same way as we investigated the virtues just discussed, i.e., according to type and so on.

888. Next [B'], at **"Apparently everyone etc.,"** he begins the investigation of justice. First [B', 1] he distinguishes particular from legal justice. Then [Lect. IV], at "One species of particular etc." (B.1130 b 30), he considers particular justice, his principal concern. He discusses the first point in a threefold manner. First [1, a] he divides justice into legal and particular. Second [Lect. II], at "Since it was said that etc." (B.1129 b 12), he shows what the nature of legal justice is.

Third [Lect. III], at "We are now investigating etc." (B.1130 a 14), he explains that, besides legal justice, there is a particular justice. He treats the initial point in a twofold manner. First [a, i] he shows what the names, justice and injustice, signify; and then [a, ii], at "It follows in most instances etc.," he distinguishes the two concepts. He develops the first under three headings. At the outset [i, x] he explains justice and injustice. Next [i, y], at "Likewise, the same etc.," he shows that the explanation is reasonable. Last [i, z], at "Oftentimes then etc.," he infers a corollary from the premises. He says in the beginning that all seem to contend that justice is the sort of habit that brings about three effects in man. The first is an inclination to a work of justice in accord with which a man is said to be disposed to just works. The second is a just action. The third is that a man wants to perform just operations. We must say the same about injustice, namely, that it is a habit by which men are disposed to unjust deeds and by which they do and will unjust actions. For that reason we must presuppose these things about justice as apparently typical in such matters.

889. Likewise, we must take into consideration that he properly explained justice after the manner of a will, which does not have passions but nevertheless is the principle of external actions. Consequently, the will is a proper subject of justice, which is not concerned with the passions.

890. At "Likewise, the same" [i, y] he shows that the preceding explanations are reasonable in this respect, viz., that justice is explained by the fact that its purpose is to will and perform just actions, and injustice to will and perform unjust actions. What is true of sciences and potencies is not true of habits, for contraries belong to the same potency (for example, white and black to sight) and to the same science

(for instance, health and sickness to medicine). But in regard to habits, contrary things are not referred to them.

891. He takes an example from habits of the body. Not the things that are contrary to health but only those in keeping with health proceed from health. In this way we say that a man walks with a vigorous step who is vigorous in health. Hence science itself, as it is a kind of knowledge, refers to contraries inasmuch as one of contraries is the reason for knowing the other; nevertheless, inasmuch as science is a certain habit, it is attributed to one act only (which is knowing the truth) and not to the contrary error. So then it was properly said that by justice we do just actions; by injustice, unjust actions.

892. Then [i, z], at "Oftentimes, then," he infers a corollary from the premises. Since contrary habits belong to contraries, and one act belongs to one object in a fixed manner, it follows that frequently one contrary habit is known by another and oftentimes by its object which is, as it were, matter subject to the operation of the habit. He illustrates this by an example. If *evexia* or a healthy condition is known, *cachexia* or an unhealthy condition is also known. In this way a habit is known by its contrary. Likewise it is known from its object because from the things that make a man healthy, a healthy condition becomes known. This is further illustrated in a more particular way. If the fact that a man has very firm flesh is a characteristic of a healthy condition, then the fact that he has flabby flesh—as it were loosely compressed by reason of disordered humors —is necessarily characteristic of an unhealthy condition. Again, that which makes a man healthy is necessarily a condition making him have firm flesh.

893. Next [a, ii], at "It follows in most instances," he distinguishes justice and injustice. First [ii, x] he gives the division; and then [ii, y], at "Since the unjust man etc.," the parts of the division. He treats the first point in three ways. At the outset [x, aa] he shows that various meanings of injustice indicate various meanings of justice. The reason is that it follows in most instances that if one of opposites may be spoken of in diverse ways, then the other can be. This is the case, too, with what is just and unjust.

894. Second [x, bb], at "Justice and injustice," he explains the nature of their various meanings. He says that both justice and injustice can be spoken of in diverse ways, but their many meanings lie concealed because the things making for equivocation are close to one another in their agreement among themselves. But in widely separated things equivocation is evident, if the same name be given them, because their great difference in concept, i.e., in the essential element of the proper species, is immediately apparent. In this way the name key [1] is used equivocally of an instrument which locks doors and of the clavicle (clavicula i.e. little key) which covers the artery in the shoulder of animals.

895. Third [x, cc], at "The unjust man," he explains in how many ways the previously mentioned habits may be signified, saying that first we must consider the unjust man in as many ways as he is designated. He is spoken of in three ways: in one way as the lawbreaking man, i.e., one who acts contrary to the law; in another way as the covetous man who wants too much prosperity; in the last way as the unfair man who determines to have too few burdens.

896. It is obvious then that the just man is taken in two ways: in one way as a law-abiding person, i.e., as one who observes the law; in the other

[1] In the text of Aristotle *kleis*. St. Thomas uses *clavis* with the same meaning.

way as the fair person who is willing to have the smiles and frowns of fortune in equal measure. The equal is opposed to both, i.e., to what is excessive and to what is deficient. From this he draws a further conclusion that what is just is said to be according to the law and fair; and what is unjust, contrary to the law and unfair inasmuch as objects are made known by habits, as was said before (892).

897. At "Since the unjust man" [ii, y] he makes clear the parts of the division just given. First [y, aa] he shows in what way the covetous man is said to be unjust. He affirms that since the covetous person who wants to have too much is unjust, it follows that he will be concerned about an abundance of goods which men desire. However, he will not be solicitous about all goods but only those pertaining to fortune and adversity. Goods of this kind are beneficial if we do not make qualification, i.e., they are good considered independently and in themselves. But they are not always beneficial for an individual because they are not always proportionate to him nor always expedient for him. However, men seek these goods from God, and pray for and desire them as if such things were always beneficial. By reason of this they become covetous and unjust. It should not be this way, but a man ought to pray that those things that are in themselves good be made good for him, so that each may choose what is good for him, i.e., the proper exercise of virtue.

898. Then [y, bb], at "But the unjust man," he shows how the unjust person is said to be unfair, stating that a man is not always called unjust because he chooses too much but because he chooses too little of the things that simply and considered in themselves are burdensome—like labors, lack of necessities, and so on. However, since lesser evil apparently is in some way a good precisely as it is eligible—covetousness regards a good as was just said (897)—it seems for this reason that a person who desires too little of what is arduous is in some way covetous. But it is nearer the truth to say that he is unfair—a term that contains both and is common to excess and defect.

899. Last [y, cc], at "Besides, the unjust," he explains how the unjust man is said to be lawbreaking, affirming that he who is unlawful is also called unjust. A person is designated a lawbreaker by reason of unlawfulness which is also an inequality inasmuch as a man is not equal to the norm of the law. This unlawfulness contains in general all injustice and something common in respect of every kind of injustice, as will be made clear later (911, 919, 922).

LECTURE II

Legal Justice

ANALYTICAL OUTLINE
OF ST. THOMAS

TEXT OF ARISTOTLE
(*B.1129 b 12*)
Chapter 1

A. He treats the legally just itself.

I. THE LEGALLY JUST IS DETERMINED BY LAW.

Since it was said that the lawless person is unjust and the law-abiding person just, obviously lawful acts are in some measure [1] just acts. Likewise, what is determined by the positive law is lawful, and we say that such a determination is just. **900-901**

2. THE NATURE OF LEGAL ENACTMENTS.

a. For whose sake a law is enacted.

But laws aim to touch on everything which contributes to the benefit of all, or of the best, or of the rulers, either on account of virtues or something else. Therefore, for one such reason we call those laws just that bring about and preserve happiness and the things that make for happiness in the civic community. **902-903**

b. On what matters laws are made.

A law commands deeds of bravery, for instance, that a soldier should *20* not leave the battle line nor throw away his arms. It commands things belonging to temperance, for example, that no one should commit adultery, that no one should be guilty of outrage. It commands things that pertain to meekness: no one should strike another, no one should contend with another. It is the same with other virtues and vices, the law ordering the former and forbidding the latter. In accord with this, a law rightly drafted will be ex-

[1] The text used by St. Thomas had *aliqualiter* not *aequaliter*.

cellent but one insufficiently considered will be bad.   **904-905**

B. He considers legal justice.

   1. THE NATURE OF LEGAL JUSTICE.

Justice itself then is a perfect virtue, not in itself but in relation to another. For this reason justice seems to be the most excellent among the virtues. Hence we have the proverb: "neither evening star nor morning star is so wonderful as justice."   **906**

   2. IN WHAT WAY IT IS RELATED TO THE VIRTUES.

a. He sets forth his intention.

But under justice every virtue is *30* included at the same time, and it is especially the perfect virtue because it is the exercise of perfect virtue. **907**

b. He explains his proposition.
   i. *Legal justice is an especially per-fect virtue.*

Legal justice is perfect because the person who has this virtue can exercise it in relation to another and not in relation to himself alone. Some people can apply virtue to their own affairs but not to affairs per- *B.1130* taining to others. Because of this, the saying of Bias seems to be commendable that authority tests a man, for the prince is already engaged in communication with others. Therefore, justice alone among the virtues seems to be another's good because it refers to another. It produces goods useful to another, viz., the prince or the common good. Consequently, the man who practices vice in regard to himself and his friends is most wicked. On the other hand the man who practices virtue in regard to himself and toward others—a difficult thing to do—is most honorable.   **908-910**

   ii. *(Legal justice) includes every virtue.*

This virtue, therefore, is not a particular but a general virtue, Like- *10* wise, the opposite injustice is not a particular vice but a general one. **911**

c. He settles a point which could be called in question.

How virtue and justice differ from one another is evident from what has been said, for they are the same in substance but different in concept. Vir-

tue as related to another is justice; as
this kind of habit it is virtue without
qualification.   **912**

COMMENTARY OF ST. THOMAS

900. After the Philosopher has given
the division of justice, he now considers legal justice. First [A] he treats
the legally just itself, which is the
object of legal justice. Second [B], at
"Justice itself then etc.," he considers
legal justice. He discusses the first point
in a twofold manner. First [A, 1] he
shows that the legally just is determined by law. Now [A, 2], at "But
laws aim etc.," he explains the nature
of legal enactments. He affirms first
that, since it was said above (895-896,
899) that the lawless man is unjust and
the law-abiding man just, it clearly
follows that all lawful acts are just in
some measure.

901. He says "in some measure" because every law is determined in relation to some state. Now, not every
state possesses what is simply just but
some states have only what is partially
just, as is evident in the third book of
the *Politics* (Ch. 9, 1281 a 10; St. Th.
Lect. VII, 413). In a democratic state
where all the people govern, what is
partially just is observed but not what
is simply just, so that because all the
citizens are equal in one respect (i.e.,
in liberty), therefore they are considered equal in every respect. Consequently, acts that are prescribed by
law in a democracy are not simply but
only in some measure just. But Aristotle says that those enactments are
lawful that have been fixed and determined by positive law, which is
within the competence of legislators,
and that each enactment so decreed is
said to be just in some way.

902. Next [A', 2], at "But laws
aim," he explains with what the decrees of law are concerned. He considers this point from two aspects.
First [2, a] he shows for whose sake
a law is enacted. Then [2, b], at "A
law commands," he shows on what
matters laws are made. He says first
that laws touch on everything that can
be of any possible utility for the community (as in the ideal states where
the common good is kept in mind),
or for the utility of the best (i.e., certain elders of the state who govern it
and are called nobles), or for the
utility of the rulers (as happens in
states ruled by kings and tyrants). In
the framing of laws attention is always given to what is useful to the
affair of chief importance in the city.

903. Some may be considered as best
or as ruling either because of virtue
(as in an aristocratic state where certain ones rule on account of virtue),
or for the sake of something else (as
in an oligarchy where the few rule on
account of riches or power). Since
human utility of every kind is finally
ordered to happiness, obviously the
legal enactments that bring about happiness and the means to it (i.e., the
things that are ordered to happiness
either principally, like the virtues, or
instrumentally like riches and other
external goods of this kind) are called
just in some fashion. This is by comparison with the civic community to
which the framing of a law is directed.

904. At "A law commands" [2, b]
he explains on what matters laws are

made, saying that a law commands what belongs to individual virtues. It commands deeds of bravery, for instance, that a soldier should not leave the battle line, nor take flight, nor throw away his arms. Likewise, it commands things pertaining to temperance, for example, that no one should commit adultery, that no one should dishonor the person of a woman. Also it commands the things belonging to meekness: no one should strike another in anger, no one should contend with another by insults. It is the same with other virtues whose acts the law commands, and with other vices whose acts the law forbids.

905. If the law is rightly drafted according to this, it will be declared an excellent law. Otherwise it is called *aposchediasmenos* (from *a* meaning without, *poschedias* meaning knowledge, and *menos* meaning a searching) as if the law was drafted without a thorough knowledge, or the expression may come from *schedos* signifying a decree published without being thoroughly scanned, from which we have *schediazo,* i.e., I am doing something off-hand. Hence a law is said to be *aposchediasmenos* which lacks proper forethought.

906. Then [B], at **"Justice itself then,"** he determines how legal justice is constituted, showing first [B, 1] the nature of legal justice; and then [B, 2], at "But under justice," in what way it is related to the virtues. He says first that justice itself is a certain perfect virtue not in terms of itself but in relation to another. Since it is better to be perfect not only in oneself but also in relation to another, therefore it is often said that this justice is the most excellent among all virtues. This is the origin of the proverb that neither Hesperus nor Lucifer, the brightest of the morning and evening stars, shine with such brilliance as justice.

907. Next [B, 2], at **"But under justice,"** he shows from our discussion thus far how legal justice is related to the virtues. He treats this point under three headings. First [B, 2, a] he sets forth his intention. Then [B, 2, b], at "Legal justice is perfect etc.," he explains his proposition. Lastly [B, 2, c], at "How virtue and justice etc.," he settles a point which could be called in question by the present discussion. He states first that justice itself comprehends every virtue at the same time and is even the perfect virtue in a special way. The reason is that legal justice consists in the exercise of virtue having to do with another and is in agreement with every virtue prescribed by the law.

908. At **"Legal justice is perfect"** [B, 2, b] he explains what was set forth: first [b, i] that legal justice is an especially perfect virtue; and then, at "This virtue, therefore" [B, ii], that it includes every virtue. He says first that legal justice is a perfect virtue because a man who has this virtue can employ it in relation to another and not to himself only—something not characteristic of all virtuous people. Many can practice virtue in things pertaining to themselves but not in the things pertaining to others. To make clear the previous statements he introduces two common sayings or proverbs.

909. Bias, one of the seven wise men, said that authority tests whether a man is perfect or deficient. The man who rules is already engaged in communication with another because it is his business to arrange the things which are ordered to the common good. So from this we see that the perfection of virtue is indicated by the fact that one person is in touch with another. He proposes another saying to show that legal justice refers to another. For this reason legal justice alone seems to be the good of another (that is, relates to our neighbor) inasmuch as it aims to perform actions useful to another, viz., to

the community or the ruler of the community. But some virtues aim to achieve an individual's good, for instance, temperance strives to quiet the disgraceful desires of the soul. The same is true of other virtues.

910. He draws the conclusion that, as that man is most wicked who practices vice not only in regard to himself but also in regard to his friends, so that man is most honorable who practices virtue in relation not only to himself but also to others. This is especially difficult. So then it is clear that the law-abiding just man is most virtuous and legal justice is the most perfect of virtues.

911. Then [b, ii], at **"This virtue, therefore,"** he infers that legal justice embraces every virtue, for it pertains to legal justice to exercise virtue in regard to another. But a person can practice every virtue in his relation with another. Hence obviously legal justice is not a particular virtue but has a connection with virtue in general. Likewise, the opposite vice is not a particular vice but a general vice, since in a similar way man can exercise every vice in his relations with his neighbor.

912. Next [B, 2, c], at **"How justice and virtue,"** he clarifies something that may be doubtful from the premises. He says that it is clear, from what has been said, the way in which virtue and legal justice differ since they are the same in substance but different in concept. However, virtue in its relation to another is called justice, but precisely as it is a habit operative of such good, it is a virtue simply. This must be understood in regard to the act itself of justice and virtue, for an act identical in subject but diverse in concept is produced by legal justice and by virtue simply so called, for instance, not to commit adultery. But where a special formal aspect of an object exists even in general matter, there a special habit must be found. For this reason it follows that legal justice is a definite virtue taking its species from this, that it tends to the common good.

LECTURE III

Particular Justice

ANALYTICAL OUTLINE
OF ST. THOMAS

TEXT OF ARISTOTLE
(*B.1130 a 14*)
Chapter 2

A. He indicates his proposition.

> We are now investigating that justice which is a part of the general virtue. As we have remarked, there is such a virtue. We also intend to speak in a similar way about particular injustice. **913**

B. He explains (the proposition).

I. THERE IS A JUSTICE WHICH IS A PARTICULAR VIRTUE.

a. First argument.

> The proof for the existence of a particular justice is that a man who practices other vices acting unjustly, nevertheless does not act covetously, for example, one who throws away his shield out of cowardice, or who speaks ill of another out of anger, or who refuses financial help because of stinginess. On the other hand, a *20* person often sins by covetousness, although not by one or all of the other vices, but he does sin by this particular vice, for we reproach him for being unjust. There is then another kind of injustice, a part of injustice in general. Likewise, there is a certain unjust thing that is a part of that which is legally unjust. **914-915**

b. Second argument.

> Moreover, if one man commits adultery for the sake of gain and makes money by this act, while another commits adultery for the sake of concupiscence and pays, thus sustaining a loss; the second man seems to be more lustful than the first who is unjust rather than lustful, for obviously he acted for gain. **916**

c. Third argument.

Yet in all other kinds of injustice [1] there is always a reference to some particular vice, for instance, if a man commits adultery it is ascribed to lust. If a soldier deserts his leader, it is *30* referred to cowardice. If anyone strikes another, it is attributed to anger. But if a person makes an exorbitant profit, it is not reduced to any other vice but only to injustice. Hence it is clear that over and above general justice, there is a particular justice.   917

2. WHY IT HAS A NAME IN COMMON WITH LEGAL JUSTICE.

a. The reason for this.

This justice has the same name because defined under the same genus, since both agree in a relation to *b* another.   918

b. The difference between them.

But particular justice is concerned with honor, money, security, and all other things of this kind whatever name they may have, and also with the pleasure that follows upon possession. But general justice touches upon everything by reason of which a man can be called virtuous.   919

C. He sums up what has already been said and shows what remains to be discussed.

I. HE SETS THIS FORTH IN A GENERAL WAY.

Obviously then there is more than one justice, there is another justice besides the general virtue. What this other justice is and its characteristics will be considered now.   920

2. HE TAKES IT UP IN A SPECIFIC WAY.

a. What was said about the distinction between justice and injustice.

We have determined that the unjust thing is both the illegally unjust and the unjust simply, but the just *10* thing is both the just corresponding to the law and the just that is equal or fair.   921

b. There is a twofold justice.

Therefore, in accord with the illegally unjust thing, there is an injustice that we previously discussed. Now, the unjust thing that consists in a desire

---

[1] *Justificationes* in the text should be *injustificationes* or *injustitias*.

for inequality is not the same, but is related to the other as a part to the whole, for every unjust thing consisting in a desire for inequality is an illegally unjust thing but not the reverse. Besides, the excessive is unequal but not the reverse. Because one unjust thing is not the same as another, so also one injustice is not the same as another but different from it as a part from the whole. The same comparison holds for one injustice with the other. 922

c. Which . . . we must discuss.
   i. We must treat particular justice
   after this.

We must then discuss particular justice and injustice, and also the just and the unjust thing taken in the same sense. 923

   ii. Here we are not going to treat
   legal justice.

Justice that corresponds to all 20 of virtue and injustice that corresponds to all of vice, as their exercise pertains to our neighbor, are both to be passed over for the present. It is evident in these cases how the just thing must be determined. Nearly all legal enactments are prescribed by the general virtue, for the law commands us to live according to every virtue and forbids us to live according to any vice. 924

   iii. He raises a doubt.

However, positive laws are productive of virtue in general in regard to instruction which pertains to the common good. But that instruction according to which a man is good simply, whether it belongs to political science or some other science, must be determined afterwards. Perhaps, to be a good man and to be a good citizen are not the same thing in any state. 925-926

COMMENTARY OF ST. THOMAS

913. After the Philosopher has shown what is the nature of legal justice, which is a general virtue, now he shows that besides this there is a particular justice. He treats this point under three headings. First [A] he indicates his

proposition; and then [B], at "The proof for etc.," he explains it. Last [C], at "Obviously then etc.," he sums up what has already been said and shows what remains to be discussed. He says first that, while legal justice is a general virtue, we are not principally investigating this at present, but that which as a part of the general virtue is a particular virtue. As is commonly held, there is such a virtue. Also we intend to speak about particular injustice in a similar manner.

914. Then [B], at **"The proof for,"** he explains the proposition. He discusses this point from two aspects. First [B, 1] he shows that besides legal justice, which is a general virtue, there is a justice that is a particular virtue. Next [B, 2], at "This justice etc.," he assigns the reason why it has a name in common with legal justice. On this question we must consider that to prove there is a justice that is a particular virtue, he takes for granted that there is an injustice that is a particular vice, for we said above (892) that habits are made known by their contraries. He proposes three arguments for this. The first argument [B, 1, a] is taken according to the real distinction of injustice from other vices inasmuch as injustice is found without the others and conversely. From this it is evident that injustice is a particular vice distinct from other vices.

915. He says that we have this proof that there is a particular justice and injustice because a man, who practices other particular vices acting unjustly according to legal injustice, nevertheless does not act covetously in taking something from his neighbor, for example, when a soldier throws away his shield because of cowardice, or a man casts opprobrium on someone because of anger, or a person refuses financial help to a friend because of the vice of stinginess. So other vices can exist without covetousness which is a spe-

cial kind of injustice. Sometimes, on the contrary, it happens that a person sins by covetousness in taking another's goods; although he does not sin by some one or all of the other vices, he does sin by a particular vice. This is clear because he is reproached as unjust for that reason. Hence obviously there is another justice—a part of the virtue—that is a special virtue. So evidently there exists also a certain unjust thing that is a part of what is legally unjust—the legally unjust being the unjust thing in general.

916. At **"Moreover, if one man"** [B, 1, b] he gives the second argument, which is taken from the order to the end. Clearly, if a vicious or evil act is ordered to another unbecoming end, from this fact it will obtain a new species of vice. This is so when a man commits adultery for the sake of gain, for example, to rob a woman or to take from her in any way whatsoever. Also it happens sometimes that a man commits adultery entirely because of concupiscence, so that he not only does not gain but rather gives something of his own and suffers a loss of his goods. A man of this sort seems to be lustful, essentially speaking (*per se*), since the vice of lust is strictly ordered to the satisfaction of concupiscence. But the man who commits adultery to take a woman's goods does not seem to be lustful, absolutely speaking, because he does not intend lust as his end. He seems rather to be unjust since he sins against justice for the sake of gain. So it is clear then that injustice is a special vice.

917. At **"Yet in all"** [B, 1, c] he assigns the third argument, which is taken by comparison with legal justice. As nothing is contained in a genus that is not contained in some species, so anything that is done according to legal injustice is reduced to a particular vice. If a man acts contrary to legal justice by committing adultery, this will be referred to the vice of lust. If

a soldier deserts his general in battle, this will be attributed to the vice of cowardice. If anyone immoderately strikes his neighbor, this will be ascribed to the vice of anger. But if a person inordinately enriches himself by pilfering another's goods, this will not be ascribed to any other vice except injustice. Hence it remains that there is a particular injustice over and above the other injustice that is a general vice. For a like reason there is another particular justice besides legal justice that is a general virtue.

918. Then [B, 2], at **"This justice has,"** he shows why a particular virtue of this kind is also named justice. First [B, 2, a] he assigns the reason for this from the agreement of particular with legal justice. Next [B, 2, b], at "But particular justice," he explains the difference between them. He says first that particular justice is univocal, that is, has a common name with legal justice. The reason is that they agree in definition according to the same genus inasmuch as both are concerned about what relates to another. However, legal justice is taken into account in relation to what is the common good, while particular justice is ordered to another as pertaining to a private person.

919. Next [B, 2, b], at **"But particular justice,"** he explains the difference between justice and injustice on part of the matter. He says that particular justice regards those things that take into account social intercourse, like honor, money, whatever pertains to the safety or harm to the body, and so on. Likewise, particular justice is concerned not alone with external things but also with pleasure consequent on the profit by which a man takes his neighbor's goods beyond what he ought. But legal justice and injustice treat all moral matters in general in whatsoever way a man may be said to be good or virtuous about a thing.

920. At **"Obviously then"** [C] he

summarizes what has been said and shows what remains to be discussed. First [C, 1] he sets this forth in a general way; and then [C, 2] at "We have determined etc.," he takes it up in a specific way. He says first that it is clear from the premises (913-919) that there is more than one justice, viz., legal justice and justice aiming at equality, and that over and above legal justice, as a general virtue, there is a particular justice. But we must determine later on (927-1077) the nature and characteristics of particular justice.

921. Then [C, 2], at **"We have determined,"** he shows in detail what has been treated and what remains to be discussed. First [C, 2, a] he resumes what was said about the distinction between justice and injustice. He affirms that we have determined that the unjust thing is called illegal and unequal either by excess or defect. On the contrary, the just thing is called legal and equal.

922. Next [C, 2, b], at **"Therefore, in accord with,"** he resumes what he has said, viz., that as there is a twofold just thing, so there is a twofold justice. He affirms that in accord with the illegally unjust thing there is a certain injustice, previously discussed (911, 919), which is a general vice. Likewise, in accord with the just corresponding to the law, there is a certain justice that is a general virtue. Now, the unjust thing consisting in a desire for inequality and the illegally unjust thing are not altogether the same, but one is related to the other as a part to the whole so that every unjust thing consisting in a desire for inequality is an illegally unjust thing, but not the reverse. Again, every thing that is excessive is unequal but not the reverse, since there is a certain illegal injustice in having too few burdens. Because (I say) one unjust thing is a part of the other unjust thing, and they are not entirely the same;

in a similar way, therefore, the injustice called inequality is not entirely the same as illegal injustice but is compared to it as a part to the whole. Also the justice aiming at equality is compared to legal justice in a similar manner.

923. Last [C, 2, c], at **"We must then,"** he shows which of these things we must discuss. On this point he does three things. First [c, i] he says that we must treat particular justice after this (927-1077), and similarly the just and the unjust thing particularly so called.

924. Then [c, ii], at **"Justice that corresponds,"** he explains that here we are not going to treat legal justice. He affirms that legal justice—which conforms to all of virtue inasmuch as the use of the whole of virtue referring to our neighbor pertains to it—is to be passed over for the present. Likewise, the opposite injustice (inasmuch as the use of the whole of vice pertains to it) is to be passed over. It is clear how what is just and unjust ought to be determined according to justice and injustice of this kind, because they are the precepts as laid down by the law. The greater part of legal prescriptions are enjoined in agreement with the whole of virtue inasmuch as the law commands us to live according to every virtue and forbids us to live according to any vice. However, there are certain determinations of the law that do not belong directly to the exercise of any virtue but to some disposition of external goods.

925. Last [c, iii], at **"However, positive law,"** he raises a doubt. It is evident that positive laws are productive of virtue in general by the instruction given a man in reference to the common good. But there is another kind of instruction by which a man is trained in virtuous actions as applicable to him individually, i.e., to his proper good inasmuch as in this way a man becomes virtuous in himself. Therefore, there can be a doubt whether instruction of this kind should belong to political science or to some other science.

926. He says that this question must be settled afterwards in the work on *Politics*. It is proved in the third book of the *Politics* (Ch. 4, 1276 b 16-1277 b 33; St. Th. Lect. III, 365-377) that to be a good man simply and to be a good citizen are not the same in every state. There are some states not worthy of honor in which a person can be a good citizen yet not be a good man. But in the most worthy state no one is a good citizen who is not a good man.

LECTURE IV

Distributive and Commutative Justice

ANALYTICAL OUTLINE
OF ST. THOMAS

TEXT OF ARISTOTLE
(B.1130 b 30)
Chapter 2

I. HE CONSIDERS PARTICULAR JUSTICE IN A GENERAL WAY.

A. He makes a division of particular justice.

A'. He indicates a species of particular justice.

> One species of particular justice—and of the just thing corresponding to it—consists in the distribution of honor, money, and other common goods that are to be apportioned to people sharing in social community, for in these matters one man as compared with another may have an equal or unequal share. **927**

B'. He gives a second kind of particular justice.

> Another species gives direc- **B.1131** tions for use in private transactions. **928**

C'. He subdivides commutative justice.

1. THERE ARE TWO PARTS.

> There are two parts of this species, as some types of transaction are voluntary and others involuntary. Examples of the voluntary are selling, buying, bail, loan, deposit, rent. They are called voluntary because the origin of these exchanges is voluntary. **929**

2. THE OTHER DIVISION OF TRANSACTIONS.

> Some kinds of involuntary transaction are occult, like theft, adultery, poisoning, procuring,[1] enticement of a

---

[1] *Proagogia* in the text, but *paragogia* in the Commentary.

slave, assassination, false testimony.
Others are done with manifest violence, for example, beating, imprison-
ment, murder, robbery, despoiling *10*
parents of children, reproach, outrage.
930-931

B. How a mean may be taken in this virtue.

  A'. The just thing is a mean.

  I. IN WHAT WAY THE JUST THING . . . MAY BE DETERMINED.

a. The just thing may be taken as a
mean according to distributive
justice.
  i. He proves that the mean . . .
  should be taken according to a
  . . . relationship of proportions.
  X. FROM THE VERY CONCEPT OF
  JUSTICE.

  aa. The just thing is a certain
  mean.

Chapter 3

Since the unjust person is unfair
and the unjust thing is unequal, it is
clear that there is a mean corresponding to what is unjust. This is the equal,
for in operations of this kind where
there is more or less, there is also an
equal. Therefore, if the unjust thing
is the unequal and, the just thing the
equal—and this is evident in all situations without need of proof—then the
just thing will be the mean since the
equal is the mean.   **932-933**

  bb. The mean is according to
  a certain relationship of
  proportions.

However, the equal implies at least
two things. Therefore, since the just
thing is both a mean and an equal,
it necessarily is related to another and
pertains to certain matters of equality.
As a mean it will be between two
things which are more and less. As it
is an equal it will be between two
things. As it is a just thing it will
concern matters in relation to other
persons, for justice regards an- *20*
other. Therefore, the just necessarily
involves at least four objects, viz., two
persons by whom justice is observed
and two things about which justice is
done. There will be the same equality
between persons and between things
in such a way that, as things are re-

lated to one another, so are persons. If they are not equal they will not have equal shares, and from this source quarrels and complaints will arise when, either persons who are equal do not receive equal shares in distribution, or persons who are not equal do receive equal shares.

934-935

Y. FROM THE CONCEPT OF MERIT.

Moreover, this is clear from the fact that bestowal should be made according to merit, for the just thing in distribution has to be done according to a certain merit. But all do not agree that merit consists in the same thing. People of a democracy place it in a condition of freedom, people of an oligarchy in one's riches or nobility of birth, and people of an aristocracy in a state of virtue.   **936-937**

COMMENTARY OF ST. THOMAS

927. After the Philosopher has differentiated particular justice from legal justice, he now begins to investigate particular justice without treating legal justice. He divides the investigation into two parts. In the first part [I] he considers particular justice in a general way by comparison with its proper object, and in the second part [Lect. XI], at "Since someone etc." (B.1134 a 16), he considers it in its application to the subject. In regard to the first part, he does two things. Initially [A] he makes a division of particular justice. Next [B], at "Since the unjust person etc.," he explains how a mean may be taken in this virtue. He discusses the initial point from three aspects. First [A'] he indicates a species of particular justice. He says that one species—the same holds for the unjust thing corresponding to it—consists in the distribution of certain

common goods (either honor or money or any other thing belonging to external goods or even to external evils, like labor, expenses and so on) that are to be apportioned among people who share in social community. He proves that this should belong to particular justice because in matters of this kind, equality and inequality—which belong to particular justice and injustice, as was stated before (922)—of one person to another are taken into consideration.

928. Next [B'], at "Another species," he gives a second kind of particular justice. He says that another species establishes a measure of justice in transactions, by which a thing is transferred from one person to another —in the first species the transfer of a thing from the community to the individual was considered.

929. Last [C'], at "There are two

parts," he subdivides commutative justice according to the different kinds of transactions, making a twofold division. He says first [1] that there are two parts of commutative justice because there are two kinds of transactions. Some are voluntary, others involuntary. The voluntary are so-called because the principle of transaction is voluntary in both parties, as is evident *in selling and buying,* by which one man transfers the dominion over his own property to another as compensation for a price received; *in barter,* by which someone gives what is his to another for something of equal value; *in bail,* by which a person voluntarily appoints himself a debtor for another; *in a loan,* by which a man grants the use of his property to another without recompense but reserves ownership of the thing to himself; *in a deposit,* by which one commits something of his to the custody of another; *in rent,* by which a person accepts the use of something belonging to another for a price.

930. Then [2], at **"Some kinds of involuntary,"** he subdivides the other division of transactions, saying that some involuntary transactions are occult: like theft, by which one takes a thing belonging to another who is unwilling; adultery, by which a man secretly approaches the wife of another for sexual intercourse; poisoning, by which a person poisons another with intent either to kill or injure in some way. Also they are especially called poisoners who by some sorcery bring about murder or harm. *Paragogia* is a derivation or a leading away, for example the occult diversion of a stream belonging to one person to the property of another. The enticement of a slave takes place when someone induces another's slave to flee from his master. Assassination is that slaying which happens from wounds inflicted by trickery. Testimony is false in which a person conceals the truth

by lying. Other transactions are involuntary and done by manifest violence. Thus a man may use violence either upon a person by beating, fettering, murdering, or upon things by robbing another of his goods, by despoiling parents of their children through murder. Likewise, a man may use violence through infamy by using reproachful words, or through injury by inflicting outrage.

931. We must consider that the voluntary and involuntary in transactions make a difference in the species of justice because voluntary transactions cause the subtraction of only a thing which must be repaid according to the equality of justice. But involuntary transactions cause a certain injury. Hence the robber is forced not only to return the thing plundered but to undergo punishment because of the affront inflicted. Since the involuntary is twofold, viz., arising from force and from ignorance, he divides involuntary transactions into those which are occult, as it were through ignorance, and those that are done openly through violence.

932. Next [B], at **"Since the unjust person,"** he shows how a mean is understood in these matters. He discusses this point from two aspects. First [B, A'] he explains how the just thing is a mean; and then [Lect. X], at "From these discussions etc." (B.1133 b 30), how justice is a mean. He treats the first point in a twofold manner. First [A', 1] he shows in what way the just thing, consisting in a mean according to either justice, may be determined. Next [Lect. VIII], at "Some philosophers seem to think etc." (B.1132 b 21), he rejects an error. He further discusses the first point in two stages. First [1, a] he explains how the just thing may be taken as a mean according to distributive justice; and second [Lect. VI], at "There remains another etc." (B.1131 b 25), according to commutative justice. He considers the first

point in two ways. First [a, i] he proves that the mean of distributive justice should be taken according to a certain relationship of proportions. Next [Lect. V], at "Therefore, the just thing etc." (B.1131 a 30), he shows what the nature of that relationship of proportions is. On the initial point he does two things. First [i, x] he proves the proposition from the very concept of justice; and then [i, y], at "Moreover, this is clear etc.," from the concept of merit. He treats the first point under two headings. First [x, aa] he shows from the very notion of justice that the just thing is a certain mean. Second [x, bb], at "However, the equal etc.," he explains that the mean is according to a certain relationship of proportions.

933. He says first that, as was said previously (898, 921), the unjust man is one who desires an inequality of good and evil, and the unjust thing is that which consists in an inequality, and concerns both too much and too little. But wherever there is more and less, there the equal must be found, for the equal is the mean between the greater and the less. Hence wherever we find equality, there we find a mean. It is clear then that the unjust thing is a kind of unequal thing, and the just thing is a kind of equal thing. That the just thing is a kind of equal thing is obvious to everyone without any proof. Therefore, since the equal is a mean between more and less, as has been shown (310, 896, 898), it follows that the just thing is a kind of mean.

934. At **"However, the equal"** [x, bb] he explains that the just thing is a mean according to a certain relationship of proportions. To prove this he takes for granted that the equal consists in at least two things between which an equality is considered. Therefore, since the just thing is both a mean and an equal, inasmuch as it is just, it is necessarily a relation to some-

thing, i.e., with respect to another, as is evident from what has been indicated (922); but inasmuch as it is an equal it pertains to certain matters in which equality between two persons is taken into account. Thus it is evident that if we consider the just thing precisely as a mean, it will then be a mean between two things that are more and less. But precisely as the just thing is an equal, it must be between two things (as a just thing, of course, it must concern some matters in relation to other persons, because justice regards another person). However, justice insofar as it is a mean, an extrinsic thing, considers more or less; but as something intrinsic it considers two things and two persons in which justice is established. So it is clear that what is just, necessarily consists in at least four objects, viz., two persons by whom justice is observed and two things about which justice is done.

935. In the concept of justice there must be the same equality between persons who practice justice and between things about which justice is done, so that as the things are related to one another, so are the persons. Otherwise they will not have shares proportional to themselves. But, by reason of this, quarrels and complaints arise as if justice had been neglected because, either persons who are equal do not receive equal shares in the distribution of common goods or persons who are not equal do receive equal shares, for example, if laborers are paid wages for doing an unequal amount of work, or are paid unequal wages for doing an equal amount of work. So then it is evident that the mean of distributive justice is taken according to a certain relationship of proportions.

936. Then [i, y], at **"Moreover, this is,"** he shows that it is obvious also by reason of merit that the just thing

consists in a certain relationship of proportions. In this way a thing is said to be just in distributions inasmuch as allotment is made according to merit as each is worthy to receive. A certain relationship of proportions is designated by this—that as one person is deserving of one thing, so another is deserving of another thing.

937. However, all do not judge merit in distribution in agreement with the same norm. In a democratic state where everyone governs, they judge merit according to a condition of freedom. Because the common people are the equal of others in freedom, therefore they think it proper that equal distribution be made to them. In an oligarchy where some few rule, they measure merit according to a man's riches or according to nobility of birth, so that men who are more eminent by birth or riches should have more of the common goods. In an aristocracy where certain men govern because of their virtue, they measure merit according to a state of virtue, so that a man should have more who practices virtue more perfectly. Thus it is clear that the mean of distributive justice is understood according to a relationship of proportions.

LECTURE V

Proportionality

ANALYTICAL OUTLINE
OF ST. THOMAS

TEXT OF ARISTOTLE
(*B.1131 a 30*)
Chapter 3

A. He explains in what way the just thing should be taken according to a certain proportionality.

I. SOME GENERAL COMMENTS ABOUT PROPORTIONALITY.

a. The just thing is fittingly said to be according to proportionality.

Therefore, the just thing is something belonging to proportion, for the proportional is proper not only to abstract number but to all enumerations. Proportionality is an equality of ratios. **938-939**

b. The second comment.

Proportionality consists of four parts at least. It is clear that discrete proportionality has four terms, but so does continuous proportionality, for we use one term in two different aspects and state it twice, for ex- *b* ample, A is in proportion to B as B is to G. So B has been stated twice. Wherefore if B is used twice there will be four proportioned terms. **940**

2. HOW THE JUST THING CONSISTS IN A CERTAIN PROPORTIONALITY.

Like proportionality, what is just is also found in four terms at least, for both the things and persons are divided according to a similar proportion. Therefore, as the term A will be to B, so G will be to D. Hence, alternating, as A is to G, B will be to D. Therefore, the whole will be related to the whole, and this is what distribution conjoins.

If adjustment be made in this way, it will be justly done. Therefore, *10* the union of term A with G, and of B with D will be the just thing and the mean guiding distribution. But the un-

just thing is outside of what belongs
to proportion, for the proportional is
a mean and the just thing belongs to
proportion.   **941-943**

3. THE NATURE OF PROPORTIONALITY.

a. The above-mentioned proportiona-
ality . . . is called geometrical.

Mathematicians call this proportionality geometrical, for in geometry it
happens that the whole is compared
to the whole as part to part.   **944**

b. This proportionality . . . cannot be
continuous.

But this proportionality is not continuous because there is no numerically common term for the person and
the thing.   **945**

B. He shows how the unjust thing is outside that proportionality.

This just thing then is a proportional. But the unjust thing is outside
the proportional either by excess or
defect. This occurs in distributions
where a man acts unjustly when he
accepts too much and a man suffers
unjustly when he has too little of *20*
good. The reverse is true in regard to
evil. By comparison with a greater evil
a lesser evil has the aspect of good, for
a lesser evil is preferable to a greater
one. Good is preferable, and a greater
good is more to be preferred. This then
is one kind of the just thing.   **946**

COMMENTARY OF ST. THOMAS

938. After the Philosopher has
shown that the mean of distributive
justice is taken according to proportionality, he now shows according to
what proportionality and in what way
it is understood. He considers this
point in a twofold manner. First [A]
he explains in what way the just thing
should be taken according to a certain
proportionality. Second [B], at "This
just thing etc.," he shows how the unjust thing is outside that proportionality.
He discusses the initial point under

three aspects. First [A, 1] he presents
in advance some general comments
about proportionality. Then [A, 2], at
"Like proportionality etc.," he explains
how the just thing consists in a certain
proportionality. Last [A, 3], at "Mathematicians call etc.," he shows the nature of proportionality by which a
thing is judged just in distributive justice. On the first point he premises
two comments. The first [1, a] is that
the just thing is fittingly said to be
according to proportionality, because

proportionality is found not only in the enumeration of units (which is number simply taken and here called abstract number), but the quality of being proportionate is met with wherever number is found.

939. This is so because proportionality is simply geometrical equality, i.e., this to this and that to that contains the proportion of equality. Proportion is only a relation of one quantity to another. But quantity has the nature of a measure. It is found in numerical unity and is transferred from there to every kind of quantity, as the tenth book of the *Metaphysics* indicates (Ch. 1, 1052 b 20 sq.; St. Th. Lect. II, 1938). Therefore, number primarily is found in the enumeration of units, and thence is attributed to every genus of quantity which is measured according to the idea of number.

940. He makes the second comment at "**Proportionality consists**" [1, b], saying that every proportionality consists of four parts at least. It has a twofold division, one of which is a disjunctive proportionality and the other a continuous proportionality. The disjunctive proportionality is an equality of two proportions not alike in any term. Therefore, when any proportion exists between the two, it is evident that the disjunctive proportionality consists of four terms, as when I say: as six is to three so ten is to five. There is a double proportion on both sides. The continuous proportionality is an equality of two proportions alike in one term, for instance, if I say: as eight is to four so four is to two. There is a double proportion on both sides. Therefore in this continuous proportionality there are in some measure four terms inasmuch as we use one term in two different aspects, declaring it twice, i.e., in either proportion as when I say: the proportion of A to B (or eight to four) is the same as the proportion B to C (or four to two). There is a double proportion

from both sides. In this way B is used twice. Hence, although B is one in subject, nevertheless because it is taken in two different aspects there will be four proportioned terms.

941. Then [A, 2], at "**Like proportionality**," he shows how the mean of distributive justice is taken according to proportionality. He says that, like proportionality, the just thing is found in four terms in which the same proportion is observed, because the things that are distributed and the persons to whom distribution is made are divided according to the same proportion. Therefore, let A be one term, for example, two pounds, and B one pound. But let G be one person, for example, Socrates who has worked two days, and D, Plato, who has worked one day. Therefore, as A is to B so G is to D, because a double proportion is found on the one side and the other. Hence by alternation, as A is to G, so B is to D. Whatever things are proportionable one to another are proportionable by alternation, as is evident in the preceding example (940), for instance, as ten is to five so eight is to four. Therefore, by alternation, as ten is to eight, so five is to four, for there is a ratio of five to four on one side and the other. In this way then, by alternation, it will be true to say that as A is to G, i.e., two pounds to the man who worked two days, so B is to D, i.e., one pound to the man who worked a day.

942. In such matters we must also consider that in the things proportionable in this way, the ratio of one to the other is the ratio of the whole to the whole. For example, if the ratio ten to eight is the same as five to four, it follows further that the ratio ten to eight and five to four will be the same ratio as ten and five taken together, i.e., fifteen to eight and four taken together, i.e., twelve. The reason is that here we have also the ratio of five to four. How does this happen? Because

fifteen contains twelve and its fourth part, i.e., three.

943. In the proposition it follows that, if as this thing is to this person, so that thing is to that person, then also the whole will be to the whole in the same way, i.e., both things taken together will be to both persons taken together. This is as distribution connects them. If in distribution man unites the things to the persons in this way, he acts justly. It is plain then that the union of A with G, i.e., of a thing doubled with a person doubly more deserving, and of B with D, i.e., of a half thing with a person deserving only half is the just thing in distribution and such a just thing is a mean. But the unjust thing is outside this proportionality. The proportional is a mean between excess and defect because the proportionality is an equality of proportion, as has been remarked (939). So the just thing is a mean since it is a certain proportional.

944. At "Mathematicians call" [A, 3] he explains the nature of proportionality according to which this just thing is understood. On this point he does two things. First [3, a] he says that the above-mentioned proportionality, which is considered according to the equality of proportion, is called geometrical by mathematicians. In this it happens that as the whole is to the whole so one part is to another, as we have pointed out in previous discussions (939-940). But this does not take place in arithmetical proportionality, which we will treat later (950).

945. Next [3, b], at "But this," he says that this proportionality, which is observed in distributive justice, cannot be continuous because on one side are the things and on the other the persons. So it is not possible to take for a common term a person to whom distribution is made and the thing which is distributed.

946. Then [B], at "This just thing," he considers what is unjust in distributions. He says that, since the just thing is proportionable, it follows that the unjust thing is outside the proportionable. This happens either by reason of more or less than the equality of proportion demands, as is evident in the very operations of just and unjust distribution. That man acts unjustly who accepts for himself too many goods, but he suffers unjustly who has too few. The reverse is true in regard to evils. Since a lesser evil has the aspect of good by comparison with a greater evil, the lesser evil is more to be preferred than the greater evil. Everything is chosen under the aspect of good, and for this reason the thing which has the aspect of greater good is more to be preferred. So then this is one species of justice that has been discussed.

LECTURE VI

The Mean of Commutative Justice

ANALYTICAL OUTLINE
OF ST. THOMAS

TEXT OF ARISTOTLE
(*B.1131 b 25*)
Chapter 4

A. He shows that there is a species of justice in addition to distributive.

> There remains another kind of justice directive of what is done both in voluntary and involuntary transactions.
> 947

B. This differs from the other justice.

I. HE SETS FORTH HIS PROPOSITION.

> This differs in species from the preceding justice.
> 948

2. HE PRESENTS THE DIFFERENCE.

a. He reviews something relative to distributive justice.

> What is just in the distribution of common goods is always in conformity with proportionality previously *30* discussed, for when distribution is made of common wealth, it will be made according to the proportion contributed by each one. On the other hand the unjust thing opposed to this just thing is outside the proportional.
> 949

b. What pertains to commutative justice.
  i. *A fact relative to commutative justice.*

> However, in transactions *B.1132* the just thing is an equal—and the unjust thing an unequal—not according to geometrical but according to arithmetic proportion. Here it does not matter whether the good man steals from the wicked man or the wicked from the good, whether the good or wicked man commits adultery. But the law looks at only the nature of the damage done, and treats the parties as equals, if indeed one does an injustice

and the other suffers an injustice, if this one injures and that one is injured. Therefore, the judge attempts to reduce to equality the unjust thing which has an inequality.   950-951

ii. *He clarifies this by an example.*
x. THE EXAMPLE.

If one of two contestants receives a wound and the other inflicts a wound or even one commits murder and the other is murdered the division of action and passion brings about inequality. However, a judge tries to remove inequality by awarding damages. 952

y. HE RESOLVES A DOUBT.

In the interest of plain talk, we   10 speak of gain in these matters, even though the name is not appropriate to some cases, for example, to the person who strikes another or to the person injured. But when passion is measured, one thing is called loss and another gain.   953

iii. *Some corollaries.*
x. ON THE PART OF THE JUST THING ITSELF.

Therefore, that which is just is an equal, a mean between more and less in such a way that gain is taken as more, and loss as less. Gain is understood in contrary ways, for it is more in relation to good and less in relation to evil, while the opposite is true of loss. Between gain and loss stands a mean, the equal which we call the just. This then is a directive, and will be the mean between gain and loss.
954

y. ON THE PART OF THE JUDGE.

For this reason when men are in doubt they have recourse to a judge. But going to a judge is going to   20 justice, for a judge ought to be living justice. Men approaching a judge are seeking an intermediate, and this is why judges are called intermediaries or mediators, as if they touch the mean when they attain what is just. Therefore, the just thing is a mean as also is the judge who brings about an equality.   955

COMMENTARY OF ST. THOMAS

947. After the Philosopher has shown how the mean should be taken in distributive justice, he now explains in what way the mean should be understood in commutative justice. He discusses this point under three aspects. First [A] he shows there is a species of justice in addition to distributive. Then [B], at "This differs etc.," he says this differs from the other justice. Third [Lect. VII], at "It is as though etc." (B.1132 a 25), he shows how a mean should be understood in this kind of justice. He says first that in addition to the preceding species of justice which exists in distributions, there remains one that is directive of transactions both voluntary and involuntary.

948. Then [B], at "This differs," he shows the difference between this species and the preceding. He treats this point under two headings. First [B, 1] he sets forth his proposition, saying that the just thing existing in transactions belongs to another species than distributive justice.

949. Second [B, 2], at "What is just," he presents the difference. First [2, a] he reviews something relevant to distributive justice. Then [2, b], at "However, in transactions etc.," he shows what pertains to commutative justice. He says first that the justice mentioned before always directs the distribution of common goods in conformity with proportionality, i.e., the geometrical which is observed in the equality of proportion. This is clear because if wealth belonging to the city or to certain men must be distributed to individuals, the distribution will be made in such a way that each may receive from the community in that ratio according to which he contributed to the community. We suppose in business ventures that the more a man invests in a company the greater is his return. As the just thing directing distributions consists in this proportionality, so the opposite unjust thing consists in disregarding proportionality of this kind.

950. At "However, in transactions" [2, b], he shows what pertains to commutative justice. He gives a threefold consideration of this notion. First [b, i] he explains a fact relative to commutative justice. Next [b, ii], at "If one of two contestants etc.," he clarifies this by an example. Third [b, iii], at "Therefore, that which etc.," he deduces some corollaries from the premises. He says first that the just thing that exists in transactions agrees somewhat with the just thing directing distributions in this—that the just thing is equal, and the unjust thing, unequal. But they differ in the fact that the equal in commutative justice is not observed according to that proportionality, viz., geometrical, which was observed in distributive justice, but according to arithmetical proportionality which is observed according to equality of quantity, and not according to equality of proportion as in geometry. By arithmetical proportionality six is a mean between eight and four, because it is in excess of the one and exceeds the other by two. But there is not the same proportion on the one side and the other, for six is to four in a ratio of three to two while eight is to six in a ratio of four to three. On the contrary by geometrical proportionality the mean is exceeded and exceeds according to the same pro-

portion but not according to the same quantity. In this way six is a mean between nine and four, since from both sides there is a three to two ratio. But there is not the same quantity, for nine exceeds six by three and six exceeds four by two.

951. Therefore, in commutative justice the equal is observed according to arithmetic proportion. This is clear from the fact that here the different relations of persons are not considered. It does not matter, insofar as commutative justice is concerned, whether a good man has stolen or robbed an evil man of his property or an evil man has done it to a good citizen. Likewise, it does not matter whether a good or evil man commits adultery. The law takes into account only the nature of the injury, so that the man who has done more damage, whatever his condition, must make more restitution. So it is evident that if one of two contestants does an injustice and the other suffers an injustice, one injures and the other is injured, the law treats them as equals, however much they may be unequal. Hence a judge, who is a dispenser of the law, attempts to reduce that injustice—by which one man injures another and which has a certain inequality—to an equality by establishing an equality in the very quantity of things and not according to the relation of different persons.

952. Next [b, ii], at **"If one of two contestants,"** he clarifies what he had said, by an example. First [ii, x] he presents the example; and then [ii, y], at "In the interest of plain talk etc.," he resolves a doubt. First he sets forth the example of a personal injury about which too little is clear. He says that if one of two contestants receives a wound and the other inflicts it, or even if one commits murder and the other is murdered, this division of action and passion brings about inequality because the assailant and the murderer have more of what is es-

teemed good, inasmuch as they have done their own will and so seem as it were to have gained. But the man who is wounded or murdered has more of evil insofar as he is deprived against his will of well-being or life, and so he seems as it were to have suffered loss. The judge tries to equalize this by subtracting from the gain and allotting compensation for the loss, inasmuch as he takes away something from the assailant and the murderer contrary to their will and bestows it to the gain or honor of the person wounded or murdered.

953. Then [ii, y], at **"In the interest of plain talk,"** he resolves a certain doubt that could arise from the words "gain and loss." He says that, in the interest of plain talk, the terms "gain and loss" are used in matters where a person has more or less. Strictly these words refer to what we possess, and sometimes they do not seem suitable, for example, in the case of personal injuries (as when one person receives a blow and another inflicts it, some injury results) because a fixed measure of action and passion cannot be taken in injuries of this kind so that what is more can be called gain and what is less, loss. But when passion is measured, i.e., according to the measure of justice, then what is more is called gain and what is less, loss.

954. At **"Therefore, that which is just"** [b, iii], he deduces two conclusions: the first [iii, x] on the part of the just thing itself; and the second [iii, y], at "For this reason etc.," on the part of the judge. He says first that the just thing in transactions is a kind of equal that is a mean between more and less in such a way that gain is taken as more and loss as less. However, they are understood in different ways in good and evil, for to have more of good and less of evil belongs to the nature of gain. But the contrary pertains to the idea of loss. Between

these two, gain and loss, stands a mean, that equal which we call the just thing. Consequently that just thing, which gives directions in transactions, is a mean between gain and loss as both these terms are commonly understood.

955. Next [iii, y], at "For this reason," he draws a conclusion on the part of the judge of whom it was said (952) that he tries to bring about an equality. Aristotle affirms that because the just thing is a mean between gain and loss, it follows that when men are in doubt about the mean they have recourse to a judge. A judge ought to be, as it were, living justice, so that his soul is entirely possessed by justice. But the people who go to a judge seem to be seeking a mediator between parties who quarrel. Consequently, judges are called intermediaries or mediators as if they may attain the intermediate or the mean, and lead the way to what is just. So then it is evident that what is just, the subject of our discussion, is a certain mean because the judge, who determines this just thing, is the middle inasmuch as he proposes what is equal between the parties. But the equal is the mean or middle between more and less, as we have pointed out (310, 933).

LECTURE VII

Finding the Mean of Commutative Justice

ANALYTICAL OUTLINE
OF ST. THOMAS

TEXT OF ARISTOTLE
(*B.1132 a 25*)
Chapter 4

C. He shows how the mean of that justice which regulates transactions is understood.

1. HE DISCLOSES HIS PROPOSITION.

a. How we may discover the mean of commutative justice.
  i. *An example to show how the mean is applied.*
    x. THE EXAMPLE.

It is as though the judge were dealing with a line divided into unequal sections, and took from the greater section the length exceeding the half and added it to the smaller section. When a whole belonging to two men is divided by the *dicha* or measure, then it is said that each has what is his inasmuch as each receives an equal portion—the equal portion being a mean between something greater and something less according to arithmetic proportionality. **956-957**

    y. THE APPROPRIATENESS OF THE EXAMPLE.

Therefore, this mean is called *dicheon* (*dikaion*)—since it is a *30* *dicha* (measure)—in the way they say *dicheon* (just thing) and *dichastes* (just man) and *dichaste* (justice).[1] **958**

  ii. *He clarifies what he has said.*
    x. HE EXPLAINS HIS STATEMENT.

If there are two equals and the half of one is taken from it and added to the other, the other will exceed it *b* by two. But if what was taken away

---

[1] Thus St. Thomas seems to have understood the sentence. W. D. Ross translates it: "It is for this reason also that it is called (*dikaion*), because it is a division into two equal parts (*dicha*), just as if one were to call it (*dichaion*); and the judge (*dicastes*) is one who bisects (*dichastes*)." (New York: Random House, page 1009.)

413

was not added to the other, the other would exceed the half by one. Therefore, the half taken is equal to one, and the half from which subtraction was made is equal to one. From this we know both what must be taken from the person with too much, and what must be added to the one with too little. The amount exceeding the mean must be awarded to the man with too little and taken from the one with too much. **959-960**

Y. HE EXPRESSES IT BY TERMINALS.

Let us take three equal lines and mark them by the terms A A, B B and G G. Subtract A E (the half of A) from A A, and add it to G G and call it G D. Therefore the whole line D G G exceeds the line A E by that which is G D and by that which is G B (the half of G),[1] but it exceeds line B B by that which is G D. **961**

b. He shows how we may discover (the mean) in the matter of the different arts.

This is true also in other arts, for they would be destroyed if the *10* craftsman doing the quality and quantity of work which he should is not supported accordingly.[2] **962**

2. HE EXPLAINS THE ORIGIN OF THE NAMES, GAIN AND LOSS.

The names, gain and loss, have their origin in voluntary transactions. When a man owns more than he did own he is said to have profit, but when less he is said to have loss, as in buying, selling, and other exchanges permitted by law. However, when men have neither more nor less but the same after their transactions they are said to have what is theirs, neither gaining profit nor suffering loss. Therefore, jus- *20* tice is a mean between some kind of gain and loss arising in involuntary transactions; it is having an equal amount of these both before and after the transaction. **963-964**

[1] "B" is evidently "3." See diagram in n. 961.
[2] W. D. Ross omits this paragraph in his translation.

COMMENTARY OF ST. THOMAS

956. After the philosopher has shown the difference between the mean of justice regulating transactions and the mean of justice regulating distributions, now [C] he shows how the mean of that justice which regulates transactions is understood. He handles this point in a twofold fashion. First [C, 1] he discloses his proposition. Then [C, 2], at "The names etc.," he explains the origin of the names, gain and loss, which he has used. He discusses the initial point from two aspects. First [1, a] he shows how we may discover the mean of commutative justice in these things; next [1, b], at "This is true etc.," how we may discover it in the matter of the different arts. He treats the first point in two ways. First [a, i] he introduces an example to show how the mean is applied in commutative justice. Then [a, ii], at "If there are etc.," he clarifies what he has said. In regard to the initial point he first [i, x] gives the example to explain his proposition. Then [i, y], at "Therefore, this mean etc.," he shows the appropriateness of the example from the very manner of speaking.

957. Aristotle says that this is the way a judge expresses a reduction to equality. If he wishes to reduce to equality a line divided into unequal parts, he takes away from the larger part that portion by which it exceeds the half of the whole line and adds it to the smaller part so that the half of the whole line is a certain *dicha*, i.e., rule or measure for reducing unequal portions to an equality. So when a whole thing belonging to two men is divided by such a *dicha* or measure, then it is said that each one has what is his inasmuch as he receives equality —which is the mean between more and less—according to arithmetic proportionality. The reason is that the mean of justice is exceeded by the one with more to the extent that it exceeds the person with less—this pertains to arithmetic proportionality, as we pointed out before (944,950).

958. Then [i, y], at "Therefore, this mean," he shows that the preceding example is suitable according to Greek usage. He says that since the mean of this justice is a certain *dicha,* hence it is that the just thing is called *dicheon* by the Greeks, as if a person wanting to vary the names should say that *dicheon* is the just thing, *dichastes* the just man, and *dichaste* justice.

959. Next [a, ii], at "If there are two equals," he makes clear what he has said, viz., that it is necessary to take from one with more in the amount exceeding the mean and to give to one with less. First [ii, x] he explains his statement; and then [ii, y], at "Let us take etc.," he expresses it by terminals. He says first, let us take two equal lines both of which are two measures long, for example, two palms breadth or two feet; let us subtract half from one line and add it to the other. Obviously, the line receiving the addition exceeds the other by two units because the line from which the subtraction was made has only one unit remaining, and the line to which the addition has been made has three units. But if the section subtracted from one line is not added to the other, there will be an excess of only one unit. By that line, to which nothing is added or from which nothing is subtracted, we understand the mean of justice, having as it does neither more nor less than what belongs to it. By the line to which addition has been made we understand the

person who has too much. By the line from which subtraction has been made we understand the person who has too little.

960. In this way then it is evident that the man who has too much exceeds the mean by one unit, which has been added to it over and above, but the mean exceeds by one—which has been taken from it—that from which subtraction has been made. Therefore, we will know by this mean what we ought to take from him who has more and give to him who has less. Besides, we will know that we ought to take from the greater, i.e., from him who has more, the amount by which he exceeds the mean because we ought to give him who has less in the amount the mean exceeds him.

961. At "Let us take" [ii, y] he sets forth in figure what was said. Let us take three equal lines and mark the terminations of one A A, of another B B, of the third G G. Then let B B remain undivided, but divide A A in half at the point E, and divide G G in half at the point 3. Next, take away from line A A a section A E, add it to the line G G and call the addition G D. It is clear then that the whole line D G exceeds the line A E by two units, viz., by that which is G G and by that which is G D, but it exceeds the line B B by one unit only, viz., G D. Therefore, obviously, that which is longest exceeds the mean by one unit and the shortest by two units after the manner of arithmetic proportionality.

A ——————— E ——————— A

B —————————————— B

G ——————— 3 ——————— G ————— D

962. Then [1, b], at "This is true," he shows that what has been said must be observed in transactions having to do with the different arts. The arts would be destroyed if the craftsman, who works at some handicraft, would not be supported, i.e., would not receive for his workmanship according to the quantity and quality of what he produced. For that reason the work of one craftsman must be commensurate with the work of another to the extent that there is a just transaction.

963. Next [C, 2], at "The names," he explains the origin of the names, gain and loss, saying that they come from voluntary transactions in which names of this kind were first used. When a man owned more than he previously had owned, he was said to have gained; but when less, he was said to have suffered loss, as in buying, selling and in all other transactions which are permitted by law. However, when men have neither more nor less than they had in the beginning, but bring back in equal quantity the same as they had taken by their transactions, then they are said to have what belongs to them, neither gaining nor losing.

964. He draws the final inference that he had principally intended. It is evident from the premises that the justice we are now discussing is a mean between gain and loss, that justice is simply the possession of an equal amount before and after a transaction even an involuntary one, as we see in the person who, when constrained by a judge, restores to another what he had in excess.

LECTURE VIII

The Opinion of Pythagoras

ANALYTICAL OUTLINE OF ST. THOMAS	TEXT OF ARISTOTLE (*B.1132 b 21*) Chapter 5

I. HE STATES THE ERRONEOUS OPINION.

> Some philosophers seem to think that, generally speaking, justice is reciprocation, as the Pythagoreans held; in this way they defined justice without qualification. **965**

II. HE REJECTS IT.

A. In regard to distributive justice.

> However, reciprocation does not belong to distributive justice. **966**

B. In the case of commutative justice.

1. HE PROPOSES WHAT HE INTENDS TO DO WITH COMMUTATIVE JUSTICE.

> Likewise, it is not suited to the justice that regulates all transactions, although Rhadamantus wished to say that it was, holding that if a man suffers what he himself did to another, justice is attained. **967**

2. HE REJECTS THIS VIEW FOR TWO REASONS.

a. First.

> Such justice is at variance with true justice in many situations, for example, if a prince strikes another it is not required that the prince be struck, but if another strikes a prince such a *30* man should not only be struck but also punished in addition. **968-969**

b. Second.

> Moreover, it makes a great deal of difference whether the offender acts voluntarily or involuntarily. **970**

417

III. HE SHOWS WHERE AND HOW THE TRUTH MAY BE FOUND.

A. There must be reciprocation in exchanges according to proportionality.

1. HE STATES HIS INTENTION.

But in dealings of exchange justice is such that it includes reciprocation according to proportionality but not according to equality. **971-972**

2. HE PROVES HIS STATEMENT.

By reason of proportional reciprocation the state continues to exist, for either the citizens seek to return evil (for evil)—if not, a kind of *B.1133* servitude seems to be present when revenge may not be taken—or they seek to return good (for good) and if not, proper recompense will not be made. It is by return of favors that men live together. Because of this they promptly express gratitude as if it were a sacred duty to make repayment—a thing characteristic of gratitude. It is fitting that a man should be of service to one who has done him a favor and in return begin to do a greater favor. **973-974**

B. He explains the form of this proportionality.

1. HE GIVES AN EXAMPLE.

A conjunction by means of a diagonal shows how to make that compensation which is according to proportionality. Let A be a builder, B a shoemaker, G a house, and D a sandal. It is necessary that a builder should take from the shoemaker his product and in return give what he himself makes. *10* If first an equality according to proportionality be found and then reciprocation be made, it will be as we have said. But if not, there will not be an equality—and the state will not continue to exist—because nothing hinders the work of one craftsman from being of more value than the work of another. Therefore these things must be equated. **975-976**

2. THE SAME IS FOUND IN OTHER ARTS.

This is to be observed also in the other arts, for they would be destroyed if a workman did not receive according to the quantity and quality of what he produced. Between two doctors an exchange does not take place but between a doctor and a farmer who are altogether different and unequal. These then must be equated. 977

COMMENTARY OF ST. THOMAS

965. After the Philosopher has shown how the mean should be understood in both kinds of justice, now he rejects a false opinion about the understanding of the mean of justice. He discusses this point under three headings. First [I] he states the erroneous opinion. Next [II], at "However, reciprocation etc.," he rejects it. Third [III], at "But in dealings etc.," he shows where and how the truth may be found. He says first it seems to some that, generally speaking, justice is nothing other than reciprocation, viz., that a man should suffer according to what he has done. This was the opinion of the Pythagoreans who decided that justice is the same as reciprocation.

966. Then [II], at "However, reciprocation," he rejects this opinion on two accounts; and first [II, A] in regard to distributive justice, he says that reciprocation does not correspond to what is just distributively. The reason for this is evident. The just thing in distributions is not judged according to what one of two, who must be equated by justice, does against the other or suffers from the other. This is necessary for the nature of reciprocation; but in distribution a share of the common goods is given to each by an equality of proportion.

967. Next [II, B], at "Likewise, it is not," he rejects the preceding error in the case of commutative justice. First [II, B, 1] he proposes what he intends to do with commutative justice. He says that reciprocation does not coincide with all the processes in justice that regulate transactions, although the philosophers who expressed the foregoing opinion meant that in transactions justice is the same as reciprocation. This is clear from the fact that a legislator named Rhadamantus maintained that this justice is of such a nature that if a man suffers those very things he inflicted on others, justice is vindicated.

968. Then [II, B, 2], at "Such justice," he rejects this view for two reasons. In regard to the first [2, a] he says that in many situations vengeance of this kind is found to be at variance with true justice, for instance, if a ruler strikes a private person justice does not require that the ruler be struck. But if a person strikes a ruler it is necessary that such a person not only be struck but be more gravely punished.

969. This seems to contradict what the Philosopher said before (951) that in commutative justice the different rank of persons is not taken into ac-

count—all being equal under the law. But it should be noted what the Philosopher had said was this: in commutative justice the law considers only the nature of the damage. It is clear that when damage is considered in the taking of an external thing—money for instance—the amount of damage does not vary according to a person's rank. Still when the injury is personal, the extent of the injury necessarily changes according to the rank of the person. Obviously, worse damage is done when someone strikes a ruler, by reason of the fact that injury is done not only to the person of the ruler but also the whole commonweal. Therefore, reciprocation simply taken is not suitable for justice in matters of this kind.

970. At **"Moreover, it makes"** [2, b] he gives the second reason. He says in the matter of imposing punishment, it makes a great deal of difference whether the offender inflicted the injury voluntarily or involuntarily, i.e., because of ignorance or violence or fear. The man who sinned voluntarily ought to be punished more severely than the man who sinned involuntarily, for two reasons. First, because in regard to punishments, consideration is given to the restoration of equality of justice not only by a person restoring what he has taken but also by his being punished for the crime. For this reason some are punished by law even for sins causing no injury or damage to another. Likewise a thief is compelled not only to restore what he took —by which the equality of justice is reestablished—but beyond that he is punished for the offense perpetrated. But the offense is increased or diminished by the fact that a man sins voluntarily or involuntarily. Hence the voluntary offender is punished more severely than the involuntary offender. The second reason is that the injury of the deliberate transgressor is greater, for internal contempt is added to the external damage.

971. Next [III], at **"But in dealings,"** he explains in what matter and manner the statement is true that reciprocation is justice. He discusses this point from three aspects. First [III, A] he shows that there must be reciprocation in exchanges according to proportionality. Then [III, B], at "A conjunction by means etc.," he explains the form of this proportionality. Last [Lect. IX; C], at "Therefore all etc." (B.1133 a 18), he shows how such a form can be observed. On the initial point he does two things. First [III, A, 1] he states his intention. Next [III, A, 2], at "By reason of proportional etc.," he proves his statement. He says that in dealings of exchange it is true that justice is of such a nature that it includes reciprocation not according to equality but according to proportionality.

972. It seems this is contrary to what was said before (950), that in commutative justice the mean is taken not according to geometrical proportionality, which consists in an equality of proportion, but according to arithmetic proportionality, which consists in a quantitative equality. We must say that, in regard to commutative justice there should always be an equality of thing to thing, not, however, of action and passion, which implies corresponding requital. But in this, proportionality must be employed in order to bring about an equality of things because the work of one craftsman is of more value than the work of another, e.g., the building of a house than the production of a penknife. Hence, if the builder exchanged his work for the work of the cutler, there would not be equality of thing given and taken, i.e., of house and penknife.

973. Then [III, A, 2], at **"By reason of proportional,"** he proves his statement, saying that justice in exchanges includes reciprocation according to proportionality. This can be shown by the fact that the citizens live to-

gether amicably because they have a proportionate kindliness towards one another. Accordingly, if one does something for another, the other is anxious to do something in proportion in return. Obviously, all citizens desire that reciprocation be done to them proportionately. By reason of this all men can live together because they do for one another what they themselves seek. Therefore, they never seek in regard to evil that corresponding requital be done to them proportionately. But if they do not seek this in regard to evil, for example, when one man does not take vengeance on another who injures him, a kind of servility seems to result. Indeed it is servile when a man cannot gain by his own activity something that he does not desire in an evil way.

974. We may even say that men not only do not desire that corresponding requital, when unjust, be done to them proportionately, but they do not desire that it be done when just. In this way if corresponding requital is not done them in a proportionate way, proper retribution will not be effected. But men live together because one makes a return to another for the favors he has received. So it is that virtuous men promptly express gratitude to their benefactors as if it were a sacred duty to make them a return in this way—repaying a favor is characteristic of gratitude. It is fitting that a man should be of service to one who has done him a favor, i.e., bestowed a gratuitous kindness, and that he be not content to give only as much as he received but that in return he begins to offer more than he got so that he himself may do a favor.

975. Next [III, B], at "A conjunction by means," he makes known the form of proportionality according to which reciprocation ought to be made. First [III, B, 1] he gives an example in the shoemaker and the builder; then [III, B, 2], at "This is to be observed etc.," he shows that the same is found in other arts. He says first that a conjunction by means of a diagonal shows how to make compensation or reciprocation according to proportionality. To understand this draw A B G D, make two diagonals intersecting one another, viz., A D and B D. Let A represent a builder, B a shoemaker, G a house that is the work of the builder, and D a sandal that is the work of a shoemaker. It is necessary at times that the builder should take from the shoemaker his product, a sandal. But the builder himself ought to give his product as a recompense to the shoemaker.

976. Therefore, if first an equality according to proportionality is found so that on one side a certain number of sandals be fixed as equal to one house (for a builder incurs more expense in building one house than a shoemaker in making one sandal), next, corresponding reciprocation is had so that the builder may receive many sandals equal to one house and the shoemaker one house, there will be recompense—as was said—made according to proportion by a diagonal conjunction.

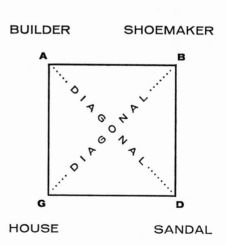

BUILDER   SHOEMAKER

A   B

G   D

HOUSE   SANDAL

The reason is that a proportionate number of sandals are given to the builder, and the house to the shoemaker. But if compensation is not made in this way, there will not be an equality of things exchanged—and so men will not be able to live together—since nothing hinders the work of one craftsman from being worth more than the work of another, a house than a sandal. For this reason these things must be equated one with the other according to the previously mentioned proportionality, so that a just exchange may take place.

977. Then [III, B, 2], at **"This is to be observed,"** he shows that the same thing is found in the other arts. He affirms that what was said (975, 976) about the builder and the shoemaker must be observed also in the other arts, so that reciprocation and exchange may take place according to diagonal proportionality. Indeed the arts would be destroyed if a workman did not receive according to the quantity and quality of what he produced—a thing that must be discovered in the way indicated. It is not common for men practicing one art, for example, two doctors, to communicate their work with one another, but very often men practicing different arts do, for instance, a doctor and a farmer, both entirely different and unequal. These must be equated in the preceding way.

LECTURE IX

Money

ANALYTICAL OUTLINE
OF ST. THOMAS

TEXT OF ARISTOTLE
(*B.1133 a 18*)
Chapter 5

(III) C. He shows in what way this form of proportionality can be observed.

I. HE EXPLAINS HIS INTENTION.

a. It is necessary to make everything commensurate.

  i. The nature of that which measures all things.

Therefore all things capable of exchange ought to be compared in some way. For this purpose money was invented and became a kind of me- *20* dium measuring everything including excess and defect. **978-979**

  ii. How such a commensuration is established in exchanges.

A certain number of sandals are equal in value to a house or to a quantity of food. Therefore, as many sandals must be exchanged for a house or a quantity of food in proportion as the builder contributes more than the shoemaker (or the farmer). If this is not observed, there will be neither exchange nor sharing. But this reciprocation will not be possible unless things are equated. **980**

  iii. He indicates the nature of this commensuration.

Therefore, it is reasonable to measure all things by one norm, as has been pointed out previously. This norm in reality is demand which connects all things. If men were not in need there would be no exchange, or if they did not have a similar demand, exchange would not be the same. Money *30* originated by agreement on account of necessary exchange. Hence money (*numisma*) has the name because it is a norm not by nature but by law (*nomos*). We have the power to change money and to make it useless. **981-982**

b. How a just reciprocation in exchanges may be effected.
    i. *He explains his proposition.*

When things have been equated
there will be reciprocation, so that as
the farmer is to the shoemaker, the
amount of the shoemaker's work is to
the amount of the farmer's work.
When things are to be exchanged they
ought to be represented in a figure *b*
showing proportionality. If this is not
done one extreme will have both excesses, but when all have what is theirs
they will be equal and will do business
with one another because this equality
can be brought about for them. **983**

    ii. *(He) puts it in a diagram.*

Let A represent the farmer, G the
food, B the shoemaker and D his
equated work. If there is no such
reciprocation, there will not be any
sharing of goods.   **984**

2. HE CLARIFIES THE PREVIOUS STATEMENTS.

a. How things are made commensurate.
    i. *Necessity is a measure according
    to reality.*

That human demand connects everything as by a kind of measure is evident because when men are so mutually
situated that both or at least one is
not in need, they do not exchange
their goods. But they engage in exchange when one needs what the other
has, e.g., wine, and they give grain
for it. An equation then must be *10*
made between these goods.   **985**

    ii. *Currency is a measure according
    to the provision of law.*

For future exchanges money is as
it were a guarantee that a man, who
has no present need, will be helped
when he is in want later on. The man
who offers currency should receive
what he needs. However, currency
suffers like other things, for it is not
always of the same value; although it
tends to be more stable than other
things.   **986-987**

b. How the things made commensurate may be exchanged.
    i. *In what manner there is ex-
    change of goods . . . meas-
    ured in currency.*

Everything then must be evaluated
in money, for in this way exchange
will always take place and consequently
association among men. Money equates

424

goods making them commensurate after the manner of a measure. Indeed association is not possible without exchange, nor exchange without equality which cannot exist unless there is commensuration. **988**

ii. Under what aspect currency serves as a measure.

It is impossible that things so greatly different be made commensurate according to reality, but they agree sufficiently by comparison with the needs of man, and so there must be one measure determined by man. And this is called money, which makes all things commensurate inasmuch as they are measured by money. **989**

iii. He puts in terminals what was said.

Let A represent a house and B five minae. Let G represent a bed worth one mina. The bed then will be one fifth the value of the house. Therefore it is obvious how many beds equal a house, viz., five. Likewise it is obvious that barter took place before money existed. But it makes no difference whether five beds or the value of five beds are given.

We have now discussed the nature of what is just and what is unjust.
990-991

COMMENTARY OF ST. THOMAS

978. After the Philosopher has proposed the form of proportionality, with which reciprocation is identified in exchange, he now shows [III, C] in what way this form of proportionality can be observed. First [C, 1] he explains his intention. Then [C, 2], at "That human demand etc.," he clarifies the previous statements. He discusses the initial point in a twofold manner. First [1, a] he shows that to preserve the form of proportionality perfectly it is necessary to make everything commensurate. Next [1, b], at "When things have been etc.," he explains how a

just reciprocation in exchanges may be effected by a commensuration of this kind. He treats the first point under three aspects. Initially [1, a, i] he explains the nature of that which measures all things. Then [1, a, ii], at "A certain number etc.," he shows how such a commensuration is established in exchanges. Last [1, a, iii], at "Therefore, it is etc.," he indicates the nature of this commensuration.

979. He says first, in order that the products of the different workmen be equated and thus become possible to exchange, it is necessary that all things

425

capable of exchange should be comparable in some way with one another so that it can be known which of them has greater value and which less. It was for this purpose that money or currency was invented, to measure the price of such things. In this way currency becomes a medium inasmuch as it measures everything, both excess and defect, to the extent that one thing exceeds another, as was pointed out before (955, 959-960). It is a mean of justice—as if someone should call it a measure of excess and defect.

980. Next [1, a, ii], at "A certain number," he shows how exchange takes place according to the preceding commensuration. Although a house is worth more than a sandal, nevertheless a number of sandals are equal in value to one house or the food required for one man during a long period. In order then to have just exchange, as many sandals must be exchanged for one house or for the food required for one man as the builder or the farmer exceeds the shoemaker in his labor and costs. If this is not observed, there will be no exchange of things and men will not share their goods with one another. But what has been said, that a number of sandals are exchanged for one house, is not possible unless the sandals are equated with the house in some way.

981. At "Therefore, it is" [1, a, iii] he indicates the nature of this commensuration made by means of money. He states that for this reason it is possible to equate things because all things can be measured by some one standard, as was pointed out (957). But this one standard which truly measures all things is demand. This includes all commutable things inasmuch as everything has a reference to human need. Articles are not valued according to the dignity of their nature, otherwise a mouse, an animal endowed with sense, should be of greater value than a pearl, a thing without life. But they are priced according as man stands in need of them for his own use.

982. An indication of this is that if man were not in need there would be no exchange, or if they did not have a similar need, i.e., of these things, exchange would not be the same because men would not exchange what they have for something they did not need. That demand really measures everything is evident from the fact that money originated by arrangement or a kind of agreement among men on account of the necessity of exchange, i.e., exchange of necessary goods. There is an agreement among men that what a person needs will be given him in exchange for currency. Hence currency is called money (numisma)—nomos means law—since currency is not a measure by nature but by law (nomo). It is in our power to change currencies and make them useless.

983. Then [1, b], at "When things have been," he shows how just reciprocation takes place in exchanges according to the preceding commensuration. First [1, b, i] he explains his proposition; and then [1, b, ii], at "Let A represent etc.," puts it in a diagram. He says first that the norm measuring all things by need according to nature and by currency according to human convention will then become reciprocation when everything will be equated in the way just mentioned. This is done in such a manner that as the farmer (whose work is raising food for men) excels the shoemaker (whose work is making sandals), in the same proportion the work of the shoemaker exceeds in number the work of the farmer, so that many sandals are exchanged for one bushel of wheat. Thus when exchange of things takes place, the articles to be exchanged ought to be arranged in a proportional figure with diagonals, as was stated previously (957). If this was not done, one extreme would have both excesses; if a farmer gave a bushel of wheat for a

426

sandal, he would have a surplus of labor in his product and would have also an excess of loss because he would be giving more than he would receive. But when all have what is theirs, they are in this way equal and do business with one another because the equality previously mentioned is possible for them.

984. Next [1, b, ii], at **"Let A represent,"** he puts in a diagram what has been said about the proportional figure. Take then (as in the previous example) a square A, B, G, D, and two diagonals A D and B G intersecting one another. Let A represent the farmer and G the food, his product, e.g., a bushel of wheat. Let B represent the shoemaker and D his equated product, i.e., as many sandals as have the value of a bushel of wheat. There will then be a just reciprocation if A be joined with D and B with G. If there is not such a compensation men will not share their goods with one another.

FARMER   SHOEMAKER

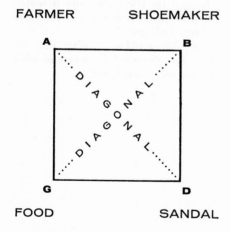

FOOD   SANDAL

985. At **"That human demand"** [C, 2] he explains more fully what has already been mentioned. First [2, a] he shows how things are made com-

mensurate; and next [2, b], at "Everything then," how the things made commensurate may be exchanged. He discusses the first point from two aspects. First [2, a, i] he shows that necessity is a measure according to reality; and then [2, a, ii], at "For future exchanges etc.," how currency is a measure according to the provision of law. He says first the statement (981-982) that human need contains everything as a certain measure is explained in this way. When men are so situated among themselves that either both, or at least one, do not need a thing possessed by the other, they do not engage in mutual exchange. But exchange does take place when a man owning grain is in need of wine which his neighbor has, and thus gives the grain for the wine, so that a quantity of grain is alloted according to the value of the wine.

986. Then [2, a, ii], at **"For future exchanges,"** he shows clearly how currency serves as a measure. On this point we must consider that if men always needed immediately the goods they have among themselves, they would have no need of any exchange except of thing for thing, e.g., wine for grain. But sometimes one man (who has a surplus of wine at present) does not need the grain that another man has (who is in need of wine), but perhaps later he will need the grain or some other product. In this way then for the necessity of future exchange, money or currency is, as it were, a surety that if a man has no present need but may want in the future, the thing he needs will be available when he presents the currency.

987. The particular virtue of currency must be that when a man presents it he immediately receives what he needs. However, it is true that currency also suffers the same as other things, viz., that it does not always obtain for a man what he wants because it cannot always be equal or of

the same value. Nevertheless it ought to be so established that it retains the same value more permanently than other things.

988. Next [2, b], at **"Everything then,"** he explains how, by the measure of currency, there is exchange of things which are made commensurate in currency. He discusses this point from three aspects. First [2, b, i] he shows in what manner there is exchange of goods that are measured in currency. Then [2, b, ii], at "It is impossible," he discloses under what aspect currency serves as a measure. Last [2, b, iii], at "Let A represent a house," he puts in terminals what was said. He states first that, because currency as a measure ascertaining quantity retains its value longer, all goods must be evaluated in currency. In this way exchange of goods can take place and, consequently, association among men. Money equates commutable goods, as a certain measure making them commensurate. He clarifies what has been said by stating that association is not possible if there is no exchange. But exchange is impossible unless an equality is established in goods, which in turn cannot exist without commensuration.

989. Then [2, b, ii], at **"It is impossible,"** he shows in what way cur-rency is used as a measure. He says that it is impossible that things so greatly different be made commensurate according to reality, i.e., according to the peculiar nature of the things themselves. But they can be sufficiently contained under one measure by comparison with the needs of men. Hence there must be some one criterion that measures all things of this kind and is not a measure by reason of nature but because so fixed by men. Therefore, this is called money owing to the fact that it makes all things commensurate insofar as they are measured by money.

990. At **"Let A represent a house"** [2, b, iii] he explains in terminals what has been said, stating: let A be a house worth five minae, B a bed worth one mina, and in this way the bed will be one fifth the value of the house. Hence it is obvious how many beds are equal in value to one house, viz., five. Likewise it is obvious that barter took place before there was currency, since five beds have been exchanged for one house. But it makes no difference whether five or the value of five beds are given.

991. He concludes saying that we have now discussed the nature of what is just and what is unjust.

LECTURE X

Just Action as a Mean

ANALYTICAL OUTLINE OF ST. THOMAS	TEXT OF ARISTOTLE (*B.1133 b 30*) Chapter 5

1. HE STATES HIS INTENTION.

a. The operation of justice is a mean.

From these discussions it is clear that a just action is a mean between doing what is unjust and suffering what is unjust. To be unjust is to have too much, to be injured is to have too little.   **992**

b. How justice itself is a mean.

But justice is a mean, not in the same way as the preceding virtues but in the sense that it produces a mean. However, injustice pertains to extremes.   **993**

2. HE PROVES HIS STATEMENT.

a. The nature of justice.
   i. *What justice is.*

Justice is also a habit by *B.1134* which the just man is said to operate by choosing what is just and to distribute both to himself in relation to his neighbor and to one man in relation to another.   **994-995**

   ii. *What injustice is.*

He does not act in such a way that he bestows more desirable things on himself and less desirable things on his neighbor, and on the contrary less hurtful things on himself than on his neighbor, but he distributes equally according to proportion. Likewise, he observes a rule regarding one man in relation to another. On the other hand injustice is a habit operative of what is unjust. This takes place by excess and defect of useful or hurtful things contrary to what is proportional. Hence injustice is called excess and defect because it brings about excess and defect, the unjust man assigning *10*

429

himself an excess of what is simply useful and a deficiency of what is harmful. In a similar way he attributes both an excess and a deficiency to others. But this too is contrary to what is proportional in whatever way it takes place. **996**

b. Some remarks to bring his subject to a conclusion.

One injustice, which is to have too little, is to suffer what is unjust. Another injustice, which is to have too much, is to do what is unjust. **997-998**

3. HE RECAPITULATES WHAT HAS BEEN SAID.

We have then discussed justice and injustice, and the nature of both. Likewise we have treated in a general way what is just and unjust. **999**

COMMENTARY OF ST. THOMAS

992. After the Philosopher has shown how the just thing is a mean, now he shows how justice is a mean. On this point he does three things. First [1] he states his intention. Then [2], at "Justice is also etc.," he proves his statement. Finally [3], at "We have then discussed etc.," he recapitulates what has been said. Since habits are known by acts, he treats two aspects of the initial point. First [1, a] he proposes that the operation of justice is a mean; and second [1, b], at "But justice etc.," how justice itself is a mean. He says first that, from previous considerations (978-991), it is evident that a just operation, that is, an operation of justice, is a mean between doing what is unjust and suffering what is unjust. The first is to have more than is due to oneself, i.e., to do an unjust action; but the other, viz., to suffer an unjust thing, is to have too little by reason of the fact that a person has been deprived of what is due him. The act of justice is to do

what is equal, i.e., the mean between too much and too little. Obviously then it follows from the premises that a just action is a mean between doing what is unjust and suffering what is unjust.

993. Then [1, b], at "But justice," he explains how justice is a mean, saying that justice is not a mean in the same way as the other moral virtues. Their mean lies between two vices; liberality is a mean between parsimony and extravagance. But justice is not a mean between two vices. However, it can be called a mean by reason of its effect inasmuch as it constitutes a mean, since its act is a just operation which is a mean between doing what is unjust and bearing the unjust. The first of these, active injustice pertains to a vice of injustice which is a habit of extremes inasmuch as it takes for itself too many goods and too few evils. But the other, i.e., the toleration of the injustice is not a vice, but a suffering.

994. Next [2], at **"Justice is also,"** he proves what was said, viz., that justice is not a middle course between two vices, as is the case with other moral virtues. He treats this point in a twofold manner. First [2, a] he takes up the nature of justice; then [2, b], at "One injustice etc.," he adds some remarks to bring his subject to a conclusion. He discusses the first point from two aspects. Initially [a, i] he states what justice is; and next [a, ii] at "He does not act etc.," what injustice is. He says first that justice is a habit by which the just man does the just thing—and this by deliberate choice because, as was previously pointed out in the second book (305, 308, 382), a moral virtue is a habit of correct choice. Doing the just thing can be referred to justice directing exchanges, in which the nature of justice is more apparent by reason of the equality of the thing. Hence he adds "and to distribute" in order to include also distributive justice, which consists in the equality of proportion.

995. A man can do the just thing by choice, both in exchanges and in distributions, in two ways. In one way he does this between himself and another, and touching this point Aristotle says "both to himself in relation to his neighbor." In the second way a man does this between two others— this pertains to a judge or an arbiter— and so the Philosopher adds "and to one man in relation to another." He explains, by exclusion of the contrary, how the just man does a just deed. He adds that the just man does not so act that in regard to desirable things (for example, riches and honors) he bestows more on himself and less on his neighbor, and in regard to harmful things (i.e., burdensome and painful), on the contrary, more on his neighbor than himself; but he makes an equal distribution according to proportion—a thing he observes not only between himself and another but also between two others.

996. At [1] **"He does not act"** [a, ii] he presents the nature of injustice. He affirms that on the contrary injustice is a habit which does by choice what is unjust. This happens by excess or defect of useful or harmful things which the just man accepts according to due proportion. Hence, as justice is called a mean because it produces a mean, so also injustice is called excess and defect because it produces excess and defect in such a way that the unjust man bestows on himself an excess of things which are simply useful but a deficiency of things which are harmful. In a similar way he attributes to others both excess and defect, however not of the same things, but a defect of the useful and an excess of the harmful. Nevertheless, it has not been determined in what way injustice may depart from the proper proportion, i.e., how much more or how much less it may accept than is due. But injustice does this, howsoever it may happen.

997. Next [2, b], at **"One injustice,"** he adds some remarks required to conclude the subject. He says there is a twofold injustice: one consists in a lack of beneficial things, and indicates an excess of onerous things—which amounts to the same. This is to suffer what is unjust. The other injustice is to have an excess of beneficial things and a lack of onerous things—and this is to do an injustice.

998. From what has been said we can come to three conclusions. To do an unjust act pertains to injustice. However, to have a lack of benefits or an excess of burdens is not to do what is unjust but to suffer what is unjust. Therefore this does not pertain to the vice of injustice. But justice is a mean between having too much and too little, as was pointed out before (992,

[1] More specifically at "On the other hand injustice."

993). Consequently, injustice is not a mean between two vices.

999. Then [3], at **"We have then discussed,"** he concludes by recapitulating what has been said. He affirms that we have discussed justice and injustice and the nature of both. Likewise we have treated what is just and what is unjust in a general way, for he will determine afterwards (1000-1108) certain particular modes of what is just and unjust.

LECTURE XI

The Unjust Man

ANALYTICAL OUTLINE   TEXT OF ARISTOTLE
   OF ST. THOMAS   (*B.1134 a 16*)
                           Chapter 6

I. HE DETERMINES THE TRUTH (SHOWING HOW A MAN . . . BECOMES UNJUST).

A. He asks a question.

A'. He presents the question.

> Since someone doing an unjust act may not be unjust himself, we will investigate the nature of the unjust actions that show the doer—for example, a thief or an adulterer or a robber—already unjust according to the injustice proper to each case. Or does not this make any difference? If a man having sexual intercourse with a woman knows with whom he sins *20* and acts not by choice but by passion, he does an unjust act but is not unjust. So neither is a man a thief although he steals, nor an adulterer although he commits adultery. The same is true in other cases. **1000-1001**

B'. He shows that another question was settled previously.

> We have previously discussed how reciprocation is related to what is just. **1002**

B. He interposes some subjects necessary for a solution of the question.

A'. What is justice in the absolute sense.

    I. HE STATES HIS INTENTION.

> We must not forget that we seek what is just in the absolute sense and political justice. **1003**

2. HE CARRIES OUT HIS INTENTION.

a. What political justice is.
  i. *What he intends.*
    X. WHAT POLITICAL JUSTICE IS.

The latter consists in a community of life for the purpose of having a self-sufficiency among free men equal according to proportionality or arithmetical equality.   **1004-1005**

    Y. THERE ARE OTHER KINDS OF JUSTICE.

Therefore, among those persons in whom this does not exist we find not political justice but a special kind of metaphorical justice.   **1006**

  ii. His intention.
    X. IN REGARD TO POLITICAL JUSTICE.
      aa. He clarifies his statement.

For justice exists between those very persons whose relations are gov- *30* erned by law. But the law is enacted for those among whom injustice is found, because punishment is a judgment of what is just and what is unjust. Among these there is unjust action, but injustice does not exist in everyone who does an unjust action, which is to attribute to oneself too many of the things good in themselves and too few of the things onerous in themselves.   **1007-1008**

      bb. He draws some corollaries.
        a'. First.

For this reason we do not permit the rule of man but of reason, for a man rules for himself and becomes a tyrant. But a prince is the guardian *b* of justice and of equality.   **1009**

        b'. Second.

Since a prince, if he is just, attributes nothing excessive to himself, it follows that he does not give himself more of what is simply good, except according to proper proportion, and on this account he works for others. Therefore it is said that justice is the good of another, as was previously pointed out.   **1010**

        c'. Third.

Consequently a reward should be allotted to him, namely, honor and glory. Rulers who are not satisfied with these are tyrants.   **1011**

Y. IN REGARD TO THE JUSTICE OF
A MASTER OR A FATHER.
   aa. . . . Of a master and of
   a father.
      a'. What he intends.

      b'. (This) justice is not
      unqualified.

      c'. (This) justice is not
      political justice.

   bb. . . . (Of) a husband in
   relation to a wife.

However, the justice of a master and
of a father are not the same as but
similar to those we have examined.
1012
Toward one's own things injustice
does not exist in an unqualified 10
manner. But a chattel and a son, until
he is a certain age and acts in his own
right, are as it were a part of a man.
Now no one chooses to injure himself.
Therefore, there is no injustice done
to oneself, and consequently no injustice simply speaking.   1013
Nor is political justice observed here
which is according to the law and is
found in men naturally bound by the
law. Such are the persons who have
equality in regard to ruling and being
ruled.   1014
Hence justice concerns rather a wife
than children and chattels. In the first
there is domestic justice, and this is
also different from political justice.
1015

COMMENTARY OF ST. THOMAS

1000. After the Philosopher has
treated justice and the unjust thing in
themselves together with their opposites, now he treats them in comparison
with their subject, showing how a man
in doing an unjust action becomes unjust. He handles this point under two
headings. First [I] he determines the
truth. Then [Lect. XIV, II], at "Someone may raise etc." (B.1136 a 10), he
raises some doubts about matters previously settled. He discusses the initial point from three aspects. First [A]
he asks a question. Next [B], at "We
must not forget etc.," he interposes

some subjects necessary for a solution
of the question. Finally [Lect. XIII,
C], at "Since just and unjust etc."
(B.1135 a 15), he answers the question.
He treats the first point in a twofold
manner. First [A, A'] he presents the
question. Then [A, B'], at "We have
previously etc.," he shows that another
question was settled previously. He
says first that a person who does an
unjust action still may not be unjust.
Therefore, we must inquire into the
characteristics of injustice, i.e., the actions of unjust men must be of such
a type that the man who does unjust

435

deeds is already unjust in that particular species of injustice, for example, theft or adultery or robbery. Or, passing over the cases just mentioned, can it be said that for a man to be unjust it makes no difference in what actions he may act unjustly?

1001. For this reason we ask with what kind of injustice it occurs, because the doing of an unjust action takes place in many ways. A man may have sexual intercourse with a woman, the wife of another, and not be ignorant who the person is (ignorance could cause an involuntary) but know with whom he is having intercourse, and still not perform the act by deliberate choice but by passion. Such a man does an unjust act although he does not seem to be unjust because he does not act by deliberate choice. So also we can say in a particular case that a man is not a thief although he has stolen, since he did not commit theft by deliberate choice. In a similar way a man is not an adulterer although he has committed adultery. The same idea is found in other matters.

1002. Then [A, B'], at **"We have previously,"** he shows that a particular doubt has already been solved, viz., in what way reciprocation is related to justice—a point we discussed previously (971-972).

1003. Next [B], at **"We must not forget,"** he interposes some subjects that are necessary for the solution of the proposed question: first [B, A'] what is justice in the absolute sense; and second [Lect. XII; B, B'] at "There is a difference etc." (B.1135 a 9), what is unjust action. He handles the initial point in a twofold fashion. First [A', 1] he states his intention. Then [A', 2] at "The latter consists etc.," he carries out his intention. He says first that for a clear understanding of the question (in which we seek by what actions a man who does a just or an unjust act is said to be just or unjust) we must not forget the fact that the justice sought is justice in the absolute sense which is political justice.

1004. Then [A', 2], at **"The latter consists,"** he carries out his intention. First [2, a] he shows what political justice is. Then [Lect. XII; 2, b], at "One kind of political justice etc." (B.1134 b 18), he divides it. He treats the initial point under two aspects. First [a, i] he proposes what he intends, viz., what political justice is. Next [a, ii], at "For justice exists etc.," he explains his intention. He discusses the first point under two headings. Initially [i, x] he shows what political justice is. Second [i, y], at "Therefore, among those persons etc.," he concludes that there are other kinds of justice differing from this. He says first that political justice consists in a community of life that is ordered to a self-sufficiency of the things pertaining to human living. And the state-community should be such that everything sufficient for the needs of human life is found in it. This justice is found in free men, not slaves, because masters exercise towards slaves not political justice but the justice of dominion, of which more later (1006-1012). However, political justice is encountered with persons who are equal, i.e., one of whom is not subject to the other in the natural or political order, as a son to a father between whom there is no question of political justice but of paternal right.

1005. This political justice is either according to proportionality, i.e., proportional equality pertaining to distributive justice, or numerical equality, i.e., the equality of numerical quantity pertaining to commutative justice.

1006. Next [i, y], at **"Therefore, among those persons,"** he concludes there are other kinds of justice differing from that just mentioned. He states that—since political justice exists among the free and equal—in people who do not have this (that they are free and equal) there is not found political justice, which is unqualified justice, but a peculiar justice, viz., of a master or father, which is a qualified justice inasmuch as it has some likeness to political justice.

1007. At "For justice exists" [a, ii], he clarifies his statement: first [ii, x] in regard to political justice, which is unqualified justice; second [ii, y] in regard to justice of a master or a father, which is qualified justice, at "However, the justice of a master etc." First [x, aa] he clarifies his statement, viz., that political justice is in free and equal persons. Next [x, bb], at "For this reason we do not etc.," he draws some corollaries from the premises. He says first—as has been pointed out (1004)—that political justice is in the free and equal because, being determined by law, it necessarily is found in those for whom the law is enacted. But law is enacted principally not for slaves who are restrained by masters nor for children who are restrained by fathers but for the free and equal. That political justice exists in men of this kind, for whom law is enacted, is obvious from this that justice and injustice exist in them. Now, law extends to persons in whom there can be injustice. This is clear from the fact that punishment, which is fixed by law, is nothing other than a judgment about what is just and unjust.

1008. From this statement—the law exists for those between whom justice exists—it follows that it is for those between whom there is unjust action and for those between whom there is just action. The reason is that in whomsoever there is injustice, in these the performance of an unjust act is found but not the reverse. It was pointed out in the second book (252-253) that the doing of a virtuous action may take place without virtue, and likewise the doing of vicious actions without the habit of vice. An unjust act arises from the fact that a person should attribute to himself too many

of those things which are absolutely and of themselves good, like riches and too few of those things which are simply and of themselves evil, as the opposite of these.

1009. Next [x, bb], at "For this reason we do not permit," he draws three corollaries from the premises. First [bb, a'] he says that because injustice consists in this that a man attributes to himself too many of the benefits and too few of the burdens, it follows that in good government of the multitude we do not permit that men should rule, that is, according to whim and human passion but that the law, which is a dictate of reason, should rule man, or that man who acts according to reason should rule. The explanation is that if a prince follows human passions he will do this for himself; he will take more of the good things and less of the burdensome and so become a tyrant, although this is contrary to the concept of a prince. A prince was given the office to observe justice, and consequently equality, which he passes over when he usurps for himself too many beneficial and too few onerous things.

1010. He gives the second corollary [bb, b'] at "Since a prince." He affirms that since a prince—if he is just—attributes no more of the good things to himself than to others (unless perhaps according to a proper ratio of distributive justice), it follows that he does not labor for the advantage of himself but of others. Because of this it was said before (909) that legal justice, by which the prince rules the multitude of the people, is the good of another.

1011. He presents the third corollary at "Consequently a reward" [bb, c']. It is clear that everyone should reward the man who labors for him. Therefore, since the prince labors for the multitude, a reward should be given by the multitude, namely, honor and glory, which are the greatest goods that can be offered by men. But if there are some princes who are not satisfied with these for a reward but seek wealth, they are unjust and tyrannical. Over and above this reward proffered by man, good princes look for a reward from God.

1012. Then [ii, y], at **"However, the justice of a master,"** he explains what was indicated previously about the fact that this is not justice in the absolute sense but by similitude. First [y, aa] (he explains) in regard to the justice of a master and of a father; and second [y, bb], at "Hence justice concerns etc.," in regard to justice which belongs to a husband in relation to a wife. On the prior point he does three things. First [aa, a'] he proposes what he intends, saying that the justice of a master, i.e., of a lord over a slave, and paternal justice, i.e., of a father over a son, are not the same as political justice but have some likeness to it according as it has a relation to another in a way.

1013. Second [aa, b'], at **"Toward one's own things,"** he explains what was pointed out regarding this that the justice of a master or of a father is not justice without qualification. It is evident that injustice cannot exist in an unqualified way for a man in regard to the things belonging to him, and neither can justice, because both have a relation to another. But the slave belongs to the master as a chattel, and a son is—so to speak—a part of the father until he is a certain age or mature and separated from the father by emancipation. That there is no injustice toward oneself is clear from the fact that no one chooses to injure himself. Hence it is obvious that absolutely speaking there is no justice or injustice towards a son or a slave.

1014. Third [aa, c'], at **"Nor is political justice,"** he explains that even if the justice of a master and of a father would be justice without qualification, it would not be political justice because political justice is according to the law and in those for whom the law is designed by its nature. Such are those persons who have equality in regard to ruling and being ruled; but of these one is subject to another, e.g., a slave to a master and a son to a father. Hence political justice does not exist in these matters.

1015. Then [y, bb], at **"Hence justice concerns,"** he treats justice pertaining to a wife. He says that because a wife is less subject to a husband than a slave to a master or a son to a father, therefore the relation of a husband to a wife has more of the nature of justice than the relation of a father to his children, and of a master to his chattels or slaves. The justice that belongs to a husband in regard to a wife is domestic because the husband is the head of the home, as the prince of the state. However, domestic justice is different from political, as the home is different from the state.

LECTURE XII

A Division of Political Justice

ANALYTICAL OUTLINE OF ST. THOMAS	TEXT OF ARISTOTLE (*B.1134 b 18*) Chapter 7

b. He makes a division of it.
  i. He divides political justice into species.
    X. HE PROPOSES THE DIVISION.

One kind of political justice is natural and the other is legal.　**1016-1017**

    Y. HE EXPLAINS IT.
      aa. First he explains natural justice.

Natural justice is that which *20* has the same force everywhere and is not affected by what men may or may not think.　**1018-1019**

      bb. He explains legal justice.

That is called legal justice which in the beginning is indifferent about a thing being done this way or that. But when something just is decreed a difference arises, for example, a mina for redeeming a captive, a goat but not two sheep for sacrifice; also when things are mentioned individually in the law, for instance, sacrifice to Brasidas; and again when sentences are passed by judges.　**1020-1024**

    Z. HE REJECTS AN ERROR OPPOSED TO THE DIVISION.
      aa. He proposes the error.

Some people were of the opinion that all justice is of this kind because what is by nature is unchangeable and has the same force everywhere (fire, for instance, burns both here and in Persia). But just things are looked upon as variable.　**1025**

      bb. He refutes it.

However, that opinion is not true universally but in some respect, although there may be no change at all among the gods. But with us there is something natural and this is changeable because everything in us is *30* changeable. Moreover, there is in us something natural and something not natural.　**1026**

cc. He asks a question occasioned by the refutation.
*d'. First he asks the ques-
tion.*

Among the things subject to change,
what kind is just by nature and what
kind is just not by nature but by law
and agreement, if both kinds are
changeable in a similar way?   1027

b'. Then he answers it.
   a. THINGS JUST BY NA-
      TURE ARE CHANGE-
      ABLE.

Obviously, the same determination
applies to other natural things. Now
by nature the right hand is stronger,
although some people are ambidex-
trous.   1028-1029

   b. THINGS JUST BY LAW
      ARE CHANGEABLE.

Those things that are just according
to agreement and utility are *B.1135*
similar to the measures of commodities.
But the measures of wine and grain
are not equal everywhere, for where
these articles are bought (wholesale)
the measures are greater, where sold
(retail), smaller. Likewise, things just
not by nature but by agreement among
men are not the same everywhere, as
neither is the form of government. But
one form only is best everywhere by
nature.   1030

*ii. The division of this justice into
individual parts.*

Particular just and legal things hold
the place of universals in regard to
singulars, for there are many actions
performed but each of the just things
is one and a universal.   1031

B'. What just action and unjust action are.

1. WHAT UNJUST ACTION IS.

There is a difference between an unjust action and an unjust thing, between a just action and a just thing.
The unjust thing is something un-   *10*
just by nature or ordinance of man,
but when it is performed it becomes
an unjust action. Before a thing has
been done it is not an unjust action but
something unjust.   1032

2. WHAT JUST ACTION IS.

It is the same with just action. In
general it is more often called the
doing of a just thing (*diceopragma*)
but it means the correction of unjust

action. In regard to each of these we must see afterwards of what nature they are, what are their species and how many they are.   **1033-1034**

COMMENTARY OF ST. THOMAS

1016. After the Philosopher has shown the nature of political justice, i.e., unqualified justice, now [b] he makes a division of it. First [i] he divides political justice into species. Then [ii], at "Particular just and legal things etc.," he touches upon the division of this justice into individual parts. He discusses the first point from three aspects. First [x] he proposes the division. Next [y], at "Natural justice etc.," he explains it. Last [z], at "Some people were etc.," he rejects an error opposed to the division. He says first that there is a twofold division of political justice: natural justice, and legal justice. This is the same as the division that the jurists make, namely, that one kind of right is natural and the other positive. They call right the very thing that Aristotle calls the just object. Isadore too says in *Libri Etymologiarum* (Bk. V, Ch. III) that right is as it were what is just. But there seems to be inconsistency in that political is the same as civil. In this way what the Philosopher considers the whole division seems to be considered by the jurists as a part of the division, for they make civil law a part of positive law.

1017. But we must take into account that political or civil is taken here in one way by the Philosopher and in another way by the jurists. The Philosopher here calls justice political or civil from the usage the citizens are accustomed to, but the jurists call right political or civil from the cause, viz.,

that some city has decreed for itself. For this reason the Philosopher appropriately designates legal or posited by law that which they call positive. Political justice then is properly divided by means of these two, for the citizens use justice to the extent that it is imparted to the human mind by nature and to the extent that it is posited by law.

1018. Then [y], at "**Natural justice,**" he indicates the parts of the preceding division. First [y, aa] he explains natural justice in two ways: in one way according to its effect or power, saying that that justice is natural which everywhere has the same force and power to induce to good and prevent evil. This happens because nature, the cause of this justice, is the same everywhere among all men. But justice by the decree of a state or prince has force only among those who are subject to the jurisdiction of that state or prince. In the other way he explains this justice according to its cause, when he says that natural justice does not consist in what seems or does not seem to be, i.e., it does not arise from human conjecture but from nature. In speculative matters there are some things naturally known, like indemonstrable principles, and truths closely connected with them; there are other things discovered by human ingenuity, and conclusions flowing from these. Likewise in practical matters there are some principles naturally known as it were, indemonstrable principles and truths related to them, as evil must be avoided, no one is to be unjustly injured, theft must not be committed and so on; others are devised by human diligence which are here called just legal enactments.

1019. We must consider that that justice is natural to which nature inclines men. But a twofold nature is observed in man. One, is that which is common to him and other animals. The other nature belongs to man properly inasmuch as he is man, as he distinguishes the disgraceful from the honorable by reason. However, jurists call only that right natural which follows the inclination of nature common to man and other animals, as the union of male and female, the education of offspring, and so forth. But the right which follows the inclination proper to the nature of man, i.e., precisely as he is a rational animal, the jurists call the right of the peoples (*jus gentium*) because all people are accustomed to follow it, for example, that agreements are to be kept, legates are safe among enemies, and so on. Both of these, though, are included under natural justice as it is here taken by the Philosopher.

1020. Next [y, bb], at **"That is called legal justice,"** he explains legal justice and seems to give three differences in justice of this kind. The first is this: when something is universally or commonly imposed by law it becomes legal. Regarding this he says that that justice is called legal which in the beginning, i.e., before it becomes law, is indifferent whether something is done in this way or that, but when it is laid down, i.e., enacted into law, then a difference arises because observing it is just, disregarding it is unjust. Thus in some state it has been decreed that a prisoner may be redeemed at a fixed price and that a goat should be offered in sacrifice but that two sheep are not to be sacrificed.

1021. The second difference in legal justice is that something is stated by law in a particular case, for instance, when a state or a prince grants some privilege—called a private law—to an individual person. Touching this point he says there are also legal enactments, not those that are decreed in a general way but whatever are prescribed by legislators as law in individual cases. It was enacted, for example, in a particular state that sacrifice should be offered to a woman[1] named Brasidas who rendered great service to the state.

1022. The third difference in legal justice is that sentences passed by judges are called a kind of legal justice. In regard to this he adds that the decrees of judges are also legal enactments.

1023. But here we must take into consideration that legal or positive justice always has its origin in natural justice, as Cicero says in his *Rhetoric*.[2] Origin from natural right can occur in two ways: in one way as a conclusion from a principle, and in such a manner positive or legal right cannot originate from natural right. The reason is that once the premises are stated the conclusion necessarily follows. But since natural justice exists always and everywhere, as has been pointed out (1018), this is not applicable to legal or positive justice. On this account it is necessary that whatever follows from natural justice as a conclusion will be natural justice. Thus, from the fact that no one should be unjustly injured it follows that theft must not be committed—this belongs to natural justice. In the other way something can originate from natural justice after the manner of a determination, and thus all positive or legal justice arises from natural justice. For example, that a

---

[1] Correction: "man." Brasidas was worshipped as a hero by the citizens of Amphipolis (in Sparta) in whose defense he fell, 424 B.C.

[2] *Rhetorica, De Inventione*, Lib. II, Cap. LIII.

thief be punished is natural justice but that he be punished by such and such a penalty is legal justice.

1024. Also we must consider here that legal justice has its origin in two ways from natural justice in the preceding manner. In one way it exists with an admixture of some human error, and in the other without such error. Aristotle explains this by examples. It is natural justice that a citizen who is oppressed without any fault on his part should be aided, and consequently that a prisoner should be ransomed, but the fixing of the price pertains to legal justice which proceeds from natural justice without error. Likewise it is natural justice that honor be bestowed on a benefactor but that divine honor be given him—that he be offered sacrifice—arises from human error. But the just decrees of judges are applications of legal justice to particular cases.

1025. At **"Some people were of the opinion"** [z] he rejects an error opposed to this division. On this point he does three things. First [z, aa] he proposes the error together with the reason for it. Second [z, bb], at "However, that opinion etc.," he refutes it. Last [z, cc], at "Among the things etc.," he asks a question occasioned by the refutation. He says first that some were of the opinion that all justice is that which is established by law and there is then no natural justice. This was the opinion of the followers of the Socratic philosopher Aristippus. They were influenced by this reason: that which is according to nature is invariable, and wherever it is it has the same force, as is obvious fire burns in Greece as well as in Persia. Apparently this is not true of justice because all just things seem to be changed at times. Nothing seems to be more just than that a deposit should be returned to the owner. Nevertheless the return must not be made to a madman demanding his sword or to a traitor

to his country demanding money for arms. So then it seems that there is nothing just by nature.

1026. Then [z, bb], at **"However, that opinion,"** he provides a refutation, saying that the statement that natural things are unchangeable is not so universally but is true in some respect. The reason is that the nature of divine things never changes, for example, the nature of separated substances and of the heavenly bodies, which the ancients called gods. But with us humans, who are counted among perishable things, there is something according to nature and yet whatever is in us is changeable either intrinsically or extrinsically. Moreover, there is in us something natural like having two feet, and something not natural like having a coat. Undoubtedly all the things that are just among us are variable, although some of them are naturally just.

1027. Next [z, cc], at **"Among the things,"** he raises a doubt occasioned by the preceding refutation. He handles the first point in a twofold manner. First [cc, a'] he asks the question. Then [cc, b'], at "Obviously, the same," he answers it. First he proposes this question. If all just human things are changeable the question remains: of the things that change, what kind is just by nature and what kind is just not by nature but by the decision of the law and agreement among men, if both are changeable in a similar way?

1028. At **"Obviously, the same"** [cc, b'] he answers the question just asked. He considers this point in a twofold manner. First [b', a] he shows how things just by nature are changeable. Then [b', b], at "Those things that are," he shows how things just by law are changeable. He says it is obvious that the arrangement found in other natural things, likewise applies to things just by nature. Those things that are natural with us occur in the same way in the greater number of cases but fail in a few. Thus it is natural that the right hand is stronger than the left, and this is so in the greater number of instances, although it happens occasionally that some men are ambidexterous since their left hand is as strong as their right. So also the things that are just by nature, for example, that a deposit ought to be returned must be observed in the majority of cases but is changed in the minority.

1029. However, we must keep in mind that the essences of changeable things are immutable; hence whatever is natural to us, so that it belongs to the very nature of man, is not changeable in any way, for instance that man is an animal. But things that follow a nature, like dispositions, actions, and movement, are variable in the fewer instances. Likewise those actions belonging to the very nature of justice cannot be changed in any way, for example, theft must not be committed because it is an injustice. But those actions that follow (from the nature of justice) are changeable in a few cases.

1030. Then [b′, b], at **"Those things that are,"** he shows how the legally just are changeable without exception. He says that regulations that are just according to arrangement and advantage, i.e., by what is agreed among men for some utility, are similar to measures of salable commodities, wine and wheat. These are greater where products are bought wholesale but smaller where products are sold retail. So also things that are not naturally just but fixed by men are not the same everywhere, thus the same punishment is not inflicted everywhere for theft. The reason is that civil life and the administration of the state are not the same everywhere. All laws are framed as they are needed for the end of the state, although only one form of government is everywhere best according to nature.

1031. Next [ii], at **"Particular just and legal things,"** he treats the division of justice in regard to the individual parts. He says that each particular just and legal thing is related to human affairs as a universal to singulars. The reason is that actions which are done according to justice are many but each just thing is one, as it were a kind of universal. Thus, that a deposit must be returned is one which has a reference to many cases.

1032. At **"There is a difference"** [B′] he shows what just action and unjust action are. First [1], what unjust action is. Then [2], at "It is the same etc.," what just action is. He says first that unjust action and unjust thing differ, for an unjust thing is something that is contrary to justice either by nature or by human decree, as theft. But the doing of an action by someone, for instance, stealing is called unjust action, the execution of injustice so to speak. However, before this is done by anyone it is not called an unjust action but an unjust thing.

1033. Then [2], at **"It is the same,"** he shows what just action is. He says that in a similar way just action is present when a person does a thing which is just by nature or by regulation of law. But with the Greeks the doing of a just thing in general is rather called *dicaeopragma* or doing of what is just, but every doing of a just thing does not seem to be called justifying action but only when a person is corrected in the justifying action, i.e., by restoring what is unjust to justice.

1034. Finally, he says that we must discuss later, in the *Politics* (Bk. I, Ch. 6, 1255 a 3-1255 b 15; St. Th. Lect. IV, 75-88), the nature, the number, and the species of each type of justice, viz., natural and legal.

LECTURE XIII

Actions Which Make a Man Just or Unjust

ANALYTICAL OUTLINE   TEXT OF ARISTOTLE
OF ST. THOMAS   (*B.1135 a 15*)
                            Chapter 8

C. By what just or unjust actions may a man become just or unjust?

A'. He explains his plan.

> I. WHEN A JUST OR UNJUST THING MAY EXIST WITHOUT A JUST OR UNJUST ACTION.

a. He explains his intention.

Since just and unjust acts are such as have been described, a man acts unjustly or justly when he acts voluntarily. But when he acts involuntarily he works neither injustice nor justice except incidentally, for it is incidental that the actions are just or unjust. An act of justice and a just action 20 are indicated by reason of a voluntary and an involuntary. When a voluntary is done and a person is blamed, then there is at the same time an unjust action. Wherefore something unjust may be present but an unjust action never exists if there is no voluntary. **1035-1036**

b. He clarifies what he said.
    i. He indicates his intention.

As has been pointed out previously,[1] I call voluntary any of the actions within a man's power, which he does knowingly and without ignorance of the what, how and why; for example, whom he struck, with what instrument, and with what intention—none of these being unintentional. Also the act must be done without violence, thus when one takes a person's hand and strikes another, that person does not act voluntarily because it was not in his power to hinder this. It can happen that the one struck is the man's father,

---

[1] Bk. III, Ch. 1, 1111 a 22 sq.

445

the striker knowing the person is a
human being or someone present *30*
but not recognizing his father. Likewise the same should be determined
in what concerns the intention and the
whole operation. Certainly the act done
without knowledge, or knowingly and
not being in our power, is like an involuntary. We knowingly do and experience many natural things none *b*
of which are either voluntary or involuntary, for example, growing old
and dying.   **1037-1038**

ii. The previous explanation is ap-
plicable to both just and unjust
acts.

The same is true even when the act
is just or unjust incidentally, because
if someone restores a deposit unwillingly and on account of fear his act
is not said to be just, nor is it an act
of justice except incidentally. In a similar way a person forced against his
will not to restore a deposit is said
to do an unjust thing or an act incidentally unjust.   **1039**

2. THERE IS JUST OR UNJUST ACTION WITHOUT THE AGENT BEING JUST OR
UNJUST.

a. First he premises a division necessary to explain the statement.

We perform some voluntary actions
by choice and others without de- *10*
liberation. When we make a choice of
anything we first deliberate, but things
we do without choice[1] are without
previous deliberation.   **1040**

b. He explains the statement.
    i. He repeats when there may be
    an unjust thing without an un-
    just action.

Injury may occur in dealings among
men in three ways. Through ignorance
sins are committed in which neither
the person against whom, nor the
what, nor the how, nor the end are
known, and they take place for an end
not considered, for example, a man
intends not to wound but to tap, not
this person or not in this way. When
therefore (1) injury is inflicted unintentionally, we have an unfortunate
accident, but when (2) the injury is
not unintentional although without

[1] The text used by St. Thomas evidently
had the word *ineligibilia* and not *intelligibilia*
as given in the Pirotta and Spiazzi editions.

ii. He restates when there is unjust action without the agent being unjust.

evil intent, we have a sin certainly since the principle of the cause is in the agent. But what happens incidentally has an external cause.   **1041-1043**

However, when (3) injury is *20* inflicted knowingly but without deliberation, we have unjust action, thus whatever is done through anger or other passions which are necessary or natural to man. Under these circumstances persons sinning and injuring others act unjustly and their actions are unjust but they are not unjust or evil on account of this, for they do not inflict injury from wickedness.   **1044**

iii. He shows when one is unjust by the injustice and wickedness of the agent.

But when injury is inflicted by choice the perpetrator is unjust and evil.   **1045**

c. He clarifies some things which have been said.

  i. He explains . . . what is done from weakness or passion (by two reasons).

    x. FIRST.

Therefore, it is in their favor that the things done out of anger are judged not to arise from premeditation,

for it is the man who gave the provocation that began it and not he who acted in sudden anger.   **1046**

    y. SECOND.

Besides, it is not a question of whether the act is done but whether it is done justly, for anger indicates some injustice which is obvious. The case is different when the fact is questioned as in transactions *30* where the alternative is necessarily evil if the action is not done through forgetfulness. But angry people, acknowledging the fact, are uncertain in what way there is injustice. However, those who act deviously are not ignorant on this point. Therefore the cunning, but not the angry, know that the *B.1136* injured party suffered unjustly.   **1047**

  ii. He explains . . . what is done by deliberate choice.

If a man inflicts injury by deliberate choice, he acts unjustly and he is now called unjust because of those unjust acts since they are contrary to the proportional or the equal. In a similar way a person is called just when he acts justly by deliberate choice, but he is said to be a doer of a just act only if he acts voluntarily.   **1048**

B'. He introduces a division to explain things mentioned previously.

Some involuntary acts deserve pardon, others do not. Whatever sins men commit not only in ignorance but also because of ignorance are excusable. However, the sins they commit not by reason of ignorance but in ignorance because of passion, which is neither natural nor human, are inexcusable.
1049

COMMENTARY OF ST. THOMAS

1035. After the Philosopher has shown what justice in itself is, and what just action and unjust action are, now [C] he answers a question that he previously asked, viz., by what just or unjust actions may a man become just or unjust? He treats this point in a twofold manner. First [A'] he explains his plan. Then [B'], at "Some involuntary acts etc.," he introduces a division to explain things mentioned previously. He discusses the initial point from two aspects. First [1] he shows when a just or unjust thing may exist without a just or unjust action. Next [2], at "We perform some voluntary etc.," he shows that there is just or unjust action without the agent being just or unjust. He discusses the first point under two headings. Initially [1, a] he explains his intention. Second [1, b], at "As has been pointed out etc.," he clarifies what he said. He affirms first that since just and unjust acts are such as have been described before (1000-1001), then a man acts unjustly or justly in this way: there is an act of injustice or a just action when he voluntarily does these very things, i.e., what is just and unjust. But when a man does them involuntarily he does not act justly or unjustly except perhaps incidentally; it happens contrary

to his intention that the acts he does are just or unjust.

1036. Those things that we intend to do are said to be done in themselves and not incidentally. However, nothing is specified by what is incidental but only by what is in itself (*per se*). Therefore the act of justice and the *dicaeopragma* or the just operation, and likewise the act of injustice are indicated by a voluntary or involuntary, in such a way that when something is voluntary a person is praised or blamed. Hence, obviously, on the part of the thing done there will be something unjust, but there will not be an unjust action as regards the species of the operation if there is not a voluntary on the part of the agent. The same holds for just action.

1037. Then [1, b], at **"As has been pointed out,"** he clarifies some things that have been said, what a voluntary and an involuntary are. He handles this point in a twofold fashion. First [1, b, i] he indicates his intention. Second [1, b, ii], at "The same is true etc.," he shows that the previous explanation is applicable to both just and unjust acts. He says first that a voluntary, as has been pointed out in the third book (382, 391, 427, 435, 436), is said to be present when a person knowingly does a thing that is in his power and is not ignorant either of what is done, or by what means, or for what end he does this. For example, he knows whom he struck, how he delivered the blow—as by an instrument—and the purpose of it; so too he knows each of these in themselves and not incidentally. In order that there be a voluntary it is necessary that the thing not happen by violence, for instance, if one takes a person's hand by force and strikes another, he whose hand it is does not do this voluntarily, because it is not in his power to avoid being forced.

1038. After this, he explains how a thing may be known incidentally. It is possible that the man struck is his father. He who delivers the blow knows that a human being or someone present was struck but not that his father was; thus he knows incidentally that this was his father inasmuch as he knows that the person to whom this happened was his father. As we have discussed the man who delivers the blow, similarly we must investigate the purpose of the whole operation, i.e., all the circumstances of the operation. From the statement of what the voluntary is we can know what the involuntary is. The reason is that if something is done through ignorance or (after ignorance has ceased) is not in the power of the agent, or still more is done through violences it will be an involuntary. On this account it was added "by violence" [1] because many things that are in us are not involuntary, for there are many natural things we knowingly do and experience, for example, growing old and dying. Nevertheless none of these is voluntary or involuntary because each one of them concerns the

things which are in us by nature. But if it happens through violence that one of them is not in us, then it is called an involuntary.

1039. Next [1, b, ii], at "**The same is true,**" he explains what was said about just and unjust acts. In regard to just acts, for example, if a man hands over a deposit to its owner not willingly but on account of fear, we do not say there is just action in this case except incidentally. Likewise if a person forced against his will abstains from restoring a deposit, we say he does an unjust thing or acts unjustly by accident.

1040. At "**We perform some voluntary actions**" [2] he shows when there is just or unjust action and yet the agent himself is not just or unjust. First [2, a] he premises a division necessary to explain the statement. Next [2, b], at "Injury may occur etc.," he explains the statement. Last [2, c], at "Therefore, it is etc.," he clarifies some things that have been said. He states first that we do some voluntary actions by deliberate choice and others without deliberate choice. Whatever we do by deliberate choice we do with preceding counsel or deliberation; but whatever is not subject to choice or is performed without choice we do without previous counsel or deliberation.

1041. Next [2, b], at "**Injury may occur,**" he explains the statement. First [2, b, i] he repeats when there may be an unjust thing without an unjust action. Then [2, b, ii], at "However, when etc.," he restates when there is unjust action without the agent being unjust. Last [2, b, iii], at "But when injury etc.," he shows when one is unjust by the injustice and wickedness of the agent. He says first, as appears from what has been stated previously (1037-1038), that injury may occur in dealings among men in three ways: in one way by ignorance and involuntarily, in another way voluntarily but without

---

[1] The text given in the Spiazzi and Pirotta editions does not have "per violentiam" or any equivalent expression. Cf. *L'Éthique à Nicomaque* by Gauthier and Jolif, Vol. 1, p. 144, line 4: " . . . ou est fait par contrainte." (Publications Universitaires, Louvain, 1958.)

choice, and in a third way voluntarily and with choice.

1042. Those sins are committed through ignorance that are done by a man who does not know what he is doing, nor against whom he acts, nor with what means, nor for what end even if he was aware of performing an act. Thus a man thought that he landed a blow not with this instrument, e.g., a piked lance but with a rounded one; or he thought that he struck not this man, viz., not his father but an enemy; or he did not think he was about to strike for this objective but an objective was achieved he did not think of, for example, when he intended to strike not to wound but to tap. The case is similar when ignorance exists in regard to the way a man landed a blow, mightily or lightly.

1043. But on this point we must consider that when injury is inflicted unintentionally, i.e., contrary to plan or intention, then an altogether unfortunate accident happens. For instance, a man means to brandish a spear and instead throws it. But when someone inflicts injury not unintentionally, that is, not without the intention of injuring but without malice in the sense that he does not mean to injure much or injure such a person, then there is some sin, although not so great a one. A man sins when the principle of an inordinate act is in his power in this that he intends to perform the act. But when the principle of operation is entirely external so that it works contrary to the intention, then an unfortunate accident occurs since fortune is an intellectual cause acting outside of reason, as is explained in the second book of the *Physics* (Ch. 5, 196 b 10-197 a 8; St. Th. Lect. VIII, 207-216).

1044. Then [2, b, ii], at "**However, when,**" he shows when there may be unjust action without wickedness or injustice of the agent. He says that when a man inflicts injury knowingly but not with previous counsel, i.e.,

without deliberation, then there is a kind of injustice, as there is in any action that a person commits through anger and other passions—provided these passions are not natural and necessary to men, like desire for food and drink in extreme necessity which excuses the taking of what belongs to another. Therefore, those who injure others because of these passions sin and do an unjust thing and their acts are unjust actions. Nevertheless by reason of this they are not unjust and evil because they do not inflict injury from wickedness but from passion. Such people are said to sin from weakness.

1045. At "**But when injury**" [2, b, iii] he shows when there may be unjust action with injustice on the part of the agent. He says that when a man by deliberate choice causes injury to another, he is unjust and evil. Such a one is said to sin out of sheer wickedness.

1046. Next [2, c], at "**Therefore, it is,**" he clarifies what has been said. Because the first of the three things mentioned previously (which treats of what is done from ignorance) was commented on before (1042-1043), in the beginning [2, c, i] he explains the second, which deals with what is done from weakness or passion. Then [2, c, ii], at "If a man inflicts injury by choice etc.," he explains the third, which treats of what is done by deliberate choice. He says first that when people sin from anger they are not evil or unjust because of this. Therefore we are well able to judge from this proof of previous statements that what is done from anger is not considered to be done with premeditation. He proves this afterwards, at "for it is the man" [i, x], by two reasons. The first is this, that it is not the man himself who does something in anger that begins the process of injuring but the person who provoked him. So it does not seem that the injury arose with premeditation.

1047. Then [i, y], at **"Besides, it is not,"** he gives the second reason. He says that when a man inflicts injury in anger there is no question whether he does the act or not but whether he does it justly, for by anger some injustice is obvious, i.e., operates openly. And the angry man wishes the punishment to be obvious but it seems to him that he is justly provoked. It is not the same thing with unjust dealings, like theft and so forth in which there is doubt whether the act should have been done. One of the things must be evil, for instance, giving or not giving; for we sin sometimes by omission, other times by transgression unless we are excused by reason of forgetfulness, as when a person forgets to pay a debt to a creditor at an agreed time. But people acting in anger admit the thing, or the fact, but doubt whether what they did is unjust. This does not happen to those who act deviously by choice and are not ignorant that they act unjustly. Wherefore, the insidious person judges that the man he injured suffers unjustly; but the angry person does not think this. So it is evident that he who does an unjust thing in anger does not act with premeditation.

1048. At **"If a man inflicts injury"** [2, c, ii] he explains the third reason concerned with acts done by deliberate choice. He says that if a man inflicts injury by deliberate choice, it is obvious that absolutely speaking he acts unjustly, because he operates voluntarily. He who acts according to an injustice of this kind is called unjust since this action is contrary to the proportional, i.e., against distributive justice, or contrary to the equal, i.e., against commutative justice. In a similar way a man is called just when he acts justly by deliberate choice. However, if he should act voluntarily and not by choice he will be called the worker or doer of what is just.

1049. Then [B'], at **"Some involuntary things,"** he gives a division to explain things mentioned previously. He says that some involuntary acts are venial, i.e., deserving of pardon, and others are not. Those sins deserve pardon that men commit not only in ignorance, that is, when they have concomitant ignorance, but on account of ignorance, viz., when ignorance is the cause so to speak—this happens to those who are sorry when they become aware. But those sins do not deserve pardon that men commit not on account of causative ignorance but in ignorance because of passion, which is neither natural nor human nor according to right reason. In actions of this kind passion is the cause of ignorance and sin; these have been more fully treated in the third book (406-424).

LECTURE XIV

Suffering Injustice, an Involuntary

ANALYTICAL OUTLINE OF ST. THOMAS	TEXT OF ARISTOTLE (*B.1136 a 10*) Chapter 9

II. SOME DOUBTS ABOUT THE QUESTIONS JUST DISCUSSED.

  A. He raises the doubts and solves them.

  A'. The first part is divided into two.

    I. HE PROPOSES THE QUESTION.

a. He proposes the matter of the question.	Someone may raise a doubt whether suffering and doing injustice have been treated sufficiently. Does Euripides speak the truth when he unseemly says: "I killed my mother: briefly, willingly or unwillingly I killed her who was willing to be put to death?" [1]
	1050
b. He puts the questioning into form. *i. One question.*	Is it true or not that a person willingly suffers injustice? Or is this an involuntary, as every doing of injustice is a voluntary? **1051**
ii. Another question.	Is suffering injustice always voluntary or always involuntary, or is it sometimes voluntary and sometimes involuntary? The same question can be asked about the reception of justice.[2]
	1052

    2. HE FOLLOWS UP THE QUESTION.

a. He argues that every reception of justice is voluntary or every reception is involuntary.	Every doing of justice is a voluntary. Therefore it is reasonable that suffering injustice and the reception of justice, in a similar way, are opposed *20* according to both, viz., the voluntary and the involuntary (so that all of the one are voluntary, and all the other are involuntary). **1053**

[1] From a lost play by Euripides.
[2] *Justum* seems called for in place of *injustum*. Cf. Commentary.

b. He argues that not every suffering of injustice is voluntary.

   i. He argues for the proposition.

It seems unreasonable that every suffering of injustice is voluntary, for some people unwillingly suffer injustice. **1054**

   ii. He asks a question on this point.

Wherefore, doubt can arise whether a person who has undergone damage suffers injustice. **1055**

   iii. He answers the objection.

In regard to what is incidental the same holds for receiving as for doing, since clearly we take one for the other in matters concerning justice and injustice alike. Acting unjustly is not the same as doing something unjust, nor is suffering unjustly the same as suffering something unjust. Likewise, doing an unjust thing and suffering an unjust thing are not the same. It is impossible to suffer unjustly with- *30* out someone doing what is unjust, or receive justice without someone doing what is just. **1056**

c. He argues that not every suffering of injustice is involuntary.

   i. He argues for the proposition.
     X. HE OFFERS TWO REASONS. IN
     . . . THE FIRST HE PRESENTS
     THREE CONSIDERATIONS.
      aa. He gives a definition of doing injustice.

Doing an injustice in itself is present when a man voluntarily inflicts injury, that is, knowing who is injured, by what means, and in what manner. **1057**

      bb. He argues from the definition given.

The incontinent person who voluntarily injures himself also voluntarily suffers an injustice and does an injustice to himself. **1058**

      cc. He asks an incidental question.

But this is one of the doubtful *b* points whether it is possible for a man to do an injustice to himself. **1059**

     Y. HE GIVES THE SECOND REASON.

Moreover, it happens by reason of incontinence that a man is voluntarily injured by another acting voluntarily. Hence someone willingly suffers an injustice. **1060**

   ii. He solves the proposition.
     X. HE CORRECTS THE DEFINITION
     . . . GIVEN ABOVE.

Perhaps the definition is not correct, and we should add to the words "knowing who is injured, by what means, and in what manner" the further qualification "contrary to the will

453

Y. HE ANSWERS THE FIRST REASON.

Z. HE ANSWERS THE SECOND
REASON.

of the injured person." Anyone, then, can have an unjust thing done to him voluntarily, but no one can suffer injustice voluntarily.   **1061**

No one wants to suffer injustice—not even the incontinent person unless he acts contrary to his will. No one wishes what he does not think is good. But the incontinent person performs actions he thinks he ought not to perform.   **1062**

Anyone who gives what is his,   *10* as (according to Homer's story)[1] Glaucus gave Diomede golden armor for brass armor and a hundred oxen for nine oxen, suffers no injustice. It is in this man's power to give but not in his power to suffer injustice—there must be someone who inflicts the injustice. Therefore it is obvious that suffering injustice is not voluntary.

1063-1064

[1] *Iliad* vi. 236.

COMMENTARY OF ST. THOMAS

1050. After the Philosopher has shown by what just actions a person may be called just or unjust, now [II] he raises some doubts about the questions just discussed. He treats this point from two aspects. First [A] he raises the doubts and solves them. Then [Lect. XV, B], at "Men are of the opinion etc." (B.1137 a 5), he refutes the errors of some philosophers about these subjects. The first part [A'] is divided into two according to the two questions he answers. The second part begins at [Lect. XV, B'] "There are still etc." (B.1136 b 15). He handles the initial part under two headings. First [1] he proposes the question. Then [2], at "Every doing of justice," he follows up the question. He discusses the first point in a two-

fold manner. First [1, a] he proposes the matter of the question. Next [1, b], at "Is it true or not etc.," he puts the questioning into form. In the first place the matter of the question is taken from material that was settled earlier (1035-1049). Hence he says that someone can raise a doubt whether the suffering and doing of injustice have been sufficiently discussed by reason of what has been said already. It was stated (1035) that doing justice is voluntary. So it can be questioned whether this must be referred to suffering injustice. In the second place the matter of the doubt is taken from the words of the poet Euripides who somewhat unbecomingly introduced a character saying: "I killed my mother—to make the story short, either I voluntarily

454

killed her who wished to be put to death or else I killed her involuntarily."[1] In either case we understand that the mother had expressed a wish to be killed.

1051. Then [1, b], at **"Is it true or not,"** he puts the questioning into form. He considers this in two ways. First [1, b, i] he proposes one question, viz., whether it is really proper to say that a man voluntarily suffers injustice or whether this is untrue, but that every suffering of injustice is involuntary, as every doing of injustice is voluntary.

1052. Second [1, b, ii], at **"Is suffering injustice,"** he proposes another question. The question is whether every suffering of injustice is constituted in this way or in such a way that every suffering of injustice is either voluntary or involuntary. As this question can be asked about doing injustice—whether every such action is voluntary or whether some are voluntary and others involuntary—so in a similar way the same question can be asked about the reception of justice.[2]

1053. Next [2], at **"Every doing of justice,"** he follows up the question previously asked. He develops this in a threefold fashion. First [2, a] he argues that every reception of justice is voluntary or every reception is involuntary. Then [2, b], at "It seems unreasonable," he argues that not every suffering of injustice is voluntary. Last [2, c], at "Doing an injustice," he argues that not every suffering of injustice is involuntary. He argues in this way for the first point. Every doing of justice is voluntary, as is clear from what has been pointed out (1035). But doing justice is the opposite of receiving justice. Therefore it seems reason-

able that receiving justice or injustice should be opposed similarly according to both, i.e., voluntary and involuntary, so that all of the one is voluntary and all of the other involuntary.

1054. At **"It seems unreasonable"** [2, b] he argues that not every suffering of injustice is voluntary. He treats this point from three aspects. First [2, b, i] he argues for the proposition, saying it seems unreasonable to hold that every suffering of injustice is voluntary. Obviously some people unwillingly suffer injustice, like those who are flogged or whose possessions are taken by others.

1055. Second [2, b, ii], at **"Wherefore, doubt can arise,"** he asks a question on this point: whether everyone who suffers injustice materially and incidentally can be said to suffer injustice formally and in itself. Thus someone may readily object that the man who unwillingly suffers robberies or blows, suffers injustice incidentally, nevertheless he is not, so to speak, simply a victim of injustice.

1056. Last [2, b, iii], at **"In regard to what is incidental,"** he answers the objection. He says that the same holds for doing as for receiving. The reason is that in both cases it is possible to take one for the other: to understand what is incidental about justice in a similar way to what is incidental about injustice. He gives this explanation, that performing acts incidentally unjust is not the same as doing an act unjust in itself. It was pointed out (1035-1036) that sometimes a person in ignorance does by chance what is unjust, nevertheless, absolutely speaking, he does not act unjustly. Similarly, undergoing things that are incidentally unjust is not the same as undergoing what is simply unjust. Likewise it is impossible that these things are the same in the doing of justice and in receiving justice; and that the same reason holds for the doing and receiving both in regard to just

---

[1] Thought to be from Euripides' lost play called *Alcmaeon*.

[2] *Injustum* should be *justum*, it seems. Cf. *L'Éthique à Nicomaque*, Vol. I, p. 148, line 7: Gauthier and Jolif.

things and unjust things. He explains this afterwards by the fact that it is not possible to suffer something just or unjust simply speaking because passion is an effect of action. If then a man does what is unjust incidentally and does not become unjust simply, it follows that neither does he suffer injustice simply who suffers an unjust thing. The same argument holds for justice.

1057. Then [2, c], at **"Doing an injustice,"** he argues against the idea that suffering injustice is involuntary. First [c, i], he argues for the proposition. Second [c, ii], at "Perhaps the definition etc.," he solves the proposition. Concerning the initial point he offers two reasons. In regard to the first [i, x] of these he presents three considerations. First [x, aa] he gives a definition of doing injustice, which was defined previously (1035, 1045): doing injustice simply and in itself is simply the voluntary inflicting of injury. By voluntary is meant that one knows who is injured, what inflicts the injury, and how, i.e., in what manner together with other circumstances of this kind.

1058. Second [x, bb], at **"The incontinent person,"** he argues from the definition given. It is obvious that the incontinent person voluntarily injures himself, inasmuch as he does voluntarily what he knows is harmful to him. If then suffering injustice resembles doing injustice, it follows that the person acting voluntarily himself may suffer injustice from himself, so it is possible for someone to do injustice to himself. Thus it follows that not every suffering of injustice is involuntary.

1059. Third [x, cc], **"But this is one,"** he asks an incidental question: whether in fact someone can do an injustice to himself. But he takes up this question later (1091-1108).

1060. At **"Moreover, it happens"** [i, y] he gives the second reason. If it

happens that anyone by reason of incontinence is knowingly and willingly injured by another (for example, a man ensnared by love of a prostitute allows himself to be robbed) then it is possible that a person may willingly suffer injustice. So, not every suffering of injustice is involuntary.

1061. Then [c, ii], at **"Perhaps the definition,"** he gives the solution. He discusses this point from three aspects. First [ii, x] he corrects the definition of doing injustice given above (1057), and from it he infers the truth of the question. He says that the definition of doing injustice, stated without qualification, is not correct. But the statement should be added that doing injustice is present when someone with a knowledge of the circumstances inflicts injury on another against his will. From this it follows that although a person voluntarily may be injured and suffer incidentally what is unjust; nevertheless, no one voluntarily suffers injustice, absolutely speaking, because in itself doing injustice is to inflict harm on another against his will.

1062. Next [ii, y], at **"No one wants,"** he answers the first reason. No one wishes with a complete will to suffer injustice, not even the incontinent person, although he does things harmful to himself against his will. Essentially he wills good, but by concupiscence he is drawn to evil. Aristotle proves this statement from the fact that, since the will desires what appears good, no one wills what he does not think is good. But the incontinent person in a passionless moment does not think what he does is good and therefore he does not will it absolutely; nevertheless he does what he thinks he ought not to do, on account of concupiscence which is in the sensitive appetite, the will being in the reason.

1063. Last [ii, z], at **"Anyone who gives,"** he answers the second reason concerning the person who is willingly injured by another. He says that a man does not suffer injustice absolutely speaking who voluntarily gives what is his own, as Homer narrates [1] about an individual named Glaucus that he gave Diomede golden armor for brass armor and a hundred oxen for nine oxen. Therefore this type does not suffer injustice because it is in the man's power to give what belongs to him. However, suffering injustice is not in the power of him who suffers

[1] *Iliad* vi. 236.

injustice, but there must be someone who does the injustice. Consequently suffering injustice is involuntary, and doing injustice is voluntary because the principle of action is in the agent— this belongs to the nature of a voluntary. However, the source of suffering is not in the patient but in another —and this belongs to the nature of an involuntary.

1064. He concludes by way of summary that suffering injustice obviously is involuntary.

LECTURE XV

Who Does Injustice in Distributions?

ANALYTICAL OUTLINE OF ST. THOMAS	TEXT OF ARISTOTLE (B.1136 b 15) Chapter 9

B'. He comes to another (doubt).

    1. HE PROPOSES IT.

        There are still two questions we wish to discuss. Who does an injustice, he who distributes more than one's share or he who receives it? And does a person do injustice to himself? **1065**

    2. HE FOLLOWS IT UP.

a. First he objects to the false part.

        If the first proposal is true, viz., he who distributes but not he who receives commits injustice; then when a person knowingly and willingly *20* gives more to another than to himself, he does injustice to himself, as moderate men seem to do, for the person who keeps within measure takes what is of less value for himself. **1066**

b. Next . . . he solves it:
    i. By two reasons. The first.

        But it does not seem entirely true, for in this case he abounds in another good, namely, glory or moral good. **1067**

    ii. The second reason.

        Again we can answer in accord with the definition of doing injustice, for the distributor suffers nothing contrary to his will. Therefore he does not suffer injustice by reason of this but only damage. **1068**

c. Last he determines the truth.
    i. The man who distributes more than one's share does an injustice.

        However, it is obvious that he who distributes too much, but not always he who receives it, does an injustice. **1069**

*ii. He proves the proposition by
three reasons.*

x. FIRST.

Not the man in whom the unjust
thing exists does injustice but the man
who wills to do it. He is the one who
is the principle of action. This is in
the distributor, not in the recipient.
1070

Y. SECOND.

Action is said to occur in vari- *30*
ous ways: in one way as inanimate
things or the hand or servant of the
owner are said to take life. These do
not act unjustly but do unjust things.
1071

z. THIRD.

Moreover, he who has formed a
judgment through ignorance of what
is legally just does not do an injustice nor is his judgment unjust
but it resembles injustice, for legal
justice differs from primary *B.1137*
justice. But if a person knowingly
forms an unjust judgment, he acts
covetously to obtain favor or avoid
punishment. Hence—just as if he
shares in the injustice—the man, who
judges unjustly for that purpose, has
more than his due; for in such cases
the man who awards a field does not
receive a field but silver.   **1072-1073**

B. He refutes some errors.

I. HE REFUTES SOME FALSE OPINIONS CONCERNED WITH ONE DOING JUSTICE OR
INJUSTICE.

a. The first.

Men are of the opinion that they
are unjust when they do what is unjust, and for this reason they think it
easy to become unjust. But this is not
true. It is easy and within their power
to have carnal intercourse with a
neighbor's wife, to strike another, and
to hand over silver, but doing these
things as a habit is not (immediately)
in their power.   **1074**

b. Second he refutes a false opinion
about the knowledge of just and
unjust things.

Similarly, some people think *10*
that no wisdom is needed to know
what things are just and unjust because it is not difficult to understand
what the law says. However, these
things are only incidentally just but
become truly just when done and dis-

tributed in a particular way. Now to know this way is a more difficult task than to know the things that are healthful because there it is easy to know the virtue of honey, wine, and hellebore, to know the effect of cautery and surgery, but how they ought to be prescribed for health, for what patient, and when is as great an accomplishment as that of being a doctor.   **1075**

c. Third . . . concerning the facility in doing justice and unjust things.

For this very reason it is thought also that the just man is not less able to do injustice but rather can do *20* any unjust thing: for example, he can have carnal intercourse, strike a blow, and a brave man can throw away his shield, can turn and run away. However, perpetration of a cowardly action or of something unjust is doing these things only incidentally, but the doing is absolute for one having the permanent facility, just as healing and restoring to health do not consist in cutting or not cutting, in giving medicine or not giving it, but in prescribing these things as they should be. **1076**

2. HE SHOWS IN WHOM JUST AND UNJUST ACTS EXIST.

Just acts are found among people who participate in things good in themselves but have both defect and excess of them. For some persons there is no excess in regard to such goods (possibly so with the gods). For others, the hopelessly evil, no particle of these goods is useful but every one of them is harmful. In still others the goods become harmful at a deter- *30* mined point; and this is human.
1077

COMMENTARY OF ST. THOMAS

1065. After the Philosopher has solved one doubt, now [B'] he comes to another. First [1] he proposes it,

then [2], at "If the first proposal etc.," he follows it up. He says first that in the matter of justice and injustice two questions still remain which he wishes to treat in preference to others. The first of these is, which of the two persons does an injustice in regard to distribution: he who gives to someone without regard to worth or he who accepts? The second—Can a person do injustice to himself?—is a question he asked before (1059) and resolves later (1091-1108).

1066. Then [2], at "If the first proposal," he follows up the question previously asked. First [2, a] he objects to the false part. Next [2, b], at "But it does not seem," he solves it. Last [2, c], at "However it is," he determines the truth. He says first that if what was just said (1065) is true, viz., that the dishonest distributor does injustice and not he who receives too much, something inappropriate seems to follow. It can happen that a person knowingly and willingly gives more to another than to himself, and so it seems that he may do injustice to himself—a thing that is inappropriate. The reason is that moderate men apparently do this, as they retain things of less value for themselves. It is characteristic of the virtuous man that he belittles himself, i.e., accepts things of less value for himself.

1067. Next [b, i], at "But it does not seem," he solves this by two reasons. The first is that sometimes it is not entirely true that the distributor retains things of less value for himself. Although he keeps the less valuable external goods for himself, he nevertheless has an abundant share of another good, viz., glory, and of moral or honorable good.

1068. At "Again we can answer" [b, ii] he gives the second reason proceeding from the definition of doing justice given before (1061). To this an addition was made indicating that it is contrary to the will of him who suffers. But the distributor suffers nothing contrary to his will. Consequently

he does not suffer injustice but only undergoes some damage.

1069. Then [2, c], at "However it is obvious," he determines the truth. He says [c, i] that obviously the man who distributes more than one's share does an injustice, yet this is not always true of him who accepts too much but only when he works to bring about this object.

1070. Next [c, ii], at "Not the man in whom," he proves the proposition by three reasons. The first [ii, x] is that the man in whom the unjust thing exists is not said to do injustice, because in this way the one who is injured would do injustice; but he does injustice who wills to do it—he is the principle of action. This is the case of the person who distributes but not so with the recipient. Therefore the distributor does injustice and not the receiver.

1071. Aristotle gives the second reason at "Action is said" [ii, y], affirming that a man is said to act in various ways. In one way he acts as a principal agent, and in another, as instruments act. In the latter way it can be said that inanimate things, like stones, swords, or arrows cause death, and that the hand or the servant of the one who commands brings about death. None of these, absolutely speaking, does injustice although they are the means by which unjust actions are done. The reason is that doing injustice, since it is voluntary, is attributable to the agent in whom the principle of action lies, as has been pointed out (1063). But it is clear that in distribution the distributor holds the place of the principal agent while the recipient holds the place of an instrument after the manner of one obeying. Hence it remains that the distributor does the injustice.

1072. At "Moreover, he has formed" [ii, z] he gives the third reason. He says that if a person by reason of ignorance of legal justice wrongly judges, he does not do injustice, absolutely speaking, nor is the judgment by which his action is done unjust in itself; but it is unjust in a way because the thing judged is unjust. Therefore we spoke of legal justice because one kind of justice is legal which can be unknown, another is natural which cannot be unknown because it is impressed by nature on the human mind. But if someone knowing legal justice judges unjustly, then he acts greedily, that is, unjustly either for the sake of acquiring the favor of another or to avoid a penalty.

1073. If a man wishes to share injustice in unfair portions, he who judges unjustly to curry someone's favor has more good than belongs to him. So he acts greedily, although he may not have more of that good in which he injured another. The reason is that in such affairs a man who unjustly awarded a field to someone obviously for profit, did not get the field but money. And so a distributor is situated in distribution as a judge in exchanges. Therefore as a judge wrongly judging with full knowledge does an injustice, so too does he who distributes unjustly.

1074. Then [B], at **"Men are of the opinion,"** he refutes some errors. Regarding this he does two things. First [B, 1] he refutes some false opinions concerned with one doing justice or injustice. Next [B, 2], at "Just acts are found," he shows in whom just and unjust acts exist. In regard to the first point he refutes three false opinions. The first of these [1, a] concerns the facility in becoming unjust. He says that many people are of the opinion that they are ready to do even injustice immediately. Hence they think that it is easy to be habitually unjust. Certainly it is easy, and immediately in a man's power, to do unjust things: to have sexual intercourse with his neighbor's wife, to strike his neighbor, to take money from the hand of another, or to hand over money to have

murder or some crime done. But that men should do actions of this kind in such a way that they act promptly and with pleasure is not easily nor immediately in a man's power, but they come to this point through persistent habit.

1075. Second [1, b], at **"Similarly, some people,"** he refutes a false opinion about the knowledge of just and unjust things. He says some people think great wisdom is not needed for a man to discern just and unjust acts because it is not difficult to understand the decrees of the law determining legally just acts. However, such people are self-deceived because these acts simply considered are just only accidentally inasmuch as it is an accident that such things are just. But they become genuinely just when in some way they are performed and distributed (i.e., attributed) in some way to affairs and persons. But proper adaptation to affairs and people is more laborious and difficult than knowing remedies in which the whole art of medicine consists. There is a greater diversity among voluntary acts about which justice is concerned than among the humors about which health is concerned. Also it is easy to know the virtue of honey, wine, and hellebore, and the effect of cautery and surgery, but to prescribe these things for the restoration of health in the right way, for the right person, and at the right time is as great an accomplishment as being a doctor, for one who has this knowledge is a doctor.

1076. Third [1, c], at **"For this very reason,"** he refutes a false opinion concerning facility in doing justice and unjust things. He affirms that, on account of what has been said, people also are of the opinion that the just man can do injustice as readily as anyone else, because from the fact that he is just he knows not less but more and can do any one of the things called unjust, like having **sexual inter-**

course with another's wife, striking another, throwing away his shield in battle; and a man can attack anyone he pleases. But they deceive themselves because the perpetration of cowardly actions and the doing of what is unjust is doing these things only incidentally inasmuch as it happens that the acts are unjust, but to do what is simply unjust is for someone to do these things in such a way that he is willing and prompt at it. So it is in medicine—healing and restoring to health do not consist in operating or not operating, in prescribing or not prescribing a drug, i.e., a laxative, but in a person prescribing them as he ought.

1077. Then [B, 2], at "**Just acts are found,**" he shows to whom they are attributable. We say that just acts are attributable to the people among whom are found things simply and in themselves desirable, like riches and so on, although these persons (as is common among men) have excess and defect in this matter. For some there is no excess in such things that are used most laudably, as becomes men perfect in virtue and perhaps the gods (according to the error of people who hold that gods use things of this nature). For others, viz., the very wicked and the incurably evil no particle of these goods is useful but everything is harmful. For still others not everything is harmful but it becomes so at a certain fixed point. Hence it is evident that justice is a human good because it regards the general condition of man.

LECTURE XVI

Equity

ANALYTICAL OUTLINE
OF ST. THOMAS

TEXT OF ARISTOTLE
(*B.1137 a 31*)
Chapter 10

I. HE INDICATES HIS INTENTION.

Next we will treat equity and the equitable thing; we will consider in what way equity is related to justice, how the equitable is related to the just thing.   **1078**

II. HE PROCEEDS WITH HIS PROPOSITION.
A. He determines the object of equity.
1. HE RAISES A DOUBT.

When we stop to think of it, they are not absolutely the same nor do they altogether differ in kind. Sometimes we praise a thing and a man as equitable, and hence transfer "equitable" as a greater good to the things *b* we praise, showing that it is better. Other times it seems unfitting, to those following reason, that the equitable—as something beyond the just—is praiseworthy. Either the just thing or the equitable (which is other than the just) is not good. Or if both are good then they are the same. The doubt generally arises because of the things said about the nature of what is equitable.   **1079-1080**

2. HE SOLVES IT.

a. He sets forth the truth.

Everything said is true in a certain way and contains no latent contradiction. The equitable is something just and is better than some other just thing, but it is not better as another genus separated from the just. Therefore the equitable is the same as the just *10* thing and when both are good the equitable is better.   **1081**

b. He assigns the reason.
   i. He assigns the reason for doubt.

ii. He indicates the reason for the truth proposed.
   X. A DEFECT IN LEGAL JUSTICE.

Y. THIS DEFECT DOES NOT DESTROY THE RECTITUDE OF LEGAL JUSTICE.

Z. THE NECESSITY FOR DIRECTION.

iii. He infers the truth intended.

What raises the doubt is that the equitable is a just thing, yet it is not something legal but is a directing of the legally just.   1082

The reason for this is that every law is proposed universally, but it is not possible to deal with some things in a universal way. Where the necessary exists we can speak universally but it is impossible to apply this rightly where the law understands the application to be valid in the majority of cases, while being clearly aware that a defect is present.   1083-1084
Nevertheless the law is good, for the defect is not in the law nor the making of it but in the nature of the thing. And clearly the matter of human actions is such that they are not always done in the same way.   1085
Therefore, when the law pro- 20 poses something universally and a particular thing happens contrary to this, then, where the legislator has left a gap and erred in speaking absolutely, it is right to correct what is deficient. The legislator would have spoken on the point in this way if he had been present, and if he had known he would have filled this gap in the law. 1086
For this reason what is equitable is just and is something more excellent than one kind of just thing, not better than that which is absolute but better than that which errs by reason of being proposed absolutely. This thing that is the equitable is the directing of the law where there is deficiency because of faulty universal application. The reason why everything cannot be judged according to the law is that it is impossible to make a law for certain cases. Hence there is need of passing judgment, for the rule of indeterminate matter is itself flexible, like the 30 leaden rule used by builders in Lesbos; just as that rule conforms to the shape of the stone, and does not remain the

same, so also the sentence is adapted to the conditions. In this way then it has been made clear what the equitable is, that it is both the just and better than the just thing.   **1087-1088**

B. (He determines) the subject of (equity).

From this it is obvious who the equitable man is. He is one who chooses and does the things spoken of; he is not a zealous enforcer of justice in the worse sense, but a mitigator although he recognizes the law as a deterrent.   **1089**

C. He determines the habit.

And this habit of equity is a species of justice and not another kind of habit.   **1090**

COMMENTARY OF ST. THOMAS

1078. After the Philosopher has finished the consideration of justice in general, he now begins to consider equity which is a general directive of justice. First [I] he indicates his intention. Then [II], at "When we stop to think etc.," he proceeds with his proposition. He says first that following what has been said, we should discuss equity that designates a certain habit and the equitable thing that is its object. In the discussion we should declare how equity is related to justice and how its object, which is called the equitable thing, is related to the just thing, the object of justice. In Greek *epiiches* is understood as what is reasonable or becoming; it is derived from *epi* meaning "above" and *ikos* meaning "obedient," because by equity a person is obedient in a higher way when he follows the intention of the legislator where the words of the law differ from it.

1079. Then [II], at **"When we stop to think,"** he proceeds with his proposition. He discusses it under three headings. First [II, A] he determines the object of equity. Second [II, B], at "From this it is obvious etc.," the subject of it. Last [II, C], at "And this habit etc.," he determines the habit. He considers the initial point in a twofold manner. First [A, 1] he raises a doubt; then [A, 2], at "Everything said is true," he solves it. He says first that if we look closely, it does not seem that the equitable thing is absolutely the same as the just, because the equitable sometimes departs from what is legally just; nor does it seem to be altogether different in species from what is just. He assigns a reason for these things: sometimes we praise what is equitable and declare that it is well done. Likewise we praise the kind of man who does it—we even call him a manly and perfect individual. So it is evident that, when we transfer praise to what is equitable, or to a person, as if to a greater good, we show what is equitable as something better than what is just. Hence the equitable does not seem to be the same absolutely as the just thing.

1080. On the other hand (if we wish to follow reason) it seems inappropriate if what is equitable is praiseworthy and something over and above the just. It seems necessary that either the just thing is not desirable, i.e., good, or that if what is equitable is different from the just, it is not good because good (in the law) is achieved in one way, as was pointed out in the second book (319-321); or it is necessary that if both are good, they are identical. So he infers that a doubt arises about what is equitable on account of the things just stated. On the one hand it seems that it is not the same inasmuch as it is praised as better than the just thing, on the other it seems that it is the same as the just thing, for what is beyond the just apparently is not good and praiseworthy.

1081. Next [A, 2], at "Everything said is true," he solves the question raised. He handles this point in two ways. First [2, a] he sets forth the truth. Then [2, b], at "What raises the doubt etc.," he assigns the reason. He says first that everything that has been said for either side of the doubt is in some way right, and if correctly understood no opposition lies hidden there. It is true that what is equitable is one kind of just thing and is better than another just thing because, as was noted before (1016-1017), justice which citizens practice is divided into natural and legal. But what is equitable is better than what is legally just but is contained under the naturally just. Consequently it is not said to be better than the just thing as if it were some other kind of norm distinct from the genus of just things. Although both, viz., the legally just thing and

the equitable, are good, the equitable is better.

1082. At "What raises the doubt" [2, b] he assigns the reason, treating it in a threefold manner. First [b, i] he assigns the reason for doubt. Second [b, ii], at "The reason for this etc.," he indicates the reason for the truth proposed. Third [b, iii], at "For this reason what is equitable etc.," he infers the truth intended. He says first that this is what raised the doubt: that the equitable is a just thing, yet it is not something legal. But it is a certain directing of legal justice, for we said (1023) that it was contained under natural justice from which legal justice has its origin.

1083. Then [b, ii], at "The reason for this," he assigns the reason for the truth proposed, i.e., why legal justice has need of direction. He discusses this point from three aspects. First [ii, x] he points out a defect in legal justice. Next [ii, y], at "Nevertheless the law," he shows that this defect does not destroy the rectitude of legal justice. Last [ii, z], at "Therefore, when," he infers the necessity for direction. He says first that the reason why legal justice has need of direction is that every law is proposed universally. Since particulars are infinite, our mind cannot embrace them to make a law that applies to every individual case. Therefore a law must be framed in a universal way, for example, whoever commits murder will be put to death.

1084. It is evident that our intellect can predicate something universally true about some things, in the case of what is necessary where no defect can occur. But about other things it is not possible that something true be predicated universally, in the case of what is contingent. Here even though something is true in most instances, nevertheless it errs as we know in a few instances. And of such a nature are human acts about which laws are framed. In these things the legislator necessarily speaks in a universal way on account of the impossibility of comprehending particulars; however, he cannot be correct in all the situations for which he legislates since error arises in some few cases. For this reason the legislator accepts what happens in most cases, and nevertheless he is not ignorant that defect is possible in some cases. Thus the anatomist says that man has five fingers, although he knows that by a mistake of nature it happens that man has more or less in rarer cases.

1085. Next [ii, y], at "**Nevertheless the law,**" he shows that the previously mentioned defect does not destroy the rectitude of law or of legal justice. He says that, although a fault may be committed in some cases by the observance of the law, nevertheless the law is good because that fault is not on the part of the law (since it was made according to reason) nor on the part of the legislator (who legislated according to the condition of the material), but the fault arises from the nature of the thing. Such is the nature of human actions that they are not done always in the same way but are done otherwise in certain infrequent instances. For example, the return of a deposit is in itself just and good, as it happens in most cases, but in a particular situation it can be bad, for instance, if a sword is returned to a madman.

1086. At "**Therefore, when**" [ii, z] he infers the necessity for directing legal justice. He says that when the law proposes something in a universal way, and the observance is not beneficial in a special instance, reason rightly dictates that a person should correct what is deficient in the law. Where the legislator evidently left indeterminate a particular case (in which the law falls short) he is at fault, i.e., he proposed a defective proposition in speaking absolutely or universally. The reason is that even the legislator himself, had he been present where such a case happened, would have determined in this way and the correction would have been made. Moreover, had he foreseen this from the beginning he would have put it in the law. But he could not comprehend all particulars; in a certain city it was decreed under penalty of death that strangers were not to climb the walls of the city for fear they would usurp the civil government. But during an enemy invasion some strangers by climbing the walls defended the city from the invaders. They do not deserve to be punished by death; it would be against the natural law to reward benefactors with punishment. Therefore in this case legal justice must be directed by natural justice.

1087. Then [b, iii], at "**For this reason what is equitable,**" he infers the truth intended, affirming that by reason of what has been said it is clear what the equitable is. It is a just thing and it is better than one kind but not better than what is naturally just that is laid down absolutely, that is, universally. Hence the nature of the equitable is that it be directive of the law where the law is deficient for some particular case. Indeed the law does fail in particular cases. The reason why not everything can be determined according to the law is that the law cannot possibly be framed to meet some rare particular incidents, since all cases of this kind cannot be foreseen by man. On account of this, after the enactment of the law, a decision of the judges is required by which the universal statement of the law is applied to a particular matter. Because the material of human acts is indeterminate, it follows that their norm, which is the law, must be indeterminate in the sense that it is not absolutely rigid.

1088. He offers an example of a norm for building in Lesbos. In this island there are certain hard stones that cannot easily be dressed by chisel so they may be arranged in an entirely correct position. Therefore the builders there use a leaden rule. Just as this leaden rule conforms to the shape of the stone and does not stay in the same form, so the sentence of the judge must be adapted to things according to their suitableness. In this way then he ends by way of summary that it is clear from the premises what the equitable thing is, that it is something just which is better than one kind of just thing, viz., the legally just.

1089. Next [B], at **"From this it is obvious,"** he determines the subject of equity. He affirms that it is evident from what has been proposed (1078-1088), who the equitable man is: he who chooses and does the things which have been discussed. He lays down a certain characteristic of this kind of virtuous person. He says that such a one is not *acribodikaios,* i.e., a zealous enforcer of justice in the worse sense, for vengeance, like those who are severe in punishing, but rather like those who mitigate the penalties although they may have the law on their side in punishing. The legislator does not intend punishments in themselves but as a kind of medicine for offenses. Therefore the equitable person does not add more punishment than is sufficient to prevent violations.

1090. At **"And this habit"** [C] he determines the habit of virtue. He says that this habit, called equity, is a particular species of justice and is not a habit different from legal justice; we said the same about its object, for habits are known by reason of their objects.

LECTURE XVII

Injustice to Oneself

ANALYTICAL OUTLINE
OF ST. THOMAS

TEXT OF ARISTOTLE
(*B.1138 a 4*)
Chapter 11

I. NO ONE, PROPERLY SPEAKING, CAN DO HIMSELF AN INJUSTICE.

A. No one can do himself an injustice nor suffer an injustice from himself.

A'. A question of this kind can be settled from what has been said before.

Whether or not it is possible to do injustice to oneself is clear from what has been discussed. **1091**

B'. Certain grounds on which it seems that a person can do himself an injustice.

1. HE GIVES TWO REASONS . . . THE FIRST.

There are certain just acts arising from every virtue that are ordained by law. Hence, for example, the law never commands a man to kill himself. But what it does not command it forbids. **1092**

2. THE SECOND REASON.

Again, however, when someone inflicts damage contrary to the law (it being not against one resisting injury from another) he voluntarily does injustice. By "voluntary" is meant the agent knows both the nature of what he does and the circumstances. But *10* the man who voluntarily kills himself in anger does an act contrary to a just law by willing what the law does not permit. Therefore he does an injustice. **1093**

C'. He determines the truth.

I. FIRST HE PRESENTS AND CONFIRMS THE SOLUTION.

a. He solves the doubt raised before regarding legal justice.
  i. He proposes the solution.

But to whom? Does he not injure the state rather than himself? **1094**

  ii. He confirms the solution given.
    X. ONE DOES NOT DO HIMSELF AN INJUSTICE.

He voluntarily suffers what is unjust but no one voluntarily suffers injustice. **1095**

    Y. (HE DOES) INJUSTICE TO THE STATE.

For this reason the state imposes punishment and a certain disgrace on the person who commits suicide as on one who does an injustice to the state. **1096**

b. He solves the doubt regarding particular justice.
  i. He proposes what he intends.

Besides, inasmuch as a man is called unjust not as being entirely evil but only as performing particular injustice, he does not do injustice to himself. This is different from the other kind of injustice because a person unjust in a limited way—like the coward is evil—does not possess total perversity. Hence he does not do injustice to himself according to this injustice. **1097**

  ii. He proves the proposition by four reasons.
    W. FIRST.

Indeed something will be given to and taken from one and the same person at the same time. This is impossible, for it is necessary that justice and *20* injustice be found in different persons. **1098**

    X. SECOND.

Again, doing injustice is voluntary and with choice and happens previous to suffering injustice. A man who first suffers injustice and resists it does not seem to do an injustice. But the person receiving injustice from himself suffers and does the same injustice at the same time. **1099**

    Y. THIRD.

Moreover, he will be voluntarily suffering injustice. **1100**

    Z. FOURTH.

Besides, no one does injustice to himself in regard to particular injustice. No one, for example, commits adultery with his own wife, nor breaks into his own home, nor steals his own goods.   **1101**

2. SECOND HE GIVES THE ROOT OF THE SOLUTION.

This question of doing injustice to oneself is completely solved according to the definition that suffering injustice is contrary to the will.   **1102**

B. Whether it is worse to do an injustice or suffer an injustice.

A'. First . . . both of them are evil.

Obviously both are evil, that is, suffering injustice and doing injustice— for the former is to have less and the latter to have more than the mean, (this corresponds to what produces *30* health in medicine and good condition in physical training.)   **1103**

B'. Next . . . in itself it is worse to do injustice.

However, to do injustice is worse because it is blameworthy and wicked either completely and absolutely, or for the most part (not every voluntary injury takes place with injustice). But a man suffers injustice without being guilty of wickedness or injustice. Therefore in itself suffering injustice is a lesser evil,   **1104**

C'. By chance the contrary can be true.

although nothing hinders it from being by chance a greater evil. But *b* art does not care about what is by chance, for example, medicine considers pleurisy a worse ailment than an injured foot, even if it should happen that the latter may be worse. An example of this would be the case when the one so injured falls and so is captured and put to death by enemies.   **1105**

II. (ONE CAN DO HIMSELF AN INJUSTICE) IN A METAPHORICAL SENSE.

By metaphor and likeness, there is justice not of a man toward himself but among the parts of man toward one another. However, not every kind of justice is found here but the justice of master or administrator. According to these concepts, one part of the soul has been divided as against the irrational part (irascible and concupiscible). Looking at these, some *10* people think that injustice to oneself is present because in them it is possible to suffer something contrary to one's own desire. Here a kind of injustice is found as between master and slave. We have, then, finished the treatise on justice and the other moral virtues according to the preceding plan.

1106-1108

COMMENTARY OF ST. THOMAS

1091. After the Philosopher has finished the treatise on justice in the proper sense, he now intends to treat justice in the metaphorical sense. Because justice of this kind exists in things that relate to oneself, therefore, he first [I] shows that no one, properly speaking, can do himself an injustice. Second [II], at "By metaphor etc.," he shows how this takes place in a metaphorical sense. He develops this point in a twofold manner. First [A] he shows that no one can do himself an injustice nor suffer an injustice from himself. Then [B], at "Obviously both are evil etc.," he shows whether it is worse to do an injustice or suffer an injustice. He considers the first under three aspects. Initially [A, A'] he suggests that a question of this kind can be settled from what has been said before. Next [A, B'], at "There are certain just acts etc.," he proposes certain grounds on which it seems that a person can do himself an injustice. Last [A, C'], at "But to whom? etc.," he determines the truth. He says first

that from the premises it can be made clear whether a man may do an injustice to himself. He raised this question before (1059-1064). But here he follows it up because of the connection it has with an understanding of justice taken in a metaphorical sense.

1092. Then [A, B'], at **"There are certain just acts,"** he gives two reasons from which it seems that someone can do himself an injustice. The first is this [B', 1]. Obviously from what has been said before, the things that are just according to any virtue are ordered by law. Hence what is not ordered at all by law does not seem to be just in terms of any virtue and hence is unjust. In no case does the law command a man to take his own life. But those acts that the law does not command as just, it forbids as unjust. This is not to be understood as if no mean exists between the command and the prohibition of the law, since there are many acts that are neither commanded nor forbidden by the law but are left to man's will, for example, buying or not buying a particular thing. But this is to be understood in the sense that it is only those things which are forbidden as unjust in themselves that the law in no case commands. So it seems that to take one's own life is of itself unjust, since the law never commands it.

1093. At **"Again, however"** [B′ 2] he gives the second reason, saying that one who injures another contrary to the precept of the law (as when the law commands that an action be punished provided it is not against a person defending himself, i.e., resisting injury inflicted on oneself by another), such a one, I say, willingly does injustice. When I say "willingly," it is understood the person should know what he does, in what manner, and the other circumstances. But he who takes his own life because of anger acts contrary to a good law in willing something the law does not permit. Therefore he does injustice. Consequently it seems that a man can do himself an injustice.

1094. At **"But to whom"** [A, C′] he solves the previously mentioned doubt. First [C′, 1] he presents and confirms the solution. Second [C′, 2], at "This question," he gives the root of the solution. He treats the first point in two ways. Initially [1, a] he solves the doubt raised before, regarding legal justice. Second [1, b], at "Besides, inasmuch etc.," he solves the doubt regarding particular justice. On the initial point he does two (three) things. First [a, i] he proposes the solution saying that the man who commits suicide does some injustice. But we must consider against whom he acts unjustly. Certainly he does an injustice to the state, which he deprives of a citizen, even if he does no injustice to himself.

1095. Next [a, ii], at **"He voluntarily suffers,"** he confirms the solution given; first [a, ii, x] in regard to the fact that one does not do himself an injustice. He may willingly endure the

slaying but no one willingly suffers injustice, as was said before (1094). Therefore this person does not suffer an injustice and does not do himself an injustice.

1096. Then [a, ii, y], at **"For this reason,"** he confirms the solution in regard to the injustice to the state—this by a certain sign. We see that the state imposes what punishment is possible, dishonor or censure on the suicide; that it has his body dragged or left unburied. In this way we are given to understand that this man committed injustice against the state.

1097. At **"Besides, inasmuch"** [1, b] he shows that no one does himself an injustice according to particular justice. First [b, i] he proposes what he intends. He says that inasmuch as a person is called unjust not as being completely perverse in evil but only as doing particular injustice, according to this injustice it is not possible for a person to do injustice to himself. This particular injustice, which we discussed before (913-926), is different from legal injustice. A man may be called unjust in some measure not as being completely evil but as being partially evil, for example, someone is called cowardly according to a particular evil. Hence neither according to particular injustice can anyone do injustice to himself.

1098. Next [b, ii], at **"Indeed something,"** he proves the proposition by four reasons. The first [b, ii, w] is that one who does injustice according to particular injustice has more than is due him, and he who suffers injustice has less. If then someone could do injustice to himself, it would follow that something could be taken from him and added to him at one and the same time—things that are opposites. Therefore it is impossible for the same person to be the one doing injustice and suffering injustice from himself. But justice and injustice necessarily implies more than one person.

1099. At **"Again, doing injustice"** [b, ii, x] he gives the second reason saying that doing injustice must be voluntary and with choice, and must be previous to suffering injustice. That man, who first has suffered injustice and reacts against it according as the law allows, does not seem to do injustice, for example, if he repossesses a thing taken from him. But if a person injures himself, he suffers and inflicts the same act at the same time. Therefore he does not seem to do injustice to himself.

1100. Then [b, ii, y], at **"Moreover, he will,"** he offers the third reason. Certainly a person voluntarily does harm to himself. If then such a one suffers injustice from himself, it follows that suffering injustice is a voluntary. This we disproved before (1094-1096).

1101. Next [b, ii, z], at **"Besides, no one,"** he gives the fourth reason. If we look at particular injustice, that is, the species of particular injustice, it is apparent that no one does himself an injustice. One particular species of injustice is fornication, i.e., adultery. But no man fornicates or commits adultery with his own wife. No one is called a burglar—burglary belongs to another species of injustice—because he breaks into his own home, nor a thief if he secretly takes his own goods. Obviously then it is not possible to do oneself injustice.

1102. At **"This question"** [C', 2] he gives the principal root of the previously mentioned solution. He says that this question about doing injustice to oneself is completely solved in accord with what was determined before (1063, 1071, 1099) on the point that it is impossible to suffer any injustice voluntarily. From this it clearly follows that no one unwillingly does injustice, since doing injustice is a voluntary, as was pointed out previously (1063, 1071, 1099).

1103. Then [B], at **"Obviously both,"** he compares these two things with one another. In regard to the comparison he takes up three points. First [B, A'] he shows that both of them are evil. Next [B, B'], at "However, to do injustice etc.," he shows that in itself it is worse to do injustice. Last [B, C'], at "although nothing hinders etc.," he shows that by chance the contrary can be true. He says first that both, doing injustice and suffering injustice, are evil. He proves the statement from the fact that to suffer injustice is to have less than the mean of justice requires. But the first, to do injustice, is to have more than the measure of justice. Now the mean of justice, called the just thing, is related to exchanges and distributions as the healthful is to medicine and the well-conditioned to gymnastics. Consequently, as in medicine and gymnastics what is too much or too little is evil, so also in regard to justice.

1104. Next [B, B'], at **"However, to do injustice,"** he shows that it is worse to do injustice than to suffer injustice. This he proves from the fact that to do injustice is blameworthy and evil— a thing that is to be understood either as complete and absolute evil (for instance, when someone does injustice not only voluntarily but by choice) or as coming close to complete evil (evident in the person who acts unjustly not by choice but by anger or some other passion). It has been explained before (1041) that not every voluntary accompanies injustice, because sometimes a man does an unjust act and nevertheless is not unjust, although he is blameworthy. But a person's suffering injustice is entirely without evil and injustice, for he who suffers injustice can in no way be considered unjust or evil. But, obviously, that by which a man is called evil is worse than that by which he is not called evil, an actual whiteness by which a person is called white is whiteness in a greater degree than potential whiteness by which a person is not called white. It follows then that suffering injustice is in itself less evil than doing injustice.

1105. At **"although nothing hinders"** [B, C′], he shows that the contrary can be true by chance. He says nothing prevents suffering injustice from being more evil by chance than doing injustice, as when a man is provoked to do greater injustice by the fact that he suffers unjustly. But this is by chance, and art does not care about what is by chance but judges only according to what is essential. Thus the art of medicine calls pleurisy, a dangerous and deadly abscess under the ribs, a worse ailment than a sore foot that nevertheless can by chance be worse, for instance, when a man falls because of an injured foot and so by accident is captured and slain by an enemy.

1106. Next [II], at **"By metaphor and likeness,"** he shows of what nature metaphorical justice is. He says that by a kind of metaphor and likeness, it is possible to have, not justice or injustice of the whole man toward himself, but a certain species of justice among the parts of man. However, this is not justice in the full sense but only the justice of a master or an adminis-

trator (viz., the head of a household), because corresponding to these reasons of dominion and administration the rational part of the soul seems to be distinguished from the irrational part, which is divided into irascible and concupiscible. The reason is master of the irascible and concupiscible parts and governs them.

1107. In view of such consideration some people think that a man's justice extends to himself because, by reason of these parts, he can suffer from his own desires, for instance, when he acts against reason out of anger or concupiscence. Hence, among the parts a kind of justice and injustice is found, as between one who commands and one who obeys. However, it is not genuine justice because it is not between two, but it has a resemblance to justice inasmuch as the diversity in the soul is like the diversity between persons.

1108. Finally, as a summary, he concludes that we have finished the treatise on justice and the other moral virtues according to the preceding plan. With this the teaching of the fifth book is completed.

LIST OF WORKS CITED AND CONSULTED

List of Works Cited

ARISTOTLE: *The Works of Aristotle,* translated into English under the editorship of W. D. Ross and J. A. Smith, Oxford: 1908-1931.
Ethica Nichomachea (Vol. IX)
Metaphysica (Vol. VIII)
Rhetorica (Vol. XI)
De Anima (Vol. III)
Politica (Vol. X)
Physica (Vol. II)
De Caelo (Vol. II)
De Sensu (Vol. III)
De Memoria et Reminiscentia (Vol. III)
Categoriae (Vol. I)
Analytica Posteriora (Vol. I)
De Somno et Vigilia (Vol. III)
De Generatione Animalium (Vol. V)
De Anima, translated by Kenelm Foster and S. Humphries, New Haven: Yale University Press, 1951.
The Nicomachean Ethics, translated by R. Rackham, Cambridge, Mass.: Harvard University Press, 1956.
L'Éthique à Nicomaque (2 Vols.), Introduction, Traduction et Commentaire. Ed. Gauthier and Jolif, Louvain/Paris: Publications Universitaires, 1958-1959.
AUGUSTINE, SAINT: *The Confessions of St. Augustine,* translated by F. J. Sheed, New York: Sheed and Ward, 1942.
AVERROES: *Commentarium Magnum in Aristotelis De Anima Libros,* recensuit F. S. Crawford, Cambridge, Mass.: Mediaeval Academy of America, 1953.
CICERO: *Cicero's Tusculan Disputations,* ed. Charles Anthon, New York: Harper and Brothers, 1897.
De Oratore, Eldredge and Brothers, Philadelphia, 1879.
Cicero, Marcus Tullius, "De Inventione." With an English translation by H. M. Hubbell, Cambridge, Mass.: Harvard University Press, 1949.
EURIPIDES: *The Phoenician Maidens.* Great Books of the Western World, Vol. 5, pp. 378-393, Chicago: Encyclopaedia Britannica, Inc., 1952.
GILBY, THOMAS: *St. Thomas Philosophical Texts.* London: Oxford University Press, 1951.
HESIOD: *The Works of Hesiod, Callimachus and Theognis,* translated by Rev. J. Banks, London: Henry G. Bohn, 1856.
HOMER: *Homer's Odyssey,* translated by H. B. Cotterill, London: George H. Harrap and Company, 1911.
Iliad of Homer, translated by Richmond Lattimore, Chicago: University of Chicago Press, 1951.
ISIDORE: *Libri Etymologicarum,* J.-P. Migne, Vol. 82 (199), Parisiis: 1850.
ISOCRATES: *Isocrates* (3 Vols.), translated by George Norlin, New York: G. P. Putnam's Sons, 1928.

List of Works Cited

Johnson, Charles, and J. H. Baxter: *Medieval Latin Word List,* London: Oxford University Press, 1934.

Plato: *The Dialogues of Plato* (2 Vols.), translated by B. Jowett, New York; Random House, 1939.
Protagoras
Laws
Philebus

Shorey, Paul: *Platonism Ancient and Modern,* Berkeley, California: University of California, 1938.

Sophocles: *Philoctetes,* Great Books of the Western World, Vol. 5, pp. 182-195, Chicago: Encyclopaedia Britannica, Inc., 1952.

Theocritus: *The Idylliums of Theocritus,* translated by Francis Fawkes, London: Dryden Leach, 1767.

Thomas Aquinas, Saint: Marietti publications, Turin/Rome:
In Duodecim Libros Metaphysicorum Aristotelis Expositio, ed. Cathala-Spiazzi: 1950.
In Aristotelis Librum De Anima Commentarium, ed. Pirotta: 1948.
In Libros Politicorum Aristotelis Expositio, ed. Spiazzi: 1951.
In Octo Libros Physicorum Aristotelis Expositio, ed. Maggiola: 1954.
In Aristotelis Libros De Coelo et Mundo Expositio, ed. Spiazzi: 1952.
In Librum Beati Dionysii De Divinis Nominibus Expositio, ed. Pera: 1950.
In Aristotelis Libros De Sensu et Sensato, De Memoria et Reminiscentia Commentarium, ed. Pirotta: 1928.
In Aristotelis Libros Peri Hermeneias et Posteriorum Analyticorum Expositio, ed. Spiazzi: 1955.
Opera Omnia, ed. Fretté, Parisiis: Vivès, 1875.
Opuscula Theologica (Vol. I), ed. Raymond A. Verardo, Turin/Rome: Marietti, 1954.
Summa Theologica, translated by the Fathers of the English Dominican Province, New York: Benziger Brothers, Inc., 1947.

Vegetius, Flavius Renatus: *Epitoma rei militaris.* Recensuit Carolus Lang, ed. 2, Lipsiae: In aedibus G. B. Teubneri, 1885.

Xenophen:*The Greek Historians,* New York: Random House, 1942.

Works Consulted

Aristotelis Opera Omnia (Vol. II), ed. Mauro-Beringer, Parisiis: P. Lethielleux, 1886.

The Ethics of Aristotle, translated by J. A. K. Thomson, London: Whitefriars Press, 1953.

Commentary on the Metaphysics of Aristotle (2 Vols.), translated by John P. Rowan, Chicago: Henry Regnery Company, 1961.

Nicomachean Ethics, translated by R. W. Browne, London: George Bell and Sons, 1901.

The Nicomachean Ethics. A Commentary by H. H. Joachim. Edited by D. A. Rees, Oxford: Clarendon Press, 1951.

Love and Friendship. St. Thomas Aquinas on Aristotle's—, a translation of Books VIII-IX of the Nicomachean Ethics, by Pierre Conway, O.P., Providence, R. I.: Providence College Press, 1951.

Sancti Thomae Aquinatis Opera Omnia. Parma: Petri Fiaccadori, 1852-1869.

INDEX OF NAMES

Index of Names

(Numbers refer to sections of *Commentary*)

AESCHYLUS, 417
AGAMEMNON, 1689
AGATHON, 1138, 1159
ALCMAEON, 395
ALCMAEONA, 395
ANAXAGORAS, 1191, 1192, 2131
ANAXANDRIDES, 1464
ANACHARSIS, 2077
ANDRONICUS, 78
APOLLO, 161
ARGIVES, 581
ARISTOTLE, 7, 68, 79, 83, 157, 181, 182, 193, 196, 206, 211, 339, 347, 363, 367, 376, 387, 400, 416, 522, 523, 553, 556, 610, 671, 676, 680, 739, 745, 771, 777, 782, 824, 839, 851, 860, 876, 901, 955, 957, 995, 1016, 1024, 1062, 1071, 1300, 1329, 1343, 1388, 1415, 1422, 1423, 1430, 1472, 1491, 1502, 1504, 1536, 1549, 1619, 1634, 1635, 1670, 1809, 1811, 1829, 1875, 1876, 1937, 1973, 1974, 1979, 1980, 1981, 1984, 1994, 1997, 2064, 2084, 2098, 2099, 2107, 2126, 2128, 2135, 2143, 2171, 2179
ATHENIANS, 179, 765, 1834
BIAS, 909
BRASIDAS, 1021
CARCINUS, 1415
CELTS, 551
CICERO, 222, 337, 376, 415, 778, 1023
CIRCE, 372
CRETES, 225
CYCLOPES, 2155
CYPRIAN, 1394
CYPRUS, 1394
DELOS, 161
DIOMEDE, 563, 1063
DIONYSIUS, 320
EMPEDOCLES, 1344, 1352, 1546
EPICHARMUS, 1843
EPICUREANS, 57, 2002
EUDOXUS, 221, 1964, 1965, 1966, 1967, 1968, 1969, 1974, 1980
EURIPIDES, 395, 1050, 1204, 1546
EVENUS, 1467
GLAUCUS, 1063
GREECE, 119, 1302
GREEK, 345
GREEKS, 314, 485, 563, 581, 732, 765, 958, 1033, 1472
HECTOR, 563, 565, 1300
HELEN, 377
HERACLITUS, 278, 1337, 1546, 2058

HESPERUS, 906
HOMER, 178, 485, 563, 565, 572, 620, 765, 1063, 1300, 1394, 1682 1689
ISIDORE, 1016
JOVE, 765, 1682, 1780.
JULIUS CAESAR, 778
JUPITER, 765
LAWRENCE, SAINT, 395
LESBOS, 1088
LUCIFER, 906
MEGARIANS, 732
MELOPES, 1415
MEROPE, 418
MILO, 314
NEOPTOLEMUS, 1322, 1445
NIOBE, 1365
OLYMPIC, 152, 153
PERICLES, 1168
PERIPATETICS, 143, 196
PERSIA, 1025
PERSIANS 1683
PHALARIS, 1372, 1382
PHILOCTETES, 1322, 1415, 1445
PHILOXENUS, 615
PHOENISSAE, 1835
PINDAR, 1834
PLATO, 75, 78, 79, 81, 82, 88, 230, 268, 1501, 1971, 1972, 1973
PLATONISTS, 9, 49, 74, 75, 79, 80, 83, 84, 86, 87, 89, 1503, 1887, 1974, 1980, 1985, 1989, 1993, 1997, 2005
POLYDAMAS, 563
PRIAM, 178, 1300
PROTAGORAS, 1765
PYTHAGORAS, 88
PYTHAGOREANS, 87, 88, 319, 965
RHADAMANTUS, 967
SARDANAPALUS, 61
SATYRUS, 1365
SCYTHIANS, 464, 1416
SENECA, 337
SICYONIANS, 581
SIMONIDES, 683, 2107
SOCRATES, 78, 567, 847, 1281, 1282, 1284, 1286, 1313, 1314, 1328, 1341, 1345, 1352, 2144
SOLINUS, 314
SOLON, 179, 180, 181, 201, 2130
SOPHISTS, 1766, 2167, 2168, 2172
SOPHOCLES, 1322, 1445
SPARTA, 2155
SPARTANS, 225, 464, 765, 847, 1302, 1834

Index of Names

ALPHABETICAL INDEX OF SUBJECTS

Alphabetical Index of Subjects

(Numbers refer to sections of *Commentary*)

Accident:
offspring of substance, 80
Acribodikaios:
an enforcer of justice in the worse sense, 1089
Acrocholoi:
people excessive in anger, 809
Act:
determined by object, 322, 423
diversified by objects, 1563
Act, External:
object of—is its matter, 390
Act, Human:
principles of—, 8, 496
Act, Internal:
object of—is its end, 390
Action:
immanent and transient, 144
concerned with particulars, 390, 452
judged in its particularity, 390
from violence accompanied by sadness, 429
principle of—is in the agent, 1063
differs from making, 1150
an operation remaining in agent, 1151
sometimes its own end, 1167
good of—in the agent, 1167
has to do with singulars, 1194
and passion cannot be treated with certitude, 1779
in the thing moved, 1846
Action, Evil:
pleasurable to evil men, 156
performed out of desire for pleasure, 268
Action, Good:
harmonizes with right reason, 257
itself is the end in immanent action, 1136
Action, Immanent:
a perfection of the agent, 144, 282
Action, Moral:
contingent and changeable, 259

Action, Vicious:
dominant in unhappiness, 187
Action, Virtuous:
pleasurable in itself, 158
dominant in happiness, 187, 198
most lasting, 188, 191
Activity (*see also* Operation, Action, Function, Act):
kinds of—, 13, 98
an additional perfection, 1486, 1491
use of a natural form or habit, 1493
desirable prior to pleasure, 2038
perfection of—, 2024
most perfect—is most pleasant, 2024-2026
perfected by different pleasures, 2040
of mind and of sense, 2041
stimulated by its own pleasure, 2042, 2045
impeded by alien pleasures, 2045
more pleasant—drives out the less pleasant, 2046
affected by proper pleasure and pain, 2049
act of a perfect thing, 2052
differs according to virtue and vice, 2055
more immaterial—is purer, 2056
follows the forms of things, 2057
and agreeable amusement, 2070
more productive of happiness, 2078
and the active virtues, 2112
Activity, External:
performed by the body, 2117
and the perfection of moral virtue, 2119
Activity, Virtuous:
desirable in itself, 2070
Admiration:
concerns great things, 777
Adultery:
sexual intercourse with another's wife, 930

489

Aristocratic State:
  defined, 903, 937
  in—merit is measured according to virtue, 937
Art:
  definition of—, 8
  in the practical intellect, 8
  produces concrete and individual good, 101
  progresses with time, 133-134
  right plan of things to be made, 282, 1496
  requires only the thing made be good, 282
  as related to chance, 1105, 1159
  a habit concerned with making, 1153, 1160, 1166
  has a threefold operation, 1154
  an intellectual virtue, 1155, 1177
  distinguished from divine science and mathematics, 1156
  distinguished from natural science, 1157
  distinguished from prudence, 1158, 1172
  concerned with the thing wrought, 1167
  requires moral virtue, 1172
  deals with external goods, 1172
  differs from wisdom, 1180
  the power to bring about a process, 1496
Artist:
  strives for universal knowledge, 2162
Ascesis:
  companionship in virtue, 1899
Assassination:
  slaying by trickery, 930
Associations:
  agree in something useful, 1665, 1668
  contained under civic association, 1657, 1665, 1667, 1669, 1671
  some—directed to a particular interest, 1667
  directed by civic association, 1669
Autocastos:
  possesses the mean of veracity, 835
Autophastos:
  one who manifests himself as he is, 835

Authority:
  of husband and wife is aristocratic, 1684
  brothers'—in a household is timocratic, 1686
Average:
  (*Aequale*) a mean between the great and small, 360, 741

Bad Man:
  performs evil actions by choice, 1294
  delighted by evil things, 1470
  wants bodily pleasures excessively, 1520
  does a favor thinking to make a profit, 1778
  at odds with himself, 1814
  lacks beneficence towards himself, 1814
  lacks goodwill towards himself, 1815
  lacks concord within himself, 1816, 1817
  cannot converse with himself, 1816
  is filled with remorse, 1818
Bail:
  by—a person appoints himself a debtor for another, 929
Banausia:
  excess in magnificence, 344, 711
Banausos:
  person immoderate in grand outlays, 732
Barter:
  exchange of things equal in value, 929
  used before currency existed, 990
Beatitude (*see* Happiness):
  perfect, not attainable in this life, 202
Beauty:
  a fitting arrangement of parts, 159, 320
Beloved:
  takes pleasure in favors from lover, 1587
Benefactor:
  loves his beneficiaries more than the reverse, 1840, 1845, 1848, 1853
  his good consists in bestowing benefits, 1848
  feels love for beneficiary, 1844, 1845, 1854

Demonstration (Cont.):
  possible about contingent things, 1123
  deals with things whose principles are certain, 1164
  proceeds from indemonstrable principles in speculative matters, 1253
  proceeds from demonstrable principles in practical matters, 1253
Deposit:
  defined, 929
Desirable:
  a greater good is more—, 116
Desire (see also Concupiscence, Sensual Desire):
  increased by need of good, 48
  of agent moved by the end, 108
  when undisturbed by lack of unnecessary things, 116
  a movement of the appetite, 293
  differs from concupiscence, 294
  concerns future goods, 618, 2052
  division and definition of—, 619, 620, 621
  for food in general is natural, 620, 1390
  of pleasure is insatiable, 646
  for superfluous objects follows the imagination, 1391
  for pleasure arises insidiously, 1394
  tends to object as apprehended, 1555
  for good objects praiseworthy, 2051
  separated from activity by time, 2052
  an act of something imperfect, 2052
Desire, Natural:
  defined, 21
  cannot be frustrated, 21, 202
Dicaeopragma:
  doing what is just, 1033, 1036
Dicha:
  a measure determining equality, 957
Dichaste:
  justice, 958
Dichastes:
  the just man, 958
Dicheon:
  the just thing, 958
Disgraceful Pleasures:
  not pleasant in the absolute sense, 1998, 2063

Dissembler:
  sins by defect of veracity, 835
  more pleasing than the boaster, 846
Dissembling:
  practiced in different ways, 847
Dissimulation:
  pretends contemptible things about oneself, 352
Distributive Justice:
  an equality of proportion, 932, 935, 941-943, 957, 994
  directs distribution of common goods, 949
Divine:
  comes from God or makes us like God, 169
Divine Good:
  is the essence of goodness, 1973
Divine Virtue:
  perfection beyond usual mode, 1298, 1299
  the opposite of brutishness, 1300
  found in some men, 1300
  more noble than human virtue, 1301
Domestic Justice:
  differs from political justice, 1015
Domestic Prudence:
  holds a middle place between prudence and civic prudence, 1196
  administers a household, 1199
  necessary for good of the individual, 1206
Domestic Society:
  antecedent to civil society, 1720
  arises from union of man and wife, 1720
  ordered to acts necessary for life, 1720
Duration:
  outside the nature of good, 85

Effeminacy:
  censured when concerned with pain, 1304
  worse than incontinence, 1413
  shuns all weariness inordinately, 1414
  innate tendency in Scythian kings, 1416
Effeminate Person:
  concerned with pleasure and pain, 1355, 1360

Equitable Thing (Cont.):
a kind of just thing, 1246
Equity:
directs ordinary justice, 886
designates a habit, 1078
follows intention of the legislator, 1078
a directing of legal justice, 1082
contained under natural justice, 1082
a species of justice, 1090
Equivocation:
evident in widely separated things with the same name, 894
Essential:
what is predicated absolutely, 1439
Etairicia:
friendship between persons of same age, 1695
is like friendship corresponding to timocracy, 1695
Eternal:
how the—differs from the non-eternal, 85
Ethics (Moral Science) (*see also* Moral Philosophy):
definition of—, 2, 3
division of—, 6
treats acts of the will, 35
young men not good students of—, 38
role of experience in—, 38
teaches men to follow reason, 39
end of—not knowledge, but action, 40, 256
procedure used in—, 52
a principle of—, 53
principal object of—is happiness, 224
gives the principles of political science, 225
purpose of—is virtuous activity, 351, 369
Eubulia:
excellent deliberation, 1217, 1218
a kind of rectitude, 1217, 1222
is not *eustochia,* 1218
is not science, 1218
associated with inquiry, 1218, 1219, 1226, 1239
not concerned with the end, 1220
is not opinion, 1221, 1226

Eubulia (Cont.):
not rectitude of science or opinion, 1223-1226, 1227
conditions of—, 1228-1233
is rectitude of deliberation, 1229, 1234
about good end and by good means, 1231
of two kinds: unqualified and particular, 1233
Eugnomonas:
men who pronounce fair judgments, 1243
Evexia:
a healthy condition, 892
Evil:
desired under aspect of good, 10
cannot be complete, 140, 808
comes from any single defect, 140
a deviation from reason, 326
future—terrifying, 584
present—distressing, 584
a privation of good, 808
opposed not only to good but also to evil, 1978
as such is to be avoided, 1979
Evil Habits:
differ like evil acts, 510
withdraw men from good, 510
already formed not subject to the will, 513
difficult to overcome, 513
are voluntary, 514
caused by man's continual sinning, 520
Evil Men:
lack steadfastness or stability, 1651
do not long remain like-minded, 1651
friendship of—not lasting, 1652
always act for gain, 1857
do nothing for the good of others, 1857
diversified by their connection with vice, 1977
should be punished by pain, 2152
Excellence:
twofold: absolute and relative, 214
Excess:
and defect pertain to vice, 321
Exchange (*see also* Transaction):
includes reciprocation, 973
how—is made just, 980

Fortitude (Cont.):
can be deficient in three ways, 559, 560
of the soldier, 567-569
soldier's—compared with citizen's, 570
has a likeness to rage, 571
not found in animals, 574
operating through anger, 576
concerned differently with daring and fear, 583
how—is concerned with pain, 584, 585
more praiseworthy than temperance, 585
how—is related to pleasure, 586
not lessened by sorrow of death, 591
defined, 594
properties of—, not found in soldier's fortitude, 593
resides in the irascible part, 596
primarily concerned with sorrows following the presence of harmful things, 627
proximate matter of—, fear and recklessness, 652

Fortitude, Civic:
similar to real fortitude, 562, 564
motivated by honor and avoidance of disgrace, 564
three kinds of—, 564-566
practiced on account of punishment, 565

Fortune:
an accidental cause, 466

Fortunes:
influence a man's happiness, 205
of friends affect a person, 206
of friends do not change the condition of the dead, 208, 209

Fraternal Friendship:
why brothers love one another, 1712
resembles friendship between persons of the same age and rearing, 1713
is like friendship of comrades, 1717

Friend:
another self, 1543, 1811, 1896, 1909
wishes good to friend, 1637, 1638
does good for the sake of a friend, 1798

Friend (Cont.):
best—is to be loved best, 1858
a man's best—is himself, 1860
to be loved above money or honors, 1881, 1882
how—loves himself more, 1881, 1882
is the greatest of external goods, 1888
gives rather than receives benefits, 1889
a prosperous—is to be approached modestly, 1942

Friends:
useful in good fortune and adversity, 1539
a refuge in poverty, 1540
useful to the old, 1540
perform like services for each other, 1584
for utility parted when utility ceases, 1590
characteristic of—, to live together, 1600
many—possible in friendships for utility and pleasure, 1612
virtuous—pleasant to one another, 1616
chief external sign of honor, 1644
praised because they love, 1648
those sharing a common undertaking are—, 1659
share the same sorrows and joys, 1800
characteristically make the same choices, 1829
needed by the unfortunate and the fortunate for different reasons, 1890
should be neither too many nor too few, 1913
a few—are enough for pleasantness, 1916
number of—limited in virtuous friendship, 1918, 1920
necessary in prosperity and adversity, 1925
are pleasant in good and bad fortune, 1927, 1936, 1937
reluctantly summoned to share misfortunes, 1939
suffering misfortune are to be helped, 1940

Habit (Cont.):
a disposition determining a power, 298
twofold: good and bad—, 298
distinguished by act and object, 322, 327, 713, 992, 1151
of moral virtue defined, 494
known by its object, 892, 896
is known from its contrary, 892, 914
the best—insures best action, 1125
in reason alone can be forgotten, 1174
difficult to change, 1467
an initial perfection, 1486
terminates at activity, 1646

Habits:
order of—, 16
praiseworthy—called virtues, 244
good and bad—produced by actions, 253, 256, 259
of the soul are voluntary, 509
produced by operations, 511
produced by the same actions which caused the—, 526
are in our power and voluntary, 526
three—, 558
some—natural, others unnatural, 1371
diversified by objects, 1371
evil—incline more to lower pleasures, 1407
good—incline more to higher pleasures, 1407
acquired and preserved by practice, 1597

Habituation:
to virtuous living required to make a man good, 2138, 2139, 2143
for—legislation is required, 2138
must pre-exist for exhortation to have effect, 2147

Happiness:
highest good of human activity, 45, 105, 128, 131, 224
men differ about the nature of—, 46-49
among the goods of this life, 55
placed by some in pleasure, 57-61; in honor, 62-63; in virtue, 66; in money, 70; in a separated good, 74

Happiness (Cont.):
not sought for something else, 65, 67, 2097
goal of voluntary actions, 71, 98
the ultimate end of man, 103, 106, 118
absolutely perfect, 111
the most perfect good, 111, 112, 118
a self-sufficient good, 112, 114, 118
as attainable in this life, 113
activity proper to man, 119
nature of—, 119
consists in some vital operation, 123
not in the goods of the body, 124-125
activity according to virtue, 128, 173, 1889, 2075, 2129
perfect—cannot be had in this life, 129
more properly in the life of thought; in an act of reason; in the rational by nature, 126
the most proper good of man, 126
extends to a complete life, 129
from a continued performance of good deeds, 129
continuity and perpetuity required for—, 129
among the goods of the soul, 143, 150
an operation and not a product, 144, 1267, 1894
identified with living a good life, 145
views on—, 147
and pleasure, 148
and virtue, 151
the best, most beautiful, and most pleasant, 160, 161
needs external goods, 162, 163, 164
gift of the supreme God, 167
something especially divine, 169
the reward and end of virtue, 169, 1953
the end of political science, 174
greatest of perfections, 180
can last a lifetime, 191
impeded by loss of reason, 197
definition of—, 201
a good to be honored, 215, 222
the principle of all human good, 223
consists more in the operation of wisdom, 1267, 2096, 2135

Happiness (Cont.):

an unimpeded activity, 1505, 1506

consists in the highest pleasure, 1505

needs good fortune, 1508

not identical with good fortune, 1508

is the highest good, 1509, 2078

consists in continual living and doing, 1895

the end of all human activity, 2065

is not a habit, 2066, 2067

an activity desirable in itself, 2068,
2069

does not consist in amusement, 2076,
2077

is the ultimate end, 2076

not attributed to the bestial man,
2079

not in physical pleasures, 2079

activity of the highest virtue, 2080

the goal of all human goods, 2080

an activity of the best element, 2085,
2087

consists in activity of contemplative
virtue, 2086

perfect—consists in the contemplation of suprasensible objects, 2087

especially continuous and lasting,
2088

found most of all in the contemplation of truth, 2089, 2097

involves a kind of leisure, 2098

perfect—not in the activities of the
moral virtues, 2102

perfect—in contemplation of the intellect, 2104

of contemplative living attributed to
wisdom; of active living to prudence, 2111

how—arises from the moral virtues,
2111

in the life of prudence and the moral
virtues, 2115

of contemplative living is more excellent than that of active living,
2116

principally in some form of contemplation, 2125

Happy Man:

acts virtuously, 187, 188, 192, 200

possesses perfect virtue, 192, 193

Happy Man (Cont.):

bears changes of fortune becomingly,
193, 198, 199

condition of the—, 200, 201

cannot attain perfect beatitude, 202

needs goods of the body, 1507

necessarily virtuous and beneficent,
1889

needs friends he can benefit, 1889,
1891

is not a solitary, 1891

does not need useful and pleasant
friends, 1893

needs virtuous friends, 1894, 1896,
1912

should live pleasantly, 1897

existence of—naturally good and
pleasant, 1911

a friend is desirable to—, 1911

needs external goods, 2126

in contemplating,—most pleasing to
God, 2133

Harshness:

opposed to gentleness, 1379

Heavenly Bodies:

do not directly change intellect or
will, 508

can cause a disposition in human
body, 523

better than men, 1192

Honor:

extrinsic and superficial, 64

why—is sought, 65

differs from praise, 214, 219

testimony of a person's excellence,
214

the reward of virtue, 539, 742, 756

desired by men in high places, 742

the best of external goods, 742

a kind of reverence due an excellent
good, 756

due to the more worthy, 1639, 1693

a mark of goodness in the one
honored, 1641

desired not for itself but incidentally,
1642

sought from two classes of men, 1642-
1643

a suitable compensation for acts of
virtue and kindness, 1749, 1751

is a common good, 1750

Alphabetical Index of Subjects

Law-Breaker:
is unjust, 895, 899
Lawful Acts:
are just in some way, 900, 901
Laws:
deal with what is useful for the community, 902
excellent—impel to good by a kind of necessity, 2148
needed throughout a man's life, 2150
public—in states are like paternal precepts in families, 2158
are rules for activities of the state, 2176
Learning:
proper order of—, 1211
Legal Enactments:
principles devised by human diligence, 1018
decrees of judges, 1022
Legal Justice:
the perfect virtue, 906, 907, 908, 910
in agreement with every virtue prescribed by law, 907, 911
a general virtue, 911, 913
as a definite virtue tends to the common good, 912, 918
treats all moral matters in general, 919
is the good of another, 1010
three differences in—, 1020-1022
origin of—in natural justice, 1023, 1082
can be unknown, 1072
the direction of—, 1083, 1087
Legally Just Thing:
the object of legal justice, 900
determined by law, 900
is changeable, 1030
Legally Unjust Thing:
the unjust thing in general, 915
Legal Utility:
two kinds: formal and liberal, 1735
Legislation:
required for virtuous habituation, 2148
needed for training and activities of citizens, 2155
is a part of political prudence, 2165
principal part of political science, 2165, 2174

Legislation (Cont.):
for—a man must devise new laws, 2175
a part of government, 2179
Legislative Prudence:
called architectonic, 1197
prudence in making laws, 1199
is principal about actions to be done, 1201
Legislator:
habituates men to virtuous works, 251
should consider voluntary and involuntary, 385
decrees honors and punishments, 504
has zeal for maintaining friendship, 1542
aims to obtain the general welfare, 1666
to be a—pertains principally to an official, 2156
needs experience, 2177
Leisure:
when a person is said to have—, 2098
is rest in the end, 2099
a special property of happiness, 2099
not in the activities of the practical virtues, 2099, 2101
Liberality:
mean between extravagance and miserliness, 324, 993
a mean in regard to wealth, 343, 651
differs from magnificence, 346
has to do with wealth, 649, 658, 679
moderates the desire for external goods, 650, 652
act of—is the proper use of wealth, 658
virtue of—consists rather in giving than receiving, 661-665
properties of—, 672-675
Liberal Man:
praised for giving of wealth, 651
characteristically distributes wealth, 660, 682
especially loved, 665
gives in conformity with reason, 666, 672, 677, 679, 680
gives cheerfully, 667, 669

Material Goods (Cont.):
sought to satisfy desires and passions, 1864
Matter:
object of external act, 423
Mean:
objective and relative—, 311, 312, 313
in arithmetic and geometric proportion, 312
pertains to virtue, 321
cannot be of any excess or defect, 322
good and praiseworthy, 335, 381
in virtue—is difficult to discover, 370, 379
how to attain the—, 371
what suffices for the—, 380
in virtue—is judged according to right reason, 741, 1109
Meanness:
defect opposed to magnificence, 344, 711
Means:
reason for—found in the end, 23, 223
proportionate to end, 55
sought as things ordered to the end, 446
investigated by reason, 1131
Measure:
principal element in a genus, 1743
Meekness:
a mean for anger, 800
Meek Person:
defined, 800
inclined to forgive and remit punishments, 801, 802
Megalocindinos:
braves great dangers for great things, 760
Melancholic Persons:
seem particularly inclined to anger, 810
hold firmly to what they accept, 1440
continually need a remedy for sadness, 1532
frequently become intemperate and depraved, 1532
Memory:
of virtuous deeds is pleasant, 1850
of useful goods less pleasant than of honorable goods, 1850

Metaphorical Justice:
exists in things related to oneself, 1091
nature of—, 1105
Method:
of understanding in human things, 24
of manifesting truth in a science, 32, 36
Microcindinos:
exposes himself to danger for trifles, 760
Mildness:
a mean in regard to anger, 349
Miser:
deficient in giving; excessive in taking, 685
Miserliness (*see also* Illiberality):
defect in the use of wealth, 654
Miserly Persons (*see also* Illiberal Persons):
too solicitous about keeping wealth, 655
Misery:
increased by reduction from prosperity to wretchedness, 178
Misfortune:
inconsistent with happiness, 2067
Mocker:
tries to put another to shame, 864
Modesty (*see also* Shame):
not a virtue but a laudable passion, 355
Moral ("moralis"):
sometimes means custom; sometimes, vice or virtue, 247
Morals:
teaching on—even in general aspects is uncertain and variable, 259
Moral Science (*see also* Ethics):
completed by knowledge of particulars, 832
treats pleasure, 1955, 1957
Moral Virtue:
consists principally in regulation of the appetite, 1956
Monarchy:
the rule of one, 1673
best form of government, 1674
corruption of—called tyranny, 1675

Operation (Cont.):
 more perfect than virtue itself, 152
 virtuous—is pleasurable, 155, 156,
  158, 592
 more delightful than other pleasures,
  156
 perfect—proceeds from a perfect
  agent, 308
 concerned with particulars, 339, 1339
Opinion:
 common—cannot be entirely false,
  203
 what—deals with, 448, 452, 1143,
  1174
 divided into true and false, 449
 pertains to the intellect, 451
 perfection of—, 453
 rectitude of—is truth, 453, 1225
 lacks certitude, 454
 precedes choice, 456
 not an intellectual virtue, 1143
 defect in—is called falsity, 1225
 not an inquiry but a declaration,
  1226
 a person's—may be changed in two
  ways, 1442
Opportune:
 the—differs in different acts, 82
Orakizontes:
 rulers of households, 1955
Order:
 twofold in things, 1
 to know—pertains to reason, 1
 related to reason in a fourfold way, 1

Pain:
 the nature of—, 636, 637, 642
 twofold, 1498
 in itself to be avoided, 1498, 1514,
  1967, 1979
 opposed to pleasure as a good, 1499
 not contrary to excessive physical
  pleasure, 1521
 is evil, 1521
 eliminated by vehement pleasure,
  1523
 no—opposed to intellectual pleasure,
  1523
 arising from natural movements and
  activities, 1529

Pain (Cont.):
 caused by continual seeing and
  hearing, 1530
 not opposed to pleasure as evil to
  evil, 1979
 not the correlative of every pleasure,
  1996
 from an activity destroys it, 2048
Paragogia:
 definition of—, 930
Pardon:
 due to person acting involuntarily,
  383
 distinguished from pity, 384
Parents:
 love of—for children, 1706-1709,
  1711
 special benefactors of their children,
  1715
Particular Cases:
 judged by prudence, 259
Particular Injustice:
 differs from legal injustice, 1097
Particular Justice:
 existence of—, 913-917, 920
 agrees with legal justice in genus,
  918
 ordered to another as a private person, 918
 takes into account social intercourse,
  919
 twofold, 927
 establishes a measure of justice in
  transactions, 928
Particular Reason:
 collates particular impressions, 1123
 the sensory power of judgment, 1123,
  1249
 deals with particular ultimates, 1255
Passion:
 definition of—, 269, 272, 292, 302,
  869, 1351
 terminated at pleasure and sorrow,
  296, 441, 1571
 neither virtue nor vice, 299
 precedes the deliberations of reason,
  301
 a certain—implies vice, 329
 contrary to reason in two ways, 336,
  367
 aroused by external things, 426

Politicians:
activities of—, 2168, 2169, 2170
Polity:
a kind of justice is found in every—, 1688
Polyphiloi:
are real friends of no one, 1923
Positive Law:
right reason by which rulers frame just laws, 1197
Potential Intellect:
the power of becoming all things, 1119
Potentiality:
becomes determinate by means of act, 1904
without act is potentiality with privation, 1904
Power:
motive—manifested through motion, 9
Powerful:
the—have different kinds of friends, 1618
Powers:
exist according as we are capable of experiencing the passions, 297
Practical Affairs:
in—our aim is not knowledge but conduct, 2132
Practical Arts:
called sciences and aptitudes, 2166
taught by the people practicing them, 2166
Practical Intellect:
good of the—is the conformable truth, 1130
truth of the—is the rule of rectitude for the appetite, 1131
terminates at an individual operable, 1132, 1135
same in subject with the speculative intellect, 1132
governs immanent and transient operations, 1135
is for the sake of something made or done, 1136
Practical Sciences:
end of—is action, 255
deals with particular contingent things, 1152

Praise:
verbal testimony of another's excellence, 214
differs from honor, 214
given for virtue of mind and strength of body, 216, 217, 222
and blame due to virtue and vice, 384
Precept:
of a father does not have full coercive power, 2159
Predication:
equivocal and analogical, 95, 96
Pretense:
the wickedness of the—of virtue, 1788
Prince:
orders things for the common good, 909
rules by legal justice, 1010
should be rewarded by the multitude, 1011
office of the—is to observe justice, 1099
Principle:
should be thoroughly understood, 139
is the ultimate end in practical matters, 139
Principles, First:
of reason given by nature, 286
of demonstration are indemonstrable, 1177
immediately understood from a knowledge of their terms, 1179
in themselves most known, 1181
Principles:
conform to conclusions, 35
how—are understood, 137
cannot be reduced to anything previous, 137
knowledge of—are a great help in understanding conclusions, 138
no science of—but understanding, 219
within our power make actions voluntary, 502
cannot be weaker than the inferences drawn from them, 1164
of practicable things are ends, 1170
more certain than necessary conclusions, 1177, 1182, 1254

Reproach (Cont.):
   use of—in amusement and in correction, 862
Rest:
   taken for the sake of activity, 2099
   in the end is leisure, 2099
Return:
   equivalent—cannot be made to teacher, 1768
   made according to appraisal of recipient, 1771
   to a benefactor to be made before a present to a friend, 1775
Rhetoric:
   deals with variable matter, 36
   gives persuasive arguments on a threefold basis, 2173
Riches (see also Wealth):
   not the end of domestic economy, 15
   use of—, 658
   abundant—not needed for happiness, 2132
Rich Men:
   have no need of useful friends, 1615
Right:
   the just object, 1016
Right Choice:
   not without prudence and moral virtue, 1289
Right Plan (Reason):
   of prudence, the guide in morals, 1111
Right Reason:
   defined, 1110
   determines the mean in all habits, 1110
   use of—, 1111
Rule:
   of a father is a kind of kingship, 1682
   of brothers in a household is timocratic, 1695

Sadness:
   how—is increased at loss of goods, 589
   a feeling of injury, 804
Scents:
   considered in two ways, 608

Science (see also Knowledge):
   concerned with conclusions known by reason of principles, 219, 1176, 1177
   every operative—perfects its work, 315
   treats of the true and necessary, 1118, 1224
   deals with the necessary and eternal, 1145
   based on universal reasons, 1146
   every—can be taught, 1147
   a demonstrative habit, 1149
   not concerned with things to be done, 1165
   proceeds demonstratively from principles to conclusions, 1176, 1177
   the principle of—is neither a science, nor an art, nor prudence, 1176
   better—deals with better subject, 1186
   has to do with universals, 1213, 1352, 2162
   and prudence have some agreement with understanding, 1214
   in no way is synesis, 1256
   the principal consideration in any—, 1470
   end of—in practicable matters is not to know but to do, 2138
Science, Demonstrative:
   object of—, necessary things, 189
Science, Political:
   definition of—, 6
   truly architectonic, 25-28
   dictates to practical and speculative sciences, 26, 27
   end of—, 29, 30, 43
   develops good citizens, 174, 225
   a study of virtue and its attainment, 225
   placed above all other sciences, 225
Science, Practical:
   called skill, 24
   proceeds in a deductive manner, 35
   in—we must know a determined effect follows a determined cause, 255
Science, Speculative:
   called science (disciplina), 24
   proceeds in an analytical manner, 35

Alphabetical Index of Subjects

Science, Speculative (Cont.):
seeks only knowledge of the truth, 255
in—it suffices to know the cause of a determined effect, 255
Sciences:
all—and acts tend to some good, 8, 100
division of—, 2
role of architectonic—, 26, 28, 29
not the same certitude in all—, 32, 36, 258
have been lost gradually, 134
practical and speculative—differ, 136
take their principles from wisdom, 1184
how some—are bad, 1504
Seeing:
completed in the first instant of time, 2006
not a process of generation, 2021
and hearing, when most pleasant, 2029
Self-Indulgence (see also Intemperance):
more opposed to temperance than insensibility is, 386
Self-Lovers:
men criticize—, 1856
take more than their share of material goods, 1863, 1865
Self-Sufficiency:
definition of—, 115
understood in two ways, 115
necessary for happiness, 2093
found most of all in contemplation, 2093
for happiness does not consist in a superabundance of riches, 2128
Senses:
apprehend a particular being, 129
do not establish a mastery of action, 1127
judge good only in its immediacy, 1976
the active principle of sensitive activity, 2023, 2024
requirements for functioning of—, 2023
Sensitive Appetite:
movements of—are the passions, 508

Sensitive Faculties:
operate by means of bodily organs, 1250
Sensory Power of Judgment:
passes judgment on singulars, 1255
Sensual Desire (see also Concupiscence, Desire):
common to men and brutes, 438
accompanied by pleasure or sorrow, 441
brings sorrow when object not attained, 628
satisfied, becomes master, 646
increases what is innate, 646
faculty of—should conform to reason, 647
does not move by reasoning, 1388, 1389
binds reason, 1394
Separated Substances:
called gods, 1634
seem supremely happy and blessed, 2121
moral virtues not ascribed to—, 2121, 2122
have only intellectual life, 2125
Servility:
results from not taking vengeance, 973
Shame (see also Modesty):
fears disgrace, 564, 868, 2141
not properly a virtue, 867, 870
accompanied by a bodily change, 869, 870
becoming to adolescence, 871-872
unbecoming to old age, 873
does not belong to the virtuous, 874, 876, 878
properly regards only voluntary defects, 878
Shameless Person:
falls short in modesty, 355
does not fear a bad reputation, 533
Shrewdness (Dinotica):
definition of—, 1272
differs from prudence, 1272, 1458
Shrewd People:
may be either prudent or crafty, 1272
Sight:
the purest of all sensitive activities, 2056

526

Sin:
  arises from any inordinate circumstance, 320
  contrary to right reason, 546
  through ignorance, 1042
  when—is said to occur, 1043
  of weakness, 1044, 1046-1047
  from wickedness, 1045
  of omission and transgression, 1047
  from ignorance deserves pardon,
  1049
Singulars:
  judgment about—made by internal
  sense, 381
  judgment of—belongs to prudent
  man, 399
  voluntariness of—in temperance, 641
  not perceived by reason, 1214
  as principles, 1249
Sketch:
  defined, 131
Slave:
  a living tool, 1699
Slow:
  when a thing is called—, 1991
Small-Mindedness:
  effects of—, 787
  more opposed to magnanimity than
  conceit is, 790
Small-Souled Person (see also Pusillanimous):
  characteristics of the—, 744, 784, 786,
  788
Sorrow:
  has to do with present evil, 618
  affects the brave and the temperate
  differently, 626
Soul:
  act of the body, 122, 1847
  form of man, 123
  has two kinds of operations, 144
  survival of the—not treated in Ethics,
  212
  one part rational, the other irrational,
  229, 1114
  irrational part, the cause of assimilation and growth, 231
  vegetative—especially active during
  sleep, 234
  irrational—participates in reason, 236,
  239, 241

Soul (Cont.):
  irrational is twofold, 240
  rational part is of two kinds, 242
  three principles in the—, 290
  parts of the—correspond to objects,
  1116
  scientific and estimative, 1118, 1123
  the same power of the—knows perfect and imperfect things of the
  same genus, 1120
  human—between the higher substances and animals, 1299
  man acts by means of the—, 2024
Speculative Intellect:
  what constitutes the good and evil of
  the—, 1130
  does not move anything, 1135
Speculative Matters:
  in—we inquire about conclusions,
  474
Speculative Sciences:
  how—deal with contingent things,
  1146, 1152
  sought as honorable in themselves,
  1185
Spendthrift (see also Extravagant Person):
  how—sins, 343, 684, 685
  the over-indulgent person sometimes
  called a—, 656
  less evil than the miser, 686, 689, 690
  how a—is cured of his vice, 687
  compared with the liberal man, 688
  sometimes takes from the wrong
  sources, 691, 692
  does not give according to right reason, 693, 694
  why a—is intemperate, 695
  resembles the generous soul, 1441
State:
  the good citizen and the good man
  in a—, 926
Statesman:
  must know the things belonging to
  the soul, 227
Subject:
  admits of degrees in two ways, 1983
Substance:
  defined, 80
  more excellent than accidents, 1549

Substances, Separated:
    attain truth without investigation, 132
    may bestow something on man, 168
Suicide:
    an injustice to the state, 1094, 1096
    strictly not an injustice to oneself, 1095, 1097
Sullen Persons:
    keep anger pent up, 810
Supervision:
    good—exercised according to good laws, 2157
Suspicion:
    cause and nature of—, 1143
Swift:
    when a thing is called—, 1991
Swiftness and Slowness:
    not proper to motion in itself, 1990
Sycophant (see also Flatterer):
    overdoes affability for profit, 354
Syllogism:
    proceeds from universal principles, 1148
    only the demonstrative—causes science, 1148
Sympathetic Friends:
    a consolation in sorrow, 1928, 1929, 1930, 1932
    bring gladness in two ways, 1931
    presence of—has an admixture of pleasure and sorrow, 1933
Synesis:
    not the same as science or opinion, 1235, 1236
    judges about matters deliberated, 1236, 1239, 1240
    more excellent than eubulia, 1240
    compared with prudence, 1238, 1240, 1241, 1242
    deals with singular ultimates, 1246
Syngnome:
    judges what is equitable, 1244

Taste:
    most common of all the senses, 616
Teaching:
    definition of—, 8
    proceeds from previous knowledge, 1147
    is twofold, 1148

Temperance:
    how—is destroyed and preserved, 263
    treats of pleasures and sorrows, 267
    regards things preservative of life, 267, 340, 595
    restrains desires and pleasures of touch, 339, 342
    resides in the concupiscible part, 596
    deals with physical pleasures, 597, 603
    a mean for pleasure and sorrow, 598
    not concerned with the pleasures of the soul, 601-603
    deals only with certain sensitive pleasures, 604, 605-608
    has to do with pleasures common to all animals, 612, 613, 759
    deals with the sense of touch, 616, 651, 1385
    primarily concerned with pleasures following the presence of pleasurable things, 627
    how—is acquired, 639
    moderates the desires of tactile pleasures, 650
    the matter of—, 652
    taken for any moderation, 738
    moderates pleasure and pain, 1169
    called sophrosyne in Greek, 1169
    and continence agree in matter, 1330
    and intemperance, 1357, 1359, 1399, 1400
Temperate Man:
    how to become a—, 239, 264, 266, 287
    praised for refraining from pleasures, 626
    follows the golden mean, 632
    saddened by shameful things, 632
    desires necessary pleasures, 633
    how the—desires unnecessary pleasures, 634
    seems continent and persevering, 1307
    does not permit concupiscence to master reason, 1346
    and intemperate man act with deliberate choice, 1361, 1400
    follows a middle course in pleasure, 1409

Vice (Cont.):
taken in two senses, 1359
unqualified—is according to human mode, 1383
unnatural—called brutish or pathological, 1383
the nature of brutish—, 1403
compared to long sicknesses, 1424
sins with deliberate choice, 1428
destroys a principle of action, 1431
a corruption of nature, 1977
Vices:
are contrary to one another, 1977
Violence:
excludes appetitive movement, 386, 387
actions resulting from—are accompanied by sadness, 429
Virginity:
is not a vice, 263
Virtue:
cause of honor, 65
makes its possessor good, 65, 81, 128, 222, 1575
habit of—firmly fixed, 189, 1577
inclines the appetite, 190
makes good use of misfortunes, 195
proper work of—done according to reason, 243
two kinds of—, 243
produces actions similar to the actions that caused it, 260, 264
destroyed by pleasure and sadness, 268
works what is best in pleasures and sorrows, 272
is choice or not without choice, 301, 322
a habit, 305, 308, 322
of a thing judged by the best it can do, 308
a mean, 309, 316, 324, 325, 327, 1110, 1435
treats the more, the less, and the equal, 310
more certain and better than art, 315, 316
seeks the mean in regard to us, 322
principal act of—is choice, 322
how—is an extreme, 326, 327
root of—is rectitude of reason, 335

Virtue (Cont.):
opposed to both extremes, 359, 361, 362
ought to restrain vice, 368
chooses the mean in passions and actions, 369
works by means of choice, 382
within our power and voluntary, 496, 499
bestows rather than receives benefits, 661
concerned with the difficult, 663, 768
operates according to right reason, 737
good of—exceeds external goods, 751
is praised, 804
renders work of a thing good, 1124, 1575
perfects characteristic operation, 1125
work of—needs two things, 1269
and prudence, 1283
opposed to vice, 1297, 1359
not attributed to God, 1301
in the complete and incomplete sense, 1359
preserves a principle of action, 1431
cause of true friendship, 1538
more proper to friendship than money is, 1792
a standard for everyone, 1803
the proper perfection of man, 1803
makes its possessor and his work good, 1805, 1807, 1809
is a perfection of nature, 1977
the measure for all human affairs, 2062
Virtue, Intellectual:
the nature of—, 246
Virtue, Moral:
not in us by nature, 245, 248
derived from customary activity, 247
pertains to the appetite, 248, 322
how called natural, 249
concerned with pleasures and pains, 266, 267, 269, 276
concerns passions and operations, 267, 317, 383
deals with actions, 269
perfection of—, 283, 286
makes its possessor and his work good, 307, 309